Marginalization, Development and Resistance

Essays in Tribute to S.R. Sankaran

S.R. Sankaran

Marginalization, Development and Resistance

Essays in Tribute to S.R. Sankaran

Vol. 2: Dalits and Tribals

Edited by
K.B. Saxena
G. Haragopal

AAKAR

Marginalization, Development and Resistance Vol. 2
Edited by K.B. Saxena and G. Haragopal

First Published, 2016

ISBN 978-93-5002-285-6 (Set)
ISBN 978-93-5002-435-5 (Vol. 2)

Published by
AAKAR BOOKS
28 E Pocket IV, Mayur Vihar Phase I, Delhi 110 091
Phones: 011 2279 5505, 2279 5641
aakarbooks@gmail.com

Printed at
D. K. Fine Art Press (P) Ltd. Delhi - 110 052

Contents

Acknowledgements *vii*

Introduction *ix*

PART 1 : DALITS: THE QUESTION OF MARGINALIZATION AND DISCRIMINATION

1. Rural Poor and Access to Land: The Case of Scheduled Castes in Andhra Pradesh 3
   D. Narasimha Reddy

2. Of Caste and Institutions of Higher Education: A Case Study of AIIMS 28
   Vikas Bajpai and Anoop Saraya

3. Untouchability and the Right to Personal Liberty 65
   Kalpana Kannabiran

4. Manual Scavengers: A Struggle for Retrieving India's Soul 94
   P.S. Krishnan

5. Atrocities Against Scheduled Castes and Tribes: Implementation Prevention of Atrocities Act and Proposed Amendments 113
   S.D.J.M. Prasad

6. Meanwhile, We Refuse to Die! 130
   Deepti Sukumar

7. Dalit Movement and Dalit Literature in Andhra Pradesh: A Survey of the Pre-dandora Movement Period 138
   K.Y. Ratnam

8. Economic Reforms, Impetus to Aquaculture and Implications for Land Reforms 163
   K. Gopal Iyer

PART 2 : MARGINALIZATION AND ALIENATION OF THE TRIBALS

9. Culture, Economy, and Power: Roots of Disparities between Adivasis and Others 183
K.B. Saxena

10. The Rights of Tribals over Their Land 234
T.L. Sankar

11. Irrelevance of Land Reforms Policies to the Tribals of Jharkhand 245
B.K. Sinha

12. Wages of Sin: Tribals and Excise Policy 276
B.D. Sharma

13. Subsistence Economy in a Subverted Development: Re-rethinking Development Concretely 298
G. Vijay

14. Adivasi Militancy and Land Relations: The Context of Central and Eastern India 328
Joseph Marianus Kujur

15. Adivasi Awakening and Emergence of New Politics 347
Manoranjan Mohanty

16. Bleeding Manipur: Repeal the Armed Forces (Special Powers) Act, 1958 355
K.S. Subramanian

17. Land and Tribals in Andhra Pradesh 373
K. Raju

About the Contributors 386

Acknowledgements

The idea of presenting a collection of papers of S.R. Sankaran was mooted by some of his close associates and admirers to honour his work as a civil servant and a social activist for the under privileged sections of society around four years ago. Before we could progress sufficiently in the matter, sadly, S.R. Sankaran passed away. It was therefore decided to convert the proposed volume into a tribute to him.

We invited papers from former and serving civil servants, social activists, academics and those associated with social movements under the broad theme of Marginalization, Development and Resistance.

The response to our invitation was so overwhelming that it was decided to cover the contributions in two volumes. The first volume was devoted to the Crisis of Development and was published in 2014. The second volume dealing exclusively with the two marginalized groups Dalits and Adivasis which was to have come out soon after but was delayed due to unavoidable is now being brought out.

We are sad that Dr B.D. Sharma one of our esteemed contributors and a very close associated of S.R. Sankaran also passed away recently.

We wish to express our gratitude to the Council for Social Development, New Delhi and its Chairman and Director for their support and interest in this work and for the secretarial support received from Ms Gurmeet Kaur, Ms Lovely Nagpal and Mr Dev Dutt.

We also thank Shri K.K. Saxena of Aakar Books for his perseverance and keenness and Shri K.P. Kannan and Ms Padma Malini Rao for the editing.

The Editor

Introduction

I

Marginalized social groups refer to social collectivities who have been pushed to the margin of society where they fail to get the dignity, the sense of security and the treatment as equal citizens due to them. This usually gets manifested in exclusion from the formal productive process, benefits of the system and decision making process of the polity. Pejorative characteristics are ascribed to them which they are unable to fight or erase (Cox, 2001). These specific characteristics are associated with caste, ethnicity, religion, colour, gender or race of the groups. The discrimination which this marginalization unleashes is in respect of access to opportunities for economic advancement, social goods, enjoyment of civil rights, legal entitlements, exercise of political rights, and share in political power and process of governance (Thorat, 2009). This leads to multiple deprivation, low incomes, a high degree of poverty, and, in extreme conditions, to their alienation from the government and the mainstream society.

Historical Roots

The two social groups in India, the Dalits and the Adivasis, are examples of entrenched marginalization of the pathetie variety in Indian society. The marginalization of Dalits is rooted in caste-based hierarchical Hindu social order which assigns to them the lowest position in it based on birth which cannot be changed. This order structurally denies any access to productive assets for earning a decent livelihood, and social freedom of mobility; permanently condemns them to engage in degrading occupations and assigns a subordinate status which requires them to provide labour and services to the higher castes. They are left with no means to shed this stigmatized existence and lead a dignified social life. They also face varying degrees of violence but failed to get effective protection from the State. The other social group called the Adivasis or the Tribals are regarded as inferior, lazy and as drunkards and backward by the larger society due to their occupation, pattern of living, social organization and cultural values. There are also racial overtones in the pejorative characterization of their colour and facial structure which in Hindu scriptures are associated with 'demons'. Their marginalization is rooted in the loss of their control over productive resources, distinctive way of life, and deligitimization of autonomy of internal governance. This process is traced by some scholars to the Aryan invasion which pushed them out of their fertile land in river valleys and integrated those who could not escape to forests at a very low position in their society. As for the larger part of Tribal population which settled in the distant forests, their marginalization crystallized during the colonial rule which incorporated them in the State and triggered the process of economic domination of the non-Tribal communities over them and political control through structures of governance. The process has been further consolidated by the post-colonial state through its paradigm of development and governance and processes of their aggressive integration in the national mainstream society. The marginalized status of the two groups has resulted in their underdevelopment, poverty, inequality vis-à-vis dominant social groups and inter-group conflicts (Thorat and Kumar, 2008).

Under Development: Defining Characteristics

Assets and Livelihood

Let us take the underdevelopment aspect first. This is conveyed by the nature of their participation in the national economy, employment, level of skills, income and status of social development. Both Dalits and Adivasis have high labour participation rates (more than two-thirds) and high worker population ratio compared to the general population. But an overwhelmingly large number of their workers are engaged in agriculture primarily as labourers. The proportion of self-employed in agriculture among Dalits is small compared to Adivasis. Both have very low percentages of population in non-agricultural employment in rural areas. In urban areas too, the percentage of self-employed is very low in respect of both the groups but self-employed Adivasis are even lower than Dalits. Both have much lower presence in urban labour compared to others and among them casual workers are much higher than regular workers. Adivasis have lower participation than even Dalits in both categories. Only 27% of Dalits have some access to land but in most cases it is largely homestead land with an additional few decimal points in some cases. A larger number of Adivasis had land earlier but they lost it as a result of alienation to non-Tribals and to the State through acquisition for development projects. There has been an unprecedented increase in landlessness among Adivasis particularly during the last two to three decades. The percentage of households among them owning other assets is negligible in the case of Adivasis and very low among the Dalits compared to other groups. The Access Index in this respect is 0.47 in case of

Dalits and 0.51 in the case of Adivasis compared to 1.60 in respect of others in rural areas and broadly the same in urban areas. The average value of assets among Dalits and Adivasis is nearly one-third of assets owned by other groups. The unemployment rate as a percentage of labour force (CDS) is much higher in them than in other groups both in rural and urban areas. Rural and urban employment rates for Dalits and Adivasis have declined. There is a reduction in government jobs for SCs by -7.25% compared to 0.7% in the case of non SCs/STs (Thorat, 2009).

Both Adivasis and Dalits are in the lower end occupations, largely as casual labourers which carry low incomes and wages. This is because of their lack of skills which constrain mobility for better paying jobs and lack of certainty of work. The lack of access to fixed assets – land, capital and education constrains their ability to improve income. Their participation in higher education is also very low and presence in vocational courses miniscule. This explains the high incidence of poverty. Adivasis still have higher access to land compared to Dalits but the variation between owned land and cultivated land is very high in their case. This is because a large part of owned land is barren and uncultivable and unsuitable for giving high returns on investment. The lack of adequate irrigation facilities in their area is responsible for mono-cropping. Adivasis are located in dry land areas which are highly vulnerable to climate fluctuations. The average sizes of land being small, most of them are marginal farmers (Radhakrishna and Ray, 2005). Dalits are virtually landless or near landless. Both depend upon wage labour in agriculture and outside it to survive.

Poverty

As a result, Head Count Ratio of Poverty is much higher in Dalits and Adivasis, the highest in the latter, and the pace of reduction lower than in the other groups. Large scale displacement from land and absence of rehabilitation are responsible for accentuating the poverty of Adivasis. The Adivasis in the Northeastern states are better off than their counterparts in the rest of India due to protection of their land, autonomy of governance and higher educational development. The other dimension of their poverty is food insufficiency which is higher among them than Dalits even after taking into account their use of wild products of forest as edibles. This explains why most cases of starvation deaths or selling children to overcome desperate situations come from Adivasi areas. Nearly 71-61% Adivasi households are food deficient for 2-3 months and 5% for 6 months (Radhakrishna and Roy, 2005). The worst period for food availability is between post Rabi harvest and prior to Kharif sowing when there is no work in rural areas and they have to resort to distress migration where they get entangled in debt bondage. Food insufficiency also explains the high level of malnutrition among both Dalits and Adivasis, higher among the latter, leading to stunted growth and being underweight as also mortality among children and anaemia among adults, particularly women. Yet another dimension of poverty among both these groups is the incidence of child labour. The working children (5-14) years is 2.8% among Dalits and 3.8% among Adivais compared to 2.0% among others. There is high incidence of trafficking of children from Adivasi areas.

Monthly per capita expenditure (MPCE), a proxy for income, is another indicator of their economic status. The average MPCE of Dalits and Adivasis both in rural and urban areas is much lower than that of others. A large part of their population is concentrated in the lowest consumption bracket (Sengupta, et al 2008). There is also a spatial dimension of poverty which affects Adivasis as they are located in geographically far-flung, forests and hilly areas which are poorly served by availablity of infrastructure and employment opportunities. This explains why despite the high economic growth registered during the last decade, the incidence of poverty is still very high among 'Dalits and Adivasis' compared to others. It is 20.6% (rural) and 22.8% (urban) among Dalits and 25.3% and 20.6% among Adivasis compared to 6.3% and 7.3% among others. The percentage gap is 16 and 21 in respect of Dalits and 18 and 21 in respect of Adivasis (IAMR, 2011). In the NCEUS four-fold classification of poor and vulnerable – 'extremely poor', 'poor' 'marginal' and 'vulnerable' Dalits and Adivasis have an overwhelmingly large presence at the lower ends indicating that historically entrenched inequalities have not changed even with high economic growth rates (Sengupta, et al, 2008).

Poverty is also accentuated by the low level of human development, primarily reflected in the status in respect of education and health. This is an area which reflects continuing disparities between Dalits /Adivasis and other groups in respect of all major indicators such as the rate of literacy (male and female), access to safe drinking water and sanitation facilities, participation in education at different levels, health status reflected in Infant Mortality Rate/ Maternal Mortaligy Rate (IMR/MMR), level of malnutrition, sex ratio at birth, access to institutional delivery and level of immunization, access to housing and electricity etc. (IAMR, 2011) These disparities are showing no signs of getting bridged. There is, however, a claim made in IAMR report (2011) about convergence of SCs/STs with all India average on health and education and income indicators with the exception of nutrition and sanitation. But this claim is strongly contested (Chakravarty, 2012, Oomen, 2012) (Mehrotra and Gandhi, 2012). These disparities are indicative of the discriminatory processes at work which constrain access to these social goods. But the access is also affected by the economic status of these groups. Poverty forces households in those groups to push their children to labour market, thereby adversely affecting their attendance in schools and increasing their vulnerablity to trafficking.

Lack of employment forces households from these groups to migrate in search of work for survival which not only entangles them in debt bondage but also deprives them of access to social services in their home place. The harsh working conditions and unhealthy living environment at their place of work worsen their health condition and exposes them to communicable and non-communicable diseases. The discriminatory treatment of Dalit and Adivasi children in school forces them to drop out. The indifferent attitude of service providers, overcrowding, non-availability of doctors and drugs in health centres force them to either go without any treatment or approach quacks exposing them to further health risks. The introduction of user charges and privatization of some social amenities also restrict their ability to access such amenities.

Discrimination and Exclusion

The high level of economic inequalities manifested in income distribution and asset holding between them and others is a significantly contributive factor in the continuing poverty and the slower speed of its reduction in their case. These economic inequalities existed even before but have worsened with the onset of economic reforms and changeover to market economy. But when these economic inequalities intersect with historically entrenched social inequalities, this leads to an unbridgeable divide. The patterns of social inequalities manifested in social exclusion/discrimination have not ceased or even significantly reduced. One of the markers of entrenched social inequality is the practice of untouchability leading to the exclusionary social relations between these marginalized groups and higher castes which is particularly acute in the case of Dalits. Their most visible pattern is the segregation of Dalit settlements away from the centre of the village with its rules of social intercourse between residents of the two segments of the village. Another pattern can be observed in denial of access to and discriminatory treatment in access to public spaces and services such drinking water facility, cinema hall, entry into village shops and mode of transactions therein, denial of barbers and washermen to serve Dalits, conditions of entry and access to service in tea shops, etc. The third pattern is restrictions in public behaviour and sanctions imposed on their violation such as taking out marriage processions followed by the related celebrations, expected norms of behavior with the upper caste residents, dress code, walking through the upper caste areas etc. The fourth pattern is restriction in market participation such as selling milk to milk cooperatives or buying milk from them, selling their products in the local market, etc. (Thorat, 2009). These practices are most conspicuous in respect of Dalits because they live in the socially composite settlements unlike Adivasis who usually live in areas of their concentration with larger number and greater homogeneity in the social composition of the village. The economic discrimination in respect of both operates in hiring for jobs, sale and purchase transactions, use of Common Property Resources (CPRs) and various market and non-market transactions. Labour market discrimination is practised, besides hiring, in assignment of work, denial of work, wage payments, access to irrigation facilities, grazing and fishing grounds.

Victims of Violence: Societal and State

Historically, transgressions of the customary social code and norms imposed on Dalits were considered serious crimes and were punished by the dominant castes controlling the governance structure and this mode of social sanction was upheld by the higher dispensations. These atrocities against them were an integral part of the prevailing justice administration system. Adivasis were relatively spared of it where they were not incorporated in the State and integrated with the dominant ethnic groups of Hindus or Muslims. However, the incorporation of Adivasis in the state was enlarged by the colonial government which also increased their interface with dominant social groups. This process was intensified in the post-colonial state, subjecting Adivasis to the same status as the Dalits except where their interface with non-Adivasis was negligible. The Northeast remained relatively free from this status degradation. In the post-colonial polity, despite abolition of untouchability and guaranteed civil rights, the social relations have not witnessed any significant change. Rather, not only violence is inflicted on them, but social and economic sanctions are also imposed. The incidents of violence increase where members of these groups through their own efforts improve their economic position or assert their rights—civil, social, economic and political. These include the refusal to comply with the social norms embedded in caste order, and the demand for equality of treatment both in public spaces and social relations in respect of civil rights. Economic rights related atrocities cover attempts to cultivate the assigned land, use of CPRs, demand for minimum wages, recognition of tenancy status, entitlement to homestead land, and selling their products in the local market. Atrocities relating to political rights occur when these groups vote as per their own choice, seek public office, resist capture of booths or mobilize themselves socially for collective action. Atrocities concerning cultural rights are committed when they celebrate festivals, hold marriage festivities, or make their entry into temples etc. Atrocities on women are committed with a view to humiliating them into submission. Atrocities include not only physical violence but also psychological violence reflected in their undignified treatment. Atrocities are committed not only against individuals by individuals but also collective reprisals are resorted to by higher caste groups. This pattern of violence is followed pronouncedly in respect of Dalits for reasons already explained.

Strategy for Addressing Marginalization

Constitutional Provisions

The Government has an impressive architecture of policies for addressing marginalization of Dalits and Adivasis. Its foundation has been laid in the Constitution of India which provides for several safeguards to neutralize the historical discrimination. Most important among them are the Fundamental Rights which guarantee equality before law (Article 14), equality of opportunity for seeking employment (Art 16) empower the State to make provisions for reservation in appointments to the Government (Article 16.4) abolish untouchability and make its practice an offence (Art 17) and authorize the State to make special provisions for advancement of SCs and STs and any socially and educationally backward classes (Article 15.4). Further the Constitution also provides for reservation of seats in elective democratic institutions (Central and state legislatures as well as Panchyati Raj Institutions) (Article 330 and 332 and 243d). The Constitution in addition includes provisions for appointment of a commission each for SCs and STs to act as watchdog bodies to safeguard the interests of the SC and ST communities respectively (Articles 338 and 339). The Directive Principles of State Policy enjoin the State in Article 38 to minimize inequalities and undertake other welfare measures for the poor and specifically empower the State to promote the educational and economic interests of weaker sections of society and protect them from social injustices and all forms of exploitation (Article 46). Both SCs and STs are covered within the ambit of socially and educationally backward classes and are thereby considered as weaker sections of society.

In respect of governance, the Constitution itself has laid down a special governance structure for Tribals different from the non-Tribal areas taking into account their vulnerabilities by demarcating territories where they are concentrated as the Fifth and Sixth Schedule areas. In the Fifth Schedule areas, the Governor of the state has been given extraordinary powers to protect the interests of the Tribes against laws and policies which may have adverse implications for them. There is also a provision for constituting a Tribal Advisory Council to advise the concerned state governments on matters concerning the Tribes. The Sixth Schedule areas have a provision for autonomous councils with considerable powers of self-governance.

Besides the two National Commissions under the Constitution one each for Dalits and Adivasis to safeguard their interests, a separate commission exclusively for Safai Karamcharis has also been setup. In respect of Adivasis besides a standing commission, another commission has been provided to periodically review the conditions of the Tribals in Scheduled Areas.

Policy Architecture

In pursuance of these overarching constitutional provisions, the State has also built a comprehensive policy structure to combat marginalization of these groups covering four parameters: protection, reservation, development and participation. The protective dimension covers laws to abolish untouchability and protect civil rights, prevent acts of violence on these groups, and eliminate practices of manual scavenging and Devdasi system. These laws not only contain punitive provisions for their violation but also include rehabilitation of victims. The second component of the protective strategy consists of laws relating to protection against labour exploitation. Though not specific to these groups, their benefits largely accrue to them due to their overwhelming presence in the labour market. This includes a number of labour welfare legislations such as those relating, to payment of minimum wages, and payment of equal remuneration to men and women, abolition of bonded labour system, regulation and protection of child labour, regulation of contract labour and terms and conditions of employment of migrant labour. The second dimension of this strategy lies in the provision of reservation in public employment to be effected in proportion to the population of SCs and STs at the Centre and states/UTs. This reservation also extends to admission into institutions of higher learning.

The third dimension of the strategy covers a wide range of development measures. These include land reforms which seek to redistribute land to the landless and confer security of tenure on tenants to prevent their dispossession. In respect of Adivasis, land reforms also provide protection against alienation of their land to non-Tribals and recognition of their right of access to forest resources. The second component of development measures is a special financial arrangement for allocation of resources for accelerated development of Dalits and Adivasis called the SC Component Plan for Dalits and Tribal Sub-Plan for Adivasis. The two groups also have earmarked shares in coverage and accrual of benefits from various developmental schemes which have a beneficiary component. The welfare measures which focus on students of the two communities include provision of residential schools, scholarships, textbooks, and hostels. Two separate agencies have also been established for providing subsidized capital to entrepreneurs belonging to the two communities to set up their own self-employment ventures. There is also a coaching scheme which provides training to aspirants to compete for recruitment to various posts in the government. Besides specifically targeted development measures, the general development programmes though not exclusively focused on them are perceived to significantly contribute to the improvement in their economic conditions. These programmes relate to poverty alleviation, minimum needs and food insufficiency and malnutrion. The poverty alleviation programmes cover both wage employment and self-employment. Minimum Needs programmes includes access to drinking water, sanitation, housing, education and health facilities. The programmes to combat hunger and malnutrition consist of provision of subsidized food grains under PDS, the integrated child development scheme and mid-day meals for school children.

The fourth dimension of the strategy relates to participation. This is ensured through reservation of seats in legislative bodies and Panchayats and inclusion of usually some elected member/members from those groups in the Council of Ministers at the state and the Central level. There are Standing Committees one each for the two groups in the Parliament to deal with various issues concerning them. In respect of Adivasis, special dispensation has been provided for self-governance in the Scheduled Areas under the Panchayats (Extension to Scheduled Areas) Act 1996 to deal with matters relating to management of natural resources and development. The two groups are also usually represented in official committees for various programmes. They are also given some representation in the structure of political parties.

Status of Implementation: Protection

Security Against Violence

Has this grand strategy helped in eliminating or even significantly reducing the marginalization of these groups? Let us take the protective measures first. All protective measures suffer from poor implementation. The laws against discrimination against and violence on Dalits and Adivasis have failed to provide the desired deterrent. The implementation of Protection of Civil Rights Act (PCR Act) is so dismal that even the number of cases registered is showing a progressive decline due to the lack of interest of the enforcement agencies. There is a huge pendency in investigation of complaints, a negligible conviction rate and a large percentage of acquittal in cases caused by poor quality of investigation and prosecution. States have shown no interest in setting up special courts or in the appointment of prosecutors or even in constituting monitoring committees and in the identification of untouchability-prone areas. The discrimination against Dalits continues not only in social relations but also in public institutions. The enforcement of SC/ST (Prevention of Atrocities Act) suffers from not only apathy of the state governments but also hostility of some political parties. There are widespread complaints about non-registration of cases, shoddy investigation where cases are registered, and leaving deliberate loopholes in the investigation leading to the failure at the trial stage etc. The atrocities committed by the police and security officials are not even entertained. The disposal of cases is very low and the rate of conviction is even lower. The pendency of cases for investigation is very large and the investigation is marked by bias in the police machinery against the victims. Even in respect of payment of compensation and rehabilitation of victims of atrocities, the track record of state governments fails to inspire confidence in their sincerity (NHRC, 2004).

Liberation from Degrading Practices

As for the law against manual scavenging, there is virtually no implementation as evidenced from the absence of any information on cases registered and disposed of. Most states even deny the existence of manual scavenging in their areas. The programme of rehabilitation of liberated scavengers which has been in operation since 1980s has made little difference to the practice of manual scavenging notwithstanding the exclusive National Commission set up to look after the interests of Safai Karamcharis. The other members of the households continue to be engaged in this degrading practice even after one of their members is reported to have been rehabilitated. Recently, the law has been comprehensively revised to make it effective but is yet to show any results. The dismal impact of the rural sanitation programme is evident from the continued practice of open defecation the incidence of which in the country is the largest in the world. The practice of Devdasis/Joginis still continues due to a weak law full of loopholes and virtually no enforcement. There is no information of even one case having been registered against the practice, not to speak of any conviction. The rehabilitation of liberated Devdasis suffers from the lack of sincerity and interests, inadequate assistance provided to the victims and the failure to comprehensively address their problems (NHRC, 2004).

Exploitation of Labour

Within the ambit of the protective measures, labour laws have a great deal of significance for these groups as a large majority of their members are engaged as casual unorganized labour. The implementation of labour laws too has been very weak and is heavily tilted in favour of employers, be it in agriculture or industry. The vulnerability of labour increases manifold due to the lack of organization and lack of alternative livelihood options which forces them to accept any terms of employment for sheer survival. The victims of labour laws can be observed in the glaring instances of the widespread non-payment of Minimum Wages and Equal Remuneration to male and female labour (NCEUS, 2007). The enforcement of Bonded Labour Abolition Act faces a roadblock from unresponsive officials charged with its implementation who deny its existence despite its increasing incidence and fail to act even when social activists bring cases to their notice. This situation has not changed despite monitoring of the Act by the NHRC. The law relating to child labour suffers similarly from indifferent implementation despite its rampant violation which can be observed all around. Besides, the law suffers from structural flaws due to its untenable distinction between hazardous and non-hazardous occupations. The incidence of child labour has increased in the neo-liberal economy due to the growth-centric attitude of government which looks the other way at violation of labour laws. The brutality and violence inflicted on children by the employers shows no abatement notwithstanding the new law that has been enacted to protect children. In any case, child labour cannot be addressed unless the distress of the households which forces their children to the labour market is comprehensively addressed. The Right to Education and comprehensive Supreme Court directions on Child Labour have made no difference to the situation though occasionally raids are conducted to rescue child labour. But, in the absence of rehabilitation, the rescued children return to the labour market for survival. The Inter-State Migrant Labour Act is the least implemented of all labour laws despite the increasing incidence of migration of labour and the atrocities which are inflicted on this labour force by the employers. The migrant labour has no interlocutors as it faces indifference from the home state and unwillingness to enforce law from the host state. Worse, in the neo-liberal economy, governments at the Centre and the states are pronouncedly tilted in the favour of the employers. The enforcement of the labour laws therefore, receives no attention whatsoever. In fact, under the pressure of corporates, the labour laws are getting hugely diluted so as to give employers virtually a free hand.

Reservation: Jobs

The reservation in public sector employment has had a better record of enforcement than other measures of affirmative action. But even this positive assessment is qualified. Of the various categories of posts, the quotas in respect of Groups C and D posts only have by and large been filled up and that too in Group D more than in Group C; that is due to the large number of posts of Safai Karmcharis in that category. The quota in respect of Groups B and A continues to have many unfilled vacancies, and in Groups A more than Group B. Worse, there is virtually no enforcement of reservation in many establishments aided by government, the worst case being that of universities and institutions of science and technology. Outside the government funded establishments, it is higher caste monopoly in all spheres. The enforcement of reservation in states shows some variation with a few (in the South) performing better than others. The unfortunate aspect of this measure is that the candidates of the marginalized groups after availing of the reservation benefit face hostility and contempt of their higher caste colleagues and an unwelcome social and working environment. Besides, the courts and the government have been progressively diluting the ambit of reservation provisions. Far worse, the changes in political economy and governance measures resulting from it are snatching away even this limited opportunity of social mobility from these groups. Governance reforms have drastically reduced avenues of employment in government jobs while the private sector jobs are out of reach for these marginalized sections due to their poor quality of initial education, absence of skills and the lack of requisite cultural and financial capital. Besides, the candidates from marginalized sections face huge discrimination in recruitment and selection even where their qualifications are on par with higher caste candidates (Thorat and Newmen, 2007, Jodhka and Newman, 2007). The efforts of the government to extend some preferential treatment for candidates of these groups to the private sector employment have met with a total roadblock from the industry and business.

Reservation: Educational Institutions

The outcome in respect of reservation in higher education is far worse than reservation in jobs. The quota for them remains unfilled by large margins due to the insufficient number of eligible admission seekers and the manipulated admission process which circumvents the stipulation. Among those admitted, dropout rates are higher and completion rates are low due to the poor quality of school education and the lack of adequate support which Government has failed to address (Nayyar, 2011).

Development: Poverty Alleviation

In respect of the development dimension of the strategy, re-distribution of land through a package of land reforms was a major step towards empowerment of landless households. However, it failed to achieve its objective. In the abolition of intermediaries, Dalits and Adivasis who actually cultivated the lands owned by others failed to secure recognition of their status because they lacked any documentary proof to support their claims and therefore, were evicted from their land. Tenancy reforms too failed on similar grounds. The landowners strongly contested any attempt to record their tenancy status except in West Bengal where the ruling Marxist Government mobilized partly cadres to provide necessary support to neutralize resistance of landowners. Implementation of ceiling laws has yielded very little land for redistribution. Though a small percentage of Dalits and Adivasis did manage to get distributed land, but in many cases they failed to get possession over this land due to the resistance of local powerful landowners. In a number of cases, where they could obtain possession of land, they lacked resources to make it cultivable as the land was of poor quality. The benefits of schemes available to help such assignees of land failed to reach them. The governments at the Centre and the states have lacked the necessary political will to pursue land reforms. With the shift to a neo-liberal economy, there is no interest in this programme and the land reforms are getting hugely diluted. With regard to poverty alleviation measures such as self-employment and wage employment, there is little indication that they have led to improvement in the economic conditions of the marginalized groups on any significant scale. The wage employment programme suffered from indifferent implementation, inadequate allocation, poor targeting and the lack of comprehensive planning coverage and provision of employment round the year besides there being virtually no participation of the beneficiaries. As a result this programme has failed to alter existing relations of subordination and dependency of members of these groups on employees from higher castes even with the statutory guarantee of employment and enhanced allocations provided by MNREGS. Though relatively better implemented than earlier versions of the programme, it has failed to provide even the guaranteed hundred days of employment. The self-employment programme has fared far worse due to its flawed assumptions, lack of professional capacity to plan and implement, unwillingness of banks to provide adequate credit, poor quality of assets distributed, non-provision of supporting services etc. Its relative success in a tiny number of cases is confined to those who already had some land or traditional entrepreneurial skills. The implementation of programmes to combat hunger and malnutrition also have their negative features which have detracted from creating any significant positive impact on those who need them the most. The supply of subsidized food grains through the PDS has suffered from a large degree of exclusion of deserving Dalits and Adivasis from the BPL list which has been the pre-condition for eligibility of this benefit. The recently enacted National Food Security Act attempts to address this problem by a comprehensive survey of targeted beneficiaries and statutory entitlement. The Act is yet to be enforced by all states. But its implementation already faces inadequate financial allocation by the Central Government. As for nutritional programmes, ICDS has suffered from the lack of universal coverage for regular provision of foodgrains, poor quality of food, inadequate allocation, etc. MDM Programme faces similar problems not to speak of the discrimination children face from the service providers. As for provision of other minimum needs, the marginalized groups still face, in many places, huge discrimination in drawing water from state-financed drinking water sources, accessing health services by service providers, and in the treatment of teachers and fellow students in schools by higher castes. In respect of student welfare measures, the support structure for Dalits and Adivasis students in higher level education is quite inadequate. Ashram schools, hostels suffer perennially from poor infrastructure, indifferent services and bad management. The scholarship scheme is beset with inadequate coverage, allocation and amount of assistance. Access to health services to these groups also gets restricted due to non-availability of doctors and drugs in public health centres and lack of financial resources to avail of quality private health facilities.

Targeted Flow of Resources

The special financial arrangement in respect of these groups—SC Sub-Plan and Tribal Sub-Plan have also failed to accelerate the human development of these communities so as to bridge the wide gaps between them and the other communities. The enforcement of this special arrangement suffers from resistance of some ministries to earmark the desired resources, absence of a dedicated planning and implementation mechanism at the district level, non-utilization of available funds, their diversion and even misutilization and manipulation by a caste-biased bureaucracy to utilize funds in a manner that fails to specifically benefit these groups. There is little to show by way of outcome where expenditure has been incurred. Recently, the earnstwhile Andhra Pradesh Government enacted a law to provide a statutory basis to this financing arrangement for effective enforcement. It is to be seen whether this will lead to better outcomes. In the market economy, Dalits and Adivasis suffer greater exclusion as they are unable to participate in it due to the lack of capital and skills and discrimination encountered in the credit, labour and produce market. The market reinforces their marginalization.

Tribals: Victims of Development

While the above analysis of measures of affirmative action applies equally to Dalits and Adivasis, the marginalization of the latter has some additional features specific to them and therefore specific legal and administrative instruments are in place to arrest it. The most prominent of these instruments relate to the protection of their interest in land against its alienation by non-Tribals and recognition of forest rights enjoyed by them traditionally. In addition, Adivasis have also been provided with a modicum of self-governance though a relatively more empowering Panchayat law called PESA. The performance in respect of all the three measures is dismal. The enforcement of laws relating to the prevention of alienation of Tribal land fails to inspire confidence in Tribals that they will get justice from government agencies. This is because only a small number of land alienation cases are registered. Of the cases registered, nearly two-thirds get rejected on flimsy grounds. There are serious procedures and practice related anomalies in the disposal of cases. The land restoration courts and its procedures are weighted in favour of non-Tribals (MORD, 2004). Even in cases which are decided in favour of the Tribals, getting possession of land from the adversary is an agonizing process and Tribals often give up in despair after pursuing such cases for some time. Besides, in most such cases, the adversary goes to an appellate court and either gets the order stayed or negated. The incidence of alienation of Tribal land is increasing manifold as a result of fast pace of development, huge influx of immigrants and the increasing presence of corporates in the area and their need for land which unleash varied processes to dispossess the Tribals of their land. But the land alienation by government through compulsory acquisition far exceeds even the alienation by private individuals. The latter form of acquisition has been gaining in strength over the years and particularly so with the onset of the market economy. As a result, with more than 40% of total displacement and only 8% of population Tribals have a disproportionately high share of displacement. Three-fourths of the displaced Tribals have not received even elementary rehabilitation while the compensation they receive for their acquired land is too small due to legal restrictions on transfer of Tribal land to non-Tribals (MORD, 2004) (Fernandes, 2006). The Tribals therefore, are becoming landless at a very fast pace in comparison to other landed sections of the country.

The implementation of the recently enacted Forest Rights Act faces huge resistance and even subversion from the forest bureaucracy which is evident from the large scale rejection of the claims approved by Forest Rights Committees. In a limited number of cases, where claims have been accepted, only a miniscule portion of the claims has been conceded. There is a virtual refusal to entertain claims relating to community forest management. State governments by and large are quite apathetic to implementation of this Act as evident from the absence of any sustained campaign to make them aware due to which many Tribals have not been able to even file claims. Tribals continue to be evicted from their existing occupation of forest land in wildlife sanctuaries and national parks without even following the procedure laid down in the Act. The collection and disposal of minor forest produce has also not been transferred to the Panchayats (CSD, 2011). The enforcement of PESA, 1996 is the worst of the three instruments. States in general have been reluctant to implement it as it involves substantial decentralization of the power of decision making to the Gram Sabhas. The laws enacted by the states by way of implementation are not in tune with PESA and action taken has instead of empowering Gram Sabhas to exercise power has actually undermined it. (Bijoy et al, 2010)

Tribals have also been disempowered by the development process. This process does not merely reflect insensitive and poor implementation, but it also suffers from flawed conceptualization as it does not take into account the specificities and diversity of their situation which is totally different from the mainstream communities including Dalits. The development process has further eroded Tribals' control over natural resources management which started from the colonial period. Their communitarian living has been broken by the development process due to its approach of individual replacing the community as the unit of development which exposes them to the rapacious market forces, rent-seeking officials and intrusion of non-Tribals. This approach has been instrumental in impoverishing Tribals and marginalizing them. Further the aggressive cultural assimilation and mainstreaming of the Tribals has rendered Tribals powerless to assert their distinctive interests. The failure to use the constitutional provisions of the Fifth Schedule which confer special powers on the Governor to protect Tribal interests show total apathy towards their continuing marginalization. 'Overall, Adivasis have gained the least and lost the most from the six decades of democracy and development in India. The state has treated its Adivasi citizens with contempt and condescension' (Guha, 2007).

Participation

With regard to political participation, while reservation of seats in the Central and state legislatures and PR Institutions does ensure adequate representation in terms of population strength to these groups, this however, does not translate into power to influence policy decisions and their implementation even on matters which vitally concern these groups. Dalits' and Adivasis' elected representatives suffer from the lack of capacity, confidence and excessive control of the party to make any contribution in the debates or use the available space to raise critical issues of interest to them. They are also constrained from pursuing the cause of their fellow community members due to the mixed nature of the constituencies where, at least in the case of Dalits, they are not in majority and have to depend upon other constituents to get elected. Adivasis, more than Dalits have been unable to effectively articulate their grievances through the democratic electoral process (Guha, 2007). The lack of any genuine share in the exercise of political power is evident from the fact that there is negligible representation of these groups in the structure of political parties and distribution of portfolios where they are represented in the Council of Ministries. At the PRI levels, Dalits face overt discrimination in many places and indignities from higher caste members. In any case, both Dalits' and Adivasis' representatives elected to executive positions in Panchayates are manipulated by elected representatives from higher castes and officials to pursue their agenda.

With increasing awareness about the failure of the State to deliver on its promises and implement its own policies and programmes for them, the marginalized groups are increasingly asserting themselves in various ways peaceful as well as violent. Ordinarily, such assertions should be welcomed by the State as a wake-up call to address issues agitating them and to channelize it for creating space to enable their vigorous political participation in policy formulation and implementation. However, the State's attitude toward such assertion has been to curb the movements to maintain the existing social order which has resulted in the imposition of draconian laws, unaccountable use of force and violation of human rights and worsening of their conditions.

In view of the foregoing, it is difficult to resist the conclusion that the strategies adopted by the State have failed to neutralize the marginalized status of these groups except in respect of a tiny section of the elite. The marginal change in respect of untouchability practices is on account of assertion by Dalits even in the face of violence rather than through the efforts of the State (Mendelsohn and Vicziany 1996). The reasons are quite evident from the character of State that comes out in this paper.

Reasons for Failure

A genuine strategy to eliminate this marginalization required restructuring of the social, political and economic relations between the higher castes and Dalits on the one hand and between the state agencies, non-Tribals and Adivasis on the other. The State did not pursue this radical transformation. What emerged from the policy frame was at best mild reforms of the existing structure heavily loaded against these groups through gradual changes induced by legal entitlements and welfare programmes enforced by the bureaucracy. Quite apart from the inadequacy of the approach, the State lacked even the sincerity and determination to implement this strategy. The changed political economy has undone even the meagre benefits emerging from affirmative action policies. The marginalization of these groups, therefore, would continue to persist and in the case of the Adivasis particularly, it would increase. This is due to the imposition on them a paradigm of development, governance and nation building which has made them its victims rather than beneficiaries and has contributed to the disintegration of their social organization—their only strength in the face of adversity. It exposed them to along multifaceted forces of exploitation at a fast pace. They could not protect themselves against these onslaughts particularly in the absence of any State support.

Movements to Overcome Marginalization

Neither of the two social groups has acquiesced in their marginalized position. There have been movements against caste discrimination, economic exploitation and the unjust social order in the case of Dalits over a period of more than 100 years while the Adivasis have had a much longer history of struggles and revolts against deprivation of land and access to forest areas (Sinha, 2002). There is a fundamental difference in the nature of the two movements. While Dalits movements are directed against caste-based hierarchy and untouchability practices of Hindu social order, the Adivasi movements have directed their ire against the State for its policies which have contributed to their disempowerment. In both cases, the movements have been in response to the violence inflicted on them, by the upper castes and the State in the case of Dalits, and primarily the State in the case of Adivasis. Another aspect common to both communities is that they have to contend with the indifference if not hostility of the majority community. They also lack organization and the cultural resources to project their viewpoint through a disinterested media that is insensitive to their concerns. In the absence of effective and assertive leaders, they find it problematic if not impossible to negotiate better deals for themselves with the extant skewed power structure. Their conditions and the impact of policies and actions of the State adversely affecting them do not get truthfully reported or widely disseminated. The leaders representing them are easily manipulated by the State and dominant communities to serve their own immediate interests but there is little commitment in them to pursue even modest structural change to deliver social justice to them. Internally, the movements in respect of both communities have failed to evolve a coherent ideological basis and a consistent programme of social and economic transformation of the existing structure of inequalities (Omvedt, 2002). They have concentrated on modest concessions within the existing power structure (Nandu Ram, 2008). The struggling people in both the communities have failed to forge unity between them at the national level so as to present a united front against policies and actions of the State which hurt their interests except on the issue of job reservation. The recent period has witnessed militant struggles which, in the case of Dalits, more localized and focused on atrocities and discrimination, and in the case of Adivasis, particularly in Central India, against alienation and acquisition of their land, shrinking access to forest resources, degradation of environment and social exploitation. The militant struggles among the Northeast Tribes have, however, had a much longer history revolving around political autonomy and opposition to their incorporation in the Indian State. Between the two groups, the Dalits have displayed greater capacity and acumen in forging localized alliances with political parties for extracting some concessions and share in political power than the Adivasis. In one state (UP), Dalits have also succeeded not only in developing a strong political party of their own but also in winning the political mandate to capture political power on their own strength; the party itself has diversified its membership to accomplish this outcome but without much tangible gain for the vast majority of their members. Dalits are considered to have achieved some progress in asserting an independent cultural identity and in bringing about some changes in the traditional social relations with upper castes (Nandu Ram, 2008). There has been no comparable achievement in the case of Adivasis against aggressive cultural assimilation. Adivasis too have captured political power in Jharkhand and Chhattisgarh through forging alliances with non-

Adivasi parties but the arrangments, besides being unstable, have brought little tangible benefit to them or respite from exploitation and adverse policies of the government. Adivasis' movements despite the commonality of problems they face have failed to forge a strong united front to negotiate with the State even on such issues affecting dignified survival as the continued use of draconian laws and the un accountability of security forces for acts of violence and other human rights violations against them. Both Dalit and Adivasi movements suffer from fragmentation (Singh, 2002; Suresh, 1996) which constrain their capacity to either get concessions from the State or reduce upper caste dominance in the case of Dalits and non-Tribal dominance in the case of Adivasis. The legislators from both the communities have failed to influence political/public policy process to safeguard their interests (Suresh, 1996). Their performance in the legislature has lacked any meaningful contribution to influence the decision making process in their favour. This has been both due to the lack of skills and confidence as also their dependence on political parties for getting selected for contesting elections where party bosses exercise control over nomination of candidates. This contributes to their docile behavior and failure to assert against the decisions of the party. Besides, the electoral system also forces Dalits to subordinate their interests to those of the dominant communities as they do not constitute a majority in any constituency and pronounced pursuit of Dalit causes would alienate the non-Dalits in the area. This factor is much less important in the case of Adivasis who, in certain constituencies particularly in Central India, do constitute major groups and even a majority in some cases. But they are unable to utilise this strength to their advantage due to lack of unity. In this situation, both Dalit and Adivasi legislators ironically only look up to the State to protect their interests vis-à-vis the upper castes in the case of the Dalits and against the non-Tribals and the state agencies in the case of the Adivasis. This is most frustrating because the State from which they seek protection is the very agency responsible for their problems. But the Dalits and Adivasi legislators have even failed to unitedly exert pressure on the State to vigorously implement laws enacted for their benefit such as those relating to atrocities, forest, employment, food security protection of civil rights, and labour welfare, and even development programmes such as TSP and SCSP. Except, sometimes, for wresting a small concession like a ministership or a membership of a statutory body, there is little to show by way of effective networking practices among them for advocacy of a minimum programme of action to benefit the communities with the sole exception of the reservation issue. Even on reservation issue, they have failed to check its increasing dilution. They have even refrained from exerting pressure on their own political parties to implement the items in party manifestos concerning their interest after gaining political power. Admittedly, they are confronted with a political and social structure characterised by a highly skewed distribution of power which only gets reinforced with development, growth and modernization. The State therein would have little inclination to prioritize their concerns in policy making and even less in implementation where policies have been reluctantly conceded as a result of extensive political mobilization. This indifference is temporarily shaken when the State is confronted with militant movements (Suresh, 1996). But, here too, reliance is placed by the State on increasing use of force rather than dialogue and accommodation by way of change/reversal of policies which hurt them and vigorous implementation of programmes and laws introduced for their benefit. Even the development component of this predominantly security-centric approach to deal with such movements remains poorly implemented. The two groups are simply too powerless in the system to command attention. Democratic institutions have also failed to change this balance of power. The attempts of groups to change religion (Dalits in particular) have also not helped as their lower status follows them in the new order. The most fundamental question which confronts both Dalits and Adivasis is whether they have any trust left in the Constitution and democratic institutions to deliver what they are seeking. (Suresh, 1996) Any perceptive observer of the evolving conditions of the two communities in the Indian polity since independence would have little hesitation in giving a negative answer. The alienation of the larger masses of people in both the communities against the government and democratic institutions, far more pronounced in the case of Adivasis is too deep to provide any comfort or hope in this direction.

The papers in this volume reflect on some of the issues raised in this introduction.

REFERENCES

Bijoy, C.R., Gopalakrishnan, Shankar and Khanana, Shomona (2010): Rights of the Indigenous People Asia Indigenous Peoples fact (AIPP), Thailand 2010.

Chakrabarty, Achin (2011): 'How not to Interpret Change', *Economic and Political Weekly*, Vol. XLVI, No. 51, December 17, 2011.

Council for Social Development (2011): 'The Scheduled Tribes and Other Traditional Forest Dwellers (Recognition of Rights) Act, 2006: Status of implementation and Recommendations, New Delhi, 2011.

Cox, David Ray (2001): 'Marginalization and the Role of Social Development : The Significance of Globalization, The State and Social Movements', in Debal Singha Roy: *Social Development and the Empowerment of the Marginalized Groups: Perspective and Strategies*, Sage, New Delhi, 2001.

Fernandes, Walter (2006): 'Liberalization and Development Induced Displacement,' *Social Change*, Vol. 36, March.

Guha, Ramchandra (2007): 'Adivasis, Naxalites and Democracy' in *Economic and*

Political Weekly, August 11, 2007.

Institute of Applied Manpower Research (2011): *India: Human Development Report 2011; Towards Social Inclusion*, Planning Commission, New Delhi and Oxford, New Delhi, 2011.

Jodhka, Surinder and Newman, Katherine (2007): 'In the Name of Globalization: Meritocracy, Productivity and Hidden Language of Caste', *Economic and Political Weekly*, 42 (41).

Mehrotra, Santosh and Gandhi, Ankita (2012): 'India's Human Development in the 2005; Towards Social Inclusion', *Economic and Political Weekly*, Vol. XLVII, No. 14, April 7, 2012.

Mendelsohn, Oliver and Vicziany, Marika (1998): The Untouchables: 'Subordination, Poverty and the State in Modern India', Cambridge University Press, Delhi,, 1998.

Ministry of Rural Development (2004): Report of the Expert Group on Prevention of Alienation of Tribal Land and its Restoration, April, 2004.

Nandu Ram (2008): 'Dalit Movements in India: A Perspective from the Below' in Nandu Ram (ed): *Dalits in Contemporary India Vol. 1: Discrimination and Discontent*. Siddhant Publication, New Delhi 2008.

National Commission on Enterprises in the Unorganized Sector (2007): 'Report on Conditions of Work and Promotion of Livelihoods in the Unorganized Sector', New Delhi, August, 2007.

National Human Rights Commission (2004): 'Report on Prevention of Atrocities Against Scheduled Castes', New Delhi.

Nayyar, Deepak (2011): 'Discrimination and Justice: Beyond Affirmative Action', *Economic and Political Weekly*, Vol. XLVI, No. 42, October 15, 2011.

Omvedt, Gail (2002): 'Ambedkar and After: The Dalit Movement in India', in Ghanshyam Shah (ed): *Social Movements and the State*, Sage, New Delhi, 2002.

Oomen, M.A. (2012): 'Understanding Human Development' *Economic and Political Weekly*, Vol. XLVII, No. 7, February 18, 2012.

Radhakrishna, R and Ray, Shovan (eds.) (2005): *Oxford Handbook of Poverty in India: Perspectives, Policies, and Programmes*, Oxford, New Delhi.

Sengupta, Arjun, Kannan, K.P., Raveendran, G. (2008): 'India's Common People: Who are they, How Many they are and How do they live', *Economic and Political Weekly*, March, 2008.

Singh, K.S. (2002): 'Tribal Movements in Chhota Nagpur', in Ghanshyam Shah (ed): *Social Movements and the State*, Sage, New Delhi, 2002.

Sinha, Surajit (2002): 'Tribal Solidarity Movements in India: A Review' in Ghanshyam Shah (ed): *Social Movements and the State*, Sage, New Delhi, 2002.

Suresh, V. (1996): 'The Dalit Movement in India' in Sathyamurthy, T.V. (ed): *Region, Religion, Caste, Gender and Culture in Contemporary India*, Vol. 3, Oxford, Delhi, 1996.

Thorat, Sukhdeo and Newman, Katherine (2007): 'Caste and Economic Discrimination: Causes, Consequences and Remedies', *Economic and Political Weekly*, XLII, (41)

Thorat, Sukhdeo and Kumar, Narendra (eds.) (2008): *In search of an Inclusive Policy:*

Addressing Graded Inequality, Introduction, Rawat Publications, New Delhi, 2008.
Thorat, Sukhdeo (2009): *Dalits in India: Search for a Common Destiny*, Sage, New Delhi, 2009.

II. SUMMARIES OF THE PAPERS

Redistributive land reforms were poorly implemented in the country except in West Bengal and Kerala. This has deprived the Scheduled Castes, the largest group of landless rural poor in the country of the only avenue to access land for extricating themselves from a life of poverty, indignity and multifaceted exploitation by land owners. However, states have exercised the soft option of distributing Government and Bhoodan land to the rural landless poor to partly compensate for this failure. Andhra Pradesh and UP top the list of the states in the land distributed under the first category while Bihar, Orissa and UP were the prominent states in the second category. But these measures have had little impact on the improvement of landed assets of the SCs. Only a very small proportion of SC landowners, even with provision of irrigation, credit, and subsidized fertilizers could become self-employed cultivators due to the non-viable character of their marginal holdings.

D. Narasimha Reddy in his paper has brought out that earst while Andhra Pradesh had gone a step further to help the poor access land and put such land to productive use. It had undertaken proactive administrative initiatives for,

(a) Distribution of Government 'waste' and 'poramboke' land to the rural landless poor
(b) Convergence with existing laws and programmes which enable the rural poor to access land through purchase from the willing sellers
(c) Comprehensive projects for development of land owned by SCs/STs
(d) Development of land inventory, and
(e) Prioritizing land development work on the private land of the rural poor under MNREGS.

Priority was accorded to SC/ST lands under these programmes. Even with these creative interventions, the condition of SCs in terms of access to land continues to be precarious compared to that of the other groups of rural poor due to relatively high degree (80%) of incidence of landlessness. The average size of SC land holding household being very low (0.8 h), farming is not viable. The author, therefore, recommends that while continuing its initiative to distribute non-forest wasteland to SC households, the state should focus on provision of quality education and skill development to SCs to enable them to avail of non-farm employment opportunities for their upward economic and social mobility.

Discrimination and exclusions against Dalits and Adivasis are not confined to rural areas. They are widely practised in urban areas particularly in the institutions of higher learning and work places both in government and private. The hostility and discrimination against Dalit and Adivasi students in educational institutions where they are most marked are reservation-centric and get tacit support from faculty and establishment dominated by members of higher castes. It takes several forms—open campaigns against reservation, separate hostel rooms and seating arrangement in the classrooms and dining halls, derogatory comments against them, refusal to include them in the sports teams and cultural programmes, deliberate attempts by faculty to give lower assessment for their performance in the class and examinations, violations of reservation provisions in recruitment and promotion even after court orders. The administrative response to complaints made in this regard is characterized by the failure to take any meaningful action in such instances and to proceed against those found guilty of such practices in pursuance of recommendations of enquiry reports. Dalit and Adivasi students are also victims of violence resorted to by upper caste students when they resist such violence. **Vikas Bajpai and Anoop Saraya** in their paper have graphically brought out all these dimensions in their paper focused on All India Institute of Medical Services the most prestigious medical education centre in the country. The authors observe that the victims of these practices suffer unbearable stress leading to suicides in some cases, dropouts in some other cases and prolongation of their stay to complete their courses generally. They fail to get justice from any organ of power due to the dominance of higher castes at all levels. While institutions set up specifically to safeguard their interests are toothless to prevent recurrence of such practices or to punish those found guilty of them, even the Dalit faculty members choose to play safe to protect their careers by getting willingly co-opted by the establishment of the institution in their design to falsify such complaints. Political parties too are content with paying lip service to justice. The authors believe that resistance seems to be the only way to cope with the problem, but it comes at a huge cost to the victims. With no support from any quarter, mobilization of and resistance by victims in such situations is lessening while counter-mobilization by higher caste students is getting progressively more aggressive.

Kalpana Kannabiran in her paper brings out the crucial dimension of jurisprudence relating to untouchability and personal liberty. How the law deals with a deeply entrenched social practice is not only a challenge to the practice but to the law itself. The paper brings out very sharply the theoretical debates on liberty and untouchability. It covers Dr Ambedkar's approach and search for remedial action particularly in the realm of constitutional framework.

The practice that is so widespread, so multidimensional and so deep that the GOs issued against untouchability during the tenure of S.R. Sankaran and the comprehensive report of Justice Punnaiah in the State of Andhra Pradesh made no qualitative change. They bring out the undemocratic practices so strikingly by reminding us that the Indian society has remained far apart from the constitutional goals and the very essence of the Article 17 and the laws encoded in 1955 (Civil Rights Protection Act) and 1989 (SCs and STs Prevention of Atrocities Act).

The author characterizes S.R. Sankaran, as an insurgent civil servant who in a period of six to seven years did every thing that was possible to realize the letter and spirit of Article 17 by issuing 136 Government Orders (GOs). This was an exemplary act wherein the administrative law was used to effect social change. These GOs deal with a range of problems that the Dalits were confronting not only based on his experience and understanding but through an ingenious method of convening of conferences of SC's and ST's to take note of their demands. Kalpana observes, "That journey from the sociology of caste, through reservation to the practice of administrative law and judicial documentation of untouchability what S.R. Sankaran accomplished is an insurgent historiography of the present in all its complexity." She adds that the significance of S.R. Sankaran's GOs and Justice Punnaiah's report lies in the demonstration of the possibility of combating discrimination and curtailment of liberty through state action firmly committed to the constitutional morality.

P.S. Krishnan, in his paper on manual scavengers shares the anguish of S.R. Sankaran who fought the battle against this inhuman practice till his last breath. Krishnan produces a graphic account of the suffering and the neglect of this stigmatized section of society largely belonging to the scheduled caste community. The author himself confronted this problem in the very beginning of his service and did all that was possible, with reasonable success, for rehabilitation of members of this groups. This individual effort turned in 1980 into a vision for liberation and dignified rehabilitation of the scavengers. As a part of this initiative, various steps were taken to strike at the problem at multiple points. The enthusiasm of early 1980s gradually got diluted, if not faded out, by late 1980s and early 1990s and the measures became half-hearted and truncated and further hampered for lack of budgetary support

The paper further brings out the atrocities committed against the Balmikis in North India and exposes the duality and duplicity of the government policy. However, early in the twenty-first century there was some rethinking on the problem. Some hopeful signs were noticed particularly with the emergence of the voluntary organizations of Safai Karmacharis and activists among them during the preparation of the comprehensive Bill of 2011 on manual scavenging. There is a noticeable shift towards rights-based approach to their problems in policy making. While the Bill was comprehensive and had the potential to liberate this section from this most obnoxious practice, there was an attempt to drop certain provisions of the comprehensive Bill. (The Bill has since been possed by the Parliament and is now on the statue book). Thus the whole struggle to liberate scavengers from this abnoxious practice has had ups and downs and amply demonstrates that the commitment of the policy makers was never total to wipe out the very practice of scavenging against which S.R. Sankaran strived till the end of his life.

The institutionalized discrimination against SCs combined with the practice of untouchability is the most obnoxious feature of the Hindu social order. Though this practice in any form was abolished by the Constitution, its practice continued in public and private spaces in overt or subtle forms. The Protection of Civil Rights Act, 1955 was enacted to make it a punishable offence. But it did not curb the practice. The SCs and STs were also denied the benefits of other entilements guaranteed by law such as distribution of land, payment of minimum wages, etc. Resistane against these injustices was met with physical violence. A more stringent law, SCs and STs (Prevention of Atrocities) Act 1989 was therefore enacted. Even this Act has failed to curb acts of violence and practice of discrimination against these groups and incidence of violence has tended to increase. This was attributed to loopholes in the law, its poor implementation and the biases of the enforcement machinery. **S.D.J.M. Prasad**'s paper examines the weaknesses in the enforcement of SCs and STs (PoA), 1989 at various stages such as lodging of the complaint, registration of First Information Report (FIR), arrrest of the accused, investigations of cases, filing of chargesheet, during trial, and at the stage of judgment. He has also observed that there is resistance in official machinery even to payment of financial compensation to the victims of atroctities as per the legal provisions. SC and ST victims of atrocities face tremendous odds in seeking justice against acts of discrimination and violence. This prompted the Parliament to further strengthen the law by promulgating an ordinance, SCs and STs (Prevention of Atrocities) Amendment Ordinance 2014 which has now been formalized into a law in 2015. The author discusses the various amendments carried out in the Act amended recently. It remains to be seen whether this change would provide them the needed protection which has eluded them so far.

The hold of patriarchy in societal violence and discrimination against women is well documented. On the women of the vulnerable groups (Dalits for example) this violence is inflicied not only by the men and women of upper castes but also men of their own caste and family. What is less documented is the hold of patriarchy in development policies of the government though this is slowly changing at the macro-level. **Deepti Sukumar** unravels this dimension in her paper which specifically focuses on economic violence perpetrated on Dalit women by government in formulation of policies and implementation of programmes. This economic violence takes different forms such as denying them control of their resources and funds, not counting Dalit women as a separate unit demanding attention in their own right in the programmes, denial of access to opportunities by not addressing their difficulties and challenges, not giving them skills and knowledge; farcing them to engage in occupations or work that are undesirable, unclean and stigmatized, withholding of information that would enable access to opportunities for advancement; and not holding consultations with them while developing plans to utilize funds meant for SC welfare. Not only this, Dalit women face threats, humiliation and intimidation when they try to access credit or funds under different programmes; they are also deliberately excluded from delivery of entitlements specifically meant for them and have also to put up with allocation of inadequate resources to accomplish their tasks. Despite these heavy odds, Dalit women have refused to give up and have registered significant achievements, fighting these barriers. The author who is associated with the compaign for Dalit Women's Economic Equity calls for a sustained assault on this structural economic violence inflicted by officials through their paradigm of development, welfare and justice for Dalits.

Social and Economic oppression of Dalits sanctified by the caste-based social order and its ideological superstructure have produced varied forms of resistance the most visible forms of which are the Dalit movements and the relatively lesser known of which is the emergence of Dalit literature as a distinct category of literary works. Both have influenced each other. Dalit movements are autonomous struggles against hegemonic ideology which not only debarred Dalits from material possession but also stunted their mental development. The movements have been accompanied by Dalit literature which articulates a counter-hegemonic ideology to create an alternative socio-cultural identity. **K.Y. Ratnam** in his paper analyzes this symbiotic relationship between the two in the context of AP. The author traces the historical antecedents of Dalits literature in AP to the Buddhist culture embedded in anti-caste ideology and humanist principles and its later expressions through the works of Somnatha, Molla Vemana and Veerabramam and the influence exerted by Christian Literature Society and the works of Jyotiba Phule and Ambedkar. Early Telugu literature was dominated by writers of upper castes and did not reflect caste oppression and Dalit alienation. The later reformist literature of Appa Rao,

Suryanarain Rao, Laxminarayan, Ranga and Venketasharma did reflect the suffering of Dalits but did not convey the feelings of Dalit masses and their aspirations. The later mainstream Telegu literature also reflects protest against romanticism, idealism and individualism on the one hand and global economic depression and fascism on the other. The post-independence Telugu literature has produced a critique of agrarian system which drives the poor to destitution. But the most powerful literacy movement is Viplava Sahityam which emerged from the Naxalbari and Srikakulam movements with Marxist leanings and focused on the working poor. Yet these facets of literature failed to incorporate Dalit and feminist issues. This vacuum was filled by Dalit literature created by Dalit organic intellectuals who came from the most exploited caste and class. They developed their own historical symbols and literary concepts which focused on creating consciousness among Dalits for exhorting them to organize as agents of a new democratic revolution through their literacy and artistic creations. This literature has evolved from the works of Jashuva, Dharmamna, Chinavenkati and Abraham, etc. exposing caste oppression and has been profoundly influenced by Dalit Panther movement of Maharashtra. Present day Dalit literature is a compulsive outburst of anger, misery, resentment, injustice and displacement of Dalits, reflected in the works of Tarakamin, Gadar, Anjiah, Shambhuka etc. It represents a struggle for annihilation of caste and creation of ground for emancipation and discards pessimism, cynicism and fatalism for profound socio-politico and cultural assertion. Its most radical and revolutionary form emerged after the Karamchedu episode representing progressive evolution from the earlier literature of passive supplication. Dalit literature thus continues to evolve with great potential for its emancipatory and humanizing content, influencing Dalit movement and getting influenced by it.

The shift to a neo-liberal globalized economy post-1990, witnessed a spurt in many sectoral activities. One such activity was aquaculture development called the 'blue revolution' in the coastal areas of India responding to growing international demand and the price it fetched in the international market. This was also aided by the stagnant catch in traditional aquaculture farming and promotional activities of the Government—Central and state. The acquaculture development was primarily oriented to shrimp farming with India accounting for a sizable share in the total world shrimp production. While aquaculture was traditionally practised as a small scale activity in combination with paddy cultivation, the change in political economy brought in corporate players into the field. The land reforms laws were relaxed to incentivize them particularly in AP and Karnataka. Traditional paddy lands were converted into shrimp farms. This resulted in extensive environmental degradation comprising salinity ingress to paddyfields and drinking water sources, loss of livelihood to fisherfolk, destruction of neighbouring mangroves, pollution of seawater affecting marine organisms, depleting marine fish stock and displacement of fishing communities. **K. Gopal Iyer** has analyzed these adverse impacts and resultant social protests by affected farmers, fisherfolk and environmentalists which brought in Supreme Court's intervention barring shrimp farming in certain categories of land in coastal zones. But the author has brought out that shrimp farming in violation of Court orders has continued both in AP and Tamilnadu which has also been observed by the House Committee of AP. He has made specific recommendations to protect the interests of affected farmers, fisherfolk and the rural poor including reversal of relaxations in Land Reforms Laws.

Indian Society is characterized by wide ranging social and economic disparities which have been measured by academics, using both quantifiable and non-quantifiable indicators. **K.B. Saxena** in his paper has dealt with these disparities between Advivasis and the rest of the society to highlight their social exclusion. He has brought out that the Adivasis are at the bottom of the social pyramid in terms of quantifiable indicators, such as access to productive resources, public goods and level of employment. The non-quantifiable disparities have been analyzed with reference to the cultural differences between Adivasis and non-Adivasis which are described as 'divergent cultural perspectives'. These disparities have had an adverse impact on participation of Adivasis in economic and political activities and has led to a skewed distribution of power. It is not mainstream society alone which excludes them; the State also marginalizes them which manifests in governance characterized by laws adverse to them, unresponsive institutions and imposition of policy choices unfavourable to them.

The author argues that while the disparities can be traced to the changes in society and economy introduced during the colonial period, the post-colonial state has aggravated them through its paradigms of economy, development, conservation and modernization. Government does recognize the disparities and has sought to neutralize them by affirmative measures. These efforts have however failed to bridge the disparities due to huge gaps in implementation which are entirely due to the manner in which the ideology of State and its governance have violated the affirmative policy architecture. The author identifies key challenges for bridging these disparities which would involve certain structural changes but concludes that there is little likelihood of the State at this stage opting for such transformative alternatives.

India has treated its Tribal population very shabbily, subjecting them to displacement, dispossession from their life-supporting assets and discrimination despite constitutional and legal protection available to them. Worse, every attempt to render a modicum of justice through new legal and policy measures has been strongly resisted by those who have been getting Tribal lands very cheap for their mining and industrial projects as the recent amendments to Mines and Minerals (Regulation and Development) Act, have brought out. Tribals have been fighting to protect their assets from alienation and their way of life since the colonial period which has currently taken the form of Naxalism. **T.L. Sankar** in his paper interprets this situation of conflict as a 'clash of cultures' as evident in the paradigm of development pursued by the Indian State and the one sought by the Tribals. The two development paths cannot be reconciled. He therefore suggests by way of a solution that the Tribals should be permitted to follow in the Scheduled area their alternative development paradigm of survival and slow growth built in environmentally benign forest surroundings without disturbing ecological balance and in line with their traditions and values while the rest of society can continue to practise growth based on typical technology-big business capital accumulation measured in GDP and share market indices outside the Schedule area.

The Scheduled area could be divided into convenient regions of appropriate size and handed over to the people residing therein. All police, military and forest officials should be removed from this area. The land and its resources both over and underground should be entrusted to a regional committee, a kind of people's government to manage their development for a period of 25 years. They could be given whatever assistance sought by them in this pursuit. The arrangement could be evaluated in terms of the relative prosperity and happiness achieved as compared to non-Tribal areas.

Land and forest are central to the Tribal existence and protection of their land rights constitutes the core concern of the constitutional dispensation and legal entitlements. **B.K. Sinha**, in his paper, elaborately refers to various provisions in the laws enacted to prevent alienation of Tribal land to non-Tribals and restoration of land to the Tribals where it has been alienated in Jharkhand State. To these safeguards have been added their rights in forest areas in a recently enacted law which include those concerning occupation of forest land, collection and disposal of Minor Forest Produce and management of forest eco-system. Yet another law, Panchayats (Extension to Scheduled Areas) Act 1996 (PESA) has empowered the Gram Sabha of the village to restore encroached/alienated Tribal land and exercise a modicum of self-governance in development matters. However, non-implementation or tardy enforcement of these beneficial measures has defeated the objective behind them which has endangered the entire Tribal way of life. This mismatch between policy and implementation has led to what the author terms as 'policy incoherence'. This dismal performance is due to several reasons which include lack of knowledge and appreciation of Tribal social system and legal measures in the implementing bureaucracy, incompetence of revenue officials as also their collusion with land alienating agencies, lack of legal literacy among the Tribals, and insensitivity and disinterestedness to enforce legal provisions at all levels in the government. The author considers this state of governance as characteristic of a soft state and advises the government to erase this impression by getting down to implementation of its policies.

In a passionately written paper on 'Wages of Sin: Tribals and Excise Policy' **B.D. Sharma** highlights the ups and downs of excise policy from the days of freedom movement to the present times. The excise policy that was introduced during the colonial period itself was not without controversy. From the very beginning there was opposition to the policy and this was very forcefully expressed by Gandhi who went on record. "If I were to become a dictator for a single day prohibition will be my first decision." This sentiment got incorporated in the Directive Principles of Indian Constitution. Notwithstanding the spirit and letter of the Constitution, the prohibition policy has remained ambiguous and policy makers have been shaky on this issue.

In post-independent India, there were a few attempts to introduce prohibition but a major initiative came from Mrs Gandhi in 1975 when she imposed Emergency. Banning commercial vending of intoxicants in the Tribal areas and conceding community's control on all excise matters were fully accepted. The policy was effective for a while but soon got diluted. Above all, drinking became rampant both in Tribal and non-Tribal areas. The situation did not improve even after the enactment of PESA in 1996 which specifically envisaged control by Gram Sabha in all matters concerning preparation, storage and consumption of intoxicants.

In fact, the paper maintains, that elimination of exploitation of Tribals causesd by commercial vending of liqiour has been put in reverse gear from 1980s. By 1985, the very existence of excise policy for Tribal areas was almost forgotten. However, the promising aspect of the Tribal scene is that the community is still in a position to take a lead in the matter and there have been a number of spontaneous movements to wean away the people from drinking with commendable success in some cases. Notwithstanding this resistance, the national divide has been widening in the wake of adoption of the neo-liberal model of growth. The vested interests have always managed to contain popular resistance and continue their exploitation of the poor people through encouragement of drinking with the active connivance of the State.

There is rise of a mafia in the Tribal areas which has pushed the interests of the capitalist forces through expansion of liqour trade and continuing with the treacherous squeeze of the poor Tribals. The paper pleads that protecting Tribals from pernicious vending of intoxicants is the need of the hour and this can be accomplished only with the active involvement of the Tribal communities.

Can development intervention to propel a subsistence economy in a self-sustaining system of capitalist growth regulate its disruptive ethos and produce a consensual mode of accumulation? Kalyan Sanyal, a political theorist of contemporary development in India, answers this question in the affirmative and argues that the two apparently contradictory processes have emerged as a new feature of self-sustaining capitalist development, which has devised development as an aid to accumulation rather than an obstruction. **G. Vijay's** paper examines the validity of this theory by an empirical study covering five villages inhabited predominantly by chenchus, a socially and economically excluded primitive Tribe still in the course of transition from the hunting and food gathering stage to agriculture and wage labour, to investigate implementation of some important social development programmes and their impact on the household economy. He comes to the conclusion that such measures of rehabilitation of subsistence economy alongside an expanding accumulative economy far from producing consent to accumulation generate conflicts due to the semi-feudal roots of governance machinery implementing them. He adduces evidence to show that the processes of accumulation and rehabilitation of subsistence economy tend to be mutually exclusive. This is because implementing agencies have been captured by the accumulative interests. Only violent conflicts of the dispossessed and exploited people have produced some regulation of accumulation process. But this cannot be termed as legitimation of accumulation. The inter-face between the mode of accumulation and the mode of subsistence neither promotes co-existence nor sustainability of the latter. Rather, it creates a situation where state actively promotes primitive accumulation. This is because development is subverted by reliance of the state on the very same machinery to deliver development which is engaged in facilitating accumulation. The limited objective such development measures serve is to co-opt social elites to reinforce primitive accumulation and the power of state to exterminate any resistance to it. Accumulation rather than welfare seems to emerge as the outcome of welfare interventions in such socially excluded areas.

As brought out by reports prepared by civil society groups, security operations in the Maoist affected areas have inflicted huge human rights violations which remain officially unacknowledged let alone punished. Referring to the findings of one such report prepared by Independent People's Tribunal on Operation Green Hunt, **Joseph Marianus Kujur** locates the Adivasi militancy in Central Indian Tribal belt in the long history of deprivation of Tribals of their land by non-Tribals and the state and repression unleashed on the Adivasis when they protest against it. He constructs the Adivasi perspective on the current movement from their experience of development and governance in Tribal areas. This is attempted by analyzing the Adivasi concept of land and the history of resistance against its alienation, and their socioeconomic exploitation. The current phase of resistance is attributed to massive grabbing of their land by the state through acquisition, displacement without rehabilitation, depletion of forests, and failure to implement protective laws. What is happening today in militancy-affected areas is the continuation of structural and systemic violence unleashed against the Tribals since colonial times denying them their basic right to live with dignity. State has launched massive military operations with draconian laws to curb their protest. Democracy has failed to address their plight, respect their citizenship rights and give them a modicum of genuine participation in decision making. The author looks at the militant movement as a desperate attempt, inspired by the historical past, at assertion of their collective identity for equal citizenship, genuine democracy, participation in political power, recognition of their cultural diversity and a responsive and holistic development which empowers them and enables them to have their self-rule to determine their future in line with their vision and values.

Contemporary India has witnessed the rising trend of Adivasi assertion in defence of not only their right to land, forest and livelihood but also the right to dignity and cultural autonomy. Indian governance paradigm has failed to see the positive content in this awakening and castigated it as an anti-development sentiment and a law and order problem. This awakening also challenges civil society's patronizing attitude towards Adivasis advocating empathy for their suffering and more comprehensive welfare measures while lauding the uniqueness of their culture. **Manoranjan Mohanty** has analyzed this awakening as the outcome of many historical processes beginning with violent movements against colonization of their areas, alienation of their land, imposition of an unfamiliar governance system and, currently, culminating in the resistance against corporate plunder of their natural resources and capitalist globalization. But this latest phase of Adivasi awakening cannot be ascribed to the mobilization by Naxalites alone. Rather, this awakening signals the emergence of a new political order which has the potential of transforming the democratic politics in India and the thinking of civil society and academia. He characterizes this awakening as Adivasi Swaraj which can be summed up in the Right to Earth— i.e, right of all local inhabitants of the area to exercise control over and manage their natural and cultural resources and share them with others on terms mutually settled and to chalkout their own path of development and transformation in conformity with their socio-political goals, environmental philosophy and local culture and in a manner that does not perpetuate existing hierarchies and inequalities. Adivasi Swaraj is not confined to economic goals but extends to preserving their culture—assertion of religious identity, knowledge system and perspective on relationship of humans with nature. Maoist movement has expanded its ideological scope to accommodate some of these issues.

The specificities of the merger of Northeastern States with Indian Union after Independence gave rise to tremendous resistance from local groups opposed to it. The Indian State's response was to push in Armed Forces to suppress such resistance. These forces were given extraordinary powers of detention of suspects, the right to use violence against them if necessary and immunity against any legal challenge to their actions under special laws. This paradigm of security operations has been in existence continuously ever since it was imposed. This has led to several human rights violations: fake encounters, as also instance of enforced disappearance, arbitrary executions, torture, rape, housebreak, loot, and indiscriminate detention against which the affected persons have no relief. There has been a clamour for the repeal of the extraordinary laws investing armed forces with such unaccountable powers. Manipur most pronouncedly fits into this description. There have been commissions of enquiry, official and non-official, which have confirmed these human rights violations. The Jeevan Reddy Commission constituted by the Government of India recommended the repeal of the most draconian of all special laws—AFSPA which is a harsher version of a similar law enacted by the colonial government. But no action has been taken by the Government—Central or State to either repeal such laws or even significantly modify their crucial provisions or punish the members of security forces accused of these excesses not even after numerous protests by civil society organizations and a continuing fast by Irom Sharmila since the past many years. **K.S. Subramanian** in his paper has brought out the tragic consequences of this situation in his paper and how unaccountability for actions has corrupted security forces whose members have even resorted to extortion like the alleged militants they are fighting against. This has also failed to curb the resistance groups of armed militants who perpetrate their own violence. The fallout of sanction accorded to this State violence is that even the security forces which are not covered by such special laws also behave in a similar manner and remain unaccountable for their human rights violations. Central Government and the State Government are unmoved by reports of enquiry commissions and directions by Courts and justify the existing arrangements on grounds of continuing militancy in the State. As the least minimum first step, the author recommends that Assam Rifles, the oldest paramilitary organization and the most notorious in respect of its operations should be removed from internal security function and should be deployed for border duties only along with BSF. Its internal security function should be transferred to the State Police Forces.

Land is central to the existence of Tribals, their social system and subsistence economy. The process of alienation of Tribal land started in the colonial period which triggered protest movements. While these movements were suppressed, protective laws to prevent land alienation were enacted. But land alienation continues unabated notwithstanding these laws. The deprivation of land is a major factor contributing to the growth of left wing extremism. Focusing on the situation in AP, **K. Raju** in his paper observes that land deprivation has two dimensions— one is the lack of access to land and the other is the lack of secure titles or possession where access to it exists. Reviewing the implementation of various protective enactments and land distributing arrangements, he points out that land ownership eludes the Tribals. Land alienation takes place by circumvention of the legal provisions, encroachment, fraudulent practices, etc. due to slackness in implementation. Citing the report of Kongeru Ranga Rao Committee which went into the issue and made forty-one radical recommendations for addressing the issue of which thirty-five were accepted by the AP Government, he sadly observes that situation has not changed in any significant manner. Not all the cases of land alienation are registered. Of those registered, a larger number of cases were decided against Tribals and even those decided in favour of Tribals have not resulted in restoration of land to them due to the resistance of the adversary elements and the reluctance of officials to enforce the courts' orders. In this bleak situation, the Indira Kranthi Pratham (IKP) programme which makes available support of paralegals to the Tribals in getting back their land provides some hope. The author recommends strengthening the supply and demand mechanism as a route to stem the increasing alienation of land— strong implementation machinery on the supply side and empowering the Tribals to defend their rights through creation of awareness and ability to pursue their cases with the help of IKP and civil society organization on the demand side.

In this volume, Adivasis, Tribals and Scheduled Tribes are being used interchangeably depending upon the context. Similarly, Dalits and Scheduled Castes are being used interchangeably.

PART 1

Dalits: The Question of Marginalization and Discrimination

1

Rural Poor and Access to Land: The Case of Scheduled Castes in Andhra Pradesh

D. Narasimha Reddy

Introduction

In a rural economy dependant on agriculture and a rural society steeped in a stratified hierarchical caste system, access to land is not only a basis for livelihood, but also for a life with self-respect, security, dignity, and a better social status. It is also essential for an ability to assert one's freedom from domination as much as protest against inferiorization. Extreme poverty and exploitation in rural India are rooted in landlessness. Communities like Scheduled Castes (SCs) in rural areas have the highest incidence of landlessness and dependence on agricultural labour, which are sure signs of poverty and social deprivation. The degree of landlessness of the SCs is a quintessential characteristic of their social and economic deprivation in a rural society where land is the defining aspect of hierarchy of status. Not only is landlessness at the centre of rural poverty, but ownership and control of land is also the basis of agrarian hierarchy (Nancharaiah 1988). For Scheduled Castes, ownership of land denotes enhanced social status, self-respect, self-confidence, and a sense of equality as well (Sankaran 2000). The existence of a high degree of inequality in access to land with a large majority of those working on land suffering landlessness was the context in which progressive redistributive land reforms were conceived as an essential step towards equity. A series of legislative measures were undertaken across all the states in the country. There is a general agreement that, while most of the legislative enactments have been progressive, the implementation of these measures, with the exception of West Bengal, Kerala, and Jammu and Kashmir, were far from effective, and hence, there is a general discontentment about the success of these enactments in ensuring access to land to the landless. In this largely dismal scenario of performance of land reform legislative measures, there are instances of findings ways to provide land to the poor, particularly SCs, through administrative interventions within the constitutionally valid administrative law.

Table 1: State-wise Distribution of Ceiling Surplus Land as on 31 March 2005

(in acres)

Sl. No.	*State*	*Total Area Distributed (Acres)*	*Total Number of Beneficiaries*	*Scheduled Castes*				
				Number of Beneficiaries	*% of (5) in Col. (4)*	*Area Distributed Acres*	*% of (7) in Col. (3)*	*Average Area per Beneficiary Acres*
(1)	(2)	(3)	(4)	(5)	(6)	(7)	(8)	(9)
1	Andhra Pradesh	582188	525663	224205	42.65	226683	38.94	1.01
2	Assam	545875	445862	43723	9.81	86069	15.77	1.97
3	Bihar	306964	379528	234861	61.88	182045	59.30	0.78
4	Gujarat	146578	33312	15079	0.73	85176	58.11	5.65
5	Haryana	102388	29346	12684	45.27	44201	43.17	3.48
6	Himachal Pradesh	6167	6259	3912	62.50	2727	44.22	0.70
7	Jammu & Kashmir	450000	450000	NA	NA	NA	NA	NA
8	Karnataka	123412	33727	20356	60.36	74149	60.08	3.64
9	Kerala	68745	166814	70853	42.47	26619	38.72	0.38
10	Madhya Pradesh	186942	74705	21904	29.32	49542	26.50	2.26
11	Maharashtra	613965	135301	40707	30.09	157826	25.71	3.88
12	Manipur	1682	1258	96	7.63	128	7.61	1.33
13	Orissa	158030	141155	48382	34.28	50150	31.73	1.04
14	Punjab	104257	28582	11352	39.72	44248	42.44	3.90
15	Rajasthan	463547	82441	29932	36.61	144827	31.24	4.84
16	Tamil Nadu	183670	145608	64732	44.46	69246	37.70	1.07
17	Tripura	1598	1424	256	17.98	217	13.58	0.85
18	Uttar Pradesh	260509	300163	205104	68.33	183495	70.44	0.89
19	West Bengal	1088445	2759791	1019658	36.95	373881	34.35	0.37
20	Pondicherry	1070	1464	858	58.61	640	59.81	0.75
Total		5403277	5742403	2069179	36.03	1802199	33.35	0.87

Source: GOI (2006), p. 239.

The basic objective of this paper is to draw attention to instances where committed administrative initiatives could make significant difference in enabling the poor to access and improve their land resources. Here, the specific reference is to some of the initiatives in Andhra Pradesh, which has a tradition of creative or insurgent intervention inspired by civil servants like S.R. Sankaran, in using the power of administrative law to effect improvements in the condition of the poor, including improved access to land (Kalpana, 2012: 217–230). This paper aims at briefly documenting some of the administrative initiatives relating to access of land to the poor, especially SCs in Andhra Pradesh. The paper is divided into four sections. The introduction is followed by the second section, which briefly presents an overview of the results of the redistributive land reform measures with particular reference to the Scheduled Castes and their access to land in India. The third section deals with certain administrative initiatives relating to land access to the rural poor, particularly Scheduled Castes in Andhra Pradesh. The last section reflects up on the continued disadvantaged position of Scheduled Castes in relation to land, the changing occupational and employment structure in the country as a whole and that of Scheduled Castes, and the appropriate initiatives needed to ensure them transition to more productive livelihoods.

I
SCHEDULED CASTES AND DISTRIBUTIVE LAND REFORMS

The major land reform measures in post-independent India include abolition of zamindari or intermediaries, tenancy regulation, fixation of ceilings on ownership holdings, and consolidation of holdings. Of these, the direct redistributive reform relates to fixation of ceilings on ownership holdings, acquisition of surplus land, and distribution of ceiling surplus land to the rural land poor. Along with ceiling surplus land, land was also acquired as 'voluntary gift' under the Bhoodan Movement. In most of the states, certain types of government land were also earmarked for distribution among the landless or land poor. Ceiling surplus land, Bhoodan land and government land together are the main sources of redistribution of land. Table 1 provides state-wise details relating to the distribution of ceiling surplus land among rural poor with particular reference to Scheduled Castes.

Of the total of 54.03 lakh hectares of ceiling surplus land distributed in different States up to 31 March 2003, about one-third of the land was distributed among Scheduled Castes and of the 57.42 lakh beneficiaries, SCs constituted about 36 per cent. The average area of land per Scheduled Caste beneficiary was about 0.87 acres. Though the average area of land per SC beneficiary was only about 0.37 acres, West Bengal, with 10.9 lakh acres of distributed area and 27.6 lakh beneficiaries, was on the top of the ceiling surplus land acquired and distributed. Though much was expected from the ceiling legislation, for the country as a whole the total surplus land distributed was hardly 2 per cent of the total cultivated area of the country.

In contrast the extent of government land distributed among the rural poor households was much higher than the ceiling surplus land. Table 2 shows that by 31 March 2005, an area of 147.47 lakh acres of land was distributed among the rural poor. The government land distributed was almost three times more than the ceiling surplus land and accounted for about 6 per cent of the total cultivated area in the country.

Andhra Pradesh with 42.02 lakh acres (28.49 per cent) was on the top of the league, followed by Uttar Pradesh with 24.89 lakh aceras (28.49 per cent) Gujarat with 13.81 lakh acres (9.36 per cent), Karnataka with 13.72 lakh acres (9.30 per cent), Bihar with 13.21 lakh acres (8.96 per cent) and Maharashtra with 10.23 lakh acres (6.94 per cent). In parts of the country, Bhoodan land also was considerable in providing land to the poor. Table 2 shows that an area of 21.75 lakh acres of Bhoodan land was distributed so far. What is interesting is that almost 80 per cent of Bhoodan land was distributed in the three relatively poorer States namely, Bihar, Orissa and Uttar Pradesh.

The national data on government land assigned to the rural poor doesn't give social group-wise distribution of the land, and, therefore, we do not get any idea about the extent of government land allotted and the number of beneficiaries belonging to the Scheduled Castes. There is very little information at the national level on the extent to which the redistributed land is actually in the possession of the beneficiaries, and how much is put to productive use.

Distribution of land to the Scheduled Castes and other poorer households is only a first step towards their improvement. Often the land distributed is of marginal quality which needs land development to make it productive. If the distributed land should make a difference to the poor SC households, the related issues are: (i) whether the allotted land received supportive investment assistance to make it productive, (ii) whether the assigned households were able to retain the land, and (iii) whether the households were able to experience a shift in their employment status towards self-employed cultivators. Over the years, there has been a marginal increase in the SCs in the number of operational holdings and the area operated. Table 3 shows that the proportion of SCs in the total number of holdings increased from 11.30 per cent in 1980–81 to 12 to 13 per cent in the later period up to 2010–11. And during the same period the share of SCs in area operated also increased marginally from seven per cent to 8.60 per cent. The cause for concern, however, is that the increase in the number of holdings as well as the area is largely in the marginal holdings.

While the marginalization process is all pervasive in the landholding structure of the country, it may not be an exaggeration to say that while most

Table 2: State-wise Distribution of Government Wastelands and Bhoodan Lands as on 31 March 2005

(Area in lakh acres)

Sl.No.	*Name of State /UT*	*Waste Lands*		*Bhoodan Lands*	
		Area Distributed	*States Share%*	*Area Distributed*	*States Share%*
(1)	(2)	(3)	(4)	(5)	(6)
1	Andhra Pradesh	42.02	28.49	1.10	5.06
2	Assam	5.89	3.99	0.01	Neg
3	Bihar*	13.21	8.96	7.23	33.24
4	Gujarat	13.81	9.36	0.27	1.24
5	Haryana	0.00	0.00	0.02	Neg
6	Himachal Pradesh	0.17	0.12	Neg	Neg
7	Karnataka	13.72	9.30	0.05	0.23
8	Kerala	4.57	3.09	0.02	Neg
9	Madhya Pradesh #	0.79	0.54	1.41	6.48
10	Maharashtra	10.23	6.94	0.27	1.24
11	Manipur	0.32	0.22	-	-
12	Punjab	1.10	0.75	0.01	Neg
13	Orissa	7.26	4.92	5.80	24.28
14	Tamil Nadu	2.07	1.40	0.21	0.96
15	Tripura	1.32	0.90	-	-
16	Uttar Pradesh @	24.89	16.88	4.21	19.36
17	West Bengal	4.32	2.93	Neg	Neg
18	Goa	0.05	Negl	-	-
19	Mizoram	0.74	0.50	-	-
20	Rajasthan	0.93	0.63	1.14	5.24
21	Delhi	0.06	0.04	-	-
	Total	147.47	100.00	21.75	100.00

* including Jharkhand # including Chhattisgarh @ including Uttaranchal
Source: *GOI (2006)*, pp. 240–1.

of the SC holdings are marginal in nature, most of the holdings of others are non-marginal in size. This asymmetry between the SC landholdings and land holdings of others should be the basis for any policy towards distributive land reforms and land development. Table 4 shows that the changes in the size distribution of SC holdings is more towards marginal holdings. Of the total SC holdings, the share of marginal holdings increased from 68.9 per cent in 1980–81 to 73.8 per cent in 1995–96 to 77.5 per cent by 2010–11, and during the same period the share of marginal holdings in the area operated also increased considerably from 21.8 per cent in 1980–81 to 28.6 per cent in 1995-96 to 35.5 per cent in 2010–11. True, a similar trend is observed in the

Table 3: Changes in the Share of SCs in Operational Holdings in India 1980-81 to 2010-11

(Number: '000 Area: '000 ha)

Census Year	*Total Holdings*			*Holdings of SCs*		
Number	*Area*	*Number*	*% share in Total*	*Area*	*% in Total*	
(1)	*(2)*	*(3)*	*(4)*	*(5)*	*(6)*	*(7)*
1980-81	88,883	163,797	10,052	11.30	11,522	7.00
1995-96	115,580	163,355	14,689	12.71	13,407	8.21
2005-06	129222	158323	16073	12.44	13300	8.40
2010-11	137757	159180	17087	12.40	13695	8.60

Source: *GOI, Agricultural Census 1980-81, 1995-96 and 2010-11.*

case of 'others' as well, but it is at a much lower level from about 12 per cent to 17 per cent to 21.5 per cent in the same period. But the vulnerability of the SC marginal farms without appropriate support for land development and productive investment is likely to be much more than that of others. Together, the share of small-marginal holdings in the area operated by SCs increased from 42 per cent in 1980–81 to 60.7 per cent in 2010–11 and in the case of 'others', the increase was from about 26 per cent to 43 per cent.

As mentioned earlier, assignment of land to SCs is only one part of improving their asset base. The equally important aspect is to improve these assigned lands which are most often sub-marginal in quality, requiring considerable investment to make them productive. There were certain development programmes which had a component for the development of the lands of the poor. Of the various programmes of self-employment and wage-employment for the rural poor, some are aimed at land and irrigation

Table 4: Size Distribution of Operational Holdings among Scheduled Castes and 'Others' in India : 1980–81 to 2012–11

Size Class	*Scheduled Caste*						*Others*					
	1980-81		*1995-96*		*2010-11*		*1980-81*		*1995-96*		*2010-11*	
	H	*A*	*H*	*A*	*H*	*A*	*H*	*A*	*H*	*A*	*H*	*A*
Marginal	68.9	21.8	73.8	28.6	77.5	35.5	56.2	11.7	61.2	16.7	66.8	21.5
Small	16.4	20.2	15.5	23.7	14.4	25.2	17.9	13.7	18.6	18.3	17.8	21.7
Semi-Medium	9.5	22.4	7.5	21.9	5.9	19.5	14.0	20.8	12.5	23.6	10.2	23.6
Medium	4.4	22.2	2.7	17.1	1.9	13.7	9.3	29.8	6.3	25.6	4.4	21.6
Large	0.9	13.5	0.5	8.7	0.3	6.1	2.6	23.9	1.3	15.8	0.8	11.5
Total	**100**	**100**	**100**	**100**	**100**	**100**	**100**	**100**	**100**	**100**	**100**	**100**

Note: H – Holdings; A – Area; Others including OBC category.

Source: GoI, Agriculture Census, 1980-81, 1995-96 and 2010-11.

improvement to rural poor households. As a part of the Jawahar Rozgar Yojna (JRY) the development of private agricultural land under the Land Development Scheme, and irrigation facility under Million Wells Scheme for marginal and small farmers were also undertaken. In both the schemes, the small and marginal farmers, particularly those belonging to Scheduled Castes were given priority (Thorat, 2000: 657). Along with supply of inputs at subsidized rates, the improvements in land and irrigation facilities was expected to improve land productivity so as to make the marginal and small farmers viable and hence self-employed cultivators. There are not many studies on the impact of these programmes on the improvement of the landed assets of the SCs. The limited evidence does suggest that the impact is very little.

In an attempt to evaluate the impact of land reforms and land distribution with particular reference to SC households, Thorat looks at the NSS surveys on employment status and makes the following observations:

> It is important to note that the proportion of SC self-employed cultivating households in rural areas was the lowest in Punjab (4.31%), closely followed by Kerala (5.97%), Tamil Nadu (6.99%), Haryana (8.64%), Maharashtra (8.37%), Gujarat (7.43%), Andhra Pradesh (8.4%) and Bihar (10.08%). The situation in Punjab and Haryana is obviously quite disturbing because it was expected that new agricultural technology would have made the SC marginal and small farmers viable. However, the reasons are quite obvious. In Punjab and Haryana the proportion of scheduled castes who owned less than half a acre of land is astonishingly high, i.e. 86.84 per cent in Punjab and 87.52 per cent in Haryana in the year 1982, and 85.57 per cent in Punjab, and 73.10 per cent in Haryana in the year 1992. Even the high yielding technology with the support from the government could not have converted such a mini holdings into viable units. Same is the case of Kerala, where the holdings with less than half an acre was 77 per cent in 1982 and 79.72 per cent in 1992. The ratio of self-employed households was, however, relatively higher in Himachal Pradesh, Assam, Rajasthan, Uttar Pradesh and West Bengal. In these states the ratio varied between 31.07 per cent in Uttar Pradesh to 48.3 per cent in Himachal Pradesh. Thus, it is clear that because of the non-viable character of marginal landholding a very small proportion of SC landowners, in the end, turn out to be self-employed cultivators. Thus, the various schemes of land and irrigation improvement, credit support and subsidized inputs have benefited these households only marginally. (Thorat, 2000: 661–2).

II
ADMINISTRATIVE INITIATIVES TOWARDS IMPROVING ACCESS OF LAND TO SCHEDULED CASTES IN ANDHRA PRADESH

Andhra Pradesh, like most of the states, brought about a series of legislative enactments in carrying forward land reforms encompassing abolition of intermediaries and *inams*, enforcing ceilings on ownership holdings, regulation of tenancy, conferment of ownership on homesteads, prevention of alienation of Tribal and assigned lands, and regulations to ensure land rights. Like many other states, Andhra Pradesh, too, faced several obstacles in the implementation of these legislative measures and as elsewhere, land reforms continue to be described as an 'unfinished agenda' (GoAP, 2006: 33). The redistributive legislation in the state faced early failure. The AP (Ceilings on Agricultural Holdings) Act 1961 did not achieve its objective, since it gave more concessions and exemptions to the landlords and ended up with very meagre area declared as ceiling surplus (GoAP, 2006). This Act was replaced by AP Land Reforms (Ceiling on Agricultural Holdings) Act 1973 which came into force from 1975. Even under the revised Act, the success was limited. Initially, 16.63 lakh acres were declared as surplus, later reduced to 8.01 lakh acres, but not entirely taken possession (GoAP, 2006). As shown in Table 1, 5.82 lakh acres of ceiling surplus land was distributed to about 5.3 lakh beneficiary households. An estimated area of about 2.1 lakh acres of acquired ceiling surplus land was not distributed either because of litigation, administrative delay, or being unfit for cultivation or being used for other public purposes (GoAP, 2006: 34). Of the ceiling surplus land distributed in the State the largest proportion of (42.65 per cent) beneficiaries were SCs accounting for about 40 per cent of the distributed land, which on an average worked out to be about 1.01 acres per household. However, the extent of ceiling surplus land distributed hardly accounts for about 1.65 per cent of the total landholdings in the state, and had very insignificant effect on the access to land of the rural poor in general and Scheduled Castes in particular.

Administrative Initiatives

It is in the context of limited impact of the land reform legislations as such, that certain initiatives by committed proactive administrative measures made considerable difference. Even as it was realized that ceilings legislation was pliable and the results would not be as per the aspirations of the poor waiting for access to land, the Andhra Pradesh administrative interventions did show alternative possibilities. Though such assignments were fraught with risks of litigation and local adversarial tensions, there were determined efforts to help the poor access land through administrative initiatives not only in assigning land but also in resolving the problems which arose in the process of possessing and putting the land for productive use by the assignees. Right from the 1960s till the present, these initiatives reflect a strong belief that was well articulated in the initiation of some of these programmes of improving access of SCs to land. While recognizing the fact that in the long-run improving non-farm employment opportunities could play important role in the upward mobility of SCs, it was emphasized that in the near term, 'obtaining land ownership—even of a small amount of land—can play a crucial, incremental role in helping the poorest rural households to achieve food security, increase income, effectively utilize labour (their plentiful asset), augment wealth and status, access credit, and insure against risk' (GoAP, 2002). These initiatives were informed by the strong belief that there is no dearth of land and new opportunities do exist to provide land to the SCs. According to one estimate, an extent of 19 million acres of waste land is available in the state (Raju et al, 2006) and 'that the existing laws and programmes still offer significant scope for linking land with the landless. Government officials with substantial gross-roots, land revenue department experience reveal that concentrated efforts to fully and effectively implement existing laws and programmes could substantially enhance the rural poor's access and rights to rural land (GoAP, 2002)'.

Here, we shall analyse some of these initiatives which include (i) finding the government 'waste' and 'poromboke' land and distributing such land among rural poor, (ii) initiating active convergence of the Society for Elimination of Rural Poverty (SERP)with relevant state government departments in effectively implementing existing laws and programmes that offer potential for the rural poor's access to land, and enabling rural poor households to purchase land, both under the Andhra Pradesh Rural Poverty Reduction Project (APRPRP), (iii) the Comprehensive Land Development Project (CLDP) or *Indira Prabha,* (iv) *Indira Jala Prabha,* the development of irrigation facilities in SC/ST lands, (v) the initiative of Land Inventory under (SERP), and (vi) prioritizing land development work on the private lands of SC/ST households under MGNREGS.

(i) Government Land to the Poor and SCs

We may begin with the assignment of government land to the poor in Andhra Pradesh. What West Bengal did in the case of ceiling legislation, Andhra Pradesh did in the case of government land assignment to the poor. Though these two measures are qualitatively different in terms of ensuring equitable structure of land distribution, the AP experience shows that the limitations of legislative each could be minimized to an extent by administrative initiatives. West Bengal's success on land ceilings legislation enabled it to acquire and distribute 10.88 lakh acres which accounted for 20.14 per cent of the ceiling surplus land distributed in the entire country. The success of Andhra Pradesh was by way of administrative initiatives that enabled distribution of 42.02 lakh acres which accounted for 28.49 per cent of the entire government land distributed to the poor in the country. Table 2 shows that of the total government land of 147.5 lakh acres assigned to the poor in India, Andhra Pradesh alone accounted for

42 lakh acres or more than one-fourth (28.49 per cent). This is no mean an achievement of the administrative intervention in the state, given the fact most of the states did have such opportunities but were not realized. In Andhra Pradesh, the extent of government land assigned to the poor constitutes about 12.24 per cent of the total land holdings in the state, which is 7.4 times more than the ceiling surplus land assigned to the poor. The average area per beneficiary household under government land assigned was about 1.8 acres which was much higher than the average ceiling surplus land assigned per

Table 5: Govt. Land Assigned for Agriculture Purpose to Landless SCs and Other Rural Poor in AP (from 1.11.1969 to 30.11.2002)

Sl. No.	*Name of the District*	*Total Beneficiaries*	*Total Extent of Land Assigned in Acres*	*SCs Beneficiaries*	*% of SC Beneficiary*	*Extent in Acres to SCs*	*% of Area to SCs*
(1)	*(2)*	*(3)*	*(4)*	*(5)*	*(6)*	*(7)*	*(8)*
1	Srikakulam	75963	70787.22	16826	22.15	15591.06	22.03
2	Vizianagaram	79444	99198.87	17486	22.01	21829.91	22.01
3	Visakhapatnam	80007	161777.29	17735	22.17	36570.47	22.61
4	East Godavari	51046	55541.95	11237	22.01	12239.29	22.04
5	West Godavari	40702	82603.96	12195	29.96	18369.21	22.24
6	Krishna	66037	87430.71	14536	22.01	19242.48	22.01
7	Guntur	72061	70452.2	15857	22.00	15504.73	22.01
8	Nellore	236047	415500.5	52272	22.14	91892.55	22.12
9	Prakasam	170482	317815.79	37603	22.06	69959.48	22.01
10	Chittoor	219510	385883.68	48361	22.03	85044.53	22.04
11	Cuddapah	87970	223989.71	19407	22.06	49396.46	22.05
12	Ananthapur	203411	624653.43	45083	22.16	135892.64	21.75
13	Kurnool	37764	111893.66	8338	22.07	24694.34	22.07
14	Adilabad	72635	214373.28	15979	22.00	47161.17	22.00
15	Khammam	113495	279789.19	24494	21.58	60570.01	21.65
16	Warangal	173313	173186.5	38128	22.00	38101.03	22.00
17	Karimnagar	113699	106367.05	25031	22.02	23401.59	22.00
18	Mahaboobnagar	115234	211197.92	25430	22.07	46582.95	22.01
19	Medak	146714	239752.96	32276	22.00	52745.64	22.00
20	Nizamabad	145411	163465.68	31998	22.01	35976.25	22.01
21	Nalgonda	133224	157167.04	52959	39.75	63467.2	40.38
22	Ranga Reddy	35884	68547.78	7896	22.00	15082.92	22.00
23	Hyderabad			0	0	0	0
	Total	2398053	4321376.37	571127	23.82	979315.91	22.66

Source: *GOA, (2005) Convergence of Department of Revenue and Velugu: Physical Inventory of Government Lands, 'Velugu', Hyderabad.*

household (1.01 acres). Table 5 gives details about the district-wise beneficiaries and the area distributed as well as the share of SCs in the beneficiaries and the area assigned.

What is revealing is that the proportion of SC beneficiaries and the area allotted is fixed more or less at 22 per cent of the total in all the districts regardless of the share of SC population and SC poor in the districts. Though the proportion (22 per cent) of SC households benefiting from the land distribution is higher than the proportion of rural SC population in the State (18.45 per cent), the assignment obviously did not go by the proportion of the rural poor among whom the share of SCs is much higher at 35 per cent.

But the experience shows that assigning land to communities like Scheduled Castes is only an initial step, but ensuring actual possession is a task that requires building up responsive institutional structures without which the assignees actually may be put to more harassment than benefits. There is a certain ironic truth in the criticism that dependence on distribution of government land to the poor would end up in the distribution of litigation. It is now well documented that the first flush of extensive assignment of government land to the poor did achieve the desired effect of improving the economic condition of the poor because of three factors, namely, failure to target the poor like the SCs properly in assigning land; alienation of the land on plain paper, though not legally permitted, by the assignees due to their financial exigencies, and failure to receive actual possession of the land that was assigned on paper (Raju et. al. 2006). Besides distress transfer by the assignees, possession of assigned lands by the non-poor was also found to be the result of illegal encroachment by adjacent landowners (GoAP, 2002). To counteract both the illegal encroachment problem (Andhra Pradesh Land Grabbing Prohibition Act, 1982) and the illegal and distress transfers of assigned land (Andhra Pradesh Assigned lands Prohibition of Transfers Act, 1977) specific legislative measures were brought into force at the behest of administrative initiatives. Both Acts provide for restoration of possession back to the original assignee. However, actual implementation of these laws has not been encouraging. As a result, significant areas of government assigned lands are still in the enjoyment of the non-poor (GoAP, 2002). Again, to overcome the failure to implement these legislative measures in securing rights of the poor on their assigned lands, new administrative initiatives were designed in the project mode and one such is the Andhra Pradesh Rural Poverty Reduction Project (APRPRP) under the agency of Society for the Elimination of Rural Poor (SERP).

(ii) SERP and APRPRP

In 2002, the Andhra Pradesh Rural Poverty Reduction Project (APRPRP), under the Society for Elimination of Rural Poverty (SERP), was designed to link the rural poor with land. Two types of activities were envisaged under the project: (1) Convergence of SERP with the relevant state government departments to effectively implement existing laws and programmes that offer potential for increasing the rural poor's access and rights to land; and (2) Enabling landless households to purchase land from willing sellers under the project's Community Investment Fund (CIF) (GoAP, 2002).

The land component of the APRPRP included activities 'to provide the poor access to land previously or currently owned or controlled by the government and to strengthen or formalize legal rights to land that is possessed by poor households often under insecure tenure arrangements.' In 2003, the project entered into a partnership with the Revenue Department and the Department of Survey, Settlement, and Land Records. The objective of the convergence framework evolved between the project and the line departments emphasized three aspects namely (1) ensuring secure possession of land by poor people with legal title but not possession, (2) providing the poor with legal rights to land in their possession and regularizing rights in the revenue records, and (3) ensuring that the poor have the ability to receive physical possession and legal and alienable ownership of lands to which they were entitled by law (for a graphic description of the setting up institutional mechanism for operationalizing the framework, see Raju et al 2006).

The 'Land Purchase Component' under APRPRP was an effort to incorporate a measure that was attempted to an extent by the Scheduled Caste Development Corporation for several years but with very limited success (Raju et al 2006). But the inspiration for land purchase involving self-help groups (SHGs) seems to be from the World Bank and it was also latter widely orchestrated by the FAO as market-assisted land reform (MALR)as an alternative 'potential solution to dialatory and politically cumbersome expropriative land reform' (FAO, 2006). Since APRPRP was a World Bank funded project, incorporation of 'land purchase element' might have been a tactical ingredient of the project. The approach was premised on the theory that the market could be successfully used to redistribute land to the land poor. It was argued that if subsidies that flowed to large farmers were cut and if non-farm facilities were provided to them to move out, then there would be more land on the market and the poor could be subsidized to buy land through the market. However, the land purchase component remained an insignificant part of the project.

It is in the case of restoring the land rights of the poor through convergence of the line-departments that the agency of SERP mattered much. However, after the initial enthusiasm of the Revenue Department faded by the end of 2003, the SERP had to carry on the project much against the odds. The next push to the administrative drive towards providing land to the poor, and SCs in particular, had to wait till October 2004, when the new state government which came to power gave a new life to the initiative of land access and rights to the poor (Raju et al 2006).

(iii) Comprehensive Land Development Project (CLDP) or Indira Prabha

As discussed above, about five million acres or about 15 per cent of the area under landholdings in the state is either ceiling surplus land or government land that had been assigned to the landless and land poor households. Hardly 20 per cent of this land has been put to productive use. Most of the assigned lands were of poor quality and were often never leveled or cleared of scrubs and bushes to be put under plough. These lands required high investments for development into agriculturally productive assets, but the assignees were too poor to undertake such expenditure. Though the problem has been well recognized even from the time of assigning these lands, there were no substantive programmes to improve these lands. In November 2004, the state government launched a Comprehensive Land Development Project (CLDP), also known as Indira Prabha, for the development of assigned lands and to convert the barren and degraded lands into productive assets.

The CLDP was launched in 2004 with an estimated outlay of Rs. 670 crores to develop 6.17 lakh acres of assigned land belonging to 3.84 lakh SC, ST, BC, and other households. The broad guidelines suggested that, of the physical and financial allocation, a minimum of 50 per cent should go to SC households, 10 per cent to STs with a provision that more could be allocated to STs or BCs if their population share was higher. Of the total outlay, 95 per cent was in the form of loan from Rural Infrastructure Development Fund (RIDF) and the remaining 5 per cent from the state government. There was also a provision that assignees contribute 10 per cent of the project cost in the form of *shramadan* (voluntary work) which was to be used for maintenance.

The CLDP has been implemented in phases and is expected to be completed by 2013. During the first two phases between 2004–2010, an expenditure of about Rs. 337 crores was incurred in developing 3.49 lakh acres of land belonging to about 2.66 lakh assignee households.[1] The social group-wise distribution of the beneficiary families shows 49 per cent from SCs, 20 per cent STs, 24 per cent BCs, and 6 per cent others. The land development expenditure under the CLDP works out to an average of Rs. 9658 per acre. Each of the assignee households on an average had 1.31 acres of land developed at a cost of Rs. 12,672. The expenditure per acre appears to be low compared to the data available on the development of land belonging to SC/ST households under NREGS and it would be interesting to assess the extent of productivity improvement on these assignee lands brought under development.

(iv) Indira Jala Prabha

As a follow up to CLDP, the state government launched, in 2011, *Indira Jala Prabha* or development of irrigation facilities on 10 lakh acres of SC/ST lands with the objective of enabling more intensive and productive agriculture on the lands of the Dalit households. It is proposed to be taken up as a convergence project between MGNREGS and RIDF with an ambitious estimated budget of Rs. 1,800 crore. Under this, the expenditure for creation of irrigation sources will be from MGNREGS (Rs. 957 crore), and the cost of energisation and micro-irrigation will be met from RIDF (Rs. 844 crore). The coverage under the programme would include only lands of SC/ST farmers, which are taken up for development under MGNREGS or CLDP.[2]

(v) Society for Elimination of Rural Poverty (SERP) and SC/ST Land Inventory

The 'Land Inventory' under the Society for Elimination of Rural Poor (SERP) is an expanded initiative of what began as the 'Land Component' under APRPRP. Under Indira Kranthi Patham (IKP), a massive exercise of land inventory was launched to map the lands under 'ownership' and 'enjoyment' of SC/STs in all the 22 districts with assistance from the MGNREGS. The initiative was based on the recognition that 'apart from pro-poor land legislations, the poor, especially SCs/STs require exclusive facilitation support to get their land issues resolved' (Rajasekhar, 2012). The two main objectives of this exercise were (1) to identify SC/ST lands for development under NREGS, and (2) to identify and facilitate resolution of land issues or problems relating SC/ST lands. SERP put in place sensitive land support mechanisms in 2006-07 in place by positioning Parahgals and community surveyors (for details see Rajasekhar, 2012). The process of building up institutional machinery to undertake the challenging task received wider attention (Nielsen and Tim Hanstand, 2008). The land inventory for all SC/ST lands was completed in 954 out of a total of 1,099 mandals and 22,833 revenue villages out of 26,614 in the state. The results show that out of 30.71 lakhs of SC/ST households, 12.77 lakhs or 42 per cent are landless. The remaining 17.94 lakh households (58 per cent) possess 40.40 lakh acres of land, which is about 2.25 acres per household. But what is revealing is that 70 per cent of these households have one or the other problems relating to the record of rights of their land. Under the land inventory exercise, every parcel of land was verified with reference to how it was recorded in key revenue records like Pahani/Adangal, Record of Rights IB, Pattadar Pass Book and also the status of actual enjoyment. It was found that in 70 per cent of cases, these four aspects varied and there were huge discrepancies in the revenue records. The IKP has provided the basic information thus gathered to the Chief Commissioner of Land Administration who in turn initiated measures to resolve these issues by forming

Mandal Revenue Teams and conducting Revenue Sadassu at the village level. Under the land component of the IKP, it is reported that, during the first phase spread over 2006-10, land related issues of the 6.16 lakh poor households involving 11.86 lakh acres of land were identified and about 70 per cent of these issues were resolved (Rajasekhar 2012).

The Land Inventory helped in identifying 18.39 lakh land development works under MGNREGS over an extent of 30.14 lakh acres of SC/ST lands with an estimated investment of Rs. 9,000 crore. Land Inventory is also the basis for development of assigned land under CLDP and the provision of irrigation facilities to SC/ST lands under Indira Jala Prabha.

(vi) NREGS and the Lands of SCs/STs in Andhra Pradesh

One of the major justifications for public works, in contrast to cash transfer, as a social protection measure is that these works not only generate employment but create assets which would benefit the community as a whole. The nature of MGNREGS works are such that there is a built-in bias in favour of agriculture, due to emphasis on conservation and development of land and water resources. Of particular importance to poor farmers is the MGNREGS provision of irrigation facility, horticulture plantation. and land development on private lands of SC, ST, and BPL households or beneficiaries of land reforms and IAY, and its later extension to small and marginal farmers, (hereafter referred to as 'EGS eligible farming communities'). This provision has far reaching significance to especially the SC farming community in Andhra Pradesh.

Like many other states, small-marginal farmers constitute more than 80 per cent of farmers in Andhra Pradesh. More importantly, about 12.5 per cent of the area under cultivation is assigned land distributed by the State to the poor, either out of ceiling surplus land or government land. But, as pointed out earlier, much of the assigned land has been of very poor quality requiring substantial investment if it were to be brought under plough. However, most of these assignees could not afford such investment. Often, the State assistance for improvement of these lands was inadequate.

A sample survey of 800 beneficiaries of land assignment under land reforms in two districts of Andhra Pradesh shows that at the time of assignment only in 17 per cent of the cases the land assigned was cultivable, in about 26 per cent of cases it was all shrubs and bushes, and in 66 per cent it was barren and rocky (Rani and Rao, 2011). Considerable amount of investment had to be made to bring them under plough. Only in those cases where institutional support like that of Scheduled Tribes Development Corporation was available, investments could be made for land development and provision of irrigation facilities, and the land could be cultivated. And in most of the other cases, either the assigned land was kept fallow or used for growing some rain-fed crops or in some cases even abandoned. The Government of Andhra Pradesh saw the opportunity afforded by the provision of MGNREGS works on the lands of the 'eligible farming communities' and initiated steps to prioritize these works in the shelf of works planned for implementation under the Scheme.

Of the nine categories of works provided under the NREG Act, the fourth, 'Provision of Irrigation Facility ...' alone refers to works on private lands of certain eligible farming communities. The Government of Andhra Pradesh, specified the fourth category of works into four projects,[3] namely (1) EGS Land Development Project (EGS-LDP) to treat fallow and low productive lands of the eligible farmers with priority to SC and ST farmers, (2) Horticulture and Plantation Project (H&P), (3) Irrigation Facilities Project (IFP), (4) Sustainable Agriculture Project (SAP), and spelt out the nature of works to be taken up and priority to be assigned in selecting the farmers for implementation. The participation of self-help groups (SHGs) was enlisted in identifying lands of the poorest of the poor with special emphasis on the lands of SC and ST households. The Andhra Pradesh government has developed an ambitious plan to develop 2.5 million acres of assigned land belonging to SC, ST, small and marginal farmers under the MGNREGS at a cost of around Rs. 7,000 crore. The new works strategy evolved by the middle of 2010 emphasized completion of these works on saturation basis as could be observed from the following part of the guidelines: 'Land Development in the lands of SC/STs and Small and Marginal Farmers shall be taken up on a saturation basis. The Land Development includes various water conservation and water harvesting structures' [4]

Table 6 provides a larger picture of the efforts of the State in bringing to record the strategy of project and works planning with the highest priority accorded to the development of the lands of the eligible farming community. About 32 lakh NREGS works were planned for execution in the private lands of the SCs/STs and others. Even if each work is likely to improve farming in at least one acre of land, the impact on farming and poor peasantry would be

Table 6: Social Group-wise Prioritized MGNREGS Works on Eligible Private Lands in Andhra Pradesh 2011

(Number of Works)

Status	*SC*	*ST*	*SC + ST*	*Others*	*Total*
1. Number of works in shelf	383579	360926	977	557734	1303216
2. Number of works in sanction/start up	561547	243669	1254	484511	1290981
3. Number of works in progress	204305	132505	2237	308426	647473

Source: http://nrega.ap.gov.in (25-07-2011)

substantial. The sustained priority assigned to the works on the private land of the poor peasantry is revealed by the fact that the 'fourth category' of works alone account for almost a third of the total MGNREGS expenditure in recent years (Reddy 2012). The benefits SCs/STs and agricultural production are likely to be substantial but still remain to be systematically assessed.

Drawn from a larger study of the author (Reddy, D.N., 2011), the case of Kuppanagar village in Medak district of Andhra Pradesh is presented here with specific focus on MGNREGS works on the private lands of eligible farming communities. A sample survey was conducted in the village, and Table 7 gives the details of the caste and class distribution of the sample households. The Panchayat has been proactive in identifying MGNREGS works on the private lands of SC households.

Table 7: Caste and Class (Size of Land Holding) Based Classification of Sample Households (Kuppanagar)

Caste	*Landless*	*Marginal*	*Small*	*Semi-Medium*	*Medium*	*Large*	*All*
SC	9	6	14	13	8	Nil	50
OBC	2	3	4	5	5	-	19
Others	4	4	4	7	4	-	23*
All	15	13	22	25	17	0	92

*20 households of these 'others' belong to Muslim community which is also mainly agriculture dependant. Upper castes under 'others' in the village constitute very meagre proportion.
Source: Reddy, D.N., 2011.

Table 8 shows the NREGS development works on private lands of SCs and others in the village. Given the fact that SCs constitute almost one-fourth of the population of the village and that most of them have some land, though mostly dry and uncultivable, one of the lasting ways of improving their economic condition is to make their lands more productive. Since most of them lacked resources for investment, MGNREGS works on private lands has come as a boon.

What remained as unproductive pieces of assigned land are turning into productive agricultural assets. Application of tank silt to fallow or barren land enriches the soil, makes the land productive and ensures good crop even under rain-fed conditions. In developing of fallow lands, one of the important public works undertaken in some of these dryland areas is the removal of over grown *prosafis juliflora* with roots and stumps. Most of the assigned lands, when left fallow due to lack of resources for development turn into wild growth of *prosafis* which once sets in becomes very difficult to clear unless completely rooted out, a task which needs about Rs. 40 thousand per acre, and is beyond the means of poor farmers. There is no wonder that removal of *prosafis* overgrowth

Table 8: NREGS Development Works on Private Lands under Progress in Kuppanagar During 2010–11*

Type of Work	*Community-wise Beneficiaries* SC	OBC	Others	*All*	*Total Expenditure (Rs. Lakh)*	*Average per Household (Rs.)*
(1)	(2)	(3)	(4)	(5)	(6)	(7)
1. Tank Silt Application	103	13	1	117	13.08	11,178
2. Deep Ploughing in Hard Soil	100	16	7	123	2.21	1,800
3. Development of Fallow/ Dry-lands	103	-	-	103	61.12	59,337
4. Open Wells	4	2	-	6	2.48	41,358

*These works are approved and being implemented by the Panchayat for the years 2010–11 and 2011–12.
Source: Mandal Computer Centre, Jarasangam, Medak District, A.P.

is one of the much sought after public works by the poor farmers.

Table 9: Households Benefiting From NREGS Works on Private Lands in Kuppanagar

Community	*All House-holds*	*Landless Households*	*Households with Land*	*NREGS Private Land Improvement Work**	*Extent of Land Covered (Acres)* Total	*Average per Household*
SC	50	9	41	38 (93%)	62	1.6
OBC	19	2	17	8 (47%)	14	1.8
Others	23	4	19	8 (47%)	14	1.8
All	92	15	77	54 (70%)	89	1.6

*Households with land benefiting from NREGS improvement of private lands.
Figures in parentheses are percentages to Households with land.
Source: Reddy, D.N., 2011.

Table 9 shows the beneficiaries under the MGNREGS in private lands. SCs get top priority in these works. The preponderance of SC households benefiting from the MGNREGS in the village is because of two reasons. One is that most of the SC and other poor households in the village were assigned land out of two large tracts which were largely barren. Second, there were clear guidelines from the State that priority should be accorded to SC and ST lands in undertaking land development on private lands; and special efforts were made through SHGs to list the lands of the SC households in large number of villages for inclusion on priority in the shelf of projects prepared by the

Panchayats.[5] The state government's ambitious initiative in this regard could be guazed from the following part of the follow up guidelines circulated:

> ...prepare the land inventory of SC/ST lands in all the villages in the state and (to) identify all the possible works in these lands with the objective to achieve an annual income of Rs. 25,000 per acre. The first and second priorities of projects were given as land development project in fallow and cultivable lands of SC/ST farmers. *After saturation of the land development works in SC/ST lands* then other project shall be identified to meet the demand of the labour budget of the habitation [emphasis added].[6]

The beneficiaries included range from marginal to medium size farmers. Semi-medium or medium in dryland conditions does not indicate a better resource position. In Kuppanagar, many of the SC households are also semi-medium and medium size landholders but much of the land is without any irrigation facility and of low productivity requiring substantial investment to make it productive. Most of these households responded that they had an opportunity through MGNREGS to raise good crops on their land for the first time. Most of them obtained the benefit of tank silt application to their lands. In fact, the results of tank silt application by way of increased crop yields had a visible impact, and created a very high demand from the SC and other eligible households for this programme. The Panchayat responded by according high priority to the same.

III
SCHEDULED CASTES, ACCESS TO LAND AND BEYOND

In spite of the efforts to augment land access to Scheduled Castes, there are certain characteristics of the Scheduled Caste which persist in putting them to continued disadvantage. Table 10 shows that the incidence of poverty among

Table 10: Incidence of Poverty among Social Groups in Rural India

(Percentage)

Year	*Rural*					*Urban*				
	ST	*SC*	*OBC*	*Others*	*All*	*ST*	*SC*	*OBC*	*Others*	*All*
1	2	3	4	5	6	7	8	9	10	11
1993-94	65.7	62.2	-	43.9	50.1	40.9	51.4	-	28.0	31.7
2004-05	62.3	53.5	39.8	27.1 (35.0)	41.8	35.5	40.6	30.6	16.1 (22.5)	25.7
2009-10	47.4	42.3	31.9	21.0	33.8	30.4	34.1	24.3	12.4	20.8

Note: 1. *Tendulkar Committee Methodology* is based on MRP (Mixed Reference Period);
2. Figures in parentheses include both OBC and Others which are comparable with the 'other' in 1993-94.

Source: Estimated using NSSO Consumer Expenditure Survey unit record data.

SCs and STs is more than double that of 'others', that even in 2009–10, the share of SCs among those who are below poverty line in rural India is disproportionately higher than their share in population in almost all States (Table 11). What is surprising is that even in agriculturally better developed States like Punjab and Haryana, SCs constitute about 65 and 42 per cent of the rural poor, respectively. Overall agricultural development *per se*, without direct access to land or other enabling endowments do not seem to ensure better living for the SC population. If we consider access to land, most of the SCs are landless or near landless with less than one acre of land (GoI 2011).

Table 11: State-wise Share of Scheduled Castes (SCs) in Rural Population and Rural Poverty

Sl. No.	*States*	*SCs Share (%) in* *Rural Population* *2001*	*Rural Poor* *1993-94*	*2004-05*	*2009-10*
1	Andhra Pradesh	18.5	25.9	25.3	25.9
2	Assam	6.7	9.9	12.0	9.9
3	Bihar	16.4	29.2	32.1	29.2
4	Chhattisgarh	11.4	15.3	12.8	15.3
5	Gujarat	6.9	15.9	14.1	15.9
6	Haryana	21.4	42.1	53.6	42.1
7	Himachal Pradesh	25.6	28.2	42.6	28.2
8	Jammu & Kashmir	8.3	33.4	15.3	33.4
9	Jharkhand	12.4	17.3	15.4	17.3
10	Karnataka	18.4	26.1	31.0	26.1
11	Kerala	10.8	15.7	17.1	15.7
12	Madhya Pradesh	15.6	22.1	21.2	22.1
13	Maharashtra	14.1	20.2	20.5	20.2
14	Orissa	17.2	18.5	19.6	18.5
15	Punjab	33.0	64.8	69.6	64.8
16	Rajasthan	17.9	24.7	28.4	24.7
17	Tamil Nadu	23.8	33.4	36.9	33.4
18	Uttar Pradesh	23.4	32.5	33.7	32.5
19	Uttaranchal	19.9	26.3	30.2	26.3
20	West Bengal	26.9	36.4	28.1	36.4
All India		17.9	26.2	26.8	26.2

Note: Tendulkar Committee methodology based Poverty line used.
Source: 1. Census of India; 2. NSS Consumption Expenditure Survey unit record data.

In Andha Pradesh, in spite of the fact that redistribution of ceiling surplus land and government land together accounted for as much as 15 per cent of the total operational holdings, as against the national average of four per cent, and in spite of the creative administrative interventions to restore the assigned land and to improve the quality of land, the condition of SCs in terms of access to land continues to be much more precarious because of the historical disadvantage of relatively high incidence of landlessness of SCs in the state compared to the situation in the country as a whole. Table 12 shows that compared to the country as a whole, landlessness of SCs in Andhra Pradesh is much higher across all types of households. While landlessness among all rural households is about 57 per cent for all India, it is 75 per cent in Andhra Pradesh. The incidence of landlessness among the SC rural labour households in the state is as high as 80 per cent compared to about 70 per cent for all India.

Table 12: Different Groups of Rural Households with and without Land in Andhra Pradesh and All India: 2004–05

Social Group	*All Rural Households*			*Rural Labour Households*			*Agricultural Labour Households*		
	With Land	*Without Land*	*Total*	*With Land*	*Without Land*	*Total*	*With Land*	*Without Land*	*Total*
All Classes (A.P)	39.27	60.73	100.00	27.34	72.66	100.00	30.21	69.79	100.00
(India)	57.20	42.80	100.00	37.20	62.80	100.00	38.28	61.72	100.00
Scheduled Castes (A.P)	25.28	74.72	100.00	20.09	79.91	100.00	21.31	78.69	100.00
(India)	45.58	57.42	100.00	30.47	69.53	100.00	31.27	68.73	100.00

Source: Agricultural Labour Enquiry, Report on General Characteristics of Rural Labour Households, (61st Round of NSS) 2004-05, Labour Bureau, Shimla.

Further, almost three-fourths of SC households with land are in the category of marginal farmers (Table 13). Small-marginal size together account for 90 per cent of the holdings and 66 per cent of the area operated by the SC households in the state. The average size of all holdings has been declining over a period of time but the decline in the average size of holdings of SC households reached a very low level of 0.8 hectares by 2010–11 (Figure 1) causing serious threat to the viability of farming by SC households. It is in this context and in the light of exploding the myth that 'there is no land' for further distribution by revealing an estimated potential area of 19 million acres of non-forest wasteland available for distribution among rural poor, that the task of land to the SC households must be considered unfinished agenda that needs to be pursued through creative administrative initiatives. In this way, the state has earned a niche.

Table 13: Size-Distribution of Operational Holdings of SCs and All Social Groups in Andhra Pradesh (2005-06 – 2010-11)

	Marginal	*Small*	*Semi-Medium*	*Medium*	*Large*
2005–06					
Groups All Social (Number)	61.59	21.91	11.99	4.05	0.47
(Area)	22.69	25.75	26.47	19.04	6.06
SC (Number)	74.59	**17.42**	**6062**	**1.27**	**0.09**
(Area)	38.32	**30.21**	**2090**	**8.64**	**1.93**
2010–11					
Groups All Social (Number)	63.94	22.15	10.62	3.02	0.27
(Area)	26.08	28.82	25.78	15.45	3.87
SC (Number)	76.20	**17.00**	**5.74**	**0.99**	**0.06**
(Area)	41.44	**31.10**	**19.03**	**7.04**	**1.38**

Source: GoI (2012)

Figure 1: Changes in Average Size of Operational Holdings of SCcs and All Social Groups in Andhra Pradesh 1980–1 to 2010–11

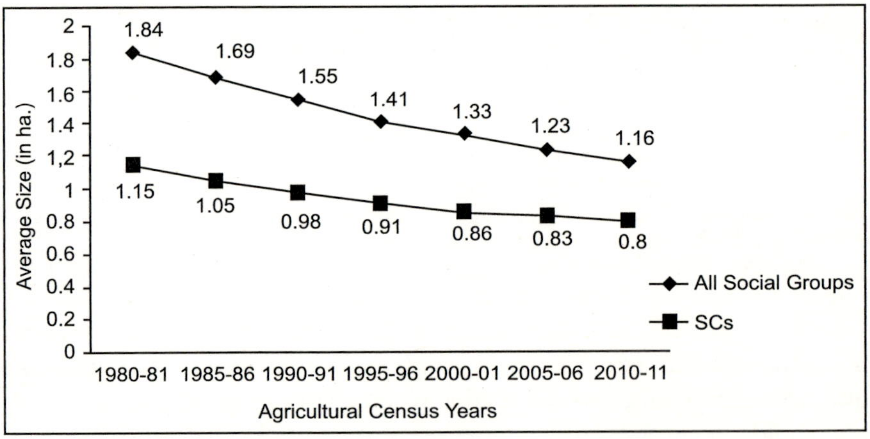

Source: GoI (2012)

It is also time to combine additional interventions in the context of changes in the economic structure and the consequent occupational structure in recent times. It is well known that SC households form the highest proportion of rural labour households and rural labour accounts for the highest source of livelihood for these households. It is interesting to observe from Table 14 that in 2004–05, in almost all social groups in rural India, about 60 per cent of the households were engaged in agriculture. By 2009–10, the dependence on agriculture had declined to an extent in almost all social groups. But, if we

Table 14: Distribution of Rural Households across Social Groups by Major Source of Livelihood – All India

	Social groups	*Self Employed in*		*Rural Labour in*			
		Agriculture	*Non-Agriculture*	*Agriculture*	*Non-Agriculture*	*Others*	*Total*
2004–05							
1	ST	39.3	6.4	34.0	11.3	8.9	100
2	SC	20.2	14.1	40.5	15.4	9.8	100
3	OBC	38.7	17.6	22.4	10.4	11.0	100
4	Others	43.3	18.1	15.6	7.7	15.3	100
	All	35.9	15.8	25.8	10.9	11.6	100
2009–10							
1	ST	37.0	7.0	33.4	13.1	9.5	100
2	SC	17.1	13.7	36.9	22.1	10.3	100
3	OBC	34.1	17.2	23.3	14.0	11.4	100
4	Others	39.4	18.1	15.9	10.3	16.3	100
	All	31.9	15.5	25.6	14.8	12.2	100

Source: NSSO Employment and Unemployment Survey Reports 61st and 66th Rounds.

examine the composition of the type of households within agriculture, then the asymmetry among the social groups comes out clearly. In almost all social groups except SCs, one-third or more households are self-employed in agriculture with less than fifteen per cent as agricultural labour households. Quite in contrast, 37 per cent of SC households were agricultural labourers and only 17 per cent were self-employed in agriculture. The direction of mobility is towards non-farm activities. As was well recognized even at the time of designing the APRPRP that over 'the long-term, the non-farm sector will play an important role in providing the majority of rural employment opportunities', it is time for administrative interventions for improving the capabilities of the young in SC households through quality education and skill formation which become essential for upward economic and social mobility.

REFERENCES

FAO (2006), 'Land and Livelihoods: Making Land Rights real for India's Rural Poor', Economic and Social Development Department, Food and Agricultural Organization, www.fao.org/docrep/007.

GOAP (2006), *Land Committee Report*, Government of Andhra Pradesh, Hyderabad.

GOAP (2006), *Land Committee Report* (Koneru Ranga Rao Committee Report), Revenue Department, Government of Andhra Pradesh, Hyderabad.

GOAP (2002), 'Increasing the Rural Poor's Access and Rights to Rural Land:

Operational Manual', AP Rural Poverty Reduction Project, Society for Elimination of Rural Poverty, Department of PR and Rural Development, Government of Andhra Pradesh, Hyderabad.

GOAP-DES (2004), *A Report on Census of Land Holdings 2000–2001*, Directorate of Economics and Statistics, Hyderabad.

GOI (2012), *Agriculture Census 2010–11*, Agriculture Census Division, Department of Agriculture and Cooperation, New Delhi.

GOI (2006), *Annual Report 2005–06*, Ministry of Rural Development, New Delhi.

GOI (2006), *Report No. 492: Some Aspects of Operational Land Holdings in India 2002–03*, NSS 59th Round, January-December 2003, NSSO, New Delhi, August 2006.

GOI (2006), *Report No. 493, Livestock Ownership Across Operational Landholding Classes in India, 2002–03*, NSS 59th Round, (January-December 2003), NSSO, New Delhi, January 2006.

GOI (2006), *Employment and Unemployment Situation Among Social Groups in India 2004–05*, Report 516, 61st Round, NSSO, MOSPI, New Delhi.

GOI (1999), *Report No. 152: Common Property Resources in India,* January-June 1998, NSS 54th Round, NSSO, New Delhi, December 1999.

Kannabiran, Kalpana (2012), *Tools of Justice: Non-Discrimination and the Indian Constitution*, Routledge, London.

Nancharaiah, G. (1988), *Land and Caste*, Himalaya Publishing House, Bombay.

Neilsen, Robin and Tim Hanstad (2008), 'Design and Implementation of a Legal Aid Component for Land Projects: Lessons from Andhra Pradesh', paper presented for the Conference on New Challenges for Land Policy and Administration, February 14–15, The World Bank, Washington, DC.

Rajasekhar, B. (2012), 'Land Para-Professionals as Last Mile Solution to Land Issues of the Poor' SERP website 6 December 2012.

Raju, K., K. Akella and K. Deininger (2006), 'New Opportunities for Increasing Access to Land: The Example of Andhra Pradesh', paper presented at MoRD and World Bank Workshop on 'Land Policies for Sustainable Growth and Poverty Reduction' January 2006, New Delhi.

Rani, Radhika Ch. and D.V.L.N.V. Prasada Rao (2011), 'Status of Land Allotment to Poor under Land Distribution Programmes: An Evaluation', Centre for Agrarian Studies and Disaster Mitigation, NIRD, Hyderabad.

Reddy, D.N. (2012), "MGNREGS and Agriculture: Opportunities and Challenges" in Ashok K. Pankaj, ed., Right to Work and Rural India, Sage, New Delhi.

Reddy, D.N. (2013), "Functioning of NREGS in Andhra Pradesh" in K.P. Kannan and Jan Breman, eds., The Long Road to Social Security, Oxford University Press, New Delhi.

Sankaran, S.R. (2000), 'Welfare of Scheduled Castes and Scheduled Tribes in Independent India – An Overview of State Policies and Programmes', *Journal of Rural Development*, Vol. 19, No. 4, October – December, pp. 507–33.

Thorat, Sukhadeo (2000), 'Programme for Empowerment and Reducing Inequality: Long way to go for untouchability', *Journal of Rural Development*, Vol. 19, No. 4, October–December, pp. 653–83.

NOTES

1. From the Website rd.cp.gov.in/CLDP/10-11-2012
2. G.O. Ms.No. 315 dt. 09 September 2011
3. There were detailed instructions in two tranches of circulars specifying projects under each category and types of works under each project (Circular No. 653/ EGS/PM(T)/2008 dated 06 October 2008 and 01 November 2008).
4. This part of the guidelines issued under the MGNREGS – New Works strategy by Commissioner of Rural Development Govt. of AP (Circular No.1192/EGS/ PM(T)/2010 dated 6 September 2010.
5. D.O. Letter No.770/IKP-EGS/2009 dated 31 October 2009 and Circular Memo No.1187/EGS/PM(T)/08 dated 04 November 2009, Commissioner of Rural Development, Govt. of AP, Hyderabad.
6. Circular No.1192/EGS/PM(T)/2010 dated 28 September 2010, Commissioner of Rural Development, Govt. of AP, Hyderabad.

2

Of Caste and Institutions of Higher Education: A Case Study of AIIMS

Vikas Bajpai
Anoop Saraya

Introduction

Different societies all over the World had to contend with a number of divisions that have bedeviled them since the beginning of history. Depending on their level of material, social, and intellectual advancement, different societies have struggled with and rationalized religion, race, ethnicity, and gender divisions differently.

Of the numerous fault lines in Indian society, divisions of caste are perhaps the most ubiquitous and prominent. Divisions of caste have a deep seated material and psychological basis that finds reflection in different spheres of life in India. It is only natural then that these divisions also find a reflection in the structure and functioning of societal institutions. This problem is compounded manifold when the institutions of higher learning become the epitome of such reactionary sentiments. In this article we shall trace and illustrate the consequences of such a degeneration of AIIMS (the All India Institute of Medical Sciences).

The Material Basis and Ideological Framework of Caste in India

- Caste is the sine qua non of Hindu religion; one cannot be a Hindu without belonging to a caste.
- Caste of a person is determined by birth and is immutable.
- Castes are hierarchical and endogamous groups broadly categorized on the basis of their occupation. In terms of occupations, hard physical labour is destined for the lower castes while the higher castes are designated for occupations concerned with the regulation and administration of society, including the ownership, control, and regulation of its principle means of production. Caste hierarchy enjoins, only upon the higher castes, the right to pursue more intellectual pursuits.

- As we move up in the caste hierarchy, the privileges of castes increase while the disabilities increase in the reverse order, with the lowest of the castes being considered as untouchables and are entitled to least material comforts.
- Caste divisions have a religious sanctity and one is enjoined by religion to follow the 'Dharma' (duties) of his caste. As the Hindu philosophy has it, it is only by the observance of one's *dharma* that a person can gain *moksha* (redemption from the cycle of life and death).
- Castes pervade all the major religions in India including Islam, Christianity, Sikhism, Buddhism, and Jainism inspite of the fact that these religions are strongly rooted in equality of all human beings and are conceptually antithetical to an institution like caste.

On the basis of these features of caste, certain consequences follow: hard physical labour is to be performed by the lower castes, and these castes have least rights and meagre material entitlements; lower castes are also more numerous; these features together with the immutability of caste render the multitudes of lower castes as a permanent source of cheap labour. Hence, caste system was a readymade mechanism for extraction of cheap labour that was too attractive for the rulers of the day to be dismantled or interfered with. Resultantly, even the Muslim and Christian rulers who came from outside used the institution of caste to establish and strengthen their rule by co-opting the higher castes in their administrative set-ups.

Even today, with the employment in the formal sector of the economy being very small, as much as 52 per cent of the country's labour force is still engaged in agriculture and allied activities. An overwhelming majority of this labour force is small and marginal farmers and the landless agricultural labourers who belong to the backward and the lower castes or the Tribes, while all the big landlords, with some exceptions, belong to the upper castes. Certain other occupations like the leather and the sanitation work and the priestly class continue to belong almost exclusively to specific castes even today.

The Dalit movement in the country under the leadership of the socially advanced Dalits have sought reservations for themselves in the legislature, in government jobs, and educational institutions rather than demand for radical redistribution of the society's productive resources, especially the redistribution of land in the villages. The ruling elite, comprising largely of the upper castes, finds it easier to accommodate these demands, to ward off a much larger and forceful political mobilization of the oppressed castes directed at a radical redistribution of society's resources.

Politically speaking, the demand for reservations does not question the exploitative nature of the present social, economic and political structure of the society, but merely seeks its greater democratization to the extent of co-opting the better off among lower castes.

A modern State, based on the principles of universal suffrage and equality of all people before law coupled with wider recognition of the rights of the oppressed under the impact of their popular political mobilization, makes the earlier kind of coercive caste oppression difficult to obtain. This coupled with factors like greater sophistication of production processes and a wider knowledge base of economy requiring higher levels of technical and intellectual capabilities has meant that forms of domination over lower castes have also become more sublime. A greater access to and control over the institutions of higher learning by the upper castes has come to acquire a crucial role in this respect.

This then lays down for us the ideological framework for the case study of caste at the All India Institute of Medical Sciences (AIIMS). Many of the instances to be discussed in the following sections are of the anti-reservation agitation that took place in the country in 2006, of which the Institute was decidedly the epicenter.

Before Caste Broke in at AIIMS: A Background

Much like any other medical or professional institution, AIIMS has very much been a repository of the elite sections of the society in India. However, there has been a prolonged phase in the history of the Institute when the political life on the campus and the mass organizations of different sections came to be dominated by people owing allegiance to the Progressive Left movement in the country between early 1970s till 1990, after which this influence gradually tapered off and remains minimal.

The different mass organizations that have existed on the campus are the Student's Union (SU) representing the undergraduate medical students, the Resident Doctor's Association (RDA), the Society of Young Scientists (SYS), the Karamchari Union of the group C and D employees, the Nurses Union and the Faculty Association of AIIMS. Apart from this there are separate associations of some sections to lobby for sectional interests, including the SC and ST association. For the last several years the only activities of the SC and ST association have been to observe the birth anniversary and the anniversary of conversion to Buddhism of the leading dalit icon of the country, Dr B.R. Ambedkar.

The crowning moment in the history of democratic struggles at AIIMS campus came when the SU boycotted and actively opposed the celebration of country's Independence Day at AIIMS in 1975 on account of the declaration of emergency in the country in that year. Two students, including the then SU president, were expelled from the institute for organizing the boycott.

This forte of progressive politics that had stood out as a shining example from among the many institutions of professional education in the country was however badly dented in the course of the first anti-Mandal agitation, which was against reserving 28 per cent seats for OBCs—other backward castes—in government jobs.

On being reduced to a minority, students and doctors owing allegiance to the Left disassociated themselves from bodies like the SU, RDA, and the SYS under the then prevailing political circumstances and formed a different organization by the name of Delhi Medicos and Scientists Forum (DMSF). From the time of its formation, the DMSF consistently took up issues of caste discrimination that had surfaced in the different medical colleges in the wake of the 1990 anti-reservation agitation and beyond.

Foregoing description lays down for us the context in which to understand the more recent upsurge in the upper caste chauvinist sentiments at AIIMS.

Ensuring the Dominance of the Upper Castes

Tensions in themselves are not the problem; they are only to be expected when the hegemony of the dominant sections is challenged by the subaltern sections. The problem is that the manner of implementation of reservations creates these tensions without commensurate empowerment of the oppressed castes, which would enable them to contend forcefully in the on-campus politics. In fact, empowerment as a social objective of 'reservation policy' is an aspect that has become increasingly obscure; rather the extent and the manner of implementation of reservations is increasingly designed to make the reserved category persons feel obliged to the upper castes for granting this concession. Quintessentially, this is reflected in the fact that rather than proudly proclaiming reservation as their right, within the four walls of these campuses, students belonging to reserved castes unsuccessfully seek to keep their caste identity obscure, especially those belonging to the Scheduled Castes (SCs) and the Scheduled Tribes (STs). Here there is a distinction between the backward castes and the SCs and STs, with the former being more assertive owing to their superior social position.

Blatant violation of constitutional reservations

The manner in which the upper caste chauvinist elements are increasingly resorting to disingenuous ways of scuttling the implementation of reservations was to be seen in the matter of filling up of faculty positions at AIIMS.

Appointment of entry level faculty at AIIMS

The denial of reservation in the appointment of entry level faculty at AIIMS is unique both for its method and scale. Between 1993 and 2003 the Institute did not conduct any regular appointment for faculty positions at entry level that is, for the posts of Assistant Professors on the plea that there was a writ petition pending in the High Court of Delhi filed by the faculty association of AIIMS (FAIIMS) against implementation of reservations in the appointments for faculty positions.

The Delhi High Court finally dismissed the petition saying that there was no reason to not 'apply the reservation rule for making regular appointment to the post of Assistant Professor' (GOI, 2007). The Court simultaneously dismissed another writ petition filed in the mean time in Delhi High Court, by the ad-hoc faculty for the regularization of their appointments (GOI, 2007).

Both the Faculty Association and the ad-hoc faculty filed special leave petitions (SLPs) in the Supreme Court against reservations in faculty appointment and for their regularization respectively. In the matter of the SLP filed by FAIMS the Supreme Court passed an interim order on the 11 of Jan 2002 saying that 'Any appointment to be made hereafter in accordance with the reservation policy will be only tentative in nature until further orders' (GOI, 2007). Seeing the criticality of the issues involved, the Court also recommended the petition to be heard by a larger bench.

In the SLP filed by the ad-hoc faculty the Supreme Court passed an interim order on the 25 November 2002 to the effect—'Let the process of selection be finalized. The application shall be put up for consideration thereafter and before any appointments are made' (GOI, 2007). In the meantime after the dismissal of the relevant writ petitions by the Delhi High Court, the Institute placed two advertisements inviting applications for the filling up of the posts of Assistant Professors purely on temporary basis. The advertisements dated 26 March 2002 and the 9 August 2002 clearly stated:

> The Appointments made against the posts of Asst Professors will be 'tentative in nature' and subject to final outcome of the SLP No. 2106/2002 pending before the Hon'ble Supreme Court of India on reservations of posts for SC/ST/OBC (GOI, 2007).

In the meantime, in a meeting held on 16 September 2002, the institute body passed the following decision:

> After detailed deliberation, it was decided that if the Assistant Professors (ad hoc) currently working at AIIMS are selected to regular faculty posts at AIIMS through regular selection process as per the recruitment rules, their period of ad hoc services will also be considered for promotion under APS as one time measure. However, Sh. B.P. Sharma, Joint Secretary opinioned that the same should be made applicable after they get selected through regular selection process (GOI, 2007).

Consequent to the aforementioned decision of the institute body, the governing body of the institute, in its meeting held on 17 April 2003 took the following decision:

> In so far as counting of the past ad hoc services rendered by the now selected Assistant Professors was concerned, the Governing Body was informed of the earlier resolution of the Institute Body for counting the period of ad hoc service. Since a case was also before the Supreme Court on the issue of regularization of ad hoc services, it was decided that the Court decision in this matter would be awaited. Further, in the circumstances where the relevant case before the Supreme Court was withdrawn by petitioners in view of the earlier decision of the Institute Body, the ad hoc period could be counted for the purpose of promotion under APS and for this purpose, DPCs would be convened (sic) subsequent date.

Subsequent to this decision the ad-hoc faculty members withdrew their SLP in the Supreme Court and finally the standing selection committee of AIIMS held interviews for the posts of Assistant Professors in April 2003.Further, it ought to be noted here that as per the Assessment Promotion Scheme of AIIMS, only those Assistant Professors who have completed four years of regular service are eligible for being promoted to the subsequent grade of Associate Professor.

Even as the aforementioned events unfolded, the ad-hoc faculty continued to swell in numbers until reaching a total of 152. As many as 45 per cent (a total of 69, kindly refer Table 1) of this ad hoc faculty had been appointed within a period of two years before the conduct of the interviews for filling up of the faculty posts in April 2003. A closer examination revealed that of these 69 ad-hoc faculty 22 had been in service for two years, while 23 had worked for a period of one year and 24 for less than a year's period. This clearly shows that even after the Delhi High Court had dismissed in 2001 the petition filed by the Faculty Association challenging the provision of reservations in faculty appointments and even after the faculty positions being advertised in 2002, AIIMS administration continued to make ad-hoc appointments.

Table 1: No. of years of service of Assistant Professors working on ad hoc basis (total=152)

No. of Asst Professors with 2 or less than 2 years of service	69 (45.3%)
No. of Asst Professors with 3 to 5 years of service	50 (33%)
No. of Asst Professors with 6 to 8 years of service	31 (20.4%)
No. of Asst Professors with more than 8 years of service	2 (1.3%)

Source: GOI, 2007.

Before it becomes too confusing to follow this trail any further, we need to make sense of the chronology of events mentioned so far without being overwhelmed by the details. We can recreate the logic of these events thus:

> In 1994 there was an acute shortage of junior level faculty at AIIMS that seriously hampered patient care as also medical teaching because as many as 219 posts of Assistant Professors in different departments were lying vacant. However, giving constitutional reservations for SCs and STs in the appointment of faculty was too

> unpalatable to the Institute administration dominated by the upper caste chauvinist elements; hence, a writ petition is got initiated on behalf of FAIMS in the Delhi High Court seeking abolition of reservations in the appointment of faculty at AIIMS.

Inspite of there being a clear cut policy on reservation in government jobs, the court entertains this writ petition and deliberates over it for seven long years before deciding that reservations have to be implemented in faculty appointments. But in the interregnum the Institute administration uses the alibi of a pending writ petition to postpone the process for regular appointment and instead allows ad-hoc appointments to be made without conforming to any set criterion, standards or credible procedures to ensure that only the deserving candidates were appointed. Procedure for regular appointments was kept in abeyance even though there was no restriction on its conduct through any court order. Over a period of ten years as many as 152 persons are appointed as ad-hoc faculty, that is, more than two third of the vacant posts.

A standard word of caution that is mentioned in any letter inviting a candidate to take an interview for any government job is that he/she should not do any canvassing or try to exercise any influence for getting himself/herself selected for the post; doing so could disqualify the candidate from being considered for the post. Apparently, such words of caution are applicable only to individuals and not to candidates organized as a group in pursuit of self promotion.

These are not mere insinuations for it does not happen every day that the highest administrative bodies (both institute body and the governing body of AIIMS) of the foremost medical institution in the country clear the decks for the promotion of ad-hoc faculty in anticipation of their regularization through a proper selection process on the basis of their ad-hoc service and in contravention of all rules and regulations. Nor was it a mere providence that soon after this decision of the institute body and its ratification by the governing body, the Institute administration decided to conduct the selection process. The brazenness and audacity of the whole process speaks from the fact that this decision was taken in spite of the fact that the Delhi High Court had already ruled that reservations have to be provided in the selection for faculty at entry level and the ad-hoc appointments had not been made in deference to this mandatory condition.

A total of 170 vacancies had been advertised for which ultimately 762 candidates had taken the interview including some from overseas and the 151 ad-hoc appointees. Of these 762 candidates 209 belonged to the reserved categories, while 553 belonged to the general categories (GOI, 2007). Ostensibly, only 162 selections were finally made. Of these 162 positions, finally 131 (81 per cent) selections were made from the pool of ad-hoc appointees, while only 28 (19 per cent) were made from the national pool of 611 candidates (GOI, 2007).

The Karan Singh Yadav Committee that was later constituted by the Ministry of Health and Family Welfare to look into the appropriateness of the process of selection of Assistant Professors and promotion of ad-hoc appointees to the next higher scale remarked in its report that—'the selection process was designed mainly to regularize the ad hoc faculty.' It also noted that 'there were several instances of highly meritorious candidates both in the reserved and in the general category who did not find place in the list of selected candidates.' It may also be noted that those ad-hoc candidates who were not selected continued to work on ad-hoc posts and were regularized in subsequent selections. Further, 64 of the selected ad-hoc Assistant Professors were promoted to the next grade of Associate Professors subsequent to their selection, in accordance with the earlier decision (in violation of the norms) taken by the Institute and Governing Bodies (GOI, 2007).

Denial of reservations

With the result of the selection process pre-destined and violation of all norms having already been sanctified at the highest political and bureaucratic level, it should be of little surprise that the rules for provision of reservations were flagrantly violated in the selection process. In fact, the implementation of reservations was in for quite some innovation.

The Government of India, Department of Personnel and Training office memorandum No. 36012/2/96-Estt. (Res.), dated the 2 July 1997 unambiguously lays down a post based roster system as the method to be followed in the implementation of reservat7ions (GOI, 1997). However, bypassing the norm, administration at AIIMS followed a unique system of 'floating reservation'. As per 'floating reservation' reservation of posts was 'to be adjusted wherever the reserved category candidates in the particular discipline/specialties/super specialties will be available. Hence the reserved category candidate who fulfils the recruitment rules for a particular discipline/specialty/super specialty will be considered against the reserved posts, subject to his/her performance in the interview' (GOI, 2007). According to the advertisement dated 26 March 2002 there were a total of 68 reserved posts out of a total of 167 advertized posts with a break up of – 9 (SC), 13 (ST) and 46 (OBC). As against these 68 posts also only 41 candidates were finally selected; this inspite of the fact that as per the Delhi High Court order dated 26 November 2001 *reservations for jobs had to be applied even for superspecialities* (GOI, 2007).

Further, in contravention of the relevant government orders no relaxation was provided for the reserved category candidates either in age or qualification or experience. The Karan Singh Yadav Committee found, on perusal of the position of the SC and ST candidates in the merit list from the documentary records of the selection process, that 'in most instances they figured in the middle or upper half of the list rather than at the bottom of the list.' Inspite of this, most reserved category candidates were adjusted against the reserved category vacancies, while the government orders regarding this explicitly state– 'in cases of direct recruitment to vacancies in posts under the Central Government, the SC/ST candidates who are selected on their own merit without relaxed standards along with candidates belonging to the other communities, will not be adjusted against the reserved share of vacancies' (GOI, 1989).

Needless to say that as a consequence of such practices, even in the past, the strength of reserved category faculty, resident doctors, nurses and even group C and D employees remains much below than what is constitutionally stipulated to be their minimum share in these jobs. Table 2 below gives the present strength of the different categories of employees as against the total strength and the stipulated minimum according to reservation criterion.

Table 2: Present strength of employees of different categories as against the total strength and the stipulated minimum as per reservation norms.

Sanctioned strength of different grades and share of posts reserved for different categories.

Name of post	*No. of sanctioned post*	*No. of reserved post*			*No. of posts filled by reservation*		
		SCs	*STs*	*OBCs*	*SCs*	*STs*	*OBCs*
Professor	119	17	8	32	-	-	-
Addl. Prof.	47	7	3	12	-	-	-
Assoc. Prof.	129	19	9	34	-	-	-
Asstt. Prof.	451	67	33	121	45	10	23

Source:

Appointment of Other Categories of Employees

A detailed description of the systematic undermining of reservations and rules in the appointment of faculty at AIIMS should give us an idea of the possibilities that exist in managing appointments for different categories of employees. Faculty positions are the most sought after and hence are likely to garner much greater public scrutiny; and if such flagrant violation of rules can take place in faculty appointments, then little need be left to imagination as regards other appointments. However, here we shall limit ourselves to the point of violation of reservation policy in appointment of different categories of doctors and medical students.

Appointment of Senior Resident Doctors

Senior residency is a three-year tenure job that is given to a person who has obtained a postgraduate degree (usually an MD or MS in a clinical, para-clinical, or pre-clinical subject. Being a proper government employment, provision of reservation is to be observed even in the appointment of senior resident doctors and they are covered by the service conditions meant for other Group B government employees. The procedure for selection of senior resident doctors is different in different hospitals/medical colleges. At most places, it is done by way of interview that is purely subjective, and as such, liable to exercise of quite some extraneous influence.

At AIIMS, the procedure followed was by way of a written examination and the candidates were selected by merit following a formal departmental interview and subject to conditions for implementation of reservations. The weightage given to the departmental interview was such that it could not undermine the candidate's performance in the written exam. However, from time to time, there have been interruptions in this procedure either on account of court cases or administrative reasons.

Importantly enough, in the wake of virulent anti-reservation agitation, as the one which took place in 2006, an atmosphere is created wherein the local administration considers it its birth right to undermine the rules for reservations and manages to do so with impunity. The attempts at such manipulation or the manner of giving reservations is such that makes these selections controversial and a subject of legal disputes, which are liberally entertained by the judiciary. This happened even in the case of AIIMS after the 2006 anti-reservation agitation. During the pendency of litigation regarding appointment of senior resident doctors, the method adopted for senior resident appointments at AIIMS was through ad-hoc appointments purely as per the whims and fancy of the departmental heads, most of whom were frankly inimical to the reserved category candidates.

The heads of different departments or senior faculty members tended to consider such ad-hoc appointments of senior residents as a matter of their paternal right rather than being subject to certain mandatory rules and regulations. In one instance, the head of the department of Obstetrics and Gynecology at AIIMS openly declared that she would not take a particular reserved category candidate so long as she was the head, even though she fulfilled the eligibility criterion and a vacancy was available in the department. Frustrated at this attitude, the candidate approached the Central Commission for Scheduled Castes, only to find little help in the matter.

The first formal selection of senior resident doctors after the 2006 anti-reservation agitation was held in June–August 2007. No roster-based earmarking of seats was done for identifying the reserved seats prior to initiating the selection process. The statutory relaxations in age and eligibility criterion due to the reserved category candidates were not included in the advertisement for the posts.

A written exam was held for selection to 106 posts of senior residency on the 20 June. In this selection, for the first time ever, a new criterion of obtaining a minimum of 50 per cent marks in the departmental assessment was introduced. This meant that even if a candidate scored 100 per cent marks in the objective written examination, he or she could easily be prevented from being selected by giving him or her less than 50 per cent marks in the totally subjective departmental assessment. This implied that a candidate who got 100 out of 100 marks in the written section, but only 49 out of 100 in departmental assessment would still fail to get selected and would be ranked lower than a candidate getting 50 out of 100 in the written portion as well as departmental assessment.

The purpose of personalized assessment, by way of an interview of a candidate who fulfills the eligibility criterion and has cleared the objective written exam, can only be in the nature of reaffirming his ability to do the required job. At a time, when the whole atmosphere in the institute seemed so vindictive towards the reserved category students and doctors, such a drastic and unjustified change in the policy was done patently with the purpose of denying reservations.

It is noteworthy that for 106 seats, as many as 84 reserved category candidates had qualified in the written examination. However, only 24 of them were finally selected after the departmental assessment as against the statutory minimum figure of 53.

Later, when the issue was raised by the Progressive Medicos and Scientists Forum, a committee was set up by the Ministry of Health and Family Welfare under the Chairmanship of the then Secretary Health & Family Welfare, Sh. Naresh Dayal, to examine the whole issue. In its report submitted on the 4 January 2008, the Committee observed that 'the selection process was not in consonance with the judgment of the Division Bench of the Hon'ble Delhi High Court (in W.A. 127 of 2003). The judgment had held that a selection process relying mainly on interview or giving minimum marks for the interview cannot be held valid' (GOI, 2008).

The Committee had annulled these selections and had given recommendations for future selections. Unfortunately, a single bench of the Delhi High Court stayed any proceedings on this selection.

Selection of Undergraduate Medical Students

After the 2006 agitation, for the first time in the history of AIIMS an occasion came that full quota of reserved category seats in the MBBS entrance examination could not be filled. Table 3 gives the year wise details of students admitted to the MBBS course at AIIMS after 2006.

Table 3: Total number of undergraduate medical seats and the proportion of students of different categories against the stipulated minimum as per the reservation norms for different years.

Position of seats advertised and filled for Junior Residents – (Students MD/MS/MDS)

Year	*Advertised Total seats*	*Gen.*	*SC*	*ST*	*OBC*
2009Filled	201	125139	2517	115	4040
2010Filled	265	173180	3336	1813	4141
2011Filled	251	163168	3131	1611	4141
2012Filled	123	7984	1416	92	2121

Sanctioned/in position seats in various courses.

Courses	*Sanctioned seats*	*In position*	*Genl.*	*SC*	*ST*	*OBC*
SR-Non Academic	769	566+119	417	52	13	84
SR-Academic	167+59	164+44	164	-	-	-
JR	702	651	410	73	26	94
MBBS	77/yr.	354	186	44	24	76

Source: Information Collected Through RTI from AIIMS Academic Section.

Consequences of Such Mechanizations

This kind of antipathy for affirmative action through reservations is not merely on account of losing out a few government jobs or prized seats in the institutions of higher learning which no doubt are scarce. Judging by the intensity of upper caste chauvinist reaction that has been on display during the anti-reservation agitations and the numerous instances of caste-based harassment of reserved category students in various professional colleges, including instances of suicides which keep surfacing every now and then, there is definitely a strong element of caste hatred involved in the opposition to reservation policy.

The unity and vociferousness of the upper castes spanning across different sections of the society; may it be the polity, the government bureaucracy, the judiciary, the academia, the media or the general upper caste masses at the time of an upsurge of upper caste chauvinist sentiment leaves nothing to doubt as to this caste hatred. During the last anti-reservation agitation, retired professors and many senior citizens whose children or even grandchildren might be well settled in life, in India or possibly abroad, came to lend their support to the anti-reservation crusaders. They possibly had no worries of the career prospects of their children or grandchildren being marred by reservations. It was their caste solidarity that motivated and moved them.

We have discussed here the sabotaging of reservations at AIIMS; but we can be rest assured that if others also decide to write of such instances we can have such examples from almost every government institution in the country. Besides being unjust and socially destructive, such mechanizations only result in poor intellectual development of our academic institutions.

Supremacy of 'merit' is the mother of all arguments that is most often foisted against reservations, but as we have seen in the case of appointments to faculty positions at AIIMS, merit is the first casualty in such frauds. Rather, in the name of opposing reservations of every rule and regulation meant to ensure selection of candidates with high caliber is violated. Once violation of one rule becomes acceptable in the zest to safeguard 'merit', then disregard for other rules is the only logical consequence.

At AIIMS, all the ad-hoc appointees ultimately got regularized. At the time of their ad-hoc appointment, they did not have to face any interview, and indeed, some of them did not even satisfy the eligibility criterion. Who then could have been the most likely of persons to be considered fit for such an appointment? Would it be a person who is proficient in his work but brooks no nonsense, or one who is critical of government's policies of commercializing health care; or would it be a person who is close to the centre/centers of authority? If the common life experience of an average Indian is anything to go by, we can be rest assured that the later kind stands a much better chance and indeed there can be any number of such persons who can be cited from among those who made it through the back door at AIIMS.

What is the worth of such persons in contributing to the intellectual growth of an Institution? Can we expect such appointees to stand up to the authorities in opposing the anti people policies of commercializing health care when they know that it is only because of these authorities that they occupy their present position? Such people can sadly be expected only to spread a culture of sycophancy. Such trends can only be suicidal for the intellectual wellbeing of an academic institution, let alone their being an instrument of alleviating people's miseries.

These are not merely ideal philosophical concepts, but are of immense relevance to what an institution contributes to a society. The kind of research that will get done, on what questions and for whose interest are some of the questions that are directly related to the kind of people who come to occupy exalted positions in institutions like AIIMS. We shall see later in the paper, how caste chauvinist sentiments, or ignorance about the role of caste in our society can cloud the orientation and academic quality of work done at these institutions.

What happens once the reserved category students/doctors make it to AIIMS?

After trying to sabotage the provisions of reservations at various levels of entry into these elite institutions, the attention gets focused on discrimination against persons of oppressed castes who do manage to get past the first obstacle, in the academic and social life of these institutions. Just like any other such institution, AIIMS has its own history in this respect; the difference is that AIIMS being the most hallowed of them all, it tends to become the trend setter of sorts.

It would indeed be most desirable that persons who face oppression on account of their caste come forward to recount their experiences with all intensity of emotion and detail, and how these experiences have dented their lives. Even as one may empathize with the plight of the oppressed castes, we wonder if it is possible to get a sense of the kind of humiliation that a person of a lower caste may be subject to and the impact that this has on his/her psychological well being; or the distortions it may effect in their personality.

It has been our experience, that unless a critical mass of people, motivated by a feeling of social injustice and hurt, as opposed to individual injustice, is materialized, the persons of lower caste may only withdraw deeper into their shells as a defensive mechanism, hoping that they shall be individually spared ignominy.

We shall not describe here all the incidents of caste discrimination at AIIMS. The attempt instead will be to elicit the processes of discrimination and their intensity through examples that are appropriate for this purpose.

The Social Divide

Among the various social fault lines existing in society and which get reflected in the campus life of the elite institutions of higher learning, caste is by far the most ubiquitous. Muslims simply aren't there in any strength to count for in these institutions. The social perception and attitude towards other religious minorities are markedly different for social and political reasons other than those having to do with the virtues of their religion.

The significance of caste needs to be brought out in terms of the fear of being ostracized that is there especially among the lower caste students, and their defense to cope with this. In this respect, an incident at the Maulana Azad Medical College (MAMC) is instructive. Every year, a Dalit organization at MAMC decided to felicitate new students of reserved category soon after their joining the college and introduce them to the reserved category faculty of the college. A day after the students had been felicitated, parents of a few of them came to see the professor who led this organization and charged him of having irreparably harmed their wards by exposing their identity. That was the first and the last open felicitation function they organized.

Caste divides in the hostels

Invariably, in the hostels, there are distinct portions that are inhabited by the general and the reserved category students. Perhaps every boys' hostel in the Delhi medical colleges has a 'shiddu' mohalla (where reserved category students live). We cannot say that it is necessarily the same in girls hostels as well, but there certainly is no reason to believe that the situation is much different. The only difference can be that in co-education colleges the proportion of girls from reserved categories is generally small compared to boys, hence, this separation of dwellings may not appear so stark in girl's hostels. From what is known generally, goings on in state medical colleges are perhaps even worse.

There are some notable exceptions to this scheme of things, that is, those reserved category students with either public school background or the few who are really from the very well to do families. This variety of reserved category students, invariably have a greater confidence about themselves. Unlike most of their other caste brethren, these are more suave, English speaking, and would generally be comfortable doing things that are up market. In keeping with the general scheme of things in our society, this lot seeks acceptance not from others of their caste; indeed they may not even bother about them. They generally mill around, and might get accepted among the better half of the divide, or just be in a limbo and form a category of their own.

Once categorization of living space in the hostels is settled, the rest follows automatically. You eat with those, with whom you live; you share your lecture notes, your hurt, your joys, your sorrows with them, and they are your pals in the thick and thin of things. In Delhi medical colleges, pals of different caste feathers even dine on different tables, or on the same table, but at different times. Nobody enforces this formally, but that is how things are. As they say, it is in the air.

These taboos seldom get broken. If they do by way of an inadvertent chance, it wouldn't be without raising at least a few eyebrows. The night of 22 February 1999 was one such ugly night at the boy's hostel of University College of Medical Sciences, for that was the night when the reserved category boys of the hostel had to face the fury of the upper caste students in full physical force. That night, the public address system of the hostel was used to summon all the general category students on the ground floor before they proceeded to pull the reserved category students out of their rooms and bash them up (Varadharajan, 1999). The bashing up was not just a few slaps and punches. To give an idea of what went on, one young Dalit boy had to save his life by hiding behind the water tank of the seven-storyed hostel all night long on a cold February night, even as all the belongings in his room were thrown out of the balcony and his motorbike set afire. From what we know from friends in other colleges, physical exchanges between the reserved and the non-reserved category students happen in other colleges as well. This incident at UCMS was however unique. The college remained closed for about a month's time after the incident with rival parties pitching their tents in the college grounds.

By virtue of having been a former General Secretary of the student's union of UCMS and as a political activist the first author of this paper went along with activists of the DMSF to the aid of the dalit students of UCMS. In the ground in front of the college building, to one side was the tent of the SC and ST Students Association and on the other side was the tent of the upper caste students who identified themselves by the banner of 'Manuwadi Chattra Morcha.' For the Dalits and the STs, caste is a condition of daily living, the ignominy of which they have to confront at every step. It is understandable that these sections form their caste organizations, but that the upper caste students should organize themselves under the banner of 'Manuwadi Chatra Morcha' is outright brazen, Manu being the ancient Indian administrator who is credited with having codified the caste hierarchy.

A comment need be reserved here for the complicity of those who choose to remain silent, or generously contribute to the situation through their studied passivity. On one of the visits to the college in that situation, the first author of this paper, along with activists of DMSF and the Democratic Students Union (DSU—a Left revolutionary student organization), led a rally of the Dalit students within the campus. Later, even as he addressed the gathering at the culmination of the rally at college gates, a particular professor, whom we know to be associated with a Left party, stood listening to us from a distance, but refused to join us saying that 'you don't know; it's a big game' and that 'these students are being manipulated by big players.' While it could definitely be possible that the oppressed dalit students went to all the big names in caste politics seeking their intervention, unable to get any protection from their college authorities. However, what the learned professor did not care to explain was—what were all the progressive people like him on the campus doing when the game was only as big as the fact that these students had been the victims of 'brazen caste violence'?

We would like to mention here another thing about this incident at UCMS that leaves us with much food for thought. On one of the days these, students of UCMS decided to hold a demonstration at the Ministry of Social Welfare, Government of India. Rather than try to impose our thinking on these students we had offered all help to them in the agitational steps that they decided even as we did give constructive suggestions. We told some sanitation workers of our then existing union at AIIMS to come along for this demonstration. They told us—'Comrade we will come if you say so, but we would like you to know that on occasions when we need some help from them, from amongst all doctors, it is these doctors who seek to avoid us the most.' We will link up with this observation later.

The hostels of AIIMS

The caste situation in hostels that has been described above, varies in different institutions only in shades; the crux of the matter is however the same. At AIIMS the caste tensions in the hostels had become particularly acute in the wake of the anti-reservation agitation of 2006. Parts of AIIMS hostels were overnight converted into SC, ST ghettos with reserved category students being 'hunted out' of their rooms. We reproduce here portions of a report published on the front page of *The Telegraph*, Kolkata, verbatim (Kasturi, 2006).

'An engraved message on the door of Room No. 49 (Hostel 1) bears testimony to their concern. The inscription, spiced with abusive language, asks the room's occupant Umakant—a scheduled caste student—to 'get out of this (hostel) wing.'

'The top floors of Hostel No. 4 and 5 of the country's premier medical school have 32 rooms in all, of which 27 are occupied by SC/ST students. Of the 250 students at the institute, 55 are SC/ST.'

'Hostel records show that 22 of the students currently in the 'ghetto' moved there only in the wake of the surcharged atmosphere of the anti-reservation agitation..........Many more want to shift but cannot because there aren't enough rooms for everyone.'

These reports appeared in many newspapers at that time, but to no avail. Neither the government nor the local authorities did anything about this. The 'Medicos Forum for Equal Opportunities', which was the successor body to the DMSF and which now goes by the name of 'Progressive Medicos and Scientists Forum' first took up this matter in the institute. A team of some senior faculty members, belonging both to the reserved and the non-reserved categories investigated the situation in the hostels and brought out a report that was widely publicized.

Some of the findings of the report are even more startling and reveal that the social division indeed goes much deeper. For example, it was found that:

> A sad example of caste based segregation occurs on the 'unequal' playing fields. Reserved category students play football and volleyball and general category students play basketball and cricket. Most general category students find it beneath their dignity to play team games dominated by the reserved category students

> and the reserved category students feel that they are demeaned and discriminated against (e.g. during team selection) while playing basketball and cricket (MFEO, 2006).

As to the segregation of living space it was found:

> While the written threats probably occurred in the aftermath of the chauvinistic anti-reservation agitation (which in no way justifies the undemocratic actions of the offenders), the segregation has been deepening for quite some time. Many reserved category students mentioned that they had opted for rooms in hostel number 4 & 5 because of the hostile milieu years before the agitation began (MFEO, 2006).

As to the role of the AIIMS administration the report said:

> While they may claim ignorance of the situation, their hypersensitive reaction to anti-reservation issues, suggests that they are taking a permissive role in the formation of the 'ghetto', by willfully turning a blind eye to the problems of the reserved category students (MFEO, 2006).

Most of the findings of the MFEO report were confirmed subsequently in the report of the Committee to Enquire in to the Allegation of Differential Treatment of SC/ST Students in All India Institute of Medical Science, Delhi, that was set up by the Ministry of Health and Family Welfare under the chairmanship of Prof SukhdeoThorat, the then Chairman of the University Grants Commission. Besides ProfThorat, the other members of the Committee were Dr Shyamprasad, Member Governing Body of AIIMS and Dr Rakesh Srivastava, Director General Health Services, Government of India (GOI, 2007). The Committee found that intimidation of the reserved category students by the general category students was common. A message on the door of a reserved category student read—'get out of this wing—you will not have peace with us. Nobody will talk to you, so you get lost and you will be thrashed' (GOI, 2007).

The situation in the girls' hostel was much the same. The Committee noted that the girls 'are not vocal about their problem because of the fear...just suffer without complaining. In case of the hostel, the SC/ST girls are not separated in one single hostel. But they do live in a group. Social isolation is as much a problem for girls as it is for boys.'

The role of the administration in all this was not confined to just being permissive; rather, it actively tried to suppress and even falsify these facts. After the submission of the Thorat Committee Report, the then AIIMS administration, headed by Dr P. Venugopal set up an eight member committee of senior faculty members of AIIMS to 'review findings, observations and recommendations of the committee' (Dhar, 2007), that is, Thorat Committee. This Committee was dominated by handpicked professors, a majority of whom belonged to the reserved category and had liberally lent themselves as a shield for the blatantly upper caste chauvinist administration of AIIMS. This AIIMS Committee, headed by Prof C.S. Pandav, the head of the department of 'Preventive and Social Medicine' rejected the findings of Thorat Committee (Dhar, 2007). It may be mentioned here that these names are not being disclosed by us over here anew and are already available in public domain in the context being talked of.

Negating the aforementioned findings, the AIIMS Committee said of the Thorat Committee that it was—'biased and unsubstantiated' and that 'The Thorat Committee acted with a clear prejudice to deliver a misleading report that relies on imaginary facts, flawed methodology and baseless conclusions apparently with the sole purpose of discrediting the AIIMS' (Dhar, 2007). It added—'allegations regarding the institute's role in the anti-reservation strike were 'baseless and unjustified' as the Youth for Equality—spearheading the agitation—did not exist' (Dhar, 2007). It further said—'The sample of students who were interviewed was miniscule and conveniently selected. Also, the questionnaire was developed in such a way that it lead to replies in a biased direction' (Dhar, 2007).

The condescending attitude of the AIIMS administration is attested to by another incident. A few weeks before the anti-reservation agitation broke out; a video shot in the AIIMS boy's hostelwas widely circulated among the students. To the tunes of background music, some of the students were shot burning the books of the biggest of the Dalit icons, Dr B.R. Ambedkar in the corridor of one of the hostels. Even as they were burning the books, they kept making obscene gestures on camera. All the students involved in the act were clearly identifiable. This video was subsequently released to the press by the MFEO. Rather than take action against the erring students some of whom were very much on the campus, reacting to the release of the video the then AIIMS spokesperson is reported to have told the press that the video was shot in the hostels a few years back and that it was released to flare up the caste tensions. There was not even a formal statement of condemnation, let alone talk of taking action against the guilty.

The question that need be asked here is what enables an administration to adopt such openly belligerent attitudes towards superior authorities, when at other times such attitudes would have seen a few heads roll? What fuels the audacity of so brazenly abusing the man who is otherwise eulogized by those in power as the 'father of the country's constitution', and above that, the official spokesperson of the country's premier government medical institute virtually gives a clean chit to the perpetrators while accusing those who brought the video to light, of spreading caste tensions? It need be known here that all of these developments were all along in the know of the Prime Minister's office and the MPs and leaders of all the principle political parties, who were informed by way of various memorandums, representations and personal meetings either by MFEO or different individuals.

We can't help but reserve greatest of scorn for the sophistry of those who argue against any affirmative action in favour of the oppressed castes and justify the expressions of upper caste chauvinism as merely an expression of frustration. But they have not a word to offer for the frustration of the oppressed caste people at being treated by the society as lesser humans, let alone condemn the reprehensible acts of upper caste chauvinism. They try to occupy a high moral ground by talking of merit and making the lower castes equal with the rest by ensuring their educational and economic uplift; and yet, they raise not even one question against the present unjust social, economic and political order that perpetuates precisely this backwardness of the lower castes and the Tribes. Rather, it is the present ordering of things in the society that ensures the privileges of the dominant castes.

Truly speaking, merit is a societal phenomenon that operates at individual level. It is the overall development of socioeconomic conditions of the society, the distribution of the societal resources and the access of different people to these resources mediated through the economic, social and political structuring of society, which brings out the merit in individuals. Variation in individual merit on account of biological or genetic factors is minimal and is again determined by the material well being of the people.

Many among the upper castes, and a good number of well meaning people among them, also start by recounting their own poor economic condition, or that of many of their relatives and friends to show that their own condition is no better than that of the oppressed castes. The implication is that social disadvantage is an economic phenomenon rather than being determined by caste; hence, why should the not so well to do among the upper castes be disadvantaged in any way by the provision of reservations for the lower castes?

While it is true that the economic condition of a large section of even the upper castes is poor, public policies are not made for considerations like who has how many poor cousins or friends. They are made based on the overall conditions of large population groups in the society. There certainly are very many whites who are poor or homeless in the US, but can that be a reason for denying the affirmative action for the blacks in that society who remain ostracized in many more ways than the poor whites. Likewise, the disabilities of lower castes go far beyond their inferior economic condition. We have already discussed the material basis of caste as being a source of cheap or usurious labour; hence, the system has a vested interest in maintaining and propagating caste disabilities.

One need only compare the relative positions of the upper and the lower castes as regards their social and economic development from large national level data sets like the National Family Health Surveys (NFHS), National Sample Surveys (NSS) and the district level health surveys to know if as caste groups these two stand at the same pedestal. Even as the disabilities of the poor among the upper castes are also considerable, the fact remains that the lower castes lag far behind (refer to Table 4).

The condition of a poor Brahmin is not the same as that of a poor Jatav (a caste of leather workers). A poor Brahmin in all likelihood has a much larger and richer social capital i.e. his community resources that might be better placed to help him as compared to that of a poor Jatav. Even if a Jatav becomes economically well off in a generation's time, his or her social milieu may still not afford them access to a number of societal resources that are necessary for their cultural and intellectual advancement. A greater democratization of our society, for which reservation in jobs and educational institutions is only a small reformative measure, is the way to ensure an all round economic, social, cultural, and intellectual advancement of the oppressed castes and Tribes.

The paucity of cultural refinement of the upper castes is further illustrated by the following statement made by a very senior professor of AIIMS in a conversation on caste with the second author of the paper. This learned professor argued that he firmly believed that the lower castes are a genetically inferior lot who are not as good as others in performance of jobs requiring greater intellectual capabilities. These words coming from a professor of biomedical sciences are amazing indeed, but certainly not exceptional, for such views might be much more common than what is otherwise portrayed. Dr James Watson, the controversial discoverer of the structure of DNA and a Nobel Prize laureate said similar thing regarding the IQ of the black people (Derbyshire, 2007).

They shall brook no opposition

Sine-qua-non of any chauvinist sentiment is that it so blinds a person with rage and belief in his or her own superiority that even smallest of dogged resistance can easily infuriate them. That a good section of students and doctors had stood up to their might became the raison d'être for the anti-reservationists to systematically unleash vengeance against those who were perceived to be closely associated with resistance. In almost every department, doctors from reserved categories or even general categories were targeted to a lesser or greater degree for their association with the pro-reservation movement.

Case of Ajay Singh and associated tensions

Ajay Kumar Singh was a reserved category student of the final semester of MBBS course at AIIMS at the time when the anti-reservation agitation broke out. We met him in the course of our investigation into cases of caste

Table 4: Health Outcome Indicators Disaggregated by Caste/Tribe.

Caste or Tribe	*Infant mortality rate*	*Under five Mortality rate*	*State of chronic malnutrition (low height for age) in children under 5yrs of age; % of children below-2SD*	*% Prevalence of anemia in children of age between 6 to 59 months*	*% of women with anemia in the age group of 15-49 yrs.*	*% of men with anemia in the age group of 15-49 yrs.*	*% of women in the age group of 15-45 yrs with BMI < 18.5*	*% of men in age group 15-45 yrs with BMI <18.5*	*% of deliveries in health facilities*	*% of house-holds covered by health scheme or health insurance*
SC	66.4	88.1	53.9	72.2	58.3	26.6	41.1	39.1	32.9	3.3
ST	62.1	95.7	53.9	76.8	68.5	39.6	46.6	41.3	17.7	2.6
OBC	56.6	72.8	48.8	70.3	54.4	23.3	35.7	34.6	37.7	3.8
Others	48.9	59.2	40.7	63.8	51.3	20.9	29.4	28.9	51.0	7.8

Source: Registrar General of India: Report of the National Family Health Survey (NFHS-3), 2005–06, India, Volume I.

discrimination in the hostels. He was very forthwith in helping us and helped in arranging a meeting with many of the affected reserved category students. Subsequently, after the MFEO and later PMSF took lead in organizing these students to fight for their rights and against their oppression, Ajay played an active role in mobilizing students from the hostels. He was the first signatory on a memorandum submitted to the AIIMS director by about 40 students against caste based discrimination in the hostels. Significantly, among the signatories a few general category students were also there.

Even as the students voiced their concerns and problems to the administration, many among them anticipated that they would be subject to discriminatory behavior by the faculty in the exam on account of the prevailing atmosphere at the campus. However, they decided to come out in open as they saw this as their only chance to protect themselves as the faculty members associated with PMSF and many others were fully supporting them.

Nonetheless, Ajay was specifically targeted in his final MBBS exam that followed soon after the anti-reservation agitation was over. He was failed in three subjects and one of the examiners made pointed remarks during his viva regarding his participation in the pro-reservation agitation. Ajay submitted his representation against this to various authorities including the President of the Institute Body, the Governing Body (GB) and the Director of the Institute. The director, Dr Venugopal ordered a reexamination for Ajay, thereby admitting that there was a problem with the first examination. However, the examination was ordered under the same set of examiners despite the fact that the Faculty Association of AIIMS had opposed the reexamination (GOI, 2007).

This matter was even discussed threadbare in the GB meeting of AIIMS and the GB directed AIIMS director to have the examination conducted under the charge of dean academics rather than dean examinations. However, defying the directions of the GB the reexamination was again conducted under dean examinations by the earlier set of examiners and Ajay was failed once again. Later, due to sustained pressure put on by PMSF, Ajay cleared all subjects subsequently; however, he lost one year in transaction.

Failing of reserved category candidates is generally a common phenomenon in various professional colleges, especially medical colleges. Often these students are made to waste many years in passing the course. In one of the meetings with the reserved category, students in the hostel we put this question to them that many of the faculty allege that these students do not wish to work hard. The reply we got is worth a consideration.

One of the students, who was otherwise a very bright boy and even doing academically well told:

> Sir, while we were in school most of us were very good students and that is why we made it to AIIMS, because inspite of provision of reservations you have to

> score really good to make it to institutions like AIIMS, which even otherwise have so few seats. However, when we come here, our scores start dropping inspite of hard work; especially in practical examinations. Soon the reasons for this become very apparent to all of us and then the students lose interest in studies; especially as they become objects of ridicule by their teachers and peers alike. Their thinking then becomes that so long as we are in college let us make merry. Though there are reserved category students who do quite well, but even their scores are much below their potential.

Those on the other side of this divide vehemently protest that there is no such thing as discrimination. It's a fallacy that is constructed to cover up the lack of merit and hard work on part of these students. While we can agree that there might be reserved category students who are insincere, there is no reason to believe that the reserved category students are any more liable to such lack of sincerity than the general category students simply because they have got the benefit of reservation and therefore the presumption that they had it too easy to realize it's worth.

Neither do our government, or the teachers, or our educationalists have the time to think of such problems, nor does the system provide for any remedial action. Under the circumstances, the simplistic and straight forward solution is to give a bad name to the dog and kill it; the question of 'merit' becomes the favored weapon of demeaning reserved category students. There is little research done on the difficulties faced by the students and faculty of the marginalized sections in these elite institutions.

Our opponents would readily come up with examples of many students who have overcome such disabilities and then seek to generalize the applicability of such exceptions. The point, however, is that systems are to be designed to cater to the general conditions and not only the exceptions; though we would agree that with little help such exceptions can become much more numerous to create general conditions of qualitatively much higher level.

Caste tensions ran high on different campuses in the aftermath of the anti-reservation agitation. The situation at UCMS once again seems to have been very difficult for the reserved category students. Such was their morbid fear that perhaps they found it difficult to even articulate their fears and concerns openly on the campus. Resultantly, a meeting of reserved category students of UCMS was organized by the Delhi SC and ST doctor's association at the Maulana Azad Medical College; that too on a Sunday. We were invited to address the meeting on behalf of PMSF.

We wondered as to why this meeting could not be organized at UCMS itself? Moreover, holding it on a Sunday when there was nobody to even notice that such a meeting was held, seemed to be of little use. Even as the meeting was in progress, a resident doctor of Lady Hardinge Medical College (LHMC), who knew some of these students informed that 'Sir, they were too scared to hold this meeting on their campus.' During the meeting most of the students expressed the fear that in the professional examinations that were soon to follow, a large number of them would be failed in one or more subjects. Seemingly offering a solution to their problems, a professor from the same campus while addressing the students started singing paeans of his own bravery, as to how in a departmental dispute with a upper caste professor he had given him a good thrashing. He actually demonstrated the method by which he brought the other fellow down. The question however was—why could he not use his bravery to challenge the upper caste chauvinist forces on the UCMS campus itself which would have enthused these students much more to get organized and resolve the questions that were bothering them, rather than having to come to another campus to listen to such crap.

Even though there was an organization of the SC and ST doctors on the UCMS campus, it could not accomplish there what PMSF could do at AIIMS. We believe that such resistance could only be organized under the banner of PMSF which has an orientation that confronts the dominant and exploitative moorings of the present system rather than seeking adjustment with them.

Speaking politically, from the perspective of the large mass of the oppressed castes; caste organizations and identity politics are a force, whose narrow political vision is guided by the dictum—*Satta hi takat ki kunji hai* (capture of political power is the key to acqure strength/cloud). These organizations are led by the better off sections of the lower castes whose politics is consummated in sharing the *satta* (power) with in is system.

The leadership of these organizations could not possibly care for the lower mass of these castes. Given this ideological framework, forming governments with the support of the upper caste dominated establishment is the farthest that caste politics can go. Their objective is not to annihilate caste, but to only join the game of the upper castes as partners (more often as junior rather than equal or senior partners) and play on. To defeat upper caste chauvinism, while fighting for the implementation of measures directed at providing partial concessions to the members of these castes, we need to take the fight to a higher moral ground from which we can dominate the upper caste chauvinist sections of the society. This requires widening the horizons of the struggle to include the alleviation of the material conditions that perpetuate caste oppression. To achieve this, we need to go much beyond implementation of 'reservations' alone, and have to strengthen the struggle for uprooting all forms of exploitation.

Case Study of a Dalit Faculty in the Radiotherapy Department

The radiotherapy department at AIIMS gained considerable notoriety during the anti-reservation agitation. The head of the department, in his capacity as the chief warden of the boys hostel had allowed ghettoization of the reserved category students to take place and when this came to public knowledge, he tried to suppress the facts as a member of the committee set up by the AIIMS director Dr Venugopal to falsify the findings of the Thorat Committee.

One of the newly appointed assistant professor in the department, who belonged to the scheduled caste category had been actively involved in pro-reservation agitation along with her husband who was at that time working as a research officer in the institute. Prior to being appointed to a faculty position she had worked as a resident doctor and then as a research officer in the same department. In the period after the agitation the tensions in the department were running high and for reasons best known to them alone the resident doctors in the department under the leadership of the RDA (Resident Doctors' Association) president, decided to precipitate the matters in May 2007 by making wild cat allegations against the dalit faculty member and her husband. In separate and collective letters written by the resident doctors of radiotherapy department allegations were made by them that the concerned faculty was not attending to her duties regularly and was discriminating against the resident doctors on *caste basis*. As many as eight individual complaints were filed on the 28 May and 2 June 2007. The resident doctors also stopped taking ward rounds with the concerned faculty member.

All complaints filed by the resident doctors individually in the month of May were promptly forwarded by the acting head of the IRCH (Institute Rotary Cancer Hospital, within which all the oncology departments are located) to the director's office on the same day for necessary action. On the instructions from the director's office, the acting chief of IRCH instituted an internal enquiry against the dalit faculty member on the basis of the complaints filed by the resident doctors. The enquiry was conducted by the head of the department of 'labouratory oncology' within a matter of just one day on 2 June 2007, without following the mandatory procedure for an enquiry or giving a chance to all accused to even present their case.

The director's office promptly constituted a high level disciplinary enquiry committee that was stuffed with heads of oncology departments of major institutes in the country and some of the faculty members of AIIMS who were the leading campaigners in the anti-reservation agitation.

Even as these events moved in quick succession PMSF moved the National Scheduled Castes Commission regarding various complaints of harassment of scheduled caste doctors and students and organized a series of programmes targeting the government for its inaction in the matter. This helped in turning the tide against the AIIMS administration.

Even as the proceedings were on in the SC Commission, the AIIMS administration fielded senior professors from reserved categories to argue its case in the Commission. These were the same luminaries who were on the committee constituted by Dr Venugopal to rubbish the findings of the Thorat Committee that enquired into cases of caste based harassment at AIIMS. They promised that no harm would come to the concerned Dalit faculty of Radiotherapy department. A senior faculty member, himself a Dalit, and who was in good books of AIIMS administration, even had the audacity to go to the house of the harassed faculty to advise her regarding the futility of complaining against the departmental authorities to the SC Commission as these people could harm her career. He advised them that it was better to sort things out amicably. Indeed, they had done all preparation to harm the career of this harrassed faculty and set an example of her. It was only the efforts of PMSF that foiled their designs.

In its special report of 2008– NCSC had recommended that:

> cases be filed under the provisions of SC/ST Prevention of Atrocities Act, against all those who made malicious, frivolous and false complaints against Dr. Suman and also against all those officials (including HOD, and Director) who failed to discharge their Constitutional duty. In addition, departmental inquiry must be instituted to investigate the role played by all those responsible for harassing Dr. Suman and appropriate disciplinary action be taken against them. Not following consultant's order is a clear case of insubordination, the HOD and the administration are duty bound to take action on this. The head of the department of Radiotherapy, Dr G.K. Rath has shown himself as having a rabidly malicious attitude towards reserved category doctors and students on more than one occasion. He should be removed from the post of Chief of the Institute Rotary Cancer Hospital and the Head of the department of Radiotherapy and placed under suspension in order to facilitate a free and fair enquiry.

But the AIIMS Governing Body and Institute Body ignored the recommendations of NCSC commission and took no action.

Such then is the quintessential *raw merit* of the upper caste chauvinist doctors of the country's premier medical institute. It is remarkable that they could manage to do all this in the premier institution of medical teaching situated in the country's capital, under the full glare of the media and against doctors who were organized and capable of defending themselves. They could do so without any sanction. One can only imagine what must be the situation in the smaller towns and cities of the country, about which the national media and the governments couldn't care less.

Role of the AIIMS Administration in Anti-reservation Agitation

All India Institute of Medical Sciences had emerged as the epicenter of the 2006 anti-reservation agitation and its director Dr P Venugopal the main hero of the agitation. With the benefit of hindsight we can say with utmost surety that this did not come about purely on the strength of a spontaneous anti-reservation reaction of the upper caste students, nor was it any divine providence. For the level of its organization and propaganda, the agitation was a government and corporate sponsored project in the public-private partnership mode.

Even as the upper caste and upper class media of India volunteered to be the willing tool of the anti-reservationists, the corporate money bags generously lent their support to fill the coffers of the 'Youth of Equality' that led the stir. But above all it was the AIIMS administration that was instrumental in establishing the institute as the epicenter of the agitation. Indeed, the agitation came in handy for the AIIMS administration led by Dr Venugopal to resolve many internal contradictions with the students, the faculty and the employees.

Given these problems, the anti-reservation agitation provided Dr Venugopal the relief which he could never have given himself. The newfound bonhomie in the electrifying atmosphere of upper caste chauvinism catapulted Dr Venugopal from being a villain to the position of becoming the poster boy of anti-reservation agitation. In this transformation, the most energetic role was played by the ad-hoc faculty; whose selection process has been dealt with in detail above.

At the time the anti-reservation agitation broke out a ban on strikes, dharnas or demonstrations was operative on the campus vide Delhi High Court's order dated 27 August, 2001 in the CWP No. 5166 of 2001. Importantly, the order was brought to bear through a suo moto notice taken by the court of an earlier agitation by the employees and the resident doctors of AIIMS. The order had been used by the administration with impunity to suppress any dissent on the campus. However, the order disappeared in thin air when the anti-reservation crusaders set their camp on the central lawns of the Institute. For the period of 20 days that the anti-reservation *dharna* went on at AIIMS no effective measure was taken by the administration to enforce this order, neither did the court seem to take a suomoto notice of the fact that the services at the premier medical institute of the country remained paralyzed and that its earlier order was being violated with impunity.

The AIIMS administration on its part facilitated electricity connection for machines dispensing cool drinking water and air coolers at the tent pitched by the anti-reservationists. The police, who on earlier occasions had come to break the strikes, dharnas or demonstrations, this time around came to provide protection to the 'freedom from reservation' agitators. The hospital paging system was used by the medical superintendent's office to relay important decisions and announcements to the faculty, resident doctors and students of AIIMS. After the strike by the resident doctors ended on the instructions of the Supreme Court, the then RDA president thanked AIIMS director Dr P. Venugopal for his support vide a letter dated 31 of May 2006. He wrote:

> We would like to inform you that following a directive from the Honorable Supreme Court, all residents shall be resuming duties with immediate effect. We would like to acknowledge the support we received from you on this issue and thank you for the same.

The resident doctors, especially the reserved category doctors who wanted to join work while the agitation was on, were prevented from doing so by the faculty members. Dr Sunil Chumber, a senior faculty in the department of surgery had to specifically write a letter, dated 18 of May 2006 to the head of department of surgery in this respect. Dr Chumber wrote:

> In regard to the ongoing anti-reservation agitation, several residents have desired to join work. Unfortunately, some consultants in the spirit of casteist chauvinism have discouraged them. I request all consultants be advised to refrain from this action as this is only this is leading to the prolongation of the current strike and the resulting misery of patients. All such residents must be assured that they shall not be victimized during their tenure in the institute.

Instances of such harassment of reserved category doctors also happened in almost all the hospitals in Delhi. In fact, the Delhi SC and ST association also filed a writ petition in the Delhi High Court seeking protection for the resident doctors of reserved category. Rather than instruct the government to uphold the rights of these doctors, the Court in its usual style prolonged the case and disposed the petition years later, passing some strictures against the government for failing to protect these residents; but this was hardly of any use.

The various instances cited during the course of our discussion till now show beyond doubt that there was a tacit agreement to brazenly open support of the government and the local administrative authorities to the anti-reservation agitation. That this was allowed to happen even at the cost of patients' interest and considerable social tensions on various campuses.

The means adopted by these crusaders were certainly far from holy. In the charged atmosphere of the agitation, with the media projecting it as a cause célèbre past all other concerns, the voice of the oppressed was totally drowned, especially as their proclaimed political representatives quietly acquiesced with the powers that be. This is a matter of grave concern for all conscientious people who care for the welfare of our people irrespective of their caste, religion, or creed. The danger is that once we become so blinded that we start identifying our wrongs as self righteous virtues, the possibility of correcting the wrongs becomes ever more distant. In this respect I would like to mention here a statement made by a senior scheduled Tribe faculty of AIIMS during the course of a private conversation; he said—'I think India is an upper caste Hindu

State and I am reminded every now and then that I am being tolerated in this country.' It is time that we started to care for such sentiments.

On the role of judiciary

Judiciary as an institution is perceived to stand apart and above the society such that it can judge various issues and adjudicate them purely on the basis of their merit. Nothing can be farther from truth, for the judges after all are human beings who belong to the same society and are afflicted by the contradictions and value system prevalent in the society. On the issue of caste, they can be as casteist as the other caste chauvinist sections albeit their caste bias is shrouded in legalese. It is pertinent to mention here the instance of a Tamil Nadu High Court judge, C.S. Karnan alleging caste discrimination against him. In a complaint filed before the National Commission for Scheduled Castes, he wrote he was being 'harassed' and 'victimised' by some 'brother Judges' on account of his being a Dalit.

The usual method adopted by the courts is that they entertain repeatedly frivolous petitions challenging the provisions of reservation even in cases where the law is settled, and try to revise the settled law by some twisted interpretation of law; else they may simply delay the matters to facilitate the violation of the provision of reservations. As we saw in the case of the appointment of faculty at AIIMS, the case filed by the Faculty Association went on for seven long years, only to reiterate the established law. However, in the interregnum the AIIMS administration appointed ad-hoc faculty. A new reality was thus created, and once created it was sought to be legitimized through patently illegal processes with impunity. Neither is there any fear of law for those who break law in such cases.

In the case of the anti-reservation agitation, there took place two instances of selective application of court's orders. The stay operative against strikes, *dharna*s and demonstrations was allowed to be broken even at the cost of the patients; and second, the court ordered the government to pay the salary for the period of the strike to the resident doctors, just because it was claimed by the resident doctors before the court that the government had promised them not to cut their salary. Tomorrow, if the government illegally promises kickbacks in some deal, probably the court will ensure that the government complies with the promised illegality.

On the role of the National Commission for Scheduled Castes

To say the least, the National Commission for Scheduled Castes is a thoroughly corrupt, inefficient and ineffective body that serves the purpose of hoodwinking the people of oppressed castes. During the time when the incidents at AIIMS took place, the Commission was headed by Sardar Buta Singh, who has been a senior leader of the Congress. Importantly, his son was caught by the Central Bureau of Investigation while taking bribe in return for keeping a case pending before the Commission in cold storage.

In the case of the complaint regarding caste-based harassment at AIIMS, the Commission virtually did nothing except for giving statements critical of the AIIMS administration from time to time and instructing the administration verbally to stop any enquiry against the dalit faculty of the radiotherapy department. It failed to make Dr Venugopal present himself before the Commission inspite of threatening to issue non-bailable warrants against him.

Bodies like the National Commission for Scheduled Castes and Scheduled Tribes only serve the purpose of giving false hope to the oppressed people of these categories, lest they go on to the path of taking their destiny in their own hands. Worse still, they may actually harm the struggles of these sections by providing sanctity to the government's policies inimical to the interests of the oppressed castes.

A Word on the Role of Different Political Forces

While those organizing themselves under the banner of 'Youth for Equality' come out clearly against reservation policy, almost no major electoral party says that they are not in favor of implementing reservations, and yet, one or the other of them, or one or the other sections of these parties are the principle political backers of anti-reservationists.

Caste-based Parties

There is however some distinction between different political parties. For the caste based parties, given their support base among specific castes, reservations is largely an issue for garnering votes of their specific caste base; but it is not an issue for sustained political mobilization of the oppressed castes by way of mass movements to build pressure for effective implementation of reservation policy and to challenge the upper caste chauvinist forces outside of the electoral arena. During the last anti-reservation agitation, none of these parties went beyond issuing an occasional statement in support of reservations and none whatsoever did anything of practical value to support the fight of the reserved category students at AIIMS and elsewhere in the country against their oppression. This was so, inspite of the fact that all of these parties were approached by various people to act on the issue.

The limited political objective of these parties is to wield political power within the system rather than seek a radical change in the system to get rid of different forms of exploitation of which caste based oppression is among the more important ones. This political character of these parties is on account of the fact that they the repositories of the more affluent sections of the oppressed castes. It is important to bear in mind that these sections do not seek annihilation of caste, but simply stake claim to their share in political power. As these parties are narrowly based on single caste groups, they very well know that they can achieve their political objectives only in collabouration with political representatives of the upper castes and if voted to power, the sustenance of their governments shall depend on the cooperation of an establishment that is dominated by the upper castes. Hence, these parties have formed electoral alliances with different parties of the mainstream ruling elite, depending on political expediency, from time to time.

In times like heightened caste tensions, their attitude appears to be one of biding time until next elections when they can again appeal to the sentiments of their caste constituency. But one thing is clear—that at the times when the general masses of the oppressed castes are the most hard pressed, these parties are of no good to them.

The Congress and the BJP

Parties like the BJP and the Congress, who have been the traditional parties of the ruling classes in the country, but under the compulsions of electoral politics, have the obligation to seek the votes of the masses of the oppressed castes, are the principle sponsors of the upper caste chauvinist forces. Among these two also, while BJP is widely perceived to be a party of mainly the upper caste Brahmins and the trading community, the SCs and the STs formed the unquestionable vote bank of Congress along with the upper castes at one time. During the last anti-reservation agitation even though both the parties supported the agitation, the Congress's role was more prominent and open. The anti-reservationists had the direct backing of the Prime Minister's Office that lent its full weight behind the then AIIMS director Dr P Venugopal who emerged as the hero of the anti-reservationists.

The Parliamentary Left

The question that need be asked of the Parliamentary Left is—why have they failed to build a consistent, determined and militant movement for the implementation of reservations in an institution where they have an unparalleled sway?

This automatically leads to the role of the other Left—the Revolutionary Left. The mass base of this Left in the country is almost exclusively among the dalits and the Tribals and the revolutionary Left has been actively involved in mobilizing the poorest of the poor of these sections on the issues of land and displacement—the two central issues confronting them.

Even at the time of the 2006 anti-reservation agitation, Medicos Forum for Equal Opportunities that was formed to organize students and doctors against the prevailing atmosphere of caste hatred consisted of a core group of doctors and faculty members who had either themselves been students or resident doctors of AIIMS in the earlier period or had a formidable background of political activism with the revolutionary movement. This group consisted of persons belonging to both the upper castes and the reserved categories. Indeed, for all the days that the anti-reservation campaigners pitched their tent on the campus, Medicos Forum for Equal Opportunities organized a lunch hour demonstration at AIIMS that over days attracted attention of people from other campuses and colleges (Varadarajan, 2006; Vij, 2006; Bhatt, 2006).

Both the authors of this paper were closely associated with the organization of this pro reservation agitation. People associated with MFEO went to other campuses in Delhi to organize demonstrations. The slogans raised by these demonstrators were—'Stop privatization of Higher Education, Down with upper caste chauvinism, and Merit equal to capitation fees plus NRI quota?' (Bhatt, 2006). A conscious attempt was made by us to ensure that these demonstrations articulated their support for reservation policy without appealing to caste sentiments of any kind. A few odd slogans that were sought to be raised by some in this respect were promptly shot down; not because someone had to stop these persons, but because the crowd would simply not respond to them as they had got attuned to different kind of slogans.

PMSF organized a day long convention at AIIMS on the issue of reservations and against the prevailing atmosphere of caste based harassment in different campuses. The convention drew a wide support from a broad section of intellectuals in Delhi. A demonstration was even organized at the Supreme Court to protest against the role of the judiciary in granting of concessions to the anti-reservationists, for example getting the salary of anti-reservation resident doctors for the strike period released from the government which virtually amounted to sanctifying and placating upper caste chauvinist forces.

These achievements become even more significant in light of the fact that unlike institutions like JNU, the students and doctors coming to AIIMS and other professional institutions are almost exclusively from the upper crust of the society that is more liable to be a fertile ground for all sorts of reactionary sentiments.

Decline in the Academic Standards

That the intellectual atmosphere of the academic institutions should provide for the free interaction of the contending ideas with as much diversity as there is in the society around them is a necessary condition for the growth and intellectual well being of these institutions. Failure to achieve such necessary conditions results in these institutions becoming an instrument in the hands of the dominant sections to justify their control over the society. The extent to which different sections of the society find representation in these institutions determines the extent to which a variety of ideas feed into the academic work being done in these institutions and contribute to the richness of their academic output. Above all, in a modern society, it is the foremost duty of these institutions to champion the cause of the subaltern sections in order to bring about their uplift.

We would like to illustrate this by way of an example. In 2009, the first author of this paper had an opportunity to visit the 'Comprehensive Rural Health Services Project' of AIIMS at Ballabgarh, Haryana as part of the short field visit arranged for the 2009 batch of the Masters of Public Health course at the Centre for Social Medicine and Community Health of the Jawaharlal Nehru University.

> The 'Comprehensive Rural Health Services Project' (CRHSP) at Ballabgarh was started as a result of the official tripartite Memorandum of Understanding signed between the then Punjab Government, the AIIMS and the Rockefeller Foundation in 1965. It was stated that, 'as there did not exist anywhere in India a satisfactory example of comprehensive health services, the project was to provide a model for such services within the framework of the health services available in the country and develop models for the future. Thus, the mandate was clearly to lead and show the way for delivery of health care services—a mandate the current vision intends to fulfill, keeping in mind the changing needs' (Anand, 2008).

The Intensive Field Practice Area (IFPA) of the project comprises of 28 villages under two Primary Health Centers, catering to a population of more than 85,000. We had a chance to visit some of the villages in the field practice area to study the social stratification in these villages and the working of the health facilities in the given social, political and economic milieu. The stratification of the rural society along caste lines was writ large on the social canvas of the IFPA. Not only were the scheduled castes in these villages socially segregated, but were also by far the poorest sections beset with proportionately much greater share of the public health problems, as it appeared on first visual impression. We have already provided some national level data in Table 4 above to show that the health indices among the SCs, STs and OBCs are by far much poorer as compared to the upper castes.

Prior to our going to the villages, a senior resident doctor of the Preventive and Social Medicine Department of AIIMS gave us a power point presentation regarding the good work being done by them in the villages of the area. The presentation included a comparison between national level and the area outcomes for indices like immunization coverage, infant mortality rate, maternal mortality rate, institutional deliveries, availability of safe drinking water, and malnutrition. Being aware of the caste wise differentials in these outcomes at the national level, I asked the doctor if he had caste wise disaggregated data on these outcomes for IFPA. He promptly replied, self-righteously—'We do not discriminate between our patients on the basis of caste.' On being told that the national level surveys did record these outcomes for different castes separately as there were substantial differences between them, his reply was—'This is what I call reverse discrimination (i.e. discrimination against the upper castes)'.

Such concepts have been taken further ahead by the faculty incharge of the CRHSP. In one of his published papers, arguing that good vaccination coverage could by itself bring down the infant mortality rate even without socioeconomic development, he along with other authors claimed that *' "Development" is not essential to reduce infant mortality rate in India'* (Anand et al, 2000). The SCs and the STs are the poorest of the segments of our society and it is their interests that are harmed the most by such prescriptions. Such prescriptions should send the alarm bells ringing in the minds of any concerned person.

Conclusion

Reflecting upon the practice of caste discrimination at AIIMS in the wake of the anti-reservation, agitation, provides us a good opportunity to reflect on those events dispassionately and draw appropriate lessons for tackling the question of caste discrimination in the elite educational institutions in the country. Not only in the society at large but even in the institutions of higher learning, the practice of caste based discrimination is common and deep seated in the style of their functioning that is hostile towards the reserved category students and faculty. Worse still, our social and political system patronizes these practices, thereby resulting in perpetuation of caste oppression.

Even as caste based reservations are crucially important for greater democratization of the social, political and economic structure of the society, our experience shows that reservations alone are grossly insufficient for uprooting caste oppression unless the fight against caste oppression is visualized as part of the struggle to uproot all forms of oppression from the society, meaning thereby that the we have to move towards a radical transformation of the society aimed at redistribution of its productive resources. It is instructive to remember that reservations only fulfill the aspirations of the better off among the oppressed castes while leaving aside the demands and aspirations of the more oppressed masses.

Among other factors, progress in this direction is constricted by the political orientation of those doing identity politics in the name of caste. Their limited objective is to mobilize the general masses of the oppressed castes to present a stronger claim to their share in power, but without questioning the present exploitative structuring of the society. The results of such a tubular thinking on caste have been most destructive. It is pertinent to note that in the AIIMS administration that followed that of Dr P Venugopal, the Institute Director, Professor In-charge examinations, Sub-Dean (Academic), Sub-Dean (Examinations), Registrar (Academic) and the Chief Administrative Officer were all from reserved categories, but they remained equally insensitive to the interests of SC/ST and OBCs.

Those belonging to reserved categories, once co-opted into the system, are motivated to prove their worth for running the present system as that alone shall determine their rise in the system; even if this came at the cost of poor masses of the oppressed castes.

We hope that this paper shall pave the way for a stronger bonding of the struggle against caste oppression with the struggle for general democratization of the society dependent upon radical redistribution of the societal resources, while in no way diluting the need for strict implementation of the provisions for caste based reservations. Failure to do so is to condemn the masses of the oppressed castes to the ignominy of perpetual exploitation in the name of caste.

REFERENCES

Anand K. (2008), 'Comprehensive Rural Health Services Project, Ballabgarh', Centre for Community Medicine, The All India Institute of Medical Sciences, Utkarsh Printers, New Delhi, March, pp. 4–5.

Anand K., Shashi Kant, Guresh Kumar, S.K. Kapoor (2000), 'Development' is not essential to reduce infant mortality rate in India: experience from the Ballabgarh project. J. *Epidemiol Community Health*; 54: pp. 247–53.

Bhatt S. (2006), 'Reservations: The other side of the story'. *Rediff News*, 27 May. Available from http://www.rediff.com/news/2006/may/27quota2.htm, on 8 November 2011.

Dhar A. (2007), 'AIIMS rejects Thorat panel report'. *The Hindu*, dated 20 September. Available from http://www.thehindu.com/2007/09/20/stories/200709206049 1300.htm, on 7 November 2011.

Derbyshire D. (2007), 'DNA scientist suspended from top lab after claiming 'white people are more intelligent than blacks'. Mail Online, 19 October. Available from http://www.dailymail.co.uk/news/article-488400/DNA-scientist-suspended-lab-claiming-white-people-intelligent-blacks.html on 8 November 2011.

Ghurye G.S. (1986), *Caste and Race in India* (Fifth edition reprint), Popular Prakashan, Bombay.

Government of India (2007a), *Report of the Committee to Examine the Selection and Promotion Process of Ad-hoc Assistant Professors in the All India Institute of Medical Sciences*, Ministry of Health and Family Welfare, November.

Government of India (1997), 'Office Memorandum No. 36012/2/96-Estt. (Res.)', Department of Personnel and Training, 2 July.

Government of India (1989), 'Office Memorandum No. 36012/13/88-Est. (Sct)', Department of Personnel and Training, 22 May.

Government of India (2008), 'Minutes of the Meeting of the Committee appointed to look into the unfairness of selection to the posts of Senior Residents of All India Institute of Medical Sciences', 4 January, Ministry of Health and Family Welfare.

Government of India (2007b), 'Committee to Enquire in to the Allegation of Differential Treatment of SC/ST Students in All India Institute of Medical Science, Delhi', Ministry of Health and Family Welfare, New Delhi.

Kasturi C.S. (2006): 'Ghetto in medical hostel – Quota student in AIIMS allege being driven to a corner.' *The Telegraph*, 5 July. Available from http://www.telegraphindia.com/1060705/asp/frontpage/story_6439173.asp, on 7 November 2011.

Medicos Forum for Equal Opportunities (2006), 'Enquiry Report into Incidents of Caste Based Harassment in Hostels at AIIMS', 20 June.

QS Top Universities, (2011), (QS Top Universities (2011): 'QS World University Rankings by Subject: Medicine.' Available from http://www.topuniversities.com/university-rankings/world-university-rankings/2011/subject-rankings/life-sciences/medicine, on 11 November 2011.

Registrar General of India, *Report of the National Family Health Survey* (NFHS-3), 2005–06, India, Volume I.

Raman A. (2010), 'Donnish Hauteur?' *Outlook*, 25 January Available from http://www.outlookindia.com/article.aspx?263782 on 8 November, 2011.

Thapar Romila (2004), 'Early India: From the Origins to AD 1300', University of California Press.

Times Higher Education (2011): 'The World University Rankings 2011–2012'. Available from http://www.timeshighereducation.co.uk/world-university-rankings/2011-2012/top-400.html, on 11 November 2011.

Varadharajan S. (1999), 'Dalit students battle prejudice and violence.' *Times of India*, 21 March. Available from http://svaradarajan.blogspot.com/1999/03/dalit-students-in-delhi-battle.html on 7 November, 2011.

Varadharajan S. (2006), 'Caste matters in the Indian media'. *The Hindu*, 3 June. Available from http://hindu.com/2006/06/03/stories/2006060301841000.htm, on 8 November 2011.........Vij S (2006): 'The Loonies'. National Highway, 1 June. Available from http://tamasha.wordpress.com/author/tamasha/page/25, on 8 November 2011.

3

Untouchability and the Right to Personal Liberty

Kalpana Kannabiran

For millennia, the practice of untouchability has marginalized, terrorized, and relegated a sector of Indian society to a life marked by violence, humiliation and indignity... Its practice is never fully defined, never fully explored and, thus, never fully understood.

—Navsarjan and RFK Centre (2010: 3)

An analysis of the caste system is central to an understanding of the law in India. The debates around caste in the courts have been confounded with the issue of reservations for the depressed classes; the debates around reservations have, in turn, become completely entangled with deliberations about the creamy layer. The reason why caste figures at all in courts, however, is that it is a source of discrimination. The history of the caste system, as we saw in the previous chapter, points to extremely persistent and violent practices of discrimination that necessitate special protections just so that people belonging to vulnerable groups can exercise the right to life and liberty. This, then, is the first linkage that must be established in the law: namely, what is the relationship between discrimination and the curtailment of liberty? Practices of reservation and the discourses of equality logically follow the establishment and entrenchment of the right to life and liberty, which non-discrimination guarantees.

At another level, when we speak of the right to personal liberty in the context of the caste system, what are the qualitative attributes of such liberty? And how may the law take note of these attributes in its operation? Clearly, in speaking of the right of the Scheduled Castes (SCs) to personal liberty, we are not speaking in the restrictive terms of personal autonomy alone. The idea of liberty needs to be spun from the visions of anti-caste philosophers, because the Constitution itself is based on this philosophical foundation. It is only after we have enunciated this idea of liberty and its relationship to non-

---

This essay is originally published as Chapter 6 in my book, *Tools of Justice: Non-discrimination and the Indian Constitution* (New Delhi: Routledge, 2012, pp. 206-241).

discrimination that we can contextualize the debate on reservations for the Scheduled Castes and Scheduled Tribes (STs). In the absence of such an endeavour, the entire debate on equality and equal opportunity—jurisprudential and public—is destined to be trapped in a reductionist mode that continues to skirt the substantive issues at hand.

While there may be a kinship between practices of reservation in India and affirmative action in the United States, attention to the specificity of context in the matter of reservations is critical. The twenty-first century opened with the demand by Dalits that caste discrimination be covered by the Convention on the Elimination of Racial Discrimination (CERD), drawing parallels between untouchability and apartheid. This, I would argue, is both a politically and a heuristically useful comparison. A point that merits reiteration at this point is that the comparison of caste with race enables an enlargement of the political kinship networks of Dalits beyond the confines of caste in India to communities across the world resisting xenophobia, racism and racism-like discrimination. Conceptually as well, this comparison opens out the possibility of looking at caste and race as analogous grounds of discrimination under international human rights jurisprudence, interlinking constitutional jurisprudence on non-discrimination on the basis of caste with radical traditions of jurisprudence on the question of race in other countries, like South Africa. Given the long history of resistance to caste on the Indian subcontinent, we could, after Baxi argue that the resistance to caste 'may be traced to a multicultural tradition of human rights that resulted decades later in the maturation of *jus cogens* of international law,' which delegitimated Enlightenment legacy in unprecedented ways (Baxi, 2002: 27).[1] How might this genealogy impact on our contemporary reading of constitutionalism? Here, we will examine judicial discourse on untouchability and the testimonies of untouchability that have been presented to competent authorities in the hope of justice being delivered. Only through an examination of these materials, relatively unexplored till today, can we redraw the parameters of the discourse on positive discrimination.

My central argument here is that articles 15(2), 17, 21, 23, and 24 of the Constitution of India lay out the context for non-discrimination. The practices proscribed in articles 15(2) and 17 provide the conditioning environment for social intercourse. Tripathi observes aptly that these articles in the Constitution, contrary to the general trend of fundamental rights, prohibit discriminatory action not only on the part of the state, but also on the part of private individuals and social groups (Tripathi, 1971: 161). Articles 15(2) and 17 resonate Ambedkar's demand for annihilation of caste:

> I am convinced that [the line of least resistance] will be ineffective in the matter of uprooting Untouchability. The silent infiltration of rational ideas among the

> ignorant mass of caste Hindus cannot, I am sure, work for the elevation of the Depressed Classes. First of all, the caste Hindu, like all human beings follows his customary conduct in observing untouchability towards the Depressed Classes. Ordinarily, people do not give up their customary mode of behaviour because somebody is preaching against it. But when that customary mode of behaviour has or is believed to have behind it the sanction of religion, mere preaching, if it is not resented and resisted, will be allowed to waft along the wind without creating any effect on the mind. The salvation of the Depressed Classes will come only when the Caste Hindu is made to think and is forced to feel that he must alter his ways. For that you must create a crisis by direct action against his customary code of conduct. The crisis will compel him to think and once he begins to think he will be more ready to change than he is otherwise likely to be. The great defect in the policy of least resistance and silent infiltration of rational ideas lies in this that they do not *compel* thought, for they do not produce crisis (Ambedkar, 2002: 362).

Echoing Ambedkar's concerns regarding 'notional change', Tripathi underscores the fact that constitutional or legal provisions, while they may deal with individual delinquency, can hardly hold out against the power of dominant communities:

> Constitutional provisions to protect the dominated communities or groups will either not be made, or, even when made they will remain ineffective. Legal provisions cannot stand against injustice all by themselves. They must be invoked and operated by people endowed with a sense of justice and equality. The real strength of the principles of justice and equality therefore lies behind the constitutional and legal provisions in the hearts of men...This requires a change of heart without which change in the text of the Constitution is neither possible nor enough (Tripathi, 1971: 185).

In a sense, then, my argument is that if we have understood the caste system and have begun to deal with it in society and in the law, we can actually map the course of justice and non-discrimination on all counts in a manner that locates the possibilities of jurisprudence in the specific social and historical context of resistance to discrimination. This chapter will examine the foundations of the constitutional category of untouchability and will look at judicial, legislative, and executive interpretations of this category with specific reference to Andhra Pradesh.

The Constitutional Category of Untouchability

The definition of untouchability is a description of the various practices that constitute the ideology of untouchability. Fairly early on, Ambedkar observed that no exact, legal definition of untouchability existed, because it was a social concept embodied in custom, which varied from one region to another. In general, however, Ambedkar observed that the population of the village was divided into the touchables and the untouchables. The untouchables lived in quarters outside the village and were a poor, dependent and subject community of hereditary bondsmen: 'In every village the Touchables have a code which the Untouchables are required to follow. This code lays down the acts of omissions and commissions which the Touchables treat as offences' (Ambedkar, 2002: 325). Or, 'the established order is the law made by the Touchables. The untouchables have nothing to do with it except to obey it and respect it' (Ambedkar, 2002: 330).

It is useful to recall Ambedkar's description of untouchability and its implications. The foundations must be the starting-point in the development of an anti-caste jurisprudence. It could, of course, be argued that Ambedkar was writing in the early twentieth century, at a time when practices of untouchability were rampant. To apply his delineation of the phenomenon to contemporary reality might be inappropriate. There are only two ways of addressing this possibility. The first is to look at recent testimonies of atrocity presented before courts and other public gatherings like citizens' tribunals. The second is to look at testimonies of untouchability offered through the medium of creative writing, which is an important form of truth-telling that must inform the jurisprudence of non-discrimination. Here, I drawn on an instance of the second kind of source, an autobiographical account of the experience of untouchability. *Joothan*, by Om Prakash Valmiki, opens with an account of the segregation of neighbourhoods:

> Our house was adjacent to Chandrabhan Taga's gher or cowshed. Next to it, lived the families of Muslim weavers. Right in front of Chandrabhan Taga's gher was a little johri, a pond, which had created a sort of partition between the Chuhras' dwellings and the village... On the edges of the pond, were the homes of the Chuhras. All the women of the village, young girls, older women, even the newly married brides, would sit in the open space behind these homes at the edges of the pond to take a shit. Not just under the cover of darkness, but even in daylight... there was muck strewn everywhere. The stench was so overpowering that one would choke within a minute. The pigs wandering in narrow lanes, naked children, dogs, daily fights, this was the environment of my childhood (Valmiki, 2007: 1).

What are the specifications, or 'code', to use Ambedkar's word, to which 'untouchable' habitations and their inhabitants must adhere?

1. Untouchables must live in segregated quarters in the south (an inauspicious location) of the village, away from Hindu habitation, and must adhere to the rule of segregation.
2. Untouchables must observe distance pollution and shadow pollution.
3. No member of the untouchable community can acquire wealth, in land, cattle, or any other form.
4. No member of the untouchable community can build a house with a

tiled roof.

5. No member of the untouchable community can put on a clean dress, wear shoes, put on a watch, or wear gold ornaments.
6. The names of members of the untouchable community must indicate contemptibility.
7. No member of the untouchable community can sit on a chair in the presence of a Hindu.
8. No member of an untouchable community can ride on a horse or a palanquin through the village.
9. Members of untouchable communities cannot move in a procession through the village.
10. Members of untouchable communities must salute Hindus.
11. No member of an untouchable community can speak in a cultured language.
12. Members of untouchable communities who come into the village at a sacred time, must not speak, because by doing so, they are held to foul the air of the Hindus.
13. No member of an untouchable community can pass himself off as a touchable.

The duties of untouchables that go along with this code include carrying messages of events in Hindu houses to their relatives even in far-flung villages; working in Hindu homes during marriages; accompanying the Hindu bride to her husband's village; performing all menial jobs preparatory to the observance of festivals; and submitting the women of their communities to indecent fun. All of these duties must be performed without remuneration (Ambedkar, 2002: 324–6).

The untouchables cannot hold land, because that would immediately put them on par with the touchable class:

> The result is that in most part, the Untouchables are forced to be landless labourers. As labourers, they cannot demand reasonable wages. They have to work for the Hindu farmers for such wages as their masters choose to give. On this issue, the Hindu farmers can combine to keep the wages to the lowest level possible for it is in their interests to do so. On the other hand, the Untouchables have no holding power. They must earn or starve. Nor have they any bargaining power. They must submit to the rate fixed or suffer violence.... When the agricultural season is over the Untouchables have no employment and no means of earning a living .... There is only one secure source of livelihood open to the Untouchables in some parts of the country.... It is the right to beg food from the Hindu farmers of the village.... This right to beg for food from the Touchables is now the principal means of livelihood for 60 millions of Untouchables in India. If any one were to move in a village after the usual dinnertime, he will meet with a swarm of

> Untouchables moving about the village begging for food and uttering the formula (Ambedkar, 2002: 328–9)

Omprakash Valmiki offers us an account of this custom, but also describes the resistance to it. He picks up from Ambedkar's idea that change will come only if thought is compelled through the creation of a crisis in the minds of the dominant castes:

> During the wedding, when the guests and the baratis, the bridegroom's party, while eating their meals, the Chuhras would sit outside with huge baskets. After the baratis had eaten, the dirty pattals or leaf-plates were put in the Chuhras baskets, which they took home, to save the joothan sticking to them... Sukhdev Singh's daughter was getting married... The barat was eating... When all the people had left after the feast, my mother said to Sukhdev Singh Tyagi ... 'Chowdhrijii, all your guests have eaten and gone... Please put something on the pattal for my children. They too have waited for this day.' Sukhdev Singh pointed at the basket full of dirty pattals and said, 'You are taking a basketful of joothan. And on top of that you want food for your children. Don't forget your place, Chuhri. Pick up your basket and get going... That night the Mother Goddess Durga entered my mother's eyes... She emptied the basket right there. She said to Sukhdev Singh, 'Pick it up and put it inside our house. Feed it to the baratis tomorrow morning.' She gathered me and my sister and left like an arrow... After that day Ma never went back to his door (Valmiki, 2007: 10–11).

Addressing the question of the citizenship rights of untouchables, Ambedkar argued that the inferior position accorded to them, as a class, was maintained by every device the majority could summon: 'This inferiority is the destiny not merely of an individual but of the whole class' (Ambedkar, 2002: 330). And there are no rights, no equal rights, there is no justice, no liberty or fraternity, no democracy, and no escape from it all in one's own generation or for the generations to come: 'Once a Touchable, always a Touchable. Once an Untouchable, always an Untouchable... Under it, those who are born high, remain high; those who are born low, remain low' (ibid.). The republic is a republic 'of the Touchables, by the Touchables and for the Touchables', 'an empire of the Hindus over the Untouchables' (ibid.: 330–1).

Starting with the Madras Removal of Civil Disabilities Act, 1938, legislations for the removal of social disabilities and for temple entry were passed in Mysore (1943 and 1948), Orissa (1946), the Central Provinces and Berar (1947), Bombay (1946 and 1947), the United Provinces (1947), West Bengal (1948), East Punjab (1948), Saurashtra (1948), Madhya Bharat (1949), Coorg (1949), Bihar (1949), Travancore–Cochin (1950), and Hyderabad (1358 Fasli). The constituent assembly debated the issue of untouchability at length in the course of drafting articles 15 and 17 of the constitution of India. The legislations just listed straddle the debates in the constituent assembly and the formulation of the constitutional protections, making the historical resistance to untouchability part of the legislative history of this constitutional category as well.

The debates on these two articles are instructive. Munshi and Ambedkar drafted the non-discrimination provision separately. Munshi's draft read:

> All persons irrespective of religion, race, colour, caste, language or sex are equal before the law and are entitled to the same rights and are subject to the same duties. Women citizens are the equal of man citizens in all spheres of political, economic, social and cultural life and are entitled to the same civil rights and are subject to the same civil duties unless where exception is made in such rights or duties by the law of the Union on account of sex. All persons shall have the right to the enjoyment of equal facilities in public places subject only to such laws as impose limitations on all persons, irrespective of religion, race, colour, caste or language. (Rao, 1968: 182–3).

Ambedkar's draft was more precise and hard-hitting:

> Whoever denies to any person, except for reasons by law applicable to persons of all classes and regardless of the social status, the full enjoyment of any of the accommodations, advantages, facilities, privileges of inns, educational institutions, roads, paths, streets, tanks, wells, and other watering places, public conveyances on land, air or water, theatres or other places of public amusement, resort or convenience, where they are dedicated to or maintained or licensed for the use of the public, shall be guilty of an offence (ibid.: 183).

In order to ensure the realization of fundamental rights in a country like India, Ambedkar felt protections were necessary against untouchability and discrimination, which were practised on a vast scale and in a relentless manner. Members brought up the need to ensure protection on grounds of political creed, language, dress and colour, all of which suggestions were dropped after debate. There was also a view that no institution should be allowed to be reserved for members of any given sect or community, and a debate on whether the word 'public' needed to be qualified further. Ambedkar responded to most of these queries: the word 'shop' was used in a generic sense to mean 'any place where the owner is prepared to offer his services to anybody who is prepared to go there seeking his service'. 'Place of public resort' was used in a specific sense (not in the sense that it is used in the penal code) to refer to facilities that were maintained wholly or partly out of state funds, including burial or cremation grounds so maintained (ibid.: 183).

With respect to the abolition of untouchability, addressed in article 17, Munshi wrote: 'untouchability is abolished and the practice thereof is punishable by the law of the Union.' Ambedkar's draft, more general in its application and more specific in its delineation, said: 'any privilege or disability arising out of rank, birth, person, family, religion or religious usage and custom is abolished' (Rao, 1968: 202). Jagjivan Ram and K.M. Panikkar observed that there was need to recognize the possibility of untouchability among Christians or other communities as well; some Christians suffered the same disabilities as Hindu untouchables. Panikkar explained this further:

> If somebody says that he is not going to touch me, that is not a civil right which I can enforce in a court of law. There are certain complex of disabilities that arise from the practice of untouchability in India. Those disabilities are in the nature of civil obligations or civil disabilities and what we have attempted to provide for is that these disabilities that exist in regard to the individual, whether he be a Christian, Muslim or anybody else, if he suffers from these disabilities, they should be eradicated through the process of law (ibid.: 202–3).
>
> The definite legal meaning of the untouchability provision, Rajagopalachari observed, was that the law would not any more recognize practices of untouchability 'as bringing into existence any right or disability' (ibid.: 203).

When the draft was adopted amidst shouts of 'Mahatma Gandhi *ki jai*', it read: '"Untouchability" is abolished and its practice in any form is forbidden. The enforcement of any disability arising out of "untouchability" shall be an offence punishable in accordance with law' (Rao, 1968: 205). The definition of untouchability was left to the statute that would be enacted in compliance with this article. However, Tripathi observes that even in the absence of legislation, article 17 'will have the effect of invalidating not only all laws, customs, usages, practices et cetera, directly or indirectly recognizing or encouraging the practice of untouchability, but even any sales, contracts, covenants or other private transactions having the effect of such recognition or encouragement' (Tripathi, 1971: 188–9).

The Protection of Civil Rights Act, 1955 (Act 22 of 1955), was enacted 'to prescribe punishment for the [preaching and practice of "untouchability"], for the enforcement of any disability arising therefrom and for matters connected therewith.'[2] Civil rights under this statute referred to any right accruing to a person by reason of the abolition of untouchability by article 17 of the constitution. The significance of this statute lies in the fact that it delineates the legal meaning of untouchability, which includes: preventing any person from entering any place of public worship that is open to other persons professing the same religion; preventing any person from worshipping or offering prayers or performing any religious service in any place of public worship, or bathing in or using the waters of any sacred tank, well, spring, or watercourse in the same manner and to the same extent as is permissible to other persons professing the same religion; enforcing social disabilities in the matter of access to or use of shops, public restaurants, hostels, rest houses, places of public entertainment, transport, or occupation of residential premises in localities; enforcing disabilities in the practice of profession, occupation, trade or business; obstructing the observance of social or religious custom, usage or ceremony, particularly taking part in processions; preventing the use of jewellery and finery; refusal of admission to any hospital, dispensary, educational institution, or hostel maintained from the general public funds; the refusal to sell goods or render services to any person at the same time and place and on the same terms and conditions applicable to other persons in the ordinary course of business; and obstructing persons from enjoying civil rights. This legislation also defines the term social boycott: the refusal to allow occupation of house or land; the refusal to enter into economic transactions; the refusal to perform or receive customary services; and abstention from social, professional or business relations, where such transactions, services and relations would ordinarily be maintained with such other persons.

The last part of the definition of untouchability contained in the Protection of Civil Rights Act deals with unlawful compulsory labour:

> 7A (1) whoever compels any person, on the ground of 'untouchability' to do any scavenging or sweeping or to remove any carcass or to flay any animal or to remove the umbilical cord or to do any other job of a similar unlawful compulsory nature, shall be deemed to have enforced a disability arising out of Labour, deemed to be a practice of 'untouchability'...
>
> Explanation: for the purposes of this section, 'compulsion' includes a threat of social or economic boycott.

This section of the Protection of Civil Rights Act, an important part of the prohibition of untouchability contained in article 17, and the prohibition of forced labour under article 23 of the Constitution, were reinforced further by the Employment of Manual Scavengers and Construction of Dry Latrines (Prohibition) Act, 1993. As late as 2003, the Supreme Court directed all state governments to file affidavits on manual scavenging within government premises, after social action groups documented this practice extensively and placed the evidence before the court (Ramanathan, 2010; Subrahmaniam, 2010). Tying forced labour to untouchability, manual scavenging represents a convergence of discrimination with the negation of liberty—in this case, by the State—in an area where extreme stigmatization guarantees impunity to state and non-state actors alike.

Sub-section (2) of the Protection of Civil Rights Act makes it an offence for anyone to deny another person of his or her own community the usual privileges of community membership, or to take part in excommunicating him or her for not practising untouchability. Drawing the crucial connection between untouchability and personal liberty, Tripathi observes that the law in India leaves little room for the practice of bigotry even within the home

(Tripathi, 1971: 191–2).

How does untouchability problematize our understanding of the fundamental right to personal liberty? This is a question that has distinct resonances in different contexts. While legal scholarship in India has equated liberty with the right to personal autonomy, what is of relevance here is not the individual's right to personal autonomy, but the right of individuals who are members of classes to the exercise of liberty and life in their fullest and most complete sense. In order to make sense of liberty, however, we must, after Orlando Patterson, look at the prior condition: namely, the condition of routine and customary denial of liberty that informs social consciousness in contemporary caste society even in the face of punitive legislation.

Insurgent Civil Servant: The S.R. Sankaran Government Orders

In looking at untouchability, our focus will be on Andhra Pradesh. The period between 1971 and 1977 saw the passage of a series of government orders that aimed at operationalizing policies of non-discrimination and the right to liberty through the systematic and planned removal of practices of untouchability through administrative fiat. A cluster of 136 Government Orders (GOs) were issued by a single officer, S.R. Sankaran, with the sole objective of realizing article 17 of the Constitution of India. Using the power of administrative law to effect social change, these GOs provide an unparalleled demonstration of the possibility of creative and insurgent administration:

> Government attach special importance to the speedy and systematic execution of the welfare and development projects for the benefit of the weaker sections in general and the SCs, STs and the BCs in particular. The speedy and efficient implementation of the programmes depend in no small measure on the total involvement of and the priority assigned by the district heads of departments entrusted with the execution of these programmes. Government wished to impress upon all heads of departments that the efficiency and the speed with which district officers implement these schemes and the involvement shown by them in the implementation of these programmes will hereafter form one of the major considerations in the matter of assessment of their work and their advancement in the career... governments have also decided that special report should be sent by collectors on such officers who do commendable work in this direction as also those whose performances is below par to enable the heads of departments and the government to take appropriate action.[3]

In 1971, the Government of India forwarded to the state governments the observation of the Parliamentary Committee on the Welfare of the Scheduled Castes and Scheduled Tribes, proposing the reservation of 15 per cent of the houses built under the low- and middle-income-group schemes for scheduled castes and scheduled Tribes.[4] The Andhra Pradesh state government ordered the implementation of this scheme in the ratio of 12:3.[5] District collectors were requested to make special efforts to see that at least some houses for Harijans were constructed in the main village, as this would help in achieving social integration.[6] Also, it was considered advisable to locate public institutions, as far as possible, either in Harijan localities and cheris or in close proximity to them: 'the site allotted for communal purposes in the land acquired for Harijans for house sites should be considered for utilization for locating these public offices or institutions.'[7] In consultation with the director of medical and health services, the government examined the feasibility of locating primary health centres, maternity and child welfare centres and sub-centres in the Harijanwadas. It decided in principle that this would be feasible if the Harijanwada was located within a distance of five kilometres from the main village. The scheme would improve social integration by making 'forward community' people go to the Harijanwadas.[8] Where house sites were allotted, authorities were instructed to make sure that actual physical possession of sites was given simultaneously.[9] It was widely acknowledged that even though statutory protections existed, the provision of access on the ground required planning and budgetary outlay.

While housing was an important need, Harijans also needed access to burial grounds and pathways, for which the budget was meagre — one lakh rupees (Rs 100,000). On a request from the director of Harijan welfare, the utilization of eight lakh rupees from the allotment of Rs 320 lakh for house sites was authorized for providing pathways and burial grounds for Harijans during 1976–7.[10] In the course of allotment of sites and acquisition of land for the same, complaints were received by the government that the lands of poor and marginal farmers were being acquired for allotment to SC persons. Cautioning the district administration to exercise discretion in this matter, since there was a possibility that the issue would get mixed up with village rivalries and factions, the government issued a directive that, as far as possible, 'special care should be taken to ensure that lands belonging to small and marginal farmers are not acquired except where it is inevitable.'[11]

The assignment of lands to persons belonging to the SCs depended on the acquisition of surplus land from landholders and the conversion of poramboke lands [unassigned land, for most part uncultivable and used as the commons] vested in the Public Works Department (PWD) and village panchayats. The acquisition of poramboke was especially fraught with procedure, which delayed the assignment of these lands considerably. Cutting through procedure, the government decided that: (*a*) notification regarding conversion of poramboke could be limited to concerned villages and the practice of publication in the district gazette could be dispensed with; (*b*) where land was vested in the PWD, a time limit would be prescribed for receiving responses on the feasibility of conversion of lands, and if no reply was received within the stipulated period, the land would be released for assignment purposes; (*c*) the panchayats would no longer control poramboke land, which would now be controlled by the revenue divisional officer with powers of revision vested in the district collector; (*d*) restrictions on the collector for excision of land from poramboke were removed with the government directing that collectors would 'exercise unrestricted powers in a matter of excision of poramboke land and its conversion into ayan [assignable land] after satisfying themselves that sufficient land has been reserved for communal needs of the village subject however to the condition that the rights in toddy trees are not disturbed'; and (*e*) as land required for communal purposes differed in extent from village to village, discretion regarding how much land to retain for communal use was vested in the collector.[12]

When the matter of separate and protected drinking water supply for scheduled caste localities was raised by the Andhra Pradesh State Harijan Conference in April 1976, the government noted that 'the provision made in the plan for welfare of scheduled castes is only supplementary in nature and that *the main thrust for their welfare should come from the general sector*.'[13] All departments were instructed to earmark 15 per cent of their plan provision for providing facilities and amenities to scheduled castes, which would include 15 per cent of the provision made for rural water supply and sanitation.

Goods and artefacts produced by persons belonging to the scheduled castes often suffered from the absence of adequate markets and networks, since existing ones were monopolized by dominant groups. The opening out of channels for the marketing of finished goods was addressed through a circular sent out to all consumers' cooperative central stores/super bazaars, directing them to purchase products from persons belonging to scheduled castes at reasonable prices and to provide good marketing facilities. At the time that the circular was sent out, some consumer cooperative stores had opened branches in scheduled caste localities; these outlets were requested to appoint only persons belonging to scheduled castes to run their branches in these areas.[14] Similarly, the Small Farmers Development Agency Programme was instructed to adhere to the priority indicated by the Government of India in the allocation of loans from financial institutions for the purchase of buffaloes: namely, that in providing loans to agricultural labourers and marginal farmers, care should be taken to ensure that 50 per cent of such loans were given to farmers from scheduled castes. Further, subsidiary occupation programmes like dairy, poultry, sheep-rearing, piggeries, and fisheries should also ensure adherence to this norm.[15]

Debates on reservation in educational institutions focus on the monopolization of seats in these institutions by the affluent sections of the scheduled castes and scheduled Tribes, that is, the 'creamy layer', discussed in the previous chapter. However, in 1973, the government of Andhra Pradesh found that a significant number of students belonging to the general category had produced false certificates in order to secure admission to institutions against seats reserved for students belonging to SCs and STs, thereby depriving the latter of their rightful claim. The education department of the Government of Andhra Pradesh issued an order setting forth guidelines for stringent action against students engaging in this form of malpractice:

> When reports are made regarding production of false caste certificates by the students, the Heads of Institutions should take immediate action to get the cases investigated through the Police and Revenue Authorities without delay. All such investigations and enquiries must be completed within a month. In all such cases, where enquiries reveal that if any of the students produced false caste certificates and secured seats reserved for scheduled castes and scheduled Tribes, the heads of institutions concerned should cancel their admissions and debar them from the institution.[16]

If it was found that candidates from the general category secured other concessions, like scholarships, or admission into hostels run by the social welfare and Tribal welfare departments, by producing false certificates, such concessions were to be cancelled immediately and the monetary value already enjoyed recovered. Further, it was notified that such students would be debarred from admission into or expelled from any educational institution for a period of not less than one year.[17] Similarly, it was found that vacancies reserved for SC and ST candidates were being appropriated by candidates belonging to the general category through the production of false certificates. No clear policy was articulated by the government on how these cases should be dealt with. The social welfare department issued a GO to the effect that all such cases should be reported to the SC and ST cell of the Department of Social Welfare, and that prosecutions were to be launched simultaneously for offences punishable under section 182 and/or section 420 of the Indian Penal Code. Such candidates were to be placed under suspension pending the completion of prosecution, and dismissed from the service if the charges were proved.[18]

Alongside safeguarding the seats reserved for students from these vulnerable groups, it was necessary to create an enabling environment that allowed them to access equality of opportunity in education and public employment. This meant supplying nationalized textbooks free of cost from the primary to the high school level,[19] ensuring through special steps the enrolment and actual attendance especially of children of 6–14 years,[20] ensuring the proper administration and monitoring of the midday meal scheme by a committee constituted where possible by parents of SC children studying in the school,[21] supplying two pairs of dresses to all boarders in government SC hostels,[22] reserving 20 per cent of seats in general hostels for SC students and five per cent for students from Scheduled Tribes, combining general and SC/ST hostels wherever possible,[23] and setting up pre-examination training centres with tuition waivers and free boarding to train scheduled caste and scheduled Tribe candidates for the All India Services Competitive Examinations.[24] At another level, the government introduced schemes for vocational training—driving, village officers, stenography, typewriting, shorthand, and so on, for individuals from these communities.[25]

Upon a recommendation made at the State Harijan conference in April 1976, the government directed that lessons on the eradication of caste and untouchability should be included in the textbooks of classes 8 to 10, and in language lessons in colleges. In addition, slogans on the eradication of untouchability were also to be included in textbooks and displayed in classrooms.[26]

Where scheduled caste persons had already completed their professional education, embarking on a professional career presented problems that were both financial and social. Law graduates from these communities, for instance, were very few and generally poor. Setting up a practice that could be sustained was a difficult proposition. The small number of lawyers from the SC also meant negligible numbers in the judiciary. Financial assistance of Rs 15,000 per year was sanctioned for 10 law graduates from across the state of Andhra Pradesh, that is, Rs 1,500 per head towards enrolment fees and purchase of law books. The condition attached to this financial assistance was that

> in addition to his own practice, the scheduled caste advocate who received the aid should take up occasionally the cases of the scheduled castes in the courts particularly in respect of untouchability cases, cases of harassment of scheduled castes etc, for at least a period of three years from the date of receipt of aid, whenever entrusted by the district collectors either free of charge or on concessional rates as decided by the district collector. The free service cases may be minimum so that the practice and earnings of the scheduled caste advocate will not suffer.[27]

The advocate-general was requested to include the names of qualified SC and ST advocates for appointment as legal advisers to government companies and corporations.[28] In government employment, where a higher qualification was a prerequisite for promotion, the government decided that SC and ST employees from the non-gazetted category would be deputed for higher studies within the country, with full pay and allowances for a period not exceeding two years, once in the career span of the employee.[29]

Since matters concerning the SCs, STs and backward classes were dispersed across different administrative sections—magisterial, land assignment, education, employment, et cetera—it became difficult to monitor the progress of action on specific government communications due to the lack of a coordinated, centralized system within the districts. The SC and ST cell in the secretariat at the state headquarters received such communications first, and coordinated action on them. In a memorandum issued to district collectors and superintendents of police, officers at the district level were directed to set up similar cells that would report to the collector or superintendent of police, who was entrusted with all matters relating to the SCs and STs. In addition to receiving all communications and referring them to the relevant departments, these cells would also be responsible for dispatching periodical reports and convening district-level committees to monitor the protection of civil rights at the local level.[30]

In 1976, panchayat *samiti*s and zilla *parishad*s were instructed to allocate 15 per cent of their general revenues to schemes benefiting the SCs. The base year for earmarking the funds was 1963–4. These bodies were to clear the backlog within a period of five years from 1975–6. Of this 15 per cent, five per cent was to be made over to the Andhra Pradesh Scheduled Castes Cooperative Finance Corporation Ltd, and 10 per cent allocated to the direct implementation of schemes, with any unspent balances made over to the corporation at the end of the financial year.[31] Guidelines were issued to panchayati raj bodies for the utilization of the 10 per cent. These bodies were directed to ensure expenditure on: construction of and repairs to drinking water wells or taps in scheduled caste localities; construction of pathways in Harijan *cheri*s [segregated hamlets/neighbourhoods of scheduled castes] connecting them to the main village; construction of social welfare school buildings and supply of furniture; electrification of scheduled caste localities; implementation of schemes for imparting training to scheduled caste candidates: for instance, training them as village officers, or in motor-driving and tractor-driving; and development of plots assigned to house sites, through levelling of land, provision of drinking water facilities, sanitary amenities, internal roads, et cetera, in the lands acquired for SCs.[32]

Given the proscription on intermarriage between castes, serious problems are faced by persons entering inter-caste marriages. The need was felt to establish a separate cell with a director 'to look after the interests of inter-caste married couples and their children and solve their problems' without delay. Non-statutory educational concessions were granted to these couples and their children. A government memorandum issued in July 1975 nominated the joint secretary to the government as the official in charge of Harijan welfare, and the director of Harijan welfare was designated to look after the problems of 'inter-caste married couples'.[33] The government also directed that, in cases where one party was an SC/ST person, his/her name should be sponsored by the employment exchange on a priority basis, as a way of alleviating the hardship that these couples underwent, given that in most cases they were disowned by their families and relatives.[34]

The eradication of untouchability requires work at different levels: enforcement, positive measures, and the creation of enabling conditions. Most often, the different levels are interwoven through administrative fiat in the hope that this would lead to the notional change that Ambedkar dreamt of. Social status is indicated through naming, especially through the affixing of prefixes and suffixes to names. The government, finding that it was a fairly common practice to attach the suffix 'gadu' to the names of Harijan men, issued a memorandum that said: 'The government direct that such suffix should be scrupulously omitted in all government records including birth registers hereafter.'[35]

In order to ensure that members of the SCs were allowed to draw water from public wells and enter hotels and places of worship without obstruction, the government directed that

> all the officers in the field including police officers, revenue officers, officers of the Panchayati Raj department, and extension officers in the blocks be held responsible to enable the members of scheduled caste community to draw water from the public wells in the villages and also make the scheduled castes use the hotels and places of worship on an equal footing with other caste people so that over a period of time this practice becomes common. Wherever the scheduled castes suffer from disability in this respect, the government officers while on tours in the villages should persuade the villagers not to obstruct the scheduled castes using the public places.

All the inspecting officers visiting the villages should make entries in their tour diaries about the practice of SCs using the public wells, hotels, and places of worship, in villages.[36]

Untouchability may escalate to heightened violence against members of SCs and STs. Members of dominant castes often resort to violent attacks against Dalits to prevent the transgression of boundaries entailed by the resistance to untouchability practices or inter-caste marriages. Apart from the penal law coming into operation in such cases, the fact of the permanent disablement or death of breadwinners in Dalit families is an issue that must be addressed with immediacy, through the immediate assignment, on a priority basis, of land, seats in schools, and hostels for children of the affected families, suitable employment for one member of the family in a government or public undertaking without the mediation of the employment exchange, or maintenance allowance to the survivor in cases where no member of the family is capable of being employed. These were some measures contemplated by the government prior to the framing of the rules under the Scheduled Caste and Scheduled Tribes (Prevention of Atrocities) Act 1989, in 1995.[37]

While several orders and memoranda have been issued, a review of the implementation of the various schemes in each district showed a lack of uniformity in implementation, with large amounts of earmarked funds remaining unutilized in some districts. The chief secretary, in his memorandum, observed that the variation reflected a lack of interest on the part of the authorities concerned. As a check on the authorities at the district level, this memorandum states that

> the government have ... considered the matter and direct that while assessing the work of the collectors, their performance in the implementation of the schemes for the benefit of the weaker sections shall also be taken into consideration and a mention of it will be made while writing the confidential reports on them.[38]

It was also found that when officers toured villages, they tended to conduct their deliberations in the main village, far away from the Harijan chery. This made it difficult for the SCs to discuss their problems with officials, and gave them the impression that they were being ignored. Collectors and heads of departments were instructed to communicate to officers up to the *firka* level the requirement that officers of all departments should visit Harijan localities during their tours to villages. These visits were to be recorded in the tour diary, which would be subjected to review with special reference to visits to Harijan cheries.[39]

Alongside administrative action, the government also recognized that:

> In the current social setting, many of the government servants may not have developed the appropriate attitude or motivation for analyzing, understanding and attending to the problems of scheduled castes and scheduled Tribes. This may not necessarily be due to any inherent bias but the result of absence of training and motivation. It is, therefore, considered that the introduction and implementation of proper training courses in this respect in various training institutions for government servants will bring about desirable improvements in the approach of government servants at different levels.[40]

A special officer in the Institute of Administration was assigned the responsibility of designing courses on the problems of SCs and STs, to enable better and more sensitive administration.

A careful examination of the micro-practices of law, particulary its implementation, points in two directions. The first of these is a methodological direction, where an understanding of the law draws not merely upon legislation and jurisprudence, but also, importantly, upon the vast field of implementation effected by the bureaucratic apparatus of the state. The governmentality of non-discrimination indicates the second direction, namely, the extent of discrimination as loss of liberty on the ground in the form of untouchability.

The Report of the Dr Justice K. Punnayya Commission

The single-member commission constituted by the Government of Andhra Pradesh, called the Dr Justice K. Punnayya Commission to Enquire into the Practice of Untouchability against the Scheduled Castes and Scheduled Tribes (hereafter the *Punnayya Report*), submitted its 2,000-page report to the government in the year 2000. The *Punnayya Report* begins with a detailed account of nationalist and Gandhian attempts at rooting out untouchability in rural Andhra, and recommendations for conciliatory practices to uproot this 'evil'. This makes our own endeavour to locate the discussion on untouchability in foundational anti-caste philosophy immediately relevant. The substantive part of the report makes no distinction between untouchability and atrocity, although in the law these are two distinct categories:

> As early as in 1970, Memo No. 1786/SC & ST Cell/70-3, dated, 2-4-1970, GAD, Government of Andhra Pradesh directed all the Collectors to ensure that fullest protection is given to the SCs in the enjoyment of the lands assigned to them. Memo No. 1816/71-2 (SC & ST) dated, 01-09-1971, GAD, was issued by Government of Andhra Pradesh stating that the Government have received many complaints of ill-treatment and harassment and beating up of SCs in various villages in the State. Collectors and Superintendents of Police are, therefore, requested to keep a special vigil and take suitable and prompt action in all such cases. In Memo No. 1299/SC & ST Cell/74-1, dated, 18th May, 1974, Employment and Social Welfare (SC & ST Cell) Department, Government of Andhra Pradesh issued instructions to all the Collectors and Superintendents of Police to keep a special vigil to take suitable and prompt action in all cases involving SCs and keep them under constant review. In spite of such clear instructions, several instances have come to the notice of the Government that no special attention is being bestowed on these cases. (*Punnayya Report* 2000: 392)

This section discusses the cases of untouchability in Andhra Pradesh that were placed before the Justice Punnayya Commission. In Srikakulam district, Golla Muthyalu and her two sons of the village Brahmana Therla in Palasa mandal stripped Thungana Damayanthi, a woman belonging to a scheduled caste in the same village, on 5 December 1999. In the village Sivvam of Veeraghattam mandal, Lakshmu Naidu beat Radhalu and his son Laxmu with a stick on 3 August 1998. Two days later, on 5 August 1998, the sarpanch of Sivvam village, Murali, beat Kinthali Ramulu, a person belonging to an SC. The sub-inspector of police, in an attempt to bring about a compromise between the Kapus and the SCs, summoned both groups to the police station. Sixty persons belonging to the SCs waited all day at the police station in vain. The following day, 2,000 Kapus led by Sarpanch Muralikrishna raided the SC colony, untethered their cows and allowed them to destroy the crops in the lands of the SCs. This was followed by a social boycott, where women from the SCs were obstructed from drawing water from the well.

In Gurandi 'B' village Bhamini mandal, 47 acres of land have been endowed in the name of Brundhavana Chandra Swamy Matam. There is no temple, however, and the idols are kept in a neighbouring village. Narvotham Goswamy of Parlakamodi of Orissa state is the *matadhipathi* (head priest) who, along with a few landlords, had occupied the lands. The 200 SC families in the village have no land, nor are they able to lease it. They put forth a proposal that they be allowed to lease the endowed lands, in return for which they would pay rent, construct a temple, and have the idols installed in their village. However, neither the district administration nor the police took note of their representations. When the Dalits persisted in trying to cultivate the lands, the police intervened through the use of force and violence, seriously injuring 70 Dalit men and women. Fact-finding missions were organized, and the collector suggested to the Punnayya Commission that the SC Finance Corporation should acquire the lands through an option and then lease it out to the Dalits of the village. The solution proposed by the collector nevertheless left unaddressed the fact of the denial of liberty with respect to access to public agricultural land in the village, and the use of state violence to actively obstruct access.

The problem of denial of access, especially to temple lands, was also reported from the Vizianagaram and Visakhapatnam districts, where Dalits were murdered by the landlords for demanding lease of temple lands. Elsewhere in the district, attempts were made to burn the sarpanch alive, Dalit women were stripped and assaulted, sometimes in public, the SC colony was raided, dwellings were destroyed, and witchcraft accusations were made, resulting in violence. Innumerable instances of social boycott were reported, along with denial of access to village commons (*banjar*), obstruction of attempts by Dalits to garland Ambedkar's statue, and violence by the police at the behest of landlords, sometimes resulting in Dalit deaths, both in custody and outside. Where the revenue administration did in fact grant banjar lands to Dalits, as in Mulapeta village of Visakhapatnam district, the dominant castes forcibly entered the lands and either destroyed the crop or carried it away. There were occasions when the Dalit families of an entire village were forced to take shelter in the police station for up to 10 days.

In some instances, specific complaints have been made by Dalits against named persons belonging to the dominant castes in the village. These complaints have ranged from accusations of lynching to sexual assault, as in Kondavaram and Chintada villages in East Godavary district. The police registered cases against those accused of offences, but did not make any arrests. In Chintada, in May 1999, the Kapus, led by the sarpanch, entered the house of Dasari Balamma, 'caught hold of her hair and threw her down and tore her blouse and outraged her modesty'. Although her husband registered a complaint, the police refused to make any arrest. The couple then filed a private complaint, whereby the sarpanch was found guilty and sentenced to one year's rigorous imprisonment plus a fine. The refusal to make arrests on the basis of complaints made by Dalits is often accompanied by the readiness of the police to arrest dalits on the basis of counter-complaints filed by the dominant castes. 'Though remedies under Sec 4 of POA Act are provided against such police officers, the SCs cannot invoke Sec 4 against the police officers' (*Punnayya Report,* 2000: 96).

Resistance to untouchability often provides the grounds for violence against dalits by the dominant castes. Such resistance includes entering hotels when dominant-caste persons are also present, sitting in banks while waiting for financial transactions to be processed, celebrating festivals, observing Ambedkar Jayanthi—in general, the Dalit claim to occupy an equal space in the public domain provides reason and justification for the perpetration of atrocities against them by the dominant castes. Krishna district reported some of the worst such cases of atrocity to the Punnayya Commission. These cases included instances of sexual assault against Pogula Jyothi, a hearing- and speech-impaired Dalit girl from Sriramapuram, Venkataramana from Pydurupadu, Bharathi from Musunuru Mandal, Nimmagadda Nagarathnamma from Singannagudem, and Gunturu Mariamma of Venuthuru Malli. Varikuri Suguna from Pydurupadu, Jhansi of the village Batla Venamarru, and another woman from Doddavevarapadu died after being gang-raped by men of dominant castes. Dalit women from Gannavaram complained of constant harassment by the landlords of their villages, to the extent that they were afraid to go anywhere alone. While cases were registered, this was not done under the Scheduled Castes and Scheduled Tribes (Prevention of Atrocities) Act, 1989. Dalit men—local leaders, farm servants, owners of telephone booths—were reported to have been killed, the accused being persons belonging to the dominant castes.

'The land lords of the Vempalli village in Ghantasala mandal unauthorisedly and forcibly dispossessed 32 Dalits of Vempalli village, 2 Dalits of Kottapalli village and 3 Dalits of Mallayya Chittoor from their lands leased out to them by the Government' (*Punnayya Report,* 2000). Appeals to the revenue and police authorities for intervention did not yield any response. The municipal commissioner sanctioned the construction of 40 shoe-shops by Dalits. However, when the dominant castes prevented the construction of these shops, no protection was provided by the government. In Thotapalli Village, the dominant groups appropriated the burial grounds of the Dalits to build their own houses.

Ambedkar believed that the 'Indian village is the very negation of a republic.

If it is a republic, it is a republic of the Touchables, by the Touchables and for the Touchables', in which there was no room for democracy, fraternity, equality, or liberty (Ambedkar, 2002: 330). Rapid urbanization and the rise of professional education, far from being an undiluted good, reproduced practices of untouchability. The *Punnayya Report* demonstrates that tied as it is to the caste system, specific practices of untouchability might vary depending on locale, but it has far from disappeared either in urban areas or even in institutions of higher education. The Students Federation of India (SFI), Vijayawada City, petitioned the commission that, in the Siddartha Engineering College and the Koneru Laxmaiah Engineering College in Vijayawada, SC and ST students were not allowed to sit in the front benches. They were provided rooms separately in the college hostels. G. Sujatha and two other female students, members of SFI, stated in their petition that the SC students resident in the hostels were subjected to 'cruel ragging by the students with caste bias and therefore the SC girls are afraid of going to colleges' (*Punnayya Report,* 2000: 1014). Dalits residing in Rajupeta of Bandar municipality charged municipal authorities of discriminating against Dalits in the provision of public facilities in their colonies. Lacking basic sanitation, electricity and metal roads, children especially in SC colonies were more vulnerable to illness and disease. The Dalit residents contrasted the lack of facilities in their colonies with the relatively better infrastructure in non-Dalit urban poor neighbourhoods (ibid.: 1017).

In the words of Bejjipurapu Anand and 34 others belonging to SCs in the village Chennuru in Kankipadu mandal:

> though we are boasting of our development, we are ashamed of the caste based discrimination on the ground of untouchability. In our village, Dalits are not allowed to draw water from the public wells and separate glass system for SCs is being maintained in the tea stalls. Not only towards Dalits who are living in the villages but also towards the Dalits Officers or Teachers and Dalit students, discrimination based on untouchability is being practised in their village. Even the elected Sarpanchs and M.P.T.Cs are being ill-treated on the ground that they are SCs. In the village Manthena in Gannavaram Mandal, the caste based discrimination is being shown towards the SC officers, teachers and students and also towards Sarpanchs and M.P.T.Cs belonging to SCs. (*Punnayya Report* 2000: 1019)

In Guntur district, several individual cases of murders of dalits were reported from different villages, as also sexual assaults on dalit women. When members of the dominant castes involved in some of these incidents were warned by the police against indulging in violence, the result was a social boycott against dalits. In Prakasam district, the conflict revolved around access to lands:

The lands of the Dalits of (1) Kalagondapadu and Chodavaram and Machavaram villages of Kanigiri Mandal, (2) of Velugonda village of Velugonda

Mandal, (3) of Mettapalem, Lingamguntla, Rasheedpuram, Ummanapalli, Nallagonda, Vemulugutta, Nelaturu and Gollapalli villages of Hanumanthunipalem Mandal, (4) of PC Palli village in PC Palli Mandal, (5) Hanumajipalem of Inkollu Mandal, (6) of Eluruvaripalem in Chimakurthi Mandal, (7) Santhamaguluru village in Santhamaguluru, (8) of Nagireddipalem in C.S. Puram Mandal and (9) the lands of the Dalits in Ragavaram, Birududanarua, Chintalantla, Bondalapadu, Thippaiahpalem, Bhupatipalli and Vemulakota in Markapuram Mandal were forcibly occupied by the Caste Hindus. No action by the Revenue authorities or by the police to restore the lands into possession was taken, (ibid.: 105).

Apart from issues relating to land, Guntur district also shares with other districts in Andhra Pradesh individual instances of rape, murder, battery, and other forms of violence, for instance, obstructing Dalit youth from playing cricket or preventing them from residing in the proximity of Reddy homes.

In Nellore district as well, the major conflicts centred around the occupation of the meagre lands of Dalits by dominant-caste persons. A petition submitted to the Punnayya Commission listed 34 dalits who had been thus dispossessed, along with the details of the dispossession (*Punnayya Report* 2000: 108–9). Contesting elections against dominant-caste candidates was another major provocation, even though the Dalit candidate lost the elections in both instances reported. The violence and battery inflicted on Dalits in this district ranged from breaking their limbs, splitting their heads causing derangement, to rape, gang-rape, and murder.

A similar pattern may be observed in the violence in Chittoor district, with the addition that dalits were not allowed to worship in the village temple in Melantham. Inter-caste marriages and inter-caste relationships, especially between dalit men and women of the dominant castes, figure as the cause of violence in several districts.

In Cuddappah district, Dalits were required to stand when caste Hindus entered their localities. Pipers and drummers refused to provide their services during dalit celebrations, dhobis and barbers also refused their services, and Brahmins did not officiate at their weddings. Dalits were denied entry to bus-stops and bus shelters, and were not allowed to participate in village fêtes. Dalit workers had to work two hours longer than other workers. They were attacked if they refused to kill he-buffaloes. Elected representatives from Dalit communities were not allowed to sit on chairs; Dalits were not allowed into temples and hotels, to draw water from wells, or to ride bicycles in the main village. They were not allowed to break coconuts at the idol of the goddess in the village *jataras* [fairs]. If, accidentally, any caste Hindu's hand touched a dalit, turmeric water mixed in cow's *panchakam* (urine) was sprinkled on their persons as a purification measure. B. Nagayya, the Dalit superintendent of the

Chekrayapet mandal revenue office, was beaten by persons belonging to the dominant caste, because he dared to question their unauthorized occupation of his mother's lands, measuring 4.35 acres in S. No. 325/1 in Maddirevula village of Lakkireddypalli mandal (*Punnayya Report* 2000: 111). Obstructing access to land and destroying Dalit houses were the major forms that untouchability and atrocities against dalits took in this district.

In Kurnool district, a Dalit *anganwadi* worker was murdered because she resisted sexual harassment by a dominant-caste man (*Punnayya Report* 2000: 112). Another worker was refused entry into a temple where the Janmabhoomi programme was being held, although participation in the programme was part of her official duties. The commission further observed that 'raids on the Dalits of Madduru, Regadaguduru, Vempenta, Gudipadu and Avukulu, demonstrate that the Dalits are leading their lives in insecurity' (*Punnayya Report* 2000: 113). Across the district of Kurnool, dalits are forced to remove carcasses and bury them, and to engage in extremely demeaning forms of labour. Any refusal to perform these tasks results in social boycott. When the Dalits of Regadagudem petitioned for the assignment of lands in the unauthorized possession of landlords, the deputy superintendent of police filed charge-sheets against 206 dalits.

In Ananthapur district bombs were hurled at dalits who were celebrating Ugadi in their neighbourhood. Dalits from 312 villages petitioned the Punnayya Commission that they were denied entry into temples, had to suffer 'the two-glass system' when they went to hotels in all these villages, were denied access to public wells and taps, were refused washing and barbers' services, were denied entry into bus shelters, were obstructed from sitting on the *rachabanda* [meeting point in the main village; usually location of village assemblies] or from riding bicycles, were not allowed to organize processions, and could not participate in village festivals. Their problems did not stop here. They were not allowed to dress well or to wear new clothes, and had to remain standing in the presence of any member of the dominant castes. After they finished their day's work in the fields, food was served to them either in their hands or on rocks nearby, and water was poured into their hands (*Punnayya Report,* 2000: 276–7). Elected Dalit mandal presidents, sarpanches or members of the panchayats were not permitted to sit on chairs alongside caste Hindu members in the meetings of these local bodies.

In Chittoor district, while Dalits were allowed into the Venkateswara Swami temple and the Sri Kalahasti temple after the Temple Entry Act came into force in 1939, the smaller temples in the district have continued to deny Dalits entry. Attempts by Dalits to force their way into temples have been met with attacks by dominant castes. Apart from the denial of temple entry, the other forms of untouchability—denial of entry into public places, restrictions on mobility and dress, and denial of services—were also routinely practised in this district (*Punnayya Report* 2000: 304). Seventeen petitions from Chittoor district spoke of how Dalits were obstructed from using or accessing burial grounds: persons belonging to the dominant castes either usurped and cultivated the lands belonging to the burial ground, or denied SCs access to the footpaths leading to these grounds. In East Godavari, on the other hand, according to Justice Punnayya, the influence of the social reform movement in bringing about the eradication of untouchability was evident in the fact that representations from only 19 mandals out of 59 were presented to the commission (ibid.: 425).

From Guntur district, with 733 villages in all, the commission received a total of 625 representations from 505 villages belonging to 57 mandals in the district. In Nalgonda, Kurnool, Khammam, and Krishna districts, the forms of untouchability reported were very similar to those reported from other districts. With regard to Mahaboobnagar district, Justice Punnayya wondered aloud whether the police machinery was doing anything at all to safeguard the civil rights of Dalits under the Constitution (*Punnayya Report,* 2000: 1274).

This is perhaps the first time that an official document lists atrocity as part of the practice of untouchability, or, rather, lists atrocity as the first and most critical part of the practice of untouchability. Up to this point, the discursive fields of untouchability and atrocity had been separate and distinct, although it is impossible to separate them conceptually. Apart from the aspect of atrocity, untouchability is reducible to three elements—the two-glass system, temple entry, and access to water—enforced by hoteliers, priests, and village elders. Untouchability, then, according to this report, consists of four elements, split into two parts, with atrocity on one side and the other three practices on the other (although these three also come within the meaning of atrocity under the law).

The solutions, likewise, are essentially two-fold: the application of the criminal law in the form of the Scheduled Castes and Scheduled Tribes (Prevention of Atrocities) Act, 1989, on the one hand, and the ritual observance of periodic intermingling under the watchful eye of the district administration on the other. But herein lies the paradox: how can intermingling be sustained in the face of atrocity? Can periodic intermingling under conditions of surveillance be deemed to be the exercise of the right to personal liberty?

Conclusion

'[U]ntouchability is not a legal term. There is no exact legal definition of untouchability whereby it could be possible to define who is an Untouchable and who is not. Untouchability is a social concept which has become embodied in a custom and as custom varies so does untouchability' (Ambedkar, 2002: 332).

This brings us back to the point at which we began this exercise. First, however, we need to underscore the criticality of insurgent ethnography, or an insurgent sociology of caste. A study of 1,589 villages spread across 11 districts in the state of Gujarat attempted to formulate an 'untouchability index' that could measure and help comprehend practices of untouchability (Navsarjan and RFK Centre, 2010). Building on Ambedkar's view of caste as a system of graded inequality, this study set out 197 variables of untouchability, divided more or less evenly between vertical discrimination (non-Dalit against Dalit) and horizontal discrimination (Dalit against Dalit). The 98 distinct variables grouped under vertical discrimination were clustered into eight categories. These included: water for drinking; food and beverage; religion; touch; access to public facilities and institutions; caste-based occupations; prohibitions and social sanctions; and private-sector discrimination (ibid.: 4). The identification of the variables and the manner of their clustering points to the significant interrelationship between the different variables, and necessitates an understanding of untouchability not as a single, isolated practice, but as a 'combination of relevant practices' (ibid.: 11).

Looking at the micro-practices of caste that form the subject-matter of both ethnography and anti-caste resistance, the significance of standpoint and its far-reaching implications are brought home in a quite startling fashion. The scope of article 17 is effectively mapped through this painstaking ethnography, extended from the sphere of vertical discrimination alone to the sphere of horizontal discrimination as well, signalling the 'complex of disabilities' that Panikkar alluded to in the constituent assembly.

The validation of dominant sociology by the courts, and the affirmation of the 'knowledge' produced about caste that privileges the experience of the dominant castes, creates a crisis of constitutional interpretation, which has drawn on a dominant knowledge base to interpret insurgent protections. The knowledge base, however, is not merely sociological/anthropological but also experiential. The imbrication of these two kinds of knowledge produces a particular common-sense about caste discrimination and its 'reasonable' remedies; it is no accident that the representation of Dalits in the judiciary has been negligible, and progress in this regard halting. Part of this dominant common-sense also truncates reservations for Dalits by negating the claims of those who convert to Christianity, excommunicating them, in a sense, from justice claims that emanate from the Hindu social order—a punitive measure for daring to aspire to a life free of oppression. In this very negation is evident the relation between non-discrimination and liberty: the guarantee of non-discrimination on grounds of caste is denied to those who assert their freedom to step outside the confines of Hinduism. While reservation is denied to Dalit Christians, is liberty guaranteed? It is here that we see a double negation: the denial of reservations to converts, and the concomitant denial of freedom manifested in the perpetration of atrocities against dalit converts to Christianity, as was the case in Chunduru in 1991.

Courts and other judicial and quasi-judicial institutions, while they have stepped in at some crucial moments, are not spaces that uniformly safeguard the spirit of non-discrimination. The first step taken in *Champakam Dorairajan* demonstrates this sharp disjuncture between the constitution and the judicial reasoning. Interestingly, in the case of caste and Tribe, the major interpretive conjuncture has been between administrative law and constitutional protections. There has been an effort to infuse constitutional morality into micro-environments through government orders and bureaucratic interventions, which in this instance have achieved an unparalleled insurgent jurisprudence.

At this moment of return to the micro-practices of caste, it is not dominant knowledge production that informs standpoints, but rather the experience of those who suffer discrimination, along with the philosophy of non-discrimination fostered and honed by the intellectual history of resistance to discrimination. While this is, in a sense, a return to the ethnographic, the landing-stage is radically different. What I hope this journey from the sociology of caste, through the judicial debates on reservation, to the practice of administrative law and judicial documentation of untouchability, has accomplished is an insurgent historiography of the present in all its complexity. The immediate relevance of the argument against concepts like the creamy layer lies in the continuing, everyday derogation of the right of dalits to non-discrimination and liberty, evidence of which derogation is contained in the government orders and the report of the Punnayya Commission. The significance of the S.R. Sankaran GOs described earlier in this chapter and the *Punnayya Report* lies in the demonstration of the possibility of combating discrimination and the curtailment of liberty through state action firmly committed to constitutional morality.

REFERENCES

Ambedkar, B.R. (2002), 'An Anti-untouchability Agenda', in *The Essential Writings of B.R. Ambedkar* ed. Valerian Rodrigues. New Delhi: Oxford University Press, 359–68.

Ambedkar, B.R. (2002), 'From Millions to Fractions', in *The Essential Writings of B.R. Ambedkar* ed. Valerian Rodrigues. New Delhi: Oxford University Press, 332-50.

Ambedkar, B.R. (2002), 'Outside the fold', in *The Essential Writings of B.R. Ambedkar* ed. Valerian Rodrigues. New Delhi: Oxford University Press, 323–31.

Baxi, Upendra (2002), *The Future of Human Rights*. New Delhi: Oxford University Press.

Navsarjan and Robert F Kennedy Center for Justice and Human Rights (2010), 'Understanding Untouchability: A comprehensive study of practices and conditions in 1589 Villages'. http://navsarjan.org/Documents/Untouchability_Report_FINAL_Complete.pdf. Last accessed on 30 January 2011.

Ramanathan, Usha (2010), 'A constitution amid dire straits'. *Seminar* 615, November, 84–8.

Rao, B. Shiva (1968), *Framing of India's Constitution: A Study*, New Delhi: Indian Institute of Public Administration.

Rodrigues, Valerian (2002), *The Essential Writings of B.R. Ambedkar*. Ed. Delhi, Oxford University Press, 473–94.

Subrahmaniam, Vidya (2010), Throwing off the Yoke of Manual Scavenging. *The Hindu*, 27 October.

Tripathi, P.K. 1971. *Some Insights into Fundamental Rights*, Bombay: University of Bombay.

Valmiki, Omprakash (2007), *Joothan*, translated from the Hindi by Arun Prabha Mukerjee. Calcutta: Samya.

NOTES

1. Upendra Baxi, *The Future of Human Rights*, New Delhi: Oxford University Press, 2002, p. 27.
2. http://Tribal.nic.in/writereaddata/linkimages/pcract955E2701676142.pdf. Accessed on 02 September 2011.
3. Government of Andhra Pradesh, General Administration (Ser. C) Department, Memorandum No. 2153/Ser/763 dated 26 August 1976.
4. Government of India, Ministry of Works, Housing letter No. 28(8)/70, 19 June 1971.
5. Government of Andhra Pradesh, Planning and Cooperation (Housing I-I) Department, G.O. Ms. No. 489, 10 September 1971.
6. Government of Andhra Pradesh, Social Welfare (B2) Department, G.O. Ms. No. 57 dated 14 July 1976. Also Government of Andhra Pradesh, Employment and Social Welfare Department, Memo No. 5092/C1/75-1, 17 December 1975; Government of Andhra Pradesh, Social Welfare (C) Department, Memo No. 5292/C1/76-1, 5 August 1976.
7. Government of Andhra Pradesh, Social Welfare (B) Department, G.O. Ms. No. 90, 25 August 1976.
8. Government of Andhra Pradesh, Medical and Health Department, G.O. Rt. No. 132, 24 January 1977.
9. Government of Andhra Pradesh, Social Welfare (C1) Department, Memo. No. 3719/C1/76-1; Government of Andhra Pradesh, Social Welfare (C) Department, Memo. No. 3788/C1/76-1, 4 June 1976.

10. Government of Andhra Pradesh, Employment And Social Welfare (C) Department, G.O. Rt. No. 393, 3 April 1976.
11. Government of Andhra Pradesh, Social Welfare (C) Department, D.O. Lt. No. 3273/C1/76-2, 20 July 1976.
12. Government of Andhra Pradesh, Revenue (P) Department, G.O. Ms. No. 87, 22 January 1975. Also Social Welfare (B) Department, Memo. No. 131/3354/B3/76-2, 16 September 1976; Government of Andhra Pradesh, Panchayati Raj (Panchayats-III) Department, G.O. Ms. No. 647, 20 November 1975.
13. Government of Andhra Pradesh, Social Welfare (B) Department, G.O. Ms. 177, 16 November 1976; emphasis added.
14. Copy of circular Rc No. 25835/76 – H2 (c), 13 August 1976 from Sri T. Lakshma Reddy, IAS, Registrar of Cooperative Societies, Andhra Pradesh, Hyderabad, addressed to all the consumer cooperative central stores/super bazaars in the state, and copy marked to Secretary, Social Welfare Department, Hyderabad.
15. Copy of Circular Lr. No. 2284/S.F./II/76-1, 26 August 1976 from S.K. Pachauri, IAS, Dy Secretary to Government, addressed to all projects officers of Small Farmers Development Agencies, and copy marked to Social Welfare Department.
16. Government of Andhra Pradesh, Education Department, G.O. Ms. No. 1134, 16 November 1973.
17. Government of Andhra Pradesh, Employment and Social Welfare (B) Department, G.O. Ms. No. 405, 13 June 1974.
18. Government of Andhra Pradesh, Employment and Social Welfare (SC & ST Cell) Department, G.O. Ms. No. 164, 15 September 1973.
19. An additional expenditure of Rs 18 lakh was approved towards this end in the year 1976–77, vide G.O. Ms. No. 488, 13 May 1976, Social Welfare (B1) Department, Government of Andhra Pradesh.
20. Government of Andhra Pradesh, Education Department, G.O. Ms. No. 141, Edn., 25 February 1977.
21. Letter from Sri P. Adinarayana, Director of School Education, AP, Hyderabad to the Secretary to Government, Education Department, AP, Hydeabad, L. Dis. No. 2714/B3-1/76, 9 July 1976.
22. Government of Andhra Pradesh, Social Welfare (E) Department, G.O. Ms. No. 73, 3 August 1976.
23. Government of Andhra Pradesh, Education (J) Department, G.O. Ms. No. 1150, 29 December 1976.
24. Government of Andhra Pradesh, Social Welfare (B1) Department, G.O. Ms. No. 523, 26 May 1976.
25. Government of Andhra Pradesh, Employment and Social Welfare (B) Department, G.O. Ms. No. 118, 14 September 1976. Also Social Welfare (B1) Department, G.O. Ms. No. 3, 5 January 1977.
26. Government of Andhra Pradesh, Education (M2) Department, G.O. Ms. No. 1120, 18 December 1976.
27. Government of Andhra Pradesh, Social Welfare (B2) Department, G.O. Ms. No. 33 dated 7 July 1976; Government of Andhra Pradesh, Social Welfare (B) Department, G.O. Ms. No. 168, 29 October 1976.

28. Government of Andhra Pradesh, Social Welfare (SC & ST Cell-B) Department, Memo No. 912/SC & ST Cell-B/76-3, 3 December 1976; Government of Andhra Pradesh, Industries and Commerce (PE Cell) Department, Letter No. 3069/PE-Cell/76-1, 29 October 1976.
29. Government of Andhra Pradesh, Social Welfare (B) Department, G.O. Ms. No. 342, 30 August 1977.
30. Government of Andhra Pradesh, General Administration (SC & ST Cell) Department, Memo. No. 4124/SC & ST Cell/74-2, 3 March, 1975.
31. Government of Andhra Pradesh, Panchayat Raj (Progs I) Department, G.O. Ms. No. 597, 22 June 1976.
32. Government of Andhra Pradesh, Panchayat Raj (Progs I) Department, G.O. Ms. No. 376, 17 May 1977.
33. Government of Andhra Pradesh, Social Welfare (B2) Department, Memo. No. 791/B2/75-1, 25 July 1975; Government of Andhra Pradesh, Social Welfare (B3) Department, Memo. No. 24 (a) 4988/B3/76-1, 3 December 1976.
34. Government of Andhra Pradesh, Labour, Employment and Technical Education Department, G.O. Ms. No. 941, 27 August 1977.
35. Government of Andhra Pradesh, Employment and Social Welfare (B2) Department, Memo. No. 873/B2/74-12, 18 July 1974.
36. Government of Andhra Pradesh, Employment and Social Welfare (B) Department, G.O. Ms. No. 178, 16 November 1976.
37. Government of Andhra Pradesh, Social Welfare (SC & ST Cell A) Department, G.O. Ms. No. 199, 9 December 1976.
38. Copy of Memorandum No. 2049/Special-A/76-1, 31 May 1976, of the General Administration (Special-A) Department.
39. Government of Andhra Pradesh, Social Welfare (B) Department, G.O. Ms. No. 136, 4 October 1976.
40. Government of Andhra Pradesh, Social Welfare (B) Department, G.O. Ms. No. 116, 13 September 1976.

4

Manual Scavengers: A Struggle for Retrieving India's Soul

P.S. Krishnan

One of the deepest and most anguished concerns that S.R. Sankaran and I shared throughout our active life pertains to the plight of the manual scavengers and other sanitation labourers or *safai karmacharis*. On the occasion of his second death anniversary, it would be appropriate to recapitulate the emergence of this class of 'slave labourers' as an expression of the caste system-with-'untouchability' or the Indian Caste System (ICS), as I have termed it, what has happened to them through history, particularly during the colonial and post-Independence periods, and understand their aspirations and their right to total liberation and the duty cast by the Constitution on the state and society to assist in fulfilling their aspirations and achieving their rights.

Introduction

Sanitary workers or *safai karmacharis* (SK) are not merely individual members of the Sanitation Work-Force but members by birth of social collectivities with inerasable identity and inter-generational continuity or *jatis* (castes), who have been forced into this 'occupation' by the inexorable evil power of the ICS and on account of the castes to which they belong. It was Dr Babasaheb Ambedkar who brought out the hierarchy of castes and the hierarchy of occupations, characteristic of the ICS.[1] The two hierarchies are matched, preserving and reserving occupations of prestige and advantage for members of castes at the top and forcing members of castes below into labourious occupations with low prestige and sometimes stigmatized, to be performed in conditions of squalor and on adverse terms.

Thus, we have in North India castes like the Balmiki which have been stigmatised as 'scavenging castes' from which the entire *safai* force is drawn and which have also spread to parts of South & East India. In the south, while there are SK communities like the Relli, much of the safai force is drawn from the poorest sections of the major Scheduled Castes (SCs), especially the Madiga caste of Andhra Pradesh and Karnataka and the Arundhatiyar caste of Tamil

Nadu, who are the same as Madigas and who have spread into Kerala also. SK castes are mostly SC. SCs have been identified and listed on the basis of the criterion of 'untouchability'. A small part of the Indian *safai* labour force is from STs like Yanadi[2] in the South and Muslim castes like Halalkhor in the North who now call themselves Dalit-Muslim. Some members of SK castes are Christian converts who continue to be identified by the same caste name as their Hindu counterparts. Escape routes for them have been sealed off not only by the ICS but, wherever possible, by statutes like the Punjab Agricultural Land Alienation Act 1901 (PALA Act), which kept the agricultural labour castes of Chamar and Churha (now Balmiki if Hindu, Mazabi if Sikh, and Masih if Christian—the name Chuhra has been deleted from the SC list, as it is derogatory and rightly resented by the community) out of the list of agricultural castes eligible to own land, resulting in tighter reinforcement of the bondage of the former, that is, Chamar, to agricultural labour and the squeezing out of the latter, that is, Balmiki (then Chuhra) into the growing cities including Delhi, as cheap and bonded safai labour in the most inhuman conditions and branded, for their services, as 'untouchables among untouchables', by a grateful society.

A word about the PALA Act will help to illustrate and understand one of the ways in which the ICS worked. This Act was conceived by the colonial rulers to prevent agricultural land from passing out of the hands of agricultural communities into the hands of moneylenders, mostly belonging to the upper caste of traders. The colonial rulers learned their lesson from the Pabna riots of Bengal and the Deccan riots in Maharashtra caused by agrarian unrest. The British rulers could not afford similar unrest to spread to a Province which supplied them a major part of the colonial army. The opportunity of the formulation of this legislation was cleverly misused by the lower Indian officers who entirely belonged to the upper castes. They manipulated its provisions to ensure that the Chamar and Churha were kept out of the schedule of agricultural communities, who alone were entitled to own land. In fact, Chamar and Churha in Punjab have been and are primarily agriculturists, though mostly landless. Therefore, they ought to have been included in the schedule of agricultural communities. As a result of the manipulation by upper caste lower-administrative Indian officers, their availability exclusively for agricultural labour, so vital for the large land-owning communities of Punjab, was ensured, and in addition, the availability of cheap scavenging labour for the growing cities was also ensured.

The Plight of 'Scavengers'

The plight of this community first came to my notice when, as a teenager, I saw a large colony of scavengers in my hometown of Thiruvananthapuram in a locality called Chengalchula (which means brick-kiln). The name of the locality was very appropriate, though unintentional, because the locality was like a burning kiln and the people living there were reduced to the status of bricks with which sanitation amenities were built in the town. At that time, a remarkable person, who deserves to be known, but whose name is forgotten even in Kerala, Ramakrishna Pillai, actively worked for them, organized them into trade unions, introduced the concept of the rights of scavengers, and led their agitations for better wages and regulated terms of service. Upper caste society derisively nicknamed him as 'Thotti' Ramakrishna Pillai—Thotti is the Malayalam and Tamil word for scavenger—though Ramakrishna Pillai himself was an upper caste non-Brahmin not born in the scavenger community. This was in the 1940s. About half century later, I met Ramakrishna Pillai at his house. He was then a very old man, and soon after our meeting, he passed away. We recalled those days. On my suggestion, the National Commission for Backward Classes, of which I was Member-Secretary, officially recommended him, with particulars of his extraordinary biodata of service, for a Padma Bhushan. Not surprisingly this recommendation was not heeded.

During the same period, two remarkable novels in Malayalam came out, which influenced my understanding of and feeling for this community. The first was *Thottiyude Makan* (Scavenger's Son) by Nagavalli R.S. Kurup and the other was *Thotti* (Scavenger) by Thakazhi Sivasankara Pillai.

Total Liberation and Dr Ambedkar's Radical Slogan

Looking at it from the point of view of the victims enslaved in this 'occupation', the national objective ought to be their liberation and their rehabilitation in occupations of social status and the cutting off of further supply by opening up occupations of social status to communities that have been the recruiting grounds of this form of slave-labour. Their total liberation can be achieved by two paths: one is to cut off demand and the other is to cut off supply. While the former is important, the latter will be most effective. No community or individual should be allowed to remain in conditions in which the community or the person is forced into this 'occupation'. This has to be achieved through a massive programme of education and training for the existing labourers and those belonging to the castes of their origin. It was this approach that is encapsulated in Dr Babasaheb Ambedkar's Slogan '*Bhangi, Jhadoo Chodo*' ('Scavenger, leave the broom').

First Three Decades of Independence—High Rhetoric

National policy, in the first three decades after Independence, was alleviation of the harsh living and working conditions of scavengers based on the compassionate vision of Mahatma Gandhi ji, the humanist-nationalist. But the controllers of India's plans and budgets, at the cutting edge of policy, enfeebled that vision and provided token lip-sympathy, high rhetoric and budgetary peanuts. Thus, for example, the Fourth Five Year Plan (1969–74) generously provided an outlay of three crore rupees at the Centre 'for improvement of the living and working conditions of those in unclean occupations .... to be additive to the general sector measures for the improvement of sanitation'. This was accompanied by a disclaimer of responsibility with the observation that 'unless the programme is considered in its totality [which was not attempted] success is bound to be limited', and postponed effective action with the observation that [F]or a lasting solution, the problem of improving scavenging conditions has to be viewed in the context of the general problem of conservancy.' This verbiage is in keeping with the almost instinctive approach of the upper caste—upper class formulators of Indian plans and plan 'literature', consisting of high-sounding rhetoric and denial of funds, programmes and organization in practical terms. The generous provision of three crore rupees was additive to general sector outlays. It is characteristic of our planning process that general sector outlays were not forthcoming for the victims and what was intended to be an additive remained the totality.

Liberation and Dignified Rehabilitation in 1980

A break from this and an SK-based vision was first unfolded by the Report of the Planning Commission's Working Group on the Development of Scheduled Castes in the VI Plan 1980–5 in September 1980 (Chairman, the present author, then Joint Secretary Scheduled Castes and Backward Classes Development, Ministry of Home Affairs, Government of India), the first such Working Group for the SCs. It declared that it is a matter of sufficient priority and importance for the nation that there should be no such thing as scavenging in the country any more, it laid down that the only meaningful objective in this field is to eliminate scavenging completely and not to accept its continuance beyond a specified date, and finally it outlined the strategy of liberating the scavengers from their profession through alternative fitment, without reduction of their income, but converting dry latrines into water-seal closets that do not require manual scavenging. Six specific measures of legislative enactment and municipal and governmental executive action to provide alternative employment for existing workers, prevention of fresh expansion of scavenging, residential education and hostels for all children of their families at government cost, and eight specific steps for conversion of dry latrines were spelt out including provision of funds on open-ended basis in this path-breaking document.

Since the controllers of the plan and budgetary resources shied away from biting the bullet, the author, as Joint Secretary, broke the ice by introducing in 1981 the scheme of Liberation of Scavengers and Construction of Low Cost, Pour-Flush Latrines in units of whole towns and providing alternative employment for the liberated scavengers as part of an existing Centrally-Sponsored Scheme (CSS). It is an indisputable fact that while the whole-town approach has helped and has show the way, manual scavenging is widely prevalent to this day, many lakhs are still forced to continue in this 'occupation' on account of lack of a comprehensive approach as well as a lack of consistent effort on the part of the political and administrative system of governance.

Growing urbanization is worsening the situation. Along with this, the recent drive to construct toilets in rural areas is adding a new dimension to the worsening of the situation. While sanitation is no doubt an important need and goal in rural as well as urban areas, failure to ensure that sanitation and toilets are provided without requiring human *safai* labour is what is contributing to the worsening of the situation. The Census of 2011 has brought out that manual scavengers are engaged in at least 7.4 lakh households in India. Another statistic from the WHO/UNICEF Joint Monitoring Programme for Water Supply and Sanitation points out that 626 million Indians are still defecating in the open. This implies the existence of scavenging to that extent, though not in the organized manner as in municipal areas. Indian open defecators account for 60 per cent of the world's open defecators.[3] Correspondingly, about 70 per cent of the world's scavengers are in India, and therefore, it may not be inappropriate to describe India as a nation of scavengers. The Indian attitude is governed by the consideration that since cheap labour for scavenging is in any case available from traditional castes bound to it, towards whom there is no feeling of fraternity in our nation and whose humiliation, therefore, does not cause a ripple in upper caste conscience, there is no need to incur great expenditure for sanitation consistent with the dignity of the scavenging castes and scavenging labourers. This all the more emphasizes the need to have at the centre of our strategy the cutting off of supply of scavenging labour by various comprehensive measures which I shall detail below.

Another important step taken in 1980 was the introduction of Special Central Assistance (SCA) to the States' Special Component Plans for Scheduled Castes (SCP)—a plan mechanism innovated by the author in 1978 to channelize population-equivalent share of plan outlays and benefits to the SCs and thereafter followed by the Central and state governments but with reduced vigour, clarity, and integrity in subsequent years. The story of how the SCP and the SCA were brought into existence is romantic; I shall recount it later in a book I am planning on the saga of the SCP and developmental autonomy for SCs. From the point of the SK, it is significant that the states' programmes for relatively weaker and more exploited groups among SCs like civic sanitation workers (sweepers and scavengers), bonded labourers, nomadic, and Vimukta Jati communities of SCs were the criteria for distribution of 10 per cent of the SCA.

The vision and new spirit of 1978 to 1982 was reflected in the plan, mid-term appraisal and plan approach documents of the VI Plan (1980–5) and subsequent plans with specific reference to the civic sanitation workers. The late 70s and early 80s also saw the introduction and commencement of a new CSS of pre-Matric scholarships for children of families in the so-called 'unclean' occupations like civic sanitation, that is, scavenging. But outlays have not been provided and organizations have not been built up to cover all children of the *safai* families.

Inadequate Plan and Budgetary Outlays

While the goal of total elimination of scavenging and education and training of SK/*safai* families for rehabilitation into alternative occupations by the end of the plan period has been spelt out, failure to provide matching outlays and organizational build-up has led to repetition of the same goal, changing the goal-post to successive plan-ending years, the last being 2012 in the XI Plan, indicating lack of seriousness and sincerity on the part of the controllers of plans and budgets. The last deadline has also passed with the situation not materially altered and threatening to worsen.

Truncated New Initiatives of 1990 to 1993

The year 1990, when the present author became Secretary Ministry of Welfare (now trifurcated into Ministry of Social Justice & Empowerment or MSJE, the Ministry of Tribal Affairs or MoTA and the Ministry of Minority Affairs or MoMA) and there were two SK-sensitive members in the Planning Commission (the late L.C. Jain and the late Rajni Kothari), who fully supported the author in these efforts, saw renewed emphasis on this, leading later to the flowering of four major initiatives for SK in 1992–93.

a. Introduction of a National Scheme of Liberation and Rehabilitation of Scavengers and their dependents in 1992 with detailed guidelines and providing for monitoring committees at the national, state, district, local body, and *mohalla* levels with representation for SK. This could have started in 1990 itself, but this was not possible on account of a certain unexpected circumstance followed by the fall of the then short-lived National Front Government headed by V.P. Singh—consequent on the recognition of and the provision of reservation for socially and educationally backward classes (BCs) on the basis of this author's note, and its well-known aftermath—and the co-eval resignation of the then Planning Commission members including the two members referred to above and my own retirement soon after, that is, in December 1990.

b. Establishment of a Central Monitoring Committee on 27 January 1993 headed by the Union Minister of Welfare and 26 official and non-official members including the author.
c. The enactment of the National Commission for Safai Karmacharis (NCSK) Act 1993 to set up the NCSK.
d. The enactment of the Employment of Manual Scavengers & Construction of Dry Latrines (Prohibition) Act 1993 or the MSCDL (P) Act.

But each of these was marked by the half-heartedness and tentativeness characteristic of the actions of the dominant elite of India, almost entirely from the upper castes (not only of Hindus but also of non-Hindu societies), and more recently, to a limited extent from the upper-middle castes, who occupy the commanding heights of Indian administration, governance, and all institutions, in respect of the SK and other people constituting the Indian masses of workers almost entirely drawn from the SC, ST, and BC. Such half-heatedness and tentativeness, and in many instances, downright negativism, was the result of the inexorable process of the ICS which has deeply infected the Indian elite mind-set gene.

Half-Heartedness in the Approach

a. The programme was disintegrated by transferring the conversion of dry latrines to the Ministry of Urban Development from 1989–90, retaining only the rehabilitation component with the Ministry of Welfare (now, after its trifurcation, with the Ministry of Social Justice and Empowerment). The status quo ante was not restored despite the recommendation of the Conference of Ministers and Secretaries of States and UTs and Mayors held on 18 and 19 September 1992. Departmentation of work and jurisdiction is inevitable for convenience of administration and governance, but it becomes a problem because administrative departmetnation is converted by the Indian genius into compartmentalizaiton of the people and programmes for them. This is what has happened in respect of SKs following the disintegration of the programme.
b. The Central Monitoring Committee met in February 1993, but thereafter, it was never convened.
c. Nearly a year was lost in operationalizing the NCSK Act by the appointment of the first team of Chairperson, Vice Chairperson and five other members as late as 12 August 1994.
d. The NCSK Act was a very diluted version of the draft prepared, on the request of Buta Singh and other SK leaders, by the author providing

considerable teeth to the commission and a chapter pertaining to the special care and measures required in respect of the communities from which the SK are drawn, so that the vulnerability on account of which they are forced into this 'occupation' are removed. The teeth and this chapter were deleted in the Act as moved and passed.

e. This is the only Act, which specified the date of its ceasure—like a horoscope prescribing the date of death of a child even before it is born. The date of its demise was set at 31 March 1997, apparently on the basis that this was the date (at the end of the VIII Plan) set for the total elimination of scavenging—without real seriousness in terms of Plan and budget outlays and organizational build-up to effectuate elimination of scavenging by that date. By the time the first team of the commission was appointed, it was left with a truncated term of only 2½ years. Thereafter, its term has been extended from time to time by amendments of the Act. In the year 2000, it is learnt that the then Minister even proposed the abolition of the commission, but this was mercifully overruled by the Prime Minister (PM). In 2004, when the last extension of its extended tenure came to an end, the government allowed the statutory base of the commission to collapse and have continued it upto 2007 by executive order, thereby downgrading and further sapping the limited effectiveness of the commission, even while new statutory commissions for various other purposes were being proliferated and upgradation to constitutional status was being considered in certain instances, sending out a negative signal about the seriousness of the government towards the SKs. Thereafter, its tenure is being extended by three years at a time.

f. The MSCDL (P) Act 1993 was related to Entry 6 (Public Health & Sanitation) of List II (State List) of the Seventh Schedule of the Constitution, making it applicable only to states which chose to adopt it, instead of relating it to Entry 24 of List III (Concurrent List) ['Welfare of Labour Including Conditions of Work'] which would have made it automatically applicable to all states and UTs. The position has not been corrected despite the advice of the National Human Rights Commission (NHRC) in 1999 and despite the recommendations of the National Commission to Review the Working of the Constitution (NCRWC) in 2002 to enact amendments to ensure its automatic applicability to all states. As a result, each state legislature had to adopt the Act. Given the insensitivity of the Indian elite at the level of states also on account of the mindset shaped by centuries of the ICS, this was a very slow process and the State of Delhi, right under the nose of the Centre brought up the rear adopting the Act as late as in 2008.

Budgetary Blows against SK

More blows came in the subsequent years. In the Budget 2003-04 an outlay of Rs. 40 Crores was provided for the Ministry of Welfare (now Ministry of Social Justice and Empowerment) for the National Scheme of Liberation and Rehabilitation of Scavengers and their Dependants. Then the Ministry of Urban Development and Poverty Alleviation (MUD&PA) was allowed to appropriate this money. In the budget for 2004–05 the MUD&PA has been provided Rs. 20 crores and an amount of Rs. 30 crores has been diverted to its Low Cost Sanitation Programme. Despite the Memorandum of the National Action Forum for Social Justice (NAFSJ) to the Chairperson NAC and Chairman UPA and the many letters of the author to the PM and FM and many other leaders, this misappropriation of the hard-earned funds of the SK has not been reversed. On the contrary, the injury has been compounded in the Budget 2005–06 by reducing the budget provision for the scheme still under the MUD&PA to nil. Simultaneously the outlay for the pre-Matric Scholarship Scheme for children of families engaged in 'unclean' occupations, namely, scavenging, tanning and flaying was reduced from Rs 16 crores in the Plan Budget 2004–05 to 0.01 crore in the Plan Budget 2005–06, along with a similar fate for the long-standing CSSs of girls and boys hostels for SCs and STs, marking the first time in the history of budget-making and plan-formulation in India that CSSs for SC, ST, and SK have been terminated or have been slated to be terminated. Efforts were made by the author and some others to reverse this. The presence of a socially sensitive member in the Planning Commission, Dr Bhalchandra Mungekar, helped in securing the reversal of this downward and negative trend. The cavalier 'plan and budgetary' approach to SKs seen between 2003 and 2006 is not an isolated instance. The see-saw of outlays and utilization of outlays has continued. For example, in the Budget 2010-11, the outlay for self-employment scheme of liberation and rehabilitation scavengers was reduced to Rs 4.5 crores from the previous year's budgetary outlay and actuals of Rs 50 crores. But, even this was not utilized and the revised outlay for 2010–11 was Rs 0.01 crore which virtually means nil. In the budget of 2011–12, an outlay of Rs 98 crores was provided of which more than two-third was left unutilized and the revised provision stood reduced to Rs 33 crores. It is in this situation of casualness and mindlessness through which the liberation and rehabilitation of SK has to move forward.

Atrocities on Balmikis in North India

Other menaces faced by the SK include the encroachment of contract labour system into the *safai* area which in effect means continuance of the same Balmiki and other SC labourers with much worse terms and conditions of service under the contractor who is an investor who invests for making the maximum possible profit and, therefore, pays as little as possible for the SK employed by him. The government needs to be sensitive to protect the SK from this SK-adverse feature of neo-laissez faire policies. Another is a spurt in the virulence of atrocities against them, as in Gohana, Haryana where 55 pucca houses of Balmikis were destroyed by arson and explosion and 97 more pucca houses were subjected to looting and destruction of household goods on 31 August 2005. One of the deep causes of this is the inability of the dominant communities to tolerate the new awareness and assertion of rights of the SK Castes (and other SC) and the material progress, though limited, achieved by them against heavy odds by dint of their hard labour and savings and shift of a small proportion (for example 25 per cent in Gohana) of them to more dignified occupations. The legislative and executive responses required to make the SC and ST (Prevention of Atrocities) Act, 1989 (POA Act) have been elabourated in the Memorandum of the NAFSJ to all leaders of the central and state government and leaders of ruling, supporting and opposition Parties following a visit to Gohana by a non-political team led by the author on 14 September 2005. Gohana has been followed by some other similar episodes, the most recent of which is the atrocity in Mirchpur, also in Haryana, where an academically bright physically handicapped Balmiki girl and her aged grandfather were burnt to death in their hut and many huts of Balmikis were destroyed. Most of the perpetrators in Gohana have been acquitted and a few have been convicted recently and awarded limited terms of imprisonment, after protracted investigation and trial, while the victims of Mirchpur are languishing in limbo, still awaiting rehabilitation.

Atrocities are a cruel response of upper caste society to the rejection of caste-based submission by the SCs. As and when any caste of SCs rises in awareness and resistance, it is subjected to atrocities. In North India, Chamars and Bihar's Dusadhs and in South India, Mala, Madiga, Adi Dravida and Pallar castes have been victims since long. In the last 20 years, it has been the turn of Balmikis in UP and Haryana, indicating the growth of resistance among them. But, the central and state governments are not able to keep pace with their legitimate aspirations and give them protection from caste violence as mandated by the Constitution. Recently, a comprehensive set of amendments in the Scheduled Castes and Scheduled Tribes (Prevention of Atrocities) Act, 1989 (POA Act) and related amendments in the RP Act, CrPC et cetera, has been prepared after wide consultations by a National Coalition of 70 Dalit and Human Rights organizations with the author as Chief Advisor, and this has been sent to the government in November, 2009. Concrete action thereon has yet to materialize.

The Two Faces of Government Policy

In brief, government policy has got two faces. One is the vision and new activity unveiled in the late 70s and early 80s in line with the ideology represented by Dr Babasaheb Ambedkar and brief spurts as in that period and in the early 90s when sincerity, patriotism, and devotion to the just rights of labourers and their castes were at the helm. But the dominant face—the face of Mr Hyde prevailing over that of Dr Jekyll—is that of the dominant elite which seeks ways to keep slaves and underdogs as slaves and underdogs only, to nip in the bud (sometimes blatantly and often subtly), any possibility of their aspirations to become equal masters, and not to allow any radical alteration of the social structure in the direction laid down by the Constitution of India. Indian governance, as it is, is unprepared to deal with the future when more and more *safai*-victims will be drawn in as urbanization gathers tempo an many rural areas, especially with regard to sanitation and scavenging. This menace of victimization of the members, particularly, women and girl children of the most vulnerable communities, almost entirely part of the SCs, is like the spread of cancer. It gets into every activity we touch. A revealing example of this came out poignantly in a public hearing at Chennai in 2012 by a panel, which included the author, of the National Commission for the Protection of Child Rights (NCPCR), which has been entrusted with the task of monitoring the implementation of the Right to Education Act. Evidence was tendered by children and their parents of instances of children belonging to the Arundhatiya caste (same as the Madiga of AP and Karnataka), which is the main source of scavenging labour in Tamil Nadu, being required to clean the classrooms and the school toilets, in school after school. Any hesitation on their part was disarmed by a reminder, not in gentle terms, of their caste and its 'occupation' of scavenging. Even some amongst the managements were aghast when the conduct of their own schools was thus brought into focus in public and the implications of such conduct were brought home to them. In conferences of SKs, in which the author participated, he questioned SK members about this practice and found, not at all to his surprise, that Tamil Nadu is not an exception, and this along with other caste-based inequities are basic features of the otherwise glorious Indian civilization. The Right to Education Act is a forward-looking legislation of considerable significance though it has to be improved in certain respects which have been detailed elsewhere.[4] But, even this Act is made an occasion to extend and impose scavenging on children admitted in terms of the Act who belong to 'traditional scavenging' communities.

Review of the Working of the Constitution (NCRWC) 2000–02

Whenever, sincerity and/or wisdom take long-term charge of the polity, it will have readily at hand the road map for the total liberation and complete rehabilitation of SK and their castes laid out in the Report of the National Commission for Review of the Working of the Constitution (NCRWC), Chapter 10, Section 10.5, titled 'Liberation and Rehabilitation of Safai Karmacharis (Scavengers)' read with para 7.1 to 7.3 of the Background Paper, both of which were drafted by the author, as desired by the Commission's humanist Chairman Justice M.N. Venkatachaliah and which was unanimously approved by the Commission and which incorporates the vision contained in the Report of the Working Group of 1980 and takes in subsequent developments up to that date.[5] This commission set up in 2000 submitted its Report in 2002 to the government, but as usual, no action was taken on its recommendations pertaining to SKs and to other deprived classes.

Recent Hopeful Developments

(a) Emergence of Voluntary Organizations and Activists of Safai Karamchari

There have been some hopeful developments in recent times emerging from the victims of this exploitative system. One is the emergence of new consciousness and spirit of resistance in the younger generation of *safai karmachari* families and the communities that are the recruiting grounds of scavengers. They have formed social organizations of their own. One of them, the *Safai Karmachari Andolan,* had the benefit of S.R. Sankaran's guidance as patron since 2003, shortly after his retirement, till his demise in 2010. This organization, led by Bezwada Wilson, a well-educated person born in a manual scavenger family of Kolar in Karnataka, works in a number of states to encourage manual scavengers to give up this 'occupation'. Success will depend on legislative and executive preparedness, but the organization, under Sankaran's guidance has been able to create much needed awareness in the *safai* communities and *safai* labourers. Another organization, which works in the same field with the same goal in a number of states especially North Indian States, is *Garima Abhiyan*, with its base in Madhya Pradesh. It is led by Ashif Shaikh. Both these organizations have conducted various campaigns and conferences in which it was the privilege of the author to participate. Both these organizations have also been able to draw the support of sensitive members of non-*safai*, non-SC society, in addition to activating SC and SK communities. A third organization in which members of the Balmiki community play a significant part along with other SC, ST, and BC activists is the National Action Forum of Social Justice (NAFSJ), which also works in a number of states and has focus on the Balmiki community and SKs, as well as on other SCs, STs, BCs, and BC minorities. This organization, too, has been able to secure the support of some enlightened leading members of upper caste society. The author has been associated with this organization also.

(b) Preparation of a Draft Comprehensive Bill, 2011

In 2010, the Ministry of Labour set up a working group for recommending legislation for sanitation workers and leather workers. The problems of sanitation workers, especially manual scavengers, and the problems of leather workers are basically different as is the approach to these two. In the case of the former, the 'occupation' of scavenging has to be terminated and the victims and the communities from which the victims originate have to be totally liberated and comprehensively and sustainably rehabilitated in occupations in which their dignity will be upheld. In the case of the latter, the occupation is not to be terminated, but it has to be modernized and technologically upgraded and the market, technology, and finance have to be placed at the disposal of those belonging to castes traditionally connected with this occupation who choose to continue in it. The working group took up the former first. The author, as a member of the working group, drafted a comprehensive bill, namely, the 'Manual Scavengers and Other Sanitation Workers (Total Liberation, Comprehensive Rehabilitation & Humanisation of Working Conditions) Bill'. This Bill, after elabourate discussions, was cleared by the working group and has been made available to the government in 2011. This has also been endorsed by the Report of the Sub-Group-I on 'Perspective Planning for Empowerment of Scheduled Castes in the XII Plan', of which the author was the chairman.

One section of a chapter of this Bill deals with the liberation of manual scavengers and another Section deals with their comprehensive rehabilitation. It requires that there shall be no manual scavenging anywhere in India from the Independence Day (of the year in which the Bill is passed) and declares all manual scavengers in the country who have been liberated from manual scavenging with effect from that day. In an effort to plug all loopholes, it requires the demolition of all latrines which require manual scavenging and are thus the symbols and instruments of perpetuation of manual scavenging, or their conversion into latrines not requiring the services of manual scavengers in any form. This task is required to be performed by municipalities, panchayats, contonment boards, notified areas and other local bodies and Authorities, all government departments, all public sector undertakings, establishments and public sector banks and other similar institutions and all private sector establishments in the respective areas of their jurisdiction/places under their control or use. Again, to plug all loopholes, the municipalities and other local bodies and authorities are required to eliminate open defecation in drains, roadsides, et cetera, which inevitably require the service of manual scavengers, by means such as enforcing and facilitating construction of water-seal latrines in every possible house, supplemented by common water-seal latrines with sufficient number of seats. The Ministry of Railways being a major employer or source of manual scavenging is specifically required to take steps to eliminate conditions requiring manual scavenging in all railway stations by adopting appropriate forms of construction or mechanization, conversion of toilets in railway coaches into eco-friendly and labour-friendly toilets, and implementation of other measures specified. Similar responsibility is placed on all other government departments, public undertakings et cetera and also private sector establishments.

Under Comprehensive Rehabilitation, the Bill requires that all manual scavengers in the employment of municipalities and other local bodies, government departments, public sector undertakings, and private sector establishments who have attained the age of 55 or more and other manual scavengers as and when they attain the age of 55, be retired with full monthly pension in recognition of the long years of service rendered to society by them under the most adverse conditions. Manual scavengers less than 55 years in age should, after their liberation, be continued on the rolls of the employer-institutions on salaries not less than and terms of employment not less advantageous than before without any break of service, and be provided by them alternative employment in the same organizations/institutions, which, in order to enhance human dignity, are unconnected with sweeping and other sanitation work. In order that no escape route be left, the Bill specifies illustratively certain services required by citizens but which are not available or are not available in adequate measure for the provision of which the liberated manual scavengers should be employed with necessary training. Among the services mentioned as illustrations are plumbing and electrical repairs services, driving including driving of modern mechanized tractor-sized street-sweepers, cooking and serving of food in mid-day meals in schools, services required in *anganwadi*s, maintenance of public gardens and parks et cetera. Similar responsibility is also placed on government departments and private sector establishments. In particular, the Ministry of Railways is required to set apart a certain proportion of its catering service contracts and catering service employment to liberated and trained sanitation workers/members of their families/members of the communities from which scavenging workers have been traditionally drawn. All of them are required to prepare detailed plans of the number of manual scavengers in their employ to be shifted to other services, identify their training needs, and provide training for the present manual scavengers and equip them for any such alternative employment before the day of liberation. Since a sizeable number of manual scavengers are privately engaged, they are required to be provided training for alternative employment or self-employment by the municipalities and panchayats and other local bodies and authorities within whose areas of jurisdiction such private manual scavengers are employed. Among other measures required by the Bill are provision of high quality residential schools upto Class XII for all their children at the cost of the central and respective state governments, and provision of proper housing with adequate drinking water, drainage, sanitation, electrification, paved internal link roads, community halls, study centres for their children, and other such facilities.

Coming to sanitation workers other than manual scavengers, sewerage including septic tank services are required to be humanized and made free from all forms of hazard and squalor by municipalities, panchayats, other local bodies and authorities, railways and other government departments, and the owners and managers of private apartment complexes and industrial and commercial complexes like malls, et cetera, by various means, some of which are illustratively specified like mechanization required to preclude the need for any person to go down into sewers, drains, and manholes, like the use of equipment for suction and removal of silt and blocks in sewers and drains. Certain safety measures, medical insurance, et cetera, are prescribed. The Bill requires the Government of India to establish an autonomous National Sanitation Workers Research Organization and a National Sanitation Technology Mission.

In respect of sanitation labourers engaged in sweeping and similar sanitation work, private contract system is prohibited and its continuance made punishable. It requires the provision of the best available technology for sweeping and similar sanitation work such as use of mechanized tractor-sized street-sweepers, and requires all such work to be given to direct employees of the respective institutions. All existing contract labourers are deemed to be the direct employees of the government, municipalities, panchayats, PSUs, or private sector industrial and commercial corporate organizations, as the case may be.

In order to prevent a relapse of liberated manual scavengers into scavenging work and in order to prevent substitution of liberated manual scavengers by others of the same communities which are vulnerable, the Bill requires all children of the families of manual scavengers—erstwhile and liberated manual scavengers—and of the vulnerable communities from which manual scavengers have been traditionally recruited to be admitted to residential schools of high quality upto Class XII with adequate infrastructure and post-graduate teachers, comparable to the best privately-run public schools. This and other measures of rehabilitation are to be provided whether or not of any member of any family of such communities is at present engaged in scavenging labour. It is necessary to re-emphasise that all rehabilitation measures shall be available not only to manual scavengers, hereafter liberated, and members and children of their families, but also to those who were earlier engaged in manual scavenging and have been liberated by their own volition or by governmental support, and to all members and families of the vulnerable communities. This is necessary because of the tendency on the part of some public servants to interpret the provision of eligibility for relief and rehabilitation narrowly and to deny their benefit to those who have ceased to be manual scavengers and their families. It is strange, but understandable in the light of the mind-set created by the ICS, that such public servants do not see the contradiction between the national policy of liberating manual scavengers from manual scavenging and at the same time insisting that they will be eligible for relief and rehabilitation only if they or any member of their family continue to live in manual scavenging!

It is also necessary to spell out that while most manual scavengers belong to SCs, converts to Islam and Christianity (who are technically not SCs only because of Clause 3 of the Presidential Orders) and any other non-SC community traditionally subjected to manual scavenging and their families shall be equally eligible for the relief and rehabilitation programmes. This is implicit in all existing programmes of the Government. Yet, there is a tendency on the part of some public servants to treat manual scavengers, erstwhile manual scavengers, and their families belonging to communities traditionally subjected to scavenging who adhere to Islam and Christianity as not eligible. Therefore, even what is obvious has to be legislatively spelt out and made binding.

The Bill also declares that it shall be the right of manual scavengers and other sanitation workers to secure the full implementation of this Act and the Act of 1993 and they shall have the right to approach tribunals and courts, if and when necessary, for which the cost including the fees of lawyers of their choice at the market rate shall be met in full by the employer at the initial stage of institution of proceedings by any of them in any tribunal or court up to the stage of its disposal by the final court. This is in keeping with the modern trend to switch over from a discretionary welfare approach of *mai-bap sarkar* (government as the mother and father) to a rights-based approach.

The Bill provides for imprisonment and fine for contravention of or failure to comply with any of the provisions of the Act and spells out who shall be punishable in the case of institutions. It also prescribes the National Monitoring and Enforcement Authority and State Monitoring and Enforcement Authorities, with adequate powers. Their members are to be selected transparently by selection committees which include representatives of the government, the opposition, and representatives of the vulnerable SC communities.

In a significant innovation, the Act opens with a Section in which the state expresses its deep regret for the humiliation and 'untouchabltiy' to which the sanitation workers of India have been subjected through centuries and for the failure to completely eradicate manual scavenging after Independence till now and expresses its determination to take all steps to immediately eradicate manual scavenging and humanise other sanitation work and make them free of all hazard and squalor.

Scuttling of the Comprehensive Bill

After consultations between the Ministry of Social Justice & Empowerment (MOSJE) and the Ministry of Labour (MOL) about jurisdiction and responsibility for moving this legislation, the two ministries have prepared two separate Bills. The Bill of the former deals with liberation and rehabilitation and the Bill of the latter deals with welfare measures. Perhaps it would have been better if there had been a single comprehensive Bill covering all aspects. This could have been done by the two Ministries in mutual consultation. The bifurcation is the result of the way in which departmentation for administrative convenience leads to compartmentation of people's issues in Indian administration and governance. Even where there are two Bills, it has to be ensured that they do not miss any of the issues relevant to the total liberation and comprehensive and sustainable rehabilitation of manual scavengers and humanization of the work of other sanitation labourers through application of the best technology. The author has seen the draft Bill of the MOSJE. While it is an improvement on the MSCDL (P) Act of 1993, many important provisions of the comprehensive Bill drafted by him, all efforts need to be made by all those concerned with the fate and future of SK and SK communities to reinstate those provisions in the Government's Bill of the MOSJE.

Need for Peaceful and Powerful Mass Movement Essential

The dynamism to ensure such effective legislation(s), thorough implementation of such legislation(s), and action required along the above lines by the government and other institutions, along with adequate and consistent plan and budgetary outlays and efficient organizational and institutional support, can be generated only by a sustained mass movement of the SK and their castes along with other SC and ST and BC especially the more, most, and extremely backward castes of the BCs including the BCs belonging to Muslim and other religious minorities in a powerful formation of unity encompassing 2/3rds to 3/4ths of India's population and contributing about 95 per cent of its physical labour force, along with all other genuine egalitarians. There is room for hope that such mass movement is building up. If those at the head of governance and administration at the centre and states seize this opportunity and voluntarily and proactively undertake the legislation(s) and other measures required with thoroughness, they will win the confidence of the historically and currently victimized communities, whose life has been full of sorrow throughout history, in the democratic process. This will be a source of great life-satisfaction for the author and others like him, and will be a fitting memorial to S.R. Sankaran's life and work in this field. If, however, those in charge of governance and administration continue to be half-hearted and less-than-sensitive, they will lose a great opportunity to contribute to the strengthening of democracy and optimum progress of this nation.

NOTES AND REFERENCES

1. Dr B.R. Ambedkar, 'Castes in India: Their Mechanism, Genesis and Development', Paper read before the Anthropology Seminar of Dr A.A. Goldenweiser at the Columbia University, New York, U.S.A., 9 May 1916. Reproduced in *Dr. Babasaheb Ambedkar Writings and Speeches*, Volume 1, Education, Department, Government of Maharashtra, 1989, pp. 5–22.
2. The author recalls his first encounter with Yanadi scavengers in Ongole when he was Sub-Collector there in 1958 to 1959. At that time, the Yanadis had not been included in the list of STs. They were classified then as a De-notified Tribe. At that time, there was much less of welfare schemes and provisions compared to today. One of those schemes was financial aid of Rs. 500 per house for construction of houses for Denotified Tribes. The author took up the Yanadi colony of Ongole which was on the slope of a hill atop which was the then Government Guest House. The meagre amount had to be stretched to the maximum to secure good pucca houses. On his request, the Municipal Chairman Sitaramaiah agreed to give them unofficial leave in groups so that they could build the Yanadi houses entirely with their own labour. In order to make the small provision go farther, the author told the lessee-contractors of the large Government quarries nearby to contribute one lorry load of stones to the Yanadi colony free of cost. They complied with this request. In order to make sure that the construction was the best possible, the author used to sit under a tree in that colony with his office files and disposed of them there, while keeping an eye on the construction. For the first time, the Yanadi scavengers had proper pucca houses of their own. About three decades later, the author visited the colony. A new generation had come up. Mutual recognition was established by the author recollecting the name of Indla Venkaiah, one of the scavengers of those days who had hurt and then lost a thumb during construction. Indla Venkaiah was one of the very few of that generation then still alive. All of them remembered their elder who had lost his thumb and brought him before the author. Since this provision was unrealistically low and was generally not being utilized, the author's request for more funds was readily complied with by the Director of Social Welfare by transferring unspent amounts to his Division. Another Yanadi colony he could take up was in Mahatma Gandhipuram in the outskirts of Bapatla town. Three decades later a Deputy Commissioner of the State Excise Department by name Venkateswara Rao came with his son, then an engineering college student, to the author's house. He proudly introduced his son and emotionally displayed, as the source of his and his son's rise, the Yanadi caste certificate which the author had signed and given to him at Mahatma

Gandhipuram when he was a small boy—it was the author's practice during village visits to issue certificates, completing the due process on the spot, to all SC, ST, and BC children so that they could be of use in their future life and, they could be free from the well-known hassles in getting certificates. A small start, a small opening given to communities like Yanadis and other Safai Karmacharis can lead to major transformation as this illustrates.

3. *Indian Express*, "Sanitation: India Can't Meet Target before 2054", 27 March, 2012.
4. Report of the Sub-Group-I on Perspective Planning for Empowerment of Scheduled Castes in the XII Five Year Plan (2012-2017), 1 August 2011.
5. Chapter 10 of the Report of the NCRWC and its Background Paper can be seen at Appendix X of the author's Book *Empowering Dalits for Empowering India: A Road-Map*. Manak Publications, New Delhi, 2009.

5

Atrocities Against Scheduled Castes and Tribes: Implementation Prevention of Atrocities Act and Proposed Amendments

S.D.J.M. Prasad

India attained independence 67 years ago in 1947. Three years later it became a republic with the self-confidence of having a government of the people, by the people and for the people. But in reality, a large section of its citizens, the Dalits and Adivasis, have been neglected by successive governments and, therefore, have been denied the full enjoyment of all the rights of citizenship assured by the Constitution. They still face subjugation, humiliation and exclusion on a daily basis from India's mainstream caste society.

This is so despite the new Constitution, which the people of India gave unto themselves in 1950, loudly proclaiming the explicit abolition of 'Untouchability' and its practice in any form (Article 17). Notwithstanding our Parliament's enactment of the Protection of Civil Rights Act (PCR),1955, 'Untouchability' based discrimination against Dalits has been rampant through all these years regardless of the gradual advancement of SCs and STs in education and economic status. Studies have revealed the prevalence of more than 150 forms of the most heinous and inhuman 'Untouchability' practices. These prevent Dalits and Adivasis from accessing civil, political, economic and cultural rights in private and public spheres, state and religious institutions, labour and consumer markets as much as they are entitled to as per the laws and policies of the land. Emerging trends show that there is an increase in the quantum of atrocities against Dalits and Adivasis even after PoA Act has come into being. During the last eighteen years (1995 to 2013), a total of 6, 57, 103 cases of atrocities were registered in police stations. A rough estimate reveals that around two crore Dalits and Adivasis have been affected by the atrocities in the last 18 years and the number is increasing day by day at the annual rate of 2.9 per cent.

According to official Indian crime statistics, every fifteen minutes four

Dalits and Adivasis are subjected to atrocities, every day three Dalit women are raped, two Dalits are murdered and eleven Dalits are beaten up, every week thirteen Dalits are murdered, five Dalits' houses are set on fire, and six Dalits are kidnapped.

The worsening situation prompted the Indian Parliament to consider the Protection of Civil Rights Act (PCR Act) 1955 and the normal provisions of the Indian Penal Code as inadequate to check and deter crimes committed by dominant caste groups. It compelled the Parliament, therefore, to enact The Scheduled Castes and Scheduled Tribes (Prevention of Atrocities) Act, 1989 (POA Act) and The Scheduled Castes and Scheduled Tribes (Prevention of Atrocities) Rules, 1995 (POA Rules).

This article is an attempt to analyze the problems of the victims of atrocities while accessing justice, the nature and extent of implementation of the PoA Act and Rules and amendments proposed in the Bill introduced in the Parliament in 2014.

I. What are the Significant Features of the Act?

The PoA Act was meant not only to prevent but also to eliminate atrocities against SCs and STs. With this in view, it defined the term 'atrocity' as 'an offence punishable under Section 3' of the Act which lists a number of offences. It formulated stringent measures for imposing heavy penalties on dominant caste perpetrators of atrocities as well as on those public servants wilfully neglecting their duties in implementing the PoA Act & Rules. In particular, this Act consists of the following significant features:

i. It addresses various offences/crimes committed against SCs/STs in the areas of social disabilities, encroachment or appropriation of property, malicious information or suit, political rights violations and economic exploitation.

ii. It establishes special procedures to prosecute the offenders booked for these offences.

iii. It mandates (i) investigation by a Dy SP; (ii) the designation of special courts and special public prosecutors for dealing with atrocities; and (iii) the setting up of State and District Level Vigilance Committees and Monitoring Committees, Special Officers, and Nodal Officers.

iv. It enjoins on the States and Union Territories to take specific preventive and punitive measures to protect Dalits and Adivasis.

v. It makes provisions for adequate relief and rehabilitation measures to the affected victims.

vi. The Act is expansive in its scope in many respects: in the list of offences, in constituting organizational mechanisms, in identifying officers for performing specific responsibilities, in defining their specific duties, in framing penalties for offences committed, and in assuring relief and rehabilitation measures to the victim-survivors. It has, indeed, promised to address the issue of discrimination and atrocities faced by Dalits and Adivasis.

II. Nature of and Extent of PoA Act Implementation

Despite the deterrence assured by the earlier PCR Act and the later SCs & STs [PoA] Act, the numerical increase in atrocities has not been checked. Nor has the response from the different governance agencies in the country (police, district and state level monitoring committees, district and state level vigilance committees, public prosecutors, special courts, et cetera) been satisfactory. The following are the problems faced by the Dalit and Adivasi Victims and witnesses at different stages while trying to obtain justice from them.

A. At the time of lodging complaint

a) Pressure is exerted on victims not to lodge the initial complaint.
b) Victims are threatened and intimidated not to speak about the incident.
c) Police officials refuse to write the complaints of the victims.
d) If police officials write the complaints, they do so in favor of the accused.
e) Police officials do not behave with the victims with proper decorum.
f) Higher officials do not visit the place of occurrence as mandated.
g) No immediate relief and protection is given to the victims.
h) Counter and false cases are registered against the victims.

B. At the time of registration of FIR

a) Victims are discouraged to register FIRs.
b) Victims are forced to compromise the case for money.
c) Victims are threatened into silence or even have to put with violence.
d) Police accept bribes from perpetrators to drop victims' complaints.
e) Police refuse to register cases specifically under PoA Act.
f) Police do not register complaints under proper sections of the Act.
g) Police do not include necessary details in FIR (facts, figures, words, names of the accused, weapons used, list of other others accused and their details).
h) Police mislead victims by registering case in the Station Diary instead of in FIR.
i) Police do not issue copy of FIR to victims.

C. At the time of arrest of the accused

a) The main accused is not arrested immediately.
b) Not all the other accused are arrested.
c) Police inform the accused before registering the case.
d) Bail and anticipatory bail are given.

e) Dalit victims are arrested in counter cases instead of the perpetrators of crime.

D. When the polices officials investigate the case

a) The case is not investigated in time.
b) Investigation is not being done by competent official as mandated.
c) All the victims and witnesses are not investigated during the investigation.
d) Investigation is often carried out sitting in the dominant caste locality, or by calling Dalits to the police station.
e) Police officials do not include all details narrated by victims and witnesses during investigation
f) Victims are not provided with protection during and after investigation
g) Victims and witnesses are not informed about the date and time of investigation officer's visits.
h) In violation of the directives of POA Act, statements are collected by lower level officials instead of the DSP who only signs the charge sheet.
i) Statements are recorded without meeting concerned victims/witnesses in person.
j) There is delay providing documents (post-mortem certificate, wound certificate) to the victims.
k) Investigation in counter cases is completed faster than in PoA Act cases.

E. When the Police file charge sheet

a) No corroboration is done between the statements collected and the contents the chargesheets.
b) Sections of SCs & STs [PoA] Act 1989 are intentionally deleted in charge sheet.
c) Getting legal opinion from prosecution department before finalizing charge sheet in deliberately delayed.
d) There is no mechanism in judiciary to monitor filing of charge sheet.
e) Charges are framed at variance with information recorded in FIR as well as in victim's statements.
f) The preparation of charge sheet is outsourced.

F. At the time of trial in the court

a) No Special Courts/PPs have been set up in all districts as mandated by the Act.
b) Inordinate delay in trial.
c) Certain witnesses are not involved on purpose at the time of trial.
d) PPs do not brief, or giving sufficient time for briefing, to victims and witnesses.

e) No information is given to victims/witnesses about the date and time of trial.

f) Victims and witnesses are made to turn hostile

G. At the stage of judgment

No appeal is mae by the Public Prosecutors in order to follow up cases of acquittals.

The abovementioned problems have resulted due to the following gaps in the implementation of the OA Act and Rules:

1. Under-reporting of the cases under the Act and victims deterred from making complaints of atrocities. Underreporting is a very common phenomenon. National Human Rights Commission (NHRC) in its report on Atrocities against Scheduled Castes 2002 observes that, "Even in respect of heinous crimes the police machinery in many States has been deliberately avoiding SCs and STs (Prevention of Atrocities) Act, 1989". The report further stated that, "Police resort to various machinations to discourage Scheduled Castes/Scheduled Tribes from registering Case, to dilute the seriousness of the violence, to shield the accused persons from arrest and prosecution and, in some cases, the police themselves inflict violence"[1]. The non-registration of cases, apart from reflecting caste bias and corruption, has also been attributed to the pressure on the police to keep reported crime rates low in their jurisdiction. With a view to presenting lower crime rates in the district, under-reporting of information is done at the **district** headquarters, which gets further diluted at the state and national level"

2. Not Registering cases under appropriate sections of the Act. It was observed from the reports of various organizations, NHRC and other Commissions of various state governments of India that FIRs were registered without reference to proper sections of the Act of 1989[2]. As per NCRB reports, 67% of cases during 1992-2000 and 64.9% during 2001-2013 were not registered under SC and ST (PoA) Act. Out of the registered cases, in 84.4 % cases wrong provisions were applied to conceal heinous, inhuman and violent nature of the atrocities.[3] That in many cases where the police do register a case under the Act, they purposely cite improper sections. For serious crimes such as murder, rape, destruction of property, dispossession of land, making foul drinking water sources, etc, the police are only citing sec. 3(1)(x) from the Act, which relates to insulting or intimidating a SC/ST person with intent to humiliate him or her in public view.[4] One of the reasons for police commonly citing this section is that this is the most minor offence under the Act and generally attracts the least punishment. In this way, they misuse the Act and allow the perpetrators, if convicted, to get away with lighter punishment.

3. Delay in filing charge sheet. Charge sheets in atrocity cases are invariably filed late. Besides non-registration of cases despite merit, there were delays in investigation, collusion with offenders and manipulation of witnesses and evidence, all of which contributed to reduce the effectiveness of legislation on atrocities.[5] The State Police Department of Andhra Pradesh in response to the query raised by the Chief Justice of the High Court of Andhra Pradesh State on the Public Interest Litigation (PIL) filed by Sakshi Human Rights Watch admitted that 14,452 cases were delayed and gave the following reasons for delay:

a. 3,281 cases were not chargesheeted due to delay in getting approval, legal opinion and superior's order;
b. 1,464 cases because of having 'more witnesses' in the case;
c. 1,873 cases due to delay in obtaining caste certificates;
d. 2,934 cases due to delay in the collection of documents and evidence;
e. 1,212 cases due to delay in receipt of Wound Certificates, Medical Certificates and Post-mortem Reports;
f. 1,006 cases due to non-apprehension of and absconding by the accused;
g. 662 cases due to delay in tracing and examining the witnesses/victims;
h. 613 cases due to delay because of the busy schedule of officers/work pressure;
i. 169 cases due to the transfer of officers;
j. 78 cases because cases investigated by the CID/CBID;
k. 48 cases because CID files were not available.

The High Court of Andhra Pradesh in an interim order on the Writ Petition observed—"The statistics furnished by the Director General of Police shows that 1 case registered under this Act is pending investigation for the last almost six years, 4 cases are pending investigation for last five years, 18 cases are pending investigation for over four years, 31 cases are pending investigation for over three yeasts. 190 cases are pending investigation for almost two years and 805 cases are pending investigation for about one year."[6] These facts are yet another admission to the gross negligence of the state machinery, especially the police. These acts of gross negligence have created a feeling that atrocities against SCs and STs can be committed with impunity.

4. Not arresting accused. The accused are invariably not arrested and are allowed to roam free. Based on the several representations presented to Justice K Punnayaya Commission of Government of Andhra Pradesh, the Commission stated that the Sub-Inspectors or Circle-Inspectors of Police did not arrest the assailants who committed the atrocities even though, the Sub-Inspectors or the Inspectors of Police, recorded FIRs and registered cases.

5. Accused are invariably released on bail. Various reports observed that the accused are invariably released on bail even in cases of serious crimes and have concluded that judicial delay and dilution of the scope and applicability of the Act of 1989 have resulted in denial of justice to the Scheduled Castes.

6. Filing false and counter cases against Dalit victims. The police deter the victims by colluding with accused persons in filing false counter cases.[7] The counter reports are indiscriminately registered against the SCs and STs and based on the counter reports the police arrest the SCs and STs, while the police do not arrest on SCs/STs complaints and in most cases do not even entertain them.

7. Compensation prescribed under the Act[8] is invariably not paid. The NHRC Report (2002) observes that "the breach of duties by Civil Administration is committed in the following manner:

a. Not conducting an enquiry, thereby evading duty to give relief and compensation,
b. Making false promises to give compensation and causing of delay in distributing cash compensation,
c. Not providing allowances, such as travel allowance relating to trial and investigation for witnesses and victims, maintenance expenses and daily allowance, medical expenses, et cetera.
d. Administration ignores social boycott of Scheduled Castes which leads to denial of employment and access to basic necessities like ration shop, refusal to buy or sell any goods in the village, et cetera to pressure Scheduled Castes into submission and cause intense suffering to them, though no physical violence may take place in the process. The attitude of district administration in such situations usually ranges from indifference to negligence".

The NHRC report further observed that,

> "It would thus be evident that even in respect of such a non-contentious matter as payment of compensation to the SC victims according to their entitlement, the subtle bias/ lack of sensitivity operates even at the highest level, both bureaucratic and political. Not only this, most states also do not provide other assistance/entitlements such as travelling allowance, maintenance expenses, daily allowance and reimbursement of medical expenditure to victims and witnesses, which are also required to be met from the funds under the Scheme. Overall, therefore, the legal framework of protection against atrocities is neither able to ensure punishment to the offenders nor payment of cash compensation and other relief to victims. This is what defines the impact of the law".

8. No access to legal aid. The Report of National Commission for Scheduled the Castes and Scheduled Tribes has found that no such special legal assistance as envisaged by the Act of 1989 was extended to SCs and STs even in one of the thousands of cases looked into by them.[9] On the other hand, the accused persons have recourse to good lawyers. A centrally sponsored financial assistance scheme[10] was introduced, initially for effective implementation of the Protection of Civil Rights Act, 1955 in the year 1974-75. The scheme was later (1990-91) extended to cover Scheduled Castes and Scheduled Tribes (Prevention of Atrocities) Act, 1989 as well. But the NHRC report states that:

a. The funds released to states bear no connection to the volume of atrocity cases committed or registered therein.
b. The withdrawal of assistance by some states is extremely low despite the sizeable percentage of SC population and also high incidence of cases of violence against SCs.
c. There is uneven distribution of assistance across years in various states, due to the unsatisfactory utilization of the assistance already provided in certain years. If this is so it would further reflect the laxity in the implementation of the Acts.
d. Some states are drawing disproportionately large amounts in certain years.
e. The lower level of demand from states, which have high percentage of SC population as well as high incidence of cases of atrocities can only be explained by the lack of interest in implementation of the Act.

9. Investigation not done by the competent authorities. Investigations are invariably done in a shoddy fashion[11] and are often not done by the Dy SP but by the junior judicial officers rendering the trial illegal[12]. An analysis of numerous cases carried by various organizations show that investigations are done by a police officer of lower rank than Deputy Superintendent of Police (DSP) or by a DSP who has not been explicitly appointed under this rule qualify under Rule 7. On this technical ground the case is vitiated and weakened.

10. Committees either yet to be formed or dysfunctional—State level and district level vigilance and monitoring Committees are ineffective. Special officers, nodal officers are not appointed nor are available for discharging their duties.

11. Non-implementation of statutory provisions. As per the Act 1989 and Rules 1995 state governments should take measures to fulfil the following statutory provisions:

a. Rule 3: Identification of atrocity prone areas and undertaking preventive measures such as review of law and order situation, cancelling arms licenses, providing arms licenses to Dalits for self-protection, setting-up vigilance committees et cetera.
b. Rule 8: Setting up Special Cells to conduct survey of the identified areas, informing nodal officer and special officer on law and order

situation of identified areas, making enquiries about the investigation and spot inspections, wilful negligence of various authorities, reviewing the position of cases registered et cetera.

c. Rule 9: Appointment of Nodal Officers
d. Rule 10: Appointment of Special Officers
e. Rule 15 (1): Contingency Plan for implementation of the provisions of the Act
f. Rule 16 and Rule 17: Vigilance and Monitoring Committees at state and district level to review the implementation of provisions of the Act
g. Section 14: Designated Special Courts and Exclusive Special Courts for speedy trial of offences under this Act

The following table shows the status of non-implementation of the provisions of SCs and STs (PoA) Act, 1989 and Rules 1995 by state governments.

Provisions	*States implemented*	*States not implemented*
Rule 3-Precautionary and Preventive Measures	11	23
Rule 8-SC/ST Protection Cell -	17	17
Rule 9-Nodal Officer	29	5
Rule 10-Special Officer	14	20
Rule 15 (1)-Contingency Plan by State Government	9	25
Rule 16-State Level Vigilance and Monitoring Committee	21	13
Rule 17- District Level Vigilance and Monitoring Committee	21	13
Section 14 Special Courts	9	25

Source: Reports of Ministry of Social Justice Empowerment

12. Seeking justice before the law. Finally, if Dalit victims are lucky enough to escape or overcome above hurdles they become part of the small percentage of cases that make it to the court. Conviction rates in the court are less than one per cent under the PoA Act. Though there is the provision of establishing Special Court under the PoA Act there is a huge pendency of cases. The judicial trends observed by NHRC report are:

(a) Technicalities often take priority over the intent of the Act and the merits of the case. In fact, the intent is lost sight of because of scrupulous pre-occupation with technicalities.

(b) The prosecutions are quashed on the ground that the offence was not committed on account of victim being an SC or an ST but on other accounts such as lust for sex, illicit intimacy in case of rape, political rivalry, enmity in case of murder, grievous hurt, et cetera.

(c) There is a tendency to accept evidence only from non-Scheduled Castes/ non- Scheduled Tribes people. An official of the National Commission on SCs/STs reported that he had studied fifty-sixty cases wherein the judge invariably concluded that SC/ST evidence was not valid because they were an interested parties. "To attribute a pattern to a community is a prejudice in and of itself. That itself is an atrocity. They do not give weightage to SC/ST evidence, but it is too much to expect evidence from a non-SC/ST when the victim is a Scheduled Caste. That is the dichotomy; if they did come forward, we would not need the Act.

(d) Personal beliefs and prejudices determine appreciation of evidence, determination of guilt and award of judgment. These beliefs have the unmistakable print of social biases, both caste and gender. "Cases at all levels have the potential to be influenced by the judge's personal perception of caste and gender that are brought to bear in determining the credibility of evidence or the likelihood of guilt..... These biases are pervasive all the way to the top of the legal system. The few cases that manage to reach the Supreme Court still do not escape these deep-seated prejudices[13]".

Despite stringent provisions of the Act, the experience shows that it has not been effective in preventing commission of offences, which is the main objective of the Act. Victims and witnesses confront hurdles at every stage of the legal process –from registration, investigation and chargesheeting, to the trial stage. The conviction rates under the Act remain low. High rate of acquittal and high rate of pendency and low disposal of cases remain issues. In this regard, the major areas of concern are:

(a) Certain forms of atrocities, though well documented, are not covered by the Act.

(b) Several offences under the Indian Penal Code are also committed frequently against SCs and STs by non SCs and non STs, on the ground that the victim was an SC or ST. Such offences need to be brought into the ambit of the Act.

(c) Public accountability provisions under the Act need to be outlined in greater detail and strengthened.

(d) Implementation of the Act suffers from the following problems, which need to be addressed.

- Procedural hurdles such as non-registration of cases
- Procedural delays -in investigation, arrests and filing charge-sheets
- Delays in trial and low conviction rate
- Procedural delays in providing relief and rehabilitation to victims, and

- Inadequate rates of compensation

It is in this context that a large number of Dalit, Adivasi and Human Rights organizations and activists came together in 2009 and formed a "National Coalition for Strengthening of the POA Act". This Coalition is a network of around 500 partners from 20 states in India. The outcome of all their campaign efforts was a set of specific and concrete proposals formulated in the light of their field experience and intended to amend the Act with a view to making it strong enough to abolish discrimination and end atrocities in the country. Based on its proposals Ministry of Social Justice introduced Bill in 2014.

III. SC/ST (PoA) Act Amendment Bill 2014

The Scheduled Castes and Scheduled Tribes (Prevention of Atrocities) Amendment Bill 2013 was introduced in Lok Sabha on 06.12.2013 and passed as an ordinance on 4.3.2014. After formation of new government, it has introduced a Bill in the parliament by carrying all the proposals made in the Ordinance and referred to the Parliamentary Standing Committee after the formation of the new government. *Proposed Amendments in the Bill 2014 can be broadly categorized as follows:*

(1) Addition of new category of offences, to the existing punishable offences, which are emerging and are frequently committed against Dalits and Adivasis. The original PoA Act lists only 22 offences under Section 3(1) and (2) as atrocities. These include forcing to drink or eat any inedible or obnoxious substance; dumping excreta, parading naked, illegally occupying or cultivating any land; dispossessing from land, forcing or intimidating to vote or to vote for a particular candidate, instituting false, malicious or vexatious suits, insulting or intimidating to humiliate in any place within public view; outraging the modesty of a woman; exploiting a woman sexually; mischief by fire or any explosive substance to cause damage to any property or destruction of any building used as a place or worship, for human dwelling. New offenses proposed in the Amendments Bill 2014 can be broadly categorized as follows:

i. Offences related to dignity- putting inedible or obnoxious substance into the mouth; garlanding with footwear , parading naked or semi-naked; removing clothes, tonsuring of head, removing moustaches, painting face or body; compelling to dispose or carry human or animal carcasses, compelling to dig graves; manual scavenging;; abusing in caste name; disrespecting any late persons held in high esteem by SCs and STs; attempting to promote feelings of enmity, hatred against SCs and STs; imposing social or economic boycott

ii. Offences related to atrocities against women- touching a women or uses words, acts or gestures of a sexual nature against women; causing physical harm or mental agony on the allegation of practising witchcraft atrocities; dedicating a SC or ST woman to a deity, idol, object of worship, temple, or other religious institution as a devadasi or any other similar practice or permits aforementioned acts

iii. *Offences related to land and housing*- dumping sewage in premises, or at the entrance of the premises; denying access to irrigation facilities, destroying the crops or taking away the produce therefrom.

iv. *Offences related to franchise* - preventing SC or ST candidates from filing nomination to contest elections or proposing the nomination; forces or intimidates or obstructs a member of a SC or a ST, who is a member or a Chairperson or a holder of any other office of a panchayat under PART IX of the Constitution or a municipality under PART IX A of the Constitution, from performing their normal duties and functions; after the poll, causes hurt or grievous hurt or assaults or imposes or threatens to impose social or economic boycott or prevents from availing benefits of any public service; commits any offence under this Act against SCs or SCs for having voted or not having voted for a particular candidate or for having voted in a manner provided by law.

v. *Offences related to Untouchability in Public sphere* - preventing from using common property resources , or burial or cremation ground or using any river, stream, spring, well, tank, preventing from mounting or riding bicycles or motorcycles or wearing footwear in public places or taking out wedding procession, entering any place of worship; entering any educational institution, hospital, dispensary, primary health centre, shop; or practising any profession or the carrying on of any occupation, trade or business or employment in any job which other members of the public, or any section thereof, have a right to use or have access to;

(2) Addition of relevant IPC offences as punishable offences under the PoA Act: Section 3(2)(v) of the principal Act defines offences punishable for more than ten years under IPC as atrocities. This formulation has excluded several offenses such as assault, kidnapping, hurt etc which are punishable for less than 10 years under IPC. New Sub Section added in the Bill as 3(2)(v)(a) without enhancement of punishment - Under a separate schedule in the amendment Bill 2014, new IPC sections are enlisted such as—punishment for criminal conspiracy, unlawful assembly, rioting, hurt; grievous hurt; throwing acid; wrongful restraint; assault or criminal force to women; sexual harassment; kidnapping; abducting and wrongfully confinement; criminal trespass; criminal intimidation et cetera.

(3) Strengthening State accountability by clearly defining the term 'willful negligence': Section 4 of the Principal Act reads as, "Whoever, being a public

servant but not being a member of a Scheduled Caste or a Scheduled Tribe, wilfully neglects his duties required to be performed by him under this Act, shall be punishable with imprisonment for a term which shall not be less than six months but which may extend to one year." The original Section 4 is now divided into three sub sections. The original text of the principal section as above is retained under sub section 4(1). New sub-sections inserted as subsection 4 (2) and 4 (3) on duties of the public servants and procedure related to the proceedings against public servants for dereliction of duties have been defined.

Section 4 (2) The duties of public servant include—reading out to an informant the information given orally and reduce it to writing, to register FIR under the Act with appropriate sections, to furnish a copy of FIR to the informant, to record the statement of victims or witnesses, to conduct the investigation and file charge sheet in the Special Court or the Exclusive Special Court within a period of sixty days, to correctly prepare, frame and translate any document or electronic record, to perform any other duty specified in this Act or the rules.

Section 4 (3) The cognizance in respect of any dereliction of duty referred to in sub-section (2) by a public servant shall be taken by the Special Court or the Exclusive Special Court and shall give direction for penal proceedings against such public servant."

(4) Establishment of Exclusive Special Courts and Exclusive Special Public Prosecutors. Under Section 14 of the Principal Act a Court of Session at the district level is deemed a Special Court to provide speedy trials for offences. Under Section 15, a Special Public Prosecutor is appointed to conduct cases in this court. The Bill substitutes this provision and specifies provisions for speedy trial such as by Exclusive Special Courts and Exclusive Public Prosecutors, Day to day trial, cognizance of trial by courts etc under section 14 (1) and section 14 A (1). Section 14(1) talks about establishment of Exclusive Special Courts with power to directly take cognizance of offences under this Act, disposal of cases within a period of two months on day-to-day basis from the date of filing of the charge sheet. Section 14. A. (1) talks about procedure and disposal of appeals in higher courts within three months after the judgment, sentence or order. Section 15 talk about the appointment of exclusive Special Public Prosecutors for every exclusive special courts.

(5) Addition of chapter on rights of victims and witnesses as Chapter IV A: The principal Act and Rules only recognize, to a limited extent the entitlements of victims and witnesses in accessing justice, as for example: a free copy of the recorded FIR, immediate relief in cash or in kind, necessary protection, relief in respect of death/injury/or damage to property, entitlement of food/water/clothing/shelter/medical aid/transport facilities, daily allowance, maintenance expenses to the victim and his/her dependents and witnesses.

But it does not talk about the rights of victims and witnesses under the Act.

The PoA Amendment Bill 2014 adds a separate chapter on the rights of victims and witnesses which includes victims and witnesses' protection, access to case documents, information on case status and right to relief, compensation and rehabilitation as well as rights during the trial. Proposed amendments mandate the state to make arrangements for the protection of victims, their dependents and witnesses. They also mandate state government to specify a scheme to ensure the implementation of rights of victims and witnesses. The courts established under the Bill may take measures such as: concealing the names of witnesses, taking immediate action in respect of any complaint relating to harassment of a victim, informant or witness, et cetera. Comprehensive sections dealing with the rights of victims and witnesses have been enlisted in the Act that include—information about their rights at the time of making complaints and registering FIR; protection from intimidation and harassment; information on status of investigation and charge sheet; rights at the time of medical examination; information regarding compensation, TA/DA etc; information in advance about dates and place of investigation and trial; adequate briefing on the case; information about legal aid; right to get experienced PPs; right to obtain copies of documents ;right to be heard at any proceeding in respect of bail, discharge, release, parole, conviction or sentence of an accused or arguments and file written submissions on conviction, acquittal or sentencing; right to take assistance from non-government organizations, social workers or advocates.

(6) Expanding the scope of presumption to minimize loopholes in the applicability of the Act. Section 8 of the Principal Act defines if in a prosecution for an offence, it is proved that—the accused rendered any financial assistance to a person accused of, or reasonably suspected of committing, an offence under this Chapter, the Special Court shall presume, unless the contrary is proved, that such person had, abetted the offence; and if a group of persons committed an offence under this Chapter and if it is proved that the offence committed was a sequel to any existing dispute regarding land or any other matter, it shall be presumed that the offence was committed in furtherance of the common intention or in prosecution of the common object.

The amendments to the Section 8 now to a limited extent also recognize that the court shall presume that the accused was aware of the caste or Tribal identity of the victim if the accused had personal knowledge of the victim or his family, unless the contrary is proved.

Conclusion

The current Government inherited two Ordinances from the previous Congress-led UPA government—The Securities Laws (Amendment)

Ordinance, 2014 and The Scheduled Castes and Scheduled Tribes (Prevention of Atrocities) Amendment Ordinance, 2014, promulgated on March 28 and March 4 respectively last year. In the first Budget session in 2014 the Government converted the Securities Ordinance into an Act of Parliament (12 August 2014) to further "protect the interests of investors and to ensure orderly development of securities markets." But the Ordinance intended to strengthen the machinery to prevent atrocities against SCs and STs was allowed to lapse even though there were strong protests by the Opposition. When the SCs and STs (Prevention of Atrocities) Amendments Bill was later placed before the Parliament by the Government on July 14, 2014, immediately it was sent to the Parliamentary Standing Committee on Social Justice and Empowerment, a procedure that was not necessary. Nonetheless, the Standing Committee is to be congratulated for submitting its report so quickly on December 19, 2014, strongly recommending the proposed amendments to this critical law. It was passed by the Lok Sabha on August 4, 2015. Passing this Bill in Rajya Sabha will go a long way to ensure basic protection to around 300 million Indian citizens.

NOTES

1. NHRC further reports that one NGO in Gujarat, in a study covered 11 atrocities-prone districts for four years. It showed that 36% of atrocities cases were not registered under Atrocities Act and 84.4% of the cases where the Act was applied, the cases were registered under wrong provisions with a view to conceal the actual and violent nature of the incidents. Victims are deterred from making complaints and as a result First Information Reports (FIR's) are rarely registered or are registered late.
2. National Commission for Human Rights (2002), One Man Commission on Untouchability and Atrocities against Scheduled Castes and Tribes, Government of Andhra Pradesh (2001) as well as civil society organizations such as Sakshi Human Rights Watch – Andhra Pradesh (2000 & 2003), National Campaign on Dalit Human Rights, Centre for Dalit Rights Rajasthan, et cetera.
3. NCRB reports (1992 to 2013)
4. Sakshi's Human Rights Watch reports show that in the State of Andhra Pradesh it was found only 17.3% of the cases under the Atrocities Act were registered under proper sections. Of the remaining 82.5 per cent of cases, 28.1 per cent were never even brought within the purview of the law due to police failure/refusal to register cases, thereby indicating neglect of their official duties and colluding with the perpetrators of atrocities.
5. A mere 4.9 per cent of cases registered under the Act of 1989 and Rules of 1995 were actually chargesheeted. Only in 9.3% cases of the 4.9%, charge sheets are filed within the stipulated time of 30 days. Even if we take the Cr.PC. time limit of 90 days, charge sheets are filed in only 31% of cases. For about 28% of

cases the investigation agency is taking more than 365 days (Affidavit of Public Interest Litigation in Supreme Court of India (2006) by NCDHR and others.

6. Writ Petition Filed by Dr S D J M Prasad representing Sakshi-Human Rights Watch on the non-implementation of the SC/ST Prevention of Atrocities Act in AP High Court, WP No. 1019 of 2006).
7. "Whenever the SC or ST victim of atrocity presents a report to the Sub-Inspector or Circle-Inspector in charge of Police Station and if he records FIR, and registers a case, the Sub-Inspector or Circle-Inspector should arrest the assailant or assailants who committed the atrocity on the complainant. But the Sub-Inspector or Circle-Inspector who recorded the FIR, and registered a case did not arrest the assailants except in rare cases. On the other hand, it is stated in their representations that those assailants against whom the SC-victims presented complaints lodge counter reports to the Police against SC-victims and the Sub-Inspectors or Circle-Inspectors register counter cases against the SCs (Victims) and arrest them. When a counter report is presented by the assailant who is the accused in the report presented by the SC-victim, it was filed obviously with the sole intention to counterblast the complaint filed by the SC-victim. As a result of the counter cases, the real SC victims of the atrocities are being arrested and subjected to criminal litigation as accused in the counter cases" (Justice Punnayya Commission, Government of Andhra Pradesh 2001).
8. Scheduled Castes and Scheduled Tribes Cell within the Social Welfare Department is to look after the implementation of relief and rehabilitation measures under the SC/ST (PoA) Act and Rules. According to Sec. 21(2)(iii) of the Act, the State should make provision for the economic and social rehabilitation of the victims of atrocities. A host of measures are then laid out in the Rules, including compensation measures—relief, rehabilitation - to be implemented by the district administration under rule 12(4). Immediate relief includes food, water, clothing, shelter, medical aid, transport facilities and other essential items necessary for the Dalit victims, while longer term relief is specified in the accompanying Schedule to the Rules in terms of compensation amounts varying according to the nature of the offence. Part payment of compensation is prescribed at either the initial stages of filing the FIR or the charge sheet, while final compensation is often only paid on the finalization of the case before the courts.
9. National SC/ST Commission Report 2000-01.
10. Under this scheme 50% financial assistance is provided by the Union Government to the State Governments and 100% to Union Territory administrations for meeting the expenses for financial assistance provided by them to Dalit victims of atrocities for the ultimate purpose of proper implementation of the aforesaid Act. Besides, the Scheme also provides assistance for strengthening the enforcement machinery and judicial administration, publicity and relief and rehabilitation of affected persons.
11. As per the NHRC report the progress of investigation of cases by police analyzed from the governmental data indicates that number of charge-sheeted cases was

53.04%, while 22.54% of cases were closed after investigation and number of cases pending with police at the end of the year constituted 24.42% and thus of total of 30,350 cases registered during the year 2000 as many as 8336 cases were closed after investigation without any trial and 9,027 cases were still pending investigation. According to another data of a total 1,43,505 cases in Courts for the year 2000, 1,32,268 cases were pending, 9996 were acquitted and 1241 ended in conviction.

12. The provision (viz. Rule 7) under the Scheduled Castes and Scheduled Tribes (Prevention of Atrocities) Rules, 1995, that, "An offence committed under the Act shall be investigated by a police officer not below the rank of a Deputy Superintendent of Police. The investigating officer shall be appointed by the State Government/Director General of Police/Superintendent of Police after taking into account his past experience, sense of ability and justice to perceive the implications of the case and investigate it along with right lines within the shortest possible time."
13. Nothing illustrates better than the following sentence quoted by Human Rights Watch from the judgement of a case of rape against an SC woman. "Rape is usually committed by teenagers and since the accused are middle-aged and therefore respectable, they could not have committed the crime. An upper caste man-28B could not have defiled himself by raping a lower caste woman". Other cases have also been referred to 28C by the same organization to illustrate the atmosphere of prejudice in courts which Dalit women face both as Dalits and as women.

6

Meanwhile, We Refuse to Die!

Deepti Sukumar

Recently, a senior High Court advocate, while speaking on the much publicized Delhi rape, 'For the first time, a rape victim said she did not want to die', which led to the public outcry of protest and supoort for her. The National Crime Records Bureau informs that 1,557 scheduled caste women were raped inh 2011. This was a 16 per cent increase from 2010. In 2006, the National Campaign for Dalit human Rights published a study report with data of 500 Dalit women survivors of sexual violence in four states. The study informs that police and judiciary responded to only 13 per cent of these cases with appropriate action. It is a well known fact that, in almost 90 per cent of instances of violence, Dalit women do not report to the police. Why! a) Because the dominant castes claim that the police are an extension of their families and communities and b) Dalit women feel threatened of being further victimzed. These different data prove beyond any doubt that only about 10 per cent of all instances of violence against Dalit women are being reported by the so called National Crime Records Bureau.

Coming back to the Delhi victim's cry 'I don't want to die', that was heard and echoed by the middle class and caste society, similar cries of Dalit women survivors and victims have been lilenced and how?!– By just not hearing them, not seeing them, and most importantly, not counting them! We Dalit women are really confused by this middle class mentality and attitudes. When the Delhi girl cried and suffered, you rightly cried and called her braveheart, India's daughter et cetera. When we cry out, we want to live you say nothing! what does this mean? Do you want us to die?!

We Refuse to Die!

Of all people in this country, it is the Dalit women who are the strongest and most resilient. The people of this country, those who enjoy the privileges of caste, have tried so systematically to make us extinct, but we still exist.....all 80.5 million in India and 5.9 millions in Tamil Nadu. Incidentally, this is the 2001 census, as the 2011 census data for Scheduled Caste could not be accessed.

Reports and statistics produced by the different governments and their departments are silent on Dalit women. This silence is deliberate to make Dalit women invisible. We call this structural violence!

What is Violence?

The United National declaration, 1993, defined violence against women as 'any act of gender-based violence that results in, or is likely to result in, physical, sexual, or psychological harm or suffering to a women, including threats of such acts, coercion or arbitrary deprivation of liberty, whether occurring in public or private life.'

Many times we are confronted with the question, 'which violence is more critical for Dalit women: cast or gender violence?' Does it matter? Violence of any kind is still violence. But then on deeper reflection, it does matter. In the Delhi gang rape case, all of the six rapists are from dominant castes. Even though the victim was not a Dalit woman, the social identity of the rapists points to the link between caste an patriarchy. But the extensive discourse that followed in the media and other elite circles was silent on this. There were even declarations that caste had no role in this rape. The analysis of the link between the perpetrators' social backgrounds and their violent behavior was kept out. It seems like there was a deliberate attempt to delink caste from patriarchy. When both are the two sides of the same coin or each has constructed the other, can this delink ever be possible?

Caste and patriarchy are sustained by violence. The forms of violence an oppression are not common to all women. Dalit women are more vulnerable and exposed to many more forms of violence and oppression. Dalit women experience violence from both men and women of dominant castes and from Dalit men. In a recent workshop, a group of Dalit women discussed that 'economic subjugation and oppression was the basis for most forms of violence and Dalit women are forced into undesirable occupationhs through caste and gender stereotyping.' This is clearly visible in the overwhelming majority of Dalit women in manual scavenging, prostitution as in the *mathamma* and *Jogini* culture, casual daily wage agriculture, construction labour, sweeping and sanitary work and domestic servitude. We did not choose these occupations but were forced into them because of being Dalit and a woman. They are called 'livelihoods', but we call it economic violence that has a lifelong impact keeping us in subordinate positions and making us depandant on the structures and systems that control us. It is critical to analyse the economic dynamics of patriarchal and caste structures while addressing violence against Dalit women. In most atrocity cases, the economic materials and possessions of Dalits are targeted for destruction. In the 2012 Dharmapuri atrocity against Dalits, the dominant Vanniyar caste targeted and destroyed all materials that were indicators of economic prosperity like wardrobes, gold, television sets, motor bikes, gas cylinders. In the 2011 atrocity against Krishnaveni, the Dalit woman panchayat president of Thalaiyuthu in Tirunelveli district of Tamil Nadu, the dominant caste men cut her on the neck, wrist, ears–wherever she was wearing gold jewelry.

The Campaign for Dalit Women Economic Equity declares that it is critical to name, define, and address economic violence in our struggle for economic justice. The systematic denial of economic equaity for Dalits is demonstrated in the apathetic and ineffective implementation of schemes and policies meant for Scheduled Caste's empowerment like the SCSP. It is even worse for Dalit women who find no significant mention in schemes for Scheduled Castes an women. There is systematic rejection of any efforts of Dalit women to involve themselves in these processes. One typical example is when, in a discussion with the State Planning Commission of Tamil Nadu on developing schemes for Dalit women within SCSP policy, we presented a set of schemes to support Dalit women in enterprises in transport, real estate, and the hotel industry. A senior IAS officer in the finance department said, 'It is really impossible for Scheduled Castes to succeed in such business models. Even I will not be able to manage such business. Only communities that are used to doing business like the Jain community will succeed in such enterprises. So please let us be practical and not waste time and money.' This was a blatant abuse of power and position to deny Dalit women opportunity to plan for and access their own rightful share in the state resources. The economic stereotyping is evident in the sustenance of providing two goats, a tailoring machine, phenol, or soap-making equipment, et cetera..

What is Economic Violence?

The campaign for Dalit Women Economic Equity defined economic violence, as being forced by structures and systems to engage in undesirable occupations and denied access to opportunities, resources, and funds to engage in occupations and livelihoods of our choice.

The Different Forms of Economic Violence

Denying us control of our resources and funds: The governments and their departments, banks, NGOs, INGOs, and families keep control of resources and funds allocated for us using their example, power and authority of position. For in the name of rehabilitation for manual scavengers, the government allocates a paltry Rs. 25,000 to Rs. 50,000 with a 25 per cent subsidy. The banks hold these funds for women. They only hand out the 25 per cent subsidy and withhold the loan amount. If at all they give the loan amount, it is tied to the salary of the male member in the household. They manage to make the process, procedures, and calculations so complicated that women just give up trying to figure it out. The amount distributed is so small that it holds no meaning and the women do not even bother to try to access it– this inspite of a RBI circular to all public sector banks that they should not ask for any guarantee or documents from the beneficiaries, should support them fully, and disburse the loans as speedily as possible.

Not counting Dalit women with disaggregated data: The government departments resposible for implementing welfare schemes for Scheduled Castes and Women do not mention Dalit women in any of their reports or plans. There is no mention of women in the SCSP plans and no mention of SC women in women related schemes. So either way, we do not figure. We are blatantly ignored in budgets and plans of governments. This indifference and not recognizing our nine per cent presence in the state is violence.

Denial of access and not addressing our difficulties and challenges in obtaining an education that would give us skills, information, and knowledge to access equity status: We are not counted in higher education. So what is the message? Knowing fully well that Dalit women are inadequately represented in higher education or industry, why are there no efforts to correct this? Again and again this country is giving us the message that we do not matter!

Forcing us to engage in occupations or work that is undesirable, unclean, and stigmatized: 90 per cent of all manual scavengers are Dalit women! Why do we occupy such an overwhelmingly large majority in daily wage casual labour, unclean labour, work by descent, and sex work? In conversations with 164 dalit women engaged in manual scavenging in Tamil Nadu, the response from all of them was that they were forced into this occupation by their own families, the caste community, and the local government. A typical experience is narrated by a Dalit woman, Satya, who studied upto 12th standard and passed in her school final examination with an above average academic record. She registered herself in the state employment exchange, but when she received her employment order, it was for a sanitation worker job. She made representations to the authorities that she had not applied for this position, only to be told, 'look, for your community this is what you will get; just take it and be satisfied!' She refused it, but her family forced her with physical and emotional violence to accept this job. Soon, the supervisor put her to work secretly cleaning out dry latrines and manual scavenging open defecation spots. The same happens to women who are exploited by the *maathamma* and *jogini* systems, or the millions of Dalit women who are engaged in daily wage labour in agriculture and construction et cetera. Was there ever a choice or even an opportunity to make a choice?

Withholding information: The same Satya did not have information that manual scavenging was prohibited and that there were rehabilitation schemes available. None of the 164 women mentioned above were aware of such a law and such rehabilitation schemes. The State does not invest in informing Dalit women on matters pertaining to them like laws, schemes, and policies.

Not holding consultations with us while developing plans to utilize our funds and resources: There is no mechanism or process to hear our opinions or views on utilization of our funds. This is why we have not moved beyond goats, typewriters, and phenol-making. None of the commissions or committees that are formed during planning and budgeting processes includes Dalit women.

Threatening humiliating, and intimidating us when we try to access credit or funds or resources: Recently, in a bank Pudukottai District in Tamil Nadu, a group of women *Safaikaramcharis* went to a nationalized bank for transacting their SHG account. An officer in the bank held his nose and said, 'Get away fast, the whole place stinks!' The women sat in protest inside the bank till the officer apologized to them in public.

Treating us with disrespect, discrimination, and humiliating us in our workplace and economic spaces: A Dalit woman sanitary worker got into an argument with the supervisor on accessing the leave she was eligible for – his comments during the argument '*pee thingire pottachikku evelo thimiruna enakku evalo thimiru irukkum!!!*' (*If a shit eating female can have such arrogance, how much more arrogance will I have!*)

Exclusion of Dalit women: To cite a typical example, in Tamil Nadu, there are about 91 all women tailoring cooperative societies. Each cooperative society has about 3000 members. There is a policy for tailoring cooperatives that one-third of the members in these cooperatives must be Dalit women. In one cooperative society in Villipuram District alone, there are 2,750 women with only 270 Dalit women. By policy there should be a minimum of 915 Dalit women in this cooperative alone. There are 91 such cooperatives all over the state. If the policy worked, there would have been 90,000 Dalit women benefitting from the tailoring cooperative schemes in the state. But, going by Villipuram District, there are only about 25,000 Dalit women benefitting by the schemes. The government gives a 25 per cent subsidy to all non-Dalit women to purchase a motorized tailoring machine valued at Rs. 17,000 per machine and a full subsidy to Dalit women. In addition, the government issues contracts to the cooperative members to stitch the school uniforms and pays the women at piece rate. The women earn an average of Rs. 20,000 every three months. This exclusion is resulting in denial of a fair share of resources and is an economic violence against Dalit women.

Allocation of inadequate resources to meet Dalit women's aspirations: Dalit women have a good track record of excelling in writing. A writer is given assistance of a measly Rs. 40,000 to write, publish, print, market, and also submit 400 copies of the book to the funding department. All of these schemes are not only unimaginative and absolutely substandard but are also insulting and derogatory to the Dalits, their creativity, and absolutely substandard but are also insulting and derogatory to the Dalits, their creativity, intelligence, and productive capacity. When the budgets of different ministries, departments, and state governments have grown tenfold over the past 10 years, the budgets for Dalits have remained almost stagnant, and the programmes have been the same traditional ones like tailoring, sewing machines, goats, vegetable vending, et cetera. There are many Dalit women who have started business enterprises and have been successful. But how many of them have started their business with government or NGO support? Why is it that both the government and the NGOs are not able to show success stories of their beneficiaries? What is the gap between the schemes and policies of government and the real situation and implementation? Why is the government not able to think or imagine beyond these minimum programmes that only go to reinforcing Dalit women as labour class, providing about Rs. 500–1,000 as income for these beneficiary families, and keep this them linked to caste-based work.

The above are typical experiences of Dalit women in the different scenarios that happen on a daily basis. These are typical examples of caste and patriarchal attitudes and behaviour. All of the above is in addition ot the usual domestic violence, sexual violence, and other forms of physical and verbal abuse that occur with such regular frequency in the lives of Dalit women. Most times, the physical, psychological, and emotional abuse is used to disempower women economically or maintain the status quo of economic power and authority of patriarchy and caste hierarchy. So, are we invisible by choice or are we forced into the shadows? In this most appalling and depressing environment, it is a wonder why there are no mass suicides of Dalit women.

We Refuse to Die! And How?!

In each of the above situations of economic violence, there are Dalit women achievers, inspite of discrimination and exclusion. Dalit women are making calculated plans and working hard to not just survive, but to prosper. Analytical data pertaining to Dalit women of this nature is missing. CAG reports, NSSO surveys, government impact surveys, et cetera, have not overed this economic dimension of Dalit women.

Safai Karamchari Andolan identified six Dalit women in Kattunaiker Street in Nagapattinam municipality and supported them with the small sum of Rs. 7,000 each. They came together and set up a coconut palm thatch weaving unit. They planned well. Two of them sourced the raw material, four of them processed and wove the palms for thatch, and then two of the six set up the thatch on the main street and marketed them. They analysed that thatch was always in demand especially in low income group housing where families would always be putting up extensions for kitchens, verandahs, and bathing spaces, and had to constantly replace them for wear and tear. In addition, all of the six women took up other activities including Amway marketing, LIC, and Peerless Insurance selling, cooking, and buying and selling of vegetables and blouse bits. The six women had done nothing but manual scavenging all of their lives. So how did this overnight transformation take place? By accessing information, social contacts, and tapping their inherent capability to succeed and thrive. They did not receive any support from government sources.

In the sweepers colony of Chinnamanur, Theni District in Tamil Nadu, 17 women are engaged in buying and selling brooms. They buy large brooms, make them into smaller ones and travel to neighbouring towns and districts by foot, lorries, and buses to do house-to-house sales. They use simple calculations and planning to ensure that they make a profit. Their hard work, sharp skills in business calculations, and mobility have sustained them.

In Villipuram District, a Dalit woman challenged the caste discrimination and exclusion practiced in the cooperative societies and became the president of 2750 women in her cooperative. She has also supported 200 women to become members, access the full subsidy sewing machine scheme, and secure the contract for school uniforms. She is determined to increase the membership of Dalit women. She has started a training institute where she trains Dalit women in tailoring, issues certificates, and makes them members in the cooperative.

A Dalit woman in Pudukottai has sold all her assets, purchased six acres of land, and plans to start a school as soon a she is able to raise resources.

In Chinnamanur of Rajapalayam, a Dalit woman is in the business of stitching and marketing of nighties. She worked for six years as a sales girl in a Xerox, mobile repair, and recharge shop. But she left the job and started her own business. She also engages in Amway marketing.

These are a few isolated cases of Dalit women. They expose the huge gap between the government schemes and Dalit women's aspirations and capabilities. The government does not have plans sand schemes to target Dalit women's empowerment or equity. The schemes are not based on capabilities or skills, but are only geared towards sustenance and keeping Dalit women in segregation and poverty. The government seems to only regard Dalit women as pregnant, lactating, or about to be married. the fact that in the last 65 years there has been no effort to assess and analyze the skills, capabilities or knowledge of Dalit women and measure the impact of government spending in different departments, points to deliberate exclusion. None of the plans and policies meant for women or Scheduled Castes articulate the caste and patriarchal violence faced by Dalit women. On the other hand, the plans and policies reinforce the caste and gender roles forced upon Dalit women to remain as labourers. This, by itself, is a clear case of structural and economic violence against Dalit women.

Justice Means.........

- to acknowledge the role of the State in the structural and economic violence against Dalit women since Independence;
- to identify and name the plans, policies, and schemes where Dalit women have been discriminated and excluded;
- to show disaggregated data for Dalit women in all government records, reports, documents, plans, policies, budgets, and schemes and measure their impact on Dalit women;
- to recognize the contribution of Dalit women to the economy;
- to recognize Dalit women as economic agents and to improve their access to markets on equitable terms;
- to address the hurdled and challenges faced by Dalit women in their economic endeavours;
- to increase Dalit women, ownership and control of property, resources, and assets;
- to consul with Dalit women in the process of planning, policy-making and budget preparations, and to ensure that all plans, policies, budgets, and schemes for SCs and women have allocations proportionate to the Population of Dalit women.

7

Dalit Movement and Dalit Literature in Andhra Pradesh: A Survey of the Pre-dandora Movement Period

K.Y. Ratnam

The Dalit movement in Andhra Pradesh was an autonomous struggle against the hegemonic ideology of the upper caste rulers, accompanied by an enormously forceful literature. As an organic collective articulation, Dalit literature has fresh, expressive comprehension and a distinct intellectual vigour. Its distinctness 'lies in its authentic unity of language and content. In it the disillusionment and disgust of young Dalits, often accompanied by a desire for revenge, come alive. It revives the memory of the pain and suffering of the past generations.' Further, 'it confronts centuries of hypocrisy, deceit and violence sustained in the name of tradition' (Satyanarayana, 1995). Hegemonic caste ideology debarred the Dalits not only from all material possessions but also systematically stunted their mental development. They were alienated from society to a space outside the purview of the social laws. Their historical sociocultural position was dissimulated and disfigured by caste as the taskmaster.

Dalit literature carries this burden of suffering, agony, and humiliation. In addition, it is encompassed by the profound objective of emancipation of all oppressed masses. It is resolutely determined to uncover the concealed contradictions of the hegemonic upper caste ideology and to make concerted efforts to create an alternative sociocultural identity.

Dalit literature has been subjected to extensive debate and discussion as a stream of Telugu literature. The purpose of this chapter is not to join that debate. Rather, it is to analyse Dalit literature as 'the counter hegemonic ideology'. The aim is to study the literature from a sociological point of view and its social origin. This chapter is divided into three sections. These deal, respectively, with the brief historical antecedents of Dalit literature, the non-Dalit writers' contribution to Dalit consciousness in the mainstream Telugu literary trends, and a random analysis of Dalit literature in Telugu produced by Dalit organic intellectuals.

Historical Background

Dalit literature in Telugu has long historical antecedents along the lines of the Dalit movement (Dangle, 1996). The numerous Buddhist inscriptions reveal that the historical legacy of Dalit literature in Telugu may be traced to the well-established Buddhist culture in Andhradesa. The Buddhist anti-caste ideology, humanist principles of liberty, equality, and brotherhood were propagated through Pali literature, which was against the hegemonic Sanskrit language (Padma Rao, 1995: 85–96). The Sufi poets, who called for the abolition of all discrimination and inequalities from contemporary society, gathered all 'men belonging to different castes and creeds speaking different languages, assembled in the Khangahs. It was but, natural that a common language was evolved as a means of communication' (Satyanarayana, 1983: 534–5). That language was Urdu. Urdu, thus, became the language of communication for the Sufi saints, against the hegemonic Sanskrit and Persian literature which got royal patronage, to propagate humanism and brotherhood, during the Muslim rule in the Deccan.

In the thirteenth century, Palkuriki Somanatha, under the influence of Basava's Veerasaivism, denounced caste divisions and explained in his poetical works, with scholarly disquisition, how Brahminism and Brahmin priests extracted the wealth of the lower caste in the name of sacrifices (Moorthi, 1977: 534–5). The Sudra poetess named Molla, daughter of a potter, wrote the *Molla Ramayanam* in simple Telugu to make it accessible to the common people. Tallapaka Annamayya, a Brahmin, disapproved of the caste system in his *kirtan*s or songs of devotion. He sang that 'the high level land of the Brahmin and the low flat level of the Chandala are the same... there is no high and low, Srihari is the soul of all' (Padma Rao, 1995: 111).

The most powerful literary voice in modern Andhradesa against upper caste hegemony was that of Vemana, a Sudra poet. Vemana chose the path of literature to fight social evils. He posed his insightful questions in the form of literary stanzas (*padyalu*) to counter the caste doctrine spread by Sanskrit *sloka*s. Vemana asked the upper castes: 'why do you again and again abuse a pariah? Are not his blood and flesh and thine one? Of what caste is he who is mingled with him? (Satyanarayana, 1983: 402)' He exhorted the upper castes:

> *Urvivarikella nokka kanchambetti, poththugudipi, kulamu*
> *Paaliyajesi, talanu cheyyibette taganammna jepparaa*

(Let everyone eat from the same plate, place their hands on their heads, and become friends) (Padma Rao, 1995: 112).

Vemana's stanzas were apparently a spontaneous reflection on social reality, disparaging the upper caste rulers, and becoming passionately cherished aphorisms for the lower castes. Vemana is said to have uttered hundreds of stanzas. One hundred stanzas among these have been published in an anthology entitled *Vemana Satakam* (100 Verses of Vemana). This work is considered to be the first Telugu text.

Veerabrahmam's teachings also became the historical inspiration for the present Dalit organic intellectuals (Satyanarayana, 1983). The Christian Literature Society in Andhra published considerable literature in both English and Telugu for the benefit of the newly converted lower castes. Among the books were: *Enlightened Teachings from the Book of Truth* (1747); *Way to Heaven* (1746); *100 Wisdom Principles* (1747); *Book of the Law* (1818). These and many other collections of hymns, pamphlets, and brochures were widely circulated, which directly or indirectly helped the emergence of Dalit literature and consciousness (Vijaya Bharathi, 1990).

The present Dalit literature also claims inspiration from Mahatma Jyotiba Phule's *Satya Shodak Samaj* movement. Phule's numerous works on education, culture, history, and literature became the fountainhead of thought for Dalit organic intellectuals. Phule's scholarly cardinal works, *Gulamgiri* (1873) and *Sarvajanik Satya Dharma Pustak* (1891) have been recognized as sources of the early organic sociological power of knowledge (Omvedt, 1994: 99). The most influential Dalit organic thinker, Ambedkar, has been the moving force for the Dalit literary movement in Andhra Pradesh. The elaborate body of his socioeconomic and politico-cultural ideas has been the guiding force and catalysing every Dalit. Ambedkarism has been regarded as an *avant-garde* of the Dalits' political and literary movement in Andhra Pradesh. Ambedkar's works such as. *The Untouchables, Who were the Sudras, the Buddha and His Dhamma, What Congress and Gandhi Have Done to the Untouchables and Castes in India; Annihilation of Caste* have become the basic frame of reference for the present Dalit organic intellectuals.

The pioneers of the early Dalit movement in Andhra Pradesh also started propaganda-cum-literary magazines to disseminate their ideas. Among these were *Bhagyanagar* by Bhagya Reddy Varma, *Jaya Bheeri* by Kusuma Dharmanna, *Navajeevan* by Vemula Kurmaiah, *Vyavasaya Kooli* by B.S. Murthy, *Jyothi* by Bojja Appala Swamy, *and Republican Jyothi*by B.V. Ramanaiah. Their speeches, essays, and poems became a part of an alternative ideological struggle against the hegemonic ideologies of both colonialism and Hinduism (Tarakam, 1987: 17).

The Dalit Sahitya Movement in Maharashtra produced an enormous amount of revolutionary Dalit literature. The first Dalit literary conference was held in 1958, which passed a resolution defining the term 'Dalit literature'. In 1967, the Milind Sahitya Parished was established at Nagsenvana, Aurangabad. Under its auspices, a quarterly known as *Asmita* (later it became *Asmithadarsha*) was published (Gangawane, 1987). These writers started a movement giving expression to their own independent identity. They declared war on the omnipresent and gigantic enemy of caste through the medium of literature (Daya Pawar, 1987).

Thus, the present Dalit literature in Telugu took much of its inspiration from different sources.

Telugu Literary Trends and the Dalit Problem

Telugu is the most Sanskritized language among the Southern languages. Though it does not belong to the Devanagari family of Northern languages it heavily borrows usage from Sanskrit texts. Starting from Nannaya in the twelfth century to the present generation, the traditional intellectuals have not created any original text in Telugu (Kalekuri Prasad, 1993). All the available major texts in Telugu were either translated from Sanskrit or were analogous creations directly from Sanskrit texts. All these early literary constructions and expressions were mostly the handiwork of the upper castes of the Telugu speaking world. The social problem of caste oppression, social alienation of Dalits and the problem of untouchability were not reflected in these writings; in fact, they helped to perpetuate caste dominance. Thus, this explains why the nineteenth century social reformers directed their anger against Sanskritized Telugu in addition to devoting attention to sociocultural reforms. It was Vemana who carefully understood social oppression and first raised his voice against the caste system.

The sociocultural problems of Telugu speaking society were reflected in some of the reformist literature in Telugu. The pioneers of the social reform movement in Andhra, Kandukuri Veereshalingam (1848–1919), Gurajada Appa Rao, Laxminarasimham (1848–1945), and Gidugu Ramamurthy worked for the reformation of orthodox social practices. They advocated women's education and widow remarriage. They also expressed sympathy for untouchables. Veereshalingam started schools for the Dalits and other working classes. Gurajada Appa Rao criticized the segregation of the Dalits on the basis their menial occupations. He said, 'Filthy occupations have been assigned to some people, looking down upon them and not even treating them as human beings' (Padma Rao, 1995: 63).

In 1911, Gurajada Appa Rao wrote a song on the Malas titled 'Malalu' in which he lamented that, 'judging people with an unclean body as Malas, and rewarding unethical people as upper caste is not at all fair. The law called caste is an un justified imposition.' Further, 'human beings have two castes, good and bad. If good is Mala I would be Mala (Satyanarayana, 1995: 107). However, these reformers' main objective was to reform certain evils of the Hindu social system and they failed to grapple with the ideological and institutional framework of Brahminical Hinduism. Their reading of classical texts and scripture was only aimed at reforming some aspects of Hindu society, but not to question and negate the *varna* system itself. Neither *Kanyasulakm* (bride-price) nor *Raja Sekhara Charitra,* written by Appa Rao and Veereshalingam respectively, addressed the basic fundamental problems of caste oppression and social alienation of Dalit masses from the mainstream society (Satyanarayana, 1995: 107).

During the anti-colonial struggle, many non-Dalit intellectuals made remarkable efforts to absorb all those masses who were socially and politically alienated into the broad terrain of the anti-colonial struggle. Most of them were immensely influenced by the growing nationalist aspirations and specifically the Gandhian 'Harijan uplift program'. They projected the Dalit problem in their literary creations from the above angle. Basavaraju Appa Rao wrote songs on the atrocities inflicted on Dalits. Among the others who dealt with the Dalit problem were Mutnuri Krishna Rao, Kamaraju Hanumantha Rao, Tapi Dharma Rao, Vemuri Ramji Rao, Adipudi Somanatha Rao, and Bandaru Achchamamba.

Tallapragada Suryanarayana Rao's *Helavati* was the first Telugu Dalit novel written by a non-Dalit in 1913. Helavati, the protagonist of the novel, was the daughter of Verabaludu, an untouchable. As a socially alienated family they lived in penury and collected grains from the porridge given to cattle. Helavati blames the caste-ridden society for their miserable plight. She refuses to marry an untouchable on the ground that she does not want to continue as an untouchable by marrying an untouchable. When Emperor Humayun is in trouble, Verabaludu renders him help. The emperor rewards him with costly gifts and money, thus enriching Verabaludu's family. But Helavati remains unmarried. Finally, she marries a Muslim, the son of a minister of the emperor. Verabaludu changes his religion and becomes Chan Mohammad. The social message of this novel was that if Hindus did not change their attitude towards the Dalits, the latter would not continue as Hindus any more (Kalekuri Prasad, 1993). Venkata Parawatisha Kavulu's novel *Matru Mandiram* (1919) also critiqued the caste system.

Unnava Laxminarayana's *Mala Palli* (Mala Hamlet, 1922) was extensively debated and discussed. The author was considerably influenced by the Gandhian reform movement and championed the rights of the working class. In this historical novel, he depicted 'the Dalits' realization of their socio-economic problems in the wake of broader national struggle under the leadership of Gandhi (Omvedt, 1994: 116). Although some of his ideas differed fundamentally from the Dalit point of view—notably those of pacifism, religiosity, and passiveness-his critique of the structured social relations and collectivism elicited wide acclaim. Summarizing the implications of the novel, Haragopal says that, 'the main reasons presented for the absence of class consciousness is the hegemony of the Hindu worldview conditioning the consciousness of the Harijans. This prevents them from revolting. This indicates not only the structural constraints in which the poor Harijans were looked upon but the cobwebs of consciousness which permitted them little concerted and organized action (Omvedt, 1994: 117).

N.G. Ranga's *Harijan Nayakudu* (*Harijan Leader*, 1933) projected the Dalit problem from the point of view of the peasantry and agricultural labour. The hero was a Dalit who 'agitates on various issues, opposing the violence against and abuse of Dalits, organizing inter-caste marriages, establishing schools, fighting for entry into the temples and use of public wells (Omvedt, 1994: 117). Adavi Bapiraju's *Narudu* (1946) depicted the problem of caste prejudice, oppression and Dalit protest at all levels. The hero of *Narudu,* a young Dalit born amidst abject poverty and social neglect, overcomes his disabilities, goes abroad for higher studies and marries an Anglo-Indian girl. Another novel of note is *Adarsham* (1946) by Anantati Narasimham.

Mangipudi Venkata Sharma's *Nirudda Bharatam* (1915) was the first anthology of poems on Dalits by non-Dalits. The first part of the anthology was devoted to the socioeconomic conditions of the Dalits and appealed to the upper castes to treat the Dalits as human beings. The second part appealed to the *panchamas* to realize their sufferings, which were brought about by the caste system rather than by mysterious fate (Vijaya Bharathi, 1990). Cherukuvada Damogipurapu Jantakavulu's song 'overlooking the Dalits is not justifiable', was published in 1921. Nelluri Venkata Ramanaidu's song 'Harijanulu' with a similar theme was published in 1928. Kondapalli Jagannatha Rao, Tirunagari Venkatasuri, Kambhampati Laximinarasimha Somayajulu, Basavaraju Appa Rao, Puripanda Appala Swamy, Karuna Sri also deplored the problems of the Dalits in their writings (Satyanarayana, 1995). One play that effectively contrasted the hegemonic upper caste ideology with the Dalit *bahujan* point of view was Tripuraneni Ramaswamy Chowdary's *Shambuka Vadha* (1922). Chowdary (1887–1943) was a father figure of the non-Brahmin movement and a literary doyen from the Sudra community. Gudapalli Rama Brahma's film *Mala Pilla* (Mala Girl) also depicted the Dalit problems. A.V. Neelakanta Sastri's play *Harijanudu* (1935) was another non-Dalit contribution to Dalit consciousness.

The main criticism about non-Dalit writings on the Dalit's plight has been that "the aspirations and emotional feelings of the Dalits masses were not adequately taken cognizance of by the middle class intellectuals, who were predominantly drawn from the upper castes" (Satyanarayana, 1995). In the post-Independence period, some of the notable non-Dalit writings on the theme were: Illandula Ranganayakulu's *Mallika* (1950), Vatti Kota Alwar Swamy's *Prajala Manishi* (1950), Muppala Ranganayakamma's *Balipeetam*

(1962), Kalipatnam Rama Rao's *Yagnam* (1964), Mahendra Ramamohan Rao's *Kollaigattitenemi* (1965). Malladi Vasunda's *Trivarna Patakam* (1965), Vachaspathi's *Antahkalahalu* (1965), Dasharathi Rangacharya's *Chillara Devundlu* (1970) and *Antaranijanta* (1973), Shiva Reddy's Three novels, *Banisalu* (1971), *Incredible Goddess* (1974) and *Swashanam Dunneru* (1974), Ellandu Saraswathi Devi's *Neebanchan Kalmokkuta* (1977), Tenneti Hemalatha's *Miss Kokila* (1978), Yerramchetti Sai's *Akari Mazili* (1978), Kethu Viswanatha Reddy's *Veerlu* (1978), Vani's *Mohanagaram* (1979), K. Ramalaxmi's *Tapobangam,* A. Kutumba Rao's *Sorojyam* (1984), N.R. Nandi's *Nymisharanyam* (1984), Bupathi Rama Rao's *Kulakanya,* and Dadala Chantabhai's *Antuleni Amavasya* (Satyanarayana, 1995). Kalipatnam Rama Rao's *Yagnam* (1964), revolving around a dispute over a loan taken by a Mala family of Appalaramudu from a petty money lender of the village, 'was the best critique of the Nehruvian phase from the point of view of the agrarian poor. Driven to destitution, within the agrarian system and without alternative employment in industry, they accumulated in members, without becoming partners in development, and became the marginalized resultants, in spite of their efforts and will (Rao, 1995: 136).

Mainstream Telugu literature witnessed another literary trend during the 1940s called *Abyudaya Sahityam* or progressive literature, in protest against the prevalent romanticism, idealism, and traditional individualism. The writings of this school also reflected on the global problems of the economic depression of the thirties and the fascist aggression in Europe. They idealized communism and propagated the communist utopia of world revolution. The writers of this school formed an organization called Abyudaya Rachayitala Sangham or Progressive Writers Association (PWA). The pioneer of this movement was Srirangam Srinivasa Rao (popularly known as Sri Sri), whose eloquent poems influenced the youth to a remarkable degree and do so even today. Sri Sri's *Maha Prasthanam* (*Great Presentation*, 1950), was an anthology of poems which basically centered on class struggle (Padma Rao, 1995).

An offshoot of the progressive writers' school was *Dibangara kavitwam* or nude poetry, which sneered at established literary traditions and advocated writing of a crude form. They resorted to unconventional practices such as having their anthologies of poems released by a rickshaw puller or a prostitute at midnight in Hyderabad. Charabanda Raju, Nagnamuni, and Nikhileswar belonged to this stream. One anthology of poems from this school was dedicated to Kanchikacherla Koteshu, a Dalit boy who was burnt alive by the upper castes in Krishna district in 1968.

The outbreak of Naxalbari and Srikakulam movements witnessed the emergence of the most powerful revolutionary literary movement in Telugu called *viplava sahityam* or revolutionary poetry. This movement was known by its organization called *Viplava Rachayitala Sangham* or Revolutionary Writers Association (RWA). Many highly talented revolutionary writers formed its core, producing a wide range of Marxist literature, which, however, is beyond the scope of the present study. The basic criticism about these writers made by Dalit organic intellectuals was that they did not take note of caste and its impact on the self-respect of Dalits. Their focus on the socioeconomic problems of the working class did not direct them to create an alternative hegemonic caste ideology and they were not able to answer Dalit and feminist issues (Padma Rao, 1995).

Other cultural-cum-literary organizations like Jana Natya Mandali (JNM), Arunodaya and Janasahiti, and journals like *Aruna Tara, Abyudaya,* and *Srujana* all played an important role in propagating pro-Dalit literature.

Dalit Literature

Dalit literature basically is a 'counter hegemonic ideology' created by 'Dalit organic intellectuals'. The ideas which they have developed reflect their own social consciousness determined by their structured social existence, which has hitherto remained neglected. Dalit organic intellectuals thus come from a most exploited class and caste origin. They necessarily share a common critical attitude towards the hegemonic upper caste ideology. In search of their new sociocultural identity and distinctness they developed their own communication system with their own historical symbols and literary concepts (Bhole and Bhole, 1977), which created an advanced necessary self-awareness and consciousness for an intended action. Dalit literature as a 'counter hegemonic ideology' is ultimately related to action is capable of organizing Dalits as agents of new democratic revolution. It is able to translate itself into a specific orientation of Dalit revolutionary practice. Dalit literature has been considered here in the Gramscian view of a positive 'organic ideology, which has a psychological validity and which organizes human masses and created the terrain on which men move, acquire consciousness of their position, struggle, etc' (Gramsci, 1996: 377).

Dalit organic intellectuals in Andhra Pradesh have evolved broadly in three stages:

- In the *first stage,* Ambedkar's anti-caste thought/ideology was not fully developed in Andhra Pradesh. The Dalit organic intellectuals were then in a stage of making appeals, but they differed from non-Dalit writers who advocated integration. They had developed a critical view about Hindu social hierarchy.
- In the *second stage*, Ambedkarism was fully received into their literature. Their arguments centered on uncritical acceptance of Ambedkar's philosophy as the base for the counter-hegemonic ideology.

- In the *third and present stage*, Dalit intellectuals have emerged with a Marxist perspective, analyzing Hindu/Indian society on the basis of historical materialism along with Ambedkar's caste annihilation theory. This new synthesis of Marxism-Ambedkarism was aimed at the successful accomplishment of a new democratic revolution in India.

In all the three stages, however, Dalit organic intellectuals have been collectively committed to reconstructing counter-hegemonic ideology through their literary and artistic creations consisting of poems, songs, essays, speeches, novels, short stories, plays, autobiographical notes, and literary criticism. An attempt has been made here to analyze available literature of the organic intellectuals. The definition of organic intellectuals is not confined to Dalits alone but has been extended to the backward classes and minority intellectuals also, because much of the Dalit literature has been created in combination with them.

The early Dalit intellectual creative expressions were mainly centered on the themes of equal treatment, self-respect and dignified living. While exposing caste exploitation and discrimination, they asserted their identity as *panchama*s and *adi-Hindus*. Their consciousness was reflected in pleading for recognition of the nature of their existence. Mahakavi Gurram Jashuva (1895–1971) was the first compelling organic Dalit voice in Telugu literature, which exposed the hypocrisy of caste ideology. Jashuva was a great creative poet, but his creative genius and literary talent were not fully recognized. Despite his intellectual establishment in Telugu literature, Jashuva was humiliated and subjected to intense mental agony and was treated as a literary outcaste by the Telugu literary world that was dominated by the upper castes (Satyanarayana, 1995). Reacting to humiliations and insults, Jashuva commented that, 'all those crack-brained crows, their prejudice, slander, can't take away my well-endowed faculty. I will bang the bells of verse, I will shower the pellets. I will chasten the crackles of Andhra voice (Jashuva, 1996: 152). He declared, in addition, that, 'I intended to pierce through caste distinction, poverty and prove that I am a human being. I wield a sword. My sword is my poetry' (Satyanarayana, 1995).

Jashuva's literary output was prolific, including poetry, short stories and plays in more than thirty works reflecting on different issues of history, society, economy, and political upheavals of his time. Basically, Jashuva was against all inequalities. Whoever fought against inhuman traditions, inequalities, and social evils, were seen by Jashuva as liberators, irrespective of caste, class, color, and ideology. His works are marked by his impartiality and rationality. Jashuva wrote poems praising Gandhi for his campaign for the untouchables' temple entry and uplift programs. He also celebrated Subhas Chandra Bose's heroic role in the national struggle. Jashuva also recognized the autonomous struggle waged by B.R. Ambedkar for the emancipation of Dalits. He asked his messenger, the Bat, whether he had got Ambedkar's blessings. Jashuva says that, 'Ambedkar my brother is there, who suffered, was victimized immensely for my community, but secured the highest position, as great as the Viceroy. Does he welcome you with a bouquet? His blessings are a must for your victory (Jashuva, 1996: 48).

Gabbilam (*The Bat*), Jashuva's magnum opus, rocked the whole Telugu world when it was published in 1941. Telugu litterateurs were until then engrossed in romanticism, without any serious social concern. *Gabbilam,* an anthology of poems, dealt with almost all socioeconomic and political issues of Dalits. Each poem reflected their agony, their despair and their anger. Each poem realistically presented the bitter daily experiences of the Dalit masses, their disgust, and misery. As Bojja Tarakam summarizes, 'the entire theme is the remorseful life as an untouchable. The language, the expression, the idiom and the style are very powerful and near to life. The depiction was very piercing' (Tarakam, 1987). The opening poem says, 'pleased with miles of penance inconsiderate. All penury just with little of morsel. Unconnected to four divisions (*varnas*) fifth born son of Mother Bharat (Jashuva, 1996: 9).

Reflecting on the economic exploitation of Dalits and how they had been mercilessly alienated from their own production by the upper caste rulers, Jashuva lamented that, 'when his (Dalit's) hands do not work, the green fields hesitate to yield crops. He (Dalit) sweats, provides food for the world. But he himself has no food (Satyanarayana, 1995). Jashuva expressed his disillusionment with Hindu social life and questioned its wisdom which treated Dalits as less than human beings. He mercilessly exposed the hegemonic caste ideology and its hypocrisy. He wrote that, 'tied my mouth with *Karma* doctrine, mean fellows are making merry at the cost of my life. Asks Eswar (the God) to reveal the truth about what is meant by *karma* and why it has a grudge against me (Jashuva, 1996: 14). Further, he explained how Hinduism was responsible for the perpetuation of caste oppression. Alienating Dalits from the mainstream society, squeezing them from all sides the upper castes regarded the Dalit's shadow itself as an offence. Jashuva asked the Dalits to be cautious about the four-hooded Hindu cobra that might attack them at any movement. He wrote that, 'by swallowing the blood of the wretched (Dalit) lives the iron ankleted Mother, upon smelling the air hisses with vengeance, the four-hooded Hindu cobra (Satyanarayana, 1995).

Naakatha (1966), Jashuva's autobiography, revealed the Dalit poet's whose integrity and honesty brought him hardship. It expressively reflected the real Dalit's inner experiences of pain and anguish and illustrated the oppressive caste social order to which Dalits were subjected.

There were many Dalit writers and activists contemporary to Jashuva who also made a mark on the Telugu literary world. Jala Ranga Swamy, Kusuma Dharmanna, Nakka China Venkaiah, Nutakki Abraham were among those organic intellectuals who exposed caste discrimination and its dominance in day to day life of Dalits. Jala Ranga Swamy wrote the first Dalit novel *Rytu Pilla* (*Farmer's Daughter*, 1938) (Tirumala Rao, 1996). In this novel, the heroine Seeta, an upper caste farmer's daughter, is progressive in her understanding of social relations. She revolts against the established tradition and boldly comes out to marry Sri Ramudu, an untouchable farm servant at Seeta's father house. Further, in his long poem, 'Who are the Untouchables' (1930), Ranga Swamy questioned the upper caste hegemony, saying that, 'some occupations were created and assigned to us, we were named as serfs, caste discrimination was introduced, we were oppressed, we were troubled with slavery/trodden, occupational differences were imposed, we were alienated (Satyanarayana, 1995).

In *Melukolupu* (*Awaken*, 1930) and *Mala Suddhi* (*Cleaning Malas*, 1930) Ranga Swamy criticised all hypocritical, pseudo-Gandhian upper caste nationalists who worked for the uplift of untouchables (Satyanarayana, 1995). In his writings, Dalit identity was symbolized as the *panchamas*. He projected the Dalit historical figures of Arundhathi, Matangi, and Sabari as Dalit women against the Aryans (Satyanarayana, 1995).

Kusuma Dharmanna, while organizing the Dalits for the national movement, also asked the Dalits to prepare for their own liberation struggle form the native hegemonic upper caste rulers. He started a propaganda-cum-literary magazine called *Jaya Bheeri*. He was said to be 'a powerful speaker, writer and organizer' (Ilaiah, 1995). Dharmanna was known for his spontaneous satires on upper caste rulers in which the Dalits identity was asserted. He noted that the Dalits participation in the freedom struggle was marginalized due to their immediate socioeconomic constrains. The upper caste leadership also failed to evolve a systematic program to ensure their socioeconomic emancipation and 'the aspirations and emotional feelings of the Dalit masses did not become an integral part of the nationalist ideology and program (Satyanarayana, 1995). Thus, the Dalits twofold struggle, against the imperial British and the hegemonic upper caste native rulers was reflected in their ideological expression. Dharmanna wrote a controversial song 'Maakoddee Nalla Doratanam' (*We Don't Want this Black/ Brown Lordship*) as a counter to the song written by Garimella Satyanarayana, an upper caste nationalist leader, *Maakoddee Tella Doratanam* (*We Don't Want this White's rule*). Portraying the pathetic living conditions of Dalit masses in this song, Dharmanna wrote:

We have only small huts outside the village
We do not have big houses
Air, light do not trifle
We have no delicious food curry
To wear we have no saree, loincloth

We have no tail ornaments
We have no land to plough, eat food
You have no sympathy on our poverty (Satyanarayana, 1995)
Despite twelve months of bonded labour
We live with hunger, Wife has no labour
Sons has to graze the animals
Despite all our drudgery, we are deficient of food and cloths
Debts are undone, God, they starved us mercilessly
We do not want this balck lordship
Sir! God! We do not want this black lordship
God, we have no equal treatment in this society
We do not want this black lordship (Vijaya Bharathi, 1990)

Nakka Chinna Venkaiah, in his *Harijana Kirtanalu* (*Harijana Hymns*, 1935) pleaded with the upper castes to forgo caste distinctions. He said that,

Why do they not forgo Untouchability
Why they have dispute on it
Why do they not forgo untouchability (Satyanarayana, 1995)

Further, he asked the upper castes to treat Dalits as fellow human beings and cease their persecutions. This tone of plea also marked the writings of Nutakki Abraham, Premaiah, Gnananda Kavi, Chodagiri Chandra Vajrapu Samba Murthy and Athota Ratna Kavi (Tarakam, 1987). Boyee Bheemanna, another Telugu Dalit literary icon reached the highest pinnacle of Telugu literary world. He wrote nearly sixty plays, stories, novels, and essays which reflected on the socioeconomic, historical, and cultural aspects of the Dalits. Two of Bheemanna's plays *Coolie Raju* (*Labour King*, 1942) and *Paleeru* (*Farm Servant*, 1946) mirrored the problems closely affecting the Dalits. *Coolie Raju* was about the struggle of Dalits for economic justice. The play was performed in every village of coastal Andhra, sometimes more than a dozen times (Tarakam, 1987). The hero of the play Nishkalaveer, says that every labourer's heart is flaring up, and that it would burn up any time. The play, written on the lines of caste-class struggle created tremendous consciousness among Dalits and other working masses. Because of its revolting content, inflammatory language against the upper castes and the British government, the play was banned by the British government (Tarakam, 1987).

Paleeru projected the problem of Dalit bonded labour. The hero Venkanna is a victim of the system of hierarchy bonded labour. Different from all previous farm servants, Venkanna wants to put an end to bonded labour as such. His solution is to educate himself and change his occupation. With the help of a school teacher and an upper-caste girl, he escapes from bonded labour and joins the Brahmo Samaj, where he is given the opportunity to study. Venkanna secures his Bachelor of Arts degree and eventually becomes deputy collector.

The play

> is an urge for social equality and the acquisition of knowledge and education by Dalit masses for a decent living as well as for a respectable place in society. In it there is a suggestion that through education and inter-caste marriage social mobility is possible. The author opined that the problems of Dalits are not only that of class, hence, Dalits should be educated first and obtain good official positions (Satyanarayana, 1995).

Ravuvri Ekambaram is another poet and organizer who moved along with Ambedkar in Andhra and together with him addressed many public meetings. Ekambaram has written many poems and songs on Dalits depicting their hatred, agony and future hope. His anthology of poems on Ambedkar tilted as *Ambedkara Samara Simha* (*Ambedkar the Warrior Lion*) created tremendous consciousness in Andhra about Ambedkar's personality and his revolutionary ideas. Ekambaram's *Ambedkar Ramayanam and Ambedkar Bharatam* contain poems that are still the most popular songs on Ambedkar (Gnaneswar, 1997).

Endluri Chinnaiah's *Ambedkar's Life History* has been the most forceful and highly influential political propaganda document on Ambedkar in Telugu. Vijaya Bharati translated many of Ambedkar's works into Telugu. Her translations into Telugu of *Ambedkar: Life and Mission* and *Mahatma Phule's* life history, both by Dananjay Keer, have inculcated a dynamic political consciousness and have heightened the Dalits' perception of Ambedkar in Telugu regions. These books have been widely read and have been responsible for the widely promoted Ambedkar cultural and youth organizations in Andhra Pradesh. Modukuri Johnson's play *Nichena Metlu* (*Ladder*) also played a significant role in building an alternative hegemonic ideology (Vijaya Bharathi, 1990). The counter-hegemonic ideology was also propagated through many media platforms as an expression by Dalit organic intellectuals. Saik Nazer (1920–97), backward class Muslim, adopted and enriched a folk form of story-telling called *Burrakatha* for his mass communication. *Burrakatha* is simple and colloquial and totally different both in form and content from the highly sanskritized *Harikatha*, which is mainly adopted by the upper castes. Suddhala Hanumanthu was another backward class singer and lyricist whose poems on *Vettii* exploitation and the heroic role of the Communists during the Telangana movement have become the main impetus for cultural movement (Ilaiah, 1995). Both Nazer and Hanumanthu played a significant role during the Telangana struggle.

Unlike Marathi Dalit literature, Telugu Dalit organic intellectuals were profoundly influenced by the Ambedkarite Dalit Panthers Movement in Maharashtra, the Marxist-Leninist Movement of Naxalbari and the armed struggle movements of Srikakulam. This remarkable change may be noticed in the Dalit literature from the seventies onwards.

K.G. Satyamurty, who was popularly known by his pen name, Shiva Sagar, was a rebel, and a revolutionary leader of peasants and proletariats. Some of his revolutionary poems, 'Gong Bells' (1969), 'Narudo! Bhaskaruda!' (1970), 'Udyamam Nelabaludu' (1971), 'Chelli Chandramma' (1971) have been classics of the Naxalbari movement. In *Udyamam Nelabaludu,* Shiva Sagar labeled himself thus:

I am Naxalbari!
I am Mushahari!
I am Srikakulam!
Renegade! I am Revolution
I am the man who sprouted
From the blood flood of those martyrs!
(Shiva Sagar, 1983: 49)

Shiva Sagar has been the bridge between the 'Progressive' writers of the forties and the 'Revolutionary' writers of the seventies, continuing the ongoing Dalit democratic revolution. As a revolutionary he sounded his revolutionary '*Gong Bells*' as early as the seventies, to unite all the working classes. His poem reveals:

Workers, Farmers
Weavers, Labours
Hamali, Kalasi
Kammari, Kummari
Oppressed, Suppressed
March on, March on!
Bang the Gong Bells
Trot out! Trot!!
Move on! Move on! (Shiva Sagar, 1983: 8)

Shiva Sagar's 'Chelli! Chandramma' became the symbolic representation of thousands of Dalit women who have silently borne the suppression by the hegemonic caste oppressors. It was a glowing tribute to all those Dalit women who were harassed and tormented by landlords. His poems 'Narudo! Bhaskaruda!' and 'O! Vilukada!' (O! Bow man, 1973) have documented the course of revolutionary struggle. Despite State repression, the revolutionary movement survived and continued, he says. The bullet (that is, the State), he asserts, hit only the thigh, which crippled movement, but not the chest, which would have killed the movement.

C. Varahala Rao, popularly known as 'CV' in Telugu literary circles, became the starting point for the present generation of Dalit poetry. His poems, 'Satyakama Jabhali', Narabhali' ('Human Sacrifice'), 'Samskritika Punarujjeevanam' ('Cultural Renaisance') and 'Varnavyavastha' ('Caste System') have been master pieces of Dalit poetry. They have played a significant role in the production of a counter-hegemonic ideology. In addition, they reflected the sorrow and anguish of the Dalits. In his poem 'Paris Commune' CV suggested an Indian variety of Marxism with the caste-class debate. His poems have given the earliest direction for the synthesization of Marxism and Ambedkarism (Shambhuka, 1992: 10).

Present-day Dalit literature is an inevitable spontaneous upsurge of the suppressed voice of the Dalit masses. Their literary expressions are a compulsive outburst of stored anger, untold misery, resentment, poverty, injustice, disillusionment, and mental and physical persecutions. They give voice to the Dalits' torments and distressful social position in the oppressive caste system. Bojja Tarakam in his poem 'I am an Untouchable' (1976), laments:

I am an Untouchable
My carcass smells dirt
My life is full of bonded cry
My eyes filled with radiance

Of sunned in Sun, of rained in Rain
My head like
Tighten Banyan suckers
....

I was told to carry the dead cows
I was told to make shoes out of it
I was told not to wear them, never
I was told to live like that (Tarakam, 1983: 78)

But he repudiates this endless prostrating life and asserts himself confidently, saying that,

I am coming...
By mutilating thy
Despotic darkness
I am erupting.
By cracking thy
Barriers and trammels
......
I am whirlwind, Gust
Mud, Pyramid
Thunder, Flash
Chasm, Ocean
Current, Deluge
Magnanimous, Inferno
Alpha, omega
I am COMING (Tarakam, 1983: 88)

Thus, the Dalit identity metamorphosed from *panchama* (fifth *Varna*), untouchable, Harijan to the Dalit. Each stage has its historical significance. In Andhra Pradesh, the Dalits further metamorphosed into a Naxalite. Salandra in his historic poem 'Dalit Manifesto' (1981) disputes and challenges all that past paradoxical record of the hegemonic caste system:

Mine!
You asked me not to enter into the Temple well, anyhow
I am happy being an theist
Mine!
Proscribed not to study
If I study you ordered to cut the tongue
Well, anyhow
I comprehend how gullible you are
How prodigious you are
......
One uttered me as an Untouchable
another affirmed as Harijan
Some rogue judged me as a Wretched
What is it for me?
Yes
What is it for me?
Whosoever calls, whatsoever manner
When I myself am a NAXALITE
(Laxmi Narasaiah and Tripuraneni Srinivas, 1995: 204-5)

In the same tone and content, Gaddar, the revolutionary singer, says that the Dalits, even if they change religion, even if they change their caste, would not be able to change their identity. The only way for them is to take up arms to capture State power. He says that,

Thy Slave! Thy Slave!
Thy Serf O lord!
Saying so
How long-O Malanna
Why don't you revolt- O Madiganna
Even if you change religion
Your life won't be changing
Even if you change caste
You won't be getting food
You without ruling the State
Your fate does not change
For the State power Malanna
Take the Rifle Madiganna
(Thirumal Rao and Kumma Ashok, 1993: 134-5)

G. Anjaiah questions the dominance of the feudal landlordism and asserts that without the labour and sweat of the Dalits there would be no such thing as village or town. Every village is sustained by their hard work, ploughing, and guarding, grazing, washing. Every task has to be done by them only. Without their contribution, every socially productive instrument designed and owned by the landlords would be of no use. Anjaiah asserts that the:

Village is ours! This street is ours!
Hamlet is ours! We are for every work!
Hammer is ours! Knife is ours!
Crowbar is ours! Spade is ours!
Cart is ours! Bullock is ours!
Why is lord and lordship?

(Jananatya Mandali 1994: 23)

Shambhuka (Pen name) in his poem '*Poyedeemi Lenoollam*' ('We Have Nothing to Lose') exposes the real picture of caste hypocrisy and how it has contaminated even the powerful Naxalite movement. He wonders how hellish caste hypocrisy is. He says that:

If Madiga wear Khadi
He is a hopeless fool
If Kamma wears it
He is simple ideal Satyagrahi
Ah! Caste!
How cruel you are?
If Brahmin says there is no caste
He is a great reformer
If Mala propagates the same
He is a dangerous casteist
Oh! Caste!
How brutal you are?
In Nagi Reddy, Pulla Reddy
You don't find caste
But in Satya Murthy, Padma Rao
Caste smell is gushing out
Ah! Caste!
How funny you are?

(Shambhuka, 1992: 33)

The present generation Dalit literature in Telugu is not a stream of pleasure, it is not regurgitation of freakish romantic memories, not even short-lived emotions. It is rather a philosophical dialogue, a socio-politico-cultural assertion. It represents the struggle among the social forces rather than individual forces (Afsar, 1995). The common contexts of the present Dalit literature are:

alienation, oppression, the nature of caste and its brutal violence, agony, perpetual atrocities, anger, pain, privations, and sorrows. At the same time, it aims at caste-class Dalit struggle, annihilation of caste, creation of ground for the revolutionary consciousness, self-respect, emancipation, and attack on all social evils. It aspires for State power. It opposes the concepts of pessimism, cynicism, stoicism, fatalism, superstition and romanticism. It is the real experience of organic life. It is for new hope, humanism, equality, fraternity, brotherhood; it endeavors a new sociocultural identity.

After the Karamchedu incident, the Dalit literature was thoroughly radicalized. Many Dalit intellectuals emerged from the Karamchedu movement. Katti Padma Rao, the leader of the movement has written many poems on Dalits. His 'Jailu Gantalu' ('Jail Bells', 1988), *Jana Geetam, Desham Dairy,*(1989). *Teluguvaari Ho chi man Shiva Sagar, Red Star and Sankaracharya* have created tremendous Dalit consciousness. His *Desham Dairy* has been the most pertinent critique of Telugu Desam government in Andhra Pradesh. He says that:

Padirikuppam, Karamchedu
Tadipatri, Kottakota
Neerukonda, Dontali
Shiraluru, Bandlapalli
Country wide bloodshed
By the oppressed Dalits
For their emancipatory struggles
Welcome! Welcome!

(Satyanarayana, 1995)

Goreeti Venkanna also asks the Dalits to revolt against the atrocities inflicted on them by upper castes: He asks that,

How many times these macabre?
How many shall we perish?
Dalitanna get organised or we can't stand
Dalitanna raise the rifle, or we can't live

(Thirumal Rao and Kumma Ashok 1993: 109)

Vanga Pandu Prasad depicts the deplorable plight of Dalits in their poverty stricken, dirty, thatched colony: He sings that,

There is Malapeta (Malas Hamlet)
At the outskirts of the Village
Of being oppressed
At the end of the Village

(Charvakudu, 1996: 70)

Masterji, singer, lyricist, dramatist, is among the leading Dalit organic intellectuals who is propagating Ambedkarism along with Marxism. Masterji's song on Ambedkar 'Salutes to Baba Ambedkar' became the chorus for the present Dalit movement. His song 'Deena Bhandavulu' ('Saviours of the Helpless') became the Dalit national anthem. Masterji sings like this:

Great many born great
But all are not saviors of the helpless
Few only could liquidate our problems
They only really gave up their lives
Among them were
Phule, Ambedkar and Periyar

(Maasterji, 1995)

Masterji responds and propagates his own theory called *moolavasi siddhantam,* (theory of aborigines). According to this theory, Madigas and Malas and other Bahujans are the real natives of this land, but in the historical process, they have been suppressed and made slaves by the Aryans who were barbarians:

Real Indians are—Adi-Hindus
Aryans invaded—fought
Weaponless—Dravidians were
Defeated and made slaves
Today they are the Dalits

(Maasterji, 1995: 7-8)

Masterji's classic poem cum song 'Neel-Lal' ('Blue and Red') seeks a synthesis of Ambedkarism and Marxism: he sings:

Under Blue Red Flag O! Sister
You and me as equals O! Sister
Be ready for the struggle O! Sister
Then only
Oppressed would get emancipation O! Sister
To dismantle the oppressor's rule O! Sister
To regain the Dalit Rule O! Sister

(Maasterji, 1995: 49)

Gaddar and Masterji were the two powerful cultural agents of the new democratic Dalit politico-cultural revolution. Gaddar represents the Marxist-Leninist Party and leads its cultural organization Jananatya Mandali (JNM). Masterji represented the Dalit Bahujan organization and in 1978 started Dalita Kala Mandali, an independent Dalit cultural organization. Gaddar's songs are dynamic, a torrent, and a powerful weapon for revolutionary movement. But his conclusions are class struggle, armed struggle, Marxism and revolution. Masterji's songs have a moving force; they represent the real organic voice of Dalit history and culture. His songs are mostly centered on Ambedkarism. U.

Sambashiva Rao, Kranti Kiran, Satish Chandra, G. Shankar, Endluri Sudhakar, Sahu, G. Anjaiah, Rama Rao, Kalekuri Prasad (Yuvaka) and many other poets and lyricists have also come up. Satish Chandar's *Panchama Vedam*, an anthology of poems, created considerable heat in Telugu literature. U. Sambashiva Rao's song on 'Dalit Muslim bhai bhai' seeks to unite the Dalit struggle.

The Dalit story and novel also occupied a distinct place in Telugu literature. The themes of these stories reveal the reality and typical depiction of the Dalits' life, centered on their daily struggle against the caste-ridden society. Similarly, they reflected the denial of public places, traditional impositions, poverty, pain, humiliations. Kolukaluri Enoch's 'Urabavi' (1969) is a short story about the denial of access to the public well in a small village. In the story, in order to protest upper caste dominance, Dalits unite and dump a carcass of an animal in the public well, which leads to retaliation by the upper castes (Chandrashekar Reddy and Laximinarayana, 1996: 99-126). Boya Jangaiah's 'Bancha Rai' (1984) is a short story about the grabbing of Dalit land by the upper caste landlords in the name of a temple or sacred place. B.S. Ramulu's *Bratukupooru* (Struggle for Existence, 1982), is a novel about the wretched *beedi* (cigar) worker's life in Telangana, written in language typical of Telangana. B.S. Ramulu has also written *Contradictions* (1990) and *Bandhi* (1995). His works are widely read in Andhra Pradesh. P. Narasaiah's *Epooratam Aagadu* (1992) is a collection of short stories about the Dalits' life in coastal Andhra. There are nine stories dealing with bonded labour, land alienation, temple entry, education, et cetera. Allam Rajaiah's *Bhoomi* (1982) and *Agnikanam* (1983), which are collection of stories, have become the primary weapons for introducing revolutionary ideas among the Tribals and Dalits in Telangana.

After Karamchedu, the first All India Dalit Writers Conference was held in 1987 at Hyderabad. Nearly 528 delegates from all over India attended. The conference was a unique effort of Bojja Tarakam. The conference unanimously took an oath saying that Dalit writers would hold the torch of liberation and participate in a people's movements. The aim of the conference was to promote a casteless and classless society based on human values, justice, liberty, equality, and fraternity. It was also emphasized at the conference that Dalit literature should not only act as a source of inspiration for the oppressed people but also become an instrument to ignite consciousness and courage (Tarakam, 1987). The establishment of the Ambedkar Memorial Trust in 1986 also helped to create a counter-ideology to caste dominance. The objectives of the Trust were to propagate the ideals of Ambedkar for establishing a casteless and classless society, to publish books, journals, periodicals, and pamphlets, and to conduct seminars mainly impressing upon the necessity to abolish the caste system and eradicate untouchability all the need to encourage writers, artists and dramatists who worked for the propagation of removal of untouchability and the caste system. In keeping with its mandate, the Trust has played a significant role in conducting seminars and memorial lectures regularly (Gnaneswar, 1997). The emergence of organic Dalit cultural and literacy organizations like Dalit Kala Mandali, Dalit Writers, Artists and Intellectuals United Forum (DWAIUF) in the post-Chundur (1991) period have brought about a perceptible change in the sociocultural milieu. 'These organizations have been instrumental in spreading the anti-caste message of Ambedkar through song, story and speech' (Srinivasulu, 1994). Further, the DWAIUF has regularly conducted workshops for Dalit young men and women to identify their inclination and talents and to train them to realize their potential (Srinivasulu, 1994). The starting of Dalits their own publications like *Lokayata, Nalupu, Edureeta,* have also played a vital role in spreading the counter-hegemonic ideology.

Dalit literary criticism of Katti Padma Rao's *Social Revolutionary Writers: A Dalitist Literary Critique* (1995) has been the best literary critique. This text has become a part of the Telugu text book syllabus for postgraduate students. His essay on reservations, entitled *Reservation and Hindu Mathonmadam* (1991) and his book *Caste and Alternative Culture* (1995) have been trenchant critiques of the hegemonic upper caste culture and ideology. Kancha Ilaiah's essays on reservations, particularly *Paranna Bukkulu Pratibanugurinch Matladutunnai* (Parasites Are Talking about Merit), which were regularly published in *Nalupu,* his highly Dalit-Bahujan organic intellectual mature work, *Why I am Not A Hindu: A Sudra Critique of Hinduta Philosophy, Culture and Political Economy* (1996) have become critical texts of the present ongoing Dalit literary movement. Bojja Tarakam's essay, *Kulam Vargham* (Caste-Class, 1996), B.S. Ramulu's *Ambedkarism and Socialism* (1994), U. Sambhasiva Rao's *Ejandani Prakkadari Pattinchi Errajandani Munduku Teesukellagalara?* (Distracting the Agenda Can We Forward the Red flag?) was a critical evaluation of the Marxist-Leninist movement from 1967 to 1987. The other literary critics from the Dalit intellectual community include G. Laxminarasaiah, Endluri Sudhakar, K.S. Chalam Shiva Sagar, Bojja Tarakam, and Vijaya Bharathi.

After Chundur, many anthologies of poems have been published by Dalit intellectuals. Some of them are: *Raktha Kheetram* (*Blood-soaked Field*, 1991), a long heart-rending poem by Katti Padma Rao is about the Chundur massacre. The *Chhikkanautunna Paata* (Solidifying Song, 1995) is an anthology of poems written by Dalits, OBCs and Minorities. These illuminating, rebellious poems were a spontaneous outpouring in reaction to the Karamchedu, Chundur, and Ayodhya events where the upper castes had instigated carnage against the Dalits. These poems are testimony to the inflating, sharpening Dalit literary tone and content in Andhra Pradesh.

Sunkara Ramesh's *Tallikodi Hechharika* (Mother Hen's Caution, 1995), is a long poem. In it, like the mother hen that is always cautious for her brood,

Dalits have to be cautious about the conspiracies hatched by the upper castes to swallow the innocent Dalits. Maddhuri Nagesh Babu's *Velivaada* (Outcast Hamlet, 1991) is an anthology of poems exposing the evil practices of the caste system and the atrocities committed by the upper castes on Dalits and other minorities. The author asks the Dalit women to conceive swords to bring on the Dalit revolution. He says that:

Tell our expectant mothers
To beget razor-sharp swords
Tell our Brothers
To make a shoe with Landlord's skin
Instead with their own skin (Nagesh Babu, 1995: 40)

Nishani (1995) is an anthology of protest poems written by promising Dalit writers, Khaza, Nagesh Babu, Teresh Babu, and Veeraiah. These poems brim with anger against the upper caste pseudo-sympathetic writers who intend to write on the Dalits only to earn a name and fame without losing their upper caste identity. The *Dalita Manifesto* (1995) is another anthology of poems written by Dalit activists, intellectuals, and young Dalit scholars. *Dalita Manifesto* has been an important trendsetter for not only Telugu literature in general but also a new generation of Dalit literary works. Shiva Sagar's famous poem 'Marching History' appeared in it. This poem has been regarded as the epoch poem of the present. Summarizing the present Dalit movement, Shiva Sagar notes:

Shambuka Sneeringly slaying Rama
Ekalavya's hatchet hewing the thumbs of Drona
Bali's tiny foot trampling Vamana underneath
Manu
of being pinned eyes
of snapping off tongue
of pouring lead in ears
rolling in the graveyard
positioned on the butchered cutter of the Epoch
the roaring Chandala
sibilating four hunter houds
on Shankara
Well done...!

The present marching history is
The history of real Chandala!
(Kesava Kumar and Satyanarayana, 1995: 114).

Thus the emergence of the Dalit movement was associated with the outpouring of prodigious and powerful literature bearing on the themes of Dalit emancipation. Dalit literature had transformed from passive supplication and pleading of an earlier generation to the higher level of revolutionary consciousness while posing a challenge to the established order. There has been a vast gulf between Dalit organic intellectuals and non-Dalit writers, in their expression and content. Though non-Dalit writers have dealt with the caste and untouchability problem in their writings, their literary expressions were not able to touch the inner psychological world of Dalit agony. At best, they remained sympathetic, but did not pose any systematic attack on the real oppressive institution, the caste.

Dalit organic literature has created a vast space for the emergence of new organic Dalit intellectuals. They were the real actors in the new democratic revolutionary movement. They were also actively involved in the construction of new ideas, and were producers of a new knowledge which was based on their real social experience. The secular form of Dalit literature could be noticed with the emergence of new Dalit-*bahujan* literature encompassing the minorities, women, and other *bahujan* oppressed castes and classes. Its secular content is not just the expression of their reflective mode of thinking but fundamentally aims at the intended new democratic revolution which would alter the present positon of Dalits and other oppressed masses. Thus, Dalit literature is evolving with a tremendous potential of emancipatory zeal and with humanizing content along with the Dalit movement.

REFERENCES

Bhole U. and Bhole A. (1977), 'The Dalit Sahitya Movement in Maharashtra: A Sociological Analysis', *Sociological Bulletin,* Vol. 26, No. 1, March.

Charvakudu, K. (1996), *Dalita Pata,* Lokayata Prachuranalu, Ponnur.

Chandrashekar Reddy and K. Laxminarayana (eds.) (1996), *Dalita Kathalu,* Vishalandra Publishing House, Hyderabad.

Dangle, A. (ed.) (1996), *Poisoned Bread: Translations from Modern Marathi Dalit Literature,* Sangam Books, Bombay.

Gangawane, K. (1987), 'Social Awareness in Dalit Literature' in Bojja Tarakam (eds.), *The First All India Dalit Writers Conference: A Commemorative Volume,* Dr B.R. Ambedkar Memorial Trust, Hyderabad.

Gramsci, Antonio (1996), *Selections from the Prison Note Books,* Orient Longman, Madras.

Ilaiah, Kancha (1995), *Caste or Class or Caste-Class: A Study in Dalit Bahujan Consciousness and Struggle in Andhra Pradesh in the 1980s,* Nehru Memorial Museum and Library, New Delhi.

Jananatya Mandali Patalu,(1994) Kranti Prachuranalu, Hyderabad.

Jashuva, Gurram (1996), *Gabblilam,* Jashuva Foundation, Vijayawada.

Jashuva, Gurram (1996), *Naa Katha,* Jashuva Foundation, Vijayawada.

Jayashree, Gokhale (1993), *From Concessions to Confrontation: The Politics of an Indian*

Untouchable Community, Popular Prakashan, Bombay.

Kesava Kumar, P. and Satyanarayana, K. (1995), *Dalita Manifesto,* Vispotana, University of Hyderabad, Hyderabad.

Laxmi Narasaiah, G. and Tripuraneni Srinivas (eds.) (1995), *Chikkanautunna Paata: Dalit Peotry,* Kavitwam Prachuranalu, Vijayawada.

Moorthi, A.V.K. (1977), *Social and Economic Conditions in Eastern India (From A.D. 1000 to 1250),* Kabir Printing Works, Secundrabad.

Nagesh Babu, M. (1995), *Velivaada, An Anthology of Poems,* Srija Publications, Narsarao Peta.

Omvedt, Gail (1994), *Dalits and Democratic Revolution: Dr Ambedkar and the Dalit Movement in Colonial India,* Sage Publications, New Delhi.

Padma Rao, Katti (1995), *Sanghika Viplava Rachayitulu: Dalita Sahitya Vimarsha,* Lokayata Publishers, Ponnuru.

Padma Rao, Katti (1995), *Caste and Alternative Culture,* GLTC Research Institute, Madras.

Prasad, Kalekuri, *Dalita Sahityam* (Telugu), Dalita Women Sahitya Parishad, Vijayawada.

Rao, R.S. (1995), *Towards Understanding Semi Feudal Semi Colonial Society,* Perspectives, Hyderabad.

Satyanarayana, A. (1995), 'Dalit Protest Literature in Telugu: A Historical Perspective', *Economic and Political Weekly,* 21 January.

Satyanarayana, K. (1983), *A Study of the History and Culture of the Andhra,* Vol. 2, People's Publishing House, New Delhi.

Satyanarayana, S.V. (ed.) (1995), *Jashuva Sahitee Prashanam,* Vishalandhra Publishing House, Hyderabad.

Shambhuka (1992), *Poyedeemi Lenoollam* (Anthology of Poems), Dalita Vimochana Samithi, Mangalagiri.

Shiva Sagar (1983), *Udyamam Nelabaludu* (Anthology of Poems), Srujana Prachuranalu, Hanumakonda.

Srinivasulu, K. (1994), 'BSP and Caste Politics', *Economic and Political Weekly,* 1 October.

Tarakam, Bojja (1983), *Nadiputtina Gontuka* (Jail Poems), Janapada Prachuranalu, Hyderabad.

Tarakam, Bojja (1983), 'Paleru-Kooli Raju' in Ganumala Gnaneswar (ed.), *Boyee Bheemanna Sahitee Shastiporrti Sanchika,* Hyderabad.

Tarakam, Bojja (1987), *The First All India Dalit Writers Conference: A Commemorative Volume,* Dr B.R. Ambedkar Memorial Trust, Hyderabad.

Thirumal Rao, Jayadhir and Kumma Ashok (eds.) (1993), *Dalita Geetalu* (2nd Part), Sahiti Circle, Hyderabad.

Tirumala Rao, Jayadhir (1996), A review article appeared in *Vaarta,* Telugu Daily, Hyderabad, 6 April.

Vijaya Bharathi, B. (1990), *Nalupu.* 1–30 April, Hyderabad.

NOTES

1. All these places where the Atrocities were committed against the Dalits, See, S.V. Satyanarayana, *Telugulo Dalita Sahityam.*
2. Compiled from S.V. Satyanarayana, 'Telugulo Dalita Sahityam' in *Adunika Sahityam: Dalita Spruha,* Yuva Bharati, Hyderabad; Kalekuri Prasad, op. cit. and Vijaya Bharati, op. cit.
3. For critical evaluation of Sri Sri see, Padma Rao, *Sanghika Viplava Rachayital* (1995).
4. For the full details see Daya Pawar's article 'History of Dalit Literature' in B. Tarakam *The First All India Dalit Writers Conference: A Commemorative Volume,* Dr B.R. Ambedkar Memorial Trust, Hyderabad,1987.
5. Interview with Ganumala Gnaneswar, 21 January 1997.
6. Jananatya Mandali (1994), *Jananatya Mandali Patalu,* Kranti Prachuranalu.
7. Maasterji (1995), *Dalita Geetalu,* Dalit Writers, Artists, Intellectuals United Forum, Hyderabad.
8. Padma Rao, (1995) For a critical evaluation of Vemana, see Katti Padma Rao, *Sanghika Viplava Rachayitalu: Dalita Sahitya Vimarsha,* Lokayata Publication, Ponnur,.
9. See B. Vijaya Bharathi (1990), *Nalupu.* 1–30 April.
10. See Bojja Tarakam (ed.), *The First All India Dalit Writers Conference.*
11. See Kalekuri Prasad (1993), *Dalita Sahityam* (Telugu), Dalita Women Sahitya Parishad, Vijayawada.
12. These historical antecedents for Marathi Dalit literature are different. See A. Dangle (ed.) (1996), *Poisoned Bread: Translations from Modern Marathi Dalit Literature,* Sangam Books, Bombay, 1992, pp. xi–xv; Eleanor Zelliot, *From Untouchable to Dalit: Essays on the Ambedkar Movement,* Manohar, New Delhi, pp. 267–317; Jayashree Gokhale (1993), *From Concessions to Confrontation: The Politics of an Indian Untouchable Community,* Popular Prakashan, Bombay, Chapter on Literature.

8

Economic Reforms, Impetus to Aquaculture and Implications for Land Reforms

K. Gopal Iyer

Globalization and Impetus to Aquaculture

The coastal shrimp farming registered the maximum growth of 400 per cent during the decade of 1990s. This was partly due to growing demand, stagnant catch in traditional marine and brackish water sources, and above all the growth of trade in the post-globalization period. Some of these developments have imposed heavy costs on ecology, environment, agriculture, and livelihoods of farmers and traditional fishermen. This paper is concerned with some of these adverse effects but the focus is on the land reforms with reference to relaxation of ceilings and the entry of corporate aquaculture.

In the wake of globalization and economic reforms the Government of India promoted active ventures in aquaculture, deep-sea fishing and marketing of value added products (Yadava, YS 1995, pp. 43-52). Aquaculture and particularly the growth of prawn or shrimp culture, often referred to as India's 'Blue Revolution', offered new vistas in the production and marketing of aquaculture products. The growing international demand for value added seafood items such as International Quality Federation (IQF) shrimps serve to boost growth of profits in this area. It is in this background that the Marine Products Exports Development Authority (MPEDA) played a key role in linking the buyers and the sellers for the Indian seafoods. Aquaculture was identified as one of the thrust sectors, and all assistance was given by the Government of India and by the MPEDA for its promotion at the national level.

Shrimp, however, continues to be the single dominant item in the seafood export accounting for almost two-thirds of the total export earnings. The world production of shrimp rose from 1.736 thousand metric tons in 1982 to 2.607 metric tons in 1995. (Coward Shrimp Farming – 1994. Shrimp News International, December 1984). The price of shrimp prawn also showed a spectacular increase from Rs. 2 lakh to Rs. 4.50 lakh per metric ton during 1997.

(Source MPEDA). It is revealing to note that of the total production of world shrimp farming in 1997, the western hemisphere contributed to only 30 per cent and the major proportion of 70 per cent was the share of eastern hemisphere. India, though a minor player in total seafood trade, enjoys a fairly prominent position in the world shrimp market. India accounts for 11 per cent of the share of the total world production of shrimp and commands 7 per cent of the share in quantity and value. In the 1960s, in fact, India enjoyed the first and second places in two of the world's leading markets i.e. Japan and the USA. Today it has slipped to the third and fourth positions respectively. The reasons for this are the capture of these markets by cultured shrimps from countries such as Thailand, Taiwan, China, and Ecuador.

Aquaculture in India historically has been a small-scale activity. Traditionally aquaculture has been practised in West Bengal and Kerala for many generations. The total brackish water area available in the country is estimated to be 1.2 million hectares, of which only 82,500 hectares are presently under shrimp farming. The traditional practice of paddy-cum-shrimp farming is being carried out mainly in West Bengal, Kerala, Karnataka and Goa in about 50,000 hectares. Productivity from this method of cultivation is very low and ranges from 200-500 kg per hectare against 5-10 tones per hectare possible through scientific farming. Aquaculture technology has been classified into four broad categories i.e. traditional, extensive, semi-intensive and intensive. Essentially the capital investment, stock density and feed management requirements go up as the scale moves up to higher levels of technology. Taiwan adopted intensive culture as land costs were high. Indonesia and the Philippines adopted semi-intensive and extensive technologies due to larger availability of suitable land. In the wake of globalization and new economic reforms fresh areas were brought under shrimp cultivation in Andhra Pradesh. Tamil Nadu, Kerala, Maharashtra, Orissa and West Bengal where production levels have reached the range of 1-4 tones per hectare by scientific method of farming. The market rules of aquaculture have also been fairly attractive over the years. Andhra Pradesh with its long coastline of 974 km and having vast potential to the extent of 1,50,000 ha for brackish water shrimp farming, has emerged as the leading state. It has developed 81,000 ha under shrimp farming with 44.500 metric ton production. (Alagirswami, K 1995). Over the years 39 Brackish Water Fish Farmers' Development Agencies have been promoted (ICAR 2012).

Since aquaculture and particularly shrimp culture is a highly paying proposition, the corporate sectors and private entrepreneurs went in a big way to buy paddy lands and brackish water lands from coastal areas in Andhra Pradesh and Tamil Nadu in particular during the 90s. Some of the state governments also relaxed the land ceiling laws and tenancy laws to promote aquaculture. In this context, it would be worthwhile to attract attention to GOMS No. 627 Revenue (L Ref) dated July 09, 1993 from the Department of Revenue, Andhra Pradesh Government which permitted the maximum limit of 200 hectares (500 acres) for purposes of setting up prawn/pisciculture units for exemption under Section 18(2) of the AP Land Reforms Act 1973 with a view to encourage companies for setting up prawn/pisciculture projects. Similarly, Karnataka Government also brought in the necessary changes in its land reforms and tenancy legislation by permitting the farmers to go in far aquaculture.

The following section refers to the amendments to land reforms legislation by the states of Andhra Pradesh and Karnataka for the purpose of aquaculture and other projects.

Andhra Pradesh

The Government of Andhra Pradesh by a mere executive order No. GO/MS/ No. 27 of January 11, 1994 (Revenue Department) issued orders for grant of exemption under Section 18/2 of the Andhra Pradesh Land Reforms Act 1973 for prawn/pisciculture projects. The background to the executive directive as stated in the above order stems from the fact that representations were received from corporate/individual entrepreneurs seeking exemption under Land Reforms Act for setting up of prawn/pisciculture projects. The order identifies the following benefits likely to accrue to the society at large by providing this exemption.

- Utilisation of uncultivable and barren lands for a gainful purpose
- Earning of valuable foreign exchange in hard currencies
- Supply of inputs and processing facilities to the fishermen for setting up small prawn ponds to improve their economic conditions.
- Creation of employment to local persons
- Exposure of local persons for improving their skills and abilities.
- Revenue to state and Central governments by way of taxes.

The executive order states that in the case of individual farmers who are intending to take up pisciculture/prawn culture, the ceiling limits of holdings would be the same as in the case of agricultural land and that in the case of individual companies, the maximum limit of holdings up to 200 ha (500 acres) will be allowed for purposes of setting up prawn/pisciculture units.

Amendment to Karnataka Land Reforms Act 1961

The Karnataka Legislature passed certain amendments to the Karnataka Land Reforms Act 1961 with the specific intention of giving support to the New Economic Policy of Liberalization (Karnataka Act No. 31/95 of October 28,

1995). The amendment provided for the following:

- Providing for the lease of land for aquaculture for a period not exceeding 20 years in the districts of Uttar Kannada and Dakshina Kannada.
- Providing for purchase of agricultural land by persons having income upto Rs. 2 lakh (which is upto Rs. 50,000 only at present).
- Providing exemptions from the provisions of the Act in respect of certain lands which are used for:

i. Industrial development, the extent of which shall not exceed twenty units.

ii. Educational institutions recognised by the state or central government to be used for non-agricultural purposes the extent of which shall not exceed four units.

iii. Places of worship too be specified by government by notification which are established or constructed by a recognised or registered body for non-agricultural purposes, the extent of which shall not exceed one unit.

iv. A housing project, approved by the state government the extent of which shall not exceed ten units.

v. The purpose of horticulture including floriculture and agro-based industries the extent of which shall not exceed twenty units.

Provision is also made enabling the state government to exempt any extent of land for any specific purpose in public interest and for reasons to be recorded in writing by a specific notification.

The thrust of the amendments is that:

- Aquaculture has acquired a lot of importance these days as it provides employment to a large section of poor people from communities living in the coastal areas.
- It enables the state to earn foreign exchange accrutry from the export of marine products.
- Enhancing the extent for land for exemption in the case of industrial development, educational institutions, horticulture et cetera is also essential for the implementation of economic liberalization policy.
- Housing is also included in the category as growth in some of the cities demands better housing facilities to the citizens. This is considered as one of the areas where there is ample scope for attracting foreign investment and there is the need to provide sufficient land for attracting such investment proposals in the state.

The note to the Amendment also states that some apprehensions have been expressed in certain quarters that the amendment might be struck down by a court of law in the absence of Presidential assent. In this context, they have referred to the previous government's four amendments to the land Reforms Act (vide Act No. 18 of 1990, Act No. 1 of 1991: Act No. 31 of 1991 and Act No. 9 of 1992) which were made with the assent of the government of the state which were neither objected to by the Government of India nor have the courts questioned their validity.

It may also be stated that the amendment to Section 2 of the Karnataka Land Reforms Act 1961 has treated 'aquaculture' as 'agriculture'. This fact was communicated to the various departments and financial institutions in the state (vide Directorate of Fisheries Karnataka circular No. FYP (1)/99/94-95 dated April 06, 1996 and State Government notification No. LAW/36/LGN/95 dated October 20, 1995. Though the Tamil Nadu Government has not initiated any amendment to their Land Ceiling or Tenancy Act for the purpose of aquaculture, yet they have permitted exemption to aquaculture farms under the existing land ceiling act which also violates the Supreme Court directives.

Impact of Aquaculture on Land Pollution of Drinking Water

As a sequel to the globalization policy the private companies and corporate entities converted considerable areas of agricultural land for aquaculture in Andhra Pradesh and Tamil Nadu. The adverse impact of aquaculture also known as the blue revolution came to the notice of the farmers and agricultural labourers in the Nagapattinam district of Tamil Nadu. Some of the environmentalists and NGOs in Tamil Nadu started an awareness campaign among the villagers and also analyzed the ecological and economic impact of the blue revolution. They came to the conclusion that it has actually aggravated the poverty of fishing and agricultural labour families.

Since the shrimp farms are set up near the coast to pump sea water into the farms they have a major ecological impact on the coastal zone ecosystem as well as on the coastal communities involved in fishing and in paddy cultivation. The stimulus to people's awareness and people's movement was provided by TN Gram Swaraj movement in the year 1974. They brought to fore the adverse environmental impact of the blue revolution:

1. The first impact of shrimp farming is on the destruction of land and forests in the coastal regions, when the land is bulldozed and converted for making gigantic fish farms. The saline belts of casuarina, palmyra and mangroves are cut to make pumping stations, aqueducts and fish ponds. The second impact is that the destruction of coastal vegetation destroys the buffer zones against destructive wind and water action increasing cyclone and floods vulnerability. The third impact is the salination of ground water. In the village Kurru, in Nellore district there was no drinking water available to the 600 fisherfolk due to

salination of the drinking water. After protests from the local women, drinking water supply was ensured in tankers. The fourth adverse impact of aquaculture is the destruction of agriculture. As the ground water salinity increases, paddy fields are destroyed. This has happened in a very large way in the coastal areas of AP and Tamil Nadu. The sixth adverse impact is the pollution of sea and coastal agriculture. The shrimp farms flush their effluents and wastes directly into the sea and neighbouring mangroves and agricultural lands. The release of water from the ponds affects estuarine and marine organisms and it causes water quality to deteriorate. The seventh impact is depleting the marine fish stock through breeding technology. The depletion of marine shrimp is due to the capture of juvenile shrimps from the mangroves for hatcheries. Intensive shrimp farming is thus a not sustainable form of shifting cultivation.

2. Since coastal ecosystem where shrimp farming has been introduced contains the regions which support the lives and livelihood of millions of fisherfolk and farmers, the environmental destruction caused by shrimp farming immediately transforms into social impacts. One of the immediate impacts is the displacement of fishing communities. The enclosure of the beaches for pumps and powerhouses has pushed fishing communities off their ancestral homes. They are reduced to the status of refugees of aquaculture development with no place to spread and mend their nets or park their catamarans (the traditional fishing vessels used by small scale fishermen) and there is no access to the sea from their villages. The depletion of marine fishing due to environmental impact of fish farms has destroyed their resources. The typical case in point is Kantamma of Ramachandrapur where Rank Aqua and Siraga Shrimp farms have affected the catch of fishermen. Since intensive farms are export oriented they do not supply to local markets. The second adverse social impact of the blue revolution is the pollution of drinking water and the increased work burden for women. The case in point is the village Kurru in the coastal belt of Nellore district where the companies owning shrimp farms were forced to spend Rs 500,000 a month to transport potable water to the village. Another adverse social impact is the destruction of agriculture and the declining food availability. As the shrimp farms render the fertile coastal region a salinated wasteland, there is destruction of agricultural land food production and livelihood of the rural poor. As people's resources and livelihood are destroyed, aquaculture development becomes a new source of social conflict. The coastal areas of Nagapattinam district in Tamil Nadu witnessed a massive mobilisation of agricultural labourers,

men and women during 1993–95 against the development of aquaculture as it affected their employment, caused pollution of drinking water and agricultural lands and caused increased burden to the women. Apart from such massive mobilization the TN Gram Swaraj Movement also field a writ petition in the Supreme Court to ban aquaculture.

Mounting Protests

As a result of these problems, protests are taking place in India, Bangladesh, Thailand, Malaysia and the Philippines, Problems in or due to aquaculture farms have also emerged in Taiwan. Disputes between farmers and landowners have often led to violent clashes with the death of at least two villagers to date. In India, a strong grassroots movement has developed in the eastern coastal states, where angry communities (helped by social groups like LAFTI (Land for Tillers' Freedom)) have organized to prevent the building of shrimp ponds and to protect themselves from gang violence caused by shrimp companies. In Andhra Pradesh, villagers of Kurru attacked aquaculture farms, uprooting the pumps and breaching the bunds of the ponds. The activists recently won a Supreme Court order prohibiting new aquaculture works in three states.

Impact of Aquaculture Farming in Ecologically Fragile Coastal Areas

The Hon'ble Supreme Court in its order of March 27, 1995 directed NEERI's team of technical experts to inspect the shrimp farms in the coastal areas of Andhra Pradesh (AP) and Tamil Nadu (TN) and to submit the investigation report on various farms and remedial measures, if necessary, for environmental restoration to the Hon'ble Supreme Court.

Accordingly, a thirteen-member team of scientists, led by Dr A.S. Bal and Dr S.N. Kaul constituted by Director, National Environmental Engineering Research Institute (NEERI) inspected the shrimp farms situated on the ecologically fragile coastal areas in the states of Andhra Pradesh and Tamil Nadu between 10 April and 19 April 1995. The coastal areas in the Union Territory of Pondicherry were also inspected by the Team due to their proximity to Tamil Nadu.

Observations of NEERI on the impacts of Aquaculture Farming on Ecologically Fragile Areas in States of Andhra Pradesh, Tamil Nadu and Union Territory of Pondicherry were as follows:

- Coastal aquaculture units are situated within 500 m of high tide line of the sea. This is not in consonance with the Ministry of Environment and Forests (MoEF) notification dated February 19, 1991.
- It is a common practice to convert agricultural land, and land under salt production, into coastal aquaculture units which infringes the

fundamental rights to life and livelihood.

- Conversion of agricultural farms and salt making lands into commercial aquaculture farms is rampant in the fragile coastal areas of Andhra Pradesh, Tamil Nadu and Union Territory of Pondicherry.
- Brackish aquaculture units have been installed in deltaic regions which is an ecologically unsound practice.
- Natural saline canals which travel from sea to the mainland are being used for brackish aquaculture farming. The flow of the natural saline canals is being obstructed due to prawn farming activity which has resulted in the spread of brackish waster over agricultural farms resulting in loss of agricultural lands, and potable water.
- Villages situated along the sea coast, deltaic regions, and natural saline canals are under threat due to diversion of land to aquaculture farms.
- Traditional fishermen have lost their landing grounds for their fish catch.
- Coastal aquaculture has resulted in the loss of mangrove ecosystems which provide protection against cyclones and other natural hazards, and which provide natural habitats for spawning of marine biota. Indiscriminate destruction of mangrove areas in and around the creeks, estuaries, and sea has resulted in loss of natural breeding grounds for shrimps.
- Natural Casuarina plantations have also been destroyed. This may result in increasing damage from cyclones, and cause intrusion of saline water into the mainland.
- Employment avenues of the contiguous population have got considerably reduced due to the commercial aquaculture farming. The unemployed villagers are seeking employment in nearby towns and cities.
- Owners of the commercial aquaculture farms are using various means to encroach upon the government lands and are also forcing the agricultural land owners/salt making villagers to sell their lands. In addition, the fishermen are also being forced to migrate to other coastal areas.

Extracts of Supreme Court Judgement in W.P. No. 561/94 filed by Shri S. Jagnannathan

- The farmers who are operating traditional and improved traditional systems of aquaculture may adopt improved technology for increased production, productivity and returns with prior approval of the 'authority' constituted by the order.
- The agricultural lands, salt pan lands, mangrove wet lands, forest lands,

lands for village common purposes, and the lands, mangrove wet lands, forest lands, elands for village common purpose, and the lands meant for the public purposes shall not be used/converted for construction of shrimp culture ponds.

- Aquaculture industry/shrimp culture industry/shrimp culture ponds other than traditional and improved traditional may be set up/ constructed outside the coastal regulations/zones as defind on the Coastal Regulation Zone (CRZ) notification.

Objectives of the Study

In spite of the Supreme Court judgment, there is continuation of aquaculture in violation of the judgment, which is the source of loss of farming land and livelihood to farmers and agricultural labourers, besides the ecological damage to fragile coastal areas. In view of the above, the present study focuses on the following issues:

- The extent to which agricultural land and other types of lands prohibited by Supreme Court order were continuing under prawn culture in Andhra Pradesh and Tamil Nadu.
- The extent of poramboke brackish water lands converted to aquaculture and also encroached by prawn farmers.
- The extent of poramboke brackish water lands distributed to fishermen, technocrats and entrepreneurs and the rationale of land lease policy.
- The present status of aquaculture industry with specific reference to land and environmental issues.

In order to examine the above objectives empirical studies were conducted in the coastal villages of East Coast comprising the states of Andhra Pradesh and Tamil Nadu. This was in particular oriented to examine the implementation of the Supreme Court directives.

Area under Aquaculture

The figures furnished by MPEDA suggest that during 1998-99, area under shrimp farming under brackish waster aquaculture was 1,41,591 hectares of which the maximum area was in Andhra Pradesh (44,500 hectares) followed by West Bengal (18,032 hectares). Kerala (7.682 hectares). Karnataka (2,650 hectares), Tamil Nadu 1,821 hectares et cetera. The length of the coastline in Andhra Pradesh is 974 KMs. As per the report of the Department of Fisheries, Government of Andhra Pradesh, the area brought under shrimp farming in the state is around 81,000 hectares out of the 1.50 lac hectares of coastal area identified as suitable for brackish water aquaculture. Over 95 per cent of the aquaculturists are marginal and small farmers operating nearly three-fourths of the total land under shrimp farming culture. Semi-medium and medium farmers constitute only 3.16 per cent and control only 7.32 per cent of the total operated area. The big farmers (above 5 hectares) constitute 2.28 per cent of the total prawn farmers and control 18.39 per cent of the total operated area. Some of the corporate sector prawn farmers are located in the district of Nellore.

Tamil Nadu also has a long seacoast. The data on the area under prawn farms in respect of Nagapattinam district furnished by the Fisheries department, indicates that out of 488 prawn farmers in this district, the majority are small farmers (438), followed by medium farmers (42); only eight are big farmers. Out of the total extent of 3,230 hectares of land operated by them. 1,256 hectares are operated by small farmers, 958 hectares are operated by medium farmers and 1,017 hectares are operated by big farmers. In Karnataka, prawn farms are spread in the two coastal district of Uttara Kannada and Dakshina Kannada. The brackish water area in the district of Uttara Kannada is 3,868 hectares and in Dakshina Kannada it is 273.25 hectares.

Conversions of Agricultural Lands and Encroachment of Government Lands

Agricultural Lands Converted into Aquaculture

The report of NEERI observed that in the Nellore district in Andhra Pradesh and in the Nagapattinam district of Tamil Nadu paddy lands were converted into prawn farms which polluted agricultural lands. The Supreme Court decision clearly forbids the conversion of agricultural lands into prawn farms. In different coastal districts of Andhra Pradesh 31,082 hectares of agricultural lands and 2,838 hectares of mangrove lands have been converted into prawn farms. This shows that 42.27 per cent of the total land under aquaculture is converted from agricultural land (38.74%) and mangroves (3.53%). (Annual Administrative Report for the year 1977-78; Directorate of Fisheries, Government of Andhra Pradesh, Hyderabad). As per the information furnished by the Revenue Divisional Officer, Bandan (letter No. ReK. 1126/99 of July 9,1999) in Bandan Mandal of Krishna district an extent of 31,447 acres of *patta* lands have been converted for prawn culture.

The District Pollution Control Board Officer, Nellore has mentioned that a lot of farmers are still converting agricultural lands into aquaculture ponds in several mandals (e.g. Muthukur, Manubolu, Indukurpet, et cetera) even after the Supreme Court judgment, has imposed restrictions on conversion of agricultural lands into aquaculture ponds. He has also stated that most of the neighbouring farmers are complaining about the adverse impact on their agriculture productivity due to salinisation of the soil and contamination of irrigation water sources.

It would be also useful to have an idea of the extent of *poramboke* brackish water lands converted into aquaculture. Nearly 25,188 acres of *poramboke* brackish water land is encroached by prawn farmers. Out of the total extent of land encroached, the major area is from Krishna district (84.37%) alone. In the district of Nellore an extent of 769.88 acres of *poramboke* lands are encroached by prawn farms. Another 1,661 acres of government *poramboke* brackish water lands are converted for aquaculture. The agricultural lands, mangrove lands and *poramboke* lands comprise approximately 54 per cent of the total land under aquaculture in the state. If we include forest land, salt land, et cetera it would consist of over 60 per cent of total land under aquaculture. As per the Supreme Court Order these lands should not be allowed to function as prawn farms. This comes within the ambit of the policy decisions of the state and Central Government.

Adverse Social Effect of Aquaculture

The villagers made the following complaints:

- The fish pond surrounding the houses of Scheduled Caste and Scheduled Tribe people of Edulavaripalem and their drinking water wills have been polluted.
- Paddy fields were adversely affected by the drainage water of prawn culture particularly in the fields of some ryots of Amudalapadu village.

In village Kurru Pattapupalem, the ground water used for drinking purposes was severely polluted due to the operation of several corporate prawn farms. At present, daily, two tankers of drinking water are being transported to meet the requirement of fresh drinking water of the villagers. Even habitation is severely affected nessitating relocation of the villagers. For this purpose, the government has acquired 12.91 acres of private land to shift the entire village and have rehabilitated 250 fishermen in the acquired land.

Complaints from Villagers of Vavilla against Formation of Ponds of Prawn Culture

The farmers of Vavilla village consisting of Nellore Gopal Reddy and 29 others complained against formation of ponds for prawn culture by B. Venugopal Reddy and others. The major complaint was that the ponds of prawn culture were damaging their paddy crops which were located adjacent to these ponds. This was investigated by the district revenue officer, environmental engineer, and assistant director (fisheries) who opined that there who the need to control the damage to paddy crops. Assistant Director (Agriculture) Kovur opined that the cultivation of fish/prawn culture in the midst of fertile land would cause irreparable loss to the paddy growers, besides contaminating drinking water.

The environmental engineer Andhra Pradesh Pollution Control Board has observed that no environmental protection measures like sedimentation tankers and biological treatment had been undertaken which was posing problems to the nearby environment.

The Assistant Director (Fisheries) pointed out that after provision of trenches around the ponds, the entire seepage water released from the pond would go through the trench to the main drainage canal. No percolation of oozing of water from the ponds would therefore affect the adjacent paddy land.

In the village Krishnapuram, the drinking water supply through the PWS scheme has been polluted. The population of this village is 822. The cost involved in the supply of their drinking water is Rs. one lakh. Similarly, in village Kudithipalem, the scheme supplying drinking water source has been affected due to saline water from prawn farms. It has affected 2,613 persons in the village and the cost involved for having fresh supply of drinking water will be Rs. 2 lakh.

In village Pottempadu alone it is estimated that supply of alternative drinking water will cost Rs. 7.50 lakh. Similarly, in respect of other villages also the supply of alternative drinking water supply would cost heavy amounts. Apart from this the villages in the Mandals of Repalle and Nizampatnam are also facing drinking water problem due to prawn farming.

Brackish water *Poramboke* Lands Distributed to Different Categories of People

The Government of Andhra Pradesh leased out brackish water lands to various categories of beneficiaries during phase 1 (vide G.O.Ms No. 233 dated June 7, 1987) and Phase-II vide notification No. 487/P2/94 dated July 13, 1994). The total extent allotted during Phase-I was 1,880.89 hectares and 2,845.93 hectares during Phase-III.

For the purpose of processing the applications, the state governments of Andhra Pradesh, Tamil Nadu and Karnataka have constituted state level committees under the chairmanship of secretaries of fisheries departments. Besides this, district-level committees under the chairmanship of district collectors with representatives drawn from the specialized fields such as fisheries, agriculture, revenue, environment, country/town planning, irrigation, ground water, state pollution control board and MPEDA have also been constituted. The constitution of an Aquaculture Authority by the Government of India is a landmark event in the history of aquaculture in the country. According to the existing procedures, even the traditional farmers who are willing to adopt the improved technology can also apply for license even if their farms are located within CRZ area; those farms located outside the CRZ and the new farms that are likely to come up have to obtain the license from the Aquaculture

Authority.

There are however, two paradoxes to the situation:

- In Andhra Pradesh only 3.70 per cent of total prawn farms operating 7.99 per cent of the total operational area of 6,290.18 ha are located outside CRZ jurisdiction and the remaining 72,412 ha are located within CRZ. This would prohibit nearly 92 per cent of the total area under prawn farms from functioning. Similar is the situation in Tamil Nadu and Karnataka as well.
- Further, out of the total 73,340 prawn farms in Andhra Pradesh only 1,903 farms have filed applications for permission of Aquaculture Authority and among them only 111 have been approved by the 'Authority'. The situation in Tamil Nadu and Karnataka is still worse.

Apart from this, the Shrimp culture activity was badly affected in 1994 due to the outbreak of a disease. The shrimp farmers in Andhra Pradesh, Tamil Nadu and Karnataka who ventured with high investment on land cost, lease, inputs, et cetera faced a near calamity because of the outbreak of the disease. Many of the farmers could not at all recover from their financial loss. In fact, many of the corporate entities and private firms who opened big aquaculture farms by converting the fertile agricultural lands to prawn farms have stopped shrimp culture. As a result, these lands which have been badly polluted and degraded are lying idle and also cannot be utilised for agriculture any more. They have done the greatest harm not only to agricultural lands but it has also affected the employment potential of fishermen and agricultural labourers who were dependant on these lands for their livelihood. The extent of damage caused to the prawn industry due to the disease in Andhra Pradesh alone is of a staggering nature. The extent of area affected and the extent of crop loss can be discerned from the following figures.

Shrimp Loss in Andhra Pradesh Due to Disease from 1994-95 to 1998-99

Sl. No.	*Year*	*Area (ha)*	*Production Loss (In Metric Tons)*
1	1995-96	15.954	4,271
2	1996-97	9,490	3,318
3	1997-98	40,483	9,388
4	1998-99	28,982	15,673

The same situation was also faced by the farmers in Tamil Nadu and Karnataka. Currently there is the expectation that constitution of Aquaculture Authority and certain precautionary measures initiated by the state governments would be effective in promoting sustainable aquaculture; It is not wholly borne out by the field situation.

Implications of Aquaculture for Land Reforms

The sustainability of aquaculture has become a major casualty due to the crop loss and the environmental problems. It poses the following major related issues:

- As per the Supreme Court direction, the agricultural lands and the government brackish water lands which have been converted into prawn farms should immediately be banned from continuing shrimp culture.
- Government brackish water lands have been encroached by rich prawn farmers to a great extent which should immediately be retrieved from them along with adequate compensation for degrading such lands.
- The land lease policy of the brackish water government lands initiated and implemented by the Andhra Pradesh and Karnataka government in particular need to be critically reviewed so that rich farmer entrepreneurs and other ineligible categories are excluded from such benefits.
- Amendments to the existing land reforms legislations made by the governments of Andhra Pradesh and Karnataka with respect to aquaculture and other allied activities should be immediately cancelled.
- An effective aquaculture sustainable policy with special provisions for protecting the interests of weaker sections should be formulated.

On the basis of the analysis of the limited data the report has tried to highlight the following points:

- The damage caused to the agricultural lands and other adverse social and environmental impacts were clearly broughtout by the Sarvodaya Organization and Environmental Groups in Tamil Nadu through their struggle and agitation. The adverse effects of aquaculture on the sea-coast of Nagapattinam district were highlighted through this agitation and supported by scientific facts were:
  - Fertile paddy lands and other agricultural lands are being converted into prawn farms.
  - It is damaging and degrading the fertile agricultural lands.
  - The government brackish water lands are being encroached by the corporate entities and the private companies.
  - It is rendering the landless labourers both men and women unemployed.
  - It is polluting the sweet drinking water in the coastal areas.
  - It is displacing the fishermen from their habitat and is also creating obstacles to their access to the sea coasts for fishing and other

activities related to their livelihood.

- In spite of the ongoing agitation, the corporate entities and private companies have continued to extend their aquaculture activities in the state. The state government also suppressed the agitation and arrested the protestors. As a consequence of this, the Sarvodaya organisation filed a writ petition in the Supreme Court of India pointing out the damages done to the weaker sections due to opening of aquaculture and requesting for banning the prawn farms.
- The Supreme Court in its interim decision gave the following directions:
  - The agricultural lands, salt pan lands, mangrove wet lands, forest lands, lands for village common purpose and the lands meant for different purposes should not be used/converted for construction of shrimp culture ponds.
  - An aquaculture authority may be set up to a regulate the implementation of the CRZ notification and to provide licenses to the aquaculture farms for running aquacultural farms.

The study has amply demonstrated that the aquaculture industry has damaged considerable areas of agricultural lands particularly in the coastal areas of Andhra Pradesh and Tamil Nadu as also in Karnataka. It needs to be particularly mentioned that a report was submitted by a House Committee to Andhra Pradesh legislature pointing out the severe damage done to the fertile paddy lands and the *poramboke* brackish water lands in Andhra Pradesh sea coast. The empirical study also gathered considerable facts in the coastal areas of Andhra Pradesh and Tamil Nadu which provides evidence of the severe damage done to agricultural lands. The pollution of drinking water, the adverse effects on employment of agricultural labourers and fishermen and also their social health and welfare are the other consequences. Over and above these, it has been found that the viral diseases have very adversely affected the industry since 1995 onwards. A large number of prawn farms as a result have been closed down rendering the lands converted into prawn farms as completely degraded. Even the formation of an Aquaculture Authority has not made any headway as less than two per cent of the prawn farmers have applied for licences.

Conversion of Agricultural Land for Prawn Culture in Andhra Pradesh (Observation of the House Committee Andhra Pradesh)

The Legislative Assembly of Andhra Pradesh constituted a House Committee on the conversion of land for prawn culture. The following are its observations:

- The committee observed that lands meant for aquaculture have been converted for prawn culture. Ground water has been drawn unauthorisedly and agricultural lands have been converted into prawn farms. The committee has welcomed the Supreme Court's interim order that the agricultural lands should not be converted into prawn farms and ground water should not be tapped for aquaculture.

- In the Bandar seashore, water is being pumped out through bore wells within 10 km of the sea shore by the farmers. The agricultural lands are being converted into prawn farms to earn more profits.
- The committee observed that forest lands are converted into prawn farms. The farmers are put to inconvenience by the forest officials. The committee directed the officials to take suitable measures to avoid inconvenience caused to the poor farmers who are cultivating prawns in the forest lands.
- The committee observed that most of the farmers have converted the agricultural lands into prawn farms in the coastal areas for earning huge profits. The committee also found that rich prawn farmers in several villagers visited by them had encroached 2074 ha of Government brackish water land, the maximum of which was in Krishna District (1764 ha).
- The committee also found that 4065.60 acres of agricultural lands in the various villages had been converted to prawn farms.

In view of the strong evidence of adverse affects of aquaculture, the study comes out with the following recommendations and suggestions in the context of the interface between economic reforms, aquaculture and land reforms:

- In view of the Supreme Court order, the agricultural lands which have been converted for aquaculture in the coastal belts of Andhra Pradesh, Tamil Nadu and Karnataka should be banned from continuing aquaculture.
- In spite of the Supreme Court order, still agricultural lands are being converted into aquaculture farms. Such conversions should also be stopped immediately.
- The state government of Karnataka and Andhra Pradesh in particular have come out with clear-cut leasing out policy of *poramboke* brackish water lands to prawn farmers, entrepreneurs and others. These lease orders also need to be cancelled in view of the Supreme Court decisions.
- A lot of *poramboke* brackish water lands have been forcibly encroached by the prawn farmers of coastal areas of Andhra Pradesh and Tamil Nadu. Some of the corporate entities and private companies have also filed writ petitions in the High Courts to obtain stay orders. All such encroachments should be immediately removed. Besides this, the prawn

farmers should be made to pay the price of such lands including the payment for permanent damage caused to such lands.

- The amendments to the Land Ceiling Act made through the executive order by Andhra Pradesh Government should immediately be made inoperative.
- The amendment of Karnataka land reforms legislation permitting both land ceiling limits and leasing out of lands for purposes of aquaculture should also be withdrawn and cancelled.

REFERENCES

Alagarswami (1981), 'Prospects for Coastal Aquaculture in India', CMFRI, Bulletin 30.

Hein, L. (2000), 'Impact of Shrimp Farming on Mangroves along India's East Coast' (FAO Corporate Document Depository).

National Environment Engineering Research Institute, Nagpur (1996), 'Impact of Aquaculture Farming and Remedial Measures in Ecologically Fragile Coastal Areas in the States of Andhra Pradesh and Tamil Nadu.'

Salim, Shyam S. and Ojha, S.N. (2002), 'Environmental and Social Issues in Coastal Aquaculture', Central Institute of Fisheries Education, ICAR, Versova, Mumbai.

Yadava, Y.S. (ed.) (1995), 'Fisheries of Floodplain Lakes: A Management Perspective', Proceedings of Conservation and Sustainable use of Flood Plains Wetland Bureau, Kuala Lampur.

PART 2

Marginalization and Alienation of the Tribals

9

Culture, Economy, and Power: Roots of Disparities between Adivasis and Others

K.B. Saxena

Social disparities characterize all human societies. In the widest sense, they relate to the diversity in personal characteristics of human beings as well as the situation (external circumstances) in which they are placed. They feature in different arenas (spaces) which can be measured through a variety of indicators—quantifiable and non-quantifiable. The methodologically assessable indicators are those whose incidence can be statistically captured such as income, wealth, access to primary goods, and utilities, which are relied upon by economists to map out inequalities. Sen has expanded this domain to the freedom to achieve and the capability to function (Sen, 1995). The sociologists and social anthropologists go beyond the statistically measurable criteria of inequalities, termed as the 'domain of fact', to non-measurable parameters belonging to the 'domain of values and norms'. The domain of fact constitutes the general/universal mode of measurement while the universe of values define the culturally specific patterns of inequality. The distribution of income, wealth, and amenities belongs to the former category (Beteille, 1969). In Weberian terms, status belongs to the realm of values which indicates how the two social groups relate to each other in the social structure. These relationships also have a bearing on the pattern of distributional development.

No other subject in the contemporary policy discourse has attracted so much attention as the existence and growing incidence of disparities among various sections of society. The incidence of disparities exercises the minds of planners who are keen to ensure that their vision of economic growth and progress is not derailed by such distortions. It is a subject that readily becomes a rallying point for political mobilizers to challenge the ethical foundations of government policies. It has the potential to become a flashpoint for violent outbursts in order to reduce them. Disparities also evoke partisan views—defended by those who stand to gain from them and fiercely opposed by those who are at the losing end—both using different sets of arguments in favour of their stands. The former justify them as a natural outcome of differential talent and merit among individuals (and groups) and as a necessary incentive for its fruition, while the latter dismiss this 'natural advantage' as a socially conditioned phenomenon produced by favourable living conditions and access to opportunities.

Disparities exist not merely between geographical regions, economies, and political systems but also within them. At a social level, disparities can be observed between people engaged in different occupations, the privileged small sections, and the large deprived sections of a society, social groups, and sections within them. The group level disparities arise from multiple factors—historical, sociological, geographical, cultural, religious, and ethnic. In the Indian context, the social groups most affected by disparities are the Dalits (intra-cultural minority) Adivasis (cultural minority) and Muslims (religious minority). Of these, the Adivasis emerge as the most vulnerable of the three. They are inheritors of a cultural tradition with a virtually different 'civilizational' perspective not shared by other social groups in the country. In their case, the geographical factors intersect with the social to reinforce their exclusion. The unique feature characterizing disparities in their case is its persistence, despite provision of comprehensive social protection available to them and the historical legacy of resistance against structures of their subjugation, exploitation, and assault on their social and cultural ethos. The extensive spread of the Naxalite movement in the areas of their concentration in Central India, challenging the legitimacy of the existing political economy and social hegemony, should be seen as a progression of the same tradition. This is so, not merely in the context of a situation existing in India, but also as a phenomenon across the counties which have Tribal/'indigenous' population because there is an underlying pattern of marginalization associated with them everywhere. (Eversole et al, 2005). Therefore, this paper has chosen to explore different dimensions of disparities affecting them and the structures of society, economy, and polity in which they are embedded.

The Adivasis account for 8.5 per cent of the country's population. They are spread over several states and union territories (UTs) except Punjab, Haryana, Delhi (leaving aside the migrant population), and UTs of Pondicherry and Chandigarh. They have traditionally lived in about 15 per cent of the geographical area which is characterized by hilly and forested topography, undulating terrain, and rich natural resources. Consisting of a large mosaic of small ethnic communities, they have remained relatively isolated for centuries from the 'mainstream' society, which has helped sustain their social organization, pattern of economy, and cultural values that are different from the rest of the population. It is precisely this isolation and distinctness which disadvantages them in their interface with the larger society and its economy. It overwhelmingly constrains 'their ability to negotiate a relationship of dignity and equality with them', and 'to cope with the adverse externalities of this 'involuntary' integration' (MTA, 2006). Despite being distributed among 700 groups, each with its separate language (dialect), customs, cultural practices, and pattern of living, 'this immense diversity is enveloped by generic similarities in the community orientation of their resource management, social relationship and lifestyle practices in harmony with nature, distinctive cultural practices, value system characterized by non-acquisitiveness, transparent and truthful interpersonal dealings lacking in complexity, abiding faith in their customary mechanism to regulate life, resolve conflicts, and cope with crisis, and a disinclination to seek outside intervention in their struggle to lead a dignified existence' (Prabhu, 2006). They have, therefore, their own norms of measurement of 'happiness', 'poverty', 'distress', and 'prosperity' which are not on par with those evolved by the 'mainstream' society. But this civilizational ethos received a rude shock from policies and practices during the colonial period, which have continued after Independence, bringing them into ever increasing, forced, and rapid contact with the outside world and the market economy. This has disrupted every aspect of their tradition, unleashed a situation over which they have little control, and produced cataclysmic changes in their lives. The disadvantages they suffer from and the disabilities resulting from these developments are rooted in this experience.

Dimensions of Disparities

The dimensions of disparities affecting Adivasis cover a large spectrum of their social existence. The measurement of disparities is never an easy task because its tools are wrapped in a great deal of contestation on whether they can meaningfully capture the differences among individuals and communities. This is because disparities are multidimensional and the factors that generate them are interently interlinked and reinforce each other (Radhakrishna and Ray, 2005). This is particularly so in the case of Adivasis. The controversy will, however, be skirted here. But to facilitate comprehensive conceptualization, it would be relevant to identify, separately, the measurable disparities in terms of facts and the non-measurable ones in terms of values embedded in culture. The two, however, are not rigidly compartmentalized as the non-measurable disparities affect the measurable ones. The investigation shall begin by first capturing measurable disparities through widely used indicators in human and social development literature—national and international—for which relatively reliable data is available. These indicators include economic parameters such as income, consumption, employment, satisfaction of elementary wants like food and clothing, and social ones, such as access to health facilities, education, utilities like drinking water, sanitation, housing, and electricity, reflecting the quality of life enjoyed. This discussion would be followed by a peep into the non-material realm of values which would be located in the dichotomy of two cultural systems providing divergent civilizational perspectives.

Economic Disparities

The economic disparities reflected in levels of income and wealth are widely accepted as significant denominators of inequality. In the country, this is readily measured in terms of the extent of poverty in various social groups. As per official data itself, poverty is disproportionately high among the Adivasis. The proportion of population below poverty line in the case of Adivasis was as high as 47.2 per cent as against 16.1 per cent in the other segments of population in 2004–05 and the headcount ratio of poverty in the Adivasis is higher even in comparison with the Dalits which was 36.8 per cent. The disparity in the ratio of poverty exists both in rural and urban areas. The proportionate reduction over the years in poverty is also slower among them. (Planning Commission 2007). The percentage decline of poverty between 1993-94 and 2004-05 is the lowest in Adivasis at 4.7 per cent as against 9 per cent in other groups and 12 per cent in the case of Dalits. This facet of deprivation is reflected in the per capita consumption expenditure. The Monthly Per Capita Expenditure (MPCE) of Adivasis is Rs 387.69 in rural areas as against Rs 418.51 for Dalits, Rs 437.65 for OBCs and Rs 577.22 for others while in urban areas, it is Rs 690.52 for Adivasis as against Rs 608.79 for Dalits Rs 734.82 for OBCs and Rs 1004.75 for others. They are worse off in this regard than the Dalits and OBCs. (Rath, 2006). The gap in poverty ratio between Adivasis and others has grown over the years. There is also spatial variation of poverty among the Adivasis across states, extremely high (>50 per cent) in Orissa, Jharkhand, Himachal Pradesh, Chhattisgarh, and low (<20 per cent) in north eastern states. This dissimilarity reflects the relative command over productive resources in the concerned states which is influenced by non-economic factors (Radhakrishna and Ray, 2005). Amongst the Adivasis, the forest-based primitive Tribal groups—hunters and food gatherers—are worse off due to declining access to forest resources, which are their main source for subsistence. Furthermore, they desist from taking to sedentary occupations in the labour market on account of cultural constraints.

The labour force participation of Adivasis, at 50.49 per cent, is the highest (2004–05), higher than the Dalits (43.75) and others (43.21). This is largely due to their poor economic conditions, multiple deprivations and essentially rural habitation. This figure, however, does not bring out the widespread underemployment and their status as workers. The latter is conveyed by the nature of work available to them. They are overwhelmingly (78.56 per cent) engaged in agriculture as against (59.61 per cent) in the case of Dalits and

(45.76 per cent) in the case of others. As against this, those belonging to the other communities have higher participation rates in sectors with better income and conditions of work. This disparity is conditioned by the social status of the Tribal communities National Commission for Enterprises in the Unorganized Sector 2009 (NCEUS, 2009). As the contribution of agriculture in the GDP is declining, this has a negative impact on income, wages, and level of work. As per the 2001 Census, cultivation is the main occupation of 44.7 per cent of the Adivasis as against 31.65 per cent overall, while 36.7 per cent of them earn their living as agricultural labourers. This percentage is 26.55 in respect of the country. In the non-farm segment, the status is illustrated by the strength of their participation and its sectoral composition. The percentage of employment is meagre, and that too, rests in the lowest category and is informal in character—5.76 per cent in construction, 4.8 per cent in manufacturing, 2.8 per cent in trade, and 1.88 per cent in transport and communication. The corresponding data, in respect of the Dalits, is 8.86 per cent, 10.68 per cent, 5.89 per cent, and 4.07 per cent. The figures in respect of 'others' are 3.32 per cent, 12.31 per cent, 14.20 per cent, and 4.86 per cent (NCEUS, 2009).

As regards access to productive resources, as per National Sample Survey Organization (NSSO), 35.5 per cent of Adivasi households were without access to land for cultivation in 2003 as against 37.8 per cent non Dalits/and Adivasis and 56.5 in the case of Dalits. The Adivasis started with the initial advantage of a higher population with landownership. But an unprecedented increase in landlessness has set in due to displacement by development projects and alienation from their land by the non-Tribals adopting diverse methods. This increase was 11.6% among Adivasis compared to 10.8% among others and 8.7% among Dalits in 2004–05 (Bakshi, 2015). In the states that have a high concentration of the Adivasis, their landholding is also lower in comparison to other communities (Radhakrishna and Ray, 2005). In fact, the percentage of large landholdings among them has came down from 4.8 per cent in 1994 to 3 per cent in 2000 (Rath, 2006). In respect of the quality of productive assets, Adivasi landholdings are characterized by an unusual distinction between the owned land and cultivated land signifying that the land owned but not used for cultivations is barren and rocky, and therefore, unfit for productive use. In fact, the Adivasi landholdings, by and large, are of low quality with poor productive capacity, largely concentrated in dry agriculture region. Only 26 per cent of their owned land is irrigated in comparison to 53 per cent in respect of the other communities (Radhakrishna and Ray, 2005). In the case of Adivasis, generally, monocropping with low productivity and least level of inputs complicated by exposure to frequent droughts define the agricultural profile. Food insecurity among them is, therefore, most widespread and acute.

Nearly 71.61 per cent of the Adivasis face food insufficiency for two to three months and five per cent for six months or above in a year (Radhakrishna and Ray, 2005). The percentage of Adivasi households facing acute food deficit for some months or the other in a year, as per NSSO 55th round, is three per cent which is an underestimate. Even so, this percentage is higher compared to other social segments. The incidence of starvation deaths is most frequently reported from Adivasi areas.

Disparities in Human Development

Besides low income and inadequate consumption, the disparities affecting Adivasis are reflected in the levels of education, health, nutrition, access to utilities, and skill development.

Literacy

The overall literacy attainment (2001) at 47.10 per cent amongst the Adivasis is also lower in comparison to the all India figure of 64.80 per cent though an improvement over 1991 estimates according to the Ministry of Tribal Affairs (MTA, 2008–09). The female literacy rate (2001) at 34.76 per cent is also lower than the all India level of 53.70 per cent. The male literacy level among them is 59.17 per cent which also reflects the huge gap when compared to the overall male literacy rate of 75.30 per cent. The male-female gap in literacy at 24.41 per cent is higher than 21.59 per cent in the case of total population (MTA, 2008–09). The attendance in schools (2001) of children 5–14 years was 61 per cent which is lower when compared to 81 per cent in respect of the others including Dalits (68 per cent) and Other Backward Classes (OBCs) (72 per cent) (Radhakrishna and Ray, 2005). Nearly two-fifths of the Adivasi children do not go to school. While the gross enrolment ratio at the primary level is slightly higher, in the case of Adivasis in comparison to the other groups, this is neutralized by dropout rates which continued to be higher (51.4 per cent) in their case than in other groups (34.9 per cent). The enrolment levels in class V–VIII (upper primary) and in secondary/senior secondary classes are also lower than those of the general population. The dropout rates in both these segments are much higher in their case than in the rest of the population. The higher dropout rates result in disproportionately low representation in higher education. The incidence of child labour (7 per cent) is also larger in comparison to the other groups including the Dalits. This is due to the engagement of Adivasi children as full-time agricultural labourers or migrant labourers, along with their family (Radhakrishna and Ray, 2005).

Health

Health indices also bring out large gaps in their status in comparison to the other communities. The sex ratio among Adivasis (2001) at 977 females per 1000 males is no doubt higher than the all-India level of 933/1000, though it has been declining. The child sex ratio in 0–6 age group of 972 girls for 1000 boys (2001) was also better than 919 for 1000 in respect of the general population but dropped from the level of 985 for 1000 prevailing in 1991. With infant mortality at 84.2 per 1000, and under-five mortality at 126.6 per 1000 and percentage of underweight children at 55.9, the health indicators were far more adverse than not only those of the general population, but also of the Dalits and the other disadvantaged sections (MTA, 2006). The same is true of neo-natal mortality at 53.3/1000 and post-natal mortality at 30.9/1000. The Adivasis also suffer from higher morbidity and receive lower level of immunization. The level of undernutrition at 56 per cent in the Adivasis is also higher compared to 42 per cent in the general population and 53 per cent in the case of Dalits. The percentage of anaemic women at 64.9 per cent is the highest among the Adivasis and way above the level of 40–50 per cent in the case of other social segments. An estimated 46.3 per cent of Adivasi women suffer from body mass <18.5 kg/m and 13.5 per cent have height <145 cm. These parameters influence the outcomes of pregnancies and percentage of children that are born with long term health consequences. Even in the short term, this is reflected in 61 per cent share of malnutrition for under five children amongst the Adivasis. Around 53 per cent of adult Tribals suffer from chronic energy deficiency. The Adivasi areas also account for the highest percentage of malarial deaths where the disease is endemic. The Total Fertility Rate (TFR), Crude Death Rate (CDR) are also higher (Mishra, et al, 2003). In terms of deficiency of health facilities and quality of care, the areas inhabited by the Adivasis are the most neglected due to their geographical isolation, nature of terrain, poor infrastructure, and the reluctance of service providers to be posted there.

The study carried out by Institute of Human Development using a composite representation of economic, health, and educational status has placed the Adivasis in low human development category while all India status has been classified as medium human development. It concluded that the human development indices and human poverty indices of the Adivasis are 30 per cent lower than the corresponding all-India indices. In terms of the Planning Commission's inflation adjusted per capita expenditure, the gap works out to 36 per cent. This level of human development is similar to the conditions in poorer countries of sub-Saharan Africa (Sarkar et al, 2006).

Drinking Water

The situation with respect to the availability of drinking water for the Adivasis is most acute. Only 15.2 per cent of Adivasi households have such a facility in their premises against 45.2 per cent among the general population. The disparity becomes most acute as 28.2 per cent of Adivasi households have drinking water sources away from their premises, while this percentage is only 14 per cent for the general population and 19.5 per cent for the Dalits. As regards sources of drinking water, 40.1 per cent of households in the general population enjoy the privilege of having piped drinking water, while only 20 per cent of the Adivasi households do so. Even the Dalits are better off in this respect with 32.2 per cent of such households benefiting from this facility. In terms of the percentage of villages having an improved drinking water source, the highest percentage of villages (23.5 per cent) where there is zero per cent improvement are inhabited by the Adivasis, while this figure is only six per cent in the case of others and 4.5 per cent in the case of Dalits. A similar disparity exists where the villages have less than 50 per cent improved drinking water source or more than or equal to 50 per cent of such sources (Planning Commission-2005).

Sanitation

The position in respect of sanitation is even more dismal. Only 17 per cent of the Adivasi households have latrine facilities compared to 42.3 per cent of general households (non SCs/STs) and 23.7 per cent of the Dalit households. In 16 states of the country, the Adivasi households have latrine facilities below the national average of 36.4 per cent. Of the 543 districts, where percentage of households having access to latrines is 15 or below, the gap between general the population and those of Dalits and Adivasis is very very wide, that is, more than 1:4. Similarly, the percentage of households with connectivity for waste water outlet is only 21.8 for the Adivasis as against 50.6 for the general households and 42.9 for the Dalits (Planning Commission, 2005). The situation may have improved slightly with the total sanitation campaign of the Ministry of Rural Development, which has pushed the cumulative coverage of percentage of rural households having access to latrines to 61 per cent as against 21.9 per cent recorded in the 2001 Census. (MOF, 2010). But the disparity continues to be large.

Housing

While 57.7 per cent of the general population and 42.8 of the Dalits have permanent houses, this percentage is only 24.4 in the case of Adivasis. The number of districts where only 15 per cent or below Adivasi households have permanent houses is 138 (highest) as against 32 of the general population which have this level of housing. The districts where 65 per cent or above of the Adivasi households have permanent houses is 71 (lowest) as against 192 districts where the general population has this level of facility (Planning Commission, 2005).

Electricity

The percentage of households belonging to the general category having access to electricity is 61.4, whereas this percentage is 36.5 in the case of the Adivasis and 44.3 in the case of Dalits. The Adivasi villages that have no electricity is a whopping 47.8 per cent while this percentage is only 19 in the case of others and 21.4 in the case Dalits. The rural electrification penetration is the slowest in the Adivasi habitations.

Disparities in Infrastructure

The disparities are not confined to human development status but extend to the infrastructure–production, communication, and social—in respect of the geographical areas where the Adivasis reside. The infrastructural disparities are even more pronounced than those of human development. The production infrastructure relates to irrigation, storage godowns for PDS, cold storage for preservation of marketable produce, outlets for supply of seeds, fertilizers and pesticides, veterinary centres, and banking units—commercial and cooperative. The communication infrastructure consists of roads, bridges, transport facilities, telecommunications, and digital networks. The social infrastructure includes schools, health centres, piped water arrangements, sanitation facilities, power distribution lines, et cetera. Geographical inaccessibility, hilly and undulating terrain, scattered habitations, and sparse population with low density have provided recurring alibis for this neglect on one pretext or another, such as economic non-viability, high cost, and difficulty in operations and maintenance. (MTA, 2006). The infrastructure is not merely inadequate but at a lower level of gradation than the rest of the country. There is a candid admission by the government that this lack of critical infrastructure, 'results in the inability of Adivasi areas to meaningfully absorb funds, including institutional support' (MTA, 2006). Not only this, the gap in infrastructure in the Adivasi areas compared to the non-Adivasi areas is widening at a fast rate. This is because, in the rest of the country, the growth of infrastructure is getting augmented in all these fields with the involvement of the private sector. The private sector does not invest on infrastructure in the Adivasi areas because it would not produce the desired returns as the people lack purchasing power for accessing facilities and services. Besides, even the meagre infrastructure that exists in the Adivasi regions is deteriorating due to poor maintenance by the concerned government agencies and is, therefore, increasingly becoming non-functional. This has been attributed to the lack of adequate funds from the government. The social sector infrastructure, such as schools and healthcare centres, is beset with problems of non-availability of essential service providers. The personnel required to provide these services avoid getting posted in 'backward' areas, and when posted, they absent themselves from duty. The Adivasi areas thus emerge as a classic case of marginalization both by the government and the non-government sector.

Non-Quantifiable Disparities

No complete picture of disparities which the Adivasis suffer from would ever emerge if we fail to look at the non-quantifiable parameters. In fact, it is the non-quantifiable parameters which would explain why the situation represented by the quantifiable indicators is so bleak. The non-measurable disparities are rooted in social relationships. These relationships can be observed at the level of formal institutions—social, political, economic, and legal. They also take shape during informal interactions, reflecting culturally internalized attitudes, assumptions, and practices and operate as all levels from international to the national and inter-personal (MCneish and Eversole, 2005). The defining characteristics of these disparities lie in the 'cultural difference' between the dominant non-Adivasi society and the marginalized Adivasi population. The factors contributing to the marginalized status of the latter are their social exclusion and discrimination against them by the members of the dominant larger society.

Divergent Civilizational Perspective

Distinctive Social Ethos

The social distinctiveness of the Adivasis from the dominant non-Adivasi population emanates from the divergent civilizational perspectives of the two social combines. This emerges from the different social structures, relationships, and practices of the two social groups and is manifested in different ways of thinking and doing things, different values which influence their behaviour, and even different languages spoken by the communities represented by the two social categories. Notwithstanding minor variations among them, the Adivasi groups across the country comprise small communities managing their own affairs according to their traditions. Within them, there are larger and smaller ethnic groups, but in relation to the size of the dominant communities of the non-Adivasi society, they are still small. The Adivasi groups are relatively self-contained with minimal contact with the outside world. The notion of personal property has not yet fully crystallized, as they have largely practised subsistence economy with relatively fewer needs. The economy is considerably non-monetized and money has not acquired high value. It is deeply embedded in the relationship to land and forests, the primary resources for production. These resources are controlled by the community and individual access to resource use has its sanction. Here, too, the accent is not on legal ownership but resource use. The motivating force in the use of natural resources is not geared towards generation of surplus or acquisitiveness but to ensure dignified survival of all its members. For this reason, it is guided by considerations of sustainability. The community's control over itself and environmental knowledge ensure this balance. At a social level, there is a greater degree of cohesion. The individual has not yet acquired a central place in social transactions. The Adivasi society is socially homogenous with greater community control over the management of its affairs. This is reflected in a great deal of social interaction and cooperation among its members. In agriculture and house construction activity, for example, the entire community helps when the individual households require it. The activity relating to the collection of forest produce also operates as a group activity. The lifestyle of Adivasis involves greater physical activity and movement. The labour activity is more evenly distributed. The Adivasis are deeply committed to conservation of natural environment. Their distinct worldview is characterized by 'a more egalitarian social system, economic life of sharing and caring, a polity of decision-making by consensus, and art and aesthetics as a celebration of collective joy and spirituality based on symbiosis between nature and culture' (Munda, 2005). This is in sharp contrast to the non-Adivasi society whose activities are entirely centred on the individual family with rare display of social solidarity, and that too, a fractured one. There are deeply embedded social divisions based on control over resources—land, labour, and capital and their distribution—which also translate into social and political control of those who have access to a larger share of these over those who have less of it or no access at all. The guiding ethos of economic activity is the acquisitive instinct, which goes beyond legitimate satisfaction of needs and towards accumulation. This generates deep-seated divisions in interests which make cooperation virtually impossible particularly across differentially endowed social groups. The productive resources stand commodified and their distribution is oriented towards individual ownership. The economic activities are guided by values of market capitalism which persuade each individual to pursue his own interests. There is little social interaction for common activities (barring religious occasions), and therefore, lesser inclination to accept any collective decision-making or control. The lifestyle is dictated by the nature of the production system which involves less of physical activity and movement and more of sedentarization. Unlike the Adivasi society where production processes necessarily involve input of personal labour, the non-Adivasi society, on account of its iniquitous nature, has created individuals who generate and acquire resources on the strength and contribution of the labour of others. The generation of wealth and its enjoyment, therefore, are not symbiotically linked but inequitably distributed which creates fissures and conflicts. The standard of living in the two societies is, therefore, vastly different. The Adivasi society is characterized by the lower level of output necessary for satisfying basic needs.

It, therefore, yields a modest standard of living but one that is better distributed, thus avoiding hunger and deprivation among its members. The non-Adivasi society produces higher levels of output in excess of the basic needs and is capable of satisfying a higher standard living. But this output is maldistributed, resulting in opulence for some and inadequate subsistence and deprivation in the case of others. This tendency also fuels efforts the towards concentration of productive resources and wealth generated from them in a smaller section of its members and, therefore, creates differentiation in status, access to facilities, and influence in governance. This ethos of the non-Adivasi society has evolved after a long period of exposure to technological development and market forces. The Adivasi society, having remained relatively isolated, could still preserve its distinct and radically different social and economic systems though changes are occurring in it under pressure of external forces.

This idealized picture of the Adivasi social system is strongly contested. It is contended that not all Tribes are small, as some major Tribes have over a million people and are scattered over extensive territories (Betteile, 1974). Leaving aside the hill Tribes, most others have also not been isolated and have had contacts with Hindu and Muslim communities. Even the religious beliefs and practices of Adivasi groups are not exclusively animistic, but have imprints of the Hindu religion. Most Adivasi groups practise settled agriculture and family farming system and there is no collective management of natural resources. There is, in fact, no way of defining an Adivasi society as distinct from the non-Adivasi one. The Adivasis represent a rural society in transition to a peasant or a caste-based one (Beteille, 1974; Corebridge, 2004). The existing Adivasi areas have also witnessed migration to and from it for a fairly long time, which brought in changes in the ethnic profiles of the communities therein. The Adivasi economy has also got transformed considerably with a large number of agricultural labourers and a notable rate of participation in mining and manufacturing industries. There has also grown differentiation in Adivasi society in land ownership with intra-Tribal transfers of land and access to jobs, positions of political power and other avenues of advancement resulting from reservation (Corebridge, 2004). These changes have led to the growth of individualism in the Adivasi communities and a declining degree of social cooperation. While not disregarding this view, the comparative picture presented here is evidently a broad generalization of the two rural societies, which in specific contexts, may carry varying degrees of deviations from it. There is also no denying that the Adivasi society is undergoing changes resulting from the policies pursued by the government and a small elite has emerged therein. Despite these changes, which have brought in some measure of inequality in its members, the elite formation is still very small and the larger Adivasi society would not defy the description presented here. The striking contrast between the ethos of two societies—Adivasi and non-Adivasi—is palpable to anyone who has had longstanding contacts with the former.

This contrasting social perspective has generated a deeply ingrained superiority in the dominant mainstream society vis-à-vis the Adivasis and their system. The numerical strength and social 'advancement' emerging from greater and varied exposure to multiple external forces over a long period of time have produced in the non-Adivasi groups a more complex society with varied skills, experience, access to knowledge systems and the capacity to deal with diverse situations and people. This has enabled them to acquire control over formal institutions—economic, social, and political and governance structures, which gets manifested in the pattern of hierarchy of dominance over the 'other' and 'different' cultures such as those represented by the Adivasis. This 'dominance' can be observed in their attitudes, behaviour, practices, and value system.

Cultural Differences

The contrasting social formations and systems emanate from two different cultures, which are reflected in the attitudes, values, beliefs, and practices of the two groups. The values of Adivasi society are diametrically opposite to those held by the mainstream dominant society. Among the values which form the Adivasi way of life is,

> the recognition of dignity and equality of all persons which includes all beings, natural, supernatural and human all bound together by complementarity for survival in a symbiotic relationship. The moral behaviour in Tribal society is not the outcome of fear of the divine but the basic belief that doing wrong to another person or take advantage of the position or to put him/her at a disadvantage is the negation of all relationship (Prabhu, 2006).

The Adivasis possess unique knowledge of their environment which is now gaining global acknowledgement and admiration (Meneish, 2005). Their attitude to 'nature' is governed by a relationship of mutual interdependence, each with rights and duties towards the other. It goes beyond environmental consciousness but reflects a collaborative relationship for survival. The society manages its affairs with trust in its members. The relationship among them is non-formal and based on the oral tradition where the spoken word' is sacred. Truth is open and unambiguous and is conveyed by a person's word. There is high valuation for the spoken word; honesty and straightforwardness are almost natural attributes (Sharma, 1978). The social ethos is embedded in the primacy of community and the collectivity of all members with its underlying egalitarian ethos, free of any exploitative relationship based either on status, age, or gender. This provides an extraordinary sense of solidarity together with mutual obligations. The abiding faith in community also influences economic and social behaviour. It also imparts to the social relations a high degree of democratic character.

In contrast, the non-Adivasi society places high value on the individual and there is little community control over individual behaviour. The morality is rooted in religious sanctions or fear of the divine. The society is highly differentiated and hierarchical. The attitude to nature is instrumental and exploitative. The social and economic transactions are governed largely by documentary tradition. The value is attached to the written matter and the word of mouth, 'the oral', is superseded by documentary proof. The individuals over a period of time have come to acquire a profound distrust of each other in their dealings. Truth and straightforwardness have, therefore, lost their value. Since individual achievement is the hallmark of non-Adivasi culture, competition rather than cooperation is the key to individual behaviour. With an inherited and sharply differentiated social structure and market-driven economic system geared to surplus production, inequalities are built into the society based on access to assets and productive resources, distribution of wealth, and consumption of goods and services. Interpersonal trust and communal solidarity are difficult to sustain in such a social environment. Equality is frowned upon because it militates against individual merit and effort. The privileged and better endowed feel no obligation towards those who are deprived and disadvantaged.

The dominance of non-Adivasi society is manifested in its characterization of Adivasis as slow, lazy, inferior, and a drag on society. They are viewed as 'backward' and their production system is considered 'inefficient'. This 'backwardness' or 'underdevelopment' is attributed to their social structure and cultural values that do not generate a higher level of aspiration, motivation for hard work, and acquisition of skills for their efficient utilization. On account of these reasons, the resources under their control or those to which they have access remain unutilized/underutilized. This neither benefits them nor the nation. These assumptions imply that the non-Adivasis who have the motivation and skills to exploit the potential of such resources should get control over them for efficient utilization in the larger societal interest.

Disparities in Participation

Economy

The contrasting civilizational perspectives have generated huge disparities in economic participation. The exposure of Adivasi society to the monetized economy is low though it is changing fast. It has traditionally been a barter economy with fewer needs, little cash, and low dependence on marketable goods. The Adivasis have traditionally exchanged their forest and agricultural produce for salt, kerosene oil, cooking oil, and cloth. This has produced an unequal exchange in transactions, which makes them extremely vulnerable to cheating and exploitation by traders, both as buyers and sellers. The non-Adivasi society is fully integrated with the monetized economy since long and has adequate capacity to handle transactions without the risk of exploitation. The Adivasis are overwhelmingly agriculturists and know no other occupation except craft production from local resources for local consumption. They have virtually no inclination for trade and business. The programmes for initiating them to trade and business have not succeded due to this cultural constraint. The non-Adivasis have had a very long history of trade and business activity not only within the country but also outside it. The Adivasis practise subsistence agriculture with low levels of production and little surplus for sale. From their meagre agricultural produce and forest collections, they take some to the market to exchange or buy essential commodities. The non-Adivasi society is pronouncedly geared to surplus production, and depending upon their access to productive resources, is motivated to produce surplus for generating greater income/wealth. For these reasons, the capacity to save and the level of available cash with the Adivasis is negligible, and therefore, the strength to mitigate risk and adversity is virtually non-existent. This forces them to borrow, much against their will, to survive. The non-Adivasis are highly inclined to save for meeting future needs and unforeseen contingencies. They are, therefore, much less vulnerable to shocks and adversity. In general, the Adivasis are disinclined to borrow, except for meeting consumption needs during lean non-agricultural season to avoid starvation. Their access to credit through formal institutions is very low. The experience of getting cheated in credit transactions even from formal institutions makes them doubly cautious about seeking access to it despite incentives provided under diverse self-employment programmes oriented to asset creation. The landless among them, in any case, have no access to formal credit as they have no collateral to offer. Whatever credit they obtain is overwhelmingly from moneylenders on highly exploitative rates of interest. The non-Adivasis virtually monopolize access to institutional credit. Even when they draw upon private institutional or informal credit sources, they are better equipped to protect themselves from fraud or exploitation by the lending agency. The skill base of Adivasis is confined overwhelmingly to agriculture and traditional crafts. That is why their participation in skill-based vocations is negligible and most of them are condemned to insecure, low paid employment in the informal sector. The non-Adivasis have diversified skills and have virtual monopoly of access to employment requiring their skills. Due to their low level of literacy and poor extension services, the access of Adivasis to technology even in the field of agriculture is very limited. This is reflected in the lower level of productivity from their land. The non-Adivasis have the requisite knowledge, cultural and financial resources, and motivation to access modern technology and obtain optimum output from their productive assets by harnessing them. These economic disparities are responsible for their continued high level of poverty and lower quality of life. These disparities make them extremely vulnerable to subjugation by the non-Adivasis who acquire control over their land and labour and exercise social dominance, which creates a spiral of impoverishment.

Political Institutions

The disparities in political participation also are acute, notwithstanding the right to vote and contest elections they enjoy on equal basis and reservation of seats in Central and state legislatures, and the Panchayati Raj Institutions (PRIs). The enthusiasm of Adivasis for electoral democracy is low. They are used to a direct, informal, transparent, and uninhibited type of democracy in their self-governance institutions where all village households participate as equals and deliberate on the subject collectively. In contrast, the non-Adivasis participate very zealously and competitively in the electoral process. Even when the Adivasis get elected as MPs, MLAs, or to positions in the Panchayati Raj bodies or get nominated to non-elective institutions, their capacity to participate in their deliberations to their advantage is very limited. They are unfamiliar with their processes, are disinclined to take part in debates or to prepare for them and have inadequate comprehension of the deliberations therein and low motivation to intervene. The non-Adivasis, in contrast, are fully conversant with their processes and are motivated to intervene in deliberations to their advantage. They have the necessary skills to network with other members, use available political spaces, devise strategies, and mobilize support for the cause they support. They, therefore, dominate politics. The capacity of elected Adivasi representatives to influence the decision-making process to protect their collective interests is negligible, notwithstanding their collective strength as a group sharing the same concerns. Often, the protection of Adivasi interests involves conflict with those of the non-Adivasis, in which battle the Adivasis rarely win, even when their case is strong. The non-Adivasis, due to their dominance in every sphere, are able to influence decision-making to protect their interests and face little competition from the Adivasis. In the distribution of political offices, the position of the Adivasis is tokenistic and does not even reflect their numerical strength. The non-Adivasis, in contrast, monopolize political offices and some sections among them, quite disproportionate to their strength. The capacity to assert in the political fora is virtually non-existent amongst the Adivasis. They are often shouted down by their non-Adivasi adversaries when they try to speak up. Their views carry no weight when compared to the views expressed by the non-Adivasis, even on subjects intimately related to them. Still worse, the Adivasis are extremely vulnerable to being used by the non-Adivasis to suit their interests. They do not have skills to negotiate the complex maze of manipulative processes of politics in defence of their interests. As for the poltics of representation, the processes of elections are equally alien to the Adivasi ethos, which works on a consensus mode across the community gatherings. While they do cast their votes, they are not very enthused to effectively participate in elections. The resources required to contest elections are beyond the capacity of even better off Adivasis. This compels them to seek help of financiers who are almost invariably non-Adivasis, thus becoming obligated to these financiers. Not surprisingly, therefore, after elections, the elected Adivasi representatives usually take up issues which are of interest to them, and at times, become unwitting victims of their manipulation. Not only the financiers, but even the voters from dominant communities in the constituencies reserved for Adivasis, though in minority, effectively use political processes for their advantage, while the Adivasi voters fail to use these mechanisms for articulating and protecting their interests. Rather, at times, political representatives from the dominant community, who empathize with the Adivasis, represent their concerns more effectively and fight for them because they know how to get through the system. This is the reason why even serious cases of violation of human rights, deprivation of entitlements, grabbing of resources, and sexual exploitation of women affecting the Adivasis go unpunished. This happens at all levels, national, provincial, and local. The situation is no different even in the states, which were recently carved out on the numerical strength of the Adivasi population. The political representatives from the dominant social groups call the shots and take decisions which are damaging to the Adivasi communities. This sums up the political marginalization of the Adivasis.

Disparities in Power Relationship

The huge disparities outlined here eventually get translated into an unequal power relationship between the two groups. The power relations can be observed in the formal institutions and their processes as well as in thoughts, processes and cultural expressions of the members of society. Power is a multi-faceted phenomenon encompassing within its ambit social, economic, political, and cultural dimensions. In all these facets, power is distributed skewedly in favour of the non-Adivasis. The factors which contribute to it are numerical strength, social and economic status, and political clout of the non-Adivasis, which enable them to exercise control over formal institutions—social, economic political, and legal—and influence decision-making process in governance, and determine the pattern of behaviour in social interactions. Power is basically an attribute of domination and control of one group/individual over another. This is an instrument by which the non-Adivasis impose their will over the Adivasis and promote their interests in the polity. The dimensions of this power relationship are manifested in different facets of life—cultural, social, economic, and political.

Manifestation of Power: Cultural

Disparaging Attitude Towards Adivasi Culture

One dimension of this power relationship lies in how non-Adivasis view Adivasis culturally, vis-à-vis their own society. The non-Adivasis, by and large, view Adivasis in disparaging terms. They treat them as racially inferior on account of the colour of their skin and texture of their bodies. This thinking is deeply embedded in Hindu mythological literature, which often forms the basis of attitudes of the Hindus towards what Prof Ram Dayal Munda calls the 'history of avoidance and non-recognition' (Munda, 2005). The dominant Aryan groups are identified with Sanskrit and Prakrit languages, while non-dominant groups are identified with other languages. Of the four levels of hierarchy observed in the ancient literary characters 1) Superhuman (*Sura, Narayana, Deva, Yaksha*) 2) Human (*Nara, Manava*), 3) Subhuman (*Vanara, Kinnara*), 4) Inhuman (*Asura, Rakshasa, Danava*), the Adivasis are bracketed with the third and fourth Their identity is perceived in pejorative terms and their physical and cultural attributes denigrated. Their contribution to the development of composite Indian culture is not recognized, though several attributes in it can be traced to Adivasi influence (Munda, 2005). Not only this, even their 'identity' as Adivasis is not accepted. While the UN and ILO conventions have characterized Tribal people as 'indigenous', the Government of India has refused to accept this nomenclature for them. It terms everybody in India as 'indigenous', as all indigenous and non-indigenous identities have disappeared in the evolution of Indian people. The Constitution concedes that the Adivasis possess a distinct cultural identity and worldview in view of their geographical isolation, historical antiquity and customary laws. But the Government and the dominant segment of society avoid using the word indigenous (the original inhabitants) and instead prefer usage of the term *Vanvasi* (forest dwellers) or Anusuchit Janjatis (Scheduled Tribes) or simply Janjati (Tribes). The Adivasis lose their status as Scheduled Tribes outside their home states. Their languages are not recognized for the purpose of teaching, communication, and formal transactions despite the recommendation of the National Policy on Education, 1986 that primary level education should be imparted through the medium of the mother tongue. Even in schools set up for Adivasis exclusively (Ashram schools), Adivasi children are neither taught in their mother tongue nor is their mother tongue taught as a subject.

Denial of Identity

The dominant segment of the society and the government have also ignored the separate faiths and belief system of the Adivasis and have tended to submerge them under the religions of the dominant communities. The Adivasi faith system has several distinguishing attributes such as the symbiosis between nature and culture, absence of formal structures like temples/churches and concepts of 'hell', and 'heaven'. Their spirits, gods, goddesses reside in nature—hills, rocks, forests, and rivers. They believe that the spirit of the dead person visits their home and watches the behaviour of the living. This creates pressures for righteous behaviour. In their value system, socially approved conduct is lauded and antisocial behaviour is denigrated (Munda, 2005). This denial of identity is particularly observed in the census operations in which the Adivasis, who do not profess to following any of the specified religions are recorded as 'Hindus'.

Strong Urge to Civilize Adivasis

Given the attitude of cultural superiority towards the Adivasis, the non-Adivasis display a strong urge to 'civilize' them. This can be observed in the statements and expressions which advocate rapid assimilation of the Adivasi communities in the mainstream society reflecting the cultural ethos of the dominant community. This move is justified on the ground that it would remove their geographical and social isolation and enable them to participate in economic and political sphere on equal terms. This majoritarian ethnocentric cultural construct defines the ideology of nation state and represents the essence of its social order. The communities which suffer from 'backwardness' have to be integrated with this social order. This is considered necessary, not only for their own advancement and modernization, but for the progress of the nation as well. The cultural values of the dominant community are viewed as modern and conducive to progress and have, therefore, to be inculcated by them. The Adiviasis have to be socialized in the languages of the mainstream communities to access their knowledge system the acquisition of which is necessary for higher level mobility and interaction with the outside world. In short, the Adivasis have to shed their values and acquire those of the non-Adivasis so that their 'separateness', which is responsible for their backwardness, poverty, and low social status, is eliminated.

Besides, Adivasis are culturally viewed in negative terms. They are considered as lazy, backward, unintelligent, dull, and inferior. They are also perceived as lacking in motivation and skills to utilize the productive potential of resources available to them. Their insularity and suspicion of outsiders is considered as a disinclination to learn from others, change and progress for the better. They are considered slow in comprehension and reaction. They are prone to be content with their existing low level of living and lack discipline and determination to transform their situation and take advantage of the opportunities that come their way. Their economy is characterized variously as moribund, stagnant, primitive, inefficient, and incapable of producing surpluses. Their social ethos is resistant to change and modernizing influences. The Adivasis society itself lacks internal dynamism to advance and progress and adopt good features of other societies. Its egalitarian ethos is antithetical to competition and is not geared to encourage and reward merit. They are considered politically disinclined and unenthused about participation in political processes. When they do articulate politically through collective mobilization, they are castigated as separatist, violent, undemocratic and even anti-national. The point to be stressed here is that these cultural traits of Adivasis are viewed as internal to the Adivasi society and not as an offshoot of their interface with the non-Adivasi world and state institutions. Also, they are evaluated by the dominant non-Adivasis in terms of their own cultural attributes which are considered superior and progressive.

Manifestation of Power: Social

The assertion of social dominance over the Adivasis is manifested in their aggressive proselytization by the dominant religions. The conversion of Adivasis to Christianity can be traced to the colonial period when the Christian missionaries induced this process through their development and social service activities such as education, health, agricultural credit, and legal aid, to help them cope with their problems. The absorption of Adivasis into Hinduism has been a slow, gradual and faltering affair over many years with varied processes in different societies in different times. The penetration of non-Adivasis into the Adivasi areas as peasants, moneylenders, and administrators exerted pressure on them to accept social practices and cultural values of the former. The adoption of technology used by the dominant (non-Adivasi) social groups and extension of state structures to the Adivasi areas were the other factors that generated in the Adivasis a feeling of inferiority and induced them to adopt the lifestyle and values of the Hindu society due to the perception of its superiority (Xaxa, 2009). While these processes of conversion were subtle, the current phase of belligerent Hinduism has aggressively steered the process in an organized manner and forced change in the belief system of the Adivasis and rules, practices, and lifestyle associated with it leading to the loss of their identity and autonomy. The state contributes to this process through its social and economic policies as well as indifference and neglect which create a favourable ambience for these forces to operate and use Adivasis to serve their political ends.

The dominant non-Adivasi society has also exerted its power over the Adivasis by manipulating differences in ethnic groups to break their social solidarity based on commonality of experience and generating inter-group clashes within them resulting in their impoverishment, exploitation, and marginalization. The Kandhmal communal flare-up reflected one dimension of it while the ethnic clashes in some parts of the North-East throw up another facet of it. This helps sustain the hegemonic social power of the non-Adivasi society and insulates it against any challenge to its position.

The manifestation of social power is not confined to the integration of Adivasis in the lowest ladder of the social order of the dominant groups but also extends to deprivation of their entitlements under various social laws, and development and welfare programmes. From reservations in jobs to acquisition of assets, skills, and technology for advancement of their social and economic status, the objective is to prevent any process of empowerment which has the potential to promote equality with other sections of society and assertion to seek rights and benefits due to them and disengage from the exploitative relationship in which they are tied up with the hegemonic larger society.

The deprivation of entitlements is effected by the non-Adivasis in diverse ways—betraying their trust, practising fraud in their dealings, and using their social clout and privileged access to governance institutions due to cultural affinity with the personnel who man them. The crudest form by which the social power is exercised is through infliction of social and physical violence on the Adivasis in day-to-day life the punitive consequences of which they manage to escape due to their ability to manipulate the justice administration system.

The unequal power relations in civil society are also reflected in the devaluation of the knowledge system of the Adivasis, trashing their social practices, denial of equality and dignity, and exertion of pressures to induce social changes in them conforming to their own society. The Adivasis have little social and political clout to defend their rights and interests against such aggressive onslaughts and negative categorization despite the constitutional protection available to them (Eversole, 2005). This is precisely what constitutes their powerlessness in the system. The state policies, attitude, and conduct of the members of the larger society complement each other in marginalizing Adivasis and causing their vulnerability (McCaskill and Rutherford, 2005).

Manifestation of Power-Economic

The economic power exercised by the dominant non-Adivasi society over the Adivasis is far more crippling as it threatens their dignified survival by increasing their vulnerability to multifaceted exploitation. This is manifested in dispossessing them of their land, their sole means of earning their livelihood besides being integral to their social and cultural ethos. The deprivation of land takes places in diverse ways. The non-Adivasis try to take away their land by practising, fraud in bilateral transactions, forcible dispossession, manipulation of land records et cetera, notwithstanding the fact that there are elaborate laws to prevent alienation of Tribal land and ensure its restoration after it has been alienated. The Adivasis fail to get justice against this deprivation due to the superior economic and social power, cultural resources, and access to governance institutions and ability to manipulate of the non-Adivasis' justice administration system. The other manner of dispossession from land is through its acquisition by the government for development projects which do not benefit them but are justified in national interest. The loss of land pushes the Adivasis into the destitute labour market in far-off places where they are completely at the mercy of employers who are all non-Adivasis leading to a level of exploitation never experienced before. They get the lowest paid work, suffer hazardous working conditions, and are denied compensation in the case of death and injury and protection against violence. Worse still, they are entangled in debt bondage and are not allowed to leave their work until the debt is cleared. Their women and children are subjected to sexual abuse and are even trafficked by their non-Adivasi employers and their intermediaries. The Adivasis suffer exclusion and discrimination in hiring for jobs even when they have requisite qualifications.

Economic power over the Adivasis is also exercised in the market place both as buyers and sellers of goods. The non-Adivasi traders and merchants who control the market cheat Adivasis in the purchase of their agri-forest produce and the sale of commodities of daily use to them against which the latter find themselves defenceless. The exclusion and discrimination are replicated in credit market and access to technology as well, which the non-Adivasis control.

Manifestation of Power: Political

Institutions

The power relations are defined by the experiences of the Adivasis in their interface with the state as well as their relationship with other social groups. The interface with state takes places through prescribed institutions rooted in the political and economic system, while the relationship with the larger society is embedded in informal interactions, thought processes, attitudes, behaviour, and cultural expressions. These authorised structures and institutions at all levels and in all spaces are dominated by the non-Adivasis because of their numerical strength, historical edge, privileged access to education, as also economic and cultural resources. Due to this reason non-Adivasis are, able to use them to their advantage and to subordinate interests of other groups to theirs. The design of these institutions and mode of their operations reinforce the unequal power relationship. Their entire ethos is hierarchical, authoritarian, and impersonal. This runs counter to the experience of Adivasis with their own institutions, where the decision-seeker and decision-maker interact with each other in a transparent and spontaneous manner which facilitates equal participation in the process, and therefore, acceptance of the decision. The processes of prescribed institutions are formalized, rule-based, document-driven and non-transparent. This helps perpetuate dominance since it puts Adivasis at a disadvantage in view of their oral tradition and great trust reposed in the spoken word. The processes also create a distance between the decision-maker and the decision-seeker, and disallow and discourage any participation. The decision-maker has a superior status in this arrangement and the seeker has to accept and abide by that decision. This places the latter in an inferior position. The transactions in institutions of the Adivasis are non-formal, oral, and carried out openly amidst a collective gathering. The decision-making process does not generate a hierarchical system in view of its participatory character. The language of communication in formal institutions also aids the process of dominance, since it is not the language of the non-Adivasis. This puts the average Adivasi in a disadvantaged position. Since his/her language is not allowed to be used for formal communication and record, he/she feels handicapped in transacting business in a language in the use of which he/she does not feel confident. The power of decision-making in all formal institutions is concentrated in the individual at the top and does not permit collective deliberations involving discussion and consultation with the complainant. It is, therefore, no surprise that those who operate the formal institutions display arrogance in their dealings with the Adivasis (as also in some situations, with poor people among sections of non-Adivasis as well). The imposition of unfamiliar structures and institutions, alien to their ethos, subject them to an indifferent, insensitive and unresponsive system which marginalizes them competently. When they do use the system to seek justice, they are bewildered by the complexity and manipulation they encounter and therefore prefer to withdraw and suffer injustice rather than pursue their cases. The legal and judicial processes are even more forbidding as they are unable to comprehend much less cope with the machinations of the adversary and cheating by the advocates. They feel that the system is not meant for them. This explains why they largely figure in court cases as the accused rather than as seekers of justice (Daghamvar, 2006).

Conceptual Framework of Liberal Democracy

State policy marginalizes Adivasis in other ways, too. The most relevant in this context is the understanding and conceptual framework within which rights and interests of Adivasis are viewed by the state. The Constitution of India recognizes and protects the distinct identity and culture of the Adivasis and the state policies affirm commitment to uphold this right. The international conventions also exhort nation states, that have indigenous population to do so (ILO connection 107 which India has ratified). The commitment is, however, conceived in terms of what has been termed as the western liberal view of citizenship and citizens' rights (McNeish and Eversole, 2005). This sets the limit of discourse because the Adivasis' own understanding of what constitutes their rights is excluded from this framework and therefore creates complications because rights sought by Adivasis cannot be accommodated in it. The liberal democratic frame revolves around a social and economic organization which recognizes individual ownership and identity as its axis in which alternative forms of organization which are embedded in community ownership, group identity and cultural values geared to collective rights are not recognized. The result is that state policies fail to integrate this specificity and uniqueness. They tend to impose mainstream society's 'individual' oriented approach on the Adivasis too. Thus, the entire legal framework of entitlements tends to exclude collective rights, collective ownership of resources and their utilization, and collective mode of contention. The collectivity implies carving out distinct areas of collective self-governance where the community should have substantial power to manage its own affairs according to its traditions not interfered with by outside forces with its own governing institutions/agencies taking decisions rather than through 'mainstream' state institutions and its officials. One significant implication of this self-governance is that Adivasis' traditional rights over resources (land, water, and forest) should not be taken away from them the state or any other authority (McNeish and Eversole, 2005). It follows that what programmes or measures would promote their development should also be settled by them rather than by any expert or an outsider and not foisted on them. The 'Rights Framework' even in the Constitution follows the model where individual rights alòne are protected, though by providing for a Sixth Schedule, the Constitution has permitted limited autonomy to the north-eastern Adivasi majority states to carry on with communitarian management of their affairs. The Adivasis stress collective rights, which recognize the Tribe as an entity rather than the Tribal individual. The constitutional provisions and numerous laws granting entitlements to citizens are unable to protect collective rights outside the Sixth Schedule. While the state does accommodate 'group' interests in its programmes and policies, these are essentially individuals coming together as functional groups. The state does not accept pre-eminence of any authority other than itself for an an individual to obey. This is the essence of the citizen-state relationship. For the Adivasis, however, the community has priority over the state in their commitment. They conceive of their relationship with state only through the collective entity called the Tribal community. Any authority that ignores this collectivity and deals with individuals directly does not have their moral and social approval (McNeish and Eversole, 2005).

This understanding strongly colours the entire behaviour pattern of the state in relation to the Adivasis. The state feels it has the ability to design policies and programmes for their welfare since their needs and wants are no different from other citizens. It also extends to the Adivasi areas' institutional arrangements for governance and development which are considered appropriate for the larger society. On the other hand, the Adivasis feel that they are 'different' from the mainstream in their cultural practices, social institutions, legal system and programmes meant for the mainstream communities which tend to create discordance with their cultural values and societal organization. This dissonance is not merely limited to the design of programmes but their implementation as well. The Adivasis feel acutely alienated while dealing with the state institutions but feel comfortable when they interface their own institutions. The state has been unwilling to concede these rights because it involves bestowing on them significant powers of decision-making which, in its perception, whittles its sovereign power. The exercise of this power may also conflict with the interests of the dominant community which controls the state. Besides, the state views the issue as a political challenge to its existence. Its entire response to collective self-governance is determined by an integrationist approach which recognizes only the right to equality of the level of citizenship conferred by the Constitution. Any deviation from this norm is perceived to encourage 'separatism' and threaten stability. The state is prepared to grant economic concessions and autonomy to pursue cultural practices and provide representation to the Adivasis in governing structures, but is not prepared to concede any alternative juridical framework of political rights and governance institutions. It has gone farthest by enacting PESA, 1996 which confers on Gram Sabha (collective assembly of villagers) in the Fifth Schedule areas decision-making powers in some matters which affect Adivasis vitally. But this does not go very far because PESA does not bestow the Adivasi community with decisive control over the management of productive resources in their jurisdiction and the power of governance through their institutions. Besides, even within the limited framework of PESA, considering the manner in which it has been diluted by the state governments in their state specific laws and lack of commitment to its implementation, there is little that the Adivasis can expect by way of getting their traditional system restored. But the issue of 'Political Rights' is central to removing disparities as it alone can bridge the cultural divide which is at the root of the marginalization of the Adivasis.

Manifestation of Power: Governance

Laws, Regulations and Implemetations

Governance is carried out by the institutions of state. The unequal power wielded by the dominant communities through the state apparatus is manifested in the enactment of laws, formulation of policies, and creation of institutional arrangements which are adverse to the interests of Adivasis and have the effect of further disempowering them. This is best exemplified by laws relating to compulsory acquisition of land, restricting/extinguishing rights of the Adivasis in the forests, and extensive commercial exploitation of resources on which Adivasis subsist et cetera. These measures unleash forces that cause loss of land and livelihood, deprive them of access to life-supporting resources, and push them out of their habitat in search of work which exposes them to multifaceted exploitation by the non-Adivasis. The imposition of structures and institutions of regulation and development alien to their ethos subject them to indifferent and insensitive governance, which destroys their system of collective and consensual self-governance and social cohesion and severely compromises their capacity to cope with adversities. The Fifth Schedule empowers the Governor of the state to evaluate the potential adverse impact of such instruments and prevent their extension to the Adivasis entirely or extend them with necessary modifications where their interests are likely to be hurt. But this power has never been utilized by any Governor. This is indication enough that even constitutional provisions for protection of the Adivasis can be ignored.

The dominance of non-Adivasis in governance is also manifested in disinterestedness to implement laws, policies, and programmes that are designed to benefit the Adivasis. These include laws relating to land alienation, moneylending, labour welfare, forest rights, empowerment of Panchayats, prevention of atrocities, and programmes relating to human and economic development. The instruments to protect the interests of Adivasis do not get any priority in the agenda of governance, and, when taken up under pressure in some cases, are executed indifferently, inefficiently, and insensitively to defeat their intended objectives.

The acid test of where the power equations between the Adivasis and the non-Adivasis in governance are tilted is provided by issues where the interests of the two conflict. On such issues, almost invariably, the interests of the dominant non-Adivasis prevail and protection of Adivasi interests are sidelined. There is no mistaking that Adivasi interests have to be subordinated to the non-Adivasi interests since the former hold the reign of political power.

Imposition of Policy Choices

Flowing from the dominance in governance, the non-Adivasis wielding the power of decision-making impose their policy choices on the Adivasis without even an attempt to consult them or evaluate their potential adverse impact on them. The most significant of these policy choices was to integrate the Adivasis rapidly with the money and market economy. This had the effect of commodifying resources for their commercial exploitation, that the Adivasis use for their subsistence. The market demand, therefore, determined the use of their resources, leading to the Adivasis' loss of access to them and their consequent impoverishment. The rapid exposure to the market also intensified processes of their exploitation both as buyers and sellers by merchants and traders. The other important policy forced on them was to utilize the natural resources in their areas (land, water, forest) extensively and rapidly with infusion of private capital and modern technology for fast economic growth. This has led to extensive mining operations, setting up of industries, development of infrastructure and services, growth of urban centres, and fast pace of economic activities that divert productive resources from the Adivasis, displace them from land, livelihood, habitat, and environment, unleash a spiral of impoverishment, degrade their natural environment affecting both livelihood and quality of life, and bring in a flood of migrants from the non-Tribal areas with attendant exploitative processes and social pathologies. Yet another policy choice thrust on them was to remove their 'social isolation' from the mainstream society, eliminate their 'backwardness' by modernizing their society, and change their social organization and cultural values to facilitate the push towards fast track development with a view to levelling them up with the rest of the population. This aggressive developmental assault has destabilized Adivasi society rendering its members increasingly more vulnerable to exploitation and violence. Far from bridging the social and economic disparities between the Adivasis and non-Adivasi population, development and modernization have increased their marginalization in the polity and economy. The policy choice to open up their areas, extend formal institutions and the reach of the state through governance apparatus also falls in this category. This has subjected them to rent-seeking administrative machinery dominated by the non-Adivasis and exposed them to a justice administration system alien to their ethos in the operation of which they are powerless to defend their interests. These adversarial policy choices starkly reflect the lack of clout of the Adivasis in the decision-making process, even on matters which vitally affect them.

Disparities Affecting Adivasis: Rooted in Colonial Policies

The political economy of disparities in relation to the Adivasis is rooted in colonial policies that introduced changes in the agrarian structure which defined rights in and access to land by ownership rather than by use. The concept of private property in land and a legal system to back it was put in place with the permanent settlement. This converted independent Adivasi landowners into tenants of Zamindars and exposed them to multifaceted exploitation by their managers and staff. The conceptual frame of rights it brought into effect was individual-centric and obliterated the traditional communal pattern of natural resource management with devastating effects on the Adivasis. It appropriated forests and made them exclusive properties of the state to be managed by forest bureaucracy and extinguished/curtailed the customary rights of the Adivasis and other communities. The theory of 'Eminent Domain' was used to acquire any land with individual possession in 'public interest', and for this purpose, the Land Acquisition Act, 1894 was enacted which provided compensation to only those with valid titles to such land. These measures were used to control natural resources for commercial exploitation. The colonial government also initiated a pattern of industrialization which diverted productive resources from the Adivasis to the mining and industrial companies and created a pool of landless, unskilled Adivasi labour to be pushed into underpaid, hazardous, and extremely arduous work (Corebridge, 1982). The influx of outsiders resulting from these developments unleashed unprecedented exploitation of the Adivasis by landlords, merchants, and moneylenders and their good land was usurped by these outsiders, forcing them to retreat to the deeper forest. The first wave of colonial industrial policy displaced a large number of people, which led to forced migration and indentured labour.

Post-Colonial State: Paradigm of Economy

These colonial policies continued in post-colonial India and were repackaged as 'development. Their ambit now extended to execution of numerous schemes, programmes, and projects, but the ideological underpinnings remained unchanged. The only difference was that they were now geared to benefit not the metropolitan colonial country but the elites of the mainstream (dominant) community in the Centre and the states of the independent country. The Adivasi areas now constituted the periphery of resource extraction and the promised land for advancement of persons from the distant centre in this structure of 'internal colonialism' (Areeparampil, 1986).

There was a systematic opening up of the Adivasi areas for varied development projects since Independence. The heavy concentration of mining and industrial projects in the area of Adivasi concentration in central India dispossessed the Adivasis from other land and displaced them from their habitat and environment. Besides compulsory acquisition of their land by the state for these projects, the huge influx of outsiders it generates into the areas inhabited by the Adivasis intensifies demand for land for diverse purposes—housing, infrastructure, business, and social utilities that push out Adivasis from their land through numerous processes leading to secondary displacement, which is much larger than the one caused by land acquisition. Industrialization has also polluted their environment—air, water, and soil—leading to loss of productivity in land, scarcity of water and numerous health problems. The benefits in terms of employment, business, investment opportunities, and other avenues of economic advancement have overwhelmingly gone to the non-Adivasi outsiders while the Adivasis have ended up in 'low paid, insecure, transient and destitute labour market' as migrant labour, where apart from getting separated from their community and its support mechanisms, they lose their identity, culture, and status as STs as well.

With the liberalization of economy and efforts to attract direct foreign private investment, the pace has grown faster and the ambit of industrial and mining expansion more extensive. The state governments of Jharkhand, Orissa, Chhattisgarh, and Andhra, which have concentrations of Tribal population as well as mineral and forest resources, have signed up investment agreements with more than 100 companies to take up mining and industrial projects requiring thousands of acres of land. The process of land acquisitions has already started in respect of some of them. In addition, several other projects relating to housing, infrastructure, social sector facilities, and power generation have been/are being proposed which would also involve acquisition of large areas of land. The establishment of SEZs would do likewise. As per the estimate of a research agency, 60 million (six crore) people were displaced due to various development projects in the country from 1947 to 2000, of which the share of Adivasis is more than 40 per cent (Fernandes, 2006 MORDs, 2004). One Tribal scholar has observed that one-fifth of the total Tribal population is already displaced (Munda, 2005). The phase of land acquisition by the state and companies since 2000 will surpass displacement in the earlier phases.

The post-colonial paradigm growth and development with market as its driving force disintegerated the holistic conceptual basis of the Adivasi economy delinking it from ethics, politics, and culture. It shattered the inter-sectoral mould of culture, economy, and governance of the Adivasis. It converted productive resources of land, labour and forest into commodities, dismantled its equity foundation reflected in reciprocity and underrated subsistence activities thus exposing the Adivasis to the onslaught of market forces which was not only in approprite for them and for which they were neither prepared nor had the capacity to accommodate. The 'instrumental attitude towards nature and people' destablized their informal economies and collective forms of economic activities and led to numerous forms of exploitation [Escobar, 1992]. Though these processes had begun in the colonial period, they became intensified after independence, and therefore, immensely contributed to the destruction of the cultural existence and identity of the Adivasi people. As Adivasi ethos was totally alien to the changes, this led to their impoverishment, marginalization, social disintegration, and powerlessness, which together widened and exacerbated the inequalities.

Post-Colonial State: Paradigm of Conservation

The post-colonial state witnessed new contestations and conflicts affecting the relationship between forests and Adivasis. The shift to commercial orientation of forest management in place of traditional social orientation introduced production forestry—a pattern of resource use which catered to the raw material needs of the industry and urban population rather than fulfilling those of the Adivasis and other rural communities. This was manifested in replacement of natural forests with diverse species by plantation of monoculture and quick growing species. Besides, huge forest lands were leased out to industries for growing species used as industrial raw material such as bamboo. This deprived the Adivasis of access to forest resources and employment in the leased areas. The other dimension of the policy was to supply forest material at very low rates to industry. This hurt the Adivasis in two ways—First, it diverted all resources to industry starving the local craftsman access to raw material for their products. Second, where the state agreed to supply such raw material to local people at a cost, the price charged was very high thereby discriminating against the traditional users. The result was slow death of the forest based tiny craft industry leading to loss of livelihood. The cumulative impact of all these policies led to greater deprivation of access to resources and impoverishment of the Adivasi people. This has damaged their economy and affected sources of food supply, causing starvation in some cases and widespread malnutrition. The alarm over huge degradation of forest lands, loss of forest cover, and growing pressure of population on forests generated an environmental movement which perceived forest dwellers as the enemies of the forest and wildlife and stressed conservation without a human face—a celebration of wilderness. This ideology delegitimized the existence of Adivasis in the forest habitat, derecognized their traditional rights, and excluded and evicted Adivasis as a means of wildlife protection and preservation. The conservation strategy now took on an adversarial relationship between the state and the forest dwellers. This took many forms. The state now viewed Adivasis as a burden on forests and a roadblock in the scientific and commercial exploitation of the forest. The rights of Adivasis to forest resources, which were reduced to 'privileges' during the colonial period, were now downgraded to 'concessions'. Greater restrictions were imposed on the Adivasis and others in accessing forest resources. The shifting cultivation, the traditional form of cultivation in hill slopes, was discouraged and measures introduced to stop it. Human interference in forests was eliminated with—introduction of Wild Life Protection Act, 1972 and setting up of biosphere reserves—National Parks and Wild Life Sanctuaries. The restrictions on movement of the Adivasis in the forests became even more stringent in these areas and, in many cases, they were forcibly evicted from land and habitat within the forests. The onslaught was further carried out through the enactment of the Forest Conservation Act, 1980 and National Forest Policy, 1988. The Supreme Court's orders in the PIL (Godavarman case) leading to the issuance of a circular by the Ministry of Environment and Forests, dated May 2002, directing state governments and UTs to evict all 'encroachers' within five months inflicted a death blow on the Adivasis. The forest departments of state governments in a span of 18 months forcibly evicted Adivasis from 1,52,000 hectares of land, destroying their dwelling units and crops, in some places, by using elephants for this purpose' (NCAS, 2008). All this while, the forest land is being liberally transferred for industrial and mining projects. Orissa leads the nation in diversion of forest land (Mishra, 2010).

Post-colonial State: Paradigm of Development

The post-colonial state was fully conscious of the pre-exiting disparities between the Adivasis and mainstream population. It, therefore, introduced a paradigm of development and welfare to reduce these disparities to enable them to catch up with the rest. This paradigm catered to three core objectives. The first related to the social goal of removing 'backwardness' of the Adivasis and to push them to the path of advancement and prosperity. The second objective envisaged upgrading their economic and social status, the former by increasing their income and the latter by improving the quality of their lives. The third focused on modernizing Tribal society by breaking its isolation and traditional mould and creating conditions for inculcation of aspirational values. Of the three, the first and third were perceived to be the outcomes of the measures taken up for the second. The measures taken up for pursuing the second goal included programmes of income generation, infrastructural development, extension of social services—health, drinking water, education and regulatory measures for protection and allotment of land, labour welfare, supply of credit, and more specifically, re-distribution of public resources so as to ensure that they received their legitimate share. The Tribal-specific 'package' also involved market intervention for their forest collections to get them remunerative prices. The conceptual frame of this 'development' suffers from serious flaws:

(a) It is premised on a standardized understanding of the causes of disparities, the requirements of a good life for an individual and dignified survival of groups and social goals they wish to achieve. It adopts standard of living as the single measure of good life and elimination of poverty and deprivation and achieving prosperity and happiness for all people as the route to achieve it which priviliges economic values and belittles other ways of life with different barometers of well being. (Lummes, 1997). It, therefore, imposes a uniform (homogenized) cultural model of development. This understanding fails to take note of the divergence of cultures and different standards of measuring their conditions and aspirations. The concept of development is viewed entirely in terms of distribution of economic resources and benefits to the neglect of environmental, social, and political issues which have a bearing on them.

(b) Its cultural frame conceives underdevelopment and poverty as the problem of an individual caused by the lack of capacity to fruitfully participate the economy, and therefore, introduces programmes of assistance to the individual to overcome it. It fails to situate poverty and marginalization in the perspective of an economy embedded in community-centric social relations and resource management.

(c) It assumes that the strategy of providing needed assistance from the outside would achieve the objective of Adivasi development and thus relies on the advice of experts rather than on the initiative of the people themselves to define their development and design programmes of mobilizing the community's own efforts for improving their conditions against the varying challenges it faces.

(d) The development model does accept the need for 'participation' of beneficiaries in the policy frame, influenced by the international discourse on poverty which seeks to counteract the indifference of people to the activities undertaken in its pursuit and to include some of their concerns. But the 'structure' of participation is insincere and lacking in genuine political engagement. It is not intended as a power sharing exercise which provides the opportunity to the Adivasis to spell out both the goals of development and the processes to achieve them. It is packaged in control of authority from above, specifed rules, bureaucratic monitoring and restraints. The participation is managed by the state machinery within the limits of prescribed methodology and state-specified policy norms in which development envisioned by Adivasis does not carry weight and the approach continues be individual-centric (McNeish and Eversole, 2005a&b; McNeish, 2005).

(e) The development is conceived solely in economic terms and directed towards expeditious economic mainstreaming of the Adivasis. It fails to be situated in the injustices Tribal people have suffered in terms of alienation of their land and loss of control over natural resources on account of expanding state activities and fails to provide for their restoration. It also does not neutralize their political subjugation responsible for their impoverishment and marginalization. (McNeish and Eversole, 2005)

(f) The overall direction of this development is defined by the consensus of the mainstream (dominant) community on what would promote progress of the country, accelerate prospects of economic advancement of people, improve their quality of life, and create a sense of well being. Its progress is measured in terms of faster economic growth, greater share in global economic and political power and fulfilling the ambition of attaining a status on par with the developed countries. The growth process underpinning it is symbolized by mega industrial and mining projects, large dams, sophisticated infrastructure, hi-tech facilities, multistoryed buildings, shopping malls, and beautification of urban landscape. This inevitably involves, besides commitment of huge resources, extensive acquisition of land, and consequent displacement of people from their rural and urban habitat with severe disruption to their life-supporting activities, social stability and opportunities for leading a dignified life. The vision of development is not neutral in terms of costs and benefits to all the people but affects them differently. The gainers are those who improve their economic status and are able to enjoy a higher quality of life resulting from these investments. Those who are dislocated from their life-supporting economic activities and stability of the existing pattern of living become losers. These externalities are justified as the necessary cost to be paid for larger benefit of the society, state, and the nation. Those who wield greater political power rationalize this vision of development and apportion costs and benefits emerging from it to various sections of the people. The Adivasis end up as losers in this arrangement beacause it does not harmonize with their economy, mode of living, and aspirations. Due to their powerlessness in the system, they get excluded from this decision-making. For them, development comes as a virtual war to deprive them of everything they value-control over productive resources, community-centric social life, identity, cultural autonomy, and a sense of contentment even amidst deprivation. They consider their existing situation, stigmatized as 'underdevelopment' in the official conception of development as benign in comparison.

Post-Colonial State: Paradigm of Modernization

The post-colonial state has also unabashedly pursued an aggressively integrationist social policy which seeks to 'remove' the isolation of the Adivasi population—physical and psychological—and speedily mainstream them. The national leaders, during the freedom movement, castigated the colonial government for treating Adivasis as a social group different from the mainstream society (Singh, 1982). The extension of mainstream administrative structures to the Adivasi areas was a concrete expression of repudiating colonial differentiation. Though the Nehruvian policy framework conceded greater cultural autonomy to the Adivasis, it was not followed in actual practice, particularly in the Fifth Scheduled areas.

The dominant integrationist approach of the ruling elite is embedded in no uncertain terms in the policy documents, the most recent being the draft of the Central Government's Tribal policy. Despite the proclaimed commitment to permit cultural autonomy to the Adivasis as guaranteed by the Constitution, this autonomy itself is conceived in the ethnocentric frame of the mainstream (dominant) society, which is assimilationist in tone and content. The ideologues of mainstream society even deny that the Adivasis had remained isolated from the larger society and aggressively assert that they were the backward segments of the Hindu social order. The project 'mainstreaming', therefore, clearly envisages that the Adivasis should progress so as to live, behave, and think as the dominant sections do. This implies that they should abandon their 'backward' practices, cultural norms, and lifestyle and become 'civilized' like the rest. This 'civilizing' mission is the hegemonic denial of their tradition, ethos, and identity. The pressure this rhetoric generates marginalizes them further because of their inability to compete on equal terms. This objective is not confined to the realm of thought process but gets enforced through formal and informal institutions which the Adivasis come in contact with as the persons governing them are deeply imbued with this philosophy. The obsession with 'mainstreaming' Adivasis is not a manifestation of ignorance but an instrument of power. It expresses dominance in the crudest form and is designed to appropriate their resources of land, water, and forest, exercise control over their labour, and subjugate them socially, economically, and politically. The Adivasis are in no position to challenge this cultural onslaught as they are confronted with non-Adivasi dominance in all spheres of life.

The mainstreaming of Adivasis has had disastrous implications. It generates in them inadequacy, infirmity and pressures for conformity. Since the Hindu society is characterized by a rigid hierarchical order governed by norms of purity and pollution with no possibilities of mobility across the ladders of hierarchy, the Adivasis can only end up as the lowest rung of it with Scheduled Castes (untouchables). The social and economic marginalization of the Adivasis is, therefore, built into the project of their integration with the larger (dominant) society which the state has been pushing. The development programmes and the nature of economy reinforce this movement towards integration.

Government Approach to Reduce Disparities

The disparities affecting the Adivasis in relation to the general population are recognized by the government and measures have been put in place to bridge them. The policy intervention to deal with disparities between the Adivasi population and the rest of the society is governed broadly by the constitutional scheme which recognizes the distinctness of Adivasis as a social category, the special nature of the problems they suffer from, and the disabilities they are likely to encounter in future. The Constitution lays down specific safeguards for their protection. The chapter on Fundamental Rights grants equality to all citizens—political and social—which are enforceable. The freedom has also been provided to conserve their distinct language, script, culture, and institutions, and directions have been given to local authorities to provide adequate facilities for instructions in the mother tongue at the primary stage of education for children belonging to linguistic minority groups. The separate governance has been enshrined in the provisions of the Fifth and Sixth Schedules to deal with administration and control of Scheduled Areas (where Adivasis have a large presence). The Fifth Schedule applies to eight states where Governors have special responsibility and powers to protect interests of the Adivasis. The provision has been made for a Tribes Advisory Council for each such State. The Governor in these states is empowered to prohibit application or permit application with modification or repeal of any Central or state law to Scheduled Areas or part thereof. He/she is also authorized to make regulations for peace and good governance, prohibit or restrict transfer of land held by any member of the Scheduled Tribes, regulate allotment of land and the business of lending money to the Tribal population. The Sixth Schedule provides for creation of autonomous district/regional councils for managing development programmes and making laws on various subjects which touch upon their lives of the people in these territories. Political safeguards are contained in the arrangement of reservation of seats in the legislatures of the Centre and state and in the PRIs in proportion to their population. The share in decision-making positions has been ensured by reservation of posts in recruitment and promotion to public services. The educational advancement of the Adivasis has been mandated by reservation of seats in institutions of higher learning. A National Commission for Scheduled Tribes has also been created as a watchdog body for investigation, monitoring and evaluation of various safeguards. The Commission is required to present a report to the President annually to be placed in the Parliament for discussion. In addition, a special commission is constituted at the interval of every 10 years to assess the pace of development and protection of the Adivasis. Political safeguards include a mandate to have a Minister of Tribal Welfare in states with a substantial Adivasi population.

The affirmative architecture of the Constitution is translated into the domains of policy and programmes. The policy instruments consist of laws to protect the vital interests of the Adivasis. The most prominent of these laws are those which provide protection against violence and civil rights violations. The Protection of Civil Rights Act, 1976 and the SCs/STs (Prevention of Atrocities) Act, 1989 are intended to achieve this objective. Laws have existed since colonial times and have been expanded and strengthened which prohibit alienation of Adivasi land to the non-Adivasis. Land reforms laws provide for distribution of land to the landless. The regulation of moneylending has been effected by laws to prevent economic and social exploitation in the disbursement of non-institutional credit. The exploitation of labour has been checked by laws relating to minimum wages, equal remuneration, abolition of bonded labour, regulation of terms of employment of migrant labour, and protection of child labour. The historical injustice that the Adivasis suffered as a result of appropriation of forests and extinguishment/curtailment of rights of access to forest resource has been undone by the Scheduled Tribes and other Traditional Forest Dwellers (Recognition of Rights) Act, 2006. The development programmes relating to asset building, skill development, poverty alleviation, employment generation earmark a specific share of benefits to be delivered to the Adivasis. With a view to effecting an equitable transfer of public resources to the Adivasis, the mechanisms of Tribal Sub-plan, Special Central Assistance, and grants-in-aid under Article 275 (1) of the Constitution and dedicated financing institutions to extend credit to the Adivasi beneficiaries for income generating projects have been put in place. Marketing support for agriculture and forest produce is sought to be provided by dedicated institutions to procure such produce at remunerative prices. Political participation takes place through representation in Central and state legislature against the reserved seats. PESA, 1996 has laid down a special dispensation of self-governance which empowers the Gram Sabha for management of local resources and control over the process of development. A minister in charge of Tribal welfare in the Cabinet at Central and state levels enables Adivasis to have representation in the decision-making apparatus at highest level.

Failure of Instruments to Reduce Disparities

Governance Structures

This elaborate policy architecture has failed to mitigate the plight of the Adivasis. The Right to Equality remains unrealised due to widespread social exclusion and discrimination. Their cultural freedom is negated by the aggressive assimilationist agenda. The governance structures designed to protect the Adivasis from violence and exploitation of have also failed to discharge their assigned role. The Governors in the Fifth Schedule Areas, for example, have also failed to use their constitutional powers to protect Tribal interests. They have acted on the advice of the Council of Ministers thereby making constitutional provisions redundant (Planning Commission, 2004). The Governor's mandatory annual report is not being submitted regularly and some states have not sent the report for years. The reports which have been submitted are routine documents, containing description of Adivasis and welfare schemes implemented for them. Neither serious problems facing the Adivasis nor the special efforts made to protect their interests are dealt with in the reports despite being required in the format prescribed. No Governor has used this power to examine Central/state laws in terms of their impact on the Adivasis with a view to preventing their application to Scheduled Areas. While Tribes Advisory Councils have been set up in the states, major policy issues, urgent legislative matters, and development issues affecting the Adivasis are not referred to them for seeking their advice. Only minor and routine matters are discussed by them.

Protective Laws

The protective laws have failed to protect the lives and interests of the Adivasis. The SC/ST Atrocities Act has had no deterrence as the conviction rate in the cases registered under it is low while the acquittal rate is very high. There are widespread complaints about non-registration of cases, pressures exerted on the victims to compromise with the perpetrators of violence, poor quality of prosecution in courts, and even bias in judgments of the trial and higher courts. The atrocities on the Adivasis are committed by the police and security agencies also. These cases rarely come on record let alone investigated and pursued. In the case of Adivasis, the atrocities also take the form of cases under the Forest and Excise Acts for petty offences under which the victims are incarcerated for months due to lack of resources to seek and furnish bail.

The alienation of Adivasi land continues unabated. Only a small percentage of cases of such alienation get registered, and out of them also, as per available statistics, more than 50 per cent are rejected (MORD, 2008). Serious procedures and practice related anomalies have also been detected in the disposal of cases by the Expert Group on Prevention of Alienation of Tribal Land and its Restoration, forcing it to describe restoration courts as no better than 'Kangaroo Courts' where justice is weighted heavily in favour of the non-Adivasis and there is large scale corruption everywhere. Even where cases are decided in favour of the Adivasis, there is endless agony and even despair in getting possessions delivered. Besides, the adversary party usually goes in appeal, thereby negating the restoration order (MoRD, 2004). Over the years, the states have connived at the dilution of these laws to protect the interests of non-Tribal encroachers (Reddy, 2006). But much greater alienation of land takes place through compulsory acquisition by the government for development projects. Of the nearly 60 million persons displaced by development projects between 1947–2000, Adivasis constituted more than 40 per cent of them. Three fourths of the displaced Adivasis have not received even the minimum of rehabilitation costs. The pace of displacement has been increasing faster in the recent years due to large-scale mining and industrial projects financed by foreign capital. The Adivasis in some states have also lost land through survey and settlement operations, in the process of which land beyond 10 degree slope in the possession of Adivasis for shifting cultivation has been declared forest and ownership recorded in the name of the government (Roy Burman, 2009). The implementation of Scheduled Tribes and other Traditional Forest Dwellers (Recognition of Rights Act), 2006 is being subverted by the forest bureaucracy. This is evident from the continued eviction of the Adivasis from their existing occupation of land, relocation from wildlife sanctuaries and national parks without consent, taking over the functions of the forest rights committee by the forest officials, and forcible plantation on land under cultivation of the Adivasis, ignoring community rights, et cetera.

The enforcement of labour welfare laws is worse than that of the land laws due to the weak position of labour, dilatory adjudicating process, and insensitive enforcement machinery. The Adivasis are overwhelmingly employed as agricultural workers. The implementation of the Minimum Wages Act in this sector is virtually non-existent. The Equal Remuneration Act is violated with impunity. Similar is the fate of laws relating to beedi workers and brick kiln workers where Adivasis are concentrated as unskilled labourers. The enforcement of the Bonded Labour Abolition Act is unabashedly resisted by the state governments who are always in a denial mode about its existence. The implementation of the Inter-State Migrant Labour Act is even worse on account of the bias of the states receiving migrant labour to protect their employers rather than render justice to the workers coming from other states. The law relating to Child Labour, despite the sensitive interventions of the Supreme Court, fares no better as is evident from frequently reported cases of child labour freed from the clutches of heartless employers. Besides, a very large part of the work force which is in the informal sector is not even covered effectively by labour welfare laws. The most glaring omission in this regard relates to domestic work where Adivasi girls are engaged and are suffering social, economic and sexual exploitation.

Tribal Sub-Plan (TSP)

On the development front, the institutional mechanism of Tribal Sub-Plan has failed to bridge the development gap between the Adivasis and others. The flow of resources to the Tribal Sub-Plan from the Central Plan has been much below the population as a proportionate percentage of STs. The Plan documents have been critical of some Central ministeries for not earmarking funds for TSP (Planning Commission, 2004). The same is true of the state governments which are reluctant to earmark the required allocation of funds and place them at the disposal of the nodal department (Planning Commission 2004 and 2007). The allocated funds remain substantially underutilised. Even the funds spent by them have been used largely for infrastructure and area development with little direct benefit to the Adivasis. Special Central assistance funds are not released to the implementing agencies in time. The access of Adivasis to credit from commercial banks is very low. The cooperative credit infrastructure has virtually collapsed. In asset building programmes, where a subsidy component is provided to the banks to induce them to lend, the credit extension is too meagre to be of effective use. The financing and development corporations exclusively meant for providing capital to the Adivasis for starting their own enterprises suffer from poor management, low recovery of loans advanced, absence of dedicated field agencies to process proposals and oversee projects, and delay in release of share capital by the Central and the concerned state governments. Overall, development efforts have failed to improve the conditions of the Adivasis due to (a) inadequate investment of public resources, (b) non-utilization, wrong utilization, and diversion of earmarked, allocated, or committed funds for their benefit, (c) deficiency in planning, and (d) unresponsive delivery system.

The efforts of the Central Government to prevent exploitation of Adivasis by traders in marketing of minor forest and agro-produce have also collapsed due to mismanagement and corruption of the apex organization, Tribal Cooperative Marketing Development Federation of India Ltd. (TRIFED) created for this purpose (Planning Commission, 2005; MTA, 2006). The situation at the state level is no better. In addition, monopoly procurement rights, exercised by the state government agencies, compound the woes of the Adivasis.

Participatory Arrangement

The participatory arrangement for enlisting the involvement of the Adivasis in democratic processes has not resulted in any effective sharing of power. The Adivasi candidates being resourceless depend upon persons with money and influence for getting elected which compromise their ability to speak up for issues that concern their communities vitally. The representation of Adivasis in the Central and state cabinets is extremely low, both in numerical terms as well as in terms of the weight of the portfolios assigned to them. Outside the arena of government, political parties provide no genuine space for sharing power beyond a tokenistic representation. There is little effort to give them leadership positions. The reality in respect of PESA-96 lays bare the illusion of self-governance conveyed by the text. The states have virtually deconstructed its provisions through numerous legal contortions, thus reducing its import and effectiveness (Prabhu, 2007). The state itself is ignoring the provisions of PESA, as for example, in obtaining the consent of Gram Sabha in the matter of land acquisition (Rao, 2006). The opposition of Gram Sabha to land acquisition is disregarded and its resistance broken with coercive tactics (Reddy, 2006). As for the reservation in the government positions, Adivasis have not attained the requisite percentage even in category C and D jobs let alone the higher ones. With the onset of neoliberal economy, this limited avenue of getting secure employment has been curtailed due to the policies of downsizing of establishment and outsourcing of work to private agencies. The reservation provisions are also subverted by non-Adivasis by obtaining false caste certificates and are also violated in many establishments. The reservation in higher educational and technical institutions remains under utilized due to financial underutilized and cultural constraints to pursue courses and the poor quality of lower level of educational system. The National Commission to protect the interests of the Adivasis are weak with no power to deliver justice in respect of the complaints received by them. Their reports are presented to the Parliament late and are rarely discussed. The successive governments have shown no enthusiasm to pursue their recommendations.

Roots of Failure

The foregoing analysis brings out that the disparities faced by the Adivasis in India are a category apart, different from those faced by other sections of the poor. These disparities are also rooted in history, going back to antiquity when the encounter with Aryans pushed them back from alluvial plains to the isolation of forested hills. This isolation shaped up a distinct cultural tradition, social organization, and more or less, a self-sufficient economy embedded in the local ecology. Over the centuries, the Adivasis managed to preserve their ethnicity, economy, social relations, and governance arrangements unhindered notwithstanding varying degrees of contact some groups had with the non-Adivasis located in the vicinity. But the colonial period shattered this arrangement. It appropriated their resources of subsistence, integrated them with market capitalism, introduced property relations, imposed centralized governance arrangements and brought them into contact with the aggressive mainstream community of a magnitude that overwhelmed them. The resulting multifaceted exploitation produced numerous revolts against the colonial authority across the Adivasi belt which were quelled by extensive use of violence. But the realization of the 'distinctness' of the Adivasis also dawned on the rulers, along with the feeling of damage that could be caused to them by their unregulated contact with outsiders. Some protective arrangements were consequently introduced. The integration of Adivasi areas through extension of administration and penetration of colonial economy continued except for frontier areas which were partially administered. Independent India continued with these arrangements while providing for safeguards to protect them from the adverse impact of development and modernization. But the intensity of state expansion in Adivasi areas, and encroachment into their resource base resulting from nation-building and development activities have exerted unprecedented pressure on their fragile social system and rendered all protective arrangements ineffective at best and irrelevant at worst. With the integration of the national economy to the global market, the ambit of disparities has widened. The Adivasis have become completely defenceless and their coping mechanism has broken down against the forces unleashed by the new economic policies while the state has turned more unresponsive to their plight. This is the perspective that informs the problem of disparities Adivasis experience in relation to the dominant majority of population.

It is evident that the state has no appreciation that the multifaceted disparities experienced by the Adivasis result from the ideology of the state itself with regard to the economy, development, modernization, nation-building and governance, and the hegemonic social relations with mainstream communities in which they are enmeshed. It blissfully ignores its own responsibility in widening disparities by disregarding the essential distinctness of Adivasis in the process of their social and economic integration with the rest of the population. Worse, its agenda of bridging these disparities and instruments devised for this purpose not only end up by reinforcing them, but even accentuating them. A government sensitive to the suffering of the Adivasis would have learnt this lesson from the expanding insurgency in the central Indian Adivasi belt which is not directed at secession from the nation state but against the injustices perpetrated on them by the system. However, the response of the government to the political articulation of this grievance is not to review its own policies and actions responsible for this situation but rather engage in retaliatory violence to maintain the very iniquitous order which generated this mobilization. There is reluctance to concede that the Adivasis are different from the mainstream community in respect of their social institutions, cultural values, economic practices, and governance arrangements. They hold a different view on what constitutes development, the structures and institutions which should govern them, regulatory arrangements which could protect them against corrosive market forces, and the cunning mainstream community and system of law which could administer justice to them than what has been imposed on them. But Adivasis do not challenge the authority of the state. Their interests can be creatively accommodated within the Constitution if there is proper appreciation of their case and the political will to do so. This poses serious challenges for policy and governance.

Challenges of Policy and Governance

The foremost of these challenges is the need to recognize that the Adivasis are culturally distinct from the mainstream communities, and this distinctness is defined not merely in terms of cultural traits such as inter-personal relations, social values, and aspirations, but also social organization, economy, governance which carve out their identity. Given the constitutional framework of protection for cultural diversity, this distinctness should get due recognition from the state as well as the larger society. This recognition requires that state policies and governance as well as societal behaviour and dealings with the Adivasis do not repudiate this democratic right and necessary institutional arrangements and an enabling social environment is created for the Adivasis to carry on with their system of life without interference. This would imply that the policies and governance arrangements which have had the effect of destroying this distinctness be revised/reversed and the interface of the Adivasis with the larger society be regulated strictly on terms which the Adivasis choose to suggest. This concession should not be perceived as a challenge to the integrity of the nation or a negation of allegiance to the state or a repudiation of 'equality' in the treatment of citizens. The Adivasis should be allowed to work out mechanisms for harmonizing their freedom to practise their 'distinctness' with the citizenship of state and creatively resolving tensions arising out of this delicate process of adjustment. The state should facilitate this process.

The second serious challenge before the state is to refrain from disturbing the traditional control of the Adivasis over natural resources—land, water, forests and their management within their territorial jurisdiction. This would imply that the state should cease to regard itself as the absolute owner of all natural resources and sole arbiter to determine the pattern of their allocation and use. This curtailment of sovereign power does not imply that the state would have no say in the use of resources and that the resources cannot be used in a manner other than how the Adivasis have traditionally used them. What this proposition entails is that the state would have to consult the Adivasis on alternative uses of resources, convince them of the benefits it would have for them and agree to the terms and conditions suggested by them if they agree to their diversion. In other words, the state would have to share decision-making with the Adivasis. This would require the state to carefully design its proposals of resource use so as to directly benefit the Adivasis and demonstrate through their execution the sincerity of its intentions with a view to obtaining their consent.

The third serious challenge before the state is to let the Adivasis decide the nature and level of contact with the non-Adivasis or even the Adivasis of other areas. This contact has two dimensions. One relates to the contact which results when the non-Adivasis or outsiders come into the Adivasi areas and the other when the Adivasis go out of their area. While taking this decision, the Adivasis would also lay down the contours of this contact where non-Adivasis come to their area and the nature and extent of protection they would require when they move out of their area. The Adivasis would also decide the pace of this contact which enables them to adjust with the cultural shock resulting from it and the corrective interventions they would require if the contact turns out to be detrimental to their interests. This would imply that this contact cannot be left to the social and economic forces to determine as at present. The state would have to design and evaluate its policies and governance arrangements taking this aspect into account and facilitate limiting of this contact in tune with the wishes of the Adivasi communities expressed through their collective decision.

The fourth challenge lies in permitting the Adivasi communities to conceptualize their paradigm of development which enables genuine participation on their own terms (Mcneish, 2005) and enhances their happiness and well being. They should also determine the mechanism and processes of this deliberation. The state should tailor its development policies in accordance with this decision irrespective of whether it deviates from the 'national norm'. Having conceptualized the model of development, the Adivasis should also be allowed to work out the strategy of its implementation, the design of its delivery arrangements and the manner of its monitoring and evaluation. This would imply that the state cannot impose a development model on them nor it can design programmes and schemes on their behalf assuming that their needs are no different from those of the other citizens. The state would have to create institutional arrangements to effect this empowerment which would go beyond Panchayat Extension to the Scheduled Areas (PESA) and may involve introducing some features of the Sixth Schedule besides other measures into their area which helps them to have greater control over natural resources and autonomy to manage their institutions.

The Adivasis are not starting from a clean slate. They are already overwhelmed by the non-Adivasi presence in many parts of their areas and are subject to multifaceted exploitation. They also move out to other areas for livelihood where they face conditions far worse than those existing in their own. The existing protective arrangements have failed to change this situation. The huge challenge is to put in place effective methods of protection. This would require not only strengthening the existing arrangements, but putting in place additional ones in line with the wishes of the Adivasis.

The issues relating to the Adivasis revolve around their identity which is related to the geographical territory in which they have an overwhelming presence. Their traditional system of governance was effective and could survive because of this demographic character within the identified territories. This has been radically disturbed by development policies, pattern of economy, and arrangements of governance. From this overwhelming presence, they are now reduced to a minority even in their own territory. The protection of

Adivasis as a distinct social entity is contingent upon the demographic balance being maintained in their favour in the areas of their concentration. This would require reversing policies which disturb this balance and regulating the pace and magnitude of their contact with the non-Adivasis. It is also necessary to bring nearly 40 per cent of the Adivasis population located outside the areas within the ambit of the concerned Schedules. A rigorous regulatory mechanism has to be put in place to check attempts of the non-Adivasi communities to obtain the status of a 'Scheduled Tribe' with a view to usurping the benefits of the latter. The process of scheduling of areas and inclusion into the list of Scheduled Tribes would have to be taken out of the ambit of political discretion for this purpose. Further, the fraudulent practice of obtaining a certificate of Tribal status has to be effectively curbed. This should include, among others, laying down methods of verification, expeditious investigation into the complaints of false certification, fast track prosecution, and trial of those found guilty and withdrawal of the wrongful benefits enjoyed by them. A comprehensive law has to be enacted for this purpose.

The more difficult challenge is to design a justice administration system which takes into account the social and cultural values as also the vulnerability of the Adivasis and inspire confidence regarding its ability to deliver justice to them. One aspect of this design would be a decentralized system where the Adivasi community adjudicates on conflicts between the members of the village and decides on the offences of lesser gravity. This would be conceptually more akin to the Nyay Panchayats, but the whole community would constitute the 'court' on the lines of traditions of Adivasi self-governance. The body would also have far greater powers and much wider jurisdiction handling the cases under different laws, regulations, et cetera, than the 'Nyay Panchayats' in the non-Adivasi areas. The other dimension of the justice administration system relates to offences and conflicts that cannot be dealt with by this Nyay Panchayat. The redesigning of this layer of the justice system would require radical changes in the judicial processes, norms of evidence, role of lawyers et cetera. This would call for jurisprudential engineering to harmonize with the social ethos of the Adivasis and make it user-friendly.

The most overarching challenge is to concede maximum self-governance to the Adivasis. Without this commitment, none of the other challenges can be faced. This would require the minimum presence of the state in terms of structures of governance and personnel managing them and the maximum degree of facilitation of the Adivasis to manage their own affairs. The nature of this minimum administration should be settled by the Adivasis collectively, which should be an evolving process. This obviously has to go much beyond the conceptual design of PESA 1996. Its details would have to be worked out in consultation with the Adivasis to give it a concrete shape.

To operationalize the changes outlined above, some constitutional changes would be required to strengthen the provisions of the Fifth Schedule, which has remained virtually ornamental, and some elements of the Sixth Schedule and/or new features would need to be introduced.

Bleak Future

It is evident that the challenges outlined above strike at the root of the approach followed so far, which views the Adivasis like any other group in society albeit with some historical disadvantages, and therefore, extends a standardized package to bridge the disparities they face to enable them to catch up with the rest of the population. This paper advocates a paradigm shift in this approach towards a model which provides maximum autonomy to these communities for self-governance and permits them to pursue their own design of development and at their own pace. The role of the state gets reduced to that of a facilitator, providing resources—finance, technology, regulation for their relations with the dominant groups and social and economic institutions, and any other help sought by the Adivasis. This approach certainly implies a considerable withdrawal of the state from the existing pattern of governance (not in the neoliberal sense) but in no way threatens the integrity of the nation or the sovereignty of the state. It would lessen conflict, strengthen peace and social harmony, enhance self-esteem of the Adivasis, promote inclusive development and responsive governance, and enrich democracy. The agenda is not utopian but it is capable of implementation within the framework of the Constitution. Would the state have the political will to bite the bullet? Past experience suggest that this is unlikely. The disparities between the Adivasis and the rest of the population would, therefore, continue and even worsen. The prospects for the Adivasis to survive with dignity are, therefore, bleak.

REFERENCES

Areeparampil, Mathew (1989). 'Industries, Mines and Displacement of Indigenous People. The Case of Chhotanagpur', in Fernandes, Walter and Thukral, Enakshi Ganguly (eds): *Development, Displacement and Rehabilitation,* Indian Social Institute, New Delhi.

Bhagat, R.B. (2013). Conditions of SC/ST Households: A Story of Unequal Improvement, *Economic and Political Weekly*, Vol. LVIII, No. 41, October.

Bakshi, Aparjita, www.ideas website.org.tdss.landownership.pds accessed on August 17, 2015.

Beteille, Andre (1974). *Six Essays on Comparative Sociology*, chapter 4 'Tribes and Peasantry', Oxford University Press, Delhi.

Beteille, Andre (1974). *Studies in Agrarian Social Structure*, Oxford University Press, New Delhi.

Beteille, Andre (ed) (1969). 'The Decline of Social Equality', in *Social Inequality. Selected Readings*, Penguin Books.

Corebridge, Stuart (1982). 'Industrial Development in Tribal India: Iron Ore Mining Industry in Singhbhum District 1900-1960' in Sengupta, Nirmal (ed): *Fourth World Dynamics: Jharkhand*, Author's Guild Publication, Delhi.

Corebridge, Stuart (2004). The Ideology of Tribal Economy and Society: Politics in Jharkhand, C 1950-1980, in Corebridge, Stuart, Jeweitt, Sarah, and Kumar, Sanjay (eds) *Jharkhand: Environment, Development, Ethnicity*, Oxford, New Delhi.

Centre for Equity Studies (2014). *India Exclusion Report 2013–14*. Books for Change, New Delhi.

Daghamvar, Vasudha (2006). *Role and Image of Law in India: The Tribal Experience in India*, Sage, New Delhi.

Deshpande, Ashwini (2015). Being Adivasi in India: Changing Economic Status of Tribal, Communities, *Critical Development Studies*, Issue 1, March, Council for Social Development, Southern Regional Centre, Hyderabad.

Escobar, Arturo (1997). 'Planning', in Sachs, Wolfgang (ed).

Esteva, Gustavo (1997). 'Development' in Sachs, Wolfgang (ed).

Eversole, Robyn (2005). 'Overview – Patterns of Indigenous Disadvantage Worldwide, in Eversole, Robyn et al (eds).

Eversole, Robyn, McNeish, John Andrew and Cimadamore Alberto D (2005). *Indigenous Peoples and Poverty, An International Perspective*, Zed books, London, New York.

Fernandes, Walter (2006). 'Liberalisation and Development Induced Displacement', *Social Change*, Vol. 36, Number 1, March, 2006.

Institute of Applied Manpower Research (2011). *India—Human Development Report 2011: Towards Social Inclusion,* Planning Commission, Government of India, Oxford, New Delhi.

Lummis, C Doughles (1997). 'Equality' in Sachs, Wolfgang (ed).

Mccaskil, Don and Rutherford Jeff (2005). 'Indigenous Peoples of South-East Asia, Poverty, Identity and Resistance', in Eversole, Robyn, et al (eds).

McNeish, John Andrew (2005). 'Overview: Indigenous Peoples' Perspectives on Poverty and Development' in Eversole, Robyn et al (eds).

McNeish, John Andrew and Eversole, Robyn (2005a). 'Overview—The Right to Self-determination' in Eversole, Robyn et al (eds).

McNeish, John Andrew and Eversole, Robyn (2005b). 'Conclusions, Poverty, People and Meaning of Change, in Eversole, Robin, et al (eds).

Ministry of Finance, Department of Economic Affairs (2010). *Annual Survey 2009–10*, Economic Division, February.

Ministry of Rural Development (2004). *Report of the Expert Group on Prevention of Alienation of Tribal Land and its Restoration*, April.

Ministry of Rural Development (2008). *Annual Report 2008–09.*

Ministry of Tribal Affairs (2006). *Annual Report 2005–06.*

Ministry of Tribal Affairs (2009). *Annual Report 2008–09.*

Ministry of Tribal Affairs (2015). *Annual Report 2014-15*, Government of India, New Delhi.

Mishra, Banikanta (2010). 'Agriculture, Industry and Mining in Orissa in Post Liberalisation Era: An Inter-district and Inter-State Panel Analysis', *Economic and Political Weekly*, Vol. XLV, No. 20, 15 May.

Mishra, Rajiv, Chatterjee, Rachel and Rao, Sujatha (2003). *India Health Report,* Oxford, New Delhi.

Munda, Ram Dayal (2005). *Globalization and the Challenges of Tribal Development,* Council for Social Development, New Delhi.

National Centre for Advocacy Studies (2005). *Advocacy Update on Land Rights*, Issue 18, October–December.

National Commission for Enterprises in the Unorganised Sector (2009). *The Challenge of Employment and Development in India, An Informal Economy Perspective*, New Delhi.

Planning Commission (2004). *Mid-Term Appraisal of the Tenth Five Year Plan.*

Planning Commission (2005). *Report of the Task Group on Development of SCs and STs,* March.

Planning Commission (2007). *Eleventh Five Year Plan.*

Planning Commission (2012). *Twelfth Five Year Plan (2012–17)* Vol. III, Government of India, New Delhi.

Prabhu, Pradip (2006). 'Development Paradigm, Praxis and Change in Tribal Society', Personal Communication from the author.

Prabhu, Pradip (2007). 'PESA and the Illusions of Tribal Self-Governance', in *Equalities.* This is our homeland, Bangalore.

Radhakrishna, R and Shovan, Ray (2005). *Hand Book of Poverty in India: Perspective, Policies and Programmes*, Oxford, New Delhi.

Rao, Palla Trinadha (2006). 'Nature of Opposition to the Polavaram Project', *Economic and Political Weekly*, 15 April.

Rath, Govind Chandra (ed) (2006). *Tribal Development in India, The Contemporary Debate* – Introduction, Sage, New Delhi.

Reddy, N. Subba (2006). 'Development Through Dismemberment of the Weak. Threat of Polavarams Project', *Economic and Political Weekly*, 15 April.

Roy Burman, B.K. (2009). 'What has driver the Tribal of Central India to Extremism', *The Mainstream*, 17 October.

Sachs, Wolfgang (ed) (1997). *The Development Dictionary: A Guide to Knowledge as Power*, Orient Longman, New Delhi.

Sarkar, Sandip, Misra, Sunil, Dayal, Harishwar and Nathan, Dev (2006). *Scheduled Tribes of India-Development and Deprivation*, Institute of Human Development, New Delhi.

Sen, Amartya (1995). *Inequality Re-examined*, Oxford, New Delhi.

Sharma, B.D. (1978). *Tribal Development–The Concept and the Frame*, Prachi, New Delhi.

Singh, K.S. (1982). 'Transformation of Tribal Society: Integration vs Assimilation', *Economic and Political Weekly*, 14 April and 21 August.

Xaxa, Virginius (2009). 'Tribes, Conversion and Sangh Parivar' in Kumar Dharmendra and Sunny Yemuna (eds) *Proselytization in India: The Process of Hinduisation in Tribal Societies*, Aakar, Delhi.

ENDNOTES

In respect of information on Economic Disparities, updated information, to the extent available, is furnished below. The gaps, if any, are due to non-availability of reliable sources or comparability of information. Information in respect of some additional dimensions is also included.

Rural Urban Distribution

In terms of Rural-urban distribution, while 91.14% of ST population is rural, it is only 60.27% in case of 'Others' and 80.04% in the case of SCs. Of the main source of livelihood, around 1/3 of ST (31.83%) households exclusively depend upon wage work as agricultural labour, it is 36% in respect of SCs and 15% in the case of 'Others'. About 42% of ST households are self-employed in Agriculture (Primary activities) as against 44.02% in the 'Others' category and 18.26% in respect of SCs. The percentage share of STs in casual labour is 23.12% compared to only 6.4% in the case of 'Others' and 26.2% in respect of SCs. Overall only 27.22% of ST households are self-employed the urban areas with 43% workers only 3% ST households are regular salaried workers through with 41% ST workers in contrast to 49 of households among 'Others'. The percentage share of STs in casual labour is 23.12% compared to only 6.4% in the case of 'Others' and 26.2% in respect of SCs. Overall only 27.22% of ST households are self-employed as against 43.07% in respect of 'Others' and 28.65% in the case of SCs (Despande, 2014)

Labour Force Participation

Labour force participation in respect of STs was 69.9% (rural) and 51.5% (Urban) compared to 60.4% (Rural) and 48.8% (Urban). The case of others and 62.4% (Rural) and 53.5% (Urban) for SCs (IAMR, 2011). STs have the highest proportion of men in the labour force (86.7%) compared to (81.01%) in respect of 'Others' and 84.69% in the case of SCs. The position of women in Labour force was 45.5% (STs) 18.6% (Others) and 30.32% (SCs) (Despande, 2014).

Employment

Unemployment rate of % of labour force (2009-10) for STs was 7.5% Current Daily Status (CDS) and 1.4% Usual Principal and Subsidiary Status (UP & SS) in Rural and 10.0% (CDS) and 4.4% (UP& SS) in Urban areas compared to 6.4 (CDS) and 1.6 (UP & SS) in Rural and 6.0 (CDS) and 3.4 (UP & SS) in Urban areas for Others. It was 11.9 (CDS) and 1.6 (UP & SS) in Rural and 10.1 (CDS) and 3.2 (UP & SS) in Urban areas for SCs. (IAMR, 2012)

Land Holding

Landlessness (2009-10) in respect of STs was the highest at 10.1% as against 8.6% for SCs and 8.3% at All India level. Among households with land, ST households with one hectare of land was also the lowest with 66.4% compared to 72.6% at All India level and 83.5% among SCs (IER, 2014)

Poverty

The incidence of Poverty (Head Count) in STs (2009-10) is 47.37% (Rural) and 30.38% (Urban) as against All India level of 33.8% (Rural) and 20.9% (Urban) and among SCs 42.26% (Rural) and 34.11% (Urban). The annual rate of decline among STs between 2004-05 to 2009-10 was 2.98% in Rural and 1.03% in (Urban) areas while it was 2.25% (Rural) and 1.29% (Urban) in respect of SCs and 1.60 (Rural) and 0.96 (Urban) for All India (Planning Commission 2012). The percentage gap among STs was 14% in Rural and 10% in Urban areas while it was 9% in Rural and 14% in Urban areas in the case of SCs.

Consumption Expenditure

The average MPCE (2007-08) of STs was 617 (Rural) and Rs. 1,221 (Urban) as against Rs. 964 (Rural) and Rs. 1,817 (Urban). Others Rs. 652 (Rural) and Rs. 1,100 (Urban) for SCs. Of this expenditure, STs spent 58.9% on food in rural and 46.0% in urban areas while this expenditure was 53.0% in rural and 45.9% in urban areas for 'Others' and 57.3% in rural and 48% in urban areas for SCs (IAMR, 2011).

Literacy

Literacy rate (2007-08) for STs was 58.8% compared to 76.9% in respect of Others, and 60.5% among Dalits. Gender wise distribution of Literacy among STs was 69.3% (Male) and 47.8% (Female) as against 84.6% (Male) and 68.8% (Female) in respect of 'Others' and 70.6% (Male) and 49.9% (Female) among SCs (IHDR, 2013). The percentage of Non Literate hhs (2009-10) among STs was 27.0% compared to 15.7% at All India level and 22.4% among SCs (IER, 2014). The position in respect of Out of School Children (2007-08) was 24.8% among STs compared to 14.3% in Others and 22.8% of among SCs. Gross Enrolment Ratio (2007-08) among STs was 129.3% at Primary, 74.4% at Upper Primary and 30.8% of Secondary and Higher Secondary level. This position at All India Level was 114.6% (Primary) 77.5% (Upper Primary) and 45.5% (Secondary and Higher Secondary) while it was 124.9

(Primary), 76.3% (Upper Primary) and 39.0% secondary and higher secondary level in respect of SCs (IAMR, 2011).

Health

On the health front, Sex-ratio among STs in 2011 was 990 as against 943 at All India level and 945 among SCs (IER, 2014). STs have infant mortality of 46 per thousand live births as against 22 in respect of Others and 39 in the case of SCs. They also have the highest child mortality under 5 at 84 per 1000 live births compared to 62 in respect of 'Others' and 83 in the case of SCs. The percentage of children with Anemia is also the highest in STs at 79 compared to 72 in respect of Others and 78 among SCs. Adivasis have 26% underweight children compared to 14% in the case of Others and 21 in respect of SCs (Planning Commission 2012). They along with SCs had in 2005-6 the highest percentage stunted children (53.9) compress to 40.7 in respect of Others. They have also the highest percentage (27.6) of wasted children compared to 18.4 in respect of 'Others' and 21.0 in the case of SCs (IER,2014). This condition is equally true of percentage of men and women with anemia. Women with anemia in STs was alarmingly high 68.5% in contrast to 51.2% in the case of 'Others' and 58.3% in respect of SCs. While Men with anemia in STs was 39.6% compared to 26.6% among SCs and 24.2% overall (IAMR, 2011). Percentage of women with BMI < 18.5 was 46.6 in STs compared to 29.3 in case of Others and 41.2 in respect of SCs. The Total Fertility Rate (2005-06) was also the highest in STs with 3.12 compared to 2.35 in 'Others' and 2.92 in respect of SCs. In respect of immunization, (2005-06) only 31.3% ST children received all vaccination in contrast to 53.8% in the case of 'Others' and 39.7% among SCs. While 10.9% of ST children received no vaccination, this position was 4.1% in respect of 'Others' and 5.4% among SCs. Only 17.7% ST women in (2005-06) had institutional deliveries compared to 52.6% women of 'other' households and 32.9% women of SC households. The working children (5-14 years) in 2007-08 were also the highest in STs with 3.8% compared to 2.0 in respect of Others and 2.8% in the case of SCs. This position was reflected in both boys and girls among working children. (IAMR, 2011).

Access to Civic Amenities

In respect of access to safe drinking water (2008- 09), households with Tap Water among STs was 24%, with hand pump/tubwell 52.2% and with well 17.9% compared to 51.6% 37.7% and 6.4% respectively in the case of 'Others' and 38.4%, 51.4% and 7.1% in the case of SCs (IAMR, 2011). As per 2011 census, only 19.7% of STs had source of drinking water within premises, 46.7% near the premises and 33.6% away from premises in contrast to All

India position of 46.6%, 35.8% and 17.6% respectively (MTA, 2014-15).

On the sanitation side, the position as per census 2011 was worse, with 77.4% ST households having no latrine within premises, 74.7% practising open defecation compared to the position at All India level of 53.1% and 49.8% respectively. A measly 6.1% ST households had waste water outlets connected to closed drainage while it was three times higher (18.1%) at All India level (MTA, 2014-15).

Housing, Electricity and Assets

In respect of housing, as per census 2011, only 10.1% ST households in 2011 had houses with a concrete roof compared to 29.6% households overall and 21.9% in respect of SCs. Access to electricity for lighting was available to 51.7% ST households compared to 67.2% at All India level and 59.0% in respect of SCs. Only 17.2% ST households had a bathroom in the premises compared to 42.0 at all India level and 27.7% in respect of SCs. In respect of electricity for lighting, 51.7% per ST households had this facility while it was 67.2% at all India level and 59.0% in respect of SCs. Only 9.2% households had access to LPG/PNG in contrast to 28.5% all India level and 16.9% in respect of SCs. These disparities can also be observed in respect of household assets such as television, telephone, mobile, computer/laptop, scooter/motor cycle/moped, car/van/jeep. The number of households with none of these assets including radio/transistor/cycle was the highest in STs with 37.3% while it was only 17.8% at All India level and 22.6% in SCs (Bhagat, 2013)

The foregoing shows that the disparities between STs and Others not only continue but, in many cases, have widened. STs have also not bridged their gap with SCs and continue to be at the lowest end virtually in all indicators of human development (Bhagat, 2013).

10

The Rights of Tribals over Their Land

T.L. Sankar

I came to know of Mr S.R. Sankaran's (SR's) very deep knowledge of Tribals, the history of their rights to their land, forests, and mineral wealth, and the long story of exploitation by almost every one who came to realise the true worth of the assets enjoyed by the Tribals. I came to comprehend the revolt and the continuing conflicts between the Tribals and the others, only when SR accepted the invitation to mediate between the Government and the Naxalites as part of the Committee of Concerned Citizens in early 2004. By then I had known SR for a long, long time. I first met SR as a fresher in the Loyola College, Madras in 1949 and till the date of his death in 2010, remained a close friend. Though, we have had endless arguments on many things from the date of our first meeting in the College (and these arguments never stopped till 2010), the subjects of our discussions were mostly relating to Scheduled Castes, their education and upliftment schemes and the pros and cons of keeping their identity separate or merging them into the mainstream. The Tribal issues were not prominent in our discussions but, in the later years, I could see that his compassion for those who were exploited for whatever reasons extended from children to women, to the untouchables and to the Tribals. With his sense of justice and human dignity he was able to see through the veil of modernity and progress which normally cloud the discussions on the displacement of Tribals, not only from their lands but from their culture and way of life and dignity which they greatly value.

Slowly, I learnt from SR many facts about Tribals and their struggles which I set forth here as a Primer on Tribals for the benefit of people like me, common people who strongly resent the 'conciliatory' policies of the government towards Tribals and peasants who stand as 'hurdles to progress and modernization' which come in the form of factories and mines. This piece is not a proper academic article appropriate for inclusion in a book comprising very deeply researched articles on this 'complex' question. It would have, however, served its purpose if at least some members of my 'Tribe', —the bureaucracy—read this and understand that persons like SR and a small band of civil servants were moved to acts of heroism in the service of the Tribals only out of their compassion for the exploited and a deep sense of justice and fair play.

Tribals are indigenous people who admittedly were in occupation of all the lands in the country, once upon a time. They are rightly called the indigenous people in many countries and in the international forums. With the advent of 'civilisation' and the migrations from other areas which brought in people with other ways of living based on cultivation of lands and rearing of animals. They by guile or force occupied the more productive areas of the land usually near the rivers and close to the sea. The indigenous people moved or were forced to move deeper into remote areas usually hills and forests which supported their very small needs. They became remote, isolated and generally forgotten in all our efforts to build a prosperous nation! While the remoteness of the Tribals provided some degree of protection and freedom to follow their culture and traditions it became an excuse for government and officials to forget and overlook them in the basic development programmes which provided basic services.

After a time, the slowly emerging knowledge about the value of what grows on the land like timber and valuable species like red sanders and the more importantly available valuables under the ground which were in the occupation of Tribals led to the more 'civilized' people occupying the valuable pieces of land nearer the rivers attempting to push back the original occupants into ever shrinking pockets of hills and barren deserts. The reluctance and refusal of the Tribals to part with their lands and rights started struggles and 'revolt'.

At this stage it may be useful to compare the numbers of the Tribals and the other 'minorities' whose needs are sought to be protected by special dispensations. How many realize that the Tribals constitute 8 per cent of India's population with over 70 million people, whereas, the total population of Christians is about 2.3 per cent only and Muslims constitute about 14.4 per cent. While the other minorities are spread all over the urban and rural India, the Tribals are confined to specific areas. The other minorities have migrated away from their ancient moorings and are able to mix and mingle with the rest of the population; Tribals who are geographically isolated remained outside the mainstream. The reasons may be many but the essential fact is that the 8 per cent Tribals with wide diversities among them are the 'Children of the Soil', and are remaining excluded from the mainstream of socio-economic progress. This state of affairs is common to all countries which have a majority of immigrant population.

While North America (USA and Canada) is an area of new immigrants, who came mainly from Europe over the last four or five centuries, India is a country of old immigrants with people who have been coming in, over the last ten thousand years or so! Probably about 92 per cent people living in India today are descendants of immigrants, who came mainly from the North-West and to a lesser extent from the North-East. It is noteworthy that in all such countries, the indigenous people were given some special rights. These primarily concerned the right to occupy some defined areas of land and enjoy the 'wealth' of the land. The wealth refers to what is naturally the available growth on the land or cultivated on the land collectively or individually and also the wealth in the form of minerals below the ground.

My interest in the rights of the indigenous people and their long struggle to retain their ownership and control of what they considered to be their heritage was kindled by the somewhat awkward twists and turns in the ownership of oil resources in 'Indian reservations' in USA. The chain of events leading to confining the indigenous people to specific areas 'Reservations' and conceding all rights within the reserved areas initially and abridging them later is closely similar in both USA and India. In both countries all the land was under the control of the indigenous people though they occupied only parts of it. Ancient folklore as well as the scriptures and old literature of these countries bear witness to the fact that the ancient occupants whom we call 'Tribals' and more accurately as 'indigenous' people of each land had fairly advanced life styles of their own which were in harmony with nature. It is also significant that much of these 'occupations of land' only refer to their use of land as a community without much of claims to permanent ownership on an individual basis over a specific piece of land. Everything that grew on the land or found under the ground was considered as common property whose benefits were to be shared by everyone in the community.

How slowly, the ideas of private ownership were seeded among the indigenous people have been very clearly set out in the history of the American Civilisation as recorded in the history of the Tribal and Indian land. Compiled from old folklore and available evidence the 'Montana Tribal History' gives some details. The history of 'Crow Tribe' says that around the year 1450 AD the Tribe found that the area under their occupation close to the great lakes of Canada and United States was too small for their growing population. The Tribes split under different chiefs. One great Chief, Red Scout elected to settle permanently taking up agriculture to grow corn, while another chief with his clan went further West and reached the regions in Wyoming, Colorado, Oakholma and possibly Missouri and continued their hunting and livestock rearing activities for their livelihood. But between 1840 and 1850, small pox epidemics wiped out much of the 'crow' Tribe population and reduced it to 2,000 from the earlier 10,000. In 1851, the treaty called the Fort Laramie Treaty was signed by the community with the US government which confined the Tribal population to an area of 38 million acres leaving the rest to the US intruders from the West. The immigrant western occupants were allowed to occupy land but subject to the condition that each farm should have a maximum of 650 acres. Within the reserved area all land was held by the community but an individual could realised occupy about 160 acres for personal cultivation. At this stage US Government Agencies realized the 'need' to develop (exploit) the wealth in the Tribal lands. US passed the Indian Re-organization Act under which money was provided in return for the support of the Tribals in the development of mineral resources under the land. The Tribes could lease the minerals for development to private agencies but with the approval of the designated government agency and subject to all the rules and conditions of the mining leases outside the reservations. It did not lead to much development of minerals, especially energy resources. In 2005 the Energy Policy Act in US provided an alternate route also for energy minerals. It provided that the Tribe could enter into a Tribal Energy Resource Agreement (TERA) with the Secretary of Interior. Under the provisions of TERA, Tribal administration could on its own lease the mineral and necessary surface rights on its own authority. The Tribe had to have its own environment protection laws and agency. The progress under this has also not been satisfactory and some further amendments are under consideration of the US legislature.

In India where there was a longer tradition of mining, gold, silver, iron, et cetra and the king had the right to apportion of this wealth leading to the concept of royalty. Western societies when they became colonial powers realized the value of minerals and precious stones underground. The started differentiating between the rights of what was above the ground which were conceded to the occupants of that piece of land, and what was found under the ground which was declared to belong to the government or the Sovereign. In India this vertical differentiation of land ownership extends to all lands in some form in all areas outside the Tribal lands. However, in some areas in North East states the British as well as other European nations in their first attempt to occupy lands which were originally under the Tribal/indigenous people agreed that the land and that everything on it and under it belonged to the original inhabitants in the areas to which they were confined. Later the government asserted its rights over the mineral resources through several legal and illegal measures.

In India, the struggles relating to land rights in Tribal areas started only when the plans for the development of forest wealth threatened their occupation of the living space or threatened to take away the common property assets which provided their livelihood.

In India, displacement of the population in vast areas due to development projects is quite historical. Since the colonial period there have been an enormous segments of displaced people. The most attractive zones for developmental projects have always been the forest resources, river systems and mineral bases and most of the developmental projects are located in the most backward areas and populated by Tribals. In India around 50 million people have been displaced due to development projects in over 50 years. Around 21.3 million development-induced displacements include those displaced by dams (16.4 million), mines (2.55 million), industrial development (1.25 million) and wildlife sanctuaries and national parks (0.6 million) (IDMC, 2007).Over 52 per cent of the displaced people are Tribals.

The difference in the treatment of Tribals and of other landowners has been brought out in a 2011 report *India and the Rights of Indigenous Peoples*, prepared by the Asia Indigenous Peoples' Pact with the ILO's support. The report states that minerals found in Adivasi or Tribal areas reportedly contribute to more than half of the national mining production. According to the report, as Indian law automatically assumes that all minerals found underground are state property. The rules framed under the Mining and Minerals (Regulation and Development) Act, 1957, while providing detailed procedures for a company or individual to obtain permission from the respective state government (and in some cases Central Government) to search for minerals, do not talk about the victims of such activity. The affected community is not required to be informed or consulted before mining leases are granted. The report observes that there is no mention of Adivasis' rights or protection in any of the procedures, although the Constitution of India has made special provisions for transfer of the lands of Tribals to non-Tribals.

Though the disaggregated data on the number of mines operating in the country or the number of people displaced by such projects does not officially exist as the information is deemed to be 'politically sensitive', the report estimates that an overwhelming majority of mines are located in the Adivasi areas. In 1991, out of the 4,175 mines in the country, 3,500 were in Tribal areas. Another estimate states that between 1950 and 1991 at least 2,600,000 people were displaced by mining projects of which only 25 per cent received any resettlement. In this background one can understand and appreciate the reasons for the poor, especially the Tribals rejecting of the proposals to take away their homes and land for building factories and mines even when the price and incentives offered in exchange appear reasonable to third parties whose sources of information on these matters are newspapers and electronic media.

While the Tribals displaced due to development projects have been treated unjustly, the Tribals still living in the lands set apart for them also undergo continuous harassment at the hands of the guardians of the forests armed with the draconian provisions of the Forest Act of 1957.

In India, the struggle for land rights began mostly on grounds of dignity and preservation of the native culture, and to assert their rights to derive a precarious livelihood from forest resources, their only source for living. In legal terms, the forest-based common pool resources (including wetlands, surface water and other water bodies in forest areas) provide access by way of property regimes outlined by the government and consist of:

a) Limited rights on reserved forests of specified communities
b) Rights as specified in protected and unclassed forests
c) The new genre of rights under evolving joint forest management schemes
d) Rights on village and panchayat forests

Upto 1980, forests were on the State List and each state had its own set of laws with respect to access to forest land. The position continues to be much the same even though forests are now on the Concurrent List and the centre too can legislate with respect to forests.

One report evaluating the management of common property assets in different countries has concluded that the ruling principle of forest management with respect to reserved forests has been 'preservation by exclusion'. The denial of the small privileges that Tribals enjoyed from time immemorial and their displacement without consent have been the principal causes for their uprisings and revolts.

Mr V. Raghavaiah in his book on *Tribal Revolts* in 1996 has listed over 70 Tribal revolts in their chronological order from 1778 to 1971; needless to say, there must have been equal number of such revolts from that day till date. Each of these troubles was caused by some denial of traditionally established rights over land in the occupation of the Tribals or high handed action of the so called forest law enforcement agencies in these agencies. But, there were also many revolts which continued for long durations turned into assertions of independence and revolts against the imposition of laws and regulations which were not in harmony with their traditional rights. Some of the earlier uprisings when they gathered wide support of the Tribals—the victims—openly espoused the cause of the freedom from colonial rule and/or imposition of state controls. In AP itself the struggles led by Alluri Seetharama Raju and later Komaram Bheem became legends which are celebrated even today in songs and festivals.

These periodic eruptions get some transient publicity; they do not project clearly the daily harassment that Tribals face for the violation of the Forest Act provisions. There are over a million-yes a million- cases pending against the Tribals for years, cases for which the compounding fees is only Rs 50 and they are pending because the Tribals do not have Rs 50 at a time to pay the compounding fees. This moved one young and effervescent minister who, when I was in service, was a valued colleague of mine- to say in an important public meeting, 'How do you prevent or address their continued victimisation, first by the state and now by the Naxals? Empowering the Tribals, who are essentially victims, by giving access to basics, by giving them what is theirs by right and by securing their livelihoods is, to my mind, an absolute undiluted must. Here, issues related to land ownership and land alienation must receive over-riding priority.' (Jairam Ramesh, 2012).

Recently I came across a recent Supreme Court decision pronounced in Kailas & Others vs State of Maharashtra [reported as AIR 2011 SC 598] which has made very interesting observations on the original inhabitants of India and their plight. It held that the historical theory that the Dravidians were the original inhabitants of India was not correct and actually the pre-Dravidian Tribals were the original inhabitants of this country. It traced the original inhabitants to some Tribes. The Supreme Court observed, 'The injustice done to the Tribal people of India is a shameful chapter in our country's history.' The Tribals were called 'rakshas' (demons), 'asuras', and what not. They were slaughtered in large numbers, and the survivors and their descendants were degraded, humiliated, and all kinds of atrocities inflicted on them for centuries. They were deprived of their lands, and pushed into forests and hills where they eked out a miserable existence of poverty, illiteracy, disease, et cetera. And now efforts are being made by some people to deprive them even of their forest and hill land where they are living, and the forest produce on which they survive.

The Court cited as an illustration, a story from the Adiparva of Mahabharat of Dronacharya and his disciple Eklavya as to how the erudite and learned upper castes exploited the Tribals. Eklavya a poor hunter wanted to learn archery, but Dronacharya who belonged to the upper caste refused to teach him, regarding him as 'low born'. Eklavya then built a statue of Dronacharya and practised archery before the statue. He might have perhaps become a better archer than Arjun, but since Arjun was Dronacharya's favourite princely pupil, Dronacharya told Eklavya to cut off his right thumb and give it to him as 'guru dakshina' (gift to the teacher given traditionally by the student after his study is complete). In his simplicity, Eklavya did what he was told by his 'Guru'.

What a shameful act on the part of Dronacharya? He had not even taught Eklavya, but knowing the ethical values of Tribals, he assumed the right to demand 'guru dakshina', and that too the right thumb of Eklavya so that the latter could not become a better archer than his favourite pupil Arjun. In fact Ekalvya the low-born with high ethical values lost the means to hunt and earn his daily meal. The story illustrates the attitude of the learned higher castes towards the lower castes and the heartless exploitation of the weaker sections . The Court itself has observed that time has come to set right these injustices.

Despite this horrible oppression against them, the Tribals of India have generally (though not invariably) retained a higher level of ethics than the non-Tribals in our country. They normally do not cheat, tell lies, and do other misdeeds which many non-Tribals do. They have generally remained simple and straightforward as compared to the non-Tribals.

Government at the centre at least has realized that it is time now to undo the historical injustice to them and slowly policy makers and the rulers started accepting that land cannot be treated as a commodity to be sold and purchased at the bidding in the market place but any land transaction should be seen as an act where some people given to elementary skills are uprooted and are pushed into an environment which cannot support their livelihoods, beliefs and culture. If there has to be a change in the utilization of land which was earlier occupied by peasants or Tribals, that their consent is a pre-requisite is now being recognized. As usual, moving through endless committees and consultations, GOI has labouriously worked out some amendments to the old Mines and Minerals Act. A bill was introduced in the Parliament and it was then referred to a Select Committee.

The amendment to the Mines and Minerals Development Act, is hailed as a great victory for the indigenous people as their rights to the land and wealth of the minerals have been conceded in two new provisions in the Amendment. One section has made it mandatory that rural lands can be acquired only in consultation with the Gram-Sabha. Another section provides that where the Tribal lands are taken over for coal mining, the Tribal population displaced have a right to 25 per cent of the profit after taxation made by the coal companies. This is over and above the other compensation and incentives But, in the case of other minerals like iron ore and bauxite (the aluminium ore) the local population are entitled to a sum of money equivalent to the royalty which the companies pay for the quantum of ore extracted. In both cases, as is usual in such bills, the proposed amendment bill drafted by officials—trained to preserve the rule of law and maintain sovereign dignity—has shown scant respect to principles of democratic participation and has prescribed the condition that the profit amount should be credited to the Government in a District Development Fund. The funds would be kept in a separate account and spent on the development of the area. The victims of the displacement are considered as incapable of designing their future and the hired help of the government which actively participated in evicting them could envision a bright future for these unfortunate victims.

At this stage, it would be appropriate to compare these grudgingly given concessions with the ILO Convention 169 which asserts that, 'The rights of ownership and possession of the peoples concerned over the lands which they traditionally occupy shall be recognised... measures shall be taken in appropriate cases to safeguard the right of the people concerned to use land not exclusively occupied by them, but to which they have traditionally had access for their subsistence and traditional activities...the rights of the people include the right to participate in the use, management and conservation of resources...any relocation shall take place only with their free and informed consent...'

Our attempts to do justice to the Tribals in the proposed bill is still miles away from what has been set out as the legitimate rights of these people by international bodies where India is an important participant.

The so-called generous provision to give the displaced 25 per cent of the post-tax profit is not an advantage given to the displaced persons; it may prove to be a disadvantage as the accounts of very large companies, especially MNCs can be manipulated in many ways to make the item 'Post-tax Profit' which is relevant for this purpose very low—much less than what it is—in a particular year. In any case, this provision can give rise to wasteful litigation as suspicions would be raised by many middlemen who can benefit which might include crafty consultants and even unethical NGOs. Even several NGOs dealing with mining issues in Jharkhand have already pointed out the level of competence of even the Government organizations and the possible manipulation of the interests of the Tribals by indifference, incompetence and the greed of officials and middlemen. The only improvement that can be done within the framework of the present draft if to make the annual compensation to be calculated in a manner easily understood by both parties and such a measure can be a multiple of the royalty. As royalty would be computed by experts of the state governments and will be the maximum estimated to be paid to the government by the miner for the rights for mining, the Tribal population need not worry over the determination of the royalty amount. Tribals will get a multiple of the royalty for giving up their homes and sources of livelihood. Second and more important amendment could be that this amount need not be credited to a distant District Development Fund but divided immediately among the concerned Panchayats in proportion to the devolution of funds fixed by the Finance Commissioner.

The provision that land can be acquired only in consultation with the Gram Sabha of the concerned villages is also not a great improvement over the existing provisions. It has not been unequivocally declared that the 'consent' of the gram-sabha is needed. Consultations and open hearings with video-graphing of the proceedings have not led to the desired results. It is important to amend the bill to substitute 'consent' in place of consultation.

As expected even the amendments with several weak links have raised a storm from the groups which had garnered huge profits from mines in Tribal lands. Industries associations, federations and individual high profile industrial leaders have drawn the attention of the Government to the adverse impact of those provisions on the industrial climate and the flow of FDI into India. Economists have started worrying about the impact on deteriorating economic environment.

It looks as though we are entering 'a new age clash of cultures' which commenced in small pockets of remote forests and hill areas and has grown into a Peoples War! Over four decades of governments in the centre and states have tried to treat the clashes as law and order issues while the other side has argued their case as a struggle for survival and preservation of the small privileges given in the Constitution of India and that they have taken to arms only in defence of their self-respect from the brutal, wanton and often motivated oppressive measures by the Forest Department officials earlier and followed later by the Armed Police Forces specially formed to fight the people of the forests in the forests itself. After four decades of this confrontation, the situation has all the attributes of a 'war' with both sides escalating violence and increasing the sophistication of the weaponry and with frequent episodes of relapse to barbarian acts in total disregard of human values. Each side later justifies each such act as a retaliation to an earlier act by the other side. The Prime Minister of the country has declared the continuing Tribal unrest officially called Naxalism as the most dangerous threat to our democracy!

A lasting solution to the preservation of the rights of the Tribals and others with legitimate rights living in the forest areas and peace and serendipity retuning to the forests is not possible by approving the provisions of the amendment even after they are discussed in great detail by the Select Committee of the Parliament and may be by other committees as well. I witnessed the anguish of SR when he was involved in the government appointed committee for Peace Talks. Talks became repeated monologues of two opposing groups reiterating their views without making any attempt to understand the other.

With my limited understanding of all the required background to these issues, I am pushed to the strange conclusion that there can be no co-existence between the two groups with such divergent aspirations –one group committed to growth based on the typical technology-big business –capital accumulation measured in GDP and share market indices and the other group, at least in theory, with aspirations towards survival and slow growth built in environmentally benign forest surroundings without disturbing the ecological balance and with great reverence to old traditions and values. The two cannot coexist within a single paradigm of development. The global economic crisis which is slowly engulfing Europe leads me to the view that it is the right time to give a chance for an alternative development paradigm to be nourished in parallel to the current paradigm followed by the Government. The technology and capital induced development could be followed in all areas outside the scheduled Tribal lands and other forest areas notified to be included in the scheduled areas. The scheduled areas should be divided into convenient regions of appropriate size and handed over to the people who are living permanently in the area or are legitimately allowed to reside in the forest areas to provide educational and medical assistance. All policing, military and forest officials should be vacated from this area. Each scheduled area or region would frame rules regarding its governance. The area, the land and all its wealth on ground and under the ground shall be given in trust to the regional committee. While entrusting the land in a trust for a period of 25 years, the number of trees will be counted and adequate number of aerial photographs will be taken to provide the base line data relating to the current ecological status. This committee of Tribals should agree to prove year by year that the trees entrusted to them increase in numbers and ensure their overall health. The Tribal development committees would draw up their own Development Plans with the guidance and help provided by persons desired by them from a pool of economists, planning experts, and technical experts in various subjects, but they would function only in an advisory capacity. The people's government in the Tribal scheduled areas will be the supreme authority. All assistance could be provided by setting up schools, colleges, technical schools and colleges by the government within this area but with funds provided by the Government; the funds saved by withdrawing the forest police and security personnel should be adequate for this. All investments in productive ventures should be by the Tribals and investments above Rs. 100 crore in industry can be made within the scheduled areas only by the Government. The laws and acts which are of great social relevance should all be extended to the Tribal areas area: at the end of the 25 years we should review the relative growth in financial prosperity and peace and happiness of people in the Tribal areas as compared to those in the non-Tribal areas.

In taking up this gigantic experiment, we would only act as per the ILO Convention 169 which categorically states that, 'The rights of the people include the right to participate in the use, management and conservation of resources... any relocation shall take place only with their free and informed consent...'

Incidentally, we will fulfil expectation of people like SR who stated even five years back that it was possible to find a long term direction for a democratic restructuring of society which alone can completely address many of the questions which are being faced by the people. He reiterated his faith in the common people who have a great stake in the move towards a just and humane society and who are willing to respond to the initiatives incorporating higher and non-negotiable standards of democracy, human rights and the rule of law.

11

Irrelevance of Land Reforms Policies to the Tribals of Jharkhand

B.K. Sinha

Policy incoherence is one of the most calamitous things to befall the governance of a country. While it gives the satisfaction to the policymakers of having done a good job, its delivery at the field level is a zero sum game. One of the consequences to flow out from this phenomenon is that it embarks the country on an endless exercise in self-delusion, getting away from the reality all the while. The same thing has gripped the mandarins in the 'magic land' of Krishi Bhavan-Shastri Bhavan where the ministries that matter for the Tribals of the Schedule V areas are located namely that of Panchayati Raj that administers the Panchayat (Extension to the Scheduled Areas) Act, 1996, the Ministry of Tribal Affairs administering the Schedules Tribes and Other Traditional Forest Dwellers (Recognition of Forest Rights) Act, 2006 and the Department of Land Resources, Ministry of Rural Development which is responsible for implementation of land reforms in the country. These ministries control the destinies of the Tribals in the central, western, south central and the middle eastern India. Yet, together these ministries have not been able to stem the erosion in the corpus of Tribal lands nor have they been able to provide a sense of security to those who live within the Tribal eco-land-social system. This, because of policy incoherence that has come to afflict the mandarins occupying inter alia the three ministries. That is where we have a cause to remember the late S.R. Sankaran, a doyen amongst the Administrator-Tribalogists of the likes of P.S. Appu, B.N. Yugandhar, K.B. Saxena, and D. Bandhopadhyay. These stalwarts had together developed an understanding of the Tribal land issues which by and large eluded their successor administrators, the present author included. Together, they formed the ABYSS (Appu-Bandopadhyay-Yugandhar-Sankaran-Saxena) School of Land Reforms. In this article, we see how compliance has deserted the policy regimen pushing the Tribal deeper into the embrace of the left radicalism.

Land is the only asset which the Tribal people are left with. The land rights of the Tribal communities are at the root of their land security. These rights are intertwined with their socio-religious institutions. Take the land away from the Tribals and they are left with nothing in their lives but toil and degradation. There has been a steady erosion in the corpus of Tribal land thereby undermining the very basis of Tribal life. The chapter reveals that numerous subterfuges that have been devised to render the protective body of laws effect and even an instrument for dispossession, the Government being the greatest culprit with using the instrumentality of land acquisition provisos for transfer of Tribal lands to the non-Tribals in the name of development. The process has been hastened after the creation of a separate Jharkhand State, purportedly to protect the Tribal land, forests, minerals and their way of life. The land security of the corpus of Tribal lands was never weaker than what it is today with worse forebodings for the future. In this context, the chapter examines the general gamut of land reforms in the country as well as in the State of Jharkhand and their relevance to the Tribal people. The chapter leaves one with the conclusion that land reforms have little relevance to the socio-economic and politically disempowered Tribal communities. In fact, every instrument of protection for their land leads to erosion in the corpus of land security and the erosion of their corpus of land. The land rights of the Tribal communities are at the root of their land security.

The Tribals: Indian Panorama

The Indian panorama encompasses a bewildering mosaic of ethnicities[1] living within a plethora of ecosystems and climatic zones[2], each replete with its wide range of biodiversities, livelihood patterns, living habits and even a philosophical framework. The term 'Tribe' has nowhere been defined in the Indian Constitution. Article 366(25) of the Constitution merely states that Scheduled Tribes means 'such Tribes or Tribal communities or parts of or groups within such Tribes or Tribal communities as are deemed under Article 342 to the Scheduled Tribes for the purposes of this Constitution.'[3] Article 342(2) of the the Constitution empowers the Parliament, by law, to include in or exclude from the list of Scheduled Tribes, specified in a notification issued under Article 342(1), any Tribe or Tribal community or part of or group within any Tribe or Tribal community.[4] Thus, the first specification of a Scheduled Tribe in relation to a particular state/union territory is by a notified order of the President following due consultation with the state governments concerned. These orders can subsequently be only modified through an Act of the Parliament. The above Article also provides for listing of Scheduled Tribes State/Union Territory-wise and not on an all India basis.

The criteria followed for specification of a community as a Scheduled Tribe include indications of primitive traits, distinctive culture, geographical isolation, shyness of contact with the community at large and economic and other kinds of backwardness.[5] These criteria are not spelt out in the Constitution, but have become well established over the course of years. Thus, the nomenclature 'Tribal' or 'Tribe' finds both common understanding and acceptance within such communities and without in the general parlance. Of the 4,635 communities in the country, so far more than 700 communities have been identified[6] as Scheduled Tribal under Article 342 of the Constitution of India and provided protection, safeguards and incentives under the Indian Constitution and the statutes arising therefrom. These would include Primitive Tribes Groups (PTGs) who are so categorised on account of their stage of sociological-anthropological development and who are in need of greater protection. In India, these people are also known by some other names such as Vanyajati (people of forest), Vanvasi (inhabitants of forest), Pahari (hill dwellers), Adimjati (primitive people), Adivasi (first settlers), Janjati (folk people), Anusuchit Janjati (scheduled Tribe) and so on (Vidyarthi, 1976).[7]

Most of these do not belong to the settled agricultural stage. The Scheduled Tribes population of the country, as per the 2001 census, is 8.43 crore, constituting 8.2 per cent of the total population. The population of Scheduled Tribes grew at the rate of 24.45 per cent during the period 1991-2001. More than half the Scheduled Tribes population is concentrated in the states of Madhya Pradesh, Chhattisgarh, Maharashtra, Orissa, Jharkhand and Gujarat. There are no communities specified as Scheduled Tribes in the states of Haryana, Punjab and the Union Territories of Chandigarh, Delhi and Pondicherry.

The Context of Land Security

Access to land continues to be of critical significance in large parts of India, and the entire economic, social and political networks revolve around it. Agriculture and primary sector activities based on land and other natural resources are the prime sources of livelihood for the vast majority of the economically vulnerable rural population. Ownership of land not only signifies livelihood, culture, identity in a Tribal society and economy but also determine the access to indices of social development like education and health. Further, land provides not only economic sustenance but also plays a key role in enhancing the prospects of asserting citizenship in much of rural India. Thus, the issue of land rights and access to natural resources is one which must be envisioned not in narrow economic terms (e.g., a unit of production) but as a basis for larger well-being of rural people.

The role of land in providing food, livelihood sustenance and surpluses for capital investment remains to be of central importance. The National Centre for Agricultural Economics and Policy Research (NCAP) forecasts that in food grains, a growth rate of 2.21 per cent is required to meet the estimated demand for the years 2003-12 and 1.85 per cent for the 2011-21. As against this the

Twelfth Plan approach paper targets an annual agricultural growth rate of 4.0 to 4.2 per cent.[8] This growth, however, cannot be achieved with a narrow institutional base, and land reforms are a precondition for the realization of these production goals. We are nowhere near exhausting the scope for fuller utilisation of our potential in many parts of the country.

The Land Tenures of the Tribals in Chota Nagpur and Santhal Parganas

In Chota Nagpur various land tenures prevailed such as Khas Land, Khorpos Tenure, Jagir Tenures, Brit Tenure, Mundari Khuntkheta Tenancies, Bhuinhari Lands, Bhutkheta Lands, Pahanai Lands, Maji has Lands and Betkheta Lands. While in Santhal Parganas the classes of tenure holders which existed were known as Ghatwali Tenures, Mul Raiyati Tenures, Ghat Chaukidari Jagir Lands and Village Headmen.

Land and Protective Laws in Jharkhand

Against the background of disintegration of the agrarian system, the British authorities tried to determine the rights of the raiyats, define the privileges of the landlords, and regulate the rent and forced labour through various legislations or through survey and settlement operations. The administrative steps, taken by the British following the revolts, did not address the issue of land security of the Tribals which was the core of the agrarian problem.

One of the earliest measures that the British took was the enactment of Chota Nagpur Encumbered Estates Act, 1876.[9] It was intended to protect the old encumbered estates. The Act empowered the Commissioner to appoint a manager to look after the Estates which could not be sold in execution of any decree. The British authorities felt that protection of the estate was a political necessity at a time when the animosities between the landlord and the raiyats were increasing. However, the Encumbered Estates Act damaged the traditional Khuntkatti system in many areas as large portions of Khuntkatti lands were converted into Majihas land of the landlords. Thus, the move favoured the estates as Tribal lands were captured and converted into Majihas or Rajhas. After three years, the British rulers enacted the Chota Nagpur Landlord and Tenant Procedure Act, 1879.[10] The main object of the Act was to regulate the relations between landlords and tenants. It was weighed heavily in favour of landlords for commutation of periodical conditions or services. Enhancement of rent in respect of such land as Bhuinhari Khuntkatti and Korkar was permissible only on certain conditions. Restriction on sale of under tenure land for arrears of rent continued. But the Act hardly satisfied the aspirations of the people of Chota Nagpur.

The British authorities tried to buy peace by introducing the settlement of Chota Nagpur Estate during 1877-86. This measure was reasonable to both the parties as it provided for a moderately enhanced rent while it abolished all labour demands and cesses. Though this particular revenue reform did not have the sanction of law, the British prevailed upon the Chota Nagpur Raja to issue rent receipts in accordance with the new government order.

The first phase of British liberalism in India also led to some revenue reforms in favour of the agricultural classes. The change of attitude of local government was clearly perceptible as a posture of ignorance was transformed into distinct kindness towards the Tribals. Another measure of reform was the Chota Nagpur Commutation Act of 1897.[11] It empowered the Governor to compulsorily commute the praedial services and conditions. However, the new measure could not quench the thirst of the Tribals. In fact, nothing short of a Record of Rights and survey based on thorough investigation of local customs could convince the people and make the legislation effective. But the absence of such provisions reduced the reform to a mere dead letter. After the Birsa movement, the violent agitation among the Mundas waned but did not die out.

The relations between the landlords and the tenants remained strained. One of the immediate effects of the uprising was the awareness among the authorities regarding the urgency of preparation of the Record of Rights. The Mundas wanted the security of tenure, recognition of their rights and the preservation of Mundari Khuntkatti system. Only a settlement operation could provide them agrarian security. In the light of above factors the Bhuinhari settlement operation in 1869-80 was limited in its scope. The settlement did not extend over the Munda area of Tamar, Khunti, Gonda and Sonahato which was the epicentre of the Birsa movement. With the beginning of new settlement operations, the Mundas welcomed them and when the Governor visited Ranchi in February, 1904 he received a submission from them for extension of operation which was done.

The Chota Nagpur Tenancy (Amendment) Act 1903[12] was the first legal recognition of the Mundari Khuntkatti system and in fact, it was precursor of the Chota Nagpur Tenant Act of 1908. The Tenancy Amendment legislation discontinued all forms of mortgage except the one known as Bhugat Bandha, recognized the customs and allowed transfer with certain conditions. In the wake of the new regulation, the Settlement Officers could not only give security to the members of Mundari Khuntkatti village but could also provide them protection. Subsequently, a revised bill was introduced in the Council and passed as Chota Nagpur Tenancy Act of 1908.[13] The Act with its modification is still in operation in the eighteen districts of Chota Nagpur comprising, Kolhan Division, North Chota Nagpur Division, South Chota Nagpur Division and Palamu Division. The Chota Nagpur Tenancy Act of 1908 marked the end of a century of agrarian strife. It was the climax of legal and administrative measures taken by the British to remove the agrarian disenchantment. The Act provided safeguards to all the Tribals in general by putting restrictions on transfer of land without permission of the Deputy Commissioner. The new law made separate provisions for protection of the interests of the Mundari Khuntkattidars. It not only defined the terms but also delineated the various provisions for regulating the land concerned.

The Deputy Commissioner was empowered under the Act to eject forcibly any person who might have acquired the land in violation of the provisos of the Chota Nagpur Tenancy Act. The Act put restrictions on the sale and transfer of Tribal lands and made provisos for the grant of rent receipts and commutation of rent. One of the most effective parts of the legislation was in respect of Mundari Khuntkattidars. The important provisos related to the Mundari Khuntkattidars are mentioned in Chapter 18. Such provisions related to restrictions on transfer of Mundari Khuntkathi Tenancy (Section 240), ejectment of persons unlawfully obtaining possession of said tenancies (Section 242) and so on. These sections incorporated safeguards for the Mundari Khuntkatti tenancies. Section 46, 47 and 48 dealt with restrictions on transfer of rights by raiyats or sale of raiyat rights in pursuance of court orders or sale of Bhuinhari tenures. The traditional Tribal right to convert the land in Korkar was recognized in section 64. In this way, the British Government transferred the Tribal agrarian system into a modern land revenue system. Certain restrictions were provided in the name of protection to Tribal lands.

After independence, some important changes were made in the Chota Nagpur Tenancy Act. After Section 71, two sections namely 71A and 71B were added to the Chota Nagpur Tenancy Act by promulgation of Bihar Scheduled Areas Regulation 1969.[14] Section 71A and 71B of the Chota Nagpur Tenancy Act empowers the Deputy Commissioner to restore position to members of Scheduled Tribes over land unlawfully transferred. The provisions are as follows:[15]

Section 71A of the Chota Nagpur Tenancy Act

"i. If at any time it comes to the notice of the Deputy Commissioner that transfer of land belonging to a raiyat [or a Mundary Khuntkattidar or Bhuinhar] who is a member of the Scheduled Tribes has taken place in contravention of Section 46 [or Section 48 or Section 240 or any other provisions of this Act or by any fraudulent method, [including decrees obtained in suits by fraud or collusion] he may, after giving reasonable opportunity to the transferee, who is proposed to be evicted to show cause and after making necessary enquiry in the matter, evict the transferee from such land without payment of compensation and restore it to the transferor or his heir and if such heir is not available or is not willing to agree to such restoration resettle it with another raiyat belonging to the Scheduled Tribes according to the village custom for the disposal of an abandoned holding:

ii. Provided that if the transferee has, within 30 years from the date of transfer constructed any building or structure on such holding or portion thereof, the Deputy Commissioner shall, if the transferor is not willing to pay the value of the same, order the transferee to remove the same within a period of six months, from the date of the order, or within such extended time not exceeding two years from the date of the order as the Deputy Commissioner may allow, failing which the Deputy Commissioner may get such building or structure removed:

ii. Provided further that where the Deputy Commissioner is satisfied that the transferee has constructed a substantial structure or building on such holding or portion thereof before coming into force of Bihar Scheduled Areas Regulation, 1969 he may, notwithstanding any other provisions of the Act validate such a transfer where the transferee either makes available to the transferor an alternative holding or portion thereof, as the case may be, of the equivalent value in the vicinity or pays adequate compensation to be determined by the Deputy Commissioner....

iii. Provided also that if after an enquiry the Deputy Commissioner is satisfied that the transferee has acquired a title by adverse possession and that the transferred land should be restored or resettled, he shall require the transferor or his heir or another raiyat as the case may be, to deposit with the Deputy Commissioner such sum of money as may be determined by the Deputy Commissioner, having regard to the amount or which the land was transferred or the market value of the land, as affected to the land which the Deputy Commissioner may deem fair and equitable. [Explanation I. In this section 'substantial structure or building' means structure or building the value of which on 4th day of initiation of enquiry, was determined by Deputy Commissioner to exceed Rs 10,000 but does not include structure or building, of any value, the material of which can be removed without substantially impairing the value of]. [Explanation II. A Bhuinhar or a Mundari Khunt Kattidar who is deemed to be a settled raiyat under the provisions of section 18 of this Act shall also be deemed to be a raiyat for the urposes of this section]."

Section 71B of the Chota Nagpur Tenancy Act

"**Penalties.** If any land is transferred in contravention of Section 46 or any other provision of this Act or by fraudulent method and is held or cultivated by any person with the knowledge of such transfer, he shall be punished with imprisonment of either description for a term which may extend to 3 years or with fine which may extend to one thousand rupees or with both and, in the case of a continuing offence, to a further fine not exceeding fifty rupees for each day during which the offence continues. [in sub-section(i) for the words 'thirty days the words ninety days' shall be substituted]"

Another important change made in the Chota Nagpur Tenancy Act relates to Section 49 which empowers the Deputy Commissioner to allow transfer of Tribal land for the purposes of charitable, religious, educational, mining, industrial purposes or any other purposes which the State Government may by general order declare as public purposes. The scope of this section was narrowed in 1996 by bringing a new legislation. According to the amendment, the Tribal land can be transferred only for those purposes namely industrial, mining and allied purposes. Now the Deputy Commissioner cannot give permission for transfer of land for religious, educational or charitable purposes.

Coming to the Santhal Pargana area, it comprises six districts. The first important enactment was the Santhal Parganas' Settlement Regulation-III of 1872.[16] The regulation provided that the government might order a settlement for the purpose of ascertaining and recording all rights pertaining to land whether belonging to the Zamindar and other proprietor or to the tenants or Headman. The regulation barred the action of civil courts during the settlement except on special references. It also provided for the reinstatement of Headman and raiyats unjustly deposed since December 31, 1858. The work of effecting a settlement under this regulation was entrusted to Mr Browne Wood, the then Deputy Commissioner of Santhal Pargana.

Subsequently, it was considered necessary that the government should keep the process of rent enhancement under its control. It was also felt that it was necessary to furnish the Zamindars information about the resettlement of rent. Accordingly the Santhal Pargana Rent Regulation-II of 1886[17] was enacted. This regulation enabled the authorities to make settlement of rent on the application of landlord or raiyats. On the other hand, the Regulation-III of 1882 provided for the preparation of record of rights as well as for determination of rent and latter Regulation-II of 1886 was further amended by Regulation-III of 1907, which provided for the enhancement of rent on account of improvements effected by or for at the expense of Zamindars and for the construction of works of improvements, buildings, et cetera.

In 1908, Santhal Parganas' Settlement Regulation-II of 1872 was further amended by Regulation–III of 1908. The main provision was the principle emphasised by the Settlement and accepted by the ordinary courts of the Santhal Pargana in the disposal of agrarian cases that raiyati land cannot be made the subject of transfer. The Regulation-III of 1908 declares the non-transferability of raiyati lands and affirms the power of the Deputy Commissioner to interfere with illegal disposition. This regulation also provided for inflicting of penalties on Proprietors, Headmen, and Raiyats who commit certain specific breaches of the record of rights.

The whole Santhal Pargana districts were settled for the first time under the provisions of Regulation–III of 1872 by Mr Browne Wood between 1873 and 1879. In 1888 resettlement operations were undertaken at the instance of proprietors entitled under Regulation–II of 1886 to have the rents of their raiyats revised after an interval of seven years. This settlement was concluded in 1894 and the next resettlement was carried out between 1898 and 1905. One of the significant effects of the Santhal Parganas' Settlement Regulation–III of 1872 was the alienation of land from moneylenders and the degradation of the raiyats. In the report of 1882, Mr Oldham, observed that the bazaar traders of Dumka had gradually absorbed all the Santhal settlements in the vicinity and a considerable proportion of lands had passed into the hands of creditors. The evil had become so great and the danger so acute that the government declared in 1887 that the occupancy rights were not saleable except where expressly so recorded at the settlement and the burden of proof was on the person who asserted to the contrary.

Finally, the Santhal Pargana Tenancy (Supplementary Provisions) 1949[18] was enacted by the Government of Bihar. The Act defined various terms as aboriginal, Khas Village, Non-original Raiyat, Mul Raiyat, Village, Village Headman and so on. It also made a detailed provision for the appointment of Village Headman of Khas Village. The Act classified the Raiyats in three categories and defined the use of land. The Act is very restrictive in nature and virtually put all restrictions on transfer of land except the land which is recorded as saleable in the record of rights. The new enactment makes various provisions for payments and collection of rent but rent is still settled as per Regulation of 1886. Similarly, the record of rights is also prepared under Santhal Pargana Regulation-III of 1872.

Land Laws and the Process of Dispossession

Failure of land laws in protecting the rights of land in Jharkhand has been one of the burning issues ever since the advent of the British on the soil of Jharkhand and even earlier. The Tribals have witnessed continuous dispossession of their land. The modes of dispossession were different in the British and the post-British period. In the British period influx of non-Tribal population in Chota Nagpur and Santhal Pargana led to dispossession of Tribal land owing to necessity of housing and commercial activities. The dispossession took place mostly through mortgage of land in the post-Independence era.

The transfer of land in Jharkhand from Tribal to Tribal and Tribal to non-

Tribal is governed by the Chota Nagpur Tenancy Act, (CNT Act) 1908 for the area falling under Kolhan, Palamu, North Chota Nagpur and South Chota Nagpur Divisions and by this Santhal Parganas Tenancy (Supplementary Provisions) Act, 1949 for the areas covering Santhal Pargana Division. Before analyzing the process of land dispossession, it is necessary to briefly narrate the provisions relating to transfer and tenures in the Chota Nagpur Tenancy and Santhal Pargana Tenancy Act.

Provisions Related to Transfer of Holdings and Tenures Section 46 (CNT Act)

Section 46 of the CNT Act which came into force in 1947 is one of the restrictive sections of the Act. It lays down restrictions on the transfer of land by an occupancy raiyat belonging to the Scheduled Castes, Schedules Tribes and Backward Classes. Under this section, a raiyat cannot sell or gift his raiyat to any other person. Moreover, he cannot lease or mortgage his holding for a period exceeding five years. However a raiyat can enter into a Bhugut Bundha mortgage for a period not exceeding twelve years, and can mortgage for a time period of fifteen years in cases of agricultural loans wherein the mortgagee is registered under Bihar and Orissa Cooperative Societies Act, 1935.[19] A bhugut bundha mortgage is defined in Section 3(II) of the CNT Act as a 'transfer of the interest of tenant in his tenancy; for the purpose of securing the payment of money advanced or to be advanced by way of loan; upon the condition that the loan, with all the interest thereon shall be deemed to be extinguished by the profits arising from the tenancy during the period of mortgage.'[20]

Thus this section permits temporary disposition of land by an Adivasi to a non-Adivasi if the above-mentioned provisions are adhered to. The competent authority that enjoys the power of the Deputy Commissioner for sanction of transfer from Tribal to Tribal includes the Sub-Divisional Officer, and the Deputy Collector Land Reforms. However, for an occupancy raiyat belonging to Scheduled Tribes, he can transfer his right to another person who is a member of the Scheduled Tribe by sale, exchange, gift and will, but only with the prior permission of the Deputy Commissioner and the other person should be within the local limits of the area of police station where the holding is situated. It is pertinent to point at this juncture that for occupancy raiyat belonging to Scheduled Caste and Backward Classes the local limits are those of the district and not of the police station.

According to section 46 (4A) of the CNT Act, the Deputy Commissioner can proceed suo moto on receiving an application by the S.T. transferor provided it is not time-barred by twelve years. If the Deputy Commissioner finds on hearing both the parties that a clause of the section is in violation, he can eject the transferee and put the transferor back into possession. If the time bar of ejectment, which is twelve years, as mentioned under this section has been exceeded then the transferee gets the adverse possession of land. These restrictions on the transfer of raiyati holding were first introduced in the amending The Chota Nagpur Tenancy (Amendment) Act 1903,[21] the object being to stop the sale of holdings by an improvident raiyat, and to restrict all forms of mortgages.

Although, this section was enacted to safeguard the interests of the Tribals, a few regressive provisions can be seen. For instance, the provisos, which specify that the local limit of a police station needs to be followed by a ST raiyat, is definitely out of time in this modern world. Moreover, the mortgage period of five years also needs to be reviewed, since an aboriginal raiyat cannot avail the different kinds of loans like the education loan and housing loan provided by the banks against his land. However, no such restriction is imposed on an occupancy raiyat who is not a member of ST, SC and Backward Classes as he can transfer his right in his holding or any portion thereof by sale, exchange, gift, will, or mortgage to any other person.

Thus, prior permission of Deputy Commissioner is a mandatory provision for any transfer of land by a member of SC/ST/BC after 1947 failing which such transfer is barred by Section 46 of the CNT Act. Thus, surrender of land by a raiyat to a landlord or any type of transfer before 1947 is valid provided it meets other requirements of the Transfer of Property Act.

Section 47 of the CNT Act, 1908

This section provides for the sale of holding of land in execution of decree of loans or recovery of land improvement and agricultural loan under certificate procedure. This section was widely used by the Zamindars who used the provisions of this Act to eject the Tribals from their land. However this section has lost much of its relevance after the abolition of the Zamindari system. It was by this method that the Tana Bhagats lost much of their land due to non-payment of the rent during the British period.

Sections 48 and 49 of the CNT Act, 1908

Section 48 of the Act deals with the restriction imposed upon the transfer of Bhuinhari tenure. The provision of Section 46, regarding the restrictions on transfer has now been made applicable to Bhuinhari tenures surveyed under The Chota Nagpur Tenures Act, 1869[22] as if they are raiyati holdings. The provision of transfer of Bhuinhari land was inserted by the (Chota Nagpur Tenancy (Amendment) Act 1938).[23] The power of granting permission for transfer of land under this section rests with the Sub-Divisional Officer and Deputy Collector Land Reforms who enjoy the powers of Deputy Commissioner. As a matter of custom, the official service tenures held by the

Pahan, Mahto and other village officials cannot be transferred by lease or mortgage even for short periods, though this custom is being broken and these tenures have been in some cases sold by the courts, in execution of decrees for debts due on the village officials and have thus been lost permanently to the village community.

There is a specific provision for restoration of Bhuinhari land under section 48(4) of the CNT Act, 1908. Power under 71A of the Act cannot be exercised for restoration because a Bhuinhari is not a raiyat; he is a tenure holder. Section 49 of the Act originally allowed transfer of raiyati and Bhuinhari land, with the Deputy Commissioner's permission, for charitable, educational, or any other such 'public purpose'. However after the 1996 amendment, (Chota Nagpur Tenancy (Amendment) Act 1995,[24] land can be transferred only for the purpose of mining or industry and that too only with the permission of the State Government.

Section 71A of the CNT Act, 1908

This section contains one of the most important provisions of the CNT Act, as it grants the power to restore possession to a member of the Scheduled Tribes whose land has been unlawfully transferred to the Deputy Commissioner. According to this section if it comes to the notice of the Deputy Commissioner that transfer of land belonging to a raiyat or a Bhuinhar or a Mundari Khuntkattidar belonging to the Scheduled Tribe has taken place, in contravention of Sections 46, 48 and 240 of the CNT Act or by any fraudulent method, he may after giving reasonable opportunity to the transferee who is proposed to be evicted, to show cause and after making sufficient enquiry in the matter, evict the transferee from such land without payment of compensation and restore it to the transferor or the heir or if both are unwilling, settle it with any other raiyat belonging to the Scheduled Tribes.

The first proviso confers power on the Deputy Commissioner to direct the transferee who has constructed a building or a structure on the holding within 30 years from the date of transfer to remove the same, failing which the same would be removed. The second proviso refers to a situation in which the transferee has constructed a substantial structure before coming into force of Section 71A (1969). The Deputy Commissioner can validate such a transfer, if the transferee either makes available to the transferor an alternative holding or portion of equivalent value in the vicinity or pays adequate compensation. Through the third proviso, even if the transferee has acquired title by adverse possession, the Deputy Commissioner is enjoined to require the transferor or his heir to deposit market value of the land alienated as well as compensation for improvements made as a condition precedent to restoration.

Section 240 of the CNT Act, 1908

This section deals with the Mundari Khuntkattidari tenancies. This section lays down that no Mundari Khuntkattidari tenancy or portion thereof is transferable by sale whether in execution of decree, order or otherwise. Furthermore no mortgage is permitted except for Bhugut Bundha mortgage not exceeding a period of seven years. This section does permit lease of the Mundari Khuntkattidari tenancy except for:

a) Mukarrari leases of uncultivated land when granted to a Mundari or a group of Mundaris for the purposes of enabling lessees or the male members of their families to bring suitable land portions under cultivation.
b) Leases of uncultivated land when granted to Mundari cultivator as a raiyat

Thus, it can be seen that the provisos related to transfer of Mundari Khuntkattidari tenancy is more stringent than the other provisos related to transfer of tenancy. A number of illegal ways of transaction of land are also prevalent in the state. People have found ways to contravene the provisions of the Chota Nagpur Tenancy Act, and Santhal Pargana Tenancy Act. However, in Jharkhand the flouting of the first two Acts are more prevalent due to restrictions on the sale of Tribal lands making transfer a difficult proposition. Thus, people have found various ways by which they evade these laws.

Section 20 of the Santhal Pargana Tenancy Act (SPT Act), 1949

This particular section of the SPT Act provides that no transfer by a raiyat of his right in his holdings or any portion thereof by sale, gift, mortgage, will, lease for any other contract or agreement shall be valid unless the right to transfer is recorded in the Record of Rights. But the Act permits the transfer of land in the following instances:

(i) A lease of raiyati land in any Sub-division for the purpose of the establishment or continuance of an excise shop may be validly granted or renewed by a raiyat for a period not exceeding one year with the permission of the Deputy Commissioner.
(ii) A Santhal raiyat may gift a part of his land to his sister or daughter with the previous written permission of the Deputy Commissioner.
(iii) An aboriginal raiyat may also make a grant of half of his land to his widowed mother or his wife for her maintenance after his death.
(iv) A raiyat may also mortgage his land in order to obtain agricultural credit with a scheduled bank within the meaning of Reserve Bank of India Act.

(v) No transfer in contravention of Sub-section 1 or 2 shall be registered or shall in any way be recognized as valid by any court.

(vi) No court or officer can pass any decree or order for the sale of a right of raiyat in his holdings or any portion thereof nor can such right be sold in execution of any decree.

By the Scheduled Area Regulations, 1969,[25] the government inserted a new Sub-section 5 to section 20. It provides for the restoration of such lands which are illegally transferred.

Panchayat (Extension to the Scheduled Areas) Act, 1996

Through the Constitution (Seventy-third Amendment) Act, 1992, a new Section (Part IX) was added to the Constitution to enshrine therein certain basic and essential features of the Panchayati Raj Institutions (PRIs) to impart certainty, continuity and strength to them. This Amendment came into force on 20-4-1993.

The bulk of the Tribal population live in the Fifth Schedule and Sixth Schedule Areas. These are described in the Constitution as Scheduled Areas and Tribal Areas, respectively. In so far as these areas are concerned, Article 243M (4)(b) in Part IX of the Constitution, provides that Parliament may, by law, extend the provisions of Part IX to these areas subject to such exceptions and modifications as may be specified in such law. There were persistent demands from prominent leaders of the Scheduled Areas for extending the provisions of Part IX to these areas so that PRIs may be established there. In the absence of such a law, the people of the Scheduled Areas had not been able to avail of the benefits of self-governance consonant with their customary law, social and religious practices and traditional management practices of community resources. A Committee of Experts including some Members of Parliament was appointed in 1994 to examine this issue. This Committee, which was known as the Bhuria Committee, gave its report in January, 2005. The Committee's Report proposed a legal framework pre-eminently suited to participatory democracy particularly at the grassroots level for the Tribal areas of the Fifth Schedule. It was contemplated that the institutions proposed to be constituted at the district level and the lower levels should have a living relationship with the self-management practices which have been in vogue in the Tribal areas.

Based on the Report of this Committee, the Panchayats (Extension to the Scheduled Areas) Act, 1996 (PESA) was passed and came into effect on December 24, 1996 (Annexure II). It may be noted that no analogous law has been passed for extending Panchayati Raj to Sixth Schedule Areas. PESA is applicable to Fifth Schedule Areas only.

PESA extends Part IX of the Constitution to Fifth Schedule Areas, subject to certain exceptions and modifications. The Act has defined a village as ordinarily consisting of a habitation or a group of habitations or a hamlet or a group of hamlets comprising a community and managing its affairs in accordance with traditions and customs. It has been laid down that every village will have a Gram Sabha which will be competent to safeguard and preserve the traditions and customs of the people, their cultural identity, community resources and customary mode of dispute resolution. The manner of reservation of seats at each level of Panchayats has been provided for in the Act. It has been stipulated that reservation for the Scheduled Tribes will not be less than half of the total number of seats and that all seats of Chairpersons of Panchayats at all levels will be reserved for the Scheduled Tribes. Further, it has been provided that the State Government will nominate persons belonging to such Scheduled Tribes as have no representation in the Panchayat at the intermediate level or the Panchayat at the district level and that such number will not exceed one-tenth of the total members to be elected in that Panchayat. Broadly, the functions, powers and responsibilities spelt out in the Act in respect of Gram Sabha and/or Panchayats can be divided into following categories:

Mandatory executive functions and responsibilities include that the Gram Sabha will approve plans, programmes and projects before they are taken up for implementation by the Panchayat at the village level, it would identify beneficiaries of poverty alleviation and other programmes and issue certification of utilization of funds by the Panchayat at the village level for the above programmes. Planning and management of minor water bodies will be done by the Panchayats.

The Act, further, provides that the Gram Sabha or the Panchayat at the appropriate level shall be consulted before making any acquisition of land in the Scheduled Areas for development projects and before resettling rehabilitated persons affected by such projects. A duty has been cast on the State Legislatures to ensure that Panchayats at the appropriate level and the Gram Sabha are endowed specifically with such powers and authority as enable them to function as institutions of self government. These include: the power to enforce prohibition; ownership of minor forest produce; power to prevent alienation of land; power to manage village markets; power to exercise control over money lending; power to exercise control over institutions and functionaries in all social sectors; and the power to control local plans and resources for such plans including Tribal sub-plans. Normally there is a tendency in the upper Panchayat bodies to encroach upon the powers of the lower Panchayats.

The Act prohibits Panchayats at the higher level to assume the powers and authority of any Panchayat at the lower level. The Act provides that any provision of any law which is inconsistent with its (PESA) provisions shall cease to be in force at the expiry of one year from the date on which the Act receives the assent of the President (24.12.1996).

Of all these powers, the most significant for the land security of the Tribals is that under Section 4(i) of PESA: 'The Gram Sabha or the Panchayat at the appropriate level shall be consulted before making the acquisition of land in the Scheduled Areas for development projects and before re-settling or rehabilitating persons affected by such projects in the Scheduled Areas; the actual planning and implementation of the projects in the Scheduled Areas shall be co-ordinated at the State level.' This power, however, enmeshed in a controversy—the kind of consultation is envisaged and whether it is to be an effective consultation or just formal information. While the protagonists of land acquisition argue for a formal consultation at any level of the Panchayat those the ABYSS School led by Shri Sankaran stood for an informed consent of the Gram Sabha wherever land is to be acquired. In PESA the basic unit is the Gram Sabha based upon the habitation of the Tribals. The issue is not yet resolved. Section 4(m) of the Act provides—

> While endowing Panchayats in the Scheduled Areas with such powers and authority as may be necessary to enable them to function as institutions of self-government, a State Legislature shall ensure that the Panchayats at the appropriate level and the Gram Sabha are endowed specifically with:
>
> (iii) the power to prevent alienation of land in the Scheduled Areas and to take appropriate action to restore any unlawfully alienated land of the Scheduled Tribe;

This provision of PESA is indeed revolutionary when viewed individually and when in consonance with others. It has been seen that the power of restoration of alienated land rests with the Deputy Commissioner both under the Chota Nagpur Tenancy Act, 1908 and under the Santal Parganas Tenancy Act, 1949. This gave rise to a good deal of amorphism in implementation. A whole genus of political economy came to grow around the aforementioned provisions attended by heavy rent seeking and sharing of spoils up and down the line. Now this power has been transferred to the Gram Sabha comprising of all voters residing in the territorial jurisdiction of the Gram Sabha. This was aimed at eliminating the rent seeking and the behavioural aspects of the process of political economy. Every individual residing at the level of the Gram Sabha has perfect information regarding the land alienated and if the powers of restoration are vested in their hands it serves to create the ideal situation.

However, the forces driving the political economic process have proved too strong. A total of nine states have Fifth Schedule Areas—Andhra Pradesh, Chhattisgarh, Gujarat, Himachal Pradesh, Jharkhand, Madhya Pradesh, Maharashtra, Orissa and Rajasthan. While all these states have enacted requisite compliance legislations by amending the respective Panchayati Raj Acts, certain gaps continue to exist. None of these states have framed rules for implementation of PESA or the amended Panchayati Raj Acts with the result that PESA is not implemented in any of these states. Further, most states are also yet to amend the subject laws, like those relating to money lending, forests, excise et cetera. Consequently, the compliance remains incomplete, perfunctory and formal in virtually all states. Vital issues like the ownership of minor forest produce, planning and management of minor water bodies, prevention of alienation of Tribal lands et cetera, which have been duly recognized in PESA as the traditional rights of Tribals living in the Scheduled Areas have still not received the warranted attention and the necessary correctives remain unapplied. There are also issues relating to powers statutorily devolved upon the Gram Sabha and the Panchayats, not being matched by concomitant transfer of funds and functionaries resulting in the non-exercise of such powers. The states have, over the years, been repeatedly urged to expedite this process and the matter has been discussed a number of times at the meetings of the Ministers of Panchayati Raj as also in the meetings of the Committee of Secretaries of Panchayati Raj of the states. It has yielded no results. PESA continues to be a dead letter of law.

The Schedules Tribes and Other Traditional Forest Dwellers (Recognition of Forest Rights) Act, 2006

This is yet another revolutionary legislation that bespeaks of the 'policy incoherence' that we have been discussing. This Act aims to redress the 'historical injustice' committed against the Tribals who mainly constitute the bulk of the people who live in or in the close vicinity of forests and who derive a significant part of their sustenance in the form of minor forest produce, water, grazing grounds and the habitat of shifting cultivation, not to speak of the wood, fuel wood and the nutritional support from the forest ecology. Moreover, vast areas of land that may or may not be forests are classified as 'forest' under India's forest laws, and those cultivating these lands are technically cultivating 'forest land'.[26] Land Acquisition, Rehabilitation and Resettlement Bill, 2011.

This is on account of application of our forest laws. India's forests are governed by two main laws, the Indian Forest Act, 1927 and the Wild Life (Protection) Act, 1972. The former empowers the government to declare any area to be a reserved forest, protected forest or village forest. The latter allows any area to be constituted as a 'protected area', namely a national park, and wildlife sanctuary, a tiger reserve or a community conservation area.[27] Under these laws, the rights of people living in or depending on the area to be declared as a forest or protected area are to be 'settled' by a 'forest settlement officer.' This basically requires that officer to enquire into the claims of people to land, minor forest produce, et cetera, and, in the case of claims found to be valid, to allow them to continue or to extinguish them by paying compensation. Studies have shown that in many areas this process either did not take place at all or took place in a highly faulty manner. Thus 82.9 per cent of the forest blocks in undivided Madhya Pradesh had not been settled as of December 2003,[28] while all the hilly tracts of Orissa were declared government forests without any survey.[29] In Orissa, around 40 per cent of the government forests are 'deemed reserved forests' which have not been surveyed.[30]

The rights which are included in section 3(1) of the Act include

- the right to hold and live in the forest land under the individual or common occupation for habitation or for self-cultivation for livelihood by a member or members of a forest dwelling Scheduled Tribe or other traditional forest dwellers;
- community rights such as 'nistar', by whatever name they are called, including those used in erstwhile princely states, Zamindari or such intermediary regimes;
- the right of ownership, access to collect, use, and dispose of minor forest produce (includes all non-timber forest produce of plant origin) which has been traditionally collected within or outside village boundaries;
- the other community rights of uses or entitlements such as fish and other products of water bodies, grazing (both settled or transhumant) and traditional seasonal resource access of nomadic or pastoralist communities;
- the rights including community tenures of habitat and habitation for primitive Tribal groups and pre-agricultural communities;
- the rights in or over disputed lands under any nomenclature in any state where claims are disputed;
- the rights for conversion of pattas or leases or grants issued by any local authority or any state government on forest lands to titles;
- the rights of settlement and conversion of all forest villages, old habitation, unsurveyed villages and other villages in forest, whether recorded, notified or not into revenue villages;
- the right to protect, regenerate or conserve or manage any community forest resource which they have been traditionally protecting and conserving for sustainable use;
- the rights which are recognized under any State law or laws of any Autonomous District Council or Autonomous Regional Council or which are accepted as rights of Tribals under any traditional or customary law of the concerned Tribes of any state;

- the right of access to biodiversity and community right to intellectual property and traditional knowledge related to biodiversity and cultural diversity;
- any other traditional right customarily enjoyed by the forest dwelling Scheduled Tribes or other traditional forest dwellers, as the case may be, which are not mentioned in clauses 1 to 11, but excluding the traditional right of hunting or trapping on extracting a part of the body of any species of wild animals.

On December 31, the Act was notified into force, and on January 1, the Rules for the Act—which provide the procedures for implementing its provisions—were also notified.[31] There have been numerous complaints regarding the manner in which the Act has been implemented after its notification. For instance, in September 2010, the Council for Social Development, a New Delhi based think tank, released a 'Summary Report on Implementation of the Forest Rights Act' which stated that: 'All of the key features of this legislation have been undermined by a combination of apathy and sabotage during the process of implementation. In the current situation the rights of the majority of Tribals and other traditional forest dwellers are being denied and the purpose of the legislation is being defeated. Unless immediate remedial measures are taken, instead of undoing the historical injustice to Tribal and other traditional forest dwellers, the Act will have the opposite outcome of making them even more vulnerable to eviction and denial of their customary access to forests... both the Central and the state governments have actively pursued policies that are in direct violation of the spirit and letter of the Act.'[32]

The progress made in the states in Forest Rights is as follows:

> It is evident from the above table that most states have taken up the implementation of this Act with mock seriousness. Despite the fact that 6 years have passed since this Act was promulgated the implementation of this Act is nowhere even 25 per cent complete. It is not only the lethargy and the mal-governance that is responsible for this state of affairs but rather the factors of political economy that dominate the implementation process. Land is a prized issue and already complains pour in that Forest Rights Act has come as a handy device for supplementing the land base of the non-Tribals, money lenders and musclemen. Thus, a very important dimension in the security and land rights of the Tribal people has proved a cropper on account of mock-implementation.

Land Acquisition, Rehabilitation and Resettlement Bill, 2011

While the Land Acquisition (Amendment) [LAA] Bill, 2007 was in the nature of making amendments to the original Land Acquisition Act, 1894, whereas Land Acquisition, Rehabilitation and Resettlement (R&R) Bill, 2011 is a new legislation which proposes to repeal the Land Acquisition Act, 1894. The issue of Rehabilitation and Resettlement was considered separately vide R&R Bill, 2007 whereas at present the issue of R&R has been integrated along with the issue of land acquisition in the comprehensive and integrated Land Acquisition, Rehabilitation and Resettlement (LARR) Bill, 2011. The R&R Bill, 2007 was applicable in all cases of the land acquisition whether under the Land Acquisition Act 1984 or any other Central or state Law. The rehabilitation benefits were also proposed to be extended to the persons affected by the natural calamities or disasters as notified by the appropriate Government. The LARR Bill, 2011 is not applicable to the persons affected by the natural calamities or disasters. Further, the land acquisition under the statutes stated out in Schedule Four of the LARR Bill, 2011 has been kept out of scope of this Bill. The Central Government may by notification direct that any of the provisions of LARR Act, 2011 shall apply or apply with such modifications as may be specified to any of the Acts listed in the Fourth Schedule.

The proposed LAAR, 2011 has many novel features. It provides for Social Impact Assessment Study, where land is to be acquired for public purposes; A Chief Secretary's Committee examines the proposal for land acquisition to determine the legitimacy of the purpose and the integrity of the area proposed; land not exceeding five per cent of the irrigated multi-cropped area will be acquired and an equivalent area will be developed; an Administrator for Rehabilitation and Resettlement will monitor the implementation of the R&R component of the programme; Gram Sabha is to be consulted in all cases of acquisition; payment of compensation will be at the market value; there is also provision for extending the facilities for private purchases and there are novel features regarding the R&R packages. However, where the Bill disappoints is on account of its ambivalent thinking on the public consultation. Consultation must imply consent and in the absence of clear provisions to that effect the changes proposed in the Bill just promise to be cosmetic. It will only serve to add to rent seeking and make it more difficult for the Tribal to protest. It does little to further the security of the Tribal lands.

Land Laws and the Connivance of State Machinery

As described in foregoing paragraphs the Tenancy Acts provide for the transfer of land by legal means but in many cases the provisions of the Act are used in connivance with the revenue functionaries for legalization the transfer of land. A glaring example is Section 46 of the Chota Nagpur Tenancy Act which imposes a complete ban on sell off rights in holding or a portion thereof by an aboriginal to an aboriginal. But the section permits temporary disposition by an Adivasi to a non-Adivasi in two cases. (i) Mortgage or lease for a period of eight years, (ii) *Bhugat Bandha* mortgage for a period not exceeding seven years or if the mortgage is a registered Society under Bihar and Orissa

Cooperative Society Act, 1935, land can be mortgaged for a period of fifteen years.

The above provision seems to provide a sufficient deterrent for the illegal transfer of land under the same section. Transfer of land is allowed from a Tribal to a Tribal with a prior sanction of Deputy Commissioner within the same thana (Police Station) area but in practice the restriction of same thana area is not followed. In Ranchi particularly many Tribals of other districts such as Chaibasa, Gumla, Lohardaga, Khuti, East Singhbum and West Singhbum and other districts simply file an affidavit that they belong to the same thana where land of the transferor is situated. In this way they are able to obtain the permission of the Deputy Commissioner. It is important to note here that the power of the Deputy Commissioner is vested in the Deputy Collector Land Reforms (DCLR) and the Sub-Divisional Officer (SDO) who openly abuse their discretion and grant permission for transfer of land.

Under Section 49 of the Chota Nagpur Tenancy Act an occupancy raiyat or any member of a Bhuinhari family could transfer his holdings for any reasonable or sufficient purpose which could be charitable, religious, educational, industrial, developmental etc in pre-1996 period. Many non-Tribals took advantage of the provisos and got permissions for transfer of land in the name of religious, educational, and industrial purposes. Such persons are occupying big chunks of land and such land is now being transferred to the non-Tribals by taking advantage of section 49(5) of the Chota Nagpur Tenancy Act. Sub-section 5 of the Section 49 of the CNT Act provides that no Tribal can file a petition for restoration of his land after a lapse of twelve years. In view of this law, the transferees have started transferring their land after the period of twelve years has lapsed. Many Tribals knocked the doors of revenue courts and some have even filed writ petitions for getting the land restored. But the provision of section 49(5) of the CNT Act has prevented them from getting any relief. Another connivance of the officials is found in the misuse of Second proviso of Section 71A of the Chota Nagpur Tenancy Act. According to this provision, if the transferee has constructed a substantial structure before coming into force of Section 71A, the Deputy Commissioner can validate such a transfer by fixing a compensation. Normally, a lower court which exercises the powers of the Deputy Commissioner is in the rank of Sub-divisional Officer or even a basic grade of Deputy Commissioner. There are only two Scheduled Area Regulation Courts (SAR Court) in Jharkhand situated at Ranchi and Latehar. In other places the Government of Jharkhand vests power to the officers mentioned above on the recommendation of the Deputy Commissioner.

Several cases have been detected in Ranchi where the SAR Court or the Deputy Commissioner exercising the power of SAR Court took wrong advantage of the second proviso of Section 71A of the CNT Act and fixed compensation amounts even for vacant lands. In other words the officers legalized the illegal transfers of Tribal land by awarding compensation and paying the same to the Tribal. Misuse of discretion has been found in case of determination of compensation also. The Tribal landowner does not get the exact market value of the land. The SAR Court or the competent court determines the value of the land on the basis of the land prices fixed by the Deputy Commissioner-cum Collector for realizing of registration fee and the stamp duty. It has been found that the prices fixed by Deputy Commissioner are lower than the exact market value. Thus, the wrong orders of the courts not only deprive the poor Tribals of the actual value of their lands but also cause huge revenue losses to the state government. The second proviso itself also provides that Deputy Commissioner can validate a transfer on the condition that the transferee has constructed a substantial structure before 1969 by ordering to make available to the transferor an alternative land of equivalent value. There are many cases of wrong validation by the competent courts through the above mentioned provision. The courts do not actually verify the nature of land and in connivance with the transferee orders for compensation of land which is of inferior quality. Various instances can be cited in the abuse of this provision. One of the glaring examples is validation of transfer of a raiyati land in exchange for a government land. In another example a Tribal was given a portion of a river (government land) for his fertile Dhandan (paddy) land.

Misuse may also be made of the first proviso of Section 71A which empowers the Deputy Commissioner to order removal of a structure within six months but the period may be extended to two years. In most of the cases the order is passed for removal of structure but the construction is not removed. The transferee by this time by conniving with the court even gets the time extended to two years. Ironically the structure is not removed but its shape and size is increased by one or two floors of building during the same period. There is a Khet Mohalla in the Hind Pira area of Ranchi district where the minorities have constructed hundreds of houses and they are not being removed despite the order of removal by the competent courts.

Thousands of acres of Tribal land have been occupied by non-Tribals by taking advantage of the provision of simple mortgage. Section 46 of the Chota Nagpur Tenancy Act permits temporary disposition by a Tribal through a simple mortgage or lease for a period of five years. Similarly, the Bhugat Bandha mortgage does not exceed seven years in case of an individual mortgage. But in practice the leased and mortgaged lands are not given back to the Tribals after expiry of the lease/mortgage period. The Tribals are not aware about the revenue loss and the protective clauses in their favour so that they can get through land restoration.

In Chota Nagpur area there is a very big racket of Tribal land in the name of *Zamindari Hukumnamas*. Most of the Hukumnamas are forged and fabricated by the land brokers to grab the transfer lands. They show that the Tribals had surrendered the land to the Zamindar and the latter settled the land in favour of the non-Tribal three or four decades back. In this way, they want to prove that the land they settled in 1950s and early 1960s when the non-Tribal took possession of the land and constructed a substantial structure in the form of building. Normally, such surrenders should be examined in the light of Section 72 of the Chota Nagpur Tenancy Act which is rarely done and the land is regulated by the competent courts.

The competent trial courts for restoration of land also take advantage of the collusive title suits. Lust for land has led to the use of several ingenuine and fraudulent methods by non-Tribals to take control of the Tribal lands. One of the most popular methods adopted by them is collusive title suits which are also known as declarative suits. In such cases the title suit is filed by the non-Tribal in the civil court and it eventually culminates in the filing of compromise petitions signed jointly by both the Tribal and non-Tribal. The civil court passes an order on the basis of compromise and issues a decree in favour of the non-Tribal but such collusive title deeds are nothing but a method for circumventing the provision of law in order to grab the Tribal land.

Another method adopted by the land broker and land *Mafias* for grabbing the Tribal land is conversion of agricultural land into *Chapperbandi* land. The *Chapperbandi* is a great misnomer. Literally it means a land with a 'chapper' or land with a house. But in actual practice even a land without a house is entered as *Chapperbandi* in the tenants ledger. The manipulation in the tenants ledger maintained by the lower revenue functionary known as Karamchari is engineered by the non-Tribals by influencing the Karamcharis. The tern *Chapperbandi* is not used anywhere in Chota Nagpur Tenancy Act, but there are several examples of the revenue courts entertaining *Chapperbandi* for turning down restoration petitions of the Tribals.

Land and the Survey and Settlement

The Survey and Settlement is conducted in Chota Nagpur on the basis of Chota Nagpur Tenancy Act and, in Santhal Pargana on the basis of Santhal Pargana Settlement Regulation, 1872[33] and Santhal Pargana Rent Regulation, 1886.[34] The head of the Survey and Settlement is the Settlement Officer who is presently in the rank of Joint Secretary of the State Civil Service. A few years back, Settlement Officers were normally posted from the IAS cadre. Below the Settlement Officer there is the Charge Officer who is in the rank of Additional District Magistrate (ADM). Below the Charge Officer there are Assistant Settlement Officers (ASOs) followed by the Kanungos and the Inspectors.

The record of rights during service operations passes through several stages. The stages are different in Chota Nagpur and Santhal Pargana areas. In Chota Nagpur area the stages are more compared to the Santhal Pargana. The preliminary record of writings is done during Khanapuri stage during which the Survey Inspectors and the Kanungos are empowered to pass orders on *Yaddast* (a note in case of a particular plot) written by the Amins (Surveyors). Most of the written orders are passed at the lowest stage by the Inspectors and Kanungos who did not have any revenue training in Jharkhand. Jharkhand does not have any Revenue Training Institute whereas other states are having several Revenue Training Institutions. Moreover, there is no course prescribed for them and they are not even required to pass any departmental examination. All these shortcomings result in very poor performance by the abovementioned revenue functionaries.

As far as Chota Nagpur Tenancy Act is concerned, restrictions on transfer of land have been mentioned earlier and every officer has to consider those restrictive provisos while passing any order on the Yaddast during Khanapuri stage. It has been found that the survey officials recorded the names of non-Tribals even on the basis of short term leases or mortgage deeds. There are instances when they regularized the transfer of land in favour of a transferee who has constructed a building in violation of the provisions of the Chota Nagpur Tenancy Act, but by playing into the hands of the encroachers of Tribal land and in spite of ousting them they pass such an order which regularizes the illegal transfer of land.

The survey authorities also ignore the provisos of Sections 46 and 48 of the Chota Nagpur Tenancy Act. The provisions lay down that an occupancy raiyat belonging to Scheduled Caste can transfer his right to another person who is also Scheduled Caste by sale, exchange, gift and will with the prior permission of the Deputy Commissioner provided that the transferee should be a resident of the local raiyat of the area of police station where the land is situated. But the survey authorities record the names of such persons who do not belong to the same area but in fact belong to different states.

Similarly, Section 48 of the Chota Nagpur Tenancy Act deals with the restrictions imposed on the transfer of Bhuinhari tenure. The provisos and restrictions are similar to those under the Section 46 of the Act. The power of creating provisos is vested with the Sub-divisional Officer and Deputy Collector Land Reforms. In case of Bhuinhari land, also the Survey authorities ignore the provisios of the Act and give recognition to the transfers which are violative at the provisos of the Act.

The survey authorities also give undue importance to the Hukumnamas which are generally an unregistered documents not recognized by the Indian Registration Act. The law provides that any land valued at more than Rs. 100

(since revised upwards several times) must be registered. It ensures that not only all the documents should be registered but also guarantees a definite source of revenue to the state government. Normally the Hukumnamas are forged and fabricated documents manufactured in the name of Zamindars and are antedated. They are created to show that the Tribal lands were transferred long before the advent of Scheduled Areas Regulation Act, 1969. By recognizing such Hukumnamas the illegal transfers of Tribal land to non-Tribals are legalized and the names of the latter are entered in the Record of Rights.

The revenue officials also tend to recognize the collusive title suits and the orders passed by the civil courts. Much has been written about these collusive title suits. It can only be said that such title suits are nothing but an ingenuine method for grabbing the land of the Tribal by gaining over him through the use of money and other methods. There are other methods also through which Tribal land is alienated and recognized by the survey officials. Some of the important methods among them are mentioned below:

(a) Transfer through forcing the Tribals to part with their lands on receipt of a small consideration without execution of any registered deed.
(b) Transfer of Tribal holdings describing them as *Chapperbandi* holdings even in cases where there was no *Chapper*. The word *Chapperbandi* is not used anywhere in the Chota Nagpur Tenancy Act and was coined by non-Tribals to defeat the provisions of the Act.
(c) Benaami purchases by rich non-Tribals also take place in the names of their poor illiterate servants, maids, concubines, wives et cetera.
(d) Taking possession of the Tribal land through marriage and then resorting to capture of the land.
(e) Through execution of Deed of Disclaimer and Deed of Relinquishment which are illegal but very often recognized by ignorant or corrupt courts.
(f) Through sale of Tribal lands on the basis of power of attorney got executed by ignorant and poor Tribal raiyats in favour of non-Tribal land brokers who transfer the Tribal lands as if these were non-Tribal lands. This is done solely to circumvent the provisions of the Chota Nagpur Tenancy Act by resorting to deception in courts. All such transfers are illegal.
(g) By showing some of Scheduled Tribes as non-Tribes. Many cases have been found in which a Lohara Tribal showed himself as a Lohar and transferred his land. Similarly Chik Baraik posing as Chik (BC) and Bedia posing as Bediya (BC).

In Santhal Pargana also the survey authorities do not act as custodians of the Tribal land but they tend to favour the non-Tribals who occupied their land through illegal means. One of the important methods of illegal transfer of land is *Dan Patra.* It is an unregistered document prepared between the Tribal and a non-Tribal for parting with a particular chunk of land of the former. In such Dan Patras the contents of the deed mention that financial difficulties of the Tribal have forced him to borrow money from the non-Tribal and the latter being a landless person, a piece of land has been given to him for domicile purposes. The amount of borrowed money is normally not entered in the Dan Patra, but separately stated in an affidavit sworn in by the Tribal either in the court of an executive magistrate or before a notary. Such transfers of land through Dan Patra are recognized by the survey officials and Khatas are opened in the names of non-Tribals on their basis.

There are several cases of abandonment in Santhal Pargana where the original raiyat or his heir leaves the village for good without making any arrangement for cultivation of land or where having made a temporary arrangement does not return at the end of the term. In such cases the law provides that a holding will be treated as abandoned after expiry of ten years. If such land is occupied by any other raiyat who is not a genuine settlee, the transfer is violative of the provisos of Santhal Pargana Tenancy (SPT) Act. The survey officials have been found to be ignorant of this provision of the SPT Act and tend to favour the illegal occupant of the land. In case of doubtful claimants, when the original raiyat or his heir comes as a claimant, the Assistant Settlement Officer should restore the land of the original raiyat or his heir.

Land and Incorrect Recording of Rights

It is common knowledge that an urban area expands at the cost of its rural fringe. It necessarily implies the transfer of land from the agriculturist to the non-agriculturist for the purposes of construction of buildings, roads and allied works. In many urban areas of Jharkhand like Ranchi, Hazaribagh, Bokaro, Jamshedpur, Chaibasa, Dumka, et cetera large areas were put to agricultural uses by the Tribals even within the municipal limits, but as urbanization increased the Tribal cultivation in urban areas gradually started vanishing and giving way to the new urban settlements. It is notable that in a large number of cases the new urban transferees did not adopt fair and legal methods acquire the Tribal land. In most of the cases it has been found that they adopted illegal and fraudulent methods to deprive the Tribals of their land without paying them fair prices.

In Chota Nagpur area advantage was taken of the provision in Chota Nagpur Tenancy Act, 1908 which allows conversion of agricultural land into homestead land and permits its transfer from a Tribal to a non-Tribal without permission of the Deputy Commissioner. Numerous antedated Hukumnamas of the erstwhile Zamindars were fabricated to establish the fact of conversion of agricultural land into homestead land. While recording the rights, the revenue officials did not examine the law in its correct perspective and passed orders in favour of the non-Tribals who adopted unfair means.

Other common fraudulent methods adopted by usurpers of the Tribal land include collusive title suits, disposition to fictitious processes and so on. In these cases also law is not properly taken into consideration and the competent authorities give their verdicts in favour of the non-Tribal transferees which encouraged the alienation of Tribal land. Instances have also come to light where land was purchased by the non-Tribal in the name of some fictitious Tribals and rent receipts were issued in the name of the purchaser after mutation. In this way the non-Tribal circumvents the provisions of Chota Nagpur Tenancy Act. In some of the cases, even regular registration deeds were effected by the Assistant Registrar though the law strictly prohibited the registration of such land which has not been transferred through legal means. Even in these two types of cases it has been found that the competent authorities who are responsible for recording of rights tend to favour the non-Tribals.

Another ignoble method of land disposition found particularly in rural areas of Chota Nagpur is by marrying a non-Tribal. There are thousands of cases in around Ranchi where the Muslims lured Tribal women in return for money and other things just for the sake of getting their land. In some of the cases even the formal marriage is not solemnized and the Tribal woman is kept in a house like a concubine. After some time their land is sold out in phases to the Muslims and non-Tribals. In such cases also the revenue officials ignore the provisions of law and favour the non-Tribals by making incorrect records of rights. As already mentioned earlier Bhugat Bandha mortgage is very common and illegal mode of transfer in Ranchi, Khunti, Simdega, Lohardaga and Gumla areas. The provisions of law stipulate that land should be mortgaged for a fixed period and then it should be returned to the Tribal but the fact remains that the land is never returned to the Tribal transferor and continues to remain in the hands of the transferees. While recording the rights of the Tribals, the competent authorities give undue weightage to the above mentioned fraudulent method and record of rights in favour of the illegal transferee.

Land and Forcible Occupation

There are many cases of Tribals losing their land in the hands of non-Tribals for petty considerations. The latter take advantage of the poverty of the Tribal families and give money for drinking and living expenses. When the Tribal does not return the money, the lender occupies his land. After taking possession of the Tribal land, the non-Tribal does not keep the land vacant and they are keen to construct their house on the Tribal land. Many college teachers and advocates have also built their houses on the lands of the Tribals in and around Ranchi.

The Tribals are poor and illiterate also. They are not conscious about the legal proceedings for restoration of their land. As a result most of them are not able to file restoration cases in the competent courts. One of the major reasons for not going to the court is the lack of legal awareness. They are not only ignorant about the provisos of the Tenancy Acts but they are also unaware about the legal aid scheme of the Government of Jharkhand under which each Tribal petitioner is provided with a amount of Rs 5,000 per case for filing land restoration petition. Restoration apart, they also get financial aid for restoring the productivity of land restored by the Government authority.

But the issue of forcible occupation of Tribal land is still unresolved. There are thousands hectares of Tribal lands under illegal occupation of non-Tribals. In many cases, the competent courts have also passed orders for eviction but in practice the non-Tribals are not being evicted because the number of such houses is in thousands. It needs strong political will for ordering demolition of such houses for returning the land to the Tribals. During the last two decades the Government of united Bihar and after the year 2000, the Government of Jharkhand have undoubtedly shown sensitivity to the problem of Tribal land disposition but have shown lack of adequate will power for ejecting others from Tribal lands.

Conclusion

Despite all attempts at modernization induced modernity, a Tribal is still a creature of his way of life sustained by five dimensions—the land including the trees, the forests, the water, the usages governed by customary laws, the social and the religious institutions and the community spirit of sharing. If any one of these elements were missing the Tribal way of life gets disrupted beyond repair. In the second place land and usages provide the rockbed of the Tribal way of life. They sustain their social and religious institutions. The Sarna is the abode of the Gods. It has to be sustained and serviced by a host of persons like the Pahans, the Pujars, the Goraits, et cetera. There is a service tenure linked to these institutions. In the third place the institutional lands or the socio-religious service tenures have prime value in the Tribal society and the Tribal way of life. It governs the usage of land and the appropriation of their produce. These tenures are inalienable and pass from service-seeker to service-provider. The Tribal way of life functions smoothly so long as these institutions are allowed to function. In the fourth place, the common lands have prime importance as they provide wood, fruits and additional means of livelihood for the expanding families. Institutions like Korkar, allow each family to bring additional land under plough by the dint of their own or family labour to meet the expanding needs of the family. It is not, however, to be equated with the Gair Majarua Aam Land. Similarly Mahtoai, Pahnai, Rjhas or Majhihas lands are not the same as the Bakasht land of the Zamindar and the community has a right to them. They cannot be eliminated. Fifthly, the Bhuinhari or Mundari-khuntkatti Tenures are unique institutions where rights vest into the descendants of the original settlers of being Mundas, Mankis or Jeth Raiyats . However, due to the lack of understanding they have been treated as tenures equivalent to Zamindari.

There is a gross lack of understanding regarding the Tribal way of life, their social-cultural, religious and land related institutions leading to trampling of their rights, uprooting of the Tribals and injuring of their ethos. By a strange quirk of fortune the bulk of the mineral resources are located in the areas inhabited by Tribals.[35] The result has been that despite having a protective set of formal laws protecting the customary laws which continue to govern the Tribal affairs they have been given the go by. Hence, the integrity of the Tribal institutions stands badly compromised thereby endangering the entire Tribal way of life based upon the land relations. In the sixth place, though not the least there have been major interventions on the side of the Tribals for the security of his lands in the form of PESA, the Forest Rights Act and the proposed Land Acquisition, Rehabilitation and Resettlement Bill, 2011. However, all of these remain non-starters qualifying the Myrdelian phrase of 'Soft State'. The question that arises here is what makes a state 'soft'? The answer, amongst many things is that it is the quality of understanding the issues and the degree of commitment to the cause by those who frame and pilot these enactments. Clearly, the fault lies not so much with the policy framework as with its implementation. This mismatch gives rise to 'policy incoherence'. That is why the Government of India have been advised not to talk but to get down to implementation. This is where we miss the guidance of stalwarts like the late S.R. Sankaran and his ilk whose understanding was deep on account of their complete identification with the cause and whose commitment was undying, beyond their physical demise.

NOTES

1. Singh, K.S. (1992), *People of India: An Introduction*, Seagull Books on behalf of the Anthropological Survey of India, Calcutta, pp. 51-52: "In all 4,635 communities have been identified and studied in all state/union territories of India....Four types of communities have been identified for study. The first consists of the very large categories of communities including caste, minorities, et cetera. The second type of communities studied by us consists of the linguistic and cultural categories or most of the speakers of the scheduled languages listed in the Eighth Schedule of the Constitution of India...Thirdly while the communities have been identified in terms of endogamy, occupations and perceptions, there are about half a dozen communities which do not conform to the three fold criteria. No religious group or sect has been studied, but there

are cases where the Kabirpanthi have been studied at a place in Bihar because they maintain that they are an endogamous community....Fourthly, the Government of India's list of the SC mentions Adi Dharmi, Adi Karnataka, Adi Andhra et cetera which represent a cluster of the SC, generally of the most backward section. Such categorie's emerged in the 1920s and 1930s in wake of the constitutional reforms and continue to figure in the listing of the SC. Therefore, while these categories have been studied, the communities which make, make up these larger/general categories have also been studied separately".

2. Singh, K.S., Ibid., p. 54: "The communities inhabit all climate zones of India. Most of them live in the warm and temperate zone (2211), followed by moderate (1853), cold (693), extreme warm (434) and extreme cold (111) zones. Some of these communities are found in more than one zone. The plains account for the largest concentration of the communities (2854), followed by the hilly terrain (1197), plateaus (804), coasts (686), valleys (236), semi-arid regions (240), high altitudes (102), deserts (69), and islands (29)".
3. Government of India. 2004. *The Constitution of India*, 6 June 2004, New Delhi: Government of India.
4. Government of India, 1961, *Report of the Scheduled Areas and Scheduled Tribes Commission*, Vol. I, New Delhi: Government of India.
5. *Annual Report*, Ministry of Tribal Affairs 2004-05, New Delhi, Government of India, 2005.
6. In this regard the Constitution (Scheduled Tribes) Order, 1950, Constitution (Scheduled Tribes) (Union Territories) Order, 1951, Constitution Andman and Nicobar Islands) Scheduled Tribes Order, 1959, the Constitution (Dadra and Nagar Haveli) Scheduled Tribes Order, 1962, the Constitution (Scheduled Tribes) (Uttar Pradersh) Order, 1967, the Constitution (Goa, Daman and Diu) Scheduled Tribes Order, 1968, the Constitution (Nagaland) Scheduled Tribes Order, 1970 and the Constitution (Sikkim) Scheduled Tribes Order, 1978 provide the additions made to the list of the Scheduled Tribes.
7. Vidyarthi, L.P. and Rai, Binay Kumar, *Tribal Culture of India*, New Delhi: Concept Publishing Company, 1976.
8. Faster, Sustainable and More Inclusive Growth: An Approach to the Twelfth Five Year Plan (2012-17), Government of India, October 2011, Planning Commission; www.planningcommission.nic.in.
9. Chota Nagpur Encumbered Estates Act, 1876 (Act VI of 1876), Bihar and Orissa, Legislative Department, Printed at the Bihar and Orissa Government Press, 1914.
10. The Chota Nagpur Landlord and Tenant Procedure Act, (Bengal Act No. 1 of 1879), Bengal, Legislative Department, Bengal Secretariat Press, 1904.
11. The Chota Nagpur Commutation Act, 1897, (Bengal Act No. IV of 1897), Bengal, Legislative Department, Bengal Secretariat Press, 1904.
12. The Chota Nagpur Tenancy (Amendment) Act (Act V of Bengal Council of 1903), Bengal, Legislative Department, Bengal Secretariat Press, 1904.
13. The Chota Nagpur Tenancy Act of 1908.

14. Bihar Scheduled Areas Regulation 1969. http://jharkhand.gov.in/DEPTDOCUPLOAD/uploads/25/D200925009.pdf)
15. The Chota Nagpur Tenancy Act of 1908, op. cit.
16. The Santhal Parganas' Settlement Regulation, (Regulation No. III of 1872). India. Legislative Department Office of the Superintendent of Government Printing, India, 1899.
17. The Sonthal Parganas Rent Regulation, 1886, (Regulation No. II of 1886), Bengal (India). Legislative Department, Bengal Secretariat Press, 1911.
18. The Santhal Parganas Tenancy (Supplementary Provisions) Act, 1949 (Bihar Act 14 of 1949).
19. The Bihar and Orissa Co-operative Societies Act, 1935, Bihar and Orissa Act VI of 1935, Bihar and Orissa (India). Legislative Department, Superintendent, Government Printing, Bihar and Orissa, 1935.
20. The Chota Nagpur Tenancy Act of 1908, op. cit.
21. The Chota Nagpur Tenancy (Amendment) Act 1903.
22. The Chota Nagpur Tenures Act, 1869: (Ben. Act II of 1869), Bengal, Legislative Department, Bengal Secretariat Press, 1909.
23. The Chota Nagpur Tenancy (Amendment) Act 1938 (Bihar Act 2 of 1938), Bihar Legislative Department, Superintendent, Government Printing, Bihar, 1938.
24. The Chota Nagpur Tenancy (Amendment) Act 1995, Act 2 of 1996 in R.N. Pandey.
25. The Bihar Scheduled Areas Regulation, 1969, op. cit.
26. Sarin, Madhu (May 5, 2005). "Scheduled Tribes Bill: A Comment" (PDF). Economic and Political Weekly 40 (21). http://www.epw.org.in/uploads/articles/637.pdf. Retrieved 2007-12-26.
27. Legislations on Environment, Forests and Wildlife, Ministry of Environment and Forests.
28. Prabhu, Pradip (August 2005), "The Right to Live With Dignity", *Seminar* (552), http://www.india-seminar.com/2005/552/552%20pradip%20prabhu.htm.
29. "Bad in Law", Madhu Sarin, World Bank website.
30. "Dispossessed and displaced: A brief paper on Tribal issues in Orissa", Kundan Kumar, Vasundhara.
31. Sethi, Nitin and Mukul, Askhaya. "Forest Act Notified, Tribals Unhappy." *Times of India*, January 2, 2008.
32. Summary Report on Implementation of the Forest Rights Act, Council for Social Development, as posted on Campaign for Survival and Dignity website
33. Santhal Parganas Settlement Regulation (3 of 1872), Bengal (India), Legislative Department, Bengal Secretariat Press, 1911.
34. The Sonthal Parganas Rent Regulation, 1886, (Regulation No. II of 1886, Bengal (India), Legislative Department, Bengal Secretariat Press, 1911.
35. Sinha B.K. (1993), "Alienation of Land in Chotanagpur-Santhal Parganans Areas" in *Administrator*, Vol. XXXVII, No. 2; April-June 1993, pp.103-104.

12

Wages of Sin: Tribals and Excise Policy

B.D. Sharma

Introduction

The British introduced commercial vending of intoxicants in the Tribal areas primarily for taming the wily Tribals and as a source of revenue from those people. They were still at pre-agricultural and 'hunting-gathering stage with nothing to do with market economy. This approach continued even after Independence. The Dhebar Commission (appointed under Article 339(1) of the Constitution in the year 1960) came down heavily on the exploitive system of colonial vintage through liquor trade continuing for more than a decade after Independence. The biggest irony is that the vital recommendation of the commission, prohibiting commercial vending of intoxicants in Tribal areas, was not implemented by the Government of India (GOI) because it got omitted, by chance, from the Summary of Recommendations. It simply remained buried in office files. In the absence of a national policy for Tribal areas, it was virtually free for all from top to bottom—astronomical targets for raising revenue, countless unauthorized outlets, huge levies in the form of obligatory purchase of *sarkaridaru* for each plough, festive occasion, marriage and such like. Sale on credit, recovery through muscle power, legendry *hafta* collected by police broke his back with virtually nowhere to go.

Pre-Independence Excise Regime

Here was an exciting world of the Tribal people set in Nature with no 'labour' to hire and no 'levy' of any description to pay. Outsiders cultivated friendship for help in need and, may be, for cherished drinks. The levy thereon, as the circle expanded, laid the foundation of a new excise policy. This virus spread very fast as was really planned by the rulers. Sensitive administrators did try to turn the tide but failed before the imperial establishment. A.O. Hume (1860), who described *abkaree* as 'wages of prohibition' as first attempted in Madras when the elected State Assembly, came to power in 1937. 'Sales Tax' was introduced to compensate the 'loss' of revenue due to prohibition. However, Tribal areas in general did not claim much attention during this period. Most of them were excluded/partially excluded areas under unequivocal command of the community. They had been managing all their affairs in accordance with their customs and tradition with regime of exotic drinks slowly expanding. Gandhiji was one of the first to realize the dangerous implications of the issue and took it up as a part of freedom struggle.

Gandhi's Perspective: Promise and Unfolding Reality

More than six decades of 'Hide and Seek' is the name of the game, which has gone on after Independence. Ironically, prohibition is about a vital matter concerning the life of the people about which—

- there was near unanimity during the freedom struggle,
- even those, who could not restrain their own craving, earnestly wished their wards not to fall its prey,
- Gandhiji was categorical, to the limit of being fanatical: If I were to become dictator for a single day prohibition will be my first decision; that is'

...the people are misled on this vital issue and continue to be misled even today by that simple statement of that wise man about prohibition.

Total identification with the ordinary people and their aspirations was the unique quality and source of limitless strength of Gandhiji. Then, could he ever dream of becoming a 'dictator'? Yet, he was a *dictator* unto himself, as he would wish every citizen to be in a real democracy of his dreams comprising *Man the Supreme*, imbued with the ideal of *'All Powers to the People'*, their representatives abiding strictly by the brief and the roles assigned to them by the people, and nothing beyond!

The people first believed that after Independence, when 'We the People' assume control over the State after establishing the same, what was so obvious would be done in the normal course. Accordingly, the goal was set, the Principle was enunciated and prohibition was enshrined in the Constitution as a Directive principle of State policy. But that was not to be. The diktat of the dictator lost its punch as those who should have led the nation as per *His Diktat* surrendered to the myths of the imperial throne and royal splendour.

The very perceptions about life and the sustaining values changed in the meantime. Whatever was done, was done by way of grudging concessions to the 'die-hards' amongst the warriors of freedom. But they themselves slowly lost their bearings in the stately confusion of institutions and authorities, their roles and responsibilities and the rituals in the name of socialism and democracy.

Nevertheless, the people expected that their representatives to assume the role of a dictator in this matter. After all what is a 'whip' in the Parliament of a democratic country? Sometimes there were upsurges as well, as the people, particularly women, lost their patience. Even when an odd dictator, be it the old Morarji or the new Bansi, came on the stage and had his say, a sort of law was enacted to bring about prohibition. But that fiat remained a mere law on paper with all its weaknesses. It was marred by skepticism galore and insincerity writ large on the part of those charged with the grave responsibility of its implementation. The ruling elite, including the politicians, would swear by it and affirm their faith over a fulsome peg, with hiccups unending.

Sabotage by the executive is unpardonable. It did not reconcile itself to the new democratic climate. It did not live up to the simple tradition of even a neutral civil service, let alone an instrument of change, committed to effective implementation with sincerity, forgetting its own preference after a political decision was taken. It is the saddest part of the administrative history of our country that it is the personal, the group, and the class interests that have plagued the system and have become the most important determinants of their action. The cause of the common man has been the worst casualty. Even the most serious issues concerning equality or even welfare of the people are handled, at best, just for the sake of form. '*Sabotage* !' is the silent cry of rulers, which begins to reverberate the entire system, the moment any of the vested interests on the other side are even obliquely affected even in pursuance of the constitutional objectives.

The way the issue of prohibition has been handled is the worst example of this nefarious design. In this case, it is not even the personal interest of these groups which has come in the way. It is hedonistic impulses and perverted self-righteousness, with arrogance of a ruler who wallows in the little world of his own, refusing even to acknowledge the reality beyond, which have been the root cause of the debacle in this vital matter concerning use and management of intoxicant. This has been so even though there is near consensus amongst the people, even after the downhill slide of half-a-century that, as a nation, we cannot afford to drink.

It is surprising that even the Gandhians of all persuasions—diehards, liberals and radicals—did not perceive the fallacy of the simple proposition of a state law on prohibition. It is true that they have been emphasizing that the real solution does not lie in the law but in the reform of Man himself. But that begs the question and does not take into account the fallacy of *individual versus the State*. The diehards and even some well-meaning persons on the other extreme, in their turn, have beleaguered the prohibitionist with a tongue-in-cheek argument, 'Why should the State be asked to intervene or even delve in this purely personal matter?' If everyone were to decide for himself to abstain from drinking, prohibition would be automatic. That is fine. But these gentlemen conveniently ignore the ugly reality of the insidious and even open and blatant collusion between the vested interests and the keepers of law on the one side and the negation of the community on the other side. In fact, community has misdeeds of a few in the name of freedom of individual.

The fact that the formal state apparatus cannot, and is not designed to intervene in social matters, is ignored on purpose. The rulers, even the elected representatives, are not prepared to shed the authority which they wield in the System which continues to be colonial not only in its frame but, what is worse, with a perverted spirit. Earlier, it was an alien power which was at the helm of affairs. Therefore, it could be targeted easily as the source of affairs. Therefore, it could be targeted easily as the source of evil. Now, it is the people's own representatives and persons under their command who are at the helm of affairs. As such, *'They can do no wrong'*, having acquired that license to rule and manage the way they like, after the ritual of vote. So we have the ridiculous spectacle of people being advised to mend their own ways even as the collusion at the top continues and evil forces are let loose to defy.

It is now generally accepted that the excise policy followed by the state Governments has resulted in exploitation. A Sub-committee of the Central Advisory Board on Prohibition comprising excise Ministers of States, which went into this question, has confirmed this finding. Some time ago, a group of Members of Parliament had represented against sale of distilled liquor in Tribal areas. They went to the extent of suggesting that the development outlays could be reduced if revenue considerations come in the way. The Central Advisory Board on Prohibition has endorsed the suggestion. At the meeting of the board, the excise Ministers did raise the question of revenue but in view of the continuing exploitation it was agreed that compensations could not be a precondition for the change. The Scheduled Areas and Tribals Commission had made similar recommendations in 1961, but it is a pity that, even though accepted by the Government, these have remained unimplemented so far. Since the matter has been gone into in detail, an early decision on the new excise policy should be taken without any further delay.

A new chapter was added in Tribal development in early 1970s with the clear object of meeting the challenge of mounting Tribal unrest. Smt. Indira Gandhi, in her minute dated 19 June 1974 (pp. 15–19 below) addressed to the Home Ministers, gave top priority to elimination of exploitation especially in matters concerning excise. The new excise policy became operational in all states in 1975 without dissent of any description. The plea for compensating the loss of revenue was rejected on the ground that there can be no compensation for exploitation.

The first phase of excise policy was a grand success, especially under the aura of emergency. All conventional *bhatties* of the *kalars* (the caste specializing in this business) were closed down in the entire Tribal tract of the country. But the crucial issue about the community in the form of the Gram Sabha managing its affairs in accordance with its customs and traditions was first camouflaged and then openly opposed by the states after change of government at the Centre. This ambivalence was taken advantage of by vested interests leading to free for all amongst the simple people.

So far as the excise policy and responsibility about its implementation are concerned, it has three clear levels, namely, (i) state legislation, (ii) PESA, and (iii) directions by the Union. The state laws in practice are too weak to counter the current avalanche of intoxicants of all descriptions. The spirit of PESA can go a long way if it is honestly pursued. But there is a lot of confusion about even the basic tenets of PESA. It is time that the 1975 Excise Policy is not left alone to fend for itself with mere paper goodwill gestures of concerned states. It is a fit case where the concerned states, as also the Union Government, must honestly admit their mistakes and omissions. How is it that even after fewer decades of the excise policy, it did not really become effective notwithstanding universal consensus in its favour.

Liquor Mafia's Rule in Tribal Territories

The author as Collector and District Magistrate of Bastar (1968–70) halted at a small village in Narayanpur for the night. In the morning, the entire village had gathered in front of my hut with a simple question: 'Why have you opened this liquor outlet in our village? You know we drink. And with this shop located here our youth, boys and girls, frequent this place and indulge in drinking at will. This fellow does not insist on cash payment either, knowing full well that we cannot refuse payment of dues of our children. In the end he will grab our land against mounting loan.' 'What can I do in this case?' I asked them. 'Please remove this shop to a distant place. Those who want to drink will go there and drink.' 'I will look into the matter,' I assured the people. That was my first rendezvous with the liquor issue in the district.

The local vendor had disappeared from the village. I went to the '*bhatti*', the authorized place for preparation and sale of *mahua* brew, in the afternoon. Admonished the *thekedar* for running illegal outlets. With no remorse about illegal activities he coolly asked me: 'Collector Sahib, when you auction the *bhattis* your officers prompt us to raise the bid. I have to make these outlets, everyone knows. Do you expect me to pay for the high bids from my pocket?' 'You have made your point,' I conceded, 'I will not blame you now, but please ensure that no complaint of this sort comes to me. No officer shall prompt the bids next year and the rule of law shall prevail leaving no scope for informal outlets.'

I informed the state government about the ugly reality of countless illegal outlets in the district with a request that no revenue targets be fixed next year. I further added that the auction shall begin with a clear statement about 'no prompting of bids and law taking its own course in dealing with illegal outlets'. There was furor in Bhopal with weighty advice to me about being practical in administration. But I stuck to my position as I was duty bound as District Magistrate to curb illegal activities. There were no bidders subsequent year for more than two-third *bhatties*. The excise revenue nose-dived from the target of rupees one crore to less than 20 lakhs. The contractors in other Tribal areas indulged in a variety of machinations that were brought to my notice, as I moved to Delhi (1972). For example, contractors in Surguja (MP, now Chhattisgarh) levied 'plough tax' of rupees two as guaranteed protection against excise raids on their domestic brew. Similarly quota for purchase of three gallons was fixed for marriage and other festive occasions.

After my morning walk in Gumla, Jharkhand, I sat for a while at a local *bhatti* and talked with a boy just 14 years old in charge. 'The business is bris, but all on credit', he said. 'What about repayment?' I asked. 'What our *lathaits*, or muscle-men are here for', he answered with pride. 'What about complaints with the police?' here came his instant unwavering replay: 'Where will the police get this much paper to write as if such complaints are ever registered?' In the context of these horrendous facts that I placed before Government of India, it was decided in 1975 to abolish vending of intoxicants as an integral part of new approach in Tribal development. The traditional *bhatties* vanished from the entire Tribal tract with great relief to the Tribal people. *But State's reluctance to enforce, nay, not even facilitate community's control over intoxicants of all descriptions has proved to be the greatest disaster for the Tribal world.*

Excise Policy–1975 with Mixed Perception

The 1975 Policy envisages

i. banning commercial vending of intoxicants in the Tribal areas;
ii. allowing preparation of traditional brews for personal consumption, but not for sale;
iii. allowing sale of intoxicants in non-Tribal enclaves exclusively through government outlets and
iv. conceding community's control on all excise matters.

The policy was implemented by all states. The Government of India did not concede any assistance for the loss of revenue to the states on the ground that *there can be no compensation for cessation of exploitation*. The message about abolition of *bhatties* that had terrorized the Tribal people for more than a century was welcomed by all with no exception. A Majhi (Chief) in Bastar confided in me that the *kochinies* (women selling traditional drinks in the market) have acquired golden bangles, please do not bring *bhatties* in our area back at any cost.

I was going from Raipur to Ranchi through a dense forest. I stopped by the road side where half a dozen people were gossiping around the fire place about abolition of *bhatties*. An old man was dramatizing the change. 'We usually drink in the company of a couple of friends. We make small cups of leaves; take the brew from the pot with a smile, wishing each other a happy bout. The second round begins with a new fervor that really epotomises in the third. And the real round is the 'fourth' where we may roar like a tiger, just a little short of pouncing on each other.' He was wondering about the wisdom of a person who might have advised Indira *ji* to abolish *bhatti*es 'honouring our tradition of 'roar' once in a while as real good friends'. The States, however, did not transfer legal control in excise matters to the community as envisaged in the policy. This exclusion resulted in continued interference by excise officials and unconcern in the community. Drinking became rampant as never before with disastrous consequences for the Tribal people.

Enactment of PESA (1996)

The situation did not improve even after the enactment of PESA, which specifically envisages full control of Gram Sabha in all matters concerning preparation, storage, and consumption of intoxicants. Madhya Pradesh has even amended its Excise Act. But the message about the community in the form of Gram Sabha having command over all excise matters has not percolated to the people. The most ludicrous situation arose in North Telangana, in people's struggle against liquor (1985). The police stations served as liquor outlets with jawans vending the same as part of their duty. The liquor shops are omnipresent in all Tribal tracts with no concern for the law and the excise policy. *Nobody even remembers the very existence of such a policy.*

The Tribal people continued to carry the cross of this obnoxious policy even after Independence. Even strong condemnation of this policy by the Scheduled Areas and Scheduled Tribes Commission in no uncertain terms was ignored by the system until 1975 when the excise policy in the Tribal areas was reviewed afresh. The Government of India issued guidelines with a clear objective of (i) removing the disconcert between the social custom and the prevailing law, (ii) demolishing the diabolic institution of liquor trade from that area, and (iii) enabling the people to manage on their own essentially what concerns their social and culture life. It envisaged stoppage of commercial vending of liquor in Tribal areas and suitable changes in the law so as to allow the people to prepare their traditional drinks for personal consumption and social purpose. It was further envisaged that a suitable provision would be made in the law to entrust the community itself its implementation and make further regulations for self-management in this regard.

It is regretted that the above policy has not been fully adopted by all the states. Even in those states where a substantive part of this policy has been accepted, there are some vital omissions. For example, in Madhya Pradesh, the state has not entrusted the responsibility of management and regulation of matters concerning local excise to the people. The result is that the Tribal people have continued to be at the mercy of the administration even regarding this vital social matter. Moreover, the vested interests are taking advantage of this situation in Maharashtra with an added handicap that commercial vending continues in many small towns deemed to be non-Tribal enclaves. These shops are being used as conduits for flow of illicit liquor as the people are helpless against the unscrupulous elements in the absence of any authority as envisaged in the guidelines. In many areas where the people are becoming conscious of the damage which drinking is causing to their health, economy, and society, are keen to rid themselves of its ill-effects through social control, an untenable situation has arisen in which the State is coming in their way. The lower officials take the cudgels to the offenders ostensibly on the premise that the community has no authority under the law to interfere with the personal freedom of any individual. The simple Tribal people are simply wonderstruck at this logic according to which they are prohibited from putting their own house in order. It is not realized that the basic social unit amongst the Tribal people is the community, not the extended family.

Whatever may be the formal postures at higher levels, the real reason for the disinclination of the State to implement excise policy is their concern for the revenue which gets the unholy support through a variety of rationalizations of lower level officials who are keen to keep their stranglehold on these people. It is rather sad that even after Independence the simple Tribal people many a time have been trapped by the modern system through the lure of liquor. It is an irony that the state should be disinclined to entrust a people who have the best tradition of responsible self-governance to manage even their social affairs and bring about desired change. The excise policy inherited from the colonial rule is all back with not one silvery spot in its favour to commend.

Elimination of Exploitation in Reverse Gear (1980s)

The highest priority item of 'Elimination of Exploitation' moved in reverse gear, while commercial vending of intoxicants was abolished reluctantly, though the states refused to empower the community to oversee excise affairs. And the Union remained unconcerned about this vital core of the holistic policy. It resulted in phenomenal unprecedented rise in drinking in Tribal areas. The Union has remained a silent spectator of the total policy reversal. Vendors have reappeared virtually everywhere in the village, near a school, or on the highway. The people's initative against liquor in North Telangana was met with force and sale of arrack was organized in police stations by policemen.

(1985) In sum, the state and its association are back in the game in amassing 'wages of sin' (excise revenue) as the very existence of an excise policy for Tribal areas has been forgotten (see *Unbroken History of Broken Promises,* p. 56).

The Government of India, in this case, did acknowledge the damage to the people caused by commercial vending of liquor. Guidelines were also issued regarding excise policy. The Government of India also kept on reminding the states for acceptance and implementation of guidelines in full. It may be noted here that these pleadings related to the year 1994, just 20 years after the formal adoption of the policy of the Government of India in 1974. It is thus clear that, notwithstanding the limitless goodwill, the Union Government, in this case, failed to adopt the path of giving directions to the concerned state under the clear provisions of Para 3 of the Fifth Schedule. It emboldened the liquor lobby that was now totally immune to the spirit of constitutional provision for effective protection of the simple Tribal people.

The adoption and implementation of excise policy in 1975, with unequivocal consensus amongst the Union, the states and even people's representatives at all levels, was a grand success. But change in leadership at the top in this period made a marked difference. The Government of India, while considering the Report of the Commissioner for Scheduled Castes and Schedule Tribes, commended 'the main guiding principle for protection against all form of exploitation.' The guidelines for excise policy had been issued. The Ministry's, 'has been following up with various State Governments for acceptance and implementation of Guidelines in full' could not be eulogized by any standards. Ironically, my proposal as Commissioner to the Government of India about 'issuing suitable directions... for ensuring effective implementation' remained unattended.

Proposition with a Difference for the Tribal People

The most promising aspect of the Tribal scene is that the community is still in a position to respond to the changing situation. A number of spontaneous movements have been occurring within the community, sometimes with stimulus from outside, to wean away the people from drinking with commendable success in some cases. But this social sanction remains valid only so long as a person voluntarily abides by it and/or the concerned officials in the System are sympathetic to the cause. An odd member of the community, in collusion with policeman, or even taking advantage of the incongruous legal frame, may directly appeal to any court of law and question the authority of the community for social sanction and portray the same as personal harassment and transgression of his rights as a citizen. Once a dent is made even in a single case, the whole edifice of social sanction, built over generations, may give way. Persons with deep concern may remain helpless witnesses in anguish to the ruination of their social and economic life, as the vested interests of contractors or bootleggers, as the case may be, rule supreme.

A new frame was prepared to enable the Tribal people to come out of this net, in which they had been trapped partly as a conscious policy of the colonial rulers to subjugate the wily Tribes of rugged wilderness, and partly because of lack of even elementary understanding about the Tribal people amongst the ruling elite after Independence. The latter, at best, indulged in meaningless rhetoric of 'museum-piece versus main stream' theories. which has no relationship with the real issues. The new excise policy frame basically comprised three elements. Firstly, commercial vending of liquor was to be totally stopped so that the vested interest of liquor contractors could be eliminated. Secondly, the traditional preparation of intoxicants for personal use was to be allowed with a clear stipulation that it could not be sold.

Thirdly, the responsibility for enforcement of the new policy was to vest with the community.

The guidelines were duly accepted by all state governments. Vending of liquor was stopped. The Tribal people were allowed to prepare their traditional drinks. But so far as the third element of the policy concerning social control was concerned, ambivalence prevailed. **Silence is the most effective weapon of the executive in such cases.** The principle was not questioned by any State. Yet, no state government took the simple decision of implementation of law, with role whatsoever for the community.

The results were predictable. Firstly, liquor shops did disappear from the Tribal scene along with the contractors and their musclemen. The people heaved a great sigh of relief. Secondly, the preparation of traditional drinks, which was being done even earlier, but in violation of law and therefore under cover, now became legal. With this change, another source of unspeakable harassment of the Tribal people by the contractor and the police, jointly and severally, was removed. There was considerable restraint on drinking itself for some time as people rejoiced in their liberation from a draconian law, which had the effect of branding every Tribal a criminal and vulnerable to legal action at the sweet-will of that law, as well as of the intruders under its cover, had one salutary effect. No one could prepare the traditional brew even for personal and social purpose without the permission of this 'gang', which, of course, could be had for a consideration. Similarly, the sale of traditional brew was kept under stringent control by the contactor, as it was a serious competitor of his liquor. On both these counts, drinking was rather restrained.

The new law had the effect of removing this constraint. The official intervention in a situation, where it is difficult to distinguish between what is for personal consumption and what is for sale, cannot be very effective. It can, at best, be notional. The community had no formal role whatsoever to play in this vital matter. In this situation, there are no restraints whatsoever on preparation and even small scale sale of traditional intoxicants in the Tribal areas. What is worse, even exotic drinks are finding their way under its cover into these areas. A new vested interest is taking root, which is interested in promotion of drinking to the very brink, with no holds barred.

It may be recalled that this policy package was envisaged as the first step towards prohibition via removal of vested interests and assertion of social will as there is realization amongst the people about its ill-effects. The full package, however, was not implemented. The end result, therefore, is just the other way round. The incidence of drinking in the Tribal society has risen sharply. A new vested interest with all associated evils has emerged and has been getting entrenched. Some people even feel that the earlier System, notwithstanding the harassment and the economic consequences, was better. There was some restraint on drinking. Now, with the incidence of drinking rising perpetually, it is disastrous for health. Moreover, the small economic gains accruing to the people on many other counts may be nullified by uninhibited drinking. It is, therefore, bound to lead to their destitution at a much faster pace than earlier. The package designed for the well-being of the Tribal people minus social control has become dysfunctional and anti-Tribal.

Here is a well-meaning excise policy, which was accepted by all. Those who are against prohibition favoured it because there is no element of compulsion in this frame. Similarly, those, who are for prohibition, supported it because that could be the first step towards prohibition. The vested interests against any scheme of prohibition would be rooted out in this process. Our logic was also very simple. There can be no case for prohibition if there is no social awareness and consensus amongst the people. 'How can one convey the idea of prohibition in a community where drinking is a norm?' I had argued while proposing the package. The community can be expected to become aware about the issue, step by step, if the community itself were to be decision-maker. Social activists can also have a decisive role in this respect as was really the case in many areas. It is unfortunate that the community, which has the real stake and vital role, had been kept out of picture for the simple reason that our ruling elite refuses to take note of its very existence. In fact, the community does not find a place at all in the formal legal frame, that is, the 'system'. The system, therefore, by its very nature, cannot take cognizance of the community comprising the people since the basic premise on which even the independent Indian State has remained unchanged ever since the Raj was founded: 'Trust the System, Not the People.' The culture of Raj came back in the incarnation of neoliberal model from early 1980s. Their entire model is unreal sing, undemocratic, unequalsing, and anti-poor people.

State Against People

Widening of the National Divide

As inequality came to be accepted as an essential condition of growth, at least in the early phase, particularly in the service of capital formation, it started acquiring demonic dimensions. Affluence got legitimacy as an engine of growth. In this milieu, not only did drinking became fashionable in the upper strata, but it also came to acquire the status of an essential condition for success. It became an insignia of modernity even for the rest. But the matter did not rest there. From mild to strong, from strong to drug-fending are just normal stages in that unrestrained progression. Accordingly, drug addiction has become rampant. This laxity is taking a heavy toll in many other spheres of social life, including increasing fragility of marriage bonds, promiscuity and last, but not the least, the spectre of AIDS. There is a quixotic search for solutions, no one caring, or daring to touch the real cause.

The situation on the other side in the dualistic system amongst the deprived also continues to deteriorate at a fast pace. While the man in distress is seeking refuge in drinking, the family is getting in deeper morass of economic catastrophe. Women are the worst sufferers. While they are in no position to understand the larger processes at the national and international level leading to deprivation and destitution, drinking is the most proximate phenomenon and the visible direct cause for the misery of the self as also their children. This they can see, feel and experience.

This has found expression, of late, in women taking the lead in anti-liquor agitations. The message or the call in this case, is so clear and near to every woman's heart in all non-elite groups that it took no time for it to spread throughout the concerned State, which happens to be the frame of reference for the ordinary people for the problems of their day-to-day life. Moreover, the State also happens to be an important frame of reference for the media, particularly the language press, which is closer to the people and also more responsive to and in turn with popular aspiration.

The first massive women's upsurge of this genre was in Tamilnadu. The government could not resist. It was forced to impose prohibition. The second upsurge, still more sharp and swift, was in Andhra Pradesh. The government had to bow before the rising women-power and impose prohibition. The third spontaneous move, again largely from women, came in Haryana. The party which promised prohibition came to power. Prohibition was imposed in this state as well.

These upsurges against liquor are qualitatively different from the early popular demands. The women particularly are convinced that the state is on the wrong in its policy on liquor. Moreover, it has no moral right to remain a silent spectator to the economic and social disaster. It must act decisively. Earlier, the stance was that the state was not doing something desirable. The pressure was moral.

Nevertheless, the end result in either case so far has been the same. The vested interests in the wake of early zeal and euphoria of success amongst the people at large lay low for some time. But as usual, the elite, particularly the ruling elite, is not really convinced about the state action which they are forced to take under what they are refusing to acknowledge even the vital difference between the two situations. The vested interests, on the other hand, reorganize themselves while the ruling elite remains unconcerned, or acquiescent. In fact, it may even collude with the former.

The State, in this frame, is rather too keen to acknowledge the failure of experiment at the slightest pretext. There is no serious and objective assessment of the real situation. The official reviews are more in the nature of specious affirmation of their faith in the failure in such misadventures than a probe into the reasons therefore. And the people are told in the style of a sermon about futility of their fight against a human failing as faulty because that suits the rulers. *The women or the people, at the end of their journey, are at square one, from where they sally forth, as a crusade but with a difference, crestfallen constantly reminded of the failing of their idealist crusades in a murky world. 'Reform the man', is the sane advice, 'but always remember, it is an ideal which one can never attain. Your effort is your reward. Never pine for the result.'*

The State and its Minions

In the formulation, which I proposed, a strong plea was made for state intervention to counter the adverse forces taking advantage of and in support of the good will, nay a very positive urge, albeit unarticulated, in favour of prohibition. I still hoped that the political executive, the representatives of the people, would see reason, respect, and the people's goodwill. They will be able to bridle the irresponsible and irresponsive executive, which was not prepared to see beyond its shell and graciously respond on its own to the people's will in the new democratic clime.

That was not to be. What is worse, the political executive, the so-called people's representatives, in the meantime, themselves learnt the tricks of the trade, trivialized all values and institutions set up and created under that great Covenant on 26 November 1949. They themselves have become a vested interest as an integral part of the rapacious inheritors. They have no concern for the people on the other side whom they are supposed to represent, so long as they can be fooled about which people have become somewhat conscious, but are unable so far to see through the games which the rulers are playing.

Moreover, in the meantime, the times have changed in a more fundamental way. The ruling elite has surrendered to what are termed as the processes of globalization and liberalization. Its means that the goals set out and values enshrined in the Constitution are no longer valid. According to new premises, we, as a nation, have to accept a place in the world economic order which may be assigned to us by the neo-Imperialist capitalist forces. The ruling elite itself has acquired a new frame for itself. It does not consider itself as a part of the Indian Nation-State. It is impelled by a vision of global citizenship for it members. The ordinary people also are sought to be captured and tamed and suitably trained. There is unprecedented cultural invasion particularly via the electronic media. The luxurious living of the rich is conditioning the people and is setting the cultural ethos of 'clicking of glasses'. What they see on the screen has now become the dream world of even the disinherited destitutes. They are made to believe through a bevy of illusions and allusions that a day shall come when they may also be partaking in the same great feast. So they are happy with the crumbs, the shadows, and even induced hallucinations with all descriptions of inebriants thrown in-between.

But this veneer is wearing off as the divide between the Inheritors and the Rest is deepening. The people are facing the harsh reality of their rejection by the System and their waning relevance in the new paradigm, notwithstanding the tall claims and still taller promises by the rulers. The Tribal people are the worst affected in this game. They are up against the logic of the eminent domain, which was forced on the 'little republics' by imperialist looters to legitimatize the plunder, and which ironically is unfolding in worse and more acute forms after Independence. Everything is currently being justified in the name of development. The rich resources in the Tribal areas, a gracious gift of nature, have become the enemy of people in the face of a sort of rapacious 'frontier spirit'. The national economy is being thrown open with no holds barred in a so-called free market in which everything, including land and forest, can be sold and purchased under suitable covers no doubt. Displacement, disorganization, and destitution are the order of the day in this *mellee* so far as the Tribal people are concerned.

The general scene in the larger rural segment of national economy is also not very different from that in the Tribal areas. The agricultural sector has been so manipulated that agriculture as an economic activity is a losing proposition for the ordinary farmers. As such, land is being taken over from farmers-in-distress by people-with-money, be it the capitalists, the corporate sector or the multinationals as such. The ordinary farmer, in this milieu, has a feeling that he cannot save; it will slip off his hands, sooner than later. He is staring at the wide blue void above with stony eyes, not even in a position to wonder about of his own, or his children.

Stark Reality Begs No Idealism

It was to meet this challenge of the so called pragmatists to the so called idealists that I had personated the analysis of the stark reality in the Essay the moral exhortations: 'To hell with idealism, I am concerned with the fate of the ordinary people', was my counter-challenge. The occasion was the Centenary year of Gandhi's birth. The All India Congress Committee, which had fought the freedom struggle and had by then ruled the country for more than two decades, was reminded of the Diktat of the Dictator about prohibition. The nation still was not ready for a *'let us forget about it'* stance. In fact, the ruling elite had not yet acquired the strangulating hold on the national scene which it is virtually enjoying now. There were still countless people on the other side whose perceptions and pursuations could not be ignored. The all India Congress Committee, therefore, was obliged to decide to work for realization of the dream of the Father of the Nation but as a phased programme of seven years in deference to the so called pragmatic considerations. This laboured resolution was really a disgrace to the centenary celebrations which no one realized because no one was even aware about the deep emotional commitment of its founder.

And much dust was raised on either side of the fence knowing full well that what had not been even seriously attempted for two long decades shall not be accomplished in seven years. It provides to be a ploy, ploy with a style of course! The reason is simple. So far as the elite was concerned, prohibition was never on its agenda. It had disappeared from the agenda of all political parties as well-right, left or centre. The rationale in each case depended on their respective situations and pursuations.

I made two basic points in my analysis. Firstly, notwithstanding the swirling dust in the sublime sky of elites, there was consensus amongst the ordinary people, who should really matter in a democracy, on the question of drinking. That drinking is undesirable is universally accepted. Even a person who drinks concede, when not under the influence of liquor, that drinking is not good. He will not like his son to drink. So far as his daughter possibly taking to drinking is concerned, it cannot be even imagined. There was only one exception to this general rule. The urban-upper class was dissenter and thought otherwise. This class, however, was minuscule and could not be taken seriously in any decision about this grave national issue, except with regard to its mischief-potential. I, therefore, urged that advantage must be taken of the most opportune social situation without losing any time before it was too late. The nation was passing through a phase of structural transformation, which was loosening the traditional social fabric. It may take a long time before a new social frame may emerge. The vested interests may take advantage of this situation of flux and destroy that climate in favour of prohibition. They may corrupt the youth and that great opportunity may be lost forever.

The second point concerned the reason for this hurry. It was quite simple. In the current phase of our national life, dedicated to the building of an egalitarian society, not only the basic needs of all citizens had to be fully met, but conditions had to be created for realization of fully met, but condition had to be created for realization of full potential of the personality of every women and man, irrespective of the accident of her/his birth and status in life. Education, health and living conditions, besides the use of leisure time, behoving a cultured people, easily come at the top of the agenda. And I demonstrated conclusively on the basis of firm data it was with regard to these vital issues that the effect of drinking amongst the ordinary people is catastrophic.

The detailed analysis, reproduced at the end in full, shows that investment on education in those poor families where farther drinks is almost zero, whereas for the same income group amongst those who do not drink, it could be as high as ten per cent. The second largest dent was in respect of expenditure on housing, that is, the living conditions of a people. It goes to determine the status of health in a family. The matter does not rest there. It is wrong to presume that drinking provides an outlet, a sort of relaxation for a person after a day's hard toil. In fact, those who drink are prone to spend more on other diversions as well such as smoking, *pan* and entertainment. And even in respect to what the pure economist may lay highest emphasis on, that is, productivity, it also is a demonstrable casualty. The sum total of diversions of income on such non-essentials could be anywhere between 15 to 20 per cent, or even more.

When there are exhortations all around to 'Invest in Man', to 'Build the future Generations', when in macro-economic system investment on social services is abysmally low and highly skewed as between the haves and the have-nots, which leaves hardly anything for the common man, can this huge diversion of family income from education, health, and housing be allowed to go unquestioned, nay, encouraged indirectly on spurious premises, since it does not affect the ruling elite? In fact, such diversion serves the purpose of the competitive frame from the very beginning. Those who can afford can see that their children are far ahead in any race for advancement from Day One, not because of their intrinsic merit and higher potential, but because of the investment which their parents can make in them. Apart from the question of social equity, this unconcern for the large majority of people is a treachery with the nation itself. The great potential of man in this nation of a phase of history when, after about two centuries of the holocaust of the imperial regime which has led the nation white, every iota of every citizen's energy needs to be harnessed for its advancement.

The fate of the poor given to drinking stands sealed. But what was happening even where the so-called development had succeeded as in Punjab?

The noted social scientist, Late Prof. Shyama Charan Dube, and myself, during our long association spanning over three decades, had agreed to disagree on the issue of prohibition from the very beginning. But after he visited Punjab sometime in the late seventies, he told me that, after what he saw in Punjab, he was obliged to agree with me. In a countryside where people took pride in taking big glasses full of milk and buttermilk, the scene had totally changed. Every third shop was a liquor shop, open or clandestine. 'Is this the society which we dream of, for which we have worked, green revolution notwithstanding?' remarked Prof. Dube with a sense of deep concern and compassion for the people he so much loved and adorned. Punjab is no longer an exception. A new India has comprising the urban organized, the inheritors of the Raj, has come of age in image of that Punjab, which Prof. Dube so passionately described, the disinherited multitude having been declared as disposable. This is the trick that market performed with considerable ease.

The Treacherous Squeeze

And the market must squeeze the man unto the last drop. Universal education has been given a goodbye. Instead, what we have is a programme of universal literacy being executed at a breakneck speed. The design is simple and transparent. The wretched of the Earth, instead of remaining glued to the wonder screen with all sorts of salacious acrobats, should be enabled to read the messages divine of corporate sponsors, national and multinational. The organized sector, which had imbibed the aura of inheritors of the Raj, is also being broken up as it is outsized as per the new global norms. A select few amongst them are being drafted into the world class of the global economy. The rest are being pushed out to what can be termed as quasi-organized sector comprising bevy of new functionaries called 'karmies'—education, health, social security, even security proper, and what not. And duped are they by the dazzle on the other side with kindled hope of crossing the *vaitarini*, if not today tomorrow, or the day after.

The worst facet of the present situation is that the democratic institutions, which should command and direct these processes, have degenerated into pressure groups ironically for the invader. Everyone who matters, the lowest *pancha* to the highest amongst them the *Prime-Panch*, has been co-opted, or outright purchased. In fact, as stated earlier, what we are witnessing is the unfolding of the Imperialist logic, which was allowed to continue in the System and adopted ostensibly for developmental goals. Equity has become a synonym of 'equitable' share is the *loot* and/or claims in the new *jagir*s sought to be established in its wake. The ground for that sham equity can be anything like class, caste, ethnicity, region, religion, gender, handicap, or anything which one can think of.

So *loot* is the order of the day. And the greatest duty of our ruling elite, now in this new *avator* as *dalals* of the neo-Imperialist-Capitalist Global Axis, is to create conditions for further facilitating that *loot*. They must project the depredations as natural and legitimate, nay, a consequence of man's own deeds. This is what *Karma* and *Punarjanma* theories have done for ages. Co-opt in the same style those who make unnecessary noices or are able to see through the game. They must convince the dissident, as also the people at large, that their suffering is not real but is like birth-pangs before a new life is born. The people must bear the same with fortitude and forbearance. And if worse comes to worst, the new angels can quote from scriptures even the greatest sages of imperialist order such as Malthus on unrestrained breeding and Darwin on the survival of the fittest.

The Kiss of Death

And promotion of drinking, or creating favorable conditions for its promotion, is the most effective and deadly weapon in the hands of the ruling elite and all anti-people forces. It creates a tiny vicious circle of expropriation, indulgence, and resignation to fate in every family. The State legitimizes even this policy on specious considerations of revenue, of futility of fighting against human nature, and of the need for investment in social services in the aid of the ravaged. It is conveniently forgotten that for every rupee of tax from liquor, the person spends five on what essentially is "the kiss of death", that the big draft on his income is at the cost of his children's education as also his own health which tells heavily on his productivity, that the government would have earned much more even by way of tax revenue *via* higher sale of other commodities, that sales tax was introduced by the first Congress Government in Tamil Nadu in 1937 in pursuance of the same logic. The most pernicious part of this entire chain of events is the denial of education for a large segment of our people. It makes them susceptible to superstitions, old and new. They also become victims of myth about their sorry state and poverty itself being a direct consequence of their lack of education. This premise has no basis in reality.

State-Managed Prohibition

The Government on its side, and the idealists on theirs, have remained engaged in the game of 'Hide and Seek'. The latter did not care even to ponder over the real nature of their demand? After all, what does a movement for Prohibition in reality mean? What the Crusaders in effect do is to pray to the government, which they feel represents the omnipotent State: *'Aye, Mai Bap Sarkar! make a law so that we, the obedient children of yours do not drink. And if some of us do not behave, adomish us, catch our ears so that we behave!'*

When these children make too much noise, the *Maibaps in sarkar* favour them with toys of law with a clear fore-warning about the fragility of those toys, the futility of the law. In fact, specious provisions are built into the same on purpose to ensure its collapse. The exclusive role and authority of the official machinery in implementation and also in overseeing the performance, which are converted into sorts of privilege, are the softest spots for the undoing of even the most earnest intentions to do the right thing, let alone the rituals concerning formal prohibition replete with insincerity and deceit. *Sarkari* prohibition is a Trojan Horse of the right make in the nefarious game of people's ruination.

Let us take the management of general excise laws. The Excise Law of MP, for example, like similar laws of all other states recognizes that drinking is injurious to health, that its sale shall not be promoted through advertisement, that its sale-points shall be strictly regulated and subject to stringent conditions under the watchful eyes of advisory committees in every town and in every district which shall include, *inter alia*, people's representatives. No retail shop, according to the rules, shall be licensed for consumption of liquor on the premises if it is

(i) at the entrance of a market place,
(ii) in the neighborhood of a mill, a factory, on such like,
(iii) near a place of worship, a bathing *ghat*, an educational institution, a hospital, a bus-stand, a railway station, a highway, a labour colony, or scheduled caste habitation.

A fine set of rules by any standards! But the State is omnipotent. The final authority not only about enforcement of the rules, but also to make exceptions, vests with the State and its officials. Moreover, the community, which is the really concerned party, is nowhere in the picture. The so-called representatives in the Advisory Committees see no fault in the System, as after all ours is democracy and, by definition, committed to the welfare of the people. A trade-off on even some important points cannot be ruled out in the context of limited frame of Excise Policy and the larger frame of overall governance of the State.

So what we find by way of the final operational point of this great law and rules made there under is the ritual of an innocuous print line at the bottom 'Liquor Is Harmful for Health' in red of course. It is in sharp contrast with the tantalizing giant-size displays of a bottle and wine with attendant glamour of all vintages, regal, mod, and ultramod, with no holds barred. Highways are studded with inviting signals for a peg, unmindful of the soaring potential for hazard. The advice of Advisory Committees is subject to the final decision of the Excise Commissioner whose main concern, nay obsession, is revenue. And the State continues to make exception after exception concerning the location on the same ground, for otherwise there would be no place for even a single shop to stand on in the growing crowded metropolises.

The result is the exception has become the rule and the rule a rare exception, which itself is waning like the Grin of Cashire Cat. The ingenuity of exception-makers is pervasive. In the case of Madhya Pradesh, the rule requires that an established shop shall not be allowed to remain on a site, should the surroundings change and any disability is acquired thereby. But lo and behold! All shops established before the rule came into force were taken out of its ambit. That was not all. A new concept of 'traditional' sites was mischievously manufactured. All shops established on or before a stipulated date, to be decided by the government, could be bestowed the honour of 'traditional' and made immune from the mischief of the law. The last notification in this regard was issued on 23 August 1986 and all shops established before 1980 were deemed to be located at 'traditional sites' and consequently raised above the mundane law of the day. That blatant transgressions are to be taken in their stride and religiously ignored by the devout can be seen any high way littered with liquor shops, *desi* and *videshi* with tantalizing sign boards even as the statue book strictly prohibits this with the provision of heavy penalty. Notwithstanding these paradoxes, the issue of prohibition was to be kept alive in the larger interest of the marginalized sections of our society.

Protecting Tribals from Pernicious Vending of Intoxicants

In a letter to Manmohan Singh—I have drawn his attention to the incalculable harm that has been caused by trade in intoxicants in the Scheduled Areas (SAs) in open violation of the Excise Policy adopted for the Tribal areas in 1974. This policy was formulated by Ministry of Home Affairs (MHA) in consultation with concerned states, in the wake of extensive Tribal unrest in the late 1960s, notably in Naxalbari, Singhbhum, and Srikakulam.

This issue was central in the comprehensive Note of Prime Minister Indira Gandhi (dated 19 June 1974). Which gave a broad frame for meeting the challenge posed by growing unrest in the Tribal areas. The Tribal Sub-plan (TSP) strategy that followed accorded highest priority to elimination of exploitation in all forms. Equitable development in harmony with egalitarian Tribal ethos was to be pursued as a co-equal goal. It was agreed that a beginning in this great task had to be made where the State itself is an exploiter. Excise came at the top of this list with no silver lining in its favour. It was also clear that unless the dark spots concerning abkari', described by A.O. Hume as 'wages of sin', are erased, the executive will have no moral authority to handle other exploitative elements plaguing the Tribal areas.

I am shocked to find a full page advertisement as recent as February 2011 for auction of 'country' and 'foreign' liquor shops in Bijapur district in Bastar in Chhattisgarh. The advertisement has set huge revenue targets with no concern about its impact on people's life. Ironically part of this district is claimed to be 'liberated area' by Maoists. It is clear that similar steps must have been taken by collectors throughout SAs in other states.

I tried to find out the state of implementation of the Excise Policy from the Ministry of Tribal Affairs. The Ministry is simply unaware even about the very existence of this policy or measures taken in this regard after enactment of Panchayat Extension to the Scheduled Areas (PESA). It has no idea of the documents of that era when Tribal affairs were in MHA in the 1970s and after PESA came to be handled by the Panchayat Raj Ministry.

The resumption of earlier practice of commercial vending of liquor in Tribal areas, as in Bijapur, has aroused no concern at any level that flouts the real spirit of TSP and PESA nurtured respectively under Indira Gandhi and Rajiv Gandhi. It is a clear case of systemic failure with divided responsibilities both at the Center and in the states, notwithstanding the strongest possible Constitutional safeguards envisaged under FS.

Anyone who has any knowledge of ground realities would realize how crucial the elements of excise policy are for protection, welfare, and development of Tribal people. It is on this realization that Smt Indira Gandhi uncompromisingly confronted this issue in her historic note as the number one item in the New Deal. The same concern was shown by Rajiv Gandhi while deciding not to extend constitutional provisions of Part IX about Panchayats in routine to the SAs, and instead, made special provisions thereof.

The Union Government has a vital role to play, so far as SAs are concerned, as it did in practice assiduously in 1970s. It must tackle this issue in terms of strong provisions of FS and also its special responsibility towards the Tribal people.It would not be out of place to mention that the Supreme Court has rightly declared that there is no protected fundamental right to trade in liquor. This being the case, the appropriate and just Excise Policy of 1974 can be enforced through executive direction.

Manmohan Singh gave a call to all concerned, especially administrators, for meeting the LWE challenge with implementation of PESA and Forest Rights Act in their true spirit. There are countless seminars, working groups, and national conventions in response to his call. Yet, the Collectors of even Maoist controlled areas like Bijapur are busy with liquor shop auctions that are undisputedly acknowledged as the worst form of state-supported exploitation in Tribal areas. Here, the greed of liquor traders has taken precedence over welfare of the Tribal people. It is sad to note that even Maoist controlled areas are being rent asunder by many factors including the State's own interest in high-target excise policy to advance the cause of liquor barons, traders, and muscle men.

The million dollar question that stares at all sensitive souls is 'what moral authority can functionaries of the State wield in tackling unprecedented crisis for which the State is directly responsible by not honouring its own promises towards the Tribal people from Day One of the adoption of Indian Constitution and thereby criminalizing the entire community?' It is imperative in the interest of peace and social welfare that Excise Policy, 1974, which was at the top of Indiraji's vision, be recognized and given effect.

The current auctions of liquor shops must be stopped forth within all SAs as an insignia of the states' determination to eliminate exploitation in all forms, on whose firm foundation alone development with equity and honour can be ensured. It is the fittest case where the Union can give directions to the states having SAs to amend their excise laws at any cost, and implement the 1974 Excise Policy in letter and spirit and erase the darkest blot on the constitutional schema for protection of the simple Tribal people.

13

Subsistence Economy in a Subverted Development: Re-rethinking Development Concretely

G. Vijay

1. Introduction

An innovative attempt to theorize the development processes underway in contemporary India has been made by Kalyan Sanyal (2007). The scholar presents various theoretical frameworks that try to present coherent analytics of understanding development as constituting different hegemonic discourses. The classical development model the scholar argues treated development as a given process which has to be theorized to understand the role of different interests or classes in the society. In contrast, the contemporary conventional approaches see neither the existence of such development-related social conflict nor the existence of an autonomous process of development. Rather, the contemporary framework adopts a technocratic approach to achieving the objective of accumulation, thus attempting to negotiate conflict technically as well as exercise control over the development process itself.

The Marxist approach, the scholar contends, inspired the dependency school which presented a framework of analysis that tried to show how both the centres of growth producing capital and consumer goods on the one hand and the underdeveloped peripheries producing raw materials and primary goods on the other, were emanating from the same development process. The contending approaches within the Marxist school challenged the dependency school's analytical frame for being rooted in international trade or circulation-based economic relations rather than on relations of production for explaining development and underdevelopment. These attempts led the scholars to theorize transition from pre-capitalist social modes of production to capitalist social modes of production. Within these attempts, while some scholars gave prominence to the changing nature of property relations, production systems, scales of production, and employment contracts to discern transition, the others gave greater significance to the role of class struggles as being crucial to all the indicators suggesting transition. In the course of these attempts, it has come to be acknowledged that there is not one but multiple paths of transition from pre-capitalist to capitalist development as experienced by different countries within Western Europe and more significantly between the Western and Eastern Europe. The conventional approaches on the other hand had adopted the categories of traditional and modern sectors to provide their narrative of transition from pre-capitalist or stagnant economic formations to capitalist or accumulating economies. The technocratic interventions aimed at transforming the traditional sector to modern sector and concluded that this required planning and systematic economic, institutional, and technological interventions to bring about this transition.

However, when for a long time underdeveloped economies experienced no such transition neither of the classical Marxist frame, nor of the multiple-paths frame nor of the traditional-modern kind of transition, alternative explanations were sought. These alternative approaches, the scholar argues, to an extent have successfully decentred development. Within the Marxist framework, this decentring is identified in terms of altering the base-superstructure relations and in dislodging the centrality of mode of production and production relations in understanding transition. From the vantage point of the conventional approaches on the other, decentring has happened by displacing the dualistic framework of tradition-modern transition which had to now confront unemployment and informality as structural realities characterizing underdeveloped economies. There was a realization that the reproduction of the social and political conditions conducive to expanded reproduction were not obvious and had to be simultaneously pursued and consciously constructed. Sanyal argues that the alternatives emerging from this phase started to recognize power and hegemony as crucial for analysis. While using these categories, some analytical frames have led to the rise of culturalism as an approach namely, orientalism, et cetera. These frames, however, did not have a clear alternative conceptualization of development. The Marxist frame on the other hand has given rise to the Gramscian concept of hegemony and passive revolution to explain why transition was not being realized in underdeveloped economies. The existence of imperialism exercising hegemonic constraints to development of underdeveloped economies under conditions of uneven development in the international context is seen as one aspect of this explanation. On the other hand, the alliance between otherwise antagonistic pre-capitalist and capitalist classes within the national context as part of an anti-colonial alliance is seen as subverting possibilities for transition to fully developed capitalism in the underdeveloped nations. Explanations for the existence of an informal sector and the chronic incapacity for transition are thus provided. Thus, while the mainstream centred itself around the objective of accumulation and treated the informal sector as a transient phase in development, the critiques centred around dispossession-exploitation and later on dominance and hegemony based explanations.

It is at this juncture that the scholar observes a major qualitative shift, which had happened in the discourse on development in the conventional frame around the early 1970s. The international monetary agencies such as the World Bank, with Robert McNamara as its chief, and the rise of the non-governmental; civil society organizations, which shifted the discourse on development from transition to addressing the issue of exclusion. The World Bank, which otherwise focussed on funding physical infrastructure and capital goods projects, changed its focus to addressing poverty issues in the poor economies. The World Bank also started to focus on funding self-employed activities in the subsistence sector. The civil society organizations also put a check on the primitive accumulative processes leading to the rise of a political society that had to regulate the primitive accumulative processes within the capitalist system. The scholar maintains that the historicism of transition was thus displaced with what is termed as Foucauldian governmentality, which in essence reinforces the hegemony of capitalism within a self-sustaining capitalist system. Such a system creates the conditions essential for accumulation and advances primitive accumulation by way of regulating the primitive accumulation in ways that it does not exterminate the subsistence sector while on the other hand, the states re-ploughs a part of the surplus generated by the accumulation processes in favour of the subsistence sector in ways that capitalist accumulation is legitimized. Kalyan Sanyal argues that Amartya Sen's capability approach which essentially focussed on the idea of entitlement regimes as playing a significant role in enhancing capabilities, thus developed tangible indicators such as nutrition, health, education, et cetera, around which governmentality could effectively function away from structural interventions around redistributing endowments. Thus, regulation of primitive accumulation, exclusion, governmentality, transfers to subsistence economy, legitimization, and hegemony of accumulation were to be seen as the new system of capitalist development.

Kalyan Sanyal argues that, with the shift in discourse, neither was the subsistence sector a constraint that needs to be transformed through modern capitalist development nor was it a sector being over exploited to produce cheap subsistence goods or inputs to compliment the capitalist accumulation. The subsistence economy in this new frame neither stands in confrontation nor outside the realm of the capitalist economy; rather it is very much part of a self-subsisting capitalist economy. The major purpose that a subsistence economy served was to legitimise the accumulation process through discursively constructed discourse involving the international monetary agencies, civil society, political society, intellectuals, and governmentality. These processes therefore end up ensuring that the subsistence economy does not completely end up being dispossessed of its means of production. The subsistence economy produces and exchanges with the capitalist economy, the only exception being that the 'subsistence' economy, something akin to simple commodity production of Marx, does not expand in size and is described as non-capitalist production where surplus generated goes towards consumption and replacement of means of production.

In the backdrop of this understanding given by Sanyal's work relating the accumulation process to the subsistence economy and these in turn to legitimization and hegemony of accumulation through regulation of primitive accumulation and governmentality, we present concrete experiences from a site of study namely, Lingala and Balmur Mandals[2] of Mahabubnagar district that are habitats for Chenchu Tribes who are located well within the subsistence economy. The subsistence economy bears a lot of similarities to the way that Sanyal characterizes a subsistence economy especially in the plains. There are also the governmentality kind of interventions one finds in the form of several welfare programmes such as employment guarantee, health insurance, food security, et cetera, The central question, however, is whether the empirical facts hold the systemic model, as imagined by Sanyal, true? Are primitive accumulation processes being regulated? Are governmentality functions causing a cost-benefit-based systematic transfers of surpluses from the capitalist economy to the subsistence economy? Are these transfers reproducing the subsistence economy along side the ever expanding capitalist economy? Is the governmentality and the interface between the accumulation processes and the subsistence economy systematically generating letimization and hegemony of the accumulative economy?

The above stated questions will be addressed by studying five villages Appapurpenta and Erlapenta, Chenchugudem, Rayavaram, and Vadde Rayavaram villages located in Lingala and Balmur Mandals of Mahabubnagar District. These villages are predominantly inhabited by primitive Tribal groups belonging to Chechus and other Tribal group namely, Lambadas as well as other non-Tribal households.

The study is based on primary household level survey carried out by the use of structured questionnaire, structured and unstructured individual interviews and group discussions. The analysis is also based on secondary data collected from Girijan Cooperative Corporation (GCC), Village Revenue Officer, Village Development Officer or Village Secretary, and Village Sarpanchs. This study also includes in its analysis several other villages belonging to Lingala and Balmur Mandals of Mahabubnagar district represented in the secondary data collected from the Mandal Revenue Offices, self-help groups, political movements such as Chenchu Seva Sangham, Indira Kranti Padam office, EGS office, and Palamur Adhyayana Vedika.

This study considers for analysis the implementation of different social security programmes, including those social security programmes implemented by the ITDA, Forest Rights Act, Indira Awas Yojana, NREGA, Programmes undertaken by SHGs (including amongst others food security), Rajiv Arogyasri, Insurance and Pension programmes. Further, this study tries to evolve a comparative perspective of the implementation and impact of these social security programmes across different social modes of production and subsistence including forest dependent hunting-gathering Tribal households in Erlapenta of Appapur in Balmur Mandal, Tribal and non-Tribal households engaging in subsistence as well as commercial agriculture, livestock trading, and those engaged in non-farm service sectors, et cetera, in Chenchugudem of Balmur Mandal. This study also focuses on the impact of social security programmes, specifically as part of its primary household survey, on a sample of indebted labour households from Rayavaram and Vadde Rayavaram villages of Lingala mandal engaged in intra and inter-state circular distress migration through middlemen contractors. An estimated million workers constitute this category of construction workers usually referred to as Palamooru labour from the district of Mahabubnagar.

2. Glimpses into the History of the Political-economy of Chengudem Village

Chenchugudem is a Tribal village located 20 kilometers from Achampet. The Girijan Cooperative Corporation (GCC) storehouse is located five kilometers away from Chenchugudem, this is the distance from the village to the main-road. The Chenchugudem, Bilakallu, Lakshmipally, and Venkatagiri villages have a common Panchayat. The lands that Tribals own today were held by landlords belonging to Velama community earlier. There were in all six landlord families who owned 200 acres of land. They were the first to introduce maize cultivation and later castor cultivation way back in 1950s. The relation between the landlords and the Tribals was still very remote during the time. Nagamma (70) recollects that land was collectively owned and labour was shared by all the Tribals. There used to be a common kitchen for the joint family. Until the 1970s, the Tribals in Chenchugudem were in their own understanding in retrospect, very fearful of people in pants. Anyone spotting a person wearing shirt and pant coming towards the village, they would alert the rest and run and hide in the jungles. Udathanoori Narasimha, who is now a contractor, recollects that the labour working with the landlords during this period were receiving as wages for their labour:

> Rs.150 per year + 8 kgs of paddy + 8 kgs of *jowar* + one woolen blanket (Gongadi) + a pair of leather footwear (*chappal*)

Nagamma recounts that the Velama landlord in Balmur, Mr Kishan Rao, who employed her, used to beat her very brutally if she reported late to work or if she questioned him. As she narrates her experience, she expresses how painful it was to be beaten and she grows very angry, starts abusing the landlord cursing him, and after a short pause, she says 'that's why he was killed'. The Balmur landlord, Kishan Rao, was shot dead by Naxalites in 2004.

In 1970, when P. Subramaniam was the collector and Mahendranath was the Member of Legislative Assembly (MLA), a Government Order (GO) was passed allowing the Tribals to clear forests and cultivate them. During this period, Nagamma recollects that land started to become monopolized and fights began within the Chenchus based on *gotram*s (family lineage). There are four main *gotram*s amongst Chenchus in Chenchugudem namely, Nimmala, Balmuri, Udathanoori, and Katraju. The Giridhari (traditional name for Revenue Officer) came and purchased these lands from Brahmin landlords and distributed it amongst the Tribals in an effort to resolve the conflict. It was partly as a consequence to this internal crisis that animosities developed, and to avert escalation of antagonisms, external migration began. When migration began in the mid to late the 70s, a section of Chenchus were taken to other states to work as construction labour by contractors. The contractors were paying workers Rs. 200–300 as advance to a *lenka (*a pair) and the labourer was expected to work for nine months. If workers wanted to come back in the middle of this contract period, they were beaten up and forced to work. Those labourer who escaped from the contractor, would borrow from another *maistry* (contractor) to repay what they owed the first contractor.

However, by the early 1980s, the forest was proclaimed as Reserve Forest. The forest land alienation from Tribals was accompanied by harassment of Tribals by forest department and revenue department becoming the major cause for the rise of Naxalite movement in this region clearly connected to the change in forest policy. The Naxalite movement distributed forest land and played an important role in settling intra-community land disputes. The presence of the Naxalite movement created fear in the minds of the forest department and revenue officials because of which the officialdom kept themselves out of the forest area, and as a consequence, there is a general perception amongst the Tribal respondents who have stated that they felt relieved.

It was in 1984, with the entry of the organization called AWARE that high agriculture was introduced into this region. AWARE introduced for the first time pesticides and new variety of seeds. Along with this, there was a rise in wage labour employment by the landlords. It was during this period that some of the Tribal leaders came to play the role of labour contractors, searching and mobilizing labour for the landlords. Two such Chenchus who associated themselves with the landlord, Mr Bagawantha Rao, namely, Veeraiah and Mutyalu, later became leaders of the Chechugudem who knew how to give representations and interact with modern state institutions. It is said that

Veeraiah, along with the landlord, got houses sanctioned for the Tribals. The rise of Tribal leadership at the local government level thus has its roots in patronage by feudal elites.

Quite clearly beginning with the early and late 1970s and into the early 1980s was the period during which the otherwise excluded Tribals were in some sense brought into the fold of the development process. This was the case especially with Tribal villages that were closer to the plains. It was also true that this process of interface between the Tribal social modes of subsistence and development was brought about through a discursive formation involving the non-government organizations, bureaucracy, and the political society. What, however, remains under-analyzed in Kalyan Sanyal's frame is that the outcomes for the subsistence economy in reality could well be in variance with the stated purpose when governmentality attempts at managing the excluded. The forms of exploitation in the so-called subsistence economy for a long time have had their origins in feudal institutions, and not only was labour attached but the expropriation of labour involved exercise of physical violence. That certain institutionalized forms of power had a lineage in the caste system and the systematic alliances between certain caste groups with the pre-modern princely states during the colonial era, which were functioning as revenue states, cannot be ignored by the analytical frame. These institutionalized forms of power, in their interface with the political economy and social development, cannot be summarily located in a self-subsisting capitalist development alone without a proper analysis of the role played by the dominant classes in the post-colonial setting. Not to grapple with these complex interactions head-on and to dismiss these analytics in the name of historicism could risk reducing the analytical frame into an a-historical approach. Further, when the otherwise 'excluded' Tribal communities came into interface with the modern state, it was not perceived as development, but rather, it led to the development of a conflict which in turn took the form of an armed resistance in the late 1980s and early 1990s. That the subsistence economy even in its rehabilitation alongside an expanding accumulative economy might not be a process without a conflict, and therefore, the analysis of the development process must reflect on both sides of this complexity, is imperative. While Sanyal acknowledges the existence of primitive accumulation as one of the aspects of the development process, governmentality and legitimacy for accumulation derived out of it overshadow any serious treatment of the conflicts innate to the interface between governmentality and primitive accumulation, especially under conditions where socially and historically agencies having semi-feudal lineages evolved to become part of governance structures itself. The real challenge of interpreting the development process is to handle these inconsistent and incongruent processes rather than to develop a systematic systemic reading based on a deductive model of governmentality and legitimization process divergent from the empirical complexities. There is no denial that the post-colonial reading of the development process constructed by Kalyan Sanyal does represent a facet of the development process. However, this framework perhaps provides a selective reading of the process failing to represent a far more complex social formation and even more complex process comprehensively. This paper attempts at addressing some of these complexities.

3. Changing Nature of the Subsistence Economy

3.1.1. Earnings from Forest Produce

The forest's minor produce collection is seasonal and includes :

a) Gum: There are several varieties of gum. However, white gum is the most valued. Gum is usually available from June-March. This quality gum is given Rs.100 per kilogram. On an average, with full time invested in searching for gum, during the entire period, a household can procure 100 kgs. The average income during this period per household is Rs.10,000.
b) Honey: Honey is available during December-January. For households that spend their full time in procuring honey, a quantity of 30–40 bottles of honey, each weighing about 700–750 ml worth Rs. 100 each can be acquired. At this rate, the average income for a household from honey is Rs. 1,500–2,000 per month for two months.
c) Soap nuts: Soap nuts can be collected during January-March. Households spending their full time on collecting soap nuts succeed in collecting 300–400 kgs during the season. Soap nuts receive Rs.10 per kg. Usually, for every 100 kgs, five kgs is set aside as waste. At this rate, on an average during this season, households collecting soap nuts earn Rs. 2,700.
d) Tamarind: Tamarind collection happens between February-March and April-May. Although during the season, 300–400 kgs of tamarind is procured, about five kgs per 100 kgs is set aside as waste. Further, the collection of tamarind is only during alternative years. At this rate on an average Rs. 2,850–4,750 are earned by the family.

Chechugudem has witnessed a change in its economic activities as a consequence to both rise in land ownership and declining forests partly caused by over-exploitation of forest produce driven by commercialization, triggered off by Girian Cooperative Corporation (GCC). The data presented in Annexure 1 shows mandal level trends in procurement of minor forest produce by Girijan Cooperative Corporation (GCC). However, villages like Chenchugudem which are showing substantial withdrawal from forest dependence in comparison to the level of dependence on forests seen in Appapur and Erlapenta would have contributed to the overall trend of falling minor-forest produce procurement.

The data suggests that, in all the commodity segments of minor forest produce, the procurement has been showing enormous variation over the years. This can be taken as a proxy for the uncertainty of finding forest produce. Further, there is a clear secular decline in the procurement of commodities like gum, which are amongst the highest valued products unlike in the case of other less valued minor forest produce. This is a result of the impact of commercialization and over-exploitation which has destroyed the source of gum itself. Gum is secreted by certain varieties of trees when small incisions are made on the trunk of these trees. Over the years, Tribals observe that the depth, width, and frequency of incisions grew leading to death of these very valuable trees.

In the recent past around 2004–05, the Chenchus settled in the settlements of Eerlapenta and Errapenta located in interior forest area have been forced by the State to move closer to the plains like Appapurpenta (police, para-military, special forces and the forest department). The reason for this has not been clear. While a section of the observers view this as part of a military strategy in the course of tackling the Naxalite movement, others view this as part of a process that has its roots in the identification of some valuable mineral deposits inside this forest area. This movement of Tribal settlements has created an ecological disaster due to excessive localized intensive dependence on the gathering of minor forest produce. This is one of the reasons why some of the most valuable gum trees seem to have gone almost extinct. This has, in turn, led to inter-settlement conflicts within the Chenchu community. Following the conflict, the Chechus of Eerlapenta and Errapenta had to return to their original habitat. In addition to the above-mentioned reason, several other processes have aggravated deforestation, as a consequence of which it has become far more time-consuming to find forest produce and there is greater effort required and higher uncertainty about incomes. The fallout has been that the young generation is no longer interested in pursuing traditional hunting-gathering activities. The ecological dimension is of immense significance in terms of understanding the process of rehabilitation of the subsistence economy since it seems to be standing outside the realm of the principles governing the governmentality. While Kalyan Sanyal does argue that the rehabilitation of the subsistence economy is contingent upon the outcomes of the usual cost-benefit analytical frames of the accumulation, overwhelmingly from the computations of capital, the costs always seem to outweigh the benefits of regulating the accumulation, thus, disapproving rehabilitation, or in other words, attempts to prevent dispossession, dislocation, and displacement of those in the subsistence economy.

The process of accumulation and the process of so-called rehabilitation in several instances seem to be mutually exclusive. Kalyan Sanyal seems to be dealing with a space where accumulation and rehabilitation of the subsistence economy could happen simultaneously, which in any case does not prove to be a contentious space. But this space is not the dominant space in economic development analysis. The valuation frames of what constitutes rehabilitation of the subsistence economy more concretely, seem to be different from the vantage point of the capital and the State as against the vantage point of those that are excluded belonging to the subsistence economy. There seems to be very little calibration of the claims made by the interests of capital by the State agencies based on other social and political consideration. Often circumventing the existing legal regulations, the regulatory institutions vested with the function of regulating accumulation seem to have been captured by the accumulative interests (G.Vijay, 2012). All the instances where accumulation processes have been regulated, have not been brought about by the autonomous political society's proactive role, but rather have been reactions to bloody battles waged by the people belonging to the subsistence economy. In effect, the question as to whether this form of regulation of accumulation which comes not by way of preempting and managing a potential conflict, but as a response to a crisis in the form of a militant resistance, which has been tackled through brutality by the state agencies can domination and control by a legitimate or illegitimate state be perceived as part of rehabilitation of the subsistence economy and bring about legitimacy for the accumulation from the population remains contestable. Is legitimacy a stock, which is being protected aggressively in the above presented experience or a flow that needs to be acquired over the years, which the state seems to be failing to secure and therefore growing brutal?

3.1.2. Increasing role for Agriculture, Indebtedness, and Circulation of Labour

Chenchugudem has approximately about 270 acres of cultivated land. The village has about 120 households. Of these 120 households, the following table gives the broad structure of land ownership under the Forest Rights Act (FRA). Private and ownership titles are quite clearly defined in Chenchugudem, unlike the case of interior hamlets of Appapurpenta and Erlapenta. However, even in Chenchugudem, the newly cleared and acquired land under the Forest Rights Act do not yet have clear titles. The Tribals have applied for approval of lands they have acquired. In the recent acquisitions of and the role of monopolization based on *gotrams* (family lineage) continues. The forest land that has been given to the Adivasis of Chenchugudem and Billakallu, is part of the village land under the local administration of the Chenchugudem Panchayat. The average land size of the newly acquired forest land is two acres. The pattern of distribution of this forest land according to *gotrams* are given below.

Table 3.1: Chenchugudem and Billakallu Villages FRA Land Beneficiaries

Caste_Chench	*No. of Beneficiaries*	*Percentage of Beneficiaries in each Gotram*
Balamoor	2	13
Katraju	3	20
Nimmala	7	47
Udthanoori	2	13
Maripally	1	7
Total	**15**	**100**

Source: VRO

It needs to be mentioned here that, in the current context, the Nimmala and Balmoori families of Chenchus are in a coalition on behalf of the Congress Party. The Udthanoori and Katraju families are in a coalition on behalf of the Telugu Desam Party. And we find from the above statistics based on official data that, together, the Balmoori and Nimmala families hold 60 per cent of the newly acquired land while Udthanoori and Katraju families hold 33 per cent of the land.

The existing clear land titles are distributed amongst 100 households.

Table 3.2: Land Distribution

Land Particulars	*Number of Households*
Landless Households	20
Land Owning Households	100
Total	120
Size of Holdings	*Number of Households*
5 acres and above	5
3-4 acres	35
2 acres	25
1 acre	35

Source: VRO

3.1. Changing Nature of Agriculture

The nature of agriculture has been changing over the years. Currently the estimated cultivated land is around 180 acres. The cropping pattern in the Tribal villages located in the plains like Chenchugudem, Rayavaram, and Vadderayavaram has been undergoing a change.

A respondent, Narasimha, states 'it was only in 1986 that he stopped working with the landlord, the crops cultivated then included food crops like taidalu, jonnallu (jowar), arkalu, and ragulu (ragi) and pedda amdalu (castor).

It was in 1990s Maize entered and in the year 2000 Tribals started cultivating Castor and Cotton as mixed crops.'

As already noted, while earlier, only food crops were cultivated predominantly, over the years, this has changed. Presently, non-food crops account for 64 per cent of the land under cultivation. Within the non-food crops, there seems to be an increased trend to opt for horticulture. Mango grooves are the predominant choice. This has been promoted by an ITDA project officer Mr Chinna Veera Bhadrudu. Mr Chinna Veera Bhadhrudu has provided the Tribals with free saplings and the necessary extension services to help the Tribals grow these trees. Some of the Tribals have been benefited by such measures. It, however, needs to be mentioned that this preference for horticulture has happened partly due to the lack of proper irrigation facilities, partly due to increasing risk due to price fluctuations of other crops, and also because of escalating labour costs.

The entry of non-food crops has also led to the entry of modern technology. A rise in the use of bore-wells in place of wells, tractors in place of traditional ploughs, and weeders in place of labour are a few illustrations.

Overview of Cropping Pattern

Type of Use	*Number of Households*	*% of Households*	*Number of Acres*	*% of Land*
Food Crops (Rice, Maize, Red Gram)	70	70	65 acres	36
Cotton	5	5	30 acres	17
Horticulture	20	20	75 acres	42
Castor	5	5	10 acres	5
Total	100	100	180	100

Source: Field Study

Technologies in use in Chenchugudem

Type of Technology	*Number*	*Cost (Rs)*
Bore Wells	35	30000
Tractors	2	Rs.500 per hour
Weeder	-	Rs.600 per hour

Source: Field Study

The movement away from food crops has involved several changes even in the social relations. Where as earlier, there were collective farming practices such as collection of best seeds from all the farmers in the community, and stocking them for the next season, which were then distributed to all the farmers, in the later period, such practices were given up. In place of this system, an increased dependence on market for seeds and other inputs has broken the old systems. The increased dependence on market for inputs also meant increased dependence on private moneylenders.

The role of credit comes into play since the cost of cultivation was beyond the means of the Tribal households. Some of the cost structures are given below:

The cost of cultivating as estimated by farmers in Vadde Rayavaram cultivating food crop like Maize was approximately Rs. 7,000 per acre. Given below is a cost breakup for Maize.

Cost Per Acre of Maize Cultivation

Inputs	*Cost (Rs.)*
Seeds	2250
D.A.P	500
Urea	400
Hiring Pair of bullocks	1200
Fodder for bulocks	1500
Labour Cost	1200
Total	7050

Source: Field Study

Returns on Maize

Quantity per acre	*Price per Quintal*	*Total Income*	*Surplus*
2-3 quintals (bad season)	Rs. 4500	Rs. 9000-13500	Rs. 2000-5000
4-5 quintals (good season)	Rs. 6000	Rs. 24000-30000	Rs. 17000-23000

Source: Field Study

With the entry of commercial crops like castor and cotton, these cost structures have drastically changed.

Cost Per Acre of Castor Cultivation

Inputs	*Quantity*	*Cost (Rs.)*
Seeds	2.5 kgs	150-250
D.A.P	1 bag	500
Urea	1 bag	400
Hiring Pair of bullocks	1	1200
Fodder for bulocks		1500
Labour Cost	(Seeding, weeding, pesticide, harvest)	7000
Pesticide	Depends on type of pest	500–3500
Total		11250–14350

Source: Field Study

Returns on Castor

Quantity per acre	*Price per Quintal*	*Total Income*	*Average Surplus*
2-3 quintals (bad season)	Rs. 12000	Rs. 24000–36000	Rs. 11200–23200
5-6 quintals (good season)	Rs. 16000	Rs. 80000–96000	Rs. 67200–83200

Source: Field Study

The cost of cultivating cotton is even higher. It costs about Rs.16,000 per acre and the returns are even greater but more uncertain.

With specific reference to the labour market in this region, in a day, the workers work from 10 am to 5 pm. Women are paid Rs. 50 and a bottle of liquor and men are paid Rs. 100 and a bottle of liquor as wages. The bottle of liquor costs Rs. 3.

The most amusing instance in this region was in the case of Chechugudem where amongst Tribal community, a grandfather was hiring a plough and bullocks from his own grandson and paying him some money. The money is used by the grandson in turn to pay the installments of the Self-Help Group of which his wife is a member. While the exposure to this reality could inflict moral indignation upon those attuned to the romanticization of Tribal societies by communitarians, the analytical significance lies in understanding how the scanty scope for monetary acquisition under conditions of enhanced significance of money has in itself become a structural pressure for altering internal social and cultural structures so crucial otherwise to the subsistence and reproduction of these economies. There is a weakening of the community without conditions for the sustenance of individualism emerging.

3.2. The Private Money Lenders; Igniting Circulation

The sources of credit was either the landlords or the Seths (merchants). A loan borrowed from landlord was repaid by rendering labour at Rs. 3,000 per year per person. Sometimes landlords also gave seeds for cultivation and this was treated as additional cost. Five per cent was the interest charged on loans. If the worker pledging his labour against the loan were to remain absent for a day, it would be treated as equivalent to a loss of wage of ten days. The Seths charged an interest rate of 2½ per cent. The transition to agriculture, far from rehabilitating the subsistence economy, in its interface with the credit markets, input markets, and quantity and price fluctuations of the output, became one path towards indebtedness.

Anthropogenic ecological changes have been the other major cause for the generation of indebtedness amongst the Chenchus. For over a decade, Mahaboobnagar, as a district, suffered drought despite the River Krishna flowing through this district. The lack of agriculture during this period, 1995–2005, caused unprecedented out-migration. An estimated million workers or one-third of the total population of the district were migrating to work as construction workers. Borrowing advances from contractors for lack of alternative means of subsistence, and thus, these continuous cycles of indebtedness and migration became part of the lives of 70 per cent of the rural populace irrespective of whether the households were landed or landlessers. The earnings of labourers in the construction sector were so meagre that even small contingencies could push households back into indebtedness. Much worse, indebtedness was also seen as a means for assured employment with contractors (to whom the labour remained indebted) in successive years, suggestive of a context characterized by complete lack of choice for labour.

What is observed is that the interface between the accumulative mode and the subsistence mode does not happen in a way that it either promotes coexistence of the accumulative mode alongside the subsistence mode or where subsistence economy in itself is reproducible sustainably. The depletion of good quality gum trees, the social differentiation within the subsistence economy that develops with changing modes of production and subsistence, the un-sustainability of cultivating food crops that surfaces with further development, and entry into non-food crops that seem to be interlinking the credit and labour markets, which in turn generate new forms of bondage in labour market, are the real challenges where, the accumulative mode is not regulated. This process usually characterized and conceptualized as primitive accumulation, accumulation through dispossession, accumulation through extra economic force predatory capital, et cetera, continues to persist wherein the State is an active party to this process rather than leaving it as an autonomous arbiter. This, however, is not to undermine the attempts made by the state to rehabilitate the subsistence economy in other sites of development process. Thus, what we have is a process with both tendencies—development seems to dispossess people in the subsistence economy at one end with State being an active party to this process, and simultaneously, there is a struggle to project governmentality and legitimization at the other end. Which process is likely to outplay itself as the dominant reality and how do these tendencies interact with one another in the course of development are the pertinent questions before analysts.

It may be apt to point out in this context that, in 2001, the Karuvu Vyatireka Porata Committee (an organization which had to be dismantled following threats from the mafia) organized an Ambali Kendram (maize porridge camp) in Achampet Mandal of Mahabubnagar District. Socially, maize porridge is food consumed by extremely poor people. Hundreds of people queued-up before these camps. In one such camp the Sarpanch of the village stood in the queue waiting for her turn to have the Porridge. There were starvation deaths for lack of any source to access food. It is in the background of these distressing conditions we must gauge the relevance and significance of the social security programmes such as NREGA, SHGs, Arogyasri, and Pension programmes, as attempts to rehabilitate the subsistence economy through governmentality, the paradox being that the distressing conditions have been a fall out of the development process to an extent. An analysis of the impact of the social security programmes is therefore twin edged—the question that needs to be asked is whether the social security programmes are reducing distress and absolute poverty of the population in question and simultaneously whether such a process is generating complex hegemony of accumulation in building a consent for accumulation in the subsistence economy.

4. Accessing Governmentality—The First Hurdle

4.1 The Problem of Tribal Life Rhythms, Formal Institutions, and Access to White Ration Cards

In various ways, the Chenchu households located deep inside the forests have been often cheated and excluded from several social security programmes implemented by the Integrated Tribal Development Agency (ITDA) and the Government.

Both in Appapurpenta and Erlapenta and especially in Erlapenta despite their poverty ridden day-to-day living conditions, large number of Tribal households do not have white ration cards. The reason for this, according to the officials, is that it is very difficult to visit these areas, and if and when the officials visit, the Tribals are usually not in their homes. The Tribals argue that like the fixed time period for GCC shops (every Thursday), if the officials can make frequent and fixed time-based visits to their *penta*s, then they can stay back at home on that day. Even if officials make announcements before they come, people often don't understand weekdays and dates. They measure the days based on the time duration between days (once every seventh day). And they are just not around because they have to hunt and gather for their survival. They suggest, 'why don't the officials visit the same day when GCC shops are open? We are all around during those days.'

As a consequence to lack of white cards, the Tribal households are denied access to certain programmes. One such case came to our notice during the course of this study. Guruvamma (58) is a Chenchu woman belonging to an extremely poor household. Guruvamma's husband had recently died. The Headmaster of Appapur Penta Ashram school, himself a Chenchu, was requesting the representative of Sangham (non-government organization), Mr Chandrashekar, who was one of those acting as a liaison between ITDA, government institutions and the Tribal households to explore the possibility of getting Guruvamma compensation from Aam-Admi Bheema. Mr Chandrashekar stated that, whereas Abhaya Hastam requires Rs.400 to be paid by a household per year, the Aam-Admi Bheema requires white ration cards. And since Tribal households living deep inside the forests do not have white cards, they could not claim this insurance. They cannot have access to the Arogyasri programme as well.

4.2 Accessing Health and Pension Programmes

In the interior Tribal areas, every 5th of the month, 108 the mobile medical service visits the *pentas*. They usually carry out medical check ups and give some routine medicines. For patients who are suffering from more serious ailments, they advice the households to visit a hospital. However, while lack of white cards is one limitation, even in the instances where people do have cards, sheer ignorance could prove to be fatal. This is where there is clearly a failure of the institution called Arogya-Mitras, who are supposed to be in the local area providing people with necessary information about the Arogyasri program.

In one such instance:

Nimmala Balamma (70) wife of Lingaiah (80) told us that Lingaiah had developed a tumor on the throat. For a very long time, the problem remained unnoticed. However, when he had developed difficulty in swallowing he was taken to Acchampet Civil Hospital, where the doctor advised that an operation was necessary and that Lingaiah must be taken to district hospital in Mahabubnagar. After being admitted to the Mahabubnagar district hospital the patient was told that they required several bottles of blood. Balamma says since they did not have sons, they thought they could not procure so many bottles of blood. Although Lingaiah was in a critical condition, he was brought back and soon he died.

For people like Balamma, there are other serious problems with using the Rajiv Arogyasri Programme. As the referral hospital's distance from the rural area increases, people do not muster enough courage to go to the cities. Finding places in the city, getting proper responses from doctors and medical staff in the corporate/private hospitals, and sustenance for the attendants during the course of treatment, it is argued, are not possibilities unless people have some contacts in the urban areas. These problems require an improvement of the scope of activity of the Arogyamitras to make them more proactive from their existing role of being nominal institutions. Although Balamma is eligible for both old age pension and widow pension, she does not receive any pension at all. The households have no idea whom to approach.

In yet another startling case, Narayana, the president of Chenchu Seva Samithi, suffered a brain hemorrhage. Subsequently, he suffered paralysis and has since lost his speech. He was operated upon at Nizam's Institute of Medical Sciences (NIMS). His hospital expenses were a whopping Rs. 5,00,000. He has received only Rs. 90,000 from Arogyasri. He mortgaged his property and paid the additional Rs. 100,000 to the hospital. Despite his social visibility and connections, he has not been able to gather the necessary resources to meet his expenses. After a lot of persuasion, the Mandal President has agreed to help.

If this is the condition of the political elite of the Chenchu community, who themselves seem to lack access to the political society and governmentality, one can imagine what would be the experiences of ordinary Chenchus, Lambadas, or other poor non-Tribals.

There are even more interesting cases with reference to other governmental interventions. These include; MGNREGA, Pashukranthi (providing livestock to Tribal households), bore-wells for Tribal households programme (aimed at providing assured irrigation), Indira Awas Yojana (homes for poor).

5. Governmentality and Subsistence Economy; The Unobvious Interface

The monetization of the Tribal economy is still very marginal in the interior forest areas. This leads to very interesting experiences. One such experience is presented below:

Chingula Papamma (54) says that after the NREGA programmes started, mobility to outside markets has increased. They go to Mannanur town about 25 kilometers away or to Appapur about 12 kilometers away for buying potatoes. Apart from the food they hunt or collect from the forest, the food they buy from the market includes rice and potatoes. A group of Chenchus usually visit the market by hiring autos or water tankers once every 3–6 months at the cost of Rs.500-Rs.1000 a trip. The NREGA programmes include construction of stone walls around cultivable land (although no cultivation happens) and water-harvesting pits. The fact that these societies are marginally monetized is evident when Papamma points out that in carrying out the NREGA programmes, they are being paid advance amounts of Rs. 500–1,000. Papamma says that the lag period between the payment of the advance and actually executing the NREGA works is anywhere between 3–6 months. This is causing problems to them because she says 'with the advances given we usually buy food from GCC stores or market and eat. If the works are carried out at the same time when we are eating purchased food, we can work. But if works are carried out afterwards then by that time we would have exhausted all the money, then where will we get the food and energy to work?' They then have to spend time gathering or hunting for food when they cannot buy food.

These local economies are in a subsistence mode. For Kalyan Sanyal, the subsistence mode is a simple commodity production system which is in interface with the capitalist economy. The subsistence economy is engaging in economic transactions with the capitalist economy. In spite of these transactions however, the subsistence economy does not expand because all the returns go towards meeting subsistence expenditures, merely reproducing the system. In this sense, when applied to the context under consideration for analysis here, some of the activities match the imagination of Kalyan Sanyal, while other activities that are completely disconnected with the market transactions would have to be characterized as being relatively 'primitive'. Kalyan Sanyal identifies those activities that fall under his concept of subsistence economy not as precapitalist economy but rather as a non-capitalist economy. There is a need to recognize that in the case of the experience under study, there is an economy that is being outside Sanyal's definition of subsistence economy which nevertheless enjoys governmentality interventions. However, these spaces seem to have some interesting insights to provide about the interaction between the accumulation process and subsistence economy (including the non-capitalist subsistence economy as defined by Kalyan Sanyal). Governmentality falls almost as an interlocutor between the requirements of accumulation economy on the one hand, and the needs of a subsistence economy on the other. The modes of governmentality have to creatively reconcile the accumulation with the needs of subsistence. The insight we get is that reproducing subsistence may place certain challenges before governmentality, as the processes of accumulation may propel forms of governmentality that could in-turn be incompatible with the structures of subsistence economy. We can foresee from the experience presented above that certain forms of governmentality, driven by the cost-benefits frame of accumulative ideology (productive asset generation as part of the MGNREGA for instance), may not succeed in reproducing the subsistence economy by taking the needs of the subsistence economy into account. This experience could be extended to what Kalyan Sanyal defines as his concept of the subsistence economy.

5.1. How to Feed the Assets? The Saga of Pashukranthi

As part of providing asset security to Tribal households, ITDA, together with the veterinary department and women's SHGs has provided the Tribal households with buffaloes. The buffaloes were however purchased from Haryana. These were extremely well-built buffaloes. Along with female buffaloes, he-buffaloes were also supplied for seeds. Each buffalo gave 6–8 liters of milk per day in comparison to local varieties which gave 1.5–4 liters of milk. However, the beneficiary Tribal households soon realized that these buffaloes were habituated to feeding only on fresh green grass as its fodder. It is very well known that Mahabubnagar is a drought-prone area. Green grass was very difficult to procure. It was very expensive in the market and transporting grass to such remote areas such as Appapurpenta would make it even more exorbitant, and this unviable. The buffaloes refused to eat either dry hay or shoots of corn or maize, which local variety of buffaloes eat. Further, the buffaloes were not used to the climate or to the tough conditions in the interior forest areas of Mahabubnagar. Temperatures in summer soar to above 42°C. The buffaloes, some of the local Tribal leaders argue, required proper hygienic conditions, which required construction of sheds with a flooring that had 1½ centimeters of slope that would allow for draining of the urine and dung of the cattle. No sheds were constructed following which the urine and dung of the buffaloes accumulated and created an unhygienic conditions making the cattle vulnerable to disease. Some of the buffaloes died as a consequence to starvation and disease. Sensing the mounting crisis, the project officer M.M. Naik, the then Programme Officer (PO), gave rice husk and green grass from ITDA. It is said that immediately he was summoned by the District Collector for explanation. The PO tried defending his action by arguing that the death of the buffaloes would be far more expensive than supplying these animals with fodder. The Collector is said to have scolded the PO for his decision. Each buffalo costs Rs. 35,000 in the market. When the buffaloes died, the Tribals did not receive any compensation, although there was an insurance coverage. In some instances where people received compensation, the amount of insurance coverage for each dead buffalo ranged from Rs. 13,000 to Rs.18,000 and not the market price. The Tribal respondents from Appapurpenta were of the opinion that to have such buffaloes it was imperative that they have irrigation facilities to cultivate green grass. Eventually, ITDA decided to initiate a program where bore-wells would be dug for Tribal households having land.

5.2 Deep Bore-Wells in Accounts

When resources are transferred from the accumulating economy to the subsistence economy, in Kalyan Sanyal's model, there are no hitches. With the exception of the cost-benefit frames, there are no other structures that come into interplay between the resources pumped into the subsistence economy from the accumulating economy through the governmentality mechanism. However, the reality seems to provide no such assurances. The resources pumped into the subsistence economy could be in turn mopped up by actors who may not part of the subsistence economy.

When the bore-well programme was undertaken in an effort to ensure that the new livestock had adequate green fodder for them to survive, the actual outcomes of this programme was a governance disaster. All along the interior hamlets of Chenchus, it is a disheartening sight to find dysfunctional bore-wells dug in tens in every Tribal *penta.* They are left as open holes or covered with stones to prevent hazards. Each bore-well costs Rs. 13,000 for digging it and Rs. 8,000 for fixing a motor at market price. The contractors hired by the ITDA dug bore-wells, fixed motors, and after getting the acknowledgement of the Tribal household, a week later, contractors would come and say that the bore-well is not being used in any case since there is no agriculture happening in the area and then they would take away the pipes and motors to reinstall them elsewhere. The new rule pertaining to the bore-wells requires that Tribal households pay Rs. 25,000 to get a bore-well. Tribal leaders, however, ask that if Tribals in these areas had access to this kind of money, why would they pay Rs. 25,000 to the ITDA when it was much cheaper (Rs. 21,000) to get a bore-well dug privately and install a motor by buying the equipment and the services on the market?

Yet another instance pointing to a similar experience was identified as part of the poor people's housing programme, the Indira Awas Yojana.

5.3 The Two Phases of Indira Awas Yojana and the Two Faces of Governmentality

During the first phase of Indira Awas Yojana, the ITDA Project Officer, Assistant Project Officer, Additional Director Agriculture, Deputy Engineer and Assistant Engineer Housing, Deputy Engineer and Additional Engineer from Tribal Welfare had visited Appapurpenta to demarcate the area where homes were being constructed for Tribals. While some of the Tribal leaders were assisting the officials, a squad of Naxalites came and encircled the officials. The officials were terrorized by what they were passing through. At this point, Tribal leaders interfered and they met the commander of the squad and criticized the Naxalites for this act. The Tribal leaders argued that officials usually do not visit the interior *pentas*. This was a rare opportunity when something beneficial was happening to the Tribals, and if the squad acted this way, it would hurt the interests of the Tribals. The squad commander was convinced with the arguments of the Tribal leaders. They checked the registers that were with the officials and told them that they must build good quality homes and that the squad would be evaluating their work. The Tribal leaders state, 'we do not know how the officials built these homes, who they robbed, but they built good quality homes'.

By the second phase of Indira Awas Yojana, terror was unleashed by the State to suppress the Naxalite movement. The State had formed 'Cobras' a Mafia terror outfit that engaged in brutal killings of Civil Rights, Dalit Rights, and Telangana activists. The 'Cobras' would attack middle class activists who were teachers, lawyers et cetera, residing in towns in broad daylight and use swords, daggers, axes, and other such crude weapons and often slice the bodies of the activists into several pieces and leave the mutilated bodies in a pool of blood. The very sight of these gruesome killings and the imagined agony of the pain and suffering such death involved were the methods through which all democratic struggles were suppressed in the State of Andhra Pradesh.

Similarly, Naxalite activists were killed by employing equally brutal methods. To kill Naxalites, the State promoted a systematic network of covert operations by converting the local militants and sympathizers by way of arresting them and torturing them and threatening them with grave consequences and by creating fear psychosis as well as by bribing these individuals. The coverts also included those youth disgruntled by the arbitrariness and the lack of deliberative or democratic participative culture of the Naxalites. For instance, a forest guesthouse meant to initiate an Eco-Tourism Project being constructed near Appapurpenta was detonated by the Naxalites. The contract of constructing the guesthouse was given to local Tribal youth. The youth were beaten up. On further query by Tribal leaders, the Naxalites gave an explanation to the Tribal leaders that eco-tourism would involve visits by foreigners and other neo-rich urban classes who would engage in the exploitation of the Tribals. Especially they thought Tribal women would become vulnerable. The Tribals in the area, however, were neither consulted in making such a decision nor was there an attempt to convince the Tribals that the act was in their interest. The bombing and razing of the Eco-Tourism Guesthouse was perceived by the Tribals predominantly as a strategic military decision by the Naxalite squads to protect itself from possible use by police and paramilitary forces of the State. A criticism of this act took the shape of covert operations in some instances when disgruntled elements started questioning whether Naxalites were basing their decision on protecting Tribal interests or promoting their organizational strategic interests. Taking advantage of the situation, the State used these elements to engage in extremely degenerated and dehumanized methods of causing losses to the Naxalite movement. Some of these methods included feeding poison to activists. In a couple of other such related instances, individuals who were very helpful to and respected by the Tribals (like GCC salesmen) were forced by the police to feed an important Naxalite activist with poison. Following this incident, the Naxalites killed this person. In this instance also, Tribals in the region were not informed about the reason for the act. The act was seen as completely immoral. The son of this GCC salesman, who was a settler from Coastal Andhra region, is said to have joined the Cobra group – an armed group enjoying a subtle patronage of the State used to assassinate activists seen as sympathetic to the Naxalite movement. For the second phase of the Indira Awas Yojana houses constructed in Appapur, this 'Cobra Contractor' was made the in-charge. By this time, the Naxalites had retreated from the region. It was amusing to observe that the second phase's Indira Awas Yojana homes do not have roofs. This was a significantly big scandal. There was, however, no serious action initiated against the culprits. Assistant Project Officer (APO) was transferred and others were suspended but local people say that these individuals had grown very rich by then and loss of job would not have mattered to them. The incomplete houses stand as monuments of corruption, criminalization and un-civility rather than as symbols of legitimization of accumulation derived from governmentality.

One of the most crucial instances that came to our notice during the course of our study was how the opposition parties and even journalists were given construction contracts so that they kept quiet about the pilferages and scandals in the implementation of the 'rehabilitation' programmes for the need economy. The social and political calibration crucial for the cost–benefit analytics founding the policy decisions around the transfers from the capitalist economy to the need economy had fallen pray to the social structures built to pursue a form of primitive accumulation or accumulation by extra economic force. To believe that these processes could be somehow decoupled and held in separate compartments seems to be an intellectual myth in social reality.

To summarize, while the first two of the programmes present above the case of incongruity between governmentality and the subsistence economy; the second two cases present a more complex problem of the role played by those social classes thrown up as part of the development process in the form of a range of middlemen and cronies complimenting accumulation by extra economic force or a form of primitive accumulation and enjoying the patronage of the powerful classes having semi-feudal lineages who are active parts of the modern State in this process. These social classes on whom the State seems to rely heavily to propel accumulation through extra economic force or a form of primitive accumulation are simultaneously deployed to deliver governmentality or rather these classes capture the institutions of governmentality. These classes try to accumulate through governmentality. These classes seem to have thus subverted this development process. So long as the State needs strategic cooption and coercion for promoting interests of accumulation and assertion of its power amidst lack of legitimacy, it cannot do away with these classes. However, these social classes are engaging in such massive pilferages and brutalities that their involvement in governmentality is bound to lead to the failure in achieving the objectives of rehabilitation of the subsistence economy and legitimization of the accumulation process.

Finally, a classic case of the interface between accumulation through extra economic force or a form of primitive accumulation and governmentality is presented by the experience of Peddulu (43) a Chenchu from Chenchugudem village. Peddulu is a small farmer with some livestock to carry out agriculture. Owning a reasonably decent home, he has a wife who does agriculture labour and two children, a girl and a boy who are studying in 8 and 10 Classes. Peddulu, like several other Tribal men, also engages in gathering of forest produce. According to the facts narrated by villagers of Chenchugudem, Peddulu went into the interior forest to procure some forest produce when he was stoked by the anti-Naxalite special police and para-military party. The police suspected him to be supplying food to Naxalites and took him into custody for interrogation. Peddulu was in police custody for over a week, during the course of which he was subjected to custodial torture. After the 'interrogation' process was over, he was dumped in the village. Peddulu has suffered severe head injuries and has lost his speech. His entire body is paralyzed and he barely manages to sit upright. He is now completely dependent on his wife and is unable to perform even ordinary functions on his own. His wife says that she has to feed him. He defecates involuntarily and she has to clean him and this care has to be provided to him round the clock. Following this tragic episode in the family's life, both the children of Peddulu had to quit school and are now going for work as part of the MGNREGA to fend for their family. The very mention of this tragedy brings uncontrollable tears to Peddulu. He is left with no other organ functioning normally, with the exception of these tears which speak silently. While what Peddulu has suffered is one side of the story of accumulation, what his children have got seems to be the process that Sanyal is trying to theorize. The processes of accumulation and rehabilitation of the subsistence economy don't seem to be connected in any sophisticated or systematic way except from the abstract vantage point of Planning Commission documents. Indeed, governmentality does rehabilitate the subsistence economy, but not quite in the way Kalyan Sanyal would like us to believe.

6. Conclusions

Mahabubnagar is one of the most backward districts of Andhra Pradesh. The Chenchu Tribes are one of the most marginalized communities who are still in the course of transition from hunter-gathering activities to agriculture and wage labour. Both regionally and socially, the categories chosen for this study belong to the excluded. Kalyan Sanyal argues that instead of treating the excluded as belonging to pre-capitalist mode in the course of a transitioning into the capitalist mode or that these sections are in a pre-modern social milieu in course of transiting into modern production and society, one must treat the excluded as a non-capitalist production and society which is very much a part of a self-sustaining capitalism. Capitalism according to Kalyan Sanyal has come of age to invent governmentality in place of unbridled primitive accumulation because it understands that capitalist accumulation would be in conflict with the excluded if these sections were to be left to the mercy of capital unaddressed. Governmentality is a strategic invention of accumulation around which a discursive discourse is constructed to reinforce the hegemony of the accumulation process. The concrete shape it takes is in the form of transfers from accumulation economy in favor of the subsistence economy (albeit within the cost–benefit frame). This process therefore leads to coexistence of a non-capitalist economy within the capitalist mode and which reproduces itself through transfers made by governmentality whose purpose would be to serve as a means for legitimizing accumulation acquiring the consent of those who are a part of the non-capitalist economy. A larger body of literature has shown that most the experiences of the subsistence economy and the social programmes carried out by the governmentality have in-fact had very different outcomes in different regions of the country (Cadéne Philpppe and Mark Holmstróm (eds), 1998; Karin Kapadia, Jan Breman and Jonathan Perry (eds.), 1999; G.Vijay, 2005; Priya Deshingkar and John Farrington (eds), 2009; Kannan and Breman (eds), 2013; Tathagata Sengupta and G. Vijay, 2015; G. Vijay, 2015. The rehabilitation of the subsistence economy through programmes of governmentality interestingly seem to be far more successful in the relatively developed regions and amongst relatively better off social groups in comparison to the performance of the programmes amongst the really excluded regions and social groups. Mahabubnagar's experience, presented here, falls into the experience of the latter category. The implications of this pattern are interesting. Accumulation as a process depends both on shades of accumulation through extra economic force or a form of primitive accumulating sites as well as sites of governmentality. This enmeshing of conflicting processes leads to more complex frames of trade-offs than what Kalyan Sanyal imagines. Accumulation through extra economic force or forms of Primitive accumulative processes and dispossession are being challenged by societies seen as being backward and excluded. The cost–benefit frames are used vis-à-vis 'handling' conflict and resistance as well as against the potential value expansion lost if the resistance succeeds. To put down or control a conflict whose existence could be seen as very costly, since it is likely to hamper or delay valuable economic projects exists alongside governmentality. To drive the requirements of accumulation through extra economic force or a form of primitive accumulation capital, State, and regional ruling elites have resorted to use of coercion. The use of coercion has in turn led to the rise of lawlessness involving criminal and corrupt bureaucracy, Mafia, and Mafia-like political elites as a formidable class nexus mediated through caste, ethnic, regional, communal, linguistic and political party based identities which in turn has led to capture of regulatory institutions. In the pockets, where such processes have besieged the development dynamics, it is not governmentality but authoritarianism that seems to be growing. These pockets of tyranny, as already pointed-out, depend on certain classes of overseers to ensure that barriers to accumulation are 'controlled', 'hunted', and 'weeded-out'. These classes neither have the sophistication to drive governmentality as imagined by Sanyal, nor do they operate well within the coherent cost–benefit frame of the accumulative order in pursuing pilferages and short-term benefits.

The need for these classes, nevertheless, exists from the point of view of the capital and the State to achieve accumulation for a pragmatic exercise of force, which simultaneously delivers another objective of reinforcing the power of the State against competing structures of power (like the Maoist movement for instance). In the course of grappling with this complexity, however, amongst those regions and social groups that are actually excluded but who are sitting in a subsistence economy on huge mountains of wealth waiting to be ploughed out, governmentality is certainly not the modus-operandi and legitimization is neither the objective nor the outcome. In these regions and amongst these social groups accumulation through extra economic force or a form of primitive accumulation rather than governmentality seems to be more relevant for analysis and reinforcing hegemony as dominance rather than as legitimization seems to be the outcome of the development process. The process of a restricted governmentality that does operate even in these backward regions and the excluded social groups, the purpose seems to be to co-opt the social elites for reinforcement of both primitive accumulation like or accumulation through extra economic force and the power of the State rather than for a larger objective of legitimization. While governmentality would require sympathetic bureaucracy, political society, civil society, political movements, and constitutional spirit being delivered by regulatory institutions including the judiciary, such processes could be perceived as ideological and economically irrational, constraining the potential expansion of value possible for capital. It is this accumulation on the edifice of which power of the State may stand on one foot. On the other hand, therefore, both the ruling elites or the dominant social groups on the one hand, and the proper agents of the State including the judiciary on the other seem to act as extensions of one another. This nexus leaves very little autonomy for regulation and they seem to have developed a vested interest in perpetuating coercive and uncivil accumulation that becomes the source of their arbitrary power, which in turn provides a niche for pilferages and privileges not deliverable by governmentality (Ajay Gudavarthy and G.Vijay, 2007). The real challenge before governmentality is to grapple with this extended State engaged in plunder, and while there seems to be too little being done, it seems governmentality has to find the means to circumvent the social elites and self-seeking regulators of the State on whose power it stands in the excluded geographical and social spaces, before it is too late for anything to be undone.

REFERENCES

Deshingkar, Priya and John Farrington (2009), *Circular Migration and Multilocational Livelihood Strategies in Rural India*, Oxford University Press, New Delhi.

Gudavarthy, Ajay and G.Vijay (2007), 'Antinomies of Political Society: Implications of Uncivil Development', *Economic and Political Weekly*, Vol. XLII, No. 29, 21 July, pp. 3051–9.

Kannan, K.P. and Jan Breman (eds.) (2013), *The Long Road to Social Security*, Oxford University Press, New Delhi.

Kapadia, Karin, Jan Breman and Jonathan Perry (eds) (1999), *The Worlds of Indian Industrial Labour,* Sage Publications, New Dehi.

Philppe, Cadéne and Mark Holmstróm (eds) (1998), *Decentralised Production in India; Industrial Districts, Flexible Specialization and Employment*, French Institute of Pondicherry and Sage Publications, New Delhi.

Sanyal, Kalyan (2007), *Rethinking Capitalist Development; Primitive Accumulation, Governmentality and Post Colonial Capitalism*, Routledge, New Delhi.

Sengutpa, Tathagata and G. Vijay (2015), A Survey of Migration from Western Odisha to Brick Kilns in Andhra Pradesh, S.R. Sankaran Chair, National Institute of Rural Development (NIRD), Hyderabad.

Vijay, G. (2005), 'Migration, Vulnerability and Insecurity in New Industrial Labour Market', *Economic and Political Weekly*, Vol. XL, No. 23, 28 May–4 June.

Vijay, G. (2013), 'Systemic Failure of Regulation: The Political Economy of Pharmaceutical and Bulk Drug Manufacturing', in Lofgren Hans (ed) *The Politics of the Pharmaceutical Industry: World Pharmacy and India,* Social Science Press, New Delhi.

Vijay, G. (2015), 'Labour Movement in Globalizing India', chapter 10 in Jayati Ghosh (ed), *ICSSR Surveys of Research and Explorations in Economics, Volume 2, India and the International Economy*, Oxford University Press, New Delhi.

ANNEXURE-1

Name of Commodity	*Gum Karaya*	*Gum Kondagogu*	*Gum Tiruman*
1995–96	350.51	104.68	1.9
1996–97	251	63.79	
1997–98	214.69	87.56	1.51
1998–99	179.71	84.48	0.91
1999–2000	193.35	127.99	
2000–01	156.22	75.64	
2001–02	140.95	99.65	
2002–03	119.84	108.08	0.16
2003–04	114.22	92.03	2.87
2004–05	126.93	143.53	2.9
2005–06	78.16	57.41	
2006–07	91.95	42.89	
2007–08	57.12	24.04	
2008–09	34.55	22.41	
2009–10	22.61	17.54	

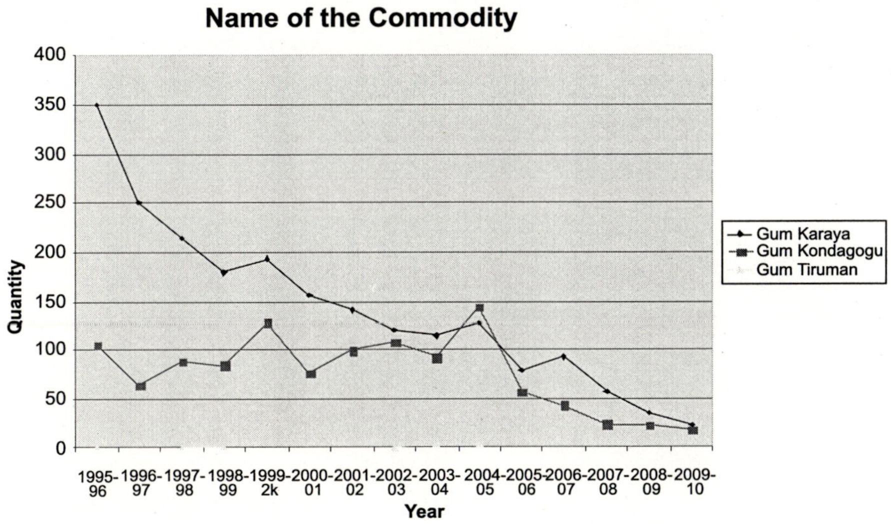

Name of Commodity	*Soap nuts*
1995–96	579.94
1996–97	817.02
1997–98	484.12
1998–99	668.91
1999–2000	1057.12
2000–01	885.13
2001–02	1621.92
2002–03	1269.66
2003–04	1507.45
2004–05	1030.29
2005–06	1375.82
2006–07	938.75
2007–08	2045.39
2008–09	378.61
2009–10	604.55

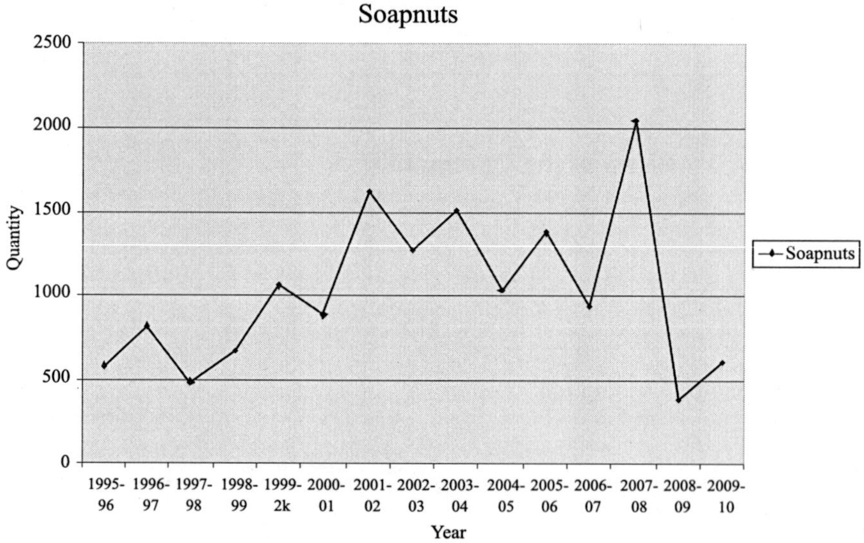

Name of Commodity	*Tamarind Seeded*	*Tamarind Deseeded*	*Tamarind Seed*
1995–96	1.2		6.1
1996–97			
1997–98	17.55		3.49
1998–99	33.58		
1999–2000	46		
2000–01	62.74		37.13
2001–02			
2002–03	13.4		3.44
2003–04	2.32		
2004–05	22.85		2.05
2005–06	7.36	1.06	32.07
2006–07	161.57	69.31	501.08
2007–08	25.29	7.09	0.6
2008–09			
2009–10			

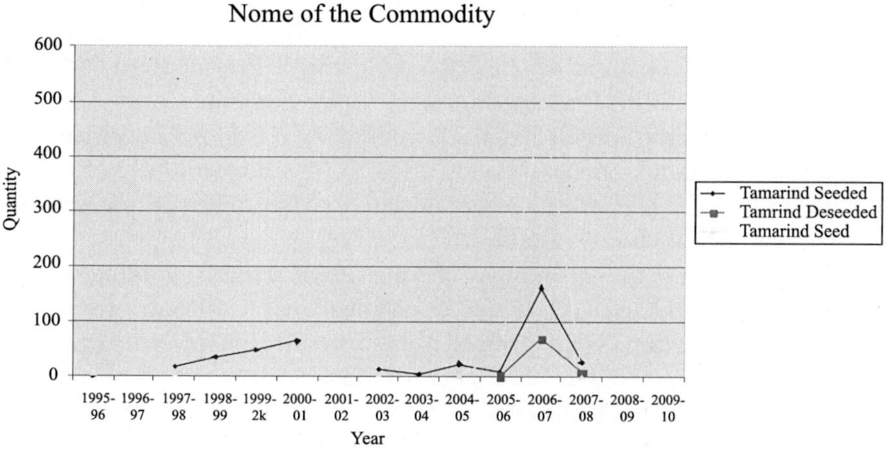

2. Some of the illustrations are also drawn from field study in Farooknagar, Achampet and Amrabad mandals of Mahabubnagar district.

14

Adivasi Militancy and Land Relations
The Context of Central and Eastern India

Joseph Marianus Kujur

The Independent People's Tribunal (IPT) on Operation Green Hunt[1] was organized in Ranchi on 25 and 26 September 2010, under the banner of the Jharkhand Alternative Development Forum with the support of the Operation Green Hunt Virodhi Nagrik Manch, Jharkhand Indigenous People's Forum, Jharkhand Initiatives Desk, Jharkhand Jungle Bachao Andolan, Jharkhand Mines Area Coordination Committee, and many other groups (Lourdswamy, 2010). The jury consisted of: Justice Vikramaditya Prasad, Retd Judge of Jharkhand High Court; Prashant Bhushan, Senior Supreme Court Advocate and Convener, Campaign for Judicial Accountability; K.S. Subramanian, IPS and former Director General of Police; and C.S. Jha, former CMD of BCCL among others. The renowned author and activist Ms Arundhati Roy was also present as a special observer in the IPT.

The Jury heard the testimonies of some social activists working among the Tribals in Jharkhand and a number of Tribal victims directly affected by Operation Green Hunt. What emerged from the testimonies presented a dismal and alarming situation of Human Rights violations against the Adivasis Driving them to unprecedented levels of desperation.

It was pointed out that, over the last 60 years, more than 20 lakh acres of land had been acquired directly by the State in the name of the so-called 'development' projects, displacing more than 15 lakh Adivasis from their homelands. This drive for land acquisition became particularly acute during the last decade when 102 MOUs were signed with large private corporations. Some of the agreements were for thousands of acres of land affecting thousands of Tribals and others dependent on the land to be alienated. Most of these MOUs were for mining or for setting up some polluting industries. However, these have met with enormous resistance from the Adivasis who have organized themselves against such 'development' projects.

The following emerged: first, there was no consent of or consultation with the Adivasis in the agreement for land acquisition; second, the MOUs were signed in haste and secrecy without any information to the affected people; and third, all this agreement was in gross violation of the Panchayats (Extension to the Scheduled Areas) Act, 1996, also popularly known as PESA.

The jury observed that the Adivasis felt disillusioned and betrayed by the State, as their constitutional right to self-rule was being flagrantly violated, thereby threatening their very identity and existence. Many of such disillusioned Tribals have taken to arms to fight the state.

The government's response to the adivasi resistance has been articulated in terms of reinforcement of the security forces trying to contain the 'rebels' in the predominantly Tribal areas of Jharkhand.

The Report of the Forum makes an interesting point that Operation Green Hunt is largely concentrated in the areas where the MOUs have been signed. The testimonies revealed that this 'Operation' caused enormous violations of Human Rights in terms of all kinds of excesses by the security forces, such as: firstly, arbitrary picking up of Adivasis and their torture; secondly, arbitrary arrests of those highlighting the abuses by the security forces; thirdly, false charges on those speaking against human rights violations by security forces; and fourthly, fake encounters in custody.

The Jury noted that courts, which were supposed to examine allegations of torture, fake encounters, and malafide arrests on false charges, had abdicated their responsibility. As a result, the innocent Adivasis had been victimized. The 15-point recommendations of the jury was focused on these issues: first, Tribal land and development; second, atrocities and human rights violations; third, accountability of the State; and fourth, compliance with international mechanisms (ibid.).

In 2004, when the United Progressive Alliance (UPA) Government came to power, the Prime Minister declaring the Common Minimum Programme (CMP) categorically stated that the problem of extremism in Tribal areas was not a law and order problem but a socioeconomic reality. Since then, six years have elapsed, and in the last six years, the position of the Government seems to have radically changed. It is clear now that the so-called extremism in Tribal areas is indeed a law and order problem for the State.

The civil society within the Tribal fraternity and outside, too, is divided in its perception and response to the above issue. Some sympathizers of the militant left radicalism blindly support the movement, as it offers solution to the problem of Tribal marginalization in the development process outside the given constitutional framework. However, while some others express their reservations about this kind of movement's viability and practicability, still others seem to be disillusioned by it when they do not see the Tribal land question being raised by the local militant leadership. They feel betrayed when they see Tribal policemen like Francis Indwar and Lucas Tete executed by the militants. They are confused when the cadres indulge in extortions even from the Tribals, and in some cases, allegedly help the industrialists to acquire land and even win elections for those who are ready to pay them the money.

Irrespective of the above confusion and disillusionment, the present paper attempts to reflect on the problem of militant left radicalism in Tribal areas from the Tribal perspective of land, within the larger framework of Tribal development in India.

The paper has four parts: firstly, the adivasi concept of land; secondly, adivasi resistance in the past; thirdly, the adivasi response to land-grabbing in the present; and fourthly, some concluding observations.

1. The Adivasis' Concept of Land

Way back in 1903, F.B. Bradley Birt, an English Officer, writing on the erstwhile impregnable vast forest tract covering the area of 43,722 square miles (Banerjee, 1993: 26) in Chotanagpur referred to it as a 'little known province' (ibid.: i) of the Empire. However, within the last ten decades that impregnable forest tract has been bored through and through from all sides by all categories of people—miners, merchants, timber mafia, forest department, administrators, politicians, left radicals, and many more kinds. There are vast stretches of land in Jharkhand now running over 74,677 square kilometers, where one wonders whether there was any forest cover at all, so bad has been the deforestation and conversion of 'Jhaadakhand'[2] into 'civilized and cultured' human habitations, harbouring on the latest technology. There have been hundreds of hectares of cultivable land for decades in some districts, but if one looked for the relevant documents regarding land transfer/conversions, there would be no surprise if that the land referred to is still entered as forest land. It means that it has not been converted into *raiyati* land[3], though it has been transferred into arable fields, and that forest had lasted for thousands of years on the place.

The nomenclature of the places and habitations on Tribal land is interesting. The names assigned to places are, most of the time, descriptions of what those places actually stood for: for example *harinchara* (the place of stags' and deer's regular grazing), *barwadih* (the jungle territory of wild dogs' hunting and undisturbed roaming), *bhalubasa* (the permanent abode of wild bears), to mention only a few. The fact is that these places were true to their names. Bhalubasa for instance, until the emergence of the city of Jamshedpur in close vicinity, engulfing all the hills and dales around, was a real den of innumerable bears because of its geographical situation. The area was completely covered with thick forest. That same *bhalubasa* today is so much in the thick of the city that no person born after 1908, the year Tata Iron and Steel Company was established in Jharkhand, would ever know why such a name was given to the place which is literally overcrowded with concrete buildings and human beings today. Ironically, the statement of Bradley Birt continues to be true to a large extent.[4]

Various interest groups, stakeholders, and institutions define 'land' differently from their own perspectives. Land, in a common parlance, is 'solid ground' or 'solid part of the surface of the earth' (http://www.thefreedictionary.com/Land). From the legal point of view, land is defined as 'any found, soil or earth whatsoever, as meadows, pastures, woods, waters, marshes, furze, and heath. It has an indefinite extent upwards as well as downwards; therefore land, legally includes all houses and other buildings, standing, or built on it; and whatever is in a direct line between the surface and the centre of the earth, such as mines of metals or fossils' (http://www.lectlaw.com/def/l063.htm 'Land').

Land, for Tribals, however, is much more than the title deed. Land is the gift of God, freely given. In their worldview, one requires only appropriating the God given gifts by the power of one's workmanship, capacity to do hard work, skillfulness in 'harnessing' nature and persistent dedication to maintain its harmony. According to the Tribal myths (Oraon, Munda, Kharia, Ho, Santhal), God gave the earth in its 'wild form' to human beings. The earth without human beings tending it yielded thorns and thistles. The prosperity and thriving of the wild plants, birds and animals, and the earth without human being's relationship with them, was called *jungli* (wild).

The earth, in the Tribal worldview, 'includes natural objects, animals, birds, water, air, sunshine and the like including human beings, and they are all bound to one another in an integral manner' (Minz, 2007: 50). According to them, there is nothing on this earth without a spirit. However, the presence of spirit in stones, waters, trees are real for the Adivasis. Their ancestors form part of a living society. This living consciousness of spirits in nature, make the adivasi perspective on ecology different from those of others (ibid.: 51–52).

The personhood for Adivasis is rooted in their concept of land. Land for them is life as Minz argues,

> Earth is mother from whom all sustenance comes to human beings and non humans. No land, no personhood of the Adivasis. Therefore ownership of land and alienation from land has theological implications for the Adivasis (for them land and forest, water and air and all nature's bounty are gifts of God. No king, no Landlord and no Government has ever created the land and the forest. Land was there, and the Adivasis have been using this gift as stewards and not as owners. Even for the custodian of these gifts of God, it is the community and not the individual who is primarily responsible for this stewardship of the earth. Only God is the king or owner and no one else. Therefore, the modern states and Governments are all deviations from the original intent of the creation of this earth (ibid.: 52).

Land defines their reciprocity and the concept of nature as their relative. This consciousness makes them treat their relatives with respect and deal with them justly, be they human beings, trees, animals and insects, water, air, or sunshine (ibid.: 53).

Some people may have misconception that Adivasis are anti-development anti-scientific and anti-technological progress. However, all that Adivasis ask is whether modern development is sustainable and what kind of technologies and industries are essential for sustaining life and nature. A Munda folk story of the Asurs smelting iron, gives an explanation of the Adivasi understanding of ecology that encompasses all forms of life—plant, animal, and human.

Myth has it that the Asurs used furnaces for smelting iron day and night without any break. The earth began to warm up more and more. It reached a point at which the life of the animals, insects, trees, was threatened. Hence, all the creatures cried to Singbonga, the Supreme Deity of the Munda Tribe, for His intervention to stop the incessant smelting of iron. God heard their cry and sent messengers in the form of birds to the Asurs not to engage in iron smelting day and night so that the earth would be able to withstand the heat and all the living beings would be happy. The greedy Asurs, however, did not listen to God's message to them, through His messengers (ibid.: 54).

Finally, God Himself, disguised as a leper boy, came down to warn the Asurs, not to pollute the earth with their iron smelting day and night. The Asurs caught hold of the boy and put him into the furnace. After some time, the Asurs thought that the boy was burnt to ashes. But to their surprise, they found him coming out of the furnace laden with gold and diamonds all over his body (ibid.).

The greedy Asurs thought that if they, like the leper boy, went inside the furnace, they too would come out laden with diamond, gold, and silver. With these ulterior motives, they entered the furnace, asking their wives to work on the bellows fast. There were loud cries inside the furnace and their women thought their husbands were fighting for the gold and diamond, and hence the noise. When the wives opened the furnace after some time they found the charred bodies of their husbands (ibid.).

The lessons of the above folk story are the following: first, industries and mining are necessary, but they cannot go on endlessly without any rest; second, balance in industry and mining is necessary if humans are to live on this earth; third, the greedy Asurs, representing the present day industrialists and miners, do not listen to the warning of God; and fourth, the greed of human beings is ultimately responsible for self-destruction of the earth and all that is in it, including the human beings (ibid.: 55). The myth also drives home the point that this earth, the environment, and ecosystem have been misunderstood as a machine, which functions by itself. It is wrong to think that human beings can manoeuvre this machine earth, as they like. There is a living organic relationship between human beings, trees, animals, insects, water, air, sunshine, and the soil of this earth. Hence, respect for one another as relatives, only will protect and sustain the earth (ibid.: 56).

Thus, the guiding principles of Tribal peoples in land tenure prior to the zamindari period can be summarized in four statements: firstly, land, the greatest gift of God for the human community, is not for an individual, but for the entire community, the clan, and hence, even if one person seems to own the land, he must understand and accept the fact that land under his possession is meant for the welfare of the community; secondly, land cannot be bought and sold like other things, precisely because it relates the people with God the Creator and the community; thirdly, land as a raw gift of God, has the potential to be converted into cultivable land for the welfare of humanity; and fourthly, nobody can claim to be a master of the land, except those who have taken the first steps to appropriate it through hard work, skillfulness and lasting dedication.

A system of land tenancy among Tribals was based on such elevated principles where there was no landlord. However, no credit was ever given to the culture attained by the non-Aryans, who prevailed long before the Aryans appeared on the scene (Banerjee, 1993: 73).

Kinds of Tribal Land

The Tribal land in the colonial period was classified into privileged land and *raiyati* land. The privileged lands could be either of the zamindars or of the permanent tenants. The lands of the permanent tenants were Bhuinhari or Khuntkatti.

The privileged land was the *manjhihas* land of the zamindars. The word *manjhihas* literally means 'the share of the Manjhi', the village chief. Strangely enough, prior to the introduction of the landlord system, the village chiefs received tributes from the villagers but no rents. When zamindars came onto the scene, they began to demand not tributes but 'remunerations', payment for their services. Since it was easier to give them land for their sustenance, the peasants readily agreed to give them some land. But very soon, the landlords claimed the best cultivation fields for themselves. To the invited guests, converted into landlords, the Raja offered the whole landmass of one area, and called it *manjhihas*. Originally, these land plots belonged to many aboriginal tenants, but in front of the Raja, the individual owners remained silent onlookers.

Manjhihas land as defined by the Act was 'Landlords privileged lands which are cultivated by the land lord himself with his own stock or by servants or by hired labourers, or are held by a tenant on lease for a term of years or year by year and which are by customs recognized as privileged land in which occupancy rights cannot accrue, have been entered as majhihas and bethkheta in the register were declared the Majhihas land' (CNT Act, 1908, Art. 118). *Manjhihas* lands were regarded as free of rent payments, and under the permanent occupancy rights of the landlords.

The *beth-kheta* lands are lands under the proprietorship of the landlords as part of the *manjhihas*, but segregated from the *manjhihas* as service land, to be cultivated by the villagers. Its yields were distributed among those who were appointed to cultivate the *manjhihas* lands of the landlords on behalf of the landlords.

The Lands of the Permanent Tenants—Bhuinhari or Khuntkatti

The very first occupation of the ancestors in the jungles of 'Jhaadakhand' who cleared the forest, and made the first settlements, they called *bhuinhari*. The reclaimer of the patch of land in the jungle was regarded as its owner. As the community progressed, he paid a light tribute or rendered a slight service to the village chief, but 'his status as a Bhuinhar or pioneer, or descendent of a Bhuinhar was always regarded as vastly higher than that of the later comers, who had settled on the land when the village was established' (Roy, 1996 & 2002: 257). Except for *mundas*, *bhuinhari* could also be called the *khuntkatti* land, though some families had their *Bhuinhari* first and generations later, *khuntkatti* was also developed away from the *bhunihari*.

According to the Chota Nagpur Tenancy Act 1908, '*Bhuinhari* includes not only lands in occupation of descendants of the first ancestors who settled in the district long before the landlords established themselves, but also lands reclaimed by more recent settlers though these cannot claim the right of Khuntkatti.' Survey Settlement restored such *Bhuinhari* lands to the original Bhuinhars from the lot of the landlords' *Manjhihas* lands, provided of course the claim was made and the justifications could be ascertained (ibid.: 327).

In course of time different pieces of the *bhuinhari* were dedicated on permanent basis to the 'service' of village Pahans, *mahto*s, and spirits. Thus new names emerged which by their very names became indicative of the special services they were engaged in. The ancestral land of the type of *khuntkatti*, pure and simple, was called *bhuinhari* proper. *Bhut kheda* land was set apart for the village spirits. If it was the property of a *khunt* (clan) and was cultivated by the *khunt*, then the proceeds of the field went to the propitiation of the family spirits. If that property was of the village community, then the Pahan took over the responsibility of sacrificing to the village spirits. *Pahnai* and *dalikatari* were lands in the village, in the name of the religious head. The Pahan had the task of appeasement sacrifices to village deities and spirits. He officiated as a priest. Lands set apart for the Pahan was known as *pahnai* and *dalikatari* lands. Panbhara was a male assistant to the Pahan. Puja required quite a bit of preparatory work for which a male assistant was appointed. Among other jobs, one of his main tasks was to get water from the wells or the water holes—the land set apart for him was panbhara land. *Mahtoi* land was set apart from the priestly work, in the name of the village headman, known as Mahto. For his services he was assigned the mahtoi land. Whenever *bhuinhari* land was talked of, implications were that all these sub-kinds of the *bhuinhari* land taken together (ibid.: 328).

When the Chotanagpur Tenancy (CNT) Act, 1908, made a special provision to safeguard the *bhuinhari* land of the Mundas and the Kurukhs, and of other Tribes, these Tribals were more than pleased. Now they knew for sure, along with their *bhuinhari* land, their *sasandiri*s and *masnas*[5] would be well protected and disturbances of family peace and harmony among the ancestors would be warded off.

Khuntkatti land was the land of the Khuntkattidars, who were 'the descendents in the male line of the original founders of a village.' They were 'recognized as the owners of the whole area included in the village boundaries' and were responsible for the 'payment to the superior landlords of a fixed annual rent', which represented the tribute which the founders of their descendents agreed to pay to the Feudal chief, when the zamindari system began (ibid.: 307).

'Raiyat having khunt katti rights' means a *raiyat* in occupation of, or having any subsisting title to land reclaimed from jungle by the original founders of the village or their descendants in the male line, when such *raiyat* is a member of family which founded the village or a descendant in the male line of any member of such family: 'Provided that no raiyat shall be deemed to have khunt-katti rights in any land unless he and all his predecessors-in-title have held such land or obtained a title there by virtue of inheritance from the original founders of the village' (Sinha, 2003: 11).

A Mundari Khunt-kattidar means a Mundari who has acquired a right to hold jungle land for the purpose of bringing suitable portions thereof under cultivation by himself or by male members of his family and includes—(a) the heirs male in the male line of any such Mundari when they are in possession of such land or have any subsisting title thereto, and (b) as regards any portions of such land which have remained continuously in the possession of any such Mundari and his descendants in the male line, such descendants' (ibid.: 12).

Raiyat means primarily a person who has acquired a right 'to hold land for the purpose of cultivating it by himself, or by members of his family, or by hired servants, or with the aid of partners; and includes the successors-in-interest of persons who have acquired such a right, but does not include a *Mundari-Khunt-Kattidar*' (ibid.: 10).

The zamindari system had been in the Tribal belt at least for three hundred years now, but the sense of belonging to the land even to the land that had slipped out of their hands had continued to deepen in the Tribal psyche. Most of the land the indigenous people was lost in the hands of the landlords, jagirdars, mahajans, and thekedars, but the attachment to the *bhuinhari*, *khuntkatti*, *kodkar*, *gaerahi*, and *nokran* kinds of land could not be weakened (ibid.). Digging work was one of the works of Tribals. Sometimes, the embankments needed to be worked on, and at other times, extra soil had to be brought to the same level as the old ones, hoping that after a few years, its fertility would be enhanced to match with the rest of the fields because of regular tending. Such land got the name of *kodkar*.

The land over which there was community ownership was known as *gaerahi* land. In Tribal society no individual possessed any land; it was always a possession of the whole clan, or family. So, the references to a particular land would be for instance, the *lakra khuntkatti* or *tigga bhuinhari*, and not *somra khuntkatti* or *birsa bhuinhari*, though Somra and Birsa could be the elders who played the major role in 'acquiring' the land. Lakra and Tigga are family names, whereas Somra and Birsa are two individuals. Still, when it comes to day-to-day speech, these pieces of land are referred to as the ownership of individuals. However, there have been several other categories of land in early Jharkhand which can cumulatively be called, 'the land pieces of community ownership'. They belong to all the people of the village as a common property. Such lands are–the village roads (*chhahur*s) the common dance and entertainment floors (*akhra*s), the common grazing grounds (*bathaan*s), the common threshing floors (*khalihan*s), common burial grounds (*nasna*s), the common places of pooja to the village spirits, or deities (*dibiguri*s), the common places of annual worship to god (*sarna*s), the common place of weekly markets (*haat*s), the common water tanks (*pokhra*s), and so on.

Some artisan communities lived for generations in the villages side by side with the Tribal peasants participating in all their joys and sorrows of life equally, but for land holding, they continued to be 'foreigners' who could not possess permanently the land as the Tribals did. The land such artisans occupied were the land of the village community known as *nokran* land.

2. Adivasi Resistance in the Past

There are normally multiple reasons behind each of the Tribal movements. Some of the factors, however, are more decisive and predominant than the others. Sachchidanand observes, 'At the root of each movement are multiple of factors, each reinforcing the other' (1990: i). In relation to the category of the rebellion type, Sinha has the following to say,

> These Tribal movements, *ulgulan*, agitation, rebellion, et cetera formed part of the whole, that is, the Tribal wrath against the system which was thrust upon them. They were mainly against economic exploitation, territorial encroachment, cultural imposition and social domination. Some of them could at best be movement for entry into existing power structure or movement for generation of alternative power structure or movement for entry into existing structure of prestige without visualizing any alternative structure of power (1990: 180).

The Tribal movements in the northeast India with the Tribal majority have primarily been political and secular in nature with a few exceptions. However, their character in Central India has been quite complex and perplexing. Tribal movements in the Northeast come under the categories of religious and social reform movements, movements for separate statehood, insurgent movements, and movements for assertion of cultural rights (Dubey, 1982: 11–12). The movements such as the Naga movement (1879, 1963–71), the Zeliangrong movement, the ethnic and script movement of Manipur, the Mizo political movement (1966–71), the cultural revivalism among the Christian Khasis, the Nativistic Seng Khasi movement, the Khasi solidarity movements, and the Brahma movements of the Bodo-Kachari, fall in one of the above categories.

In Central India, a two-pronged struggle of Tribes has primarily been for physical survival and identity assertion. Their main problems of Tribals today are: a struggle for survival, abject poverty, indebtedness, displacement, alienation of natural resources, militarization of Tribal areas, and human rights violations. These have often resulted in male and female migration, and trafficking and prostitution of women. Moreover, a sense of insecurity, crisis of identity, environmental degradation, identity and resource related conflicts, dehumanization at various levels, a breakdown of socio-political fabric, and constant exclusion from economic and political rights have given rise to numerous protests, movements, and the uprisings for self-assertion (Kujur, 2008: 139).

Sinha has categorized the Tribal movements in mid-India from 1832 to 1990 into the following seven-fold typology: first, encroachment on traditional rights, such as Birsa Rebellion (1895–1990) and Tana Bhagat Movement (1912–30); second, revolt against economic exploitation and unbearable tyranny, like Tana Bhagat Movement, Kisan Tana Rising (1918), Birsa Ulgulan (1895–1900), Khond Rebellion (1893), Gond Rebellion (1888), Santhal Discontent (1860–61), and Santhal Unrest (1871); third, revolt against cultural imposition and social domination, such as Tana Bhagat Movement, Jharkhand Movement (1950–2000), movement of Jharkhand Mukti Morcha, Kherwar Movement, Birsa Movement, Kisan Sabha Movement, and Sardari Larai; fourth, movement for generation of alternative political power structure, like Kisan Tana Rising, Jharkhand Movement, movement of Jharkhand Mukti

Morcha, Birsa Seva Dal Movement, All Jharkhand Students' Union (AJSU) Movement, and Kherwar Movement (1832–3); fifth, movement for entry into existing structure of power, such as Tana Bhagat Movement, Independence Movement among Tribes, Bhumij Movement, and Kherwar Movement; sixth, movement for entry into existing structure of prestige without visualizing any alternative, like Tana Bhagat Movement, Hari Baba Movement, Sapha Hor Movement, Coordination Committee for Jharkhand, and Sardari Movement (1889); and seventh, revolt against political encroachment, such as Bamanghati Rebellion, and Bhuiyan Rebellion of Keonjhar (Sinha, 1990: 181; Verma, 2002: 273–5).

It is obvious from the above typology that there are many factors responsible for each movement. For instance, the Birsa Rebellion emerged in protest against encroachment on Tribal rights and against economic exploitation and unbearable tyranny. Similarly, the Tana Bhagat Movement was against encroachment on traditional rights, economic exploitation and tyranny, cultural imposition, and social domination, for entry into existing structure of power, and for entry into existing structure of prestige without visualizing any alternative structure of power. The Jharkhand Movement and Jharkhand Mukti Morcha emerged primarily against cultural imposition, social domination, and for generating alternative political power structure. The 'Karticism', that is, the movement started by the late Kartik Oraon, was in protest against cultural imposition and social domination, and for entry into existing structure of power.

In Central India, practically all the Tribal movements were in protest against the colonial and neo-colonial hegemony of the exploitative and oppressive British and the Indian elites. The Tribal struggle has primarily been in relation to land, forest, and water, which are the main sources of livelihood for them The Tribal movements in Central India were in protest against injustices and oppression either by the State or the local exploiters (Tirkey, 2002: 1–3).

3. Tribal Resistance to Land Grabbing in Contemporary Times

There are constitutional provisions guaranteeing social (Articles 14, 15 (4), 16 (4), 16 (4A) and 339 (1)); economic (Articles 46, 275 (1) and 33); and political (Article 244 along with the V and the VI schedules plus 330, 332 and 243 (D)) protection, to all Scheduled Tribes in the country. However, what has been happening all these decades, even 63 years after the independence of the country, is quite disturbing. What is happening in Tribal areas today is what happened in the past. There is a parallelism between the resistance of the past and the present; only the form, intensity, and complexity have changed.

3.1 Land grabbing in the 'Tribal' states

The year 1960–1 is considered to be the initiation year of industrialization of Chota Nagpur, when the mega Project of Heavy Engineering Corporation was started at Hatia, near Ranchi. Within a few years, Bokaro Steel Plant was launched. A number of other industrial hubs in neighbouring Orissa (Rourkela Steel Plant) and Madhya Pradesh (Bhilai) Tribal belt suddenly shot up. As a result, many rural areas were urbanized. The new district headquarters sprung up everywhere.

The mines of coal, iron-ore, bauxite, cement, mica, and so on, allured crowds from different parts of the country. There was an increasing out-migration of the local inhabitants and in-migration of the 'outsiders', primarily from the state of the undivided Bihar. The demand for land skyrocketed, but the supply was limited. Hence, the usurpation of Tribal land through the manipulative designs of the land brokers and mafias emerged. Even before the Tribal owners being aware of the sale, the land tenancies of Tribal land holders were sold away to non-Tribals. In spite of the Chotanagpur Tenancy (CNT) Act, 1908, and Santhal Pargana Tenancy, Act 1949, the vested interests had their way, leaving the Tribals to fend for themselves.

This process continued in the twentieth and twenty-first centuries. In fact, with the policy of economic liberalization accelerated by the process of globalization, the alienation of Tribal land and natural resources has increased to an alarming degree.

The traditional land of Tribals was close to their heart. However, for the *dikku* (exploiters) and the land mafia, the differences among different kinds of lands, such as *bhuinhari, khuntkatti, kodkar, raiyati, pahnai*, and *mahtoi*, did not make any sense. The only thing that made any sense to them was profiteering, individual prosperity, hoarding, and centralization of power, the values which were totally different from what many Tribal communities still cherished. Even the *sarna,*[6] *masna,* and the *sasandari*, the communitarian lands, considered to be sacred, were still being encroached upon.

Some of the cases indicate that even the Government machinery is involved in the manipulations, facilitating land grabbing in the states of Chhattisgarh, Jharkhand, and Orissa.

According to the 1951 Census, there was a notification of 91 Scheduled Tribe (ST) communities in the undivided Madhya Pradesh. The number of ST communities in Chhattisgarh, according to census 2001, came down to 47 only, which was 52 ST communities less from the 1951 census (CIFTY 2010).

In the Jashpur district of Chhattisgarh, the administration launched its own website publicizing the district census updated report. According to the website, out of 765 villages of the district, 291 villages with 100 per cent ST population were shown as villages with zero Tribal population. Moreover, the district-wise Scheduled Tribe population was reduced from 4,69,953 to 36,787 persons only. Thus, tampering of the number of scheduled Tribe population, made 4,33,166 Tribal citizens non-existent entities (ibid.).

According to some reliable sources (Right to Information and others), Jashpur District's total area spreads into 6,456 square kilometers. However, the total area being acquired by the industrial companies in that district amounts to 6,022 square kilometers. If the entire land is acquired as per the agreement, 4,70,000 people of the district will be left with very few square kilometers of land. This situation has arisen because the state has signed more than 112 MOUs with various companies (ibid.).

In the Bastar District of Chhattisgarh, 644 ST dominant villages have been evacuated. Those who resisted the move of the state were branded as naxals, and those who adhered to the counsel of the state became refugees in 24 camps run by the state. There are reports that this has been done precisely to clear the land for the mining and industrial companies (ibid.).

More than 50 school buildings were permanently and 43 temporarily, occupied in Jharkhand by the CRPF and JAP. Consequently, more than ten thousand children from the ST communities were deprived of their right to education. Some of the schools were handed over to the authorities by the forces only recently under the pressure of the civil society (ibid.).

In Jharkhand, in 2009, there were MOUs signed for 9,8547 acres of land to be acquired by the Tata, ESSAR, Jindal, Mittal, and some other companies. As of now, there are more than 102 MOUs in the pipeline (ibid.).

In Orissa, which is the third major ST area in eastern-central India, the state government has signed MOUs worth 33,268 acres of land with the POSCO India, the Jindal Steel, the Mittal Steel, the Uttam Golwa Steel, the Star Light Iron, and the Steel Bhushan Steel, to name a few (ibid.).

3.2 Causes of discontent in the 'extremist' affected areas

The 16-member Expert Group set up by the Planning Commission to study 'Development Issues to deal with causes of Discontent Unrest and Extremism' in May 2006, came to a conclusion that 'excepting occasional knee jerk responses there had not been any sustained administrative and developmental action, including to eliminate the causes and reduce the discontent of the masses' (Expert Group, 2006, No. 1.6).

There is 'social and economic background to the rise of the movement' in more than 125 districts over 12 states (ibid., No. 1.1.3). These causes specific to the Naxalite Movement are part of an overall scenario of poverty, deprivation, oppression, and neglect in large parts of the country (ibid.).

There is a deep sense of exclusion, alienation, and marginalization almost all over the Tribal areas (ibid., No. 1.4.4). In the words of the Expert Committee,

Apart from poverty and deprivation in general, the causes of the Tribal movements are many the most important among them are absence of self governance, forest policy, excise policy, land related issues, multi-faceted forms of exploitation, cultural humiliation and political marginalisation. Land alienation, forced evictions from land, and displacement also added to unrest. Failure to implement protective regulations in scheduled areas, absence of credit mechanism leading to dependence on moneylenders and consequent loss of land and often even violence by the state functionaries added to the problem (ibid., No. 1.4.5).

Land is the key to the Tribal uprisings – past and present. According to the Forest Survey of India Report 2003, nearly 60 per cent of the forest covers of the country and 63 per cent of the dense forests were in 187 Tribal districts, that is, districts covered by the Fifth and Sixth Schedules to the Constitution, giving special rights to the Tribals (ibid., No. 1.4.6). It implies that any State policies legitimizing the depletion of forests and alienation of land adversely affects the Tribals. Land Acquisition Acts, Forest Laws and Special Economic Zone Act, et cetera all have contributed largely in reducing the agriculturist Tribals to sheer daily wage labourers and rickshaw pullers.

3.3 Conspiracy in amending the CNT Act, 1908

The CNT Act, 1908, for the protection of the Tribals' land from being alienated, was amended at least 26 times till 2010. Efforts are also being made in Jharkhand today to nullify the above Act, under the pretext of making it Adivasi-friendly for lifting its restrictions. The argument made by the detractors of the Act is that the absence of this Act will facilitate free sale and transfer of the Tribal land thereby making them as rich as many of the non-Tribals. The prevalent law, according to them, prohibits a Tribal land from being sold or transferred to a non-Tribal. There seems to be a conspiracy in the proposed amendment of the CNT Act facilitating thereby easy acquisition of Tribal land by unfair means, force, and allurement.

3.4 Amendment of the Jharkhand Panchayati Raj Act 2001: A ploy for de-scheduling the STs

Ever since the 73 amendment of the Constitution, Jharkhand was the only state not to have the elections. It is only before the end of 2010 that Jharkhand had panchayat elections after 32 years. To extend the panchayat law in Scheduled Areas, the panchayats (extension to the Scheduled Areas) Act, 1996, was enacted. According to the PESA 4(g), there was a provision for reservation of seats in the Scheduled Areas at every panchayat in proportion to the population of the communities in that panchayat for whom reservation is sought to be given under Part IX of the Constitution provided that the reservation for the Scheduled Tribes shall not be less than one-half of the total number of seats. There was also provision 'that all seats of Chairpersons of panchayats at all levels shall be reserved for the Scheduled Tribes' (JPRA, 2001).

To give effect to the provisions of PESA, the state legislative assembly of Jharkhand had passed the JPRA 2001, which included the following provisions: (a) JPRA, 21(B) provided reservation for the posts of Mukhia and Up-Mukhia of the gram panchayats in the scheduled areas which also providing exclusion of reserved posts 'in a prescribed manner' for Mukhia and Up-Mukhia from the gram panchayats, in the scheduled areas, where there is no population of Scheduled Tribes; (b) JPRA 40(B) provided reservation of posts of Pramukh and Up-Pramukh in panchayat samiti (in the scheduled area) for the members belonging to the Scheduled Tribes; (c) According to JPRA 55(B), the post of Adhyaksha of zila parishad in scheduled areas were reserved for the members of the Scheduled Tribes (Land Desk, 2010).

Some cases were filed against this provision in the Supreme Court. On 12 January 2010, the Supreme Court of India gave judgment on PESA (civil appeal number 484–491 of 2006 Union of India vs Rakesh and others). This verdict included section 44 (of the Judgment) the proviso of 4(g) of PESA and 21(b), 40(b) and 55(b) of JPRA 2001 were held to be constitutionally valid (ibid.).

However, an ordinance was brought by the Governor of Jharkhand, as the House was not in the session. The ordinance had to be passed by the House within six months of notification. In the meantime, the State Assembly was suspended and the state came under President Rule until the present Government came to power (ibid.).

The Ordinance proposed amendments that are likely to bring negatively dangerous effects to Adivasis and local self-governance of Scheduled Areas. They are as follows: (a) according to JPRA Ordinance 01 of 2010-2(I), the word 'and Up-Mukhiya' shall be deleted from the phrase 'Mukhiya and Up-Mukhiya' in section 21(A), 21(B) of JPRA 2001; (b) according to JPRA Ordinance 01 of 2010-4 (V), the post of Up-Pramukh shall be kept unreserved or shell be dealt with in accordance with the provision made by the state government; (c) JPRA Ordinance 01 of 2010-5(I) provided further that, if the total number of Chairpersons belonging to Scheduled Tribe in the Scheduled Areas is beyond the proportion of their population in the state, further reservation shall not be provided (for the post of Chairperson of Jila Parishad in Non-Scheduled Areas); (d) JPRA Ordinance 01, 5(V) of 2010 provided the post of Deputy Chairpersons of Jila Parishad to be kept 'unreserved' or to be dealt with in accordance with the provisions made by the state government (ibid.).

This amendment to 'unreserve' the post of Up-Mukhiya, Up-Pramukh and Up-Adhayaksh in the Scheduled Areas is a clear violation of Section 4(g) of the PESA. This amendment was tabled and introduced in Lok Sabha on 12 August 2010 and passed on 17 August after discussion and debate. It was passed in the Rajya Sabha as well. When this becomes an Act, will have a negative impact on the whole of Scheduled Areas distributed in nine states of the country (ibid.).

4. Conclusion

To close the paper, there is no better piece of oratory than the Chief Seattle's reply in 1854 to the American President who offered to buy a large area of land from the Indian people:

> How can you buy or sell the sky, the warmth of the land? The idea is strange to us if we do not own the freshness of the air and the sparkle of the water, how can you buy them. Every part of this earth is sacred to my people. Every shining pine needle, every sandy shore, every mist in the dark woods, every clearing and humming insect is holy in the memory and experience of my people. The sap that courses through the trees carries the memories of the red man. (http://www.kyphilom.com/www/seattle.html).

In the light of the above, the following observations can be made:

Firstly, what we have seen above is only the tip of an iceberg of a much larger problem. This is only a symptom of a larger root cause, which is systemic and structural. This structural and systemic violence against the Tribals began with the process of colonization with the victory of Columbus and creation of the 'new world' more than 500 years ago. The process of colonization has come back today in the form of globalization. The Salwa Judum, Operation Greenhunt, killings at Torpa, Kalinga Nagar, and Nandigram, are part of the same process of neo-colonization.

Secondly, even after 63 years of independence, if what is happening can happen to a group of human beings asking for their basic rights to live with dignity, what is the meaning of 'democracy', 'human rights', 'citizenship rights', 'fundamental rights', and Tribal/indigenous peoples' rights? The 'historical injustice' is being committed every day in the form of forced displacement, militarization of Tribal areas, trafficking of Tribal girls, alienation of Tribal land and other natural resources, legitimization of unjust structures, democratization of the undemocratic practices, and justification of the unjustified laws. Tribals do not have any participation in the decision-making process, partnership in planning, and implementation and share in the development.

Let us not forget the Australian and Canadian Governments and the people of those countries had the courage to say 'sorry' to the aborigines and native Indians for all the misdeeds of the past. The UPA Government in the CMP of 2004 did acknowledge the 'historical injustice' but as of now all that seems to be a thing of the past.

Finally, the development in India today seems to be within the framework of elite democracy. Hence, there are inner contradictions in the laws of the land. The development seems to be the monopoly of the privileged sections of the society. Though there is no denying the fact that India is progressing by leaps and bounds in areas of science and technology, it is most of the times the rich and the powerful who control and enjoy them. If only scientific and technological progress in this age of globalization were to be used to reduce discrimination against Adivasis and to alleviate poverty, hunger, and death, there is no hope that the so-called Tribal extremism would cease to exist, because, as Julius Nyrere said, 'Development is not the building up of roads, schools and hospitals. But development is when children go to school, development is when people of the place use the roads, development is when people are able to access the hospital.'

One of the ways in which a new political consciousness can come about for Tribals is to keep asserting their collective identities, collective histories, and cultural manifestations. Engaging in violent protests is certainly not the best way to do it, but it is the way some groups are trying to assert themselves.

The assertion of identity is for full citizenship, democracy and participation in the political life of the state and country. According to some scholars, the present model of development is displacing millions of Tribals is terrorizing them. True development should take care of education, health, human security, food security, and the right to sustainable dignified livelihood. The diversity of the Tribals should be recognized and respected rather than to mainstream them.

The process of development should be monitored and the Government and other agencies involved in the Tribal development should be held accountable. There is also need of joining hands with all those who truly want a holistic development and empowerment of the Tribals in India so that the latter give up their arms to give a better future for their posterity. Let Adivasis have self-rule according to their own genius, to decide their development and ultimately their own destiny.

REFERENCES

Banerjee, Mangobinda (1993), *An Historical Outline of the Pre-British Chotanagpur* [*From Earliest Times to 1765*], Educational Publications, Ranchi.

Citizens Forum for Tribal Identity (CIFTY) Delhi, a forum for more than 50 Regional and National Organizations, Indian Social Institute, New Delhi, 2010.

Dubey, S.M. (1982), 'Inter-Ethnic Alliance, Tribal Movements and Integration in North-eastern India', in K.S. Singh (ed.), *Tribal Movements in India*, Vol. 1, Manohar Publications, New Delhi.

Expert Group (2008), *Development Challenges in Extremist Affected* Areas. Report of an Expert Group to Planning Commission, Government of India, New Delhi.

http://www.kyphilom.com/www/seattle.html, Chief Seattle's Thought.

http://www.lectlaw.com/def/l063.htm 'Land' in The 1995–2010 'Lectric Law Library retrieved, 18 October 2010.

http://www.thefreedictionary.com/Land retrieved, 18 October 2010.

Jharkhand Pancyayati Raj Adhiniyam (JPRA), 2001.

Kujur, Joseph Marianus (2008), 'Human Misery and Tribal Development: Process of Globalization and the State's Response', in Sebasti L. Raj et al (eds.), *Eradicating Human Misery*, XID Publications, Jabalpur.

Land Desk - Legal Affairs Team, Ranchi, Jharkhand, August 2010.

Lourdswamy, Stan. *Report of the Independent People's Tribunal on Operation Green Hunt in Jharkhand*, held in Ranchi on 25 and 26 September 2010, organized by Jharkhand Alternative Development Forum (on behalf of Operation Green Hunt Virodhi Nagrik Manch, Ranchi, Jharkhand).

Minz, Nirmal (2007), 'The Adivasi Perspectives on Ecology', in *Pearls of Indigenous Wisdom: Selected Essays from Lifetime Contribution by Bishop Dr. Nirmal Minz, an Adivasi Intellectual*, ISI & CISRS, New Delhi.

Roy, Pandey R.N. (1996 & 2002), *Manual of Chota Nagpur Tenancy Laws*, Vol. 2, Rajpal and Company, Allahabad.

Sachchidanand (1990), 'Foreword' in S.P. Sinha, *Tribal Leadership in Bihar*, The Bihar Tribal Welfare Research Institute, Morabadi, Ranchi.

Sinha, S.P. (1990), 'Tribal Leadership in Bihar: Genesis and Development', in S.P. Sinha (ed.) *Tribal Leadership in Bihar*, The Bihar Tribal Welfare Research Institute for the Government of Bihar, Welfare Department, Ranchi, pp. 71–187.

Sinha, Satish Kumar (2003), *Chotanagpur Tenancy Act, 1908.* Malhotra Bros., Patna.

Tirkey, Mahli Livins (2002), 'Life Sketch of Shri Ignace Beck, M.P," in Ignace Beck, *Political Awakening of Tribals in Jharkhand*, Sinagi Dei Publications, New Delhi.

Verma, R.C. (2002), *Tribes Through the Ages*, Publications Division, Ministry of Information and Broadcasting, Government of India, New Delhi.

NOTES

1. This section is adapted from the report of the Operation Green Hunt Virodhi Nagrik Manch for the Jharkhand Alternative Development Forum (see Lourdswamy 2010).
2. This word is intentionally used to bring out the Tribal pronunciation and meaning of the word. The second syllable in Jhaadakhand is not 'r' as in road, reach, neither is it 'd' as in doctor or read. It is the third sound as it is in the Hindi word 'Pahadi', meaning hillock or in 'Padaav' meaning halt. This letter in Devanagri alphabet is the last but one letter which the Aryan languages try to avoid as much as possible because it is a harsh sound, whereas in Tribal languages

it is considered to be a sonorous sound; only with this word in the letter Jhaadakand the real meaning of the word comes out, 'region covered with forests' not with 'Jharkhand'.

3. After the establishment of the zamindari, the aborigines who continued to hold and cultivate, either with their own hands or through the field labourers employed, were called raiyats by the zamindars, and their lands were known as *raiyati* land.
4. Information received from an interview of J. Toppo, an Oraon Tribal from Jharkhand.
5. The burial ground of the Mundas is known as *sasandiri*s and that of the Oraons as *masna*s.
6. A place of worship for Tribals amidst the sal groves, also known as the sacred grove.

15

Adivasi Awakening and Emergence of New Politics*

Manoranjan Mohanty

S.R. Sankaran was deeply concerned with the problems of land alienation and economic and political exploitation suffered by the Adivasis of India by the state, moneylenders and commercial interests. This note is a tribute to his memory.

The rising trend of adivasi awakening is a defining characteristic of contemporary India. There is an unprecedented scale of assertion of not only the right to livelihood, but also right to dignity and the right to selfhood among the Adivasis of India. The political upsurge in Tribal India in defence of right to land and forest reflects this new awakening which is a positive sign of democratic transformation of modern India.

Yet, it is an irony that much of the intellectual and policy discourse including the media does not treat it as a positive phenomenon. Instead of making that the fundamental premise in discussing the subject, the adivasi awakening is seen as a disruption of a rising India's growth story. Indeed the adivasi movements have resisted the corporate plunder of India's natural resources and are the bulwark of people's defence against capitalist globalization.

It should be pointed out that the new political condition of adivasi awakening challenges the governance paradigm of the state that seeks to reduce the issue to one of violent challenge to state authority. It also contests the patronizing approach of the dominant sections of the civil society advocating empathy and welfare of the Tribal people. At the same time, this new trend of Tribal consciousness exposes the mobilization perspective of the major political parties who only try to build vote banks in the Tribal areas. This awakening also raises new questions about the longstanding anthropological preoccupation of much of the academia with the 'uniqueness of the Tribes', which forms the basis of many social policies.

---

* An earlier version of this paper was presented as the keynote at the national seminar on Violence and Adivasi Struggle for Livelihood organised by Vidyajyoti and Indian Social Institute, New Delhi on 18–19 February 2011.

The new awakening is the cumulative outcome of many historical processes and centuries of struggle against colonial domination. It is not the result of the naxalite movement alone. In fact, Maoist politics has been reoriented to respond to this new awakening in the adivasi areas and in the process has undergone transformation and achieved much support amongst Adivasis. I will like to argue that the new level of political consciousness in the adivasi areas demands a reconsideration of all previous formulations. It shows the emergence of a new politics that ends the era of treating adivasis as objects of welfare and assimilation and begins an era of adivasis as subjects and agency of self-determination heralding comprehensive emancipation of all oppressed people. An acknowledgement of this new phenomenon will lead to a serious indictment of prevailing state policy despite measures such as the Forest Rights Act. It also calls for the adoption of a fresh outlook on the part of the civil society and the academia on politics and development.

Questioning the Perspectives of the State, Civil Society and Academia

The present political awakening of Adivasis reconnects their history with the adivasi revolts against colonial onslaught s in the nineteenth century when the colonial state sought to penetrate Tribal areas in search of timber and minerals and established control over those territories. During the first half of the twentieth century numerous uprisings took place against the British as well as feudal autocracies. But after Independence and integration of the princely states, while most of the colonial laws continued to operate, the Tribal areas were governed under the constitutional framework of cultural protection and economic welfare. It had the clear objective of slow assimilation of the Adivasis into 'mainstream' society. Nehru's Panshasheel on adivasis welfare, the reservation of seats for Scheduled Tribes (STs) in legislatures and civil service and even the Tribal sub-plan providing for special allocation of funds in every department of government were part of this overall strategy. The vantage point for state policy was thus one of governance and welfare. This policy envisaged administering Tribal areas through state apparatus and planned development and promoting welfare activities such as education, health and building of infrastructure for economic development. This flowed from the constitutional stipulation providing special protection in the Fifth Schedule and other measures. While these welfare measures were being implemented, the exploitation of forest and mining resources by indigenous and foreign capital persisted. As the years went by, the state strategy failed to cope with the aspirations of the Tribal people who remained poor and marginalized.

The vantage point for the dominant civil society was inherited from the colonial state to treat the adivasis as the poor brethren deserving special support. The Hindu Brahmanic culture was projected as the 'automatic process' of acculturation in the history of the adivasis just as the western education was promoted as the common goal for all Indians. European colonialism had colonised the non-Western world for what it considered as its 'civilizing mission'. In the same vein, the non-Tribal upper class, upper caste elite of India considered it their duty for 'civilizing' the 'uncivilized' Adivasis. The dominant discourse is still permeated by terms like 'primitive Tribes', 'criminal Tribes' and the like. Even many of the most pro-Adivasi social workers, civil servants and intellectuals carry patronising attitudes, though with the best of intentions, to promote welfare of the adivasis. But the days of such patronage seem to be over. We are in a different era now, the era of people's rights.

Congress and the other major political parties operate within a framework that combines the state perspective of governance and welfare, and the civil society approach to patronise. The electoral system requires reservation of seats for ST a specified number of constituencies (6.5 per cent reservation in central institutions though the ST population in 2001 census was 8.2 per cent) in Parliament and proportionate number in State legislatures and panchayats according to the ST population in the area. It should be recognized that this process of reservation-based electoral politics has brought up from the grassroots level upwards two generations of adivasi politicians in India. The reservation for ST in civil services has also produced large number of adivasi officers, though many posts remain unfilled despite the monitoring by the judiciary and the National Commission on Scheduled Tribes. But even after 60 years of electoral politics none of the major political parties has allowed the emergence of a significant Tribal political leadership capable of influencing national level policy making. The adivasi leaders remain protégés of upper-caste or middle-caste leaders in the various States. After the late Jharkhand movement leader Jaipal Singh, there has not been an adivasi leader of national repute. Shibu Soren could have filled that void but for the pressures of coalition politics which severely damaged his reputation. Thus the party system has failed the Adivasis in making their voice critical in national policy-making.

Anthropologists and other social scientists, some working within government and many in the academia, generally recognized the dignity of the Adivasis and their customs while engaging in in-depth analysis of the uniqueness of various Tribal groups. While some of the colonial scholars assessed the Tribal practices against European civilization norms, a few others discovered the logic and reason behind many Tribal practices. In the post-Independence period some scholars put forward evidence to appreciate the rational practices of the Tribal communities in spheres of economy, politics and culture. Still a minority, they engaged in deeper understanding of the knowledge systems, production practices, political traditions and environmental philosophy of Adivasis and argued the case for taking them seriously and with respect, as alternative systems in the human civilization. They championed the cause of the Adivasis in public discourse as well as government forums often with great sincerity and determination. However, all their strenuous efforts ended up as inputs into the dominant policy making of the state. Their work, valuable as it certainly was, failed to persuade civil society to re-examine its patronizing attitude or the state to go beyond its welfare and assimilation strategy.

The operative consequences of these approaches did include many laudable initiatives in independent India. For example, alienation of Tribal land to non-Tribals was forbidden by law in practically all the States. But in practice, massive land transfers took place circumventing the law. The Panchayat sytem under the 73rd amendment of the Constitution was extended under PESA Act 1996, but its very important provisions were hardly implemented or were invariably manipulated to suit the state or the corporate interest. Not a single state has notified rules under the PESA Act so far. The Forest rights Act, 2006 was another major step to restore rights to land and forest to the Tribals and other forest dwellers, but its implementation has been extremely tardy. The education and health polcies did make special provisions for the Adivasis, which did have some positive consequences. But the basic social indicators show vast disparity between Adivasis and Dalits on the one hand and the rest of the society on the other, the former with distressing levels of living conditions. Thus on the whole, as a result of these approaches and policies, Adivasis remained the victims of cumulative deprivation in contemporary India.

Globalization's Aggression on Adivasis

In the early 1990s, the onset of neo-liberal policies of globalization, liberalization and privatization brought in a new wave of aggression on the Adivasis. The old colonial logic was back-arguing that capital and technology should be allowed to go freely wherever raw materials were located. On that basis European colonialism had occupied most of Asia, Africa and Latin America (ASAFLA). Indian rulers now adopted an economic growth strategy, inviting foreign capital and encouraging major Indian business houses to enter the forest areas, engage in mining and set up mineral-based industries. This put the mineral-rich states of central and eastern India, especially Chhatisgarh, Jharkhand and Odisha in the centre of attention for major investment firms. A number of proposals for steel and alumina plants came up in these states which are rich in iron ore, bauxite and coal as well as other precious metals. Steel plants by Tata were to come up in Lohandiguda in Chhattisgarh, Kalinganagar in Odisha. The Korean company POSCO signed an MOU with Odisha government to build a steel plant in Jagatsinghpur and mine iron ore in Khandadhar. Aluminium Plants by many foreign based companies were to be set up in the Tribal areas of central India; for example, by Utkal Alumina in Kashipur and Vedanta in

Lanjigarh. These are only a few illustrations of a vast number of mineral-based industries being located in adivasi areas.

This is when Adivasis woke up once again to strongly protest against the location of such projects in their land. Already, they had suffered enough due to displacement caused by dams, mining and heavy industries since Independence. According to one estimate, 80 per cent of the 60 million displaced by projects in the first 50 years since Independence were Adivasis. In each of these project areas people's movements came up challenging the rationale for these projects. The movements pointed out that the projects caused displacement, took away the sources of livelihood, destroyed the natural environment, and created cultural alienation. It should be stressed that all the movements–Kashipur, Lanjigarh, Kalinganage, Jagatsinghpur (POSCO) were peaceful democratic struggles by local people. Even though they started as protest movements against specific projects, they grew into movements raising fundamental issues of the development strategy, of the consequences of globalization for the marginalized sections of society and the larger human rights issue of self-determination. A new right thus appeared on the scene, the right to earth.

Adivasi Swaraj and the Right to Earth

The people's movements in the adivasi areas affirmed the right of the adivasis and all local inhabitants to exercise control over their land and other natural and cultural resources of their area and share it with others only on mutually agreed terms. This can be called the 'right to earth'. The entire philosophy underlying the anti-colonial struggle was indeed this. Extending Mahatma Gandhi's concept of swaraj, one can suggest that this is the right which can fulfil the urges of self-realisation of the people in an area, and Adivasis included.

It is a recognition of this right that led to the provision in the PESA that without the consultation with—it should mean the consent of—the Gram Sabha, no land can be acquired in a village in a scheduled area for any industrial purpose. But as we have seen in practice this provision exists only in violation. There are many examples in Kashipur where Gram Sabha consent has been obtained by government officials with police presence in the meetings. In Jagatsinghpur, two Gram Sabhas have clearly decreed against the POSCO project. Yet, the government succeeded in meeting the formal requirements by manipulating the process and was determined to go ahead with the project. The POSCO Pratirodh Sangram Samiti, however, persisted with its strong mobilisation of local people to resist acquisition of their land.

Right to earth is not only a narrow defense of local right to land, but is a defining right to evolve a mode of transformation and manage it according to the interests of the local people. No doubt, the local community has to be transformed at the same time so that the hierarchical structure of the village did not perpetuate existing inequalities. This is where swaraj has to go together with mutual development which is embodied in the concept of Ubuntu which in Zulu language of South Africa means 'I am because you are' and 'I can develop only if you can develop.'

The ongoing discourse on a new Land Acquisition Act and a new Rehabilitation Policy in India has clearly shown that the state and the corporate interests still do not read the writing on the wall. They do not take cognizance of the right to earth of the Adivasis and other local inhabitants. Hence the confrontation is likely to escalate.

Adivasi Awakening and Maoist Politics: Naxalbari to Narayanpatna

In the first decade of the Maoist movement in India, in Naxalbai and more so in Srkakulam two issues had come to the fore, land to the tiller and exploitation of the Adivasis. These two issues, namely land rights and multidimensional oppression, are most conspicuous in the case of the Adivasis. But more importantly, they are symptomatic of the general situation in the country. Initially during the 1970's, the Indian state took a few measures in response to these demands by treating the Naxalite challenge as essentially involving issues of agrarian structure. This policy changed in the 1980s when a new approach emerged in state policy that put it as both a law and order challenge as well as a socioeconomic problem. The era of killings in false encounters thus began. This policy continued with varying degrees of field application in different States. By the mid-2000s when globalization reached a new momentum and mega industry projects came up, a new perspective was announced. Prime Minister Manmohan Singh's statement in 2005 that naxalite threat posed the greatest challenge to India's internal security opened a new chapter on the Indian state policy towards the Maoist movement. It gave priority to liquidating the naxalites on the gound. Operation Green Hunt launched in 2009 represented this new phase of state policy on the naxalites.

During the first term of UPA, a Planning Commission Expert Group led by D. Bandyopadhyay had recommended a host of socioeconomic measures by treating the Naxalite problem essentially as a development challenge needing a political response. That perspective was relegated to the background and a fullscale militaristic offensive was on against the Maoists. As Home Minister Chidambaram put it, civil authority had to be re-established before development activity can be launched in an area. There were some initiatives such as the Integrated Action Plan in 60 Naxalite affected districts out of the 160 affected districts in 13 States of India allocating Rs 30 crores a year for each district. These were seen by the Adivasis as bureaucracy-led programmes to mainly facilitate armed operations against their movements. The new anti-Naxalite package consisted of three elements: one, the Operation Green Hunt using massive paramilitary force and giving arms and training civilians for anti-naxalite operations such as Salwa Judum in Chhattishgarh and Special Police Officers in all the affected districts; two, enacting and enforcing extraordinary laws such as UAPA, AFSPA and giving enormous powers to security forces; and three, showcasing some developmental measures. Paramilitary forces are engaged in what they call 'area domination operations' in the affected areas. These operations have been documented in detail. It involved arresting Tribals in large numbers as Maoist sympathisers, killing them if challenged, burning pro-Maoist villages, harassing and raping women, and so on. This package has failed to check the growth of the Maoist movement among the Adivasis. In fact they have extended their support base to new areas in central and eastern India. The policy of arming civilians to fight the Maoists through formations like Salwa Judum has been a clear failure and it has only increased the violent confrontation in the region. The judgement of the Supreme Court on 5 July declaring the arming of Tribal youth as SPOs, Koya Commandos, Salwa Judum, and the like as illegal and unconstitutional has discredited this tactic of the state even further. The policy package of the Indian State has failed to win over the Adivasis into the state system. That is because this did not address the basic issues underlying adivasi awakening.

This was once again demonstrated in the case of the kidnapping of Vineel Krishna, the Collector of Malkangiri in Odisha in March. The agreement worked out by the mediators, which secured the release of Krishna, stipulated the release of political prisoners (especially the Adivasis of Narayanpatna) and implementation of some development plans in the remote cut-off areas of Malkangiri. On both the fronts, the state failed to act and the violent operations by the paramilitary forces as well as the Maoists resumed in July.

The state policy also aimed at silencing civil liberty voices who challenged the coercive approach of the state and persisted in demanding comprehensive responses to the root causes of the Maoist movement. The arrest and prosecution of Binayak Sen in Chhattishgarh is the single most blatant illustration of this approach. But for the widespread protest in India and abroad and the Supreme Court intervention Binayak Sen would have languished in prison like hundreds of other activists. He is out on bail from the Supreme Court while the appeal against his life imprisonment verdict continues in court.

The naxalite movement provided substantial support to the process of adivasi awakening at a time when state policy instead of responding to their political urges, had facilitated their further exploitation through mega projects. However, Adivasis' awakening has a distinct history of its own and is wider and deeper than the Maoist movement in many ways. Their movements against exploitation by the moneylenders, against land alienation, against big dams and recently against mega industrial projects started as autonomous movements and not by the Maoists. In some of these cases when peaceful struggles were suppressed by the state, the alienated youth joined the Maoist ranks to carry on the struggle. The Narayanpatna land struggle is a clear case of this where Nachika Linga, a naib Sarpanch at one time, after failing through the panchayats to recover illegally transferred Tribal land, led a people's march to occupy the land in June 2009. His organization, Chashi Mulia Adivasi Sangh had given notice to the government giving details of the illegally alienated Tribal land.Initially the State government was considering to examine the land alienation cases. But Operation Green Hunt reached Narayanpatna in October 2009 and decided to treat it as a Maoist venture. It launched a massive operation to suppress it . The movement is still going on with a section having joined the Maoists while another section still carrying on the peaceful struggle.

The fact that the Maoist movement expanded its ideological scope to include the displacement issues showed, first of all, how Naxalites had adjusted their strategy in the light of local conditions. Second, adivasi awakening challenged the development paradigm in totality, not only its capitalist class character. That the process of change has to be decided by the local Adivasis, in conformity with their sociopolitical goals, environmental philosophy, and local culture is far broader than the industrial revolution paradigm which many Marxists still share. Third, the totality of the adivasi struggle tradition may include armed struggle, but does not ignore the vast areas of open democratic political, economic, social, and cultural struggle. They inherit great civilizational legacies of adivasi civilization, the positive elements of which they must preserve and develop. The knowledge systems of Adivasis deserve as much respect as any other knowledge system. Fourthly, the perspective on the relationship between humans and Nature, which gives rise to a host of environmental questions is yet another dimension of adivasi awakening. Fifthly, that there are local systems of religious beliefs other than the major religions of the world is emerging as yet another phenomenon in recent times. Many Adivasis are listing themselves as members of their local religious community, rather than the recognized major religions, though the Census enumerated them under 'others'. Thus, adivasi swaraj raises a number of issues which are equally significant for democratic transformation of Indian society as a whole. The Maoist movement and all other political movements can enrich themselves by fully integrating themselves with this process of adivasi awakening and participate in the new politics of people's democratic revolution in the twenty-first century.

The State, civil society and academia can find liberative possibilities if they recognize the full magnitude of the evolving process of adivasi awakening, which is much more than merely a violent challenge to authority.

16

Bleeding Manipur: Repeal the Armed Forces (Special Powers) Act, 1958

K.S. Subramanian

Historical Background

The following historical account of the situation in Manipur is based on the inputs of a Fact-finding Team which visited Manipur in November, 2009. The present writer was a member of the team.

Manipur was an independent kingdom before the British took over the state in 1891. Manipuris are ethnically and culturally distinct from the people of mainland India and are more akin to the peoples in South East Asia. The British conquest of Manipur in 1891 was preceded by stiff resistance. The first Kuki armed resistance against the colonial power broke out in 1917. In1939, a spontaneous resistance by women called the 'Second Women's War' or 'Nupilal' was organised against exploitative trade practices by the Marwari traders in the export of rice to Myanmar. The traders enjoyed the support of the corrupt feudal elite and the king.

Manipur regained independence from the British in August 1947. A constitutional monarchy was established under the Manipur State Constitution Act, 1947 and elections on the basis of universal adult franchise took place in 1948 and an elected state assembly was in place. The Maharaja, however, was forced to sign a controversial Manipur Merger Agreement with India. The elected legislative assembly was dissolved and the council of ministers disbanded followed by direct rule from Delhi. Manipur was made a union territory in 1963 and became an Indian state in 1972.

A fertile alluvial valley extends from north to south in the middle of Manipur, which is surrounded on all sides by hill ranges forming a part of the eastern Himalayas. Though it constitutes only about 12 per cent of the total geographical area, the Valley is populated by more than 75 per cent of the total population of less than 3 million.

Among the Manipuris, the Meiteis form the largest ethnic group traditionally inhabiting the fertile Valley region. The surrounding hill ranges are occupied by many Hill Tribes, mainly the Nagas and the Kukis with many subgroups within each Tribe. While the Meiteis thrive on wet cultivation, the Tribal population subsists largely on the slash-and-burn cultivation and relies heavily on the valley for basic needs.

An underground movement for independence began in 1964 with the founding of the United National Liberation Front (UNLF). Other militant outfits followed in the late-1970s: primarily, the Revolutionary Peoples' Front and its armed wing People's Liberation Army (PLA), 1978; People's Revolutionary Party of Kangleipak (PREPAK), 1977; 'Kangleipak' (original name of the state) Communist Party (KCP), 1980; and the Kanglei Yaol Kanna Lup (KYKL), 1994. In the Hills, there are Naga underground militant outfits: National Socialist Council of Nagaland (Isak-Muivah): National Socialist Council of Nagaland (Khaplang); and Kuki outfits such as the Kuki National Organization and its armed wing Kuki National Army (KNA); Kuki National Front (KNF); Kuki Revolutionary Army (KRA); Kuki Liberation Organization and its armed wing the Kuki Liberation Army (KLA) and others.

The tremors of the movement for independence in the neighbouring Nagaland spread to the Naga-inhabited districts of Senapati and Ukhrul in Manipur. As the state forces failed to contain the movement, the Army was called in. To facilitate Army operations, a legal framework was introduced in the shape of the Armed Forces (Special Powers) Act, 1958. The Act is a direct descendant of the Armed Forces Special Powers Ordinance 1942 used by the British during the Second World War to suppress the Indian freedom struggle. The present Act is more draconian but applicable only in distinct geographical regions declared 'disturbed areas' under the Act. With modifications, the 1958 Act was harsher than its predecessor Ordinance of 1942. Initially, parts of Manipur were declared 'disturbed areas'. In 1980, the whole state was declared a 'disturbed area' under the Act of 1958.

An international human rights agency in 2008 documented the failure of justice in Manipur under the AFSPA. The agency noted that, 'Security forces are bypassing the law and killing people on suspicion that they are militants instead of bringing them before a judge. In the name of national security and Armed Forces morale, the state protects abusers and leaves Manipuris with no remedy to secure justice.'

AFSPF 1958 and Its Consequences

The armed conflict between the Indian state and non-state actors in Manipur has been a long-standing affair. The Indian state tends to view the conflict as 'internal disturbances', which justified the large-scale deployment of armed forces and central paramilitary police forces and the imposition of the Armed Forces (Special Powers) Act 1958.

The AFSPA has been in force in Manipur since September 1980. However, following the fake encounter killing of Thangjam Manorama in July 2004, some municipal areas of Imphal had been freed from the operation of the Act. The place of occurrence of the incidents on 23 July 2009 was excluded from the operation of the Act. Further, Manipur Police Commandos are not protected under the provisions of the AFSPA.

The Act provides wide powers to the Armed Forces of the Indian Union, including the power to shoot on suspicion in an area declared as a 'disturbed area' under its provisions. No legal action can be initiated against the Armed Forces for misusing the law without the prior approval of the Government of India.

Many of the militant groups have factions difficult to distinguish from one another. Their brand of revolution based on extortion, kidnapping for ransom, kangaroo courts and summary executions, bomb blasts and terror tactics had led to increasing discontent among the general public directed at non-state actors.

The previously vocal civil society organizations were immobilised by the state government with charges of siding with the banned organizations. This situation gave unofficial sanction for elimination of any suspect and a killing spree by the police. In 2008 alone, the state witnessed the killing of more than 285 'suspects' by the security forces. Many of these cases remained unexplained. Families of victims or eyewitnesses said that the deceased 'suspects' were first arrested, then taken to another place and then brutally murdered. Thus, domestic laws and international human rights standards were routinely flouted by state agencies. Respect for the law on conflict and the basic tenets of international humanitarian law were ignored by both state agencies and non-state ones.

With the prolonged imposition of the Act, the cycle of violence has spread geographically and in intensity. Enforced disappearances, arbitrary executions, torture, rape, housebreak, loot, arbitrary detention et cetera have become everyday features of life in Manipur. And yet, few perpetrators of these gross violations of human rights were ever prosecuted. Thus, the Armed Forces enjoy complete impunity and immunity under the Act.

With the continuation of the AFSPA 1958, the cycle of violence has grown in geographical spread and in intensity. Contrived disappearances, arbitrary executions, torture, rape and molestation, housebreaking, looting, arbitrary detention etc have become a part of everyday life in Manipur. And yet, few violators of human rights are brought to justice. For all practical purposes, the Armed Forces enjoy complete immunity under the Act.

Though the operation of the Act was eventually withdrawn from the Imphal municipal area, the state police commandos operating along with paramilitary forces have continued killing suspects by taking advantage of the immunity provided to the Central Armed Forces.

Focusing only on the so-called 'encounters' between state forces and suspected and banned underground militant groups in 2008, the emerging pattern is one of escalation in the number of questionable killings in the state. Some distinctive features in the so-called police encounters killingsare: isolated locations; absence of casualties on the part of security forces; recovery of 9 mm pistol or hand grenades in most cases; combination of force from the police commandos units and central security forces including AR; the slain victim being taken away from home and killed at another place; theft of money, mobile phones and other valuables from the victims; and so on.

In all these cases, the police or security forces do not suffer any casualties. In most of them, security forces claim resorting to retaliatory firing and in some cases, even claim recovery of empty cases or fired cartridges. Even if claims are made by bereaved families that the victims were innocent, recoveries of the weapons are made. Such weapons are always carried by the security forces so as to plant them on victims when needed.

In most of these cases, the local 'meira paibis' ('women torch bearers') and villagers in the vicinity of the place of occurrence said that either the victims were brought there and killed or were already dead and dumped there after firing some shots in the air. There are many instances of protest by the local inhabitants against bringing and shooting of detainees at such spots. There are even instances of confrontation between the local 'meira paibis' and the security forces over bringing and shooting detainees at such locations.

The case studies in 2008 show that the security forces involved in many cases are combined teams of the Manipur Police Commandos and either Army or paramilitary forces such as the Assam Rifles set up by the British in 1835. After independence in 1947, the colonial Assam Rifles has become a historical anomaly. It is redundant since considerable state police forces were established in the period after 1972 when they were set up as an independent state government of the Indian Union.

Under the AFSPA, the Central Armed Forces and paramilitary units are immune from penalty for their acts. However, this sense of not having to answer for their actions has percolated down to the state forces as well to such an extent that the Manipur Police Commandos freely kill people on their own without fearing consequences. Such impunity has filtered down to the state security forces and created a new state-sponsored terrorist group in the form of the Police Commandos. Instituted for the purpose of containing insurgency in the state, the Manipur Police Commandos have digressed from their original purpose to embark on a path of seeking to fulfil personal agendas.

A former advisor to the Governor of Manipur states: 'In Manipur, civil policemen and officers were selected and trained as commandos. Although they did a good job initially, they soon deteriorated into a state terrorist force due to faulty leadership. They started extorting money from the business community, picking a leaf out of the insurgents' book. What were the consequences for the hapless public? Here were five to six underground groups extorting money from the traders and here was a special wing of the police force, set up to arrest the underground, who also demanded their share of the extortion pool'.

A number of case studies have revealed the Manipur Police Commandos acting independently and carrying out 'encounters' without the assistance of the Army or paramilitary forces. The state government remains a mute spectator to such killings and the usual protests and agitations which follow. Thus, the state security forces also enjoy the same immunity as the Armed Forces.

Indeed, the number of killings of 'suspects' by the police are even considered achievements and the perpetrators are rewarded with cash incentives, medals and gallantry awards by the state government which ultimately serves as stepping stones to promotion. The audacity of the state government in doling out such incentives and awards to the very perpetrators of such atrocities fuels the security forces further to indulge in even more blatant killings. These are nothing but instances of state terrorism.

Another issue of importance is the recovery of large sums of money from the person of the victim. Family members often say that the victim left home with a substantial sum of money, which is not reflected in the recovery memos of the police. Recoveries of incriminating pistols and grenades are almost always made in the aftermath of alleged encounters but recoveries of sums of money are seldom recorded. Genuine concerns thus arise as to whether the financial aspect played a vital role in the killing of the victims concerned. The situation has come to such a pass that the people of the state feel extremely insecure in carrying large amounts of cash on their persons, even for personal or business purposes.

The recruitment of personnel for the Manipur Police department is a big issue. A large number of police personnel are recruited frequently. The recruitment processes are conducted with a semblance of transparency but always reek of large scale corruption. Once the initial hurdle of selection and appointment has been overcome by a candidate, the clamour for the coveted place of posting in the state commando units begins, as these units offer useful avenues for making money by various methods including 'encounter' killings of suspected militants, which can earn the commando recognition and rewards, cash incentives, medals and gallantry awards. In other words, gaining recognition for 'devotion and dedication' to duty is more expeditious for the commando unit than the ordinary police force. As a result, a paradigm shift has occurred in the mode of operation of the police commando units contrary to the purpose for which they are set up. The police commandos are more concerned with the achievement of their personal agendas than with the main objective of maintaining public order and security of the state, thereby straying from their primary objectives.

Another disturbing trend, especially among the Tribal population in the Hill areas, is the appeasement measure usually undertaken by the security forces to subdue the hue and cry following the extra-judicial killing of an individual by resorting to the prevailing local custom of *mankad.* According to this local custom, whenever someone violates the custom and tradition of a particular Tribal community, 'mankad' allows the 'wrong' to be 'righted' by offering an elaborate feast to the members of the offended village by the offending party along with a negotiated sum of money proffered as compensation.

The security forces, especially the Army authorities, have learnt to take advantage of this local custom by offering *mankad* to the offended community whenever an extra-judicial killing is perpetrated by them after which the lips of the community are permanently sealed. In this way, any semblance of protest against such atrocities is silenced. Over and above the rampant instances of extrajudicial killings in the state, cases of arbitrary detention and torture are routine.

In almost all these cases of detention, denial seems to be the key word of the security forces. The claims of the victims are silenced with fear of reprisals or they are left persisting with their own versions and any protests or agitations are left unattended by the authorities concerned to be forgotten in the course of time.

The armed militants indulge in a 'revolution' based on extortion, kidnapping for ransom, kangaroo courts and summary executions, bomb blasts and terror tactics, opposed by the general public. The vocal sections of civil society are silenced with charges of alignment with banned organizations. Unofficial sanction is provided to elimination of suspects. In 2008 alone, the state witnessed more than 285 cases of extrajudicial killings by the security forces. Families of victims or eyewitnesses say that the deceased 'suspects' were first arrested, then taken to another place and brutally murdered.

Fact-Finding Commissions/Bodies

Numerous fact-finding commissions/bodies have been instituted to inquire into the controversial incidents attributable to the misuse of the provisions of AFSPA 1958. Some of them are as follows:

(a) Justice Jeevan Reddy Committee Year 2004

(b) Fact-finding Team of Civil and Human Rights Activists — January 2009
(c) Independent People's Tribunal of three high court judges and other organised by the Human Rights Law Network — Year 2009
(d) Justice Santosh Hegde Commission to probe extra judicial killings in Manipur — January 2013

The findings of the above bodies have not been fully revealed to the public nor have the errant officials been punished. These findings are eventually shelved.

Justice Jeevan Reddy Committee

Constituted in November 2004, the Committee opined that the AFSPA 1958 was, 'a symbol of oppression, instrument of high-handedness...' The Committee recommended that the Act be repealed. (After nearly ten years, the Ministry of Home Affairs (MHA) decided to reject the recommendation in February, 2015).

Fact-finding Team

The political situation in Manipur became explosive following a fake gun battle and extra-judicial killings by the Manipur Police Commandos of two innocents—the pregnant Rabina Devi (23) and the young ex-militant Sanjit Meitei (25)—on 23 July 2009 at the crowded Khwairamband market area in Imphal.

A fact-finding team of civil and human rights activists, including as stated earlier the present writer, visited the state from 5-10 November 2009 and assessed the human rights violations in the state. The team met a group of concerned senior citizens who blamed the Central Government for its inaction. They identified two major conflicts, which have persisted in the state ever since its merger with India in October, 1949: a 'vertical' conflict with the Government of India and a 'horizontal' conflict with the Naga people in the borderlands of the state who are seeking integration of Nagaland with the proposed 'Greater Nagaland' or 'Nagalim'. The vertical conflict arose from the deceitful methods of the Indian government in forcibly integrating the independent state of Manipur with India in 1949. This episode still rankles with sections of Manipuris who resorted to armed militant action for independence. This conflict can only be resolved by sustained tripartite negotiations between the Centre, the armed militants, and elders who have no political affiliations but speak for the people.

The horizontal conflict arising from the demand for the partition of the state by a section of the Nagas in the state can be resolved by the Centre by suitably amending Article 3 of the Constitution of India to guarantee the geographical integrity of the small-sized state of Manipur. The senior citizens identified rampant corruption and nepotism on the part of the state's ruling elites as a major problem which needs urgent attention.

Desperate to deal with the public unrest, the authorities in Manipur called for the resumption of classes in educational institutions boycotted by angry people concerned over the violence. But this required prior negotiations between the people and the government, which could not be held in the absence of the government's response to the demands of the people. If the impasse remained, the Central Government would need to intervene. Members of the public met by the fact-finding team felt that the Centre should intervene to bring peace by imposing President's Rule in the state.

The fact-finding team met and interacted with the families of those killed in the July 2009 fake encounters by the state police commandos. Harrowing and tearful tales of human rights violations were narrated. Women, whose husbands/sole breadwinners were killed, narrated their woes in the absence of their husbands whose earnings were the only support of their starving families. They demanded justice as well as income-earning opportunities to support themselves and their children. The women also demanded the resignation of the Chief Minister on moral grounds and the dismissal of the state's Director General of Police (DGP) for gross dereliction of duty in allowing fake encounters by his subordinates.

At a meeting with the Chief Minister and the state DGP, the team was told that it would not be possible for the government to provide employment opportunities to the families of all those killed since the numbers were large. The demand for the resignation of the Chief Minister and the dismissal of the state DGP were also not accepted.

The DGP informed the visiting team that about 260 people had been executed by the police since January 2006 as they were 'underground militants/activists'. When the team expressed concern over the detention of the human rights activist Jiten Yumnam, the DGP justified it by stating that he was found to have connections with the 'underground militants'. The Chief Minister stated that he was ready to have a second round of discussions with those agitating over the violent incidents, though several of their demands could not be met. He added that the repeal of the AFSPA was a matter for the Central Government. The team called for the transparent investigation of all cases registered under the National Security Act (NSA) and other laws. They declared that cases of extra-judicial executions should be transparently investigated and the guilty punished. The team learnt that about 150 persons were held in the state prison as detainees under the NSA. The team interacted with some of the former detainees.

The team met the heroic Irom Sharmila Chanu, then in the tenth year of her fast, demanding repeal of the Armed Forces Special Powers Act, 1958. It called upon the Government to provide similar access to other civil society members and recommended that her family members should be permitted to meet her on a regular basis. Being allowed only a limited number of visitors, she expressed her desire to meet, see, and speak to more people. Her strength and courage in undertaking the longest 'satyagraha' in the world, in a non-violent way was admirable.

Since the distinguished writer Ms Mahashweta Devi had been denied permission to meet her the previous day, Sharmila Chanu handed over to the team a letter addressed to the writer. She further expressed her concern over the number of innocents who were dying every day in Manipur due to the high levels of violence.

In our discussions in Imphal, the team came across repeated allegations against the security forces. The team expressed its deep concern over the deteriorating situation and the prevailing climate of impunity in Manipur. It conveyed its solidarity with the victims of violence and called for adequate recompense to the hapless women and children who had lost their husbands/fathers/sons/sole breadwinners and were denied of employment opportunities.

Many of the killings were 'fake encounters', that is, killings of innocents who perished either in custody or otherwise, but without legal sanction. Each of these cases needed transparent investigation and punishment of the guilty. Further, there were many charges on the use of preventive detention laws to curb citizens' democratic rights to protest and freely express their views. The high degree and frequency of violation of human rights in the state was a cause for alarm. Restoration of peace and order had to go hand in hand with the promotion of the rule of law and justice for the sustenance of democracy.

Official sources revealed following information about the police manpower deployed in the state as of 1 November 2009: i) 10,396 (6 battalions each) Manipur Rifles (MR) and India Reserve Battalions (IRB); 5,056 other civil police units; 10,450 (6 battalions each) Central Armed Police Forces (CRPF and BSF); 10 battalions and 26 battalions respectively of Army/Assam Rifles, which, it was reported, were meant for the entire region; and 2,312 Home Guards.

Data on cases registered and number of persons/cases convicted in the previous two years were:

2008: Number of cases registered: 3,349; Number of convicted persons: 67 persons, in 64 cases.

2009: Number of cases registered (up to 8/11/09): 3,348; Number of cases convicted: 26 persons, in 15 cases.

It was noticed that Manipur, with a population of less than 3 million, had too many military, paramilitary forces (about 60, 000) and too few civilian police forces (about 5000). The basic purpose of policing, namely service delivery to the public, was downgraded at the cost of maintenance of public order; the number of cases registered per year (including normal crime and extraordinary crime) was not large and the rate of conviction was poor. Both these features were disturbing.

The fact finding team traced the sequence of events in the violent incidents in July 2009 as follows:

> On July 23, 2009 forenoon, the Manipur police commandos during frisking operations on the arterial Khwairamband Road held a young man, allegedly with a firearm but he escaped from police custody. While chasing him, the commandos resorted to indiscriminate firing. A stray bullet from an automatic weapon hit and killed the 23-year-old pregnant woman, Rabina. Police commandos were discomfited by this unplanned killing and started looking for a scapegoat for the killing. They located the ex-militant Sanjit who was doing medical shopping for his ailing relative. The commandos caught Sanjit, dragged him to a nearby pharmacy-cum watch-repair shop, shot him dead at point blank range and planted a weapon on him to make it appear that he was responsible for shooting and killing young Rabina. Both the bodies were then placed in a truck and taken away. The police then put out the story that Sanjit, the ex-militant, had killed Rabina. However, the photographs published contemporaneously in the *Tehelka* magazine, New Delhi (Volume 6, Issue No. 31, dated August, 8, 2009), told a different story disproving the police version. The two violent killings by the police commandos and the police explanation were not credible. There was public outrage and demonstrations. At his meeting with the fact-finding team, the state police chief maintained that Sanjit was a hardened militant and that the *Tehelka* magazine photos were fabricated.

Independent People's Tribunal

An Independent People's Tribunal (IPT), organised by the Human Rights Law Network (HRLN), New Delhi met at Imphal in 2009 to take stock of the role of the Manipur Human Rights Commission on violation of human rights in the state arising from the operation of the draconian AFSPA, 1958. The Tribunal consisted of three high court judges, three district and sessions court judges and a member of the Manipur Human Rights Commission (MHRC).

A large number of victims of torture, suffering and inhuman treatment by the army (read Assam Rifles) acting under the AFSPA narrated their experience. The findings were divided into depositions, voices against oppression, observations of the jury, key findings and recommendations, the case of Irom Sharmila Chanu, critique of the Jeevan Reddy Committee Report, 2005 and annexures. Some of the important observations by the jury members are brought out below:

- Manipur is especially unsafe for women. Protective laws do exist but ordinary people are not aware of their provisions. A legal literacy programme, as in Kerala, must be carried out through the Panchayats, schools and colleges both by the NGOs and the government. If the police do not record complaints there is a provision in law for filing private complaints but for this legal assistance is necessary. A group of lawyers must be set up to assist the people.
- The immunity provisions under section 6 of the AFSPA are not applicable in seven assembly constituency areas of Imphal city from which the application of the law was done away with in 2004 after the case of the rape and murder of Thangjam Manorama by the Assam Rifles men (2004). Legal immunity is thus not available to those officers who violate human rights in this area. However, in many cases, the victims were taken away from here and the violations took place in other areas where the Act was in force.
- The MHRC does not have powers to issue any legally binding orders. It can only give recommendations for action which are not binding and can be ignored by those in authority. The powers of the MHRC must be enhanced.
- The Act was operative only in Manipur when it came into existence in 1958. Its operation was extended to the other six states of the North East in 1987 via an amendment. While ex-gratia payments have been made to the families of victims, no action has been taken against the offending security personnel. Without any reason, some boys are taken away and killed. Sometimes women too are killed. Some joint action committees are formed locally who go to the Chief Minister and he makes some ex-gratia payments. He doesn't ensure legal action against those who have committed murder. One lakh rupees is prescribed as the price of an extinguished life!
- The Act mentions only the Armed Forces but not the police who have some responsibilities when a rape or murder takes place. The Guwahati High Court has said that arrest comes first and then the extra-judicial execution. When an arrest is made, the arrested person must be produced before the local police authority. The Supreme Court of India in 1997 has issued detailed guidelines to be followed when making arrests. In 1991, the Guwahati High Court issued orders that the Army is bound to hand over the arrested persons to the local police. In our country there are laws, statutory laws, constitutional laws, and judicial laws which must be obeyed. The Act cannot overrule Supreme Court guidelines.
- There should be a mechanism for periodic review of the law as ordered

by the Supreme Court in 1998 in the case filed by the Naga People's Movement for Human Rights. Manipur is very much part of India and people's sentiments must be respected.

- Simply because there is a provision for arresting somebody, it does not mean that he can be killed. In Manipur, arrest is misused for the purpose of eliminating the arrested person.
- Affected people are not being allowed to file FIRs by various methods and by giving ex-gratia payments by local MLAs, Chief Ministers and others.
- We do not have accounts from military authorities (AR) on the incidents but have reports from others in civil society. Military authorities must be asked to give their versions.
- State police forces often coin the phrase 'combined forces' of Army and civil police to take advantage of the provisions of Section 6 of the Act, which provides immunity to Armed Forces in such cases.
- In cases where FIRs are filed by the police, the police cannot refuse to take FIRs from the public. Now, cross cases can be filed giving different versions from the police versions. The right to life and rule of law will be affected if ex-gratia payments are accepted by the families of victims. In one case, the victim's family refused to accept ex-gratia payment and asked for legal investigation of the case.
- Army men (AR) believe that militants are separatists and can be killed. Ruling political parties believe that they cannot rule without the support of the Army (AR) and AFSPA. This is the failure of politics. In reality, the militants have increased their presence. Once Nagas were called 'hostiles', Mizos 'rebels' and Manipuris 'insurgents'! Now, Manipuris are being called 'extortionists' by the authorities. Cases involving the Army are less now and cases involving the police are more than earlier.

The IPT looked into 40 fake encounter killings and gross violations of human rights and two cases of torture. The jury heard written and oral testimonies. The main points were:

- No notice of the sittings were served on the government authorities or the police; therefore, neither the alleged perpetrators nor the representatives of the government appeared before the Tribunal. In none of the cases were the copies of the FIR provided to the jury. No post-mortem reports were available. In some cases, FIRs had been filed against the victims who were no more. It was a matter of doubt if such reports of FIRs could be treated as legally valid.
- Some of the perpetrators were troops from the Assam Rifles; in others it was the Manipur Police Commandos. In one case, it was the

Rajputana Rifles. In still others, they were the combined action of the police commandos/Army/Assam Rifles.

- In seven cases, the victims were called out of the houses; in twenty-nine cases, the victims were picked up from different places in the city. In almost all cases there were allegations of encounter with the security forces. In some there were reports of recovery of arms and ammunition from the site of killing or from the persons killed. No details of criminal or political antecedents were provided except in a few cases.
- In one particular case, a twelve-year-old school boy named Mohammed Azad Khan was dragged out of his house by a combined team of police commandos and 12 AR. He was asked to run through the paddyfield adjacent to his house. When he was running the perpetrators fired at him and killed him. The victim's family was not allowed to file a police complaint. An enquiry was ordered by the State Governor but no report of findings was submitted. The writ petition filed by the mother was pending in the Guwahati High Court. The victim's uncle stated that when he wanted to file a police complaint, the police commandos asked him to withdraw his complaint if he wanted to save his life. The Chief Minister, along with the local MLA, visited the victim's family and paid them an amount of Rs 2 lakh. No further action was taken to proceed with the case. In another case, a patient of cervical spondylitis was pulled out of his house and taken to the police station. When the victim's family went to the police station the next day they were told that their relative had been killed in an encounter. A case filed in the Guwahati High Court was totally denied by the State Government. There was no reply from the Central Government to the appeal made by the victim's family. There were several other similar cases of extreme atrocities by the police commandos and AR personnel.
- Special mention was made of the killings on 23 July 2009 of Chongtham Sanjit Meitei and Thockchom Rabina Devi. The IPT took note of the report published in *Tehelka* (Vol. 6, Issue 31, 8 August 2009), which showed that Sanjit was taken by the Imphal District Police Commandos to a pharmacy by the side of the main road and later his body was brought out from the pharmacy. The photographs showed that Sanjit had not offered any resistance of the kind that could potentially justify any use of force against him. (The case of Rabina's killing has been discussed earlier under the heading 'Fact-Finding Commissions/Bodies'). The photographs showed a bystander taking photos of the dead bodies of Sanjit and Rabina being loaded in a truck. There was a prolonged State-wide agitation on the issue. The victims' families filed complaints with the police and the High Court.

> The MHRC was asked not to start an enquiry into the incident by the State Government, which said they were making an enquiry. The Guwahati High Court asked the police to register a complaint on the basis of the complaint filed by Rabina Devi's husband but the DGP and the State Government filed an appeal before the Division Bench. The matter was pending.

The IPT noted that the facts of the other cases submitted before them did not justify the extreme step of shooting people to death. The IPT concluded that unarmed people who were taken out of their houses at midnight or in daylight would not have indulged in encounters with the police/Army resulting in their death. Such unfortunate victims included invalids.

The IPT observed that the circumstances of the cases clearly indicated that if an effective machinery for investigation had been there, as it should have been in a democratic state, there would not have been any difficulty in tracing the culprits. The Government also seemed to realize the shocking injustice inflicted on innocent people. In cases in which persons had been taken into custody from or killed in public places, the police department and the investigative machinery were not doing their duty. That even the legal machinery was not allowed to function was clear from the case of Rabina Devi.

A common feature in these cases was the standard narrative by the Army/police commandos that the victims were the first to open fire and that they were killed in the retaliatory fire opened by the security forces. But when the relatives received the dead bodies from the mortuary, they found marks of severe torture inflicted on them before they were shot dead. There was evidence limbs broken and twisted, necks broken or slashed, soft flesh from the limbs slashed away, marks of injuries on the face or body, ventral side injuries with internal organs protruding outside, and in one case, the mouth of the victim was stuffed with filth. These injuries were not the result of gunfights between the Army/police commandos as claimed. Further, relatives found the dead bodies of victims with pants, trousers and shirts not fitting their body structures. They were wearing different clothes while they were taken by the security forces. Camouflage clothes were put on their bodies after they were shot dead, it was alleged. The MLAs and Chief Minister are part of a democratic government elected by the public. It cannot be assumed that they were persuaded to pay ex-gratia payments to underground extremists killed by the security forces, they must have been at least prima facie satisfied that innocent people had suffered.

The IPT concluded that the root cause of extra-judicial killings lay in the provisions of the AFSPA, which gave unlimited powers of immunity to the

Armed Forces. Section 3 empowers the governor of the state to declare an area as 'disturbed area', where Armed Forces could be used to aid the civil power. Section 4 gives very wide powers to the Armed Forces to arrest without warrant, enter and search any premises without warrant, make any arrest, open fire, or use force even to the point of causing death to any person. The provision in Section 5 that the arrested person must be taken to the nearest police station was never followed. An order passed under Section 3 is not justiciable and the right to remedy is totally taken away by the protection given under Section 6. The net effect was that even if the state government machinery was satisfied that power under the Act was exercised in excess, no action was possible against the perpetrators.

Piecemeal exclusion of an area from the operation of the Act was not sufficient. It is not difficult to fabricate stories of encounters outside the excluded areas even though as a matter of fact people were taken into custody in the excluded areas and killed. IPT noted that in 14 cases, including that of Rabina Devi and Sanjit Meitei, the perpetrators were Manipur Police Commandos who are not covered under the AFSPA with immunity under Section 6. The ordinary law of the land governed them. The IPT called for a strong and effective state Human Rights Commission. The National Human Rights Commission had to get involved in the situation in Manipur. The National Legal Services Authority should take effective steps to spread legal literacy among the common people and make available information on how free legal aid can be obtained.

The final verdict of the IPT was that the concerned area of Manipur had witnessed instances of torture, extrajudicial execution and forced disappearance of a number of people. Prima facie the excesses had been committed by the personnel of the Army/Manipur Police Commandos. The State Government cannot shirk its duty to investigate deeper into each of these incidents so as to protect the lives of innocent people. The presence of underground outfits in the area and their illegal activities cannot be used as a smokescreen for perpetrating human rights violations. The steps taken by some NGOs were useful but the 'ultimate redress is still far away'.

The IPT made a series of Recommendations including:

- Repeal of the AFSPA;
- Prevention of misuse of the provisions of special security legislations;
- Setting up of an independent Human Rights Commission in the state with no official interference in its functioning;
- Strict enforcement of procedural guidelines issued by the NHRC with regard to 'encounters' and investigation of complaints by an independent agency;
- Transparency of investigation in all such cases and public availability

of all enquiry reports;
- Prompt provision of rehabilitation and interim relief;
- Withdrawal of paramilitary forces as far as possible and sensitization programmes for such forces;
- Special attention to the Manipur situation by the NHRC; and
- Spreading of legal literacy among the people of Manipur by the National Legal Services Authority.

Justice Santosh Hegde Commission

In January, 2013, the Supreme Court of India appointed a three-member Commission led by Justice Santosh Hegde to look into the problem of extrajudicial executions in Manipur. The Commission included, reportedly at the instance of the Union Home Ministry, an IPS officer of the Karnataka cadre with no previous experience in the North East, as a member. It did not include a woman or a local civilian expert. Manipur is a state where violence against women by security forces is an established feature. The specificities of the complicated human rights scenario in Manipur are not too well known.

The Commission was an outcome of a petition submitted to the Supreme Court by the Extra-judicial Execution Victim Families (EEVFAM) Association, Manipur with Neena Ningombam as Secretary. The EEVFAM seeks justice for all those innocents killed in extra-judicial executions by security forces, including Assam Rifles (AR) and Manipur Police commandos, who often function with the AR personnel to benefit from the impunity provision of the AFSPA. EEVFAM, an organization of widows and mothers of those killed by the security forces, has asked for an independent probe into 1,528 cases of extra-judicial executions by security forces in Manipur recently (*North East Sun*, 15 November 2012). The memorandum submitted by the EEFAM Association stated that 1,528 people including 31 women and 98 children were killed in fake encounters by the security forces between 1979 and May 2012. Of these, 419 were killed by the AR and 481 were killed by combined teams of Manipur Police commandos and central armed police forces. It said that the state police forces alone killed 344 persons between 1979 and 2012. Of these, 40 were killed by Manipur Police Commandos, 90 by the Imphal East Police district commandos, 132 by the Imphal West Police district commandos, 15 by the Bishnupur Police commandos and 67 by the Thoubal Police commandos. A memorandum was also submitted to the UN Special Rapporteur on Extrajudicial, Summary and Arbitrary Executions. In almost all the cases, young boys attending to their daily chores were picked up at random and killed by the security forces. In several of these cases eyewitnesses narrated the cold established practice of picking up and gunning down of young men and women by the members of the Assam Rifles and Manipur

Police. The killings had been justified as 'encounters with militants'. Secretary Neena Ningombam's husband Michael was killed on 4 November 2008, by the Manipur Police Commandos who branded him as a terrorist. A district judge appointed by the Guwahati High Court has found that Michael was not guilty of initiating firing at the Manipur Police commandos as alleged.

Conclusion

The demands of the civilian population of the state to repeal the draconian laws and the recommendations of international bodies to review and repeal AFSPA and the failure of the Indian government to take any action on the recommendation of the Jeevan Reddy Committee to repeal AFSPA have elicited the comment: 'The Indian government has not only ignored the pleas of ordinary Manipuris and UN human rights bodies to repeal the Armed Forces Special Powers Act, but has even ignored the findings of its own committee. This reflects the sort of callousness that breeds anger, hate and further violence.' Armed conflict in Manipur has officially been viewed as largely a matter of 'internal disturbances', justifying the large-scale deployment of Assam Rifles and other central armed police forces along with the Armed Forces (Special Powers) Act 1958 (AFSPA), which provides immunity and impunity to security forces in 'disturbed areas'. The prolonged imposition of the Act to contain the violence has had the opposite effect of strengthening the cycle of violence. Contrived disappearances, arbitrary executions, torture, rape, housebreak, loot, arbitrary detention et cetera have become everyday features of life. Very few, if any, perpetrators of gross violations of human rights have been prosecuted.

Though under the AFSPA, only the Central Armed Forces and paramilitary units are immune from penalty for their actions, their sense of non-accountability has percolated down to the state police forces to such an extent that often Manipur Police Commandos kill 'suspects' on their own without fear of retribution. Such impunity appears to have created a new state-sponsored 'terrorist' group in the form of the Police Commandos. Instituted for the purpose of containing insurgency in the state, the Manipur Police Commandos have digressed from their stated purpose to embark on a path of seeking to fulfil personal agendas.The State Government remains a mute spectator to such killings and ignores the protests and agitations which follow. Indeed, the number of killings of 'suspects' by the police are considered achievements and the perpetrators are rewarded with cash incentives, medals and gallantry awards which become promotional avenues. The doling out of such incentives and awards to the perpetrators of such atrocities encourages the security forces to indulge in further such atrocities.

This discussion shows, at the very least, that the role of the Assam Rifles (AR) and the AFSPA in the North East has been controversial. The Union

Home ministry maintains that the AR is the 'oldest paramilitary force' under its control and provides increasingly large funds for it. If it is a police force under the Ministry as the other Central Armed Police Forces (CAPFs) are, then it should accountable to it but it is not! Though characterized as a central paramilitary force in the annual reports of the MHA, it works under the operational control of the Army in the North East. This is an anomaly which needs rectification. In view of the grave human rights scenario in the North East, the dual control of the AR by two central ministries, is deleterious and works to the disadvantage of the people of Manipur. It would be better to deprive the AR of its internal security functions which should be taken care of by the substantial state police forces, which have come up in the North East in the recent period. AR must be deployed for border guarding duties only along with the BSF. The Government of India's Vision North East Region:2020 document, formulated as part of its Look East Policy, appears clearly contradictory to the workings of the AR and AFSPA in the State. The contradiction must be removed to realize the real potential of the Vision.

17

Land and Tribals in Andhra Pradesh

K. Raju

Their land is not theirs. Their forests are not theirs. They do not have any say in the matters concerning their own existence. They can be just like that uprooted and displaced for greater common good. They have been relegated from their earlier 'self reliant' status to a 'reliant' one. Tribals today need a Sankaran in every Scheduled Area to reverse the injustice being done to them.

I
THE TRIBAL PARADOX

Tribal communities have a historical relationship and attachment to their lands and forests. The people who have for centuries lived in their own world of self-sufficiency with their own socio-cultural systems and have acquired great knowledge of their lands, natural resources and environment are at the mercy of the powers-that-be, either the State or the anti-State forces. Despite the existence of a plethora of laws to protect the Tribal people, they are forced to live in deprivation and disillusionment.

This deprivation, especially of land, is also known to be one of the major triggers to extremism. As land still is an emotional issue in rural areas, it is recognized as one of the key factors which have encouraged the growth of left wing extremism along with other factors like poverty, lack of access to forest resources and other deprivations. Land deprivation is two dimensional. One is the absolute lack of access to ownership or enjoyment of land and the other is the inability to enjoy the land due to the lack of the secured titles or possession.

The vision of Sri Sankaran of a wholesome and empowered development of Dalits and Adivasis is yet to be realized even after 65 years of independent existence of our country. His contribution to the governance and development of the Tribal areas of the State of Andhra Pradesh was unparalleled. His commitment and personal involvement acted as a great motivational factor to energize the administration in Tribal areas. He put in place the single line administration in the Tribal areas when he was the Principal Secretary of Social

Welfare Department in the State. The Integrated Tribal Development Agencies (ITDAs), which were expected to be the administrative and developmental nerve centres in agency areas, were empowered to be able to effectively address the problems of the Adivasis. The powers available under the Fifth Schedule of the Constitution were invoked to provide maximum benefit to the Tribals in different government appointments and a series of measures that covered education, health, agriculture, animal husbandry and so on were initiated. Despite their inadequacies, the ITDAs in AP stand out today as a fairly good model of Tribal administration.

Considering such a phenomenal contribution, with systems and laws in place, one would expect the Tribals of the State today in a better position vis-a-vis enjoyment of their lands or their forests. But unfortunately the disillusionment over the non-functioning or non-implementation of the protective laws still continues to plague the Tribals.

II
OWNERSHIP OF LAND STILL ELUDES TRIBALS

The constitutional safeguards of Schedule V and the laws made thereunder and the other laws pertaining to lands have passed through many decades of implementation and evolution. A framework for safeguards for the Tribes in respect of their land rights was put in place even before the formation of the State of Andhra Pradesh, during the British regime in the Andhra area and in the Nizam's regime in the erstwhile Hyderabad State. There has been a continual whetting and sharpening of this legal framework throughout the last century or more, following some landmark Tribal agitations and risings that served as trigger points.

In this process of evolution, the Tribals witnessed not only lots of slippages, leakages and lacunae in implementation and also blatant violations which were not uncommon. Coupled with the administrative apathy or antipathy, they found themselves in the proverbial between the devil and the deep sea situation. As if this was not enough, they were beleaguered by the process of development, roads facilitating easy inroads by non-Tribals, irrigation projects devouring their land, land acquisition displacing them from their ancestral sanctuaries, deforestation et cetera.

In spite of large scale government land distribution and protective enactments put in place, ownership of land still eludes them. The laws enacted for protection of Tribal lands in the Scheduled Areas under Fifth Schedule of the Constitution have not prevented Tribal land alienation and large scale transfers as such. Non-Tribals continue to take over Tribal lands through different methods, in spite of stringent provisions of the Land Transfer

Regulation (LTR).[1] Though the LTR prohibits transfer of lands, not only from a Tribal to a non-Tribal but also among non-Tribals in the Scheduled Areas. Non-Tribals hold as much as 48 per cent of the land in Scheduled Areas.[2]

III
VARIOUS FORMS OF LAND ALIENATION

It is an established fact that there is a large scale alienation of lands which belong to the Tribes and the grabbers invariably in all cases are the non-Tribals. Also in the process of stripping of forests by the non-Tribals, Tribals were used as labourers extensively to clear the forest area thus alienating the Tribals from the forests. Way back in 1969 itself, the Committee on Plan Projects, Planning Commission, while presenting its report on the Tribal Development Programmes noticed that Tribal lands in many areas had passed into the hands of non-Tribals, the legal prohibitions against such transfers notwithstanding. Sample studies in Andhra Pradesh, Orissa and some other states have shown that transfers took place on large scale without the permission of the collector or other competent authorities as required by law. The non-Tribals circumvented the legal provisions by entering into clandestine transactions with the native Tribals.

The non-Tribals have devised many ways and methods to usurp the Tribals' land. The first and foremost is the manipulation of land records. The unsatisfactory state of land records contributed a lot to the problem of land alienation. In the absence of evidence from the land records, the Tribals were not legally recognized as owners of the lands which they cultivated. 'Benami' transfers, and leasing or mortgaging of the land by Tribals to the local moneylenders or rich farmers to raise loans for various needs took place on a large scale.

Encroachment is another form of dispossessing the Tribals of their lands and this is abetted by the pathetic state of land records. Practices like marital alliance with Tribal women and fictitious adoption of non-Tribals by the Tribal families et cetera also are some other methods to snatch the lands of the Tribals. And finally the slackness in the implementation of the restrictive provision encourages the non-Tribals to occupy the Tribal lands.

IV
LTR-A TIGER WHOSE TEETH AND NAILS ARE REMOVED

The Andhra Pradesh Scheduled Areas Land Transfer Regulator (APSALTR), 1959, as amended in 1970, 1971 and 1978, along with the Rules framed under this Regulation in 1969, is the major enactment providing safeguards for the Tribals in Schedule V areas. Even the Panchayats (Extension to Scheduled Areas) Act, (PESA) 1996, was expected to provide an institutional bulwark to safeguard Tribals' land rights. The powers of prevention of land alienation and restoration of alienated land have been vested with the Gram Sabha and the Gram Panchayat under PESA at appropriate levels.

But when we look at the actual implementation of LTR we get a shock as to how such a strong legislation was made a paper tiger by the implementers. Look at the statistics and one will feel quite disillusioned.

Disposal of LTR Cases since inception till year 2006[3]

	Number	*(Extent in acres)*
Total cases booked	72354	323887
Total Disposed	70676	316942
Decided in favour of STs	33322	134426
Decided in favour of non-STs	33484	163598
Restored to Tribals	29786	121690

The above table shows that 3,23,887 acres of land was found to be alienated and 72,354 cases were booked. As per the field feedback, these are only half of the actual land alienations happening in Scheduled Areas. Out of the cases disposed by LTR Courts, 33,484 cases covering 1,63,598 acres (51.6%) were decided against Tribals. An LTR court which is supposed to function as a guardian of Tribal land interest giving away almost 52 per cent of the land to the non-Tribals is a great historical tragedy.

Even more pathetic is the case of Kota Ramachandrapuram agency area of West Godavari district which can be seen below:[4]

	Number	*(Extent in acres)*
Total Disposed	11507	61037
Decided in favour of STs	2584	11082
Decided in favour of non-STs	5267	30774
Cases dropped	3656	19181

In this case, not only the number of cases that have gone in favor of non-Tribals is very high, but also the number of cases dropped also is high. Dropping a case practically means disposing the case in favor of non-Tribals as primarily cases are booked against the non-Tribals. This means 78 per cent in terms of the number of cases and 81 per cent in terms of extent of land have been given away by LTR Courts of this particular agency without batting an eyelid.

In LTR courts and in various other courts, in the cases pending on Tribal land issues, more often than not, Tribals are not a party because of which the voice of the Tribals is not heard in the court. West Godavari agency has also seen incidents of fabricating bogus court judgements. The interests of Tribals are at stake because of the lack of knowledge about their rights and entitlements and the lack of legal support.

V
KONERU RANGA RAO LAND COMMITTEE RECOMMENDATION:[5] ONE MORE CHANCE TO REVERSE THE INJUSTICE

The Koneru Ranga Rao (KRR) Land Committee's report is a landmark in the history of the land struggle of the poor, especially of the Tribals, as out of the total 104 recommendations, 41 recommendations pertain to Tribal lands[6]. The Committee has observed:

> Despite the progressive constitutional safeguards in force, great injustice has been done to the Tribals and the legal mechanism evolved to address the land problems has not been able to read the laws in the light intended and construe the adjudicatory and administrative principles accordingly and the administrative apparatus presently hinders rather than furthers the objective of the laws.

The Committee has also identified a whole lot of factors that have contributed to the plight of the Tribals such as the prospective nature of LTR which has not helped the administration in having a re-look into the changes that have taken place right from 1917 to 1970, the settlement regulations formulated under the Fifth Schedule of the Constitution which had given scope to the non-Tribals to obtain *pattas* in the scheduled areas in violation of the LTR, the lack of an in-depth understanding of the special enactments and the lack of will to implement the provisions of various laws et cetera.

Along with the above, the Committee identified the major issues in the Tribal land administration such as an ineffective field machinery with inadequate staff, survey not being taken up since a long time, the lack of fresh detection of cases, the lack of investigation into the occupation by non-Tribals without verification of the bases of such occupation and assuming that these were all on valid *pattas* before 1970 or 1959 or 1950, normally subsumed under an all-pervasive phrase 'old *pattas*'. The other issues identified were:

- non-disposal of pending LTR cases for years together.
- non-restoration of land taken over under LTR decades ago
- illegal assignment of land to non-Tribals under the interpretation of the agency officers that the LTR did not apply to government lands (despite the Samata judgement laying down the implicit law that it applied to all the lands in the Schedule V areas including government lands and also to the government itself.
- an appalling armour of protection from an invalid Government Order

which was struck down by the Hon'ble High Court.

- the lack of action to evict non-Tribals from encroachments even on government land
- no settlement in the forest areas vulnerable to the threats of forest authorities at the lowest level
- growing urbanisation in the Schedule V areas pushing out the Tribals from their agricultural lands to make way for non-agricultural use of their lands, and
- making things worse by permitting more advanced Tribals from other districts or from other states to come into the areas occupied by the Primary Tribal Groups and so on and so forth.

Aggravating the grim situation, the Tribals found that the watchdogs were quite accommodative of, if not warm, towards the wolves and oblivious to the deplorable plight of Tribals.

Of the 41 revolutionary recommendations made by the Committee, 35 have been accepted by the Government. The 6 recommendations rejected by the Government are giving retrospective effect to LTR, extending the penal provision to officers who are negligent in implementation, Tribals' oral evidence to override any contrary non-Tribals' documentary evidence, changes to the definition of Gram Sabha under PESA, detection of trial of cases of lands held by non-Tribals in the name of Tribal women and acquisition of lands genuinely held by non-Tribals by the Government as a public purpose to distribute the same to the Tribals.

The State Government has also issued executive instructions on implementation of the recommendations accepted by the Government. Each and every recommendation has the potential to drastically change the nature of the land ownership and enjoyment by the Tribals, if implemented in true spirit.

To implement the recommendations, which require both legal and administrative action, the Government has to put in special efforts. The limitation period prescribed for filling appeals under both LTR and Settlement regulations has been accepted to be removed in order to facilitate appeals to protect the interests of the Tribals. Simultaneously the Government accepted to make special efforts for disposal of cases in the Hon'ble High Court and other courts by appointing Special advocates even by creating a Special Bench in the Hon'ble High Court, if need be. Another recommendation which can alter the landownership pattern in Tribal areas is the reopening and re-examining of all settlement cases where orders were passed in favour of non-Tribals and Old *Pattas* issued to the non-Tribals prior to 1950. The Settlement *Pattas* are to be cancelled if it is found that the settlement *pattadar* is an absentee or non-resident landlord.

Similarly, the unregistered documents which date back to the crucial period when LTR had not come into effect were agreed to be made inadmissible in evidence for establishing the non-Tribal's right to land.

As it was seen that the LTR courts had been functioning in favour of non-Tribals, a decision was taken that all those LTR cases in which orders were passed by the Special Deputy Collector/Agency Divisional Officer/Additional Agent/Agent to the Government, et cetera in favour of non-Tribals shall be scrutinized and appeals shall be preferred against such orders.

There are several cases where Restoration Orders passed under LTR in favour of Tribals, but actual restoration has only happened on paper. The Committee advised that such orders should be implemented proactively by the Revenue machinery within a fixed timeframe. Sri Girglani in his report mentioned that in Warangal district in Mulungu Mandal, orders were issued for restoration of 350 acres but the land could not be restored due to resistance from the non-Tribal occupants since 1980. In Tadvai Mandal also the restoration orders have not been implemented for the same reasons. In Gudur Mandal 1300 acres covered by LTR orders have not been restored and the non-Tribals continue to enjoy the land illegally and merrily. In Narsampet Mandal it was stated that in Rajivpet village all the Koyas were dispossessed of their lands. In Khammam district, in Julurpad Mandal, restoration of land taken over under LTR orders was effected only in 320 cases but was pending in 1006 cases. In Tekulapalli Mandal out of 130 LTR cases covering 353 acres restoration has been effected only in 34 cases covering 93 acres.

The Government has also agreed for eviction of non-Tribal encroachers of government land. Thousands of acres of government lands are in occupation of the non-Tribals. Sri Girglani mentioned that in Bhadrachalam Revenue Division of Khammam itself more than 25,000 acres of government lands were in occupation of non-poor and non-Tribals. Action is yet to be taken to evict them and assign the lands to the Tribals. *Pattas* issued to non-Tribals under Registered Will Deeds also are barred from consideration for transfer of land. The recommendations pertaining to action with regard to unsurveyed lands under occupation of non-Tribals, specific Scheduled Area mandals completely depleted of Tribals due to non-Tribals' influx, eviction of non-Tribals who are in illegal occupation of temple lands, assigning lands of absentee *pattadars* to the Tribals, cancellation of Protected Tenant Certificates issued to non-Tribals, et cetera have been agreed to.

Another provision which was accepted by the Government is the payment of compensation under Land Acquisition Act to the Tribal occupants although *patta* is in the name of non-Tribals after making a thorough enquiry under LTR.

Government also has agreed to issue instructions to the police not to interfere on behalf of non-Tribals against Tribals and also to the Registration Department to refrain from registering documents for transfer of immovable properties to non-Tribals.

In case of the pre-1980 settlements of the Tribals, the State Government agreed to direct the Forest and Revenue Departments to form special teams, area-wise, for completing the surveys of these settlements in a timebound manner and send the proposals to Government of India. For lands under Preliminary Notification of Reserve Forest, the Government will have to form committees consisting of Forest, Revenue and Tribal Welfare departments for conducting enquiries on the genuineness of Tribal occupations and as per law, proposals have to be formulated for denotification or withdrawal of those lands which are in possession of the Tribals.

The Government has also accepted that updating of land records has to be based on physical verification of lands and incorporation of the names of actual cultivators in revenue records shall be done meticulously. Access shall be provided to all land records and all public documents including court orders under LTR, Settlement regulations et cetera to Tribals or any interested parties at ITDA level on nominal cost by maintaining public land libraries. Basic land records must be made accessible to the Tribal parties at Gram Panchayat level to ensure greater and quicker access to information. Legal Cells have to be created with a panel of advocates with a pro-Tribal perspective at ITDA level to provide free legal support to Tribals and also assist special deputy tahsildar or any other officers who are taking up cases on behalf of Tribals.

Looking at this vast expanse of recommendations accepted by the Government, one would again expect that happy days are back again for the Tribals as now they will have more and more land coming into their hands. But in the absence of a well informed, sensitized and empowered implementing machinery, there is a danger of all these efforts going into obscurity and forgotten soon, just like the people have forgotten the existence of LTR. It is not short-term crisis management endeavours that are direly needed, but broader structural interventions that would involve Tribals themselves as participants in the development process.

VI
IKP'S COMPONENT OF ACCESS TO LAND

A right does not become a right unless the person who is intended to enjoy it, realizes its existence and demands for its fulfilment. Tribals are in this grim situation as sufficient awareness has not been created about their land rights and forest rights.[7] In the State of Andhra Pradesh, Indira Kranthi Patham[8] (IKP) has taken up the task of working on demand side empowering the communities to fight their land issues effectively.

IKP, a rural poverty alleviation project implemented by the Society for Elimination of Rural Poverty (SERP), Department of Rural Development, Government of Andhra Pradesh has a land component which is basically implemented to facilitate the members of self help groups and their federations at village, mandal and district level to have secured access to their lands. A sensitive support mechanism is put in place in DRDAs[9] in the form of Paralegals,[10] Community Surveyors,[11] Land Managers and Legal Coordinators.[12]

Kumra Mankubai, a Tribal woman gets back land from non-Tribal after 37 years of struggle...

Kumra Mankubai's father, Todsam Gangu owned 18 acres of land in Jaongon village of Adilabad district. He did not know while mortgaging this land to B. Shankar, a non-Tribal money-lender for a small loan of Rs. 1,400 in 1969 for 3 years that the non-Tribal would refuse to give the land back. In 1974, Gangu approached the Special Deputy Collector (Tribal Welfare). A long legal battle ensued. The SDC, TW, the Agent to Government, High Court and the Government have all given orders in favour of Gangu. But the non-Tribal again approached the High Court which quashed the earlier orders, holding that transfer under the agreement of sale took place when the Regulation 1/59 was not in force in Telangana area. Gangu was directed to challenge the transfer in appropriate forum. While this legal battle was going on, Gangu passed away and his family lost all hopes on the land. Kumra Mankubai became president of Mandal Samakhya (federation of SHGs at Mandal level) in 2003. She acquired knowledge about her rights and she understood that the gates were not yet closed. She approached Project Officer, ITDA, Urnoor who issued a notice to the non-Tribal on which he got a stay from High Court. IKP's Land team took up the issue, verified the records and found that the land was government land assigned to the Tribal. The land team followed up with the Tahsildar who passed ejectment orders against the non-Tribal, took over the land and handed it over to Mankubai and her family. Mankubai's 4 brothers who never dreamt of getting the land back gave her the major share of 10 out of 18 acres which is worth Rs. 30 lakh. She says she not only got the land back but also her faith in the system....

The paralegals and community surveyors of IKP have been working since 2006-07 identifying the land issues of the poor, with a special focus on Dalits and Tribals, and following up with the Revenue Department for resolving the identified issues. The State Government also has institutionalized the convergence between IKP and Revenue Department through Government Order No. 1148.

The Government of AP, since inception till date, has assigned 48.88 lakh acres of government land to 27.90 lakh landless poor of which Tribals constituted 27 per cent. 7.5 lakh Tribals were assigned 13 lakh acres of government land.[13] The field observation is that much of this land is fraught with issues regarding title and possession.

IKP has recently conducted an inventory of SC/ST lands in 90 per cent of the rural mandals in the state[14] covering 9.71 lakh Tribal households in these mandals (as per the 2011 census data, the total ST families in the state are 15.6 lakh). The inventory data reveals that 70 per cent of the lands held by the Tribals, either their own *patta* land or government land assigned to them, is having some or the other land issue. The issues range from faulty entries in critical revenue records to encroachments by non-Tribals. In many cases, the Tribals themselves are not aware that their lands are not recorded properly in the land records or their lands are legal matter in courts.[15]

The sensitive support mechanism put in place by IKP is facilitating the Tribals to get secured rights on their lands. The paralegals and Community Surveyors are creating awareness in the community, thoroughly verifying identified land allotted and finding out the facts of the case, collecting necessary evidence and documents, submitting the issues with all details to tahsildars and following them up till they are resolved.

In this way, issues pertaining to 12 lakh acres of the poor, majority of whom are Dalits and Tribals have been got resolved by them.

VII
WAY AHEAD: AGENDA FOR ACTION

In this paper I have just touched the tip of the iceberg. Every agency area has got its own history as to how the lands were administered, recorded, surveyed and settled. Gaps in this entire process as well as the apathy of implementers are responsible for the magnitude of the problems faced by the Tribals today. I have not attempted the issues plaguing the implementation of the forest rights of the Tribals under the Recognition of Forest Rights (RoFR) Act in this paper.

The need of the hour is a two-way action i.e., strengthening both the supply and demand mechanisms.

On the supply side, the government has to seriously put in place systems for implementation of the recommendation of the Koneru Ranga Rao Committee. As most of the recommendations have far-reaching implications for the governance in the Tribal areas and have the ability to alter the existing land ownership and enjoyment pattern drastically, the government has to put in place a strong implementation mechanism with sufficient protection to the field functionaries. Regular reviews and monitoring also has to happen if the functionaries have to take the work seriously. The following are the jobs the Government has to do immediately.

Firstly, action by the village revenue officers to be taken to bring on record the actual enjoyers of land. *Secondly*, as agreed to by the government, a review and re-examination of all lands under the title and enjoyment of non-Tribals by forming special teams if need be. *Thirdly*, LTR Courts have to be modernized, fairly equipped and LTR authorities have to be trained and sufficiently motivated as it is there that most of the lands are legally passed on to the hands of the non-Tribals. Here, no case shall be disposed of without a Tribal being represented and ex-parte orders should be a no-no. *Fourthly*, a strong legal assistance model has to be put in place for cases pending in civil courts by offering reasonable fees to the advocates. *Fifthly*, all the records, documents, copies of judgements have to be made available to the Tribals. The Government of AP is setting up 'mee-seva' centers[16] at every mandal where the copies of the land records can be obtained by paying some fee.

It took 28 years to restore the land back to Tribals, though court ordered so

The Mandal Samakhya of Palvancha of Khammam district, in the year 2006, requested the IKP Legal Coordinator to take up the case of a Tribal land of 10 acres for which two decrees were issued under LTR long back saying that their attempts for 25 years to get possession of the lands had been futile.

Ramulamma's husband Bollu Singaiah and another person Tati Yerraiah owned 5 acres of land each in Survey No. 62. One non-Tribal got himself recorded as an enjoyer saying that he had purchased the land. A case was registered under LTR which was disposed of in favor of Tribals and decrees were issued in 1979 and 1983 respectively. From then, the land was not restored to the Tribals. Ramulamma became the President of Palvancha Mandal Samakhya. The IKP Land Unit took up the issue and requested the Tahsildar to implement the orders. The Tahsildar accordingly ejected the non-Tribals and handed over the land to the Tribals in January, 2007. On this, the non-Tribals appealed to Hon'ble High Court. IKP Land team engaged an advocate to fight on behalf of Tribals. The High Court dismissed the Writ Petition in June, 2007. Now both the Tribal families are enjoying the land with full rights after a struggle of 28 years.

It is yet to be seen how easily accessible these services are to the Tribals keeping in view the Tribal terrain.

The Tribal community also needs to be empowered as to their land rights and made to represent competently. The civil organizations working on land issues have been making commendable efforts in this regard. But the case studies quoted while discussing IKP's land access model show as to how even though the records in one case and court orders in the other case are in favour of the Tribals, the lack of such awareness and also the inability to pursue with the administrators is hindering their access to their lands. In many such cases, small interventions could make a big difference. A project like Indira Kranthi Patham (IKP) with its strong network of women's self help groups and their federations and a dedicated cadre of land facilitators should be able to handle this task of strengthening the demand side. The advantage of such a model is that they not only work on the demand side, but also strengthen the hands of the revenue functionaries by assisting in their investigations and gathering the required evidence and documents besides assisting in conducting surveys.

The government should work hand in glove with the civil society organizations and Girijan Samakhya (federations of women SHGs) to reverse the injustice and damage done to the Tribals and follow Sri Sankaran's path that could transcend the bureaucratic systems and mindsets to help a Dalit or an adivasi and serve the larger public interest. That is the only way ahead.

REFERENCES

1. The A.P. Scheduled Areas Land Transfer Regulation, 1959 (Redulation No.1 of 1959), as amended in 1970, 1971 and 1978 is popularly known as LTR, Land Transfer Regulations.
2. Koneru Ranga Rao Land Committee Report.
3. Data collected from Tribal Cultural Research an Training Center (TCR&TI), a wing of Tribal Welfare Commissionerate of Government of AP.
4. TCR&TI data.
5. The KRR Land Committee was appointed by the Government of AP in the year 2004 to assess overall implementation of land distribution programmes/ Acts/Rules and suggest measures for their more effective implementation removing obstacles in their implementation along with action plan with time lines. The Committee submitted its report in November, 2006.
6. The Committee's recommendations were based on the study by Late J.M. Girglani, IAS (Retd.) who did a very exhaustive study in the Tribal area of (i) Warangal District, Eturunagaram Agency; (ii) Khammam District, Bhadrachalam Agency and (iii) Adilabad District, Utnoor, Agency.
7. Forest Rights are granted to the Tribals under the Scheduled Tribes and Traditional Forest Dwellers (Recognition of Forest Rights) Act, 2007
8. Indira Karanthi Patham (IKP) implemented by Society for Elimination of Rural Poverty, Department of Rural Development, Government of AP was initially funded by the World Bank and presently by National Rural Livelihoods Mission, Ministry of Rural Development, Government of India.
9. District Rural Development Agencies are implementing agencies for IKP.

10. Paralegals are graduates who were professionally trained in handling land matters
11. Community Surveyors are technically qualified youth trained in cadastral surveys to assist the community in land survey.
12. Legal Coordinators are fresh law graduates and land managers are retired revenue officers, for providing functional support to the paralegals/surveyors and to liaison with the revenue department.
13. Information taken from the office of the Chief Commissioner, Land Administration, AP.
14. Land Inventory is a process by which the land records, other land documents and the physical possession of the lands are verified. The SC/ST Land Inventory was conducted between July, 2010 to March 2011 in partnership with MGNREGA.
15. Instances have been reported where non-Tribals persuade the revenue officers to book cases against them and get the order in their favor, legitimizing their claims.
16. 'Mee Seva' literally means 'at your service'. The copies of land record, other certificates like caste, income, nativity, et cetera can be obtained from these centres, which are being established at Mandal Headquarters.

About the Contributors

Vikas Bajpai, Assistant Professor, Centre for Social Medicine and Community Health, Jawaharlal Nehru University, New Delhi.

K. Gopal Iyer, Former Professor, Department of Sociology, Panjab University, Chandigarh.

Kalpana Kannabiran, Director, Council for Social Development, Southern Regional Centre, Hyderabad.

P.S. Krishnan, Former Secretary to the Government of India and Former Member, National Commission for SCs and STs and also Member Secretary, National Commission for Backward Classes.

Joseph Marianus Kujur, Former Head of the Tribal Studies and Assistant Research Director, Indian Social Institute, New Delhi and at present Provincial Superior, Ranchi Jesuit Society.

Manoranjan Mohanty, Former Professor of Political Science, University of Delhi and currently Distinguished Professor, Council for Social Development, New Delhi.

S.D.J.M. Prasad, Founder Convenor, National Coaliation for Strengthening PoA Act and Former General Secretary, National Dalit Movement for Justice.

K. Raju, Former IAS Officer of Andhra Pradesh Cadre, he now Heads SC/ST Cell in the All India Congress Party.

K.Y. Ratnam, Associate Professor, Department of Political Science, Univeristy of Hyderabad.

D. Narasimha Reddy, National ICSSR Fellow attched to the Council for Social Development, Hyderabad and is a Former Professor of Economics, University of Hyderabad.

T.L. Sankar, Former Director General, National Institute of Rural Development, Hyderabad and former Principal, Administrative Staff College of India, Hyderabad. At present Honorary Visiting Professor

(Energy Policy), Administrative Staff College of India, Hyderabad.

Anoop Saraya, Professor, Department of Gastroenterology and Human Nutrition, All India Institute of Medical Sciences, New Delhi.

K.B. Saxena, Former Secretary to the Government of India, and at present Professor, Social Justice and Governance, Council for Social Development, New Delhi.

B.D. Sharma, Former IAS Officer, Vice Chancellor, Northeast Hill University and Commissioner for Scheduled Castes and Scheduled Tribes.

B.K. Sinha, Former Secretary, Ministry of Rural Development, Government of India and at present Member of Central Administrative Tribunal, New Delhi.

K.S. Subramanian, Former IPS Officer, was Director of the Research and Policy Division of the Union Home Ministry (1980-85) and retired as Director General of the Tripura State Institute of Public Administration and Rural Development.

Deepti Sukumar, Social Activist.

G. Vijay, Assistant Professor, School of Economics, University of Hyderabad.